Software
Engineering

Software Engineering

Edited by Merlin Dorfman and Richard H. Thayer
Foreword by Barry W. Boehm

Original contributions by:

A. Frank Ackerman
Doug Bell
Keith Bennett
Barry Boehm
Pearl Brereton
David Budgen
Mary Beth Chrissis
Bill Curtis
Merlin Dorfman
Richard E. Fairley
Stuart R. Faulk
Roger U. Fujii
Hassan Gomaa
Patrick A.V. Hall

Patricia W. Hurst
Lingzi Jin
John J. Marciniak
Ian Morrey
Linda Northrop
James D. Palmer
Mark Paulk
Roger S. Pressman
John Pugh
Robert J. Remington
Paul Rook
Richard H. Thayer
Dolores Wallace
Charles Weber

ISBN 0-8186-7609-4
Library of Congress Number 96-15910

Cover art design by Alex Torres

Contributors of Original Papers

Dr. A. Frank Ackerman, Institute for Zero Defects Software, 5130 Birkdale Way, San Jose, CA 95138-2111, USA

Dr. Doug Bell, School of Computing and Management Science, Sheffield Hallam University, Hallamshire Business Park, 100 Napier Street, Sheffield S11 8HB, England, UK

Prof. Keith H. Bennett, Center for Software Maintenance, University of Durham, Durham DH1 3LE England, U.K.

Dr. Barry W. Boehm, Center for Software Engineering, University of Southern California, Los Angeles, CA, 90089-0781, USA

Dr. Pearl Brereton, Department of Computer Science, University of Keele, Keele, Staffordshire ST5 5BG England, U.K.

Prof. David Budgen, Department of Computer Science, University of Keele, Keele, Staffordshire ST5 5BG England, U.K.

Ms. Mary Beth Chrissis, Software Engineering Institute (SEI), Carnegie Mellon University, Pittsburgh, PA 15213-3890, USA

Dr. Bill Curtis, TeraQuest Metrics, P.O. Box 200490, Austin, TX 78720-0490, USA

Mr. Jon K. Digerness (Illustrator), North Coast Graphics, 7418 Kanai Avenue, Citrus Heights, CA 95621, USA

Dr. Merlin Dorfman, Lockheed Martin Missiles & Space Company, Inc., P.O. Box 3504, Sunnyvale, CA 94088-3504, USA

Dr. Richard E. Fairley, Colorado Technical University, 4435 N. Chestnut Street, Colorado Springs, CO 80907-3896, USA

Dr. Stuart R. Faulk, Department of Computer and Information Science, Deschutes Hall, University of Oregon, Eugene, OR, 97403, USA

Mr. Roger U. Fujii, Logicon, Inc., 255 West Fifth Street, San Pedro, CA 90733-0471, USA

Dr. Hassan Gomaa, Department of Information and Software Systems Engineering, George Mason University, Fairfax, VA 22030-4444, USA

Prof. Patrick (Pat) A.V. Hall, Faculty of Math and Computing, The Open University, Walton Hall, Milton Keynes MK7 6AA England, U.K.

Ms. Patricia W. Hurst, Fastrak Training, Inc., 9175 Guilford Rd., Suite 300, Columbia, MD 21046, USA

Dr. Lingzi Jin, Department of Computer Science, Nanjing University, People's Republic of China 210093

Mr. John J. Marciniak, Kaman Sciences Corporation, 2560 Huntington Avenue, Suite 100, Alexandria, VA 22303-1416, USA

Mr. Ian Morrey, School of Computing and Management Science, Sheffield Hallam University, Hallamshire Business Park, 100 Napier Street, Sheffield S11 8HD, England, UK

Ms. Linda M. Northrop, Software Engineering Institute (SEI), Carnegie Mellon University, Pittsburgh, PA 15213-3890, USA

Dr. James D. Palmer, 860 Cashew Way, Fremont, CA 94536-2646, USA

Mr. Mark C. Paulk, Software Engineering Institute (SEI), Carnegie Mellon University, Pittsburgh, PA 15213-3890, USA

Dr. Roger S. Pressman, R.S. Pressman & Associates, Inc., 620 East Slope Drive, Orange, CT 06477, USA

Prof. John Pugh, School of Computer Science, Carleton University, Ottawa, Canada

Dr. Robert J. Remington, Lockheed Martin Missiles & Space Company, Inc., P.O. Box 3504, Sunnyvale, CA 94088-3504, USA

Mr. Paul Rook, The Centre for Software Reliability, City University, Northampton Square, London, EC1V 0HB England, U.K. (deceased)

Dr. Richard H. Thayer, Department of Computer Science, 6000 J Street, California State University at Sacramento, Sacramento, CA 95819, USA.

Ms. Dolores R. Wallace, Computer Systems Laboratory, National Institute of Standards and Technology, Gaithersburg, MD 20899-0001, USA

Mr. Charles V. Weber, Lockheed Martin Federal Systems Company, 6304 Spine Road, Boulder, CO 80301-3320, USA

Foreword

Barry Boehm
Center for Software Engineering
University of Southern California, Los Angeles, California

This tutorial volume is very timely because its subject, software engineering, is currently going through an identity crisis, leaving many people wondering where, how, and if its previous precepts still apply. When commercial-off-the-shelf (COTS) products drive the nature of a software system, what is the role of a "requirements specification?" When user interface software is developed via pointing and clicking on a screen, how relevant are metrics such as lines of code or errors per line of code? When organizations are developing software product line families, how relevant are techniques oriented toward development of a single isolated software product?

Given the magnitude of these changes, there is a temptation to toss all of the old practices out the window and either embrace one of the latest "silver bullet" solutions or reinvent processes from scratch. Unfortunately, as the Brooks article indicates, silver-bullet solutions do not address all aspects of the software problem. And, as seen in the Gibbs article, colossal software disasters such as the Denver International Airport and the FAA Advanced Automation System await projects that neglect previous wisdom in such areas as early error elimination and stabilizing software requirements.

All this is happening while software is coming onto center stage as the key empowering technology of the Information Age. Without software, one cannot enter or exit the information superhighway. Without software, a Cray supercomputer is a rather expensive loveseat and a Powerbook laptop is a rather expensive paperweight. If their software is bungled, our cars, radiation therapy machines, bank accounts—and we ourselves—can get into big trouble.

Fortunately, there is a great deal of wisdom available about how to do software projects properly. A major difficulty is that the wisdom appears in many places, without a framework of guidelines on how to apply it in changing situations.

Resolving that difficulty is what makes this software engineering tutorial volume very helpful as well as very timely. Chapter 1 provides overall perspectives on software engineering issues. Chapter 2 emphasizes a critical guideline: that software engineering needs to concentrate not just on the software, but on the system and mission that the software supports. Chapters 4 and 5 elaborate on techniques for addressing both software and systems aspects in software requirements engineering and design. These chapters particularly illuminate such key areas as concurrent systems, real-time systems, and user-intensive systems. They also address new techniques such as object-oriented system development and formal methods. Chapter 7 on verification, validation, and testing places Chapter 9 on software quality and quality assurance in proper perspective by emphasizing that quality is not tested into the software, but planned, prepared for, and sustained throughout the development cycle.

Chapter 10, software project management, covers the advantages and limitations of quantitative approaches to managing software projects. Quantitative models and methods enable software project managers and their stakeholders (users, customers, developers, maintainers, interfacers, and so forth) to reason about tradeoffs among cost, schedule, functionality, performance, and quality before committing to a course of action.

These models also provide the foundation for plans that enable managers to monitor the progress of projects and to keep them under control. However, since, software development is a people-intensive activity, strict "manage by the numbers" approaches must be tempered by people-oriented approaches. These emphasize such considerations as empowerment, delegation, and development of shared values in getting people to create systems with conceptual integrity, and in establishing organizations that enable people to fulfill their needs for belonging, achievement, recognition, and self-actualization.

The final paper in Chapter 10 and the first two papers in Chapter 11 provide perspectives on the use of risk management as the key for tailoring software projects to their particular objectives, available capabilities, and environment. Risk management offers guidelines for determining when and how much to invest in such activities as domain engineering, COTS package evaluation, prototyping, configuration management, and quality assurance; and for determining what and how much to include in successive increments of a software product. The final paper in Chapter 11 provides an overview of the Software Engineering Institute's highly influential Capability Maturity Model for assessing the maturity of one's software engineering management processes.

Chapter 12 presents some balanced views of software technology capabilities such as computer-aided software engineering (CASE) tools, reusable components, and prototyping tools, reinforcing the point in Chapter 1 that none of these serves as a silver bullet for eliminating software problems. Finally, the paper in Chapter 13 on education reinforces the point in Chapter 2 that software engineers need to learn how to deal with systems, not just the software portions of the systems.

Of course, this book is not a silver bullet either. Readers will need to exercise considerable judgment in applying its insights to their particular project situations. But it performs a valuable service in assembling and organizing the insights, and pointers to more detailed techniques, into a framework within which the appropriate insights can be recalled and applied.

Software Engineering

Merlin Dorfman
Richard H. Thayer

Preface

This tutorial describes the current state of the practice of software engineering. The purpose for writing this tutorial is twofold:

1. There is a need for a set of papers that can be used for a senior or graduate class in software engineering for those faculty members who prefer to use a set of definitive papers rather than a textbook, while relieving the instructor of the need to obtain copyright clearance from dozens of publishers.

2. There are software professionals who would like to have a preselected volume of the best papers in the field of software engineering, for self-study or for a training course in industry.

For the purposes of this tutorial, software engineering is defined as an engineering discipline that applies sound scientific, mathematical, management, and engineering principles to the successful building of large computer programs (software).

> **software engineering.** (1) The application of a systematic, disciplined, quantifiable approach to the development, operation, and maintenance of software, that is, the application of engineering to software. (2) The study of approaches as in (1).

Software systems are built within an organizational structure called a software project. A *successful* software project delivers its planned products within schedule and budget and meets its defined functional and quality requirements.

Software engineering includes software requirements analysis; software design; modern programming methods; testing procedures; verification and validation; software configuration management; software quality assurance; tools for analysis and design; corporate software policies, strategies and goals; project management planning, organizing, staffing, directing, and controlling; as well as the foundations of computer science.

In our opinion, good tutorial papers have the following characteristics:

- They define the basic terms
- They cover the state of the practice for the given topic thoroughly and evenly
- They avoid new, unproved concepts (other than to list them as future possibilities)
- They do not try to sell one tool or concept over all others
- They are easy to read
- They are organized in a hierarchical manner (top-level concepts discussed first, second level concepts discussed next, and so forth)
- They provide additional references
- They come from a refereed journal (unless written specifically for the tutorial)
- They were written by an expert in the area (to assure all of the above)

Our criteria are of course idealized. Even these "rules" can be violated if there is a good reason.

In addition, to keep the whole tutorial under 500 pages, each article should be no longer than 10–12 journal pages.

Our intent was to use the best and most current leading papers in the field. To assure that our intent was fulfilled, we sent survey forms to over 200 of the leading researchers and practitioners of software engineering in the US, Canada, Europe, and Asia, asking what papers they would like to see in a software engineering tutorial. Seventy survey forms were returned. In a surprisingly large number of the basic specialty areas of software engineering, there were no recent, high-quality overview papers identified. It appears that, as a discipline matures, people no longer write overview papers. There have been very few acceptable papers on the fundamentals of software engineering published in the last ten or so years. Therefore the editors contacted some of the leading authors and practitioners in the major subfields of software engineering and asked them to write papers for us. A list of the contributors can be found on Page v; we are grateful that they took time from their busy schedules to write for this tutorial.

Our tutorial is divided into four parts and 13 chapters.

Part One includes Chapters 1, 2, and 3 and provides an overview of software engineering in the context of current issues and the engineering of large complex systems. Chapter 1 describes the problems that occur in developing software, sometimes called the "software crisis." Chapters 2 and 3 present the concepts of system engineering of software-intensive systems, and of engineering of software products, as the solution to the "software crisis."

Part Two, Chapters 4 through 8, describes software engineering from the viewpoint of the phases of the software life cycle: requirements, design, implementation (coding), testing, and maintenance. Chapter 4, *Software Requirements Engineering and Software Design*, discusses the state of the practice in requirements and design. Originally requirements engineering and design were separate chapters, but most papers on the subject combine the two topics so we did as well. Chapter 5, *Software Development Methodologies*, also combines approaches supporting analysis and design. Because of their growing importance, special attention was paid to object-oriented and formal methods. Chapter 6, *Coding*, describes programming activities as they affect software engineering and vice versa. Chapter 7, *Software Validation, Verification, and Testing*, and Chapter 8, *Software Maintenance*, describe the state of the practice in those areas of specialization.

Part Three consists of Chapters 9, 10, and 11 and takes a phase-independent view of the software development process and its management. Chapter 9 looks at software quality assurance in the larger context of ensuring conformance to the development process, as well as in the traditional smaller-scale context. The chapter also looks at configuration management, standards, and reliability engineering as keys to building quality into software products. Chapter 10 discusses software project management and some related topics such as software cost estimation and risk management. Chapter 11 looks at the software development process and how it fits into the larger scope of the software life cycle.

Part Four discusses software technology and education. Chapter 12, *Software Technology*, discusses how technology is transitioned from theory to practice as well as software re-engineering and reuse, computer-aided software engineering (CASE), and software metrics. Chapter 13 contains a single paper on the topic of education for software professionals.

This tutorial is a companion document to the below-listed software engineering tutorials. Duplication of papers has been kept to a minimum. In a few cases, particularly important papers are duplicated in order that each tutorial can stand alone.

- R.H. Thayer, editor, *Tutorial: Software Engineering Project Management*, IEEE Computer Society Press, Los Alamitos, Calif., 1988 (revision in process).

- R.H. Thayer and M. Dorfman (eds.), *System and Software Requirements Engineering*, IEEE Computer Society Press, Los Alamitos, Calif., 1990 (revision in process).

- R.H. Thayer and A. D. McGettrick (eds.), *Software Engineering—A European Perspective*, IEEE Computer Society Press, Los Alamitos, Calif., 1993.

We would like to acknowledge the support provided by the following people.

- Ms Catherine Harris and Dr. William Sanders, managing editors of IEEE Computer Society Press

- IEEE volunteer editors under the direction of Prof. Jon Butler of the Naval Postgraduate School

- Fernando Proaño, a graduate student at Sacramento State University, who assisted us with the survey mentioned above

Merlin Dorfman, Ph.D.
Lockheed Martin Missiles and Space Company
Sunnyvale, California, USA

Richard H. Thayer, Ph.D.
California State University, Sacramento
Sacramento, California, USA

Contents

Chapter 1

Issues—The Software Crisis

1. Introduction to Chapter

The term "software crisis" has been used since the late 1960s to describe those recurring system development problems in which software development problems cause the entire system to be late, over budget, not responsive to the user and/or customer requirements, and difficult to use, maintain, and enhance. The late Dr. Winston Royce, in his paper *Current Problems* [1], emphasized this situation when he said in 1991:

> The construction of new software that is both pleasing to the user/buyer and without latent errors is an unexpectedly hard problem. It is perhaps the most difficult problem in engineering today, and has been recognized as such for more than 15 years. It is often referred to as the "software crisis". It has become the longest continuing "crisis" in the engineering world, and it continues unabated.

This chapter describes some of the current issues and problems in system development that are caused by software—software that is late, is over budget, and/or does not meet the customers' requirements or needs.

Software is the set of instructions that govern the actions of a programmable machine. Software includes application programs, system software, utility software, and firmware. Software does not include data, procedures, people, and documentation. In this tutorial, "software" is synonymous with "computer programs."

Because software is invisible, it is difficult to be certain of development progress or of product completeness and quality. Software is not governed by the physical laws of nature: there is no equivalent of Ohm's Law, which governs the flow of electricity in a circuit; the laws of aerodynamics, which act to keep an aircraft flying stably in the air; or Maxwell's Equations, which describe the radiation of energy from an antenna.

In addition, software is not manufactured like hardware; it does not have a production phase nor manufactured spare parts like hardware; it is typically custom-built, not assembled from existing components like hardware. Even in today's society, software is viewed with suspicion by many individuals, such as senior managers and customers, as somewhat akin to "black magic."

The result is that software is one of the most difficult artifacts of the modern world to develop and build.

2. Introduction to Papers

The opening paper fortuitously appeared in a recent issue of *Scientific American* as the editors were casting about for a way to incorporate a recent rash of high-publicity software problems into the motivation for this tutorial. The paper defines and presents essentially all the major issues currently plaguing software development and maintenance. The article is "popular" rather than technical in the sense that it is journalistic in style and focuses on popular perceptions of software as "black magic," but it raises many issues that software professionals need to be familiar with. It is also worth noting that many of the problems described are partly or largely due to non-software issues such as politics, funding, and external constraints, but again the software professional needs to know that problems unrelated to software engineering must overcome if software projects are to be successful.

The term "software crisis" not unexpectedly originated with the military, for that is where large, complex "real-time" software was first developed. More recently, as civilian and commercial software systems have approached and exceeded military systems in size, complexity, and performance requirements, the "software crisis" has occurred in these environments as well. It is noteworthy that the *Scientific American* article mentions military systems only peripherally.

The article begins with a discussion of the highly-publicized and software-related failure of the baggage system at the new Denver International Airport. As of the date of the article, opening of the airport had been delayed four times, for almost a year, at a cost to the airport authority of over $1 million a day.

Almost as visible in recent months, and also mentioned in the article, are failures of software development for the Department of Motor Vehicles (DMV) of the State of California, and for the advanced air traffic control system of the US Federal Aviation Administration (FAA). The DMV project involved attempts to merge existing, separately developed systems that managed driver's licenses and vehicle registrations. As

has been pointed out in the press [2], the State of California has had problems with computer projects of over $1 billion in value, and the problems resulted from the acquisition policies of the State of California (how contractors and consultants are selected and managed by the State), and from hardware-software integration difficulties, as well as from causes strictly related to software development.

The article identifies the first use of the term "software engineering" in a 1968 conference of the NATO Science Committee in Garmisch, Germany. (See also the Bauer article in this Tutorial.) Many approaches that have been proposed to improve software development are discussed; the author feels that most of these ideas have not lived up to the expectations of their originators. Also discussed is the idea that there are no "silver bullets." (See the article by Brooks in this chapter.)

The *Scientific American* article looks favorably on the use of formal specification methods to solve the problem of software quality, and on "software reuse" (the ability to use a software product developed for one application again later for another application) to solve the productivity or cost problem.

The Software Engineering Institute's Capability Maturity Model was also favorably mentioned (see the article by Paulk, Curtis, Chrissis, and Weber in this Tutorial) as a motivation to software developers to improve their practices. The paper reports an SEI finding that approximately 75 percent of all software developers do not have any formal process or any productivity or quality metrics.

Because software development depends on an educated workforce and good communications rather than on a fixed plant of any kind, software is inherently a suitable export product for developing countries. Although the US is still strong in software design and project management, the article notes that third world countries—notably India and Far Eastern countries—are capable of producing many more "lines of code" per dollar.

A sidebar by Dr. Mary Shaw provides a view of software engineering's history, and of how that history may serve as a roadmap for software engineering's future. Finally, the paper urges education of computer science students in software engineering as an essential step toward resolving the software crisis.

The second and last article in this chapter, "No Silver Bullets: Essence and Accidents of Software Engineering," is by Fred Brooks, one of the legendary figures in software engineering. He has been called the father of software engineering project management in the United States. He worked at IBM in the 1960s and was the software project manager for the OS/360 operating system.

This paper, which he wrote in 1987, states that "no single technique exists to solve the software crisis, that there is no silver bullet." The easy problems ("accidents") have been solved and the remaining difficulties are "essential." He views the solution to the software crisis as a collection of many software engineering tools and techniques that, used in combination, will reduce or eliminate software problems. Although Brooks sees no single solution to the software crisis, no single technology or management technique, he does see encouragement for the future through disciplined, consistent efforts to develop, propagate, and exploit many of the software tools and techniques that are being developed today. (In a report, also written in 1987 [3], Brooks states his belief that most software development problems of the US Department of Defense are managerial rather than technical.)

Brooks believes the hard part of building software is the specification and design of a system, not the coding and testing of the final product. As a result, he believes that building software will always be hard. There is no apparent simple solution. Brooks describes the three major advances in software development as:

- The use of high level languages
- The implementation of time-sharing to improve the productivity of programmers and the quality of their products

- Unified programming environment

Brooks also cites the Ada language, object-oriented programming, artificial intelligence, expert systems, and "automatic" programming (automated generation of code from system specification and design) as technologies with the potential for improving software. From the perspective of another eight years, the AI-related technologies for the most part have yet to fulfill the potential that Brooks saw for them in 1987.

1. Royce, Winston, "Current Problems," in *Aerospace Software Engineering: A Collection of Concepts*, edited by Christine Anderson and Merlin Dorfman, American Institute of Aeronautics, Inc., Washington DC, 1991.

2. "State Fears a Computer Nightmare: Costly 'Screw-Ups' Found in Many Government Projects," *Sacramento Bee*, Sacramento, Calif., June 16, 1994.

3. "Report of the Defense Science Board Task Force on Military Software," Office of the Under Secretary of Defense for Acquisition, Department of Defense, Washington, DC, Sept. 1987.

Software's Chronic Crisis

by W. Wayt Gibbs, *staff writer*

Denver's new international airport was to be the pride of the Rockies, a wonder of modern engineering. Twice the size of Manhattan, 10 times the breadth of Heathrow, the airport is big enough to land three jets simultaneously—in bad weather. Even more impressive than its girth is the airport's subterranean baggage-handling system. Tearing like intelligent coal-mine cars along 21 miles of steel track, 4,000 independent "telecars" route and deliver luggage between the counters, gates and claim areas of 20 different airlines. A central nervous system of some 100 computers networked to one another and to 5,000 electric eyes, 400 radio receivers and 56 bar-code scanners orchestrates the safe and timely arrival of every valise and ski bag.

At least that is the plan. For nine months, this Gulliver has been held captive by Lilliputians—errors in the software that controls its automated baggage system. Scheduled for takeoff by last Halloween, the airport's grand opening was postponed until December to allow BAE Automated Systems time to flush the gremlins out of its $193-million system. December yielded to March. March slipped to May. In June the airport's planners, their bond rating demoted to junk and their budget hemorrhaging red ink at the rate of $1.1 million a day in interest and operating costs, conceded that they could not predict when the baggage system would stabilize enough for the airport to open.

To veteran software developers, the Denver debacle is notable only for its visibility. Studies have shown that for every six new large-scale software systems that are put into operation, two others are canceled. The average software development project overshoots its schedule by half; larger projects generally do worse. And

some three quarters of all large systems are "operating failures" that either do not function as intended or are not used at all.

The art of programming has taken 50 years of continual refinement to reach this stage. By the time it reached 25, the difficulties of building big software loomed so large that in the autumn of 1968 the NATO Science Committee convened some 50 top programmers, computer scientists and captains of industry to plot a course out of what had come to be known as the software crisis. Although the experts could not contrive a road map to guide the industry toward firmer ground, they did coin a name for that distant goal: software engineering, now defined formally as "the application of a systematic, disciplined, quantifiable approach to the development, operation and maintenance of software."

A quarter of a century later software engineering remains a term of aspiration. The vast majority of computer code is still handcrafted from raw programming languages by artisans using techniques they neither measure nor are able to repeat consistently. "It's like musket making was before Eli Whitney," says Brad J. Cox, a professor at George Mason University. "Before the industrial revolution, there was a nonspecialized approach to manufacturing goods that involved very little interchangeability and a maximum of craftsmanship. If we are ever going to lick this software crisis, we're going to have to stop this hand-to-mouth, every-programmer-builds-everything-from-the-ground-up, preindustrial approach."

The picture is not entirely bleak. Intuition is slowly yielding to analysis as programmers begin using quantitative measurements of the quality of the software they produce to improve the way they produce it. The mathematical foundations of programming are solidifying as researchers work on ways of expressing program designs in algebraic forms that make it easier to avoid serious mistakes. Academic computer scientists are starting to address their failure to produce a solid corps of software professionals. Perhaps most important, many in the industry are turning their attention toward inventing the technology and market structures needed to support interchangeable, reusable software parts.

"Unfortunately, the industry does not uniformly apply that which is well-known best practice," laments Larry E. Druffel, director of Carnegie Mellon University's Software Engineering Institute. In fact, a research innovation typically requires 18 years to wend its way into the repertoire of standard programming techniques. By combining their efforts, academia, industry and government may be able to hoist software development to the level of an industrial-age engineering discipline within the decade. If they come up short, society's headlong rush into the information age will be halting and unpredictable at best.

Shifting Sands

"We will see massive changes [in computer use] over the next few years, causing the initial personal computer revolution to pale into comparative insignificance," concluded 22 leaders in software development from academia, industry and research laboratories this past April. The experts gathered at Hedsor Park, a corporate retreat near London, to commemorate the NATO conference and to analyze the future directions of software. "In 1968 we knew what we wanted to build but couldn't," reflected Cliff Jones, a professor at the University of Manchester. "Today we are standing on shifting sands."

The foundations of traditional programming practices are eroding swiftly, as hardware engineers churn out ever faster, cheaper and smaller machines. Many fundamental assumptions that programmers make—for instance, their acceptance that everything they produce will have defects—must change in response. "When computers are em-

SOFTWARE IS EXPLODING in size as society comes to rely on more powerful computer systems (*top*). That faith is often rewarded by disappointment as most large software projects overrun their schedules (*middle*) and many fail outright (*bottom*)—usually after most of the development money has been spent.

bedded in light switches, you've got to get the software right the first time because you're not going to have a chance to update it," says Mary M. Shaw, a professor at Carnegie Mellon.

"The amount of code in most consumer products is doubling every two years," notes Remi H. Bourgonjon, director of software technology at Philips Research Laboratory in Eindhoven. Already, he reports, televisions may contain up to 500 kilobytes of software; an electric shaver, two kilobytes. The power trains in new General Motors cars run 30,000 lines of computer code.

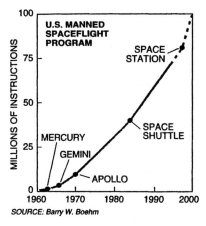

SOURCE: Barry W. Boehm

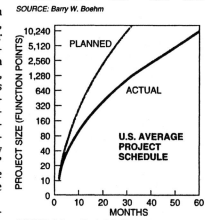

SOURCE: Software Productivity Research

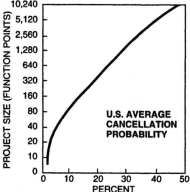

SOURCE: Software Productivity Research

Getting software right the first time is hard even for those who care to try. The Department of Defense applies rigorous—and expensive—testing standards to ensure that software on which a mission depends is reliable. Those standards were used to certify *Clementine*, a satellite that the DOD and the National Aeronautics and Space Administration directed into lunar orbit this past spring. A major part of the Clementine mission was to test targeting software that could one day be used in a space-based missile defense system. But when the satellite was spun around and instructed to fix the moon in its sights, a bug in its program caused the spacecraft instead to fire its maneuvering thrusters continuously for 11 minutes. Out of fuel and spinning wildly, the satellite could not make its rendezvous with the asteroid Geographos.

Errors in real-time systems such as *Clementine* are devilishly difficult to spot because, like that suspicious sound in your car engine, they often occur only when conditions are just so [see "The Risks of Software," by Bev Littlewood and Lorenzo Strigini; SCIENTIFIC AMERICAN, November 1992]. "It is not clear that the methods that are currently used for producing safety-critical software, such as that in nuclear reactors or in cars, will evolve and scale up adequately to match our future expectations," warned Gilles Kahn, the scientific director of France's INRIA research laboratory, at the Hedsor Park meeting. "On the contrary, for real-time systems I think we are at a fracture point."

Software is buckling as well under tectonic stresses imposed by the inexorably growing demand for "distributed systems": programs that run cooperatively on many networked computers. Businesses are pouring capital into distributed information systems that they hope to wield as strategic weapons. The inconstancy of software development can turn such projects into Russian roulette.

Many companies are lured by goals that seem simple enough. Some try to reincarnate obsolete mainframe-based software in distributed form. Others want to plug their existing systems into one another or into new systems with which they can share data and a friendlier user interface. In the technical lingo, connecting programs in this way is often called systems integration. But Brian Randell, a computer scientist at the University of Newcastle upon Tyne, suggests that "there is a better word than integration, from old R.A.F. slang: namely, 'to graunch,' which means 'to make to fit by the use of excessive force.'"

It is a risky business, for although

software seems like malleable stuff, most programs are actually intricate plexuses of brittle logic through which data of only the right kind may pass. Like hand-made muskets, several programs may perform similar functions and yet still be unique in design. That makes software difficult to modify and repair. It also means that attempts to graunch systems together often end badly.

In 1987, for example, California's Department of Motor Vehicles decided to make its customers' lives easier by merging the state's driver and vehicle registration systems—a seemingly straightforward task. It had hoped to unveil convenient one-stop renewal kiosks last year. Instead the DMV saw the projected cost explode to 6.5 times the expected price and the delivery date recede to 1998. In December the agency pulled the plug and walked away from the seven-year, $44.3-million investment.

Sometimes nothing fails like success. In the 1970s American Airlines constructed SABRE, a virtuosic, $2-billion flight reservation system that became part of the travel industry's infrastructure. "SABRE was the shining example of a strategic information system because it drove American to being the world's largest airline," recalls Bill Curtis, a consultant to the Software Engineering Institute.

Intent on brandishing software as effectively in this decade, American tried to graunch its flight-booking technology with the hotel and car reservation systems of Marriott, Hilton and Budget. In 1992 the project collapsed into a heap of litigation. "It was a smashing failure," Curtis says. "American wrote off $165 million against that system."

The airline is hardly suffering alone. In June IBM's Consulting Group released the results of a survey of 24 leading companies that had developed large distributed systems. The numbers were unsettling: 55 percent of the projects cost more than expected, 68 percent overran their schedules and 88 percent had to be substantially redesigned.

The survey did not report one critical statistic: how reliably the completed programs ran. Often systems crash because they fail to expect the unexpected. Networks amplify this problem. "Distributed systems can consist of a great set of interconnected single points of failure, many of which you have not identified beforehand," Randell explains. "The complexity and fragility of these systems pose a major challenge."

The challenge of complexity is not only large but also growing. The bang that computers deliver per buck is doubling every 18 months or so. One result is "an order of magnitude growth in system size every decade—for some industries, every half decade," Curtis says. To keep up with such demand, programmers will have to change the way that they work. "You can't build skyscrapers using carpenters," Curtis quips.

Mayday, Mayday

When a system becomes so complex that no one manager can comprehend the entirety, traditional development processes break down. The Federal Aviation Administration (FAA) has faced this problem throughout its decade-old attempt to replace the nation's increasingly obsolete air-traffic control system [see "Aging Airways," by Gary Stix; SCIENTIFIC AMERICAN, May].

The replacement, called the Advanced Automation System (AAS), combines all the challenges of computing in the 1990s. A program that is more than a million lines in size is distributed across hundreds of computers and embedded into new and sophisticated hardware, all of which must respond around the clock to unpredictable real-time events. Even a small glitch potentially threatens public safety.

To realize its technological dream, the FAA chose IBM's Federal Systems Company, a well-respected leader in software development that has since been purchased by Loral. FAA managers expected (but did not demand) that IBM would use state-of-the-art techniques to estimate the cost and length of the project. They assumed that IBM would screen the requirements and design drawn up for the system in order to catch mistakes early, when they can be fixed in hours rather than days. And the FAA conservatively expected to pay about $500 per line of computer code, five times the industry average for well-managed development processes.

According to a report on the AAS project released in May by the Center for Naval Analysis, IBM's "cost estimation and development process tracking used inappropriate data, were performed inconsistently and were routinely ignored" by project managers. As a result, the FAA has been paying $700 to $900 per line for the AAS software. One reason for the exorbitant price is that "on average every line of code developed needs to be rewritten once," be-

moaned an internal FAA report.

Alarmed by skyrocketing costs and tests that showed the half-completed system to be unreliable, FAA administrator David R. Hinson decided in June to cancel two of the four major parts of the AAS and to scale back a third. The $144 million spent on these failed programs is but a drop next to the $1.4 billion invested in the fourth and central piece: new workstation software for air-traffic controllers.

That project is also spiraling down the drain. Now running about five years late and more than $1 billion over budget, the bug-infested program is being scoured by software experts at Carnegie Mellon and the Massachusetts Institute of Technology to determine whether it can be salvaged or must be canceled outright. The reviewers are scheduled to make their report in September.

Disaster will become an increasingly common and disruptive part of software development unless programming takes on more of the characteristics of an engineering discipline rooted firmly in science and mathematics [see box on page 92]. Fortunately, that trend has already begun. Over the past decade industry leaders have made significant progress toward understanding how to measure, consistently and quantitatively, the chaos of their development processes, the density of errors in their products and the stagnation of their programmers' productivity. Researchers are already taking the next step: finding practical, repeatable solutions to these problems.

Proceeds of Process

In 1991, for example, the Software Engineering Institute, a software think tank funded by the military, unveiled its Capability Maturity Model (CMM). "It provides a vision of software engineering and management excellence," beams David Zubrow, who leads a project on empirical methods at the institute. The CMM has at last persuaded many programmers to concentrate on measuring the process by which they produce software, a prerequisite for any industrial engineering discipline.

Using interviews, questionnaires and the CMM as a benchmark, evaluators can grade the ability of a programming team to create predictably software that meets its customers' needs. The CMM uses a five-level scale, ranging from chaos at level 1 to the paragon of good management at level 5. To date, 261 organizations have been rated.

"The vast majority—about 75 percent—are still stuck in level 1," Curtis reports. "They have no formal process, no measurements of what they do and no way of knowing when they are on the wrong track or off the track altogether." (The Center for Naval Analysis concluded that the AAS project at IBM Federal Systems "appears to be at a low 1 rating.") The remaining 24 percent of projects are at levels 2 or 3.

Only two elite groups have earned the highest CMM rating, a level 5. Motorola's Indian programming team in Bangalore holds one title. Loral's (formerly IBM's) on-board space shuttle software project claims the other. The Loral team has learned to control bugs so well that it can reliably predict how many will be found in each new version of the software. That is a remarkable feat, considering that 90 percent of American programmers do not even keep count of the mistakes they find, according to Capers Jones, chairman of Software Productivity Research. Of those who do, he says, few catch more than a third of the defects that are there.

Tom Peterson, head of Loral's shuttle software project, attributes its success to "a culture that tries to fix not just the bug but also the flaw in the testing process that allowed it to slip through." Yet some bugs inevitably escape detection. The first launch of the space shuttle in 1981 was aborted and delayed for two days because a glitch prevented the five on-board computers from synchronizing properly. Another flaw, this one in the shuttle's rendezvous program, jeopardized the *Intelsat-6* satellite rescue mission in 1992.

Although the CMM is no panacea, its promotion by the Software Engineering Institute has persuaded a number of leading software companies that quantitative quality control can pay off in the long run. Raytheon's equipment division, for example, formed a "software engineering initiative" in 1988 after flunking the CMM test. The division began pouring $1 million per year into refining rigorous inspection and testing guidelines and training its 400 programmers to follow them.

Within three years the division had jumped two levels. By this past June, most projects—including complex radar and air-traffic control systems—were finishing ahead of schedule and under budget. Productivity has more than doubled. An analysis of avoided rework costs revealed a savings of $7.80 for every dollar invested in the initiative. Impressed by such successes, the U.S. Air Force has mandated that all its software developers must reach level 3 of the CMM by 1998. NASA is reportedly considering a similar policy.

Mathematical Re-creations

Even the best-laid designs can go awry, and errors will creep in so long as humans create programs. Bugs squashed early rarely threaten a project's deadline and budget, however. Devastating mistakes are nearly always those in the initial design that slip undetected into the final product.

Mass-market software producers, because they have no single customer to please, can take a belated and brute-force approach to bug removal: they release the faulty product as a "beta" version and let hordes of users dig up the glitches. According to Charles Simonyi, a chief architect at Microsoft, the new version of the Windows operating system will be beta-tested by 20,000 volunteers. That is remarkably effective, but also expensive, inefficient and—since mass-produced PC products make up less than 10 percent of the $92.8-billion software market in the U.S.—usually impractical.

Researchers are thus formulating several strategies to attack bugs early or to avoid introducing them at all. One idea is to recognize that the problem a system is supposed to solve always changes as the system is being built. Denver's airport planners saddled BAE with $20 million worth of changes to the design of its baggage system long after construction had begun. IBM has been similarly bedeviled by the indecision of FAA managers. Both companies naively assumed that once their design was approved, they would be left in peace to build it.

Some developers are at last shedding that illusion and rethinking software as something to be grown rather than built. As a first step, programmers are increasingly stitching together quick prototypes out of standard graphic interface components. Like an architect's scale model, a system prototype can help clear up misunderstandings between customer and developer before a logical foundation is poured.

Because they mimic only the outward behavior of systems, prototypes are of little help in spotting logical inconsistencies in a system's design. "The vast majority of errors in large-scale software are errors of omission," notes Laszlo A. Belady, director of Mitsubishi Electric Research Laboratory. And models do not make it any easier to detect bugs once a design is committed to code.

When it absolutely, positively has to be right, says Martyn Thomas, chairman of Praxis, a British software company, engineers rely on mathematical analysis to predict how their designs will behave in the real world. Unfortunately, the mathematics that describes physical systems does not apply within the synthetic binary universe of a computer program; discrete mathematics, a far less mature field, governs here. But using the still limited tools of set theory and predicate calculus, computer scientists have contrived ways to translate specifications and programs into the language of mathematics, where they can be analyzed with theoretical tools called formal methods.

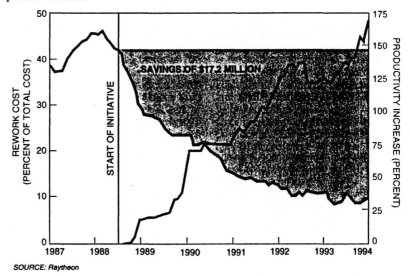

SOURCE: Raytheon

RAYTHEON HAS SAVED $17.2 million in software costs since 1988, when its equipment division began using rigorous development processes that doubled its programmers' productivity and helped them to avoid making expensive mistakes.

Progress toward Professionalism

ENGINEERING EVOLUTION PARADIGM

SCIENCE

PRODUCTION

Virtuosos and talented amateurs
Design uses intuition and brute force
Haphazard progress
Knowledge transmitted slowly
and casually
Extravagant use of materials
Manufacture for use rather than
for sale

Skilled craftsmen
Established procedure
Pragmatic refinement
Training in mechanics
Economic concern for cost
and supply of materials
Manufacture for sale

COMMERCIALIZATION

PROFESSIONAL ENGINEERING

Educated professionals
Analysis and theory
Progress relies on science
Analysis enables new applications
Market segmentation by product
variety

CRAFT

Engineering disciplines share common stages in their evolution, observes Mary M. Shaw of Carnegie Mellon University. She spies interesting parallels between software engineering and chemical engineering, two fields that aspire to exploit on an industrial scale the processes that are discovered by small-scale research.

Like software developers, chemical engineers try to design processes to create safe, pure products as cheaply and quickly as possible. Unlike most programmers, however, chemical engineers rely heavily on scientific theory, math-

ematical modeling, proven design solutions and rigorous quality-control methods—and their efforts usually succeed.

Software, Shaw points out, is somewhat less mature, more like a cottage industry than a professional engineering discipline. Although the demand for more sophisticated and reliable software has boosted some large-scale programming to the commercial stage, computer science (which is younger than many of its researchers) has yet to build the experimental foundation on which software engineering must rest.

CHEMICAL ENGINEERING

1774: Joseph Priestley isolates oxygen
1808: John Dalton publishes his atomic theory
1887: George E. Davis identifies functional operations
1922: Hermann Staudinger explains polymerization

1775: French Academy offers reward
for method to convert brine (salt)
to soda ash (alkali)

SCIENCE

PRODUCTION

COMMERCIALIZATION

PROFESSIONAL ENGINEERING

1915: Arthur D. Little refines and
demonstrates unit operations
1994: Du Pont operates chemical megaplants

CRAFT

1823: Nicolas Leblanc's industrial alkali
process first put into operation
1850s: Pollution of British Midlands
by alkali plants
1857: William Henry Perkin founds synthetic
dye industry

1300s: Alchemists discover alcohol
1700s: Lye boiled to make soap
Most dyes made from vegetables

SOFTWARE ENGINEERING

1956: IBM invents FORTRAN
1968: Donald E. Knuth publishes his theory of algorithms
and data structures
1972: Smalltalk object-oriented language released
1980s: Formal methods and notations refined

1970s: Structured programming methods
gain favor
1980s: Fourth-generation languages released
1990s: Reuse repositories founded

SCIENCE

PRODUCTION

COMMERCIALIZATION

PROFESSIONAL ENGINEERING

1994: Isolated examples only of
algorithms, data structures,
compiler construction

CRAFT

1980s: Most government and management
information systems use some
production controls

Some safety-critical systems (such
as in defense and transportation) use
rigorous controls

1950s: Programs are small and intuitive
1970s: SABRE airline reservation
system is rare success
1990s: Most personal computer software
is still handcrafted

Praxis recently used formal methods on an air-traffic control project for Britain's Civil Aviation Authority. Although Praxis's program was much smaller than the FAA's, the two shared a similar design problem: the need to keep redundant systems synchronized so that if one fails, another can instantly take over. "The difficult part was guaranteeing that messages are delivered in the proper order over twin networks," recalls Anthony Hall, a principal consultant to Praxis. "So here we tried to carry out proofs of our design, and they failed, because the design was wrong. The benefit of finding errors at that early stage is enormous," he adds. The system was finished on time and put into operation last October.

Praxis used formal notations on only the most critical parts of its software, but other software firms have employed mathematical rigor throughout the entire development of a system. GEC Alsthom in Paris is using a formal method called "B" as it spends $350 million to upgrade the switching- and speed-control software that guides the 6,000 electric trains in France's national railway system. By increasing the speed of the trains and reducing the distance between them, the system can save the railway company billions of dollars that might otherwise need to be spent on new lines.

Safety was an obvious concern. So GEC developers wrote the entire design and final program in formal notation and then used mathematics to prove them consistent. "Functional tests are still necessary, however, for two reasons," says Fernando Mejia, manager of the formal development section at GEC. First, programmers do occasionally make mistakes in proofs. Secondly, formal methods can guarantee only that software meets its specification, not that it can handle the surprises of the real world.

Formal methods have other problems as well. Ted Ralston, director of strategic planning for Odyssey Research Associates in Ithaca, N.Y., points out that reading pages of algebraic formulas is even more stultifying than reviewing computer code. Odyssey is just one of several companies that are trying to automate formal methods to make them less onerous to programmers. GEC is collaborating with Digilog in France to commercialize programming tools for the B method. The beta version is being tested by seven companies and institutions, including Aerospatiale, as well as France's atomic energy authority and its defense department.

On the other side of the Atlantic, formal methods by themselves have yet to catch on. "I am skeptical that Americans are sufficiently disciplined to apply formal methods in any broad fashion," says David A. Fisher of the National Institute of Standards and Technology (NIST). There are exceptions, however, most notably among the growing circle of companies experimenting with the "clean-room approach" to programming.

The clean-room process attempts to meld formal notations, correctness proofs and statistical quality control with an evolutionary approach to software development. Like the microchip manufacturing technique from which it takes its name, clean-room development tries to use rigorous engineering techniques to consistently fabricate products that run perfectly the first time. Programmers grow systems one function at a time and certify the quality of each unit before integrating it into the architecture.

Growing software requires a whole new approach to testing. Traditionally, developers test a program by running it the way they intend it to be used, which often bears scant resemblance to real-world conditions. In a clean-room process, programmers try to assign a probability to every execution path—correct and incorrect—that users can take. They then derive test cases from those statistical data, so that the most common paths are tested more thoroughly. Next the program runs through each test case and times how long it takes to fail. Those times are then fed back, in true engineering fashion, to a model that calculates how reliable the program is.

Early adopters report encouraging results. Ericsson Telecom, the European telecommunications giant, used clean-room processes on a 70-programmer project to fabricate an operating system for its telephone-switching computers. Errors were reportedly reduced to just one per 1,000 lines of program code; the industry average is about 25 times higher. Perhaps more important, the company found that development productivity increased by 70 percent, and testing productivity doubled.

No Silver Bullet

Then again, the industry has heard tell many times before of "silver bullets" supposedly able to slay werewolf projects. Since the 1960s developers have peddled dozens of technological innova-

tions intended to boost productivity—many have even presented demonstration projects to "prove" the verity of their boasts. Advocates of object-oriented analysis and programming, a buzzword du jour, claim their approach represents a paradigm shift that will deliver "a 14-to-1 improvement in productivity," along with higher quality and easier maintenance, all at reduced cost.

There are reasons to be skeptical. "In the 1970s structured programming was also touted as a paradigm shift," Curtis recalls. "So was CASE [computer-assisted software engineering]. So were third-, fourth- and fifth-generation languages. We've heard great promises for technology, many of which weren't delivered."

Meanwhile productivity in software development has lagged behind that of more mature disciplines, most notably computer hardware engineering. "I think of software as a cargo cult," Cox says. "Our main accomplishments were imported from this foreign culture of hardware engineering—faster machines and more memory." Fisher tends to agree: adjusted for inflation, "the value added per worker in the industry has been at $40,000 for two decades," he asserts. "We're not seeing any increases."

"I don't believe that," replies Richard A. DeMillo, a professor at Purdue University and head of the Software Engineering Research Consortium. "There has been improvement, but everyone uses different definitions of productivity." A recent study published by Capers Jones—but based on necessarily dubious historical data—states that U.S. programmers churn out twice as much code today as they did in 1970.

The fact of the matter is that no one really knows how productive software developers are, for three reasons. First, less than 10 percent of American companies consistently measure the productivity of their programmers.

Second, the industry has yet to settle on a useful standard unit of measurement. Most reports, including those published in peer-reviewed computer science journals, express productivity in terms of lines of code per worker per month. But programs are written in a wide variety of languages and vary enormously in the complexity of their operation. Comparing the number of lines written by a Japanese programmer using C with the number produced by an American using Ada is thus like comparing their salaries without converting from yen to dollars.

Third, Fisher says, "you can walk into a typical company and find two guys sharing an office, getting the same salary and having essentially the same credentials and yet find a factor of 100 difference in the number of instructions per day that they produce." Such enormous individual differences tend to swamp the much smaller effects of technology or process improvements.

After 25 years of disappointment with apparent innovations that turned out to be irreproducible or unscalable, many researchers concede that computer science needs an experimental branch to separate the general results from the accidental. "There has always been this assumption that if I give you a method, it is right just because I told you so," complains Victor R. Basili, a professor at the University of Maryland. "People are developing all kinds of things, and it's really quite frightening how bad some of them are," he says.

Mary Shaw of Carnegie Mellon points out that mature engineering fields codify proved solutions in handbooks so that even novices can consistently handle routine designs, freeing more talented practitioners for advanced projects. No such handbook yet exists for software, so mistakes are repeated on project after project, year after year.

DeMillo suggests that the government should take a more active role. "The National Science Foundation should be interested in funding research aimed at verifying experimental results that have been claimed by other people," he says. "Currently, if it's not groundbreaking, first-time-ever-done research, program officers at the NSF tend to discount the work." DeMillo knows whereof he speaks. From 1989 to 1991 he directed the NSF's computer and computation research division.

Yet "if software engineering is to be an experimental science, that means it needs laboratory science. Where the heck are the laboratories?" Basili asks. Because attempts to scale promising technologies to industrial proportions so often fail, small laboratories are of limited utility. "We need to have places where we can gather data and try things out," DeMillo says. "The only way to do that is to have a real software development organization as a partner."

There have been only a few such partnerships. Perhaps the most successful is the Software Engineering Laboratory, a consortium of NASA's Goddard Space Flight Center, Computer Sciences Corp.

and the University of Maryland. Basili helped to found the laboratory in 1976. Since then, graduate students and NASA programmers have collaborated on "well over 100 projects," Basili says, most having to do with building ground-support software for satellites.

Just Add Water

Musket makers did not get more productive until Eli Whitney figured out how to manufacture interchangeable parts that could be assembled by any skilled workman. In like manner, software parts can, if properly standardized, be reused at many different scales. Programmers have for decades used libraries of subroutines to avoid rewriting the same code over and over. But these components break down when they are moved to a different programming language, computer platform or operating environment. "The tragedy is that as hardware becomes obsolete, an excellent expression of a sorting algorithm written in the 1960s has to be rewritten," observes Simonyi of Microsoft.

Fisher sees tragedy of a different kind. "The real price we pay is that as a specialist in any software technology you cannot capture your special capability in a product. If you can't do that, you basically can't be a specialist." Not that some haven't tried. Before moving to NIST last year, Fisher founded and served as CEO of Incremental Systems. "We were truly world-class in three of the component technologies that go into compilers but were not as good in the other seven or so," he states. "But we found that there was no practical way of selling compiler components; we had to sell entire compilers."

So now he is doing something about that. In April, NIST announced that it was creating an Advanced Technology Program to help engender a market for component-based software. As head of the program, Fisher will be distributing $150 million in research grants to software companies willing to attack the technical obstacles that currently make software parts impractical.

The biggest challenge is to find ways of cutting the ties that inherently bind programs to specific computers and to other programs. Researchers are investigating several promising approaches, including a common language that could be used to describe software parts, programs that reshape components to match any environment, and components that have lots of optional features a user can turn on or off.

Fisher favors the idea that components should be synthesized on the fly. Programmers would "basically capture how to do it rather than actually doing it," producing a recipe that any computer could understand. "Then when you want to assemble two components, you would take this recipe and derive compatible versions by adding additional elements to their interfaces. The whole thing would be automated," he explains.

Even with a $150-million incentive and market pressures forcing companies to find cheaper ways of producing software, an industrial revolution in software is not imminent. "We expect to see only isolated examples of these technologies in five to seven years—and we may not succeed technically either," Fisher hedges. Even when the technology is ready, components will find few takers unless they can be made cost-effective. And the cost of software parts will depend less on the technology involved than on the kind of market that arises to produce and consume them.

Brad Cox, like Fisher, once ran a software component company and found it hard going. He believes he has figured out the problem—and its solution. Cox's firm tried to sell low-level program parts analogous to computer chips. "What's different between software ICs [integrated circuits] and silicon ICs is that silicon ICs are made of atoms, so they abide by conservation of mass, and people therefore know how to buy and sell them robustly," he says. "But this interchange process that is at the core of all commerce just does not work for things that can be copied in nanoseconds." When Cox tried selling the parts his programmers had created, he found that the price the market would bear was far too low for him to recover the costs of development.

The reasons were twofold. First, recasting the component by hand for each customer was time-consuming; NIST hopes to clear this barrier with its Advanced Technology Program. The other factor was not so much technical as cultural: buyers want to pay for a component once and make copies for free.

"The music industry has had about a century of experience with this very problem," Cox observes. "They used to sell tangible goods like piano rolls and sheet music, and then radio and television came along and knocked all that into a cocked hat." Music companies adapted to broadcasting by setting up agencies to collect royalties every time a song is aired and to funnel the money back to the artists and producers.

Cox suggests similarly charging users each time they use a software compo-

A Developing World

Since the invention of computers, Americans have dominated the software market. Microsoft alone produces more computer code each year than do any of 100 nations, according to Capers Jones of Software Productivity Research in Burlington, Mass. U.S. suppliers hold about 70 percent of the worldwide software market.

But as international networks sprout and large corporations deflate, India, Hungary, Russia, the Philippines and other poorer nations are discovering in software a lucrative industry that requires the one resource in which they are rich: an underemployed, well-educated labor force. American and European giants are now competing with upstart Asian development companies for contracts, and in response many are forming subsidiaries overseas. Indeed, some managers in the trade predict that software development will gradually split between Western software engineers who design systems and Eastern programmers who build them.

"In fact, it is going on already," says Laszlo A. Belady, director of Mitsubishi Electric Research Laboratory. AT&T, Hewlett-Packard, IBM, British Telecom and Texas Instruments have all set up programming teams in India. The Pact Group in Lyons, France, reportedly maintains a "software factory" in Manila. "Cadence, the U.S. supplier of VLSI design tools, has had its software development sited on the Pacific rim for several years," reports Martyn Thomas, chairman of Praxis. "ACT, a U.K.-based systems house, is using Russian programmers from the former Soviet space program," he adds.

So far India's star has risen fastest. "Offshore development [work commissioned in India by foreign companies] has begun to take off in the past 18 to 24 months," says Rajendra S. Pawar, head of New Delhi-based NIIT, which has graduated 200,000 Indians from its programming courses. Indeed, India's software exports have seen a compound annual growth of 38 percent over the past five years; last year they jumped 60 percent—four times the average growth rate worldwide.

About 58 percent of the $360-million worth of software that flowed out of India last year ended up in the U.S. That tiny drop hardly makes a splash in a $92.8-billion market. But several trends may propel exports beyond the $1-billion mark as early as 1997.

The single most important factor, Pawar asserts, is the support of the Indian government, which has eased tariffs and restrictions, subsidized numerous software technology parks and export zones, and doled out five-year tax exemptions to software exporters. "The opening of the Indian economy is acting as a very big catalyst," Pawar says.

It certainly seems to have attracted the attention of large multinational firms eager to reduce both the cost of the software they need and the amount they build in-house. The primary cost of software is labor. Indian programmers come so cheap—$125 per unit of software versus $925 for an American developer, according to Jones—that some companies fly an entire team to the U.S. to work on a project. More than half of India's software exports come from such "body shopping," although tightened U.S. visa restrictions are stanching this flow.

Another factor, Pawar observes, is a growing trust in the quality of overseas project management. "In the past two years, American companies have become far more comfortable with the offshore concept," he says. This is a result in part of success stories from leaders like Citicorp, which develops banking systems in Bombay, and Motorola, which has a top-rated team of more than 150 programmers in Bangalore building software for its Iridium satellite network.

Offshore development certainly costs less than body shopping, and not merely because of saved airfare. "Thanks to the time differences between India and the U.S., Indian software developers can act the elves and the shoemaker," working overnight on changes requested by managers the previous day, notes Richard Heeks, who studies Asian computer industries at the University of Manchester in England.

Price is not everything. Most Eastern nations are still weak in design and management skills. "The U.S. still has the best system architects in the world," boasts Bill Curtis of the Software Engineering Institute. "At large systems, nobody touches us." But when it comes to just writing program code, the American hegemony may be drawing to a close.

Year	India's Software Exports (millions of U.S. dollars)
1985	6
1986	10
1987	39
1988	52
1989	67
1990	100
1991	128
1992	164
1993	225
1994	360
1995	483
1996	NOT AVAILABLE
1997	1,000

INDIA'S SOFTWARE EXPORTS (MILLIONS OF U.S. DOLLARS)

SOURCES: NIIT, NASSCOM

11

nent. "In fact," he says, "that model could work for software even more easily than for music, thanks to the infrastructure advantages that computers and communications give us. Record players don't have high-speed network links in them to report usage, but our computers do."

Or will, at least. Looking ahead to the time when nearly all computers are connected, Cox envisions distributing software of all kinds via networks that link component producers, end users and financial institutions. "It's analogous to a credit-card operation but with tentacles that reach into PCs," he says. Although that may sound ominous to some, Cox argues that "the Internet now is more like a garbage dump than a farmer's market. We need a national infrastructure that can support the distribution of everything from Grandma's cookie recipe to Apple's window managers to Addison-Wesley's electronic books." Recognizing the enormity of the cultural shift he is proposing, Cox expects to press his cause for years to come through the Coalition for Electronic Markets, of which he is president.

The combination of industrial pro-cess control, advanced technological tools and interchangeable parts promises to transform not only how programming is done but also who does it. Many of the experts who convened at Hedsor Park agreed with Belady that "in the future, professional people in most fields will use programming as a tool, but they won't call themselves programmers or think of themselves as spending their time programming. They will think they are doing architecture, or traffic planning or film making."

That possibility begs the question of who is qualified to build important systems. Today anyone can bill herself as a software engineer. "But when you have 100 million user-programmers, frequently they will be doing things that are life critical—building applications that fill prescriptions, for example," notes Barry W. Boehm, director of the Center for Software Engineering at the University of Southern California. Boehm is one of an increasing number who suggest certifying software engineers, as is done in other engineering fields.

Of course, certification helps only if programmers are properly trained to begin with. Currently only 28 universities offer graduate programs in software engineering; five years ago there were just 10. None offer undergraduate degrees. Even academics such as Shaw, DeMillo and Basili agree that computer science curricula generally provide poor preparation for industrial software development. "Basic things like designing code inspections, producing user documentation and maintaining aging software are not covered in academia," Capers Jones laments.

Engineers, the infantry of every industrial revolution, do not spontaneously generate. They are trained out of the bad habits developed by the craftsmen that preceded them. Until the lessons of computer science inculcate a desire not merely to build better things but also to build things better, the best we can expect is that software development will undergo a slow, and probably painful, industrial evolution.

FURTHER READING

ENCYCLOPEDIA OF SOFTWARE ENGINEERING. Edited by John J. Marciniak. John Wiley & Sons, 1994.

SOFTWARE 2000: A VIEW OF THE FUTURE. Edited by Brian Randell, Gill Ringland and Bill Wulf. ICL and the Commission of European Communities, 1994.

FORMAL METHODS: A VIRTUAL LIBRARY. Jonathan Bowen. Available in hypertext on the World Wide Web as http://www.comlab.ox.ac.uk/archive/formal-methods.html

No Silver Bullet

Essence and Accidents of Software Engineering

Frederick P. Brooks, Jr.

University of North Carolina at Chapel Hill

Fashioning complex conceptual constructs is the *essence;* *accidental* tasks arise in representing the constructs in language. Past progress has so reduced the accidental tasks that future progress now depends upon addressing the essence.

Of all the monsters that fill the nightmares of our folklore, none terrify more than werewolves, because they transform unexpectedly from the familiar into horrors. For these, one seeks bullets of silver that can magically lay them to rest.

The familiar software project, at least as seen by the nontechnical manager, has something of this character; it is usually innocent and straightforward, but is capable of becoming a monster of missed schedules, blown budgets, and flawed products. So we hear desperate cries for a silver bullet—something to make software costs drop as rapidly as computer hardware costs do.

But, as we look to the horizon of a decade hence, we see no silver bullet. There is no single development, in either technology or in management technique, that by itself promises even one order-of-magnitude improvement in productivity, in reliability, in simplicity. In this article, I shall try to show why, by examining both the nature of the software problem and the properties of the bullets proposed.

Skepticism is not pessimism, however. Although we see no startling break-

This article was first published in *Information Processing '86*, ISBN No. 0-444-70077-3, H.-J. Kugler, ed., Elsevier Science Publishers B.V. (North-Holland) © IFIP 1986.

throughs—and indeed, I believe such to be inconsistent with the nature of software—many encouraging innovations are under way. A disciplined, consistent effort to develop, propagate, and exploit these innovations should indeed yield an order-of-magnitude improvement. There is no royal road, but there is a road.

The first step toward the management of disease was replacement of demon theories and humours theories by the germ theory. That very step, the beginning of hope, in itself dashed all hopes of magical solutions. It told workers that progress would be made stepwise, at great effort, and that a persistent, unremitting care would have to be paid to a discipline of cleanliness. So it is with software engineering today.

Does it have to be hard?—Essential difficulties

Not only are there no silver bullets now in view, the very nature of software makes it unlikely that there will be any—no inventions that will do for software productivity, reliability, and simplicity what electronics, transistors, and large-scale integration did for computer hardware.

Reprinted from *Computer*, Vol. 20, No. 4, Apr. 1987, pp. 10–19.

We cannot expect ever to see twofold gains every two years.

First, one must observe that the anomaly is not that software progress is so slow, but that computer hardware progress is so fast. No other technology since civilization began has seen six orders of magnitude in performance-price gain in 30 years. In no other technology can one choose to take the gain in *either* improved performance *or* in reduced costs. These gains flow from the transformation of computer manufacture from an assembly industry into a process industry.

Second, to see what rate of progress one can expect in software technology, let us examine the difficulties of that technology. Following Aristotle, I divide them into *essence*, the difficulties inherent in the nature of software, and *accidents,* those difficulties that today attend its production but are not inherent.

The essence of a software entity is a construct of interlocking concepts: data sets, relationships among data items, algorithms, and invocations of functions. This essence is abstract in that such a conceptual construct is the same under many different representations. It is nonetheless highly precise and richly detailed.

I believe the hard part of building software to be the specification, design, and testing of this conceptual construct, not the labor of representing it and testing the fidelity of the representation. We still make syntax errors, to be sure; but they are fuzz compared with the conceptual errors in most systems.

If this is true, building software will always be hard. There is inherently no silver bullet.

Let us consider the inherent properties of this irreducible essence of modern software systems: complexity, conformity, changeability, and invisibility.

Complexity. Software entities are more complex for their size than perhaps any other human construct because no two parts are alike (at least above the statement level). If they are, we make the two similar parts into a subroutine—open or closed. In this respect, software systems differ profoundly from computers, buildings, or automobiles, where repeated elements abound.

Digital computers are themselves more complex than most things people build: They have very large numbers of states. This makes conceiving, describing, and testing them hard. Software systems have

orders-of-magnitude more states than computers do.

Likewise, a scaling-up of a software entity is not merely a repetition of the same elements in larger sizes, it is necessarily an increase in the number of different elements. In most cases, the elements interact with each other in some nonlinear fashion, and the complexity of the whole increases much more than linearly.

The complexity of software is an essential property, not an accidental one. Hence, descriptions of a software entity that abstract away its complexity often abstract away its essence. For three centuries, mathematics and the physical sciences made great strides by constructing simplified models of complex phenomena, deriving properties from the models, and verifying those properties by experiment. This paradigm worked because the complexities ignored in the models were not the essential properties of the phenomena. It does not work when the complexities are the essence.

Many of the classic problems of developing software products derive from this essential complexity and its nonlinear increases with size. From the complexity comes the difficulty of communication among team members, which leads to product flaws, cost overruns, schedule delays. From the complexity comes the

difficulty of enumerating, much less understanding, all the possible states of the program, and from that comes the unreliability. From complexity of function comes the difficulty of invoking function, which makes programs hard to use. From complexity of structure comes the difficulty of extending programs to new functions without creating side effects. From complexity of structure come the unvisualized states that constitute security trapdoors.

Not only technical problems, but management problems as well come from the complexity. It makes overview hard, thus impeding conceptual integrity. It makes it hard to find and control all the loose ends. It creates the tremendous learning and understanding burden that makes personnel turnover a disaster.

Conformity. Software people are not alone in facing complexity. Physics deals

14

with terribly complex objects even at the "fundamental" particle level. The physicist labors on, however, in a firm faith that there are unifying principles to be found, whether in quarks or in unified-field theories. Einstein argued that there must be simplified explanations of nature, because God is not capricious or arbitrary.

No such faith comforts the software engineer. Much of the complexity that he must master is arbitrary complexity, forced without rhyme or reason by the many human institutions and systems to which his interfaces must conform. These differ from interface to interface, and from time to time, not because of necessity but only because they were designed by different people, rather than by God.

In many cases, the software must conform because it is the most recent arrival on the scene. In others, it must conform because it is perceived as the most conformable. But in all cases, much complexity comes from conformation to other interfaces; this complexity cannot be simplified out by any redesign of the software alone.

Changeability. The software entity is constantly subject to pressures for change. Of course, so are buildings, cars, computers. But manufactured things are infrequently changed after manufacture; they are superseded by later models, or essential changes are incorporated into later-serial-number copies of the same basic design. Call-backs of automobiles are really quite infrequent; field changes of computers somewhat less so. Both are much less frequent than modifications to fielded software.

In part, this is so because the software of a system embodies its function, and the function is the part that most feels the pressures of change. In part it is because software can be changed more easily—it is pure thought-stuff, infinitely malleable. Buildings do in fact get changed, but the high costs of change, understood by all, serve to dampen the whims of the changers.

All successful software gets changed. Two processes are at work. First, as a software product is found to be useful, people try it in new cases at the edge of or beyond the original domain. The pressures for extended function come chiefly from users who like the basic function and invent new uses for it.

Second, successful software survives beyond the normal life of the machine vehicle for which it is first written. If not

new computers, then at least new disks, new displays, new printers come along; and the software must be conformed to its new vehicles of opportunity.

In short, the software product is embedded in a cultural matrix of applications, users, laws, and machine vehicles. These all change continually, and their changes inexorably force change upon the software product.

Invisibility. Software is invisible and unvisualizable. Geometric abstractions are powerful tools. The floor plan of a building helps both architect and client evaluate spaces, traffic flows, views. Contradictions and omissions become obvious.

Despite progress in restricting and simplifying software structures, they remain inherently unvisualizable, and thus do not permit the mind to use some of its most powerful conceptual tools.

Scale drawings of mechanical parts and stick-figure models of molecules, although abstractions, serve the same purpose. A geometric reality is captured in a geometric abstraction.

The reality of software is not inherently embedded in space. Hence, it has no ready geometric representation in the way that land has maps, silicon chips have diagrams, computers have connectivity schematics. As soon as we attempt to diagram software structure, we find it to constitute not one, but several, general directed graphs superimposed one upon another. The several graphs may represent the flow of control, the flow of data, patterns of dependency, time sequence, name-space relationships. These graphs are usually not even planar, much less hierarchical. Indeed, one of the ways of establishing conceptual control over such structure is to enforce link cutting until one or more of the graphs becomes hierarchical.[1]

In spite of progress in restricting and simplifying the structures of software, they remain inherently unvisualizable, and thus do not permit the mind to use some of its most powerful conceptual tools. This

lack not only impedes the process of design within one mind, it severely hinders communication among minds.

Past breakthroughs solved accidental difficulties

If we examine the three steps in software-technology development that have been most fruitful in the past, we discover that each attacked a different major difficulty in building software, but that those difficulties have been accidental, not essential, difficulties. We can also see the natural limits to the extrapolation of each such attack.

High-level languages. Surely the most powerful stroke for software productivity, reliability, and simplicity has been the progressive use of high-level languages for programming. Most observers credit that development with at least a factor of five in productivity, and with concomitant gains in reliability, simplicity, and comprehensibility.

What does a high-level language accomplish? It frees a program from much of its accidental complexity. An abstract program consists of conceptual constructs: operations, data types, sequences, and communication. The concrete machine program is concerned with bits, registers, conditions, branches, channels, disks, and such. To the extent that the high-level language embodies the constructs one wants in the abstract program and avoids all lower ones, it eliminates a whole level of complexity that was never inherent in the program at all.

The most a high-level language can do is to furnish all the constructs that the programmer imagines in the abstract program. To be sure, the level of our thinking about data structures, data types, and operations is steadily rising, but at an ever-decreasing rate. And language development approaches closer and closer to the sophistication of users.

Moreover, at some point the elaboration of a high-level language creates a tool-mastery burden that increases, not reduces, the intellectual task of the user who rarely uses the esoteric constructs.

Time-sharing. Time-sharing brought a major improvement in the productivity of programmers and in the quality of their product, although not so large as that brought by high-level languages.

Time-sharing attacks a quite different difficulty. Time-sharing preserves immediacy, and hence enables one to maintain an overview of complexity. The slow turnaround of batch programming means that one inevitably forgets the minutiae, if not the very thrust, of what one was thinking when he stopped programming and called for compilation and execution. This interruption is costly in time, for one must refresh one's memory. The most serious effect may well be the decay of the grasp of all that is going on in a complex system.

Slow turnaround, like machine-language complexities, is an accidental rather than an essential difficulty of the software process. The limits of the potential contribution of time-sharing derive directly. The principal effect of time-sharing is to shorten system response time. As this response time goes to zero, at some point it passes the human threshold of noticeability, about 100 milliseconds. Beyond that threshold, no benefits are to be expected.

Unified programming environments. Unix and Interlisp, the first integrated programming environments to come into widespread use, seem to have improved productivity by integral factors. Why?

They attack the accidental difficulties that result from using individual programs *together*, by providing integrated libraries, unified file formats, and pipes and filters. As a result, conceptual structures that in principle could always call, feed, and use one another can indeed easily do so in practice.

This breakthrough in turn stimulated the development of whole toolbenches, since each new tool could be applied to any programs that used the standard formats.

Because of these successes, environments are the subject of much of today's software-engineering research. We look at their promise and limitations in the next section.

Hopes for the silver

Now let us consider the technical developments that are most often advanced as potential silver bullets. What problems do they address—the problems of essence, or the remaining accidental difficulties? Do they offer revolutionary advances, or incremental ones?

Ada and other high-level language advances. One of the most touted recent de-

To slay the werewolf

Why a silver bullet? Magic, of course. Silver is identified with the moon and thus has magic properties. A silver bullet offers the fastest, most powerful, and safest way to slay the fast, powerful, and incredibly dangerous werewolf. And what could be more natural than using the moon-metal to destroy a creature transformed under the light of the full moon?

The legend of the werewolf is probably one of the oldest monster legends around. Herodotus in the fifth century BC gave us the first written report of werewolves when he mentioned a tribe north of the Black Sea, called the Neuri, who supposedly turned into wolves a few days each year. Herodotus wrote that he didn't believe it.

Sceptics aside, many people have believed in people turning into wolves or other animals. In medieval Europe, some people were killed because they were thought to be werewolves. In those times, it didn't take being bitten by a werewolf to become one. A bargain with the devil, using a special potion, wearing a special belt, or being cursed by a witch could all turn a person into a werewolf. However, medieval werewolves could be hurt and killed by normal weapons. The problem was to overcome their strength and cunning.

Enter the fictional, not legendary, werewolf. The first major werewolf movie, *The Werewolf of London*, in 1935 created the two-legged man-wolf who changed into a monster when the moon was full. He became a werewolf after being bitten by one, and could be killed only with a silver bullet. Sound familiar?

Actually, we owe many of today's ideas about werewolves to Lon Chaney Jr.'s unforgettable 1941 portrayal in *The Wolf Man*. Subsequent films seldom strayed far from the mythology of the werewolf shown in that movie. But that movie strayed far from the original mythology of the werewolf.

Would you believe that before fiction took over the legend, werewolves weren't troubled by silver bullets? Vampires were the ones who couldn't stand them. Of course, if you rely on the legends, your only salvation if unarmed and attacked by a werewolf is to climb an ash tree or run into a field of rye. Not so easy to find in an urban setting, and hardly recognizable to the average movie audience.

What should you watch out for? People whose eyebrows grow together, whose index finger is longer than the middle finger, and who have hair growing on their palms. Red or black teeth are a definite signal of possible trouble.

Take warning, though. The same symptoms mark people suffering from hypertrichosis (people born with hair covering their bodies) or porphyria. In porphyria, a person's body produces toxins called porphyrins. Consequently, light becomes painful, the skin grows hair, and the teeth may turn red. Worse for the victim's reputation, his or her increasingly bizarre behavior makes people even more suspicious of the other symptoms. It seems very likely that the sufferers of this disease unwittingly contributed to the current legend, although in earlier times they were evidently not accused of murderous tendencies.

It is worth noting that the film tradition often makes the werewolf a rather sympathetic character, an innocent transformed against his (or rarely, her) will into a monster. As the gypsy said in *The Wolf Man*,

Even a man who is pure at heart,
And says his prayers at night,
Can become a wolf when the wolfbane blooms,
And the moon is full and bright.

— *Nancy Hays*
  Assistant Editor

The Bettman Archive

16

velopments is Ada, a general-purpose high-level language of the 1980's. Ada not only reflects evolutionary improvements in language concepts, but indeed embodies features to encourage modern design and modularization. Perhaps the Ada philosophy is more of an advance than the Ada language, for it is the philosophy of modularization, of abstract data types, of hierarchical structuring. Ada is over-rich, a natural result of the process by which requirements were laid on its design. That is not fatal, for subsetted working vocabularies can solve the learning problem, and hardware advances will give us the cheap MIPS to pay for the compiling costs. Advancing the structuring of software systems is indeed a very good use for the increased MIPS our dollars will buy. Operating systems, loudly decried in the 1960's for their memory and cycle costs, have proved to be an excellent form in which to use some of the MIPS and cheap memory bytes of the past hardware surge.

Nevertheless, Ada will not prove to be the silver bullet that slays the software productivity monster. It is, after all, just another high-level language, and the biggest payoff from such languages came from the first transition—the transition up from the accidental complexities of the machine into the more abstract statement of step-by-step solutions. Once those accidents have been removed, the remaining ones will be smaller, and the payoff from their removal will surely be less.

I predict that a decade from now, when the effectiveness of Ada is assessed, it will be seen to have made a substantial difference, but not because of any particular language feature, nor indeed because of all of them combined. Neither will the new Ada environments prove to be the cause of the improvements. Ada's greatest contribution will be that switching to it occasioned training programmers in modern software-design techniques.

Object-oriented programming. Many students of the art hold out more hope for object-oriented programming than for any of the other technical fads of the day.[2] I am among them. Mark Sherman of Dartmouth notes on CSnet News that one must be careful to distinguish two separate ideas that go under that name: *abstract data types* and *hierarchical types*. The concept of the abstract data type is that an object's type should be defined by a name, a set of proper values, and a set of proper operations rather than by its storage structure, which should be hidden. Examples are Ada packages (with private types) and Modula's modules.

Hierarchical types, such as Simula-67's classes, allow one to define general interfaces that can be further refined by providing subordinate types. The two concepts are orthogonal—one may have hierarchies without hiding and hiding without hierarchies. Both concepts represent real advances in the art of building software.

Each removes yet another accidental difficulty from the process, allowing the designer to express the essence of the design without having to express large amounts of syntactic material that add no

---

Many students of the art hold out more hope for object-oriented programming than for other technical fads of the day.

---

information content. For both abstract types and hierarchical types, the result is to remove a higher-order kind of accidental difficulty and allow a higher-order expression of design.

Nevertheless, such advances can do no more than to remove all the accidental difficulties from the expression of the design. The complexity of the design itself is essential, and such attacks make no change whatever in that. An order-of-magnitude gain can be made by object-oriented programming only if the unnecessary type-specification underbrush still in our programming language is itself nine-tenths of the work involved in designing a program product. I doubt it.

Artificial intelligence. Many people expect advances in artificial intelligence to provide the revolutionary breakthrough that will give order-of-magnitude gains in software productivity and quality.[3] I do not. To see why, we must dissect what is meant by "artificial intelligence."

D.L. Parnas has clarified the terminological chaos[4]:

> Two quite different definitions of AI are in common use today. AI-1: The use of computers to solve problems that previously could only be solved by applying human intelligence. AI-2: The use of a specific set of programming techniques known as heuristic or rule-based programming. In this approach human experts are studied to determine what heuristics or rules of thumb they use in solving problems. . . . The program is designed to solve a problem the way that humans seem to solve it.
>
> The first definition has a sliding meaning. . . . Something can fit the definition of AI-1 today but, once we see how the program works and understand the problem, we will not think of it as AI any more. . . . Unfortunately I cannot identify a body of technology that is unique to this field. . . . Most of the work is problem-specific, and some abstraction or creativity is required to see how to transfer it.

I agree completely with this critique. The techniques used for speech recognition seem to have little in common with those used for image recognition, and both are different from those used in expert systems. I have a hard time seeing how image recognition, for example, will make any appreciable difference in programming practice. The same problem is true of speech recognition. The hard thing about building software is deciding what one wants to say, not saying it. No facilitation of expression can give more than marginal gains.

Expert-systems technology, AI-2, deserves a section of its own.

Expert systems. The most advanced part of the artificial intelligence art, and the most widely applied, is the technology for building expert systems. Many software scientists are hard at work applying this technology to the software-building environment.[3,5] What is the concept, and what are the prospects?

An *expert system* is a program that contains a generalized inference engine and a rule base, takes input data and assumptions, explores the inferences derivable from the rule base, yields conclusions and advice, and offers to explain its results by retracing its reasoning for the user. The inference engines typically can deal with fuzzy or probabilistic data and rules, in addition to purely deterministic logic.

Such systems offer some clear advantages over programmed algorithms designed for arriving at the same solutions to the same problems:

- Inference-engine technology is developed in an application-independent way, and then applied to many uses. One can justify much effort on the inference engines. Indeed, that technology is well advanced.
- The changeable parts of the application-peculiar materials are en-

coded in the rule base in a uniform fashion, and tools are provided for developing, changing, testing, and documenting the rule base. This regularizes much of the complexity of the application itself.

The power of such systems does not come from ever-fancier inference mechanisms, but rather from ever-richer knowledge bases that reflect the real world more accurately. I believe that the most important advance offered by the technology is the separation of the application complexity from the program itself.

How can this technology be applied to the software-engineering task? In many ways: Such systems can suggest interface rules, advise on testing strategies, remember bug-type frequencies, and offer optimization hints.

Consider an imaginary testing advisor, for example. In its most rudimentary form, the diagnostic expert system is very like a pilot's checklist, just enumerating suggestions as to possible causes of difficulty. As more and more system structure is embodied in the rule base, and as the rule base takes more sophisticated account of the trouble symptoms reported, the testing advisor becomes more and more particular in the hypotheses it generates and the tests it recommends. Such an expert system may depart most radically from the conventional ones in that its rule base should probably be hierarchically modularized in the same way the corresponding software product is, so that as the product is modularly modified, the diagnostic rule base can be modularly modified as well.

The work required to generate the diagnostic rules is work that would have to be done anyway in generating the set of test cases for the modules and for the system. If it is done in a suitably general manner, with both a uniform structure for rules and a good inference engine available, it may actually reduce the total labor of generating bring-up test cases, and help as well with lifelong maintenance and modification testing. In the same way, one can postulate other advisors, probably many and probably simple, for the other parts of the software-construction task.

Many difficulties stand in the way of the early realization of useful expert-system advisors to the program developer. A crucial part of our imaginary scenario is the development of easy ways to get from program-structure specification to the automatic or semiautomatic generation of diagnostic rules. Even more difficult and

important is the twofold task of knowledge acquisition: finding articulate, self-analytical experts who know *why* they do things, and developing efficient techniques for extracting what they know and distilling it into rule bases. The essential prerequisite for building an expert system is to have an expert.

The most powerful contribution by expert systems will surely be to put at the service of the inexperienced programmer the experience and accumulated wisdom of the best programmers. This is no small contribution. The gap between the best software engineering practice and the average practice is very wide—perhaps wider than in any other engineering discipline. A tool that disseminates good practice would be important.

"Automatic" programming. For almost 40 years, people have been anticipating and writing about "automatic programming," or the generation of a program for solving a problem from a statement of the problem specifications. Some today write as if they expect this technology to provide the next breakthrough.[5]

Parnas[4] implies that the term is used for glamor, not for semantic content, asserting,

> In short, automatic programming always has been a euphemism for programming with a higher-level language than was presently available to the programmer.

He argues, in essence, that in most cases it is the solution method, not the problem, whose specification has to be given.

One can find exceptions. The technique of building generators is very powerful, and it is routinely used to good advantage in programs for sorting. Some systems for integrating differential equations have also permitted direct specification of the problem, and the systems have assessed the parameters, chosen from a library of methods of solution, and generated the programs.

These applications have very favorable properties:

• The problems are readily characterized by relatively few parameters.

• There are many known methods of solution to provide a library of alternatives.

• Extensive analysis has led to explicit rules for selecting solution techniques, given problem parameters.

It is hard to see how such techniques generalize to the wider world of the ordinary software system, where cases with such neat properties are the exception. It is hard even to imagine how this breakthrough in generalization could occur.

Graphical programming. A favorite subject for PhD dissertations in software engineering is graphical, or visual, programming—the application of computer graphics to software design.[6,7] Sometimes the promise held out by such an approach is postulated by analogy with VLSI chip design, in which computer graphics plays so fruitful a role. Sometimes the theorist justifies the approach by considering flowcharts as the ideal program-design medium and by providing powerful facilities for constructing them.

Nothing even convincing, much less exciting, has yet emerged from such efforts. I am persuaded that nothing will.

In the first place, as I have argued elsewhere,[8] the flowchart is a very poor abstraction of software structure. Indeed, it is best viewed as Burks, von Neumann, and Goldstine's attempt to provide a desperately needed high-level control language for their proposed computer. In the pitiful, multipage, connection-boxed form to which the flowchart has today been elaborated, it has proved to be useless as a design tool—programmers draw

18

flowcharts after, not before, writing the programs they describe.

Second, the screens of today are too small, in pixels, to show both the scope and the resolution of any seriously detailed software diagram. The so-called "desktop metaphor" of today's workstation is instead an "airplane-seat" metaphor. Anyone who has shuffled a lap full of papers while seated between two portly passengers will recognize the difference—one can see only a very few things at once. The true desktop provides overview of, and random access to, a score of pages. Moreover, when fits of creativity run strong, more than one programmer or writer has been known to abandon the desktop for the more spacious floor. The hardware technology will have to advance quite substantially before the scope of our scopes is sufficient for the software-design task.

More fundamentally, as I have argued above, software is very difficult to visualize. Whether one diagrams control flow, variable-scope nesting, variable cross-references, dataflow, hierarchical data structures, or whatever, one feels only one dimension of the intricately interlocked software elephant. If one superimposes all the diagrams generated by the many relevant views, it is difficult to extract any global overview. The VLSI analogy is fundamentally misleading—a chip design is a layered two-dimensional description whose geometry reflects its realization in 3-space. A software system is not.

Program verification. Much of the effort in modern programming goes into testing and the repair of bugs. Is there perhaps a silver bullet to be found by eliminating the errors at the source, in the system-design phase? Can both productivity and product reliability be radically enhanced by following the profoundly different strategy of proving designs correct before the immense effort is poured into implementing and testing them?

I do not believe we will find productivity magic here. Program verification is a very powerful concept, and it will be very important for such things as secure operating-system kernels. The technology does not promise, however, to save labor. Verifications are so much work that only a few substantial programs have ever been verified.

Program verification does not mean error-proof programs. There is no magic here, either. Mathematical proofs also can be faulty. So whereas verification might

reduce the program-testing load, it cannot eliminate it.

More seriously, even perfect program verification can only establish that a program meets its specification. The hardest part of the software task is arriving at a complete and consistent specification, and much of the essence of building a program is in fact the debugging of the specification.

Environments and tools. How much more gain can be expected from the exploding researches into better programming environments? One's instinctive reaction is that the big-payoff problems—hierarchical file systems, uniform file formats to make possible uniform pro-

---

Language-specific smart editors promise at most freedom from syntactic errors and simple semantic errors.

---

gram interfaces, and generalized tools—were the first attacked, and have been solved. Language-specific smart editors are developments not yet widely used in practice, but the most they promise is freedom from syntactic errors and simple semantic errors.

Perhaps the biggest gain yet to be realized from programming environments is the use of integrated database systems to keep track of the myriad details that must be recalled accurately by the individual programmer and kept current for a group of collaborators on a single system.

Surely this work is worthwhile, and surely it will bear some fruit in both productivity and reliability. But by its very nature, the return from now on must be marginal.

Workstations. What gains are to be expected for the software art from the certain and rapid increase in the power and memory capacity of the individual workstation? Well, how many MIPS can one use fruitfully? The composition and editing of programs and documents is fully supported by today's speeds. Compiling could stand a boost, but a factor of 10 in machine speed would surely leave think-time the dominant activity in the programmer's day. Indeed, it appears to be so now.

More powerful workstations we surely welcome. Magical enhancements from them we cannot expect.

Promising attacks on the conceptual essence

Even though no technological breakthrough promises to give the sort of magical results with which we are so familiar in the hardware area, there is both an abundance of good work going on now, and the promise of steady, if unspectacular progress.

All of the technological attacks on the accidents of the software process are fundamentally limited by the productivity equation:

$$time\ of\ task = \sum_i (frequency)_i \times (time)_i$$

If, as I believe, the conceptual components of the task are now taking most of the time, then no amount of activity on the task components that are merely the expression of the concepts can give large productivity gains.

Hence we must consider those attacks that address the essence of the software problem, the formulation of these complex conceptual structures. Fortunately, some of these attacks are very promising.

Buy versus build. The most radical possible solution for constructing software is not to construct it at all.

Every day this becomes easier, as more and more vendors offer more and better software products for a dizzying variety of applications. While we software engineers have labored on production methodology, the personal-computer revolution has created not one, but many, mass markets for software. Every newsstand carries monthly magazines, which sorted by machine type, advertise and review dozens of products at prices from a few dollars to a few hundred dollars. More specialized sources offer very powerful products for the workstation and other Unix markets. Even software tools and environments can be bought off-the-shelf. I have elsewhere proposed a marketplace for individual modules. [9]

Any such product is cheaper to buy than to build afresh. Even at a cost of one hundred thousand dollars, a purchased piece of software is costing only about as much as one programmer-year. And delivery is immediate! Immediate at least for products that really exist, products whose developer can refer products to a happy user. Moreover, such products tend to be much better documented and somewhat better maintained than home-grown software.

The development of the mass market is, I believe, the most profound long-run trend in software engineering. The cost of software has always been development cost, not replication cost. Sharing that cost among even a few users radically cuts the per-user cost. Another way of looking at it is that the use of *n* copies of a software system effectively multiplies the productivity of its developers by *n*. That is an enhancement of the productivity of the discipline and of the nation.

The key issue, of course, is applicability. Can I use an available off-the-shelf package to perform my task? A surprising thing has happened here. During the 1950's and 1960's, study after study showed that users would not use off-the-shelf packages for payroll, inventory control, accounts receivable, and so on. The requirements were too specialized, the case-to-case variation too high. During the 1980's, we find such packages in high demand and widespread use. What has changed?

Not the packages, really. They may be somewhat more generalized and somewhat more customizable than formerly, but not much. Not the applications, either. If anything, the business and scientific needs of today are more diverse and complicated than those of 20 years ago.

The big change has been in the hardware/software cost ratio. In 1960, the buyer of a two-million dollar machine felt that he could afford $250,000 more for a customized payroll program, one that slipped easily and nondisruptively into the computer-hostile social environment. Today, the buyer of a $50,000 office machine cannot conceivably afford a customized payroll program, so he adapts the payroll procedure to the packages available. Computers are now so commonplace, if not yet so beloved, that the adaptations are accepted as a matter of course.

There are dramatic exceptions to my argument that the generalization of software packages has changed little over the years: electronic spreadsheets and simple database systems. These powerful tools, so obvious in retrospect and yet so late in appearing, lend themselves to myriad uses, some quite unorthodox. Articles and even books now abound on how to tackle unexpected tasks with the spreadsheet. Large numbers of applications that would formerly have been written as custom programs in Cobol or Report Program Generator are now routinely done with these tools.

Many users now operate their own computers day in and day out on various applications without ever writing a program. Indeed, many of these users cannot write new programs for their machines, but they are nevertheless adept at solving new problems with them.

I believe the single most powerful software-productivity strategy for many organizations today is to equip the computer-naive intellectual workers who are on the firing line with personal computers and good generalized writing, drawing, file, and spreadsheet programs and then to turn them loose. The same strategy, carried out with generalized mathematical and statistical packages and some simple programming capabilities, will also work for hundreds of laboratory scientists.

Requirements refinement and rapid prototyping. The hardest single part of building a software system is deciding precisely what to build. No other part of the conceptual work is as difficult as establishing the detailed technical requirements, including all the interfaces to people, to machines, and to other software systems. No other part of the work so cripples the resulting system if done wrong. No other part is more difficult to rectify later.

Therefore, the most important function that the software builder performs for the client is the iterative extraction and refinement of the product requirements. For the truth is, the client does not know what he wants. The client usually does not know what questions must be answered, and he has almost never thought of the problem in the detail necessary for specification. Even the simple answer—"Make the new software system work like our old manual information-processing system" —is in fact too simple. One never wants exactly that. Complex software systems are,

moreover, things that act, that move, that work. The dynamics of that action are hard to imagine. So in planning any software-design activity, it is necessary to allow for an extensive iteration between the client and the designer as part of the system definition.

I would go a step further and assert that it is really impossible for a client, even working with a software engineer, to specify completely, precisely, and correctly the exact requirements of a modern software product before trying some versions of the product.

Therefore, one of the most promising of the current technological efforts, and one that attacks the essence, not the accidents, of the software problem, is the development of approaches and tools for rapid prototyping of systems as prototyping is part of the iterative specification of requirements.

A *prototype software system* is one that simulates the important interfaces and performs the main functions of the intended system, while not necessarily being bound by the same hardware speed, size, or cost constraints. Prototypes typically perform the mainline tasks of the application, but make no attempt to handle the exceptional tasks, respond correctly to invalid inputs, or abort cleanly. The purpose of the prototype is to make real the conceptual structure specified, so that the client can test it for consistency and usability.

Much of present-day software-acquisition procedure rests upon the assumption that one can specify a satisfactory system in advance, get bids for its construction, have it built, and install it. I think this assumption is fundamentally wrong, and that many software-acquisition problems

The Bettman Archive

spring from that fallacy. Hence, they cannot be fixed without fundamental revision—revision that provides for iterative development and specification of prototypes and products.

Incremental development—grow, don't build, software. I still remember the jolt I felt in 1958 when I first heard a friend talk about *building* a program, as opposed to *writing* one. In a flash he broadened my whole view of the software process. The metaphor shift was powerful, and accurate. Today we understand how like other building processes the construction of software is, and we freely use other elements of the metaphor, such as *specifications, assembly of components,* and *scaffolding.*

The building metaphor has outlived its usefulness. It is time to change again. If, as I believe, the conceptual structures we construct today are too complicated to be specified accurately in advance, and too complex to be built faultlessly, then we must take a radically different approach.

Let us turn to nature and study complexity in living things, instead of just the dead works of man. Here we find constructs whose complexities thrill us with awe. The brain alone is intricate beyond mapping, powerful beyond imitation, rich in diversity, self-protecting, and self-renewing. The secret is that it is grown, not built.

So it must be with our software systems. Some years ago Harlan Mills proposed that any software system should be grown by incremental development. [10] That is, the system should first be made to run, even if it does nothing useful except call the proper set of dummy subprograms. Then, bit by bit, it should be fleshed out, with the subprograms in turn being developed—into actions or calls to empty stubs in the level below.

I have seen most dramatic results since I began urging this technique on the project builders in my Software Engineering Laboratory class. Nothing in the past decade has so radically changed my own practice, or its effectiveness. The approach necessitates top-down design, for it is a top-down growing of the software. It allows easy backtracking. It lends itself to early prototypes. Each added function and new provision for more complex data or circumstances grows organically out of what is already there.

The morale effects are startling. Enthusiasm jumps when there is a running system, even a simple one. Efforts re-

Table 1. Exciting vs. useful but unexciting software products.

Exciting Products	
Yes	No
Unix	Cobol
APL	PL/1
Pascal	Algol
Modula	MVS/370
Smalltalk	MS-DOS
Fortran	

double when the first picture from a new graphics software system appears on the screen, even if it is only a rectangle. One always has, at every stage in the process, a working system. I find that teams can *grow* much more complex entities in four months than they can *build.*

The same benefits can be realized on large projects as on my small ones. [11]

Great designers. The central question in how to improve the software art centers, as it always has, on people.

We can get good designs by following good practices instead of poor ones. Good design practices can be taught. Programmers are among the most intelligent part of the population, so they can learn good practice. Hence, a major thrust in the United States is to promulgate good modern practice. New curricula, new literature, new organizations such as the Software Engineering Institute, all have come into being in order to raise the level of our practice from poor to good. This is entirely proper.

Nevertheless, I do not believe we can make the next step upward in the same way. Whereas the difference between poor conceptual designs and good ones may lie in the soundness of design method, the difference between good designs and great ones surely does not. Great designs come from great designers. Software construction is a *creative* process. Sound methodology can empower and liberate the creative mind; it cannot inflame or inspire the drudge.

The differences are not minor—they are rather like the differences between Salieri and Mozart. Study after study shows that the very best designers produce structures that are faster, smaller, simpler, cleaner, and produced with less effort. [12] The dif-

ferences between the great and the average approach an order of magnitude.

A little retrospection shows that although many fine, useful software systems have been designed by committees and built as part of multipart projects, those software systems that have excited passionate fans are those that are the products of one or a few designing minds, great designers. Consider Unix, APL, Pascal, Modula, the Smalltalk interface, even Fortran; and contrast them with Cobol, PL/I, Algol, MVS/370, and MS-DOS. (See Table 1.)

Hence, although I strongly support the technology-transfer and curriculum-development efforts now under way, I think the most important single effort we can mount is to develop ways to grow great designers.

No software organization can ignore this challenge. Good managers, scarce though they be, are no scarcer than good designers. Great designers and great managers are both very rare. Most organizations spend considerable effort in finding and cultivating the management prospects; I know of none that spends equal effort in finding and developing the great designers upon whom the technical excellence of the products will ultimately depend.

My first proposal is that each software organization must determine and proclaim that great designers are as important to its success as great managers are, and that they can be expected to be similarly nurtured and rewarded. Not only salary, but the perquisites of recognition—office size, furnishings, personal technical equipment, travel funds, staff support—must be fully equivalent.

How to grow great designers? Space does not permit a lengthy discussion, but some steps are obvious:

• Systematically identify top designers as early as possible. The best are often not the most experienced.

• Assign a career mentor to be responsible for the development of the prospect, and carefully keep a career file.

• Devise and maintain a career-development plan for each prospect, including carefully selected apprenticeships with top designers, episodes of advanced formal education, and short courses, all interspersed with solo-design and technical-leadership assignments.

• Provide opportunities for growing designers to interact with and stimulate each other. □

Acknowledgments

I thank Gordon Bell, Bruce Buchanan, Rick Hayes-Roth, Robert Patrick, and, most especially, David Parnas for their insights and stimulating ideas, and Rebekah Bierly for the technical production of this article.

References

1. D.L. Parnas, "Designing Software for Ease of Extension and Contraction," *IEEE Trans. Software Engineering,* Vol. 5, No. 2, Mar. 1979, pp. 128-138.

2. G. Booch, "Object-Oriented Design," *Software Engineering with Ada,* 1983, Benjamin/Cummings, Menlo Park, Calif.

3. *IEEE Trans. Software Engineering* (special issue on artificial intelligence and software engineering), J. Mostow, guest ed., Vol. 11, No. 11, Nov. 1985.

4. D.L. Parnas, "Software Aspects of Strategic Defense Systems," *American Scientist,* Nov. 1985.

5. R. Balzer, "A 15-Year Perspective on Automatic Programming," *IEEE Trans. Software Engineering* (special issue on artificial intelligence and software engineering), J. Mostow, guest ed., Vol. 11, No. 11, Nov. 1985, pp. 1257-1267.

6. *Computer* (special issue on visual programming), R.B. Graphton and T. Ichikawa, guest eds., Vol. 18, No. 8, Aug. 1985.

7. G. Raeder, "A Survey of Current Graphical Programming Techniques," *Computer* (special issue on visual programming), R.B. Graphton and T. Ichikawa, guest eds., Vol. 18, No. 8, Aug. 1985, pp. 11-25.

8. F.P. Brooks, *The Mythical Man-Month,* 1975, Addison-Wesley, Reading, Mass., New York, Chapter 14.

9. Defense Science Board, *Report of the Task Force on Military Software,* in press.

10. H.D. Mills, "Top-Down Programming in Large Systems," in *Debugging Techniques in Large Systems,* R. Ruskin, ed., Prentice-Hall, Englewood Cliffs, N.J., 1971.

11. B.W. Boehm, "A Spiral Model of Software Development and Enhancement," 1985, TRW tech. report 21-371-85, TRW, Inc., 1 Space Park, Redondo Beach, CA 90278.

12. H. Sackman, W.J. Erikson, and E.E. Grant, "Exploratory Experimental Studies Comparing Online and Offline Programming Performance," *CACM,* Vol. 11, No. 1, Jan. 1968, pp. 3-11.

Chapter 2

System and Software System Engineering

1. Introduction to Chapter

Figure 2.1 reflects the interfaces of three related disciplines; system engineering, software system engineering, and software engineering.

System engineering is the overall technical management of a system development project. It is a logical sequence of activities and decisions that transform an operational need to a description of system configuration. The product of system engineering is documents, not physical systems. System engineering includes:

- Problem definition
- Solution analysis
- Process planning
- Process control
- Product evaluation

Software system engineering is concerned with the development of software using the same mechanism and approach as system engineering, that is, the logical sequence of activities and decisions that transform an operational need to a description of a software system and its documentation. Software system engineering is a relatively new concept, probably less than ten years old, and as a result is not as well defined as system engineering. Software system engineering (similarly to system engineering) includes:

- Requirements analysis and specifications
- Software design
- Process planning
- Process control
- Software verification, validation, and testing

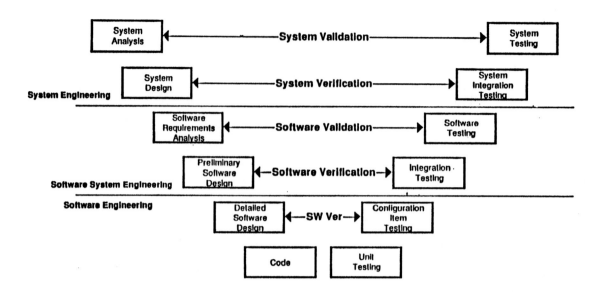

Figure 2.1. System and software system engineering process model

Software engineering has been defined as the practical application of computer science and other disciplines to the analysis, design, construction, and maintenance of the software and the associated documentation. It can also be considered to be the systematic application of methods, tools, and techniques to achieve its stated requirements objective for a software system.

Software engineering is built on the concepts of system engineering. Several authors (such as Andriole and Freeman [see paper in this chapter] and Sage and Palmer [1]) have recently argued for the use of the term *software system engineering* as a replacement for the term *software engineering*. This tutorial will take the more conservative viewpoint and refer to software development, either at the system level or at the detail level, as the more conventional *software engineering*. Much thought was given, however, to titling this IEEE tutorial *Software System Engineering*, and the importance of software system engineering in the software development process cannot be overemphasized [2]:

> System engineering and software system engineering are often overlooked in a software development project. Systems that are all software and/or run on commercial, off-the-shelf computers are often considered just software projects, not system projects, and no effort is expended to develop a system engineering approach. Ignoring the systems aspects of the project often results in software that will not run on or with the hardware selected, will not integrate with hardware and other software systems, and frequently contributes to the so-called "software crisis."

2.   Introduction to Papers

The first short paper, "Engineering a Small System," by Kurt Skytte, introduces the concept of system engineering. He argues that system engineering, once done only on government projects or by large aerospace companies, can and should be applied to small systems in the commercial arena.

Skytte's intent was to describe how system engineering can be applied to "small" systems. The author, and the editors of this Tutorial, believe that it provides a very good outline for applying system engineering to a system of any size.

The paper by Stephen Andriole and Peter Freeman on "Software System Engineering: The Case for New Discipline" is one of the few papers that shows a relationship between system engineering and software engineering. The authors propose that software engineering and system engineering be integrated into a concept called "software system engineering." As the Tutorial editors have already stated, it is clear that software engineering developed from system engineering in the early 1960s and 1970s. The editors therefore concur with the concept of developing software through the software system engineering methodology.

The third paper, "The Concept of Operations: The Bridge From Operational Requirements To Technical Specifications," was written by Richard Fairley and Richard Thayer. (Thayer is one of the Tutorial editors.) This paper presents the relatively new concept of developing a "needs" document that bridges the gap between the customer and the more formal software requirements specifications. This paper describes the role of the *concept of operations* (ConOps) document in the specification and development of a software-intensive system. It also describes the process of developing a ConOps, its uses and benefits, who should develop it, and when it should be developed. The paper compares the ConOps to other forms of operational concept documents. A detailed outline of the ConOps document is provided as an appendix to the paper.

1. Sage, Andrew P. and James D. Palmer, *Software System Engineering*, John Wiley & Sons, Inc., New York, 1990.

2. Thayer, Richard H., and Winston W. Royce, "Software System Engineering," in *"Tutorial: System and Software Requirements Engineering,"* IEEE Computer Society Press, Los Alamitos, Calif., 1990.

Engineering a small system

Once the preserve of large government projects, systems engineering can benefit commercial products, as well

"Do it right the first time" is the slogan of systems engineering. The approach can benefit all types of development projects, small as well as large, because the objective is the same: to design a high-quality product as fast and efficiently as possible.

Perhaps the most cogent definition of systems engineering is given in the *1988 Chambers Science and Technology Dictionary*: "A logical process of activities which transforms a set of requirements arising from a specific mission objective into a full description of a system which fulfills the objective in an optimum way. It ensures that all aspects of a project have been considered and integrated into a consistent whole."

In other words, systems engineering translates a customer's stated need into a set of requirements and specifications for a system's performance and configuration. The process defines all the resources and special tools needed plus the stages in the product's development. It also sets up checkpoints at each stage in the design cycle to ensure that objectives are met and that defects are identified and corrected as early as possible, thus minimizing their impact on the development schedule and on the product's cost and quality. The final system is then validated against the original requirements and specifications.

For decades now systems-engineering techniques have been standard in the U.S. Department of Defense and applied to large commercial products like airliners. But they have not been widely applied to the engineering of medium-sized or relatively small commercial products like medical diagnostic equipment or industrial test and measurement instruments. That situation, however, may be changing. Organizations such as the U.S. Food and Drug Administration (FDA) and the International Organization for Standardization (ISO) are establishing guidelines—for example, the ISO standard 9001—on how quality should be addressed during the development of products. A development process based on the analytical techniques of systems engineering also can help meet this goal.

START WITH NEEDS. Perhaps the prime assumption underpinning systems engineering is that a product should be designed to fulfill customers' actual needs; only by solving a real problem better than any competition does a product become truly successful. As identified through marketing surveys and other mechanisms, the customers' needs inspire the formal written requirements the product must fulfill. On those requirements are based the system's technical specifications, which form part of the documents that are the key references for the design.

Self-evident as this approach may seem, it is surprisingly common for companies to develop products with little or no customer input. Even when a large market exists, a product can fail when the customer's real needs are poorly understood. For example, both General Electric Ultrasound in Milwaukee, Wis., and Philips Ultrasound in Santa Ana, Calif., have introduced ultrasound medical imaging instruments that would have sold in greater numbers had the interfaces been better tailored to the needs of the intended users. The GE product put a touch screen over the image monitor—but imaging gel and other contaminants on the ultrasound technician's fingers quickly accumulated, smudging the screen and blurring the diagnostic image.

The problem with the Philips instrument was different. Ultrasound imaging instruments typically have many separate controls, and Philips sought to reduce that number by incorporating a mouse. But ultrasound technicians want to concentrate on the diagnostic image, not be distracted by computer icons, and to progress through an examination as quickly as possible. Clicking the buttons on the mouse was neither fast nor interactive enough to suit their needs.

REDUCE REDESIGN. Another assumption behind systems engineering is that the system as a whole must be carefully planned out to minimize its redesign. For a long time the largest source of project delays, redesign typically becomes necessary because the product requirements were poorly defined or changed, the engineering specifications were inferior, or the basic design's ability to meet the original requirements was not thoroughly reviewed.

The full effect of inadequate planning is rarely detected until late in the development cycle, sometimes even into the system's design validation phase. The later any design defects are detected, the more time and money any redesign will need. Moreover, late changes often compromise the product's reliability and maintenance costs, perhaps even affecting its profitability and success. Spending extra time up front completing and clarifying the basic requirements always pays high dividends in the end.

Even so, the best-written requirements can be undermined if unnecessary changes to them are allowed after design is started. During this phase, the product is often embellished in ways not specified originally. Commonly called "creeping elegance," these additions are sometimes made without an awareness that such changes may delay the schedule and add to the life-cycle costs.

In Japan, such companies as Matsushita Communication Industrial Co.'s Instrument Division in Yokohama and Toshiba American Medical Systems Inc. in Tustin, Calif., manage both to prevent and profit from creeping elegance. As new ideas or requirements surface, they are collected not for ongoing projects, but for later upgrades or new products.

To be sure, companies must at times react to market shifts or exploit some new discovery by changing product requirements, but the resulting stretchout of schedule and increase in cost should be clearly grasped and properly integrated into the product's development plan.

SPECS DRIVE DESIGN. A third essential assumption of systems engineering is that specifications for the system as a whole, as well as for the details of individual components, should direct the design process. A system-level design specification defines the system's architecture in terms of functional segments and their interfaces. Taking the time to architect the system properly can minimize the system's complexity, lower its cost, and improve its reliability, manufacturability, and serviceability. It is also important for the final top-level design and architecture to show how these objectives can be balanced in terms of life-cycle costs, not near-term objectives.

Performance specifications must also be captured so that they can be compared with measured system performance during design verification.

SCALING DOWN. Systems engineering on large government projects is rigorous and detailed. For smaller commercial applica-

Kurt Skytte   AnalySys Consulting Inc.

Reprinted from *IEEE Spectrum*, Vol. 31, No. 3, Mar. 1994, pp. 63–65.

tions, it can be streamlined to reduce the overhead while retaining the benefits.

Whatever its size, though, a company using systems engineering development must proceed through six phases: requirements development, system design, detail design, system integration, system optimization, and design validation. During each phase, formal documents are written, capturing all elements of the design. These documents then become the references that drive the design process.

Phase 1: Requirements development. The first step in designing any system is identifying the objectives it must fulfill. Since life-cycle costs hinge on this early planning, enough time and resources absolutely must be allocated to researching the system's requirements.

In a commercial environment, the product's objectives should be determined by surveying the needs of potential customers. Next, a team should be formed to develop the specification describing the product's functional requirements. This team should include representatives from marketing, engineering, manufacturing, field service, and any other group that will influence the system's functions and life-cycle costs.

The specification should cover each of the system's required functions in detail, including a description of the user interfaces with

objectives for response time, types of input and output devices (visual or auditory), and any application-specific information that relates ergonomic requirements to the typical user's environment. Each function must be associated with a specific type of control, and each requirement for user feedback must be associated with an output device. The functional-requirement specification, however, defines only *what* has to be designed into the product, not *how* it is to be designed.

One of the trickier aspects of this first phase is determining which features and functions are of the most value to the product. The first draft of a functional specification for a new product often resembles an indiscriminate list of features found in existing products. One way to identify the most valuable features is to use quality function deployment (QFD), a technique that—through developing a series of matrices—can help rank product attributes in order of their importance to the customer. Understanding which of these attributes matter most will aid the team in making sound decisions when tradeoffs must be made.

The functional-requirement specification is complete when the project team is willing to commit itself to a set of functions, recognizing that the completeness of the document describing them is vital to the quality

of the final system, and that any changes made to the document after it is released to the design engineers will directly affect product quality, production schedule, and life-cycle costs.

Phase 2: System design. The next step ' is to translate the completed functional requirements into an architecture and a set of system-level design specifications that together meet the original customer needs. It is essential now to translate all the functional requirements into design specifications, making sure that none is overlooked.

The architecture document must identify each subsystem and component, specify all the intended relationships among them, and delineate clearly how each will fulfill one of the documented functional requirements. Performance requirements should be specified quantitatively, in terms that can be measured in the final system.

For any small project, such as an instrument containing only a couple of circuit boards, writing a single system-level specification may suffice. For a larger project, such as a medical ultrasound imaging system, it is preferable to have one top-level document specify the system's architecture and performance requirements, and separate specifications define the functional and performance requirements for each subsystem. The subsystem specifications would also identify and specify the requirements for each circuit board within the subsystem.

One of the more perplexing aspects of the system-design phase is the proper allocation of functions to hardware and software. If that allocation is suboptimal, the product may end up with overly expensive hardware or overly complex software. For an intricate system such as an ultrasound imaging system, computer-aided engineering (CAE) tools are useful for comparing choices of implementation, developing critical performance specifications, and verifying signal-processing algorithms before starting the designs of subsystems and components.

Ideally, a single simulation tool would address all the necessary levels of simulation from behavior modeling through algorithm development and down to the level of hardware details. But currently, different CAE tools must address those needs [see table at right]. Any modeling or simulations begun during this phase should be revisited later to optimize the system's performance.

Part of the system-design phase is to develop a plan for the integration of the system. This plan should define the order in which the components will be assembled into larger units, whose function will be verified before proceeding to the next step in the assembly. The plan should identify the acceptance criteria for hardware (such as printed-circuit boards and other components) and software for those units, identify any needs for special test fixtures or tools, and assess the number of support personnel required to complete the assembly.

For more complex systems, a coordinated

Systems-engineering checklist

Here is a checklist of the steps essential to applying systems-engineering principles to the design of smaller commercial products:

Requirements phase
- Consult potential customers to ascertain their actual needs.
- Have a multidisciplinary project team take that statement of needs and use it to develop a detailed specification describing the product's functional requirements.

System-design phase
- Develop a system architecture that supports specified product requirements.
- Develop system-design specifications that document the system's architecture, system-level performance specifications, and the functional requirements of each subsystem and component.
- If necessary, use simulations and other analytical techniques to verify that top-level design concepts support all specified product requirements.
- Define the system's life-cycle cost model.

Detail design phase
- Design the hardware and software as described in the system-design specifications.
- Schedule several detail-design reviews to make quite sure that the hardware and software meet the specifications.
- Build and test each component to verify that the design objectives have been met.
- Develop plans for integrating the components and subsystems into the entire system, and for testing the system.
- Compare the actual costs of designing the hardware and software with the cost estimates to verify that cost objectives are being met.

System integration phase
- Integrate the components and subsystems into a prototype system and verify its functionality.

Design verification and optimization phase
- Verify that all performance specifications are met over all specified operating conditions.
- Optimize the system's design by minimizing any differences found between expected and measured performance.

System validation phase
- Evaluate the final product's configuration to ensure that it complies with the original functional-requirements specification.

test plan helps ensure that any special resources or equipment will be on hand to test and optimize the system. For efficiency, this plan should identify key performance benchmarks.

Phase 3: Detail design. Now, and only now, do engineers begin to design the hardware and software that will implement the top system-level specifications. Every aspect of these designs should be documented by drawings and written descriptions, which will ultimately support the development and manufacturing processes. From the detail-design phase emerge tested and verified components ready for integration into the system.

The design teams should use the system-level design specifications as the primary technical reference for all designs. Moreover, several times during the detail-design phase, the designs should be reviewed against the systems-level specification to see that its objectives are being met.

Phase 4: System integration. At last, it is time to put all the components and subsystems together. They should be assembled in the order defined by the integration plan, which was mapped out during the system-design phase, and verified to work.

Phase 5: Design verification and optimization. After it has been established that the system works properly, it is necessary to test that it performs just like or better than the requirements of the system-design specification. If the system was properly designed, the scope and range of the optimization parameters should be embedded within the control software or hardware so that adjustments are easy. The system is optimized when differences between the expected and measured performance of all its functions have been minimized.

Phase 6: System validation. Finally, it is time to ensure that the final system design complies with the functional-requirements specification. This is the last overall check of the system before its design is released to manufacturing.

Every state of the machine and every function described in the original functional requirements must be tested to validate the system. Since today most systems have some kind of embedded computer, functionality is usually dictated by the control software and much of the validation is bound up with the testing of the software design. Every time the software is modified or changed, the system must be re-validated. In fact, the ability to validate a system design quickly can enhance its upgradeability and maintainability. Automated test tools that can simulate user inputs and then monitor for correct responses can speed this process.

BEYOND CONCURRENT ENGINEERING. A well-conceived systems-engineering process shares some of the same development objectives as concurrent engineering. Premised on multidisciplinary project teams, concurrent engineering helps to ensure that all elements of the product life cycle are factored into the design, and overlaps development phases whenever possible to save time.

In some ways systems engineering may be viewed as a refinement of concurrent engineering. It takes the basic concept of multidisciplinary design teams and adds to it guidelines for formal development phases.

By adopting a structured approach to development that is scaled to the needs of the project, it is possible to eliminate some of the remaining sources of design defects and development risks. Development time is further shortened, and product quality and profitability are enhanced.

TO PROBE FURTHER. Because the use of system engineering principles in developing modest-sized commercial products is a fairly new concept, information on it must be taken from more general systems-engineering sources. The National Council on Systems Engineering (NCOSE) has established a working group to specifically address commercial systems-engineering practices; contact NCOSE at 333 Cobalt Way, Suite 107, Sunnyvale, CA 94086.

Benjamin S. Blanchard and Walter J. Fabrycky's textbook *Systems Engineering and Analysis* (Prentice Hall, Englewood Cliffs, N.J., 1990) is an excellent overview of systems-engineering concepts, design methods, and commonly used analytical tools.

All aspiring system architects should also read Eberhardt Rechtin's classic *Systems Architecting: Creating and Building Complex Systems* (Prentice Hall, Englewood Cliffs, N. J., 1991), which defines the role and responsibilities of the system architect and lists what knowledge, skill, and other pertinent traits are required. Rechtin's article "The Art of Systems Architecting" (*IEEE Spectrum*, October 1992, pp. 66–69) introduces a number of design heuristics that can be used, along with analytical techniques, to develop the architectures for systems.

The author wishes to thank Michael Brendel and Christopher Chapman of Siemens Medical Systems Inc. (Ultrasound Group), Issaquah, Wash., for their helpful insights. ◆

ABOUT THE AUTHOR. Kurt Skytte is the president of AnalySys Consulting, in Alamo, Calif., which specializes in consulting for the development of medical and analytical instruments. Before founding AnalySys Consulting, he was systems engineering manager at Siemens Ultrasound Inc. from 1986 to 1992. Before going to Siemens, he was a hardware design engineer and project leader for the Instrument Division of Varian Associates in Walnut Creek, Calif., for six years.

Tools for computer-aided systems-engineering design

Company	Product name	Development of requirements	Simulation and modeling	High-level software modeling and development	DSP simulations	Algorithm development
International TechneGroup Inc. Milford, Ohio	QFD/Capture	●				
Ascent Logic Corp. San Jose, Calif.	RDD		●			
I-Logix Inc. Santa Clara, Calif.	Statemate		●			
General Electric Co. King of Prussia, Pa.	OMTool			●		
Interactive Development Environments Inc. San Francisco	Software Through Pictures		●	●		
Popkin Software & Systems Inc. New York City	System Architect		●	●		
ProtoSoft Inc. Houston, Texas	Paradigm Plus			●		
Comdisco Systems Inc. Foster City, Calif.	SPW		●		●	●
Mathworks Inc. Natick, Mass.	Matlab				●	●
Mentor Graphics Corp. San Jose, Calif.	DSP Station		●		●	●
Signal Technology Inc. Santa Barbara, Calif.	NIPower		●		●	●

DSP = digital signal processing. Source: Kurt Skytte

Software systems engineering: the case for a new discipline

by Stephen J. Andriole and Peter A. Freeman

One of the hallmarks of the modern world is the creation of complex systems. The discipline of systems engineering is often utilised in this activity and, as many of these systems are also software-intensive, the discipline of software engineering becomes one of the critical technologies that must be utilised. In these cases, both disciplines address the same subject, the creation of complex software-intensive systems, albeit from different perspectives. In this paper, we examine the current state of each discipline, analyse and compare each along several dimensions, and conclude by presenting the case for a new discipline, *software systems engineering*, which combines the essential elements of both disciplines.

1 Introduction

Our working premise is simple; software-intensive systems (regardless of their application domains) are among the most important, yet hardest to create and maintain, artifacts of modern society. Thirty years ago, there were few large-scale software-intensive systems. Today they pervade the public and private sectors. We now live with a systems infrastructure that is sometimes nearly impossible to maintain. We often spend too much for too little increase in functionality and quality, and seem to learn relatively little from our mistakes. Despite every effort to enhance the process, we have, in fact, created a 'software crisis'.

Our interest here is in improving the development of software-intensive systems. As researchers, educators and practitioners, we have found that a systematic approach to the overall task, such as that provided by the discipline of *systems* engineering, is necessary. We have also observed that, when the creation or modification of software is a part of the task, additional systematic procedures, such as those provided by *software* engineering, are necessary. In short, we have found that the creation of software-intensive systems demands more than what is traditionally in either of the fields. Although there is no shortage of references that describe software engineering [1] or systems engineer-

ing [2], there are only a few [3] that have looked at the intersection. Our purpose here is to continue the analysis of the intersection; in the process, we hope to outline the terms of a productive marriage.

2 Definitions

Modern homes represent complex systems that could not have been designed or constructed by one professional. Software-intensive systems are similarly complex, although they are often designed, developed and maintained by professionals with narrow disciplinary perspectives. An information system for naïve users, who have to input, locate and route documents, should not be designed and developed by programmers, computer scientists, cognitive psychologists, or electrical engineers, but by all of these, and perhaps other professionals.

We noted above that it sometimes seems that, as a discipline, we are not learning from our experience. We believe this flat learning curve is traceable to our unwillingness to pluralise the systems design process. It is dangerous to see systems only from the bottom-up or from the top-down, only as a programmer or only as a psychologist. It is essential that we redefine the systems analysis, modelling, design, and development processes from a multidisciplinary perspective.

Systems engineering is a problem-solving process with roots in behavioural, computer, engineering, management and mathematical sciences. According to at least one source [4], the systems engineering process is a

'... *logical sequence of activities and decisions transforming an operational need into a description of system performance parameters and a preferred system configuration ...*'

The US federal government has developed a systems engineering 'standard' [4] definition:

'*Systems engineering is the application of scientific and engineering efforts to (a) transform operational need into a description of system performance parameters and a system configuration through the use of an iterating process of definition, synthesis, analysis, design, test, and evaluation; (b) integrate related technical* parameters and ensure compatibility of all physical, functional, and program interfaces in a manner that optimizes the total system definition and design; (c) integrate reliability, maintainability, safety, survivability, human, and other such factors into the total engineering effort to meet cost, schedule, and technical performance objectives.'

Eisner [5] defines systems engineering as 'an iterative process of top-down synthesis, development, and operation of a real-world system that satisfies, in a near optimal manner, the full range of requirements for the system'. In fact, most definitions of systems engineering [2, 5–9] focus on the process by which operational needs and specific requirements are converted into working systems against a backdrop of cost, time and talent constraints.

Software engineering cannot claim a widely held definition. The definition first stated by Naur and Randall [10] still captures the overall pattern of the field (and is used, for example, by Pressman [1]):

'The establishment and use of sound engineering principles in order to obtain economically software that is reliable and works efficiently on real machines.'

Boehm [11] echoes this definition:

'Software engineering is the application of science and mathematics by which the capabilities of computer equipment are made useful to man via computer programs, procedures, and associated documentation.'

Boehm's mention of mathematics foreshadows today's increasing emphasis on formal methods and, in fact, provides a tie to the non-engineering view of the creation of software as a mathematical activity. The mathematical definition of software creation is, in our view, a valid viewpoint within the realm of programming and program design, but its scope does not encompass the full range of issues with which software engineering must deal. Mills [12] notes that software engineering is between systems engineering and systems integration, is focused on software-intensive systems, and involves a mathematically disciplined design process. This view, and the work that he pioneered at IBM, is perhaps the best documented instance of a software engineering methodology.

The operational definition that we have used [13] for some years, and the one that we endorse here, is concisely stated as follows:

'Software engineering is the systematic application of methods, tools, and knowledge to achieve stated technical, economic, and human objectives for a software-intensive system.'

3 Scope of the disciplines

The creation of a complex artifact involves both time duration and a wide range of activities. These two dimensions (time and activity) provide a framework for describing the scope of a discipline.

Time duration is bounded by the time before which a system does not exist and the time after which it no longer

exists (or is out of service and of no interest). Within these extremes, there are four major time divisions:

- pre-development;
- initial development;
- operation-and-modification;
- decommissioning.

Activities present a harder subject to explicate. To provide some structure, we have chosen the following framework of activities associated with the creation of software-intensive systems:

☐ purely technical activities:
- creating technical work products (such as designs or test plans);
- modifying existing technical work products;
- studying work products to derive some information (e.g. producing a scenario from a requirements specification or testing a program);

☐ purely managerial activities:

- planning;
- acquiring resources;
- allocating resources;
- controlling;
- evaluating;

☐ ancillary/mixed activities:
- producing, modifying, studying non-technical work product (such as user documentation or needs statements);
- requirements engineering;
- acceptance testing;
- training;
- support (such as tool building, travel, physical space planning).

3.1 Time and activities scope of systems engineering

In many respects, *systems engineering* is a composite field that borrows from a wide range of areas and formal disciplines. Without these contributions, the field itself could not exist; yet without the organising systems engineering life-cycle, they remain unco-ordinated islands of expertise.

Systems engineering is also domain-independent. The design and development principles are generic. They have been applied to any number of substantive problems. Systems engineering is thus, to some people, a meta-design strategy, more than a tactical course of action. In truth, the process directly addresses both objectives.

The state-of-the-art is difficult to assess in either a methodological or applications vacuum. Some aspects of systems engineering have evolved more impressively than others. The process by which system requirements are identified, modelled and validated, for example, has evolved dramatically over the past two decades. Today it is commonplace to hear about the 'requirements engineering' process, where a set of qualitative and quantitative tools are used to elicit and represent systems requirements at all levels. Trade-off analyses are now conducted with the aid of several powerful techniques, such as computer-assisted cost-benefit and more qualitative multi-attribute utility assessment techniques. Suffice to say that the systems engineering process has evolved along with its core areas and disciplines, while maintaining a design whole greater than the sum of its methodological parts.

Eisner [5] regards the systems engineering process as consisting of the following 'elements'. These elements directly address *time duration* and *activities*:

- 1. requirements analysis;
- 2. requirements allocations;
- 3. functional analysis;
- 4. functional allocation;
- 5. specification analysis;
- 6. specification allocation;
- 7. specification development;
- 8. preliminary design:
    - A. system level;
    - B. sub-system level;
- 9. interface definition;
- 10. schedule development;
- 11. preliminary cost-analysis;
- 12. technical performance measurement;
- 13. trade-off/alternative analysis;
- 14. pre-planned product improvement;
- 15. final design:
    - A. system level;
    - B. sub-system level;
- 16. schedule update;
- 17. cost update;
- 18. fabrication;
- 19. coding;
- 20. preliminary testing;
- 21. debugging and reconfiguration;
- 22. testing and integration;
- 23. updates:
    - A. schedule;
    - B. cost;
    - C. technical performance measurement;
- 24. documentation;
- 25. training;
- 26. production.

The US government's 'Systems engineering management guide' [14] describes the process in detail. Eisner presents a graphic look at the process in Fig. 1.

In terms of the four major *time dimensions* identified above, systems engineering is concerned with all phases of the systems design and development process. Systems engineers are concerned with the pre-development phase, especially as it pertains to the identification and verification of system requirements. Systems engineers design and develop prototypes during the initial (and subsequent) development phases, especially as they pertain to the operation and modification of systems. Systems engineers are even concerned with the decommissioning of systems as decommissioned systems are the springboard to new generation systems.

The *activities* taxonomy maps directly onto the systems engineering process. Systems engineers are at once scientists, technologists and managers. In practice, of course, it is difficult to find such talent in one or two professionals.

The intersection of technical and managerial activities presumes the conversion of requirements into working systems. The systems engineering process represents the integration and synthesis of tools, techniques, methods and findings for the explicit purpose of fielding operational systems.

One of the key differences between software engineering and systems engineering is the extent to which managerial activities are pursued and integrated with technical ones. Whereas software engineers worry a great deal about software project management, they tend to restrict their concern to those technical activities connected with the design and development of software. The systems engineer, even for a software-intensive system, worries about all the system components and how to manage their technical development.

3.2 Time and activities scope of software engineering

When we look at the *time scope* of software engineering, it is no surprise to find that its focus is on the initial phase, with emerging interest in the pre-development time frame. *Pre-development* (including needs analysis, requirements analysis, project planning etc. that go on before technical development can begin) is a phase in the systems life-cycle in which software engineers are becoming increasingly involved (a phase, as suggested above, that has preoccupied systems engineering since its inception). The methods of software engineering are intended to assist in those aspects of the requirements engineering process that deal with software, especially when it comes to validating those requirements and turning them into technical specifications that trigger technical development.

Initial development is the phase in the life-cycle of a system in which it first comes into 'tangible' being. In the case of software-intensive systems, this typically involves turning requirements into software specifications, creating architectural and detailed designs for the software systems, programming, testing, and integration of the software, not only internally, but also with the hardware.

The *operation and modification* phase in a system's life-cycle is not addressed by software engineering, except with respect to the modification of existing systems about which it has a good deal to say.

Decommissioning of software-intensive systems for the most part is a relatively trivial phase (as far as the software aspect is concerned) and one of which there is very little experience. Software engineering does not address this phase of a system's life-cycle.

When we turn to the range of *activities* encompassed by software engineering, the situation is not as clear, at least in part because non-technical activities tend to be ill defined.

In the area of purely managerial activities, software engineering provides the mechanisms for dealing with project resources in some cases (estimation techniques, configuration management, performance measurement), but does not (for the most part) address how those mechanisms should be used in the overall organisation of a project. The one exception to this is in the area of technical project management, where specific techniques and models of the software development process are often

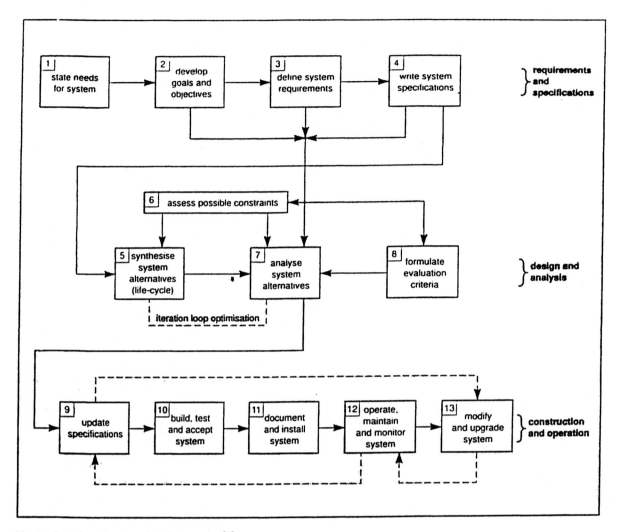

Fig. 1   Generic systems engineering process [5]

incorporated into elements of the software engineering discipline.

When we look at the ancillary/mixed activities, we find that software engineering does not, for example, address general issues of training, but clearly incorporates work on training software engineers. In the case of requirements engineering, acceptance testing and work on non-technical work products, software engineering as a discipline tries to deal with such activities from the technical aspect, without claiming total purview. In the area of support, software engineering involvement ranges from almost total in the case of tools to nothing in the case of travel or physical space planning.

A major theme of software engineering (in its short history) has been the search for the 'right' development life-cycle model to guide the process of creating software. The most widely known is the so-called 'waterfall' model shown in Fig. 2. First introduced by Royce [15] and popularised by Boehm [11], it describes the generic process that many software engineers follow, at least to some extent. Much criticism of the waterfall model has ensued, however, which has resulted in more refined models. One of the more popular of these, also from Boehm [16], is shown in Fig. 3. Boehm's 'spiral model' stresses prototyping and risk assessment, two relatively new concepts to

software engineering (although quite familiar for decades to systems engineers).

3.3   Comparative scopes

Fig. 4 compares the level of involvement of software engineering and systems engineering over the time frame of a system's life. Of particular interest here is the relative emphasis that systems engineering places on the front-end requirements analysis, modelling and validation processes (often via prototyping). Systems engineers tend to spend much more time and effort on requirements than software engineers, although it is certainly true that software engineers have begun to appreciate the importance of needs analysis, user requirements modelling, and organisational requirements profiling.

4   Structure of the disciplines

One means of analysing and understanding a discipline is to look at its structural parts, its *processes* and *objects*. It is also useful to consider *constraints*, *paradigms* and *principles*.

32

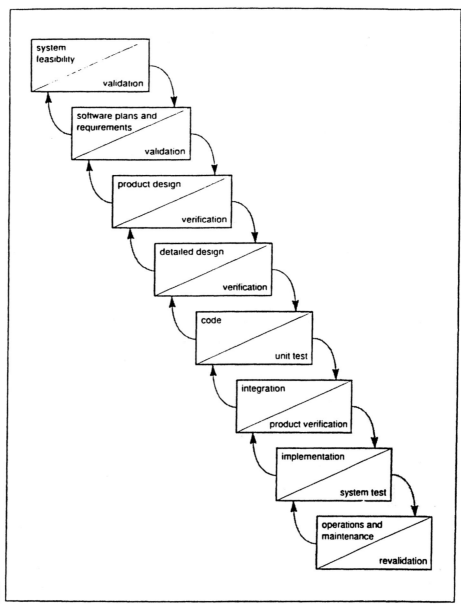

Fig. 2 Waterfall
life-cycle model [16]

4.1 Systems engineering structure

Fig. 1 from Eisner [5] presents the generic *systems engineering* process, which is reduced to three major activities: requirements and specifications, design and analysis, and construction and operation. Eisner suggests that the system engineering process is inextricably tied to technical project management, as proposed in Fig. 5. Note that Eisner locates the generic systems engineering process between technical program planning and control and a set of engineering speciality areas.

As suggested above, systems engineering is domain-independent and -driven. The systems engineering process, with its attendant 'principles' (see below), can be applied to transportation, space, weapons, command and control, urban, and, of course, information and software systems engineering problems.

The intersection between management and technology also often poses problems. What plays well in the technical 'trenches' often violates some managerial *constraints*. Systems engineers have difficulty with projecting precisely how much time and money it will take to implement design A over design B. It is also sometimes difficult to 'size up' from a prototype to a working system.

What are the systems engineering 'watchwords', the key influential *principles*? The first principle is system and user requirements specification. Multidisciplinary systems engineering (MSE) calls for the identification, definition and validation of requirements on multiple levels that suggest how requirements interrelate and how they might be satisfied through design. Note again that this is a pre-design principle.

Another key principle is iteration or the recognition that it is impossible to capture requirements the first time through a system concept. MSE assumes the need for iteration, in all phases of the design and development process. Rapid prototyping assumes the need to iterate on user requirements, alternative system concepts, software

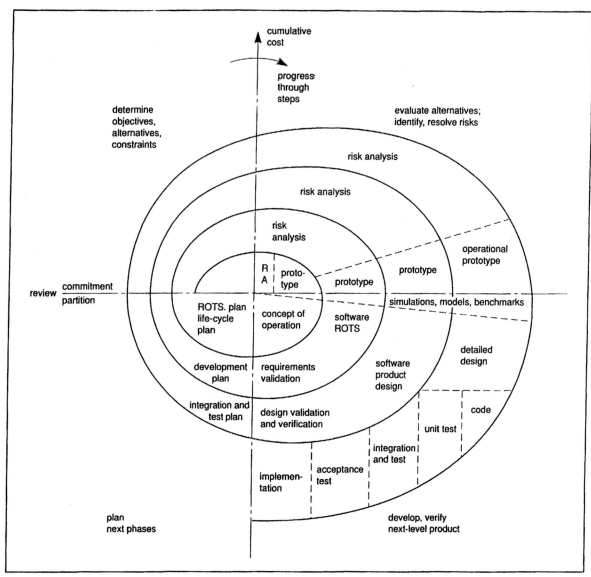

Fig. 3 Spiral model of the software process [11]

requirements, testing and evaluation and even documentation.

Yet another key concept is synthesis or the ability to integrate disparate components into a coherent cost-effective whole greater than the sum of the components. The process of creative synthesis has been described elsewhere [17] but not formally represented. Although there are steps that suggest what and where to synthesise elements of the design, there are far fewer guidelines for instructing the information systems engineer about how to proceed. Nevertheless, synthesis remains an important part of the MSE process and one that is well suited to a multidisciplinary perspective.

Trade-off analysis is always part of the MSE process. The mix among requirements, constraints and alternative designs yields a continuous need to evaluate, prioritise, and test. Which interface should we use and why? Why not use the other one? What about the software language; why C and not Ada? Which requirement is more important and why? How do we rank requirements? How do we weigh the importance of the evaluative criteria?

Last, but certainly not least, is the essential need to remain as multidisciplinary as possible. This calls for expertise that cuts across the social, behavioural, computer, mathematical, engineering, management, and even physical sciences. Note, however, that information systems engineers cannot be expected to know all there is to know about these fields and disciplines; an attitude that accepts contributions, regardless of their disciplinary race, creed or religion, is what keeps the door open to creative problem-solving. Systems engineers whose staff are clones of themselves will fail far more often than when their staff are from backgrounds of diverse experience and opinion. Maintaining inventories of analytical methods organised around the MSE cycle is another good idea. The key is to make certain that you have looked beyond the obvious or what you have done (over and over again) before; analytical inertia is not necessarily your friend.

The working *paradigm* is not Kuhnian [18] in a strict sense, nor is it easily definable from any perspective. Systems engineers practise a process that is iterative, multidisciplinary and flexible. They borrow from many

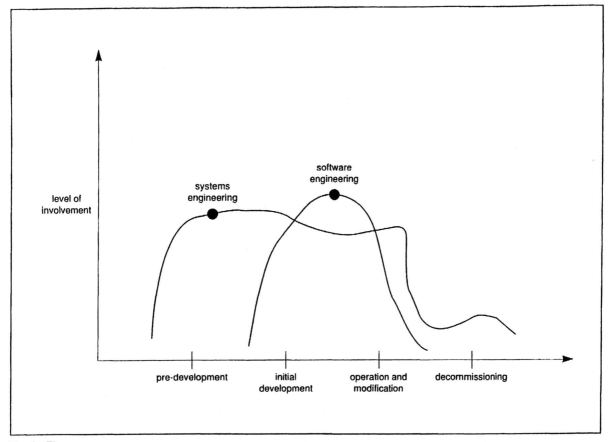

Fig. 4   Time scope

fields and disciplines. Their creed is essentially practical, although they respect the need for basic research to keep their applied tools honed.

4.2   Software engineering structure

A widely used software engineering textbook [1] implicitly specifies the *processes* of software engineering:

- needs analysis
- requirements analysis
- specification
- architectural design
- detailed design
- programming
- unit testing
- integration testing
- management
- documentation
- performance analysis
- program analysis.

The Ada Methodman study, which represented the thinking of many people in the US Department of Defense world at that time, identified eight basic processes of software development:

- ☐ analysis
- ☐ functional specification
- ☐ design

- ☐ implementation
- ☐ validation
- ☐ evolution
- ☐ management
- ☐ communication.

A more conceptual treatment [13] views all of software engineering as the following basic processes that manipulate representations:

- choose locale and operation.
- gather external information.
- change representation.
- extract information from representation.
- evaluate representation.

Lehman *et al.* [19] take a similar, but more formal, approach to model the processes of software engineering as a set of transformations. Likewise, Kerola [20] and those who have extended his work [21] focus on the intellectual activities that a system developer employs in the course of creating a system.

We try not to consolidate or reconcile these different views here. We can move forward with our structural analysis, however, by positing a set of 'basic' processes that capture the mainstream view of what is going on (at the technical level) in software engineering. They include

- ☐ *analysis*: understanding something by separating it into component parts.

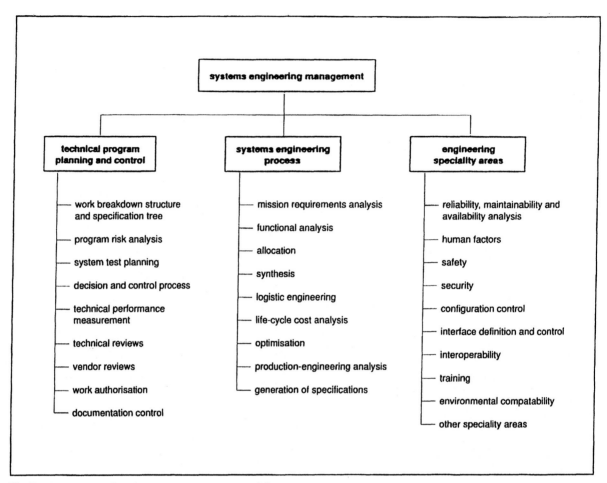

Fig. 5   A systems engineering management structure [5]

☐ *specification*: describing something by its external characteristics.

☐ *design*: devising an artifact that meets a set of objectives.

☐ *programming*: building a coherent set of instructions for a processor that will cause it to exhibit a desired behaviour.

☐ *testing*: determining empirically if an artifact meets a stated set of specifications.

☐ *verification*: determining if a step in the development process has been correctly carried out.

☐ *validation*: determining if a description of a system, or the system itself, properly meets the expectations of the customer.

☐ *modification* (*commonly called 'maintenance'*): making changes to an existing artifact.

A generally held view is that software engineering must address all of the *objects* of importance in the technical development of software, including (but not limited to) specifications, designs, programs, test results and project schedules. There is again active research underway concerned with devising effective repositories for all the 'project information' in development; this work is usually associated with work on development environments. As with processes, however, we can provide a schema for describing the objects that must be dealt with by software engineering:

● *development prologues*: needs statements, requirements specifications etc.

● *technical system descriptions*: specifications, designs, data descriptions etc.

● *system aggregations*: systems, integrated hardware and software etc.

● *installed systems*: base-line systems, versions etc.

● *derived information*: operating measurements, error reports etc.

A fundamental concern in any system of action is what are the constraints against the arbitrary application of processes to objects. In the case of software engineering, there are several generic constraints:

☐ incompleteness of most software representations.
☐ inaccuracy of many software representations.
☐ absence of robust models of standard systems.
☐ paucity of observed data concerning the results of software engineering processes.
☐ inability to observe many things of interest.
☐ incomplete and changing map between reality and models of reality.

As with the objects and processes of software engineering, the newness of the field and the relative sparsity of theoretical/conceptual work means that there is no widespread agreement on 'fundamental' *principles*. The following, however, would probably appear on most lists:

- modularity
- information-hiding
- abstraction
- step-wise refinement
- decomposition
- systematic processes.

Similarly, the *paradigms*, or overall patterns of action, of software engineering are limited at this juncture:

☐ reticulated, structured development (phases, defined work products, set relationships between activities).

☐ formal development (use of 'formal' methods wherever possible; not necessarily mutually exclusive of other paradigms).

☐ evolving development (use of prototypes; continual development).

☐ kernel development (starting with a small, central core of functionality and mechanisms, grow the desired system by accretion of additional mechanisms).

5 Depth of the disciplines

Systems engineering comprises a core process, the systems engineering technical and management life-cycle, surrounded by all of the fields and disciplines recognised by modern analytical scientists. Its depth is very much a function of the depth of the systems engineers assigned to a problem.

As a formal field, it is important to note that 'real' engineers (mechanical, electrical, chemical) sometimes wonder where systems engineering fits in the overall engineering continuum. 'Peterson's Guide to Engineering' does not place systems engineering in the engineering section; rather, systems engineering finds itself in the same section as operations research and industrial engineering.

Whereas we can date systems engineering back to the 1950s, its actual practice has come and gone over the years; there have been countless large-scale systems development projects that did not embrace the generic systems engineering (nor, for that matter, any) life-cycle. At the same time, perhaps because of some monumental failures, there is a growing appreciation for structured design and development. One measure is the number of undergraduate and graduate programs now in existence and the popularity of these programs; at the University of Virginia, for example, the systems engineering problem is the largest undergraduate program in the engineering school.

One of the problems with this field is the fear that it educates and trains professionals who are 'a mile wide and an inch deep', i.e. in its attempt to introduce as many disciplines as possible into the systems engineering process, the field has become too diffuse and too broad. Our view is that the broad, multidisciplinary perspective is precisely the strength of the field, and that practitioners who are truly free from the biases inherent in single-discipline-based solutions will always make the best problem-solvers.

As we have observed, *software engineering* is still a developing field. Specifically, there is very little 'theory' in

the sense of compact, rigorous, potentially verifiable descriptions of the essence of software engineering; very little objective data on the results of 'doing' software engineering; essentially no data describing the artifacts that are produced nor multiple paradigms for software engineers to follow; and disagreement over the value of many elements of the field. Software engineering is thus very early in its evolutionary development. Only a few ideas have been adopted and later discarded, although a few (such as structured programming) have been relegated to a position of less importance as their role became better understood. In the area of life-cycle or process modelling, there has also been a maturing in the understanding of what is needed, but in most of the technical methods of producing software, we are still dealing with first-generation ideas. (There is also disagreement over what the research agenda should contain.)

Sophistication of a field can also be evaluated in terms of the use of existing knowledge from outside the field (such as mathematics or computer science), the degree of dependence on results from other parts of the field, and the degree to which the constructs of the field address the subject matter. In this area, software engineering must also be ranked as unsophisticated (especially as compared to systems engineering, which openly trades on a multidisciplinary perspective).

Although a software engineer may use computer science extensively, the techniques of software engineering (such as structuring a system to enhance maintainability or organising testing on the basis of expected systemic payoff) do not rely heavily on any outside field. Advancement in different parts of software engineering, likewise, tend not to be too interdependent. Although we might think that producing new computer-aided software engineering (CASE) tools would be closely tied to our understanding of the nature and value of different design methods, this is not normally what happens. The last point, of how well software engineering addresses its subject, is one that must at this time (due to the lack of objective data) be largely subjective. The strongly held belief of some (including ourselves) is that the methods and principles of software engineering, when properly applied, make a significant difference and thus *do* address the problems the field is supposed to be addressing. Despite the numerous anecdotes and some quantitative data, we are nowhere near being able to assert the value of software engineering in the same way that medical science can assert the value of certain treatment protocols or drugs.

We have already noted that software engineering is not nearly as widely used as it might seem or as even the meagre objective data would indicate is sensible. A recent anonymous letter to the editor of *Software*, commenting on a previous article, provides an insight to a situation which is probably more widespread than most would care to admit:

'This project is represented to the public as state-of-the-art defense, but the simulation (and much other design) work is done in Fortran, a language originally conceived before I could drive (I'm 50 now). It runs on an operating system that was conceived before my son was (and he's a junior in dental school). It is administered by a DP group that let the default file-compare

program exist for years with a known error that caused it to report no differences for files that were in fact different. It is used by engineers who are rewarded for finding and using workarounds to get the job done rather than for fixing the real problems.'

In short, along the dimension of *usage*, software engineering is not yet very deep.

6 Requirements for a discipline to be used in the creation of software-intensive systems

The requirements for a basic and applied discipline to optimally support the design, development, testing and maintenance of software-intensive systems are many and varied. Those that we regard as essential include the following:

• the ability to indicate common alternatives for the elements of a design process over which one may have control; for example, by indicating types of design methods that can be used for detailed design or specifying what information should formally be provided to developers.
• the ability to force alternative problem-solving methods, tools and techniques onto the design process, to remain multidisciplinary in the face of single-minded solutions.
• the ability to identify, model and validate (especially user) requirements to an extent that permits communication to users and conversion to alternative forms, such as diagrams and prototypes.
• the ability to provide the means (including norms from practice) for choosing among alternatives; for example, by providing criteria that permit us to match design methods to specific types of applications, or by providing indications of current practice in building information repositories for development.
• the ability to specify in great detail, and from multiple notations, software requirements in adaptive, flexible specifications; the ability to utilise to their fullest potential available methods, techniques and computer-based tools.
• the ability to influence optimal software production methods, techniques and tools, including variants of structured programming, CASE and other environments.
• the ability to provide guidance for utilising elements, for example, by indicating how to put together multiple design methods for a complex task and what to do when they are insufficient.
• the ability to clearly delineate what subjects belong in curricula, both basic and applied, for educating/training members of the discipline; for example, by indicating that the study of design methods is included in the discipline, whereas study of the basic mathematics that may underlie them belongs to another discipline.
• the ability to characterise the artifacts that are produced by applying the discipline, both in theoretical and empirical terms; for example, designs that can be characterised in terms of prescribed properties and in terms of what is found to exist in practice.
• the ability to indicate the range and characteristics of problems (objectives) with which the approach is prepared to deal; for example, by delimiting design problems to those involving the design of software and procedures, but excluding those concerned with the design of business organisations.
• the ability to provide measures and standards by which the artifacts produced and the processes utilised can be measured; for example, by providing measurable quality criteria for a design, along with expected norms for those criteria.
• the ability to review its own theory and practice to feed the processes of metrics development, research agenda setting, and educational and training program development.

The assumption made here is that it is possible to define a field in terms of activity/process/object-based requirements; the above list attempts to develop such a set of 'living' requirements.

7 Comparative advantages and suggested syntheses

Table 1 shows how well (or badly) systems engineering and software engineering currently satisfy the above requirements. We have used a simple (H/high, M/medium, L/low) scaling of the state of each discipline's capabilities. Much more importantly, however, the Table was developed to assist in the synthesis of strengths from the two disciplines. (The two *major* differences are highlighted in **bold italic**; 'minor' differences are in **bold** only.)

It is interesting that the most diagnostic requirements for software systems engineering appear to be those that address the front-end of the systems design and development process. This is consistent with the findings of a number of field studies of why systems fail and with perceptions of major problems with the requirements analysis, modelling, prototyping and verification processes; problems that systems engineers have recognised, and addressed, for years. Where structured criteria-based qualitative and quantitative trade-off analysis has been an essential part of the systems engineering process, it is only considered critical to a handful of today's software engineers.

This 'finding' is extremely important as (perhaps harshly) it can be said that software engineers have not (lip service to the contrary) spent a great deal of time on front-end system and user requirements identification, definition, or validation. Instead, there has been a desire to 'get coding' as soon as possible. Consequently, there are a large number of 'failures' that can be traced directly to inadequate requirements analyses. Software engineers have also historically avoided the systematic development and evaluation of alternative definitions and designs throughout the software engineering process. Criteria-based alternative design evaluation, for example, is seldom conducted by software engineers; nor is there much emphasis on prioritising requirements with reference to constraints in formal (or even informal) trade-off analyses. All such activity is automatic to systems engineering; without such activity, software engineers risk proceeding prematurely to design and coding (as has often been the case).

Table 1 also suggests the ranges of methods, tools and techniques from systems and software engineering that can complement one another, which can together create a

Table 1 Systems software engineering comparative advantages

	System engineering	Software engineering
Alternative design methods	H	M
Multidisciplinary orientation	H	L
User requirements analysis and prototyping	H	L
Criteria-based trade-off analysis	H	L
Detailed software specifications	M	H
Optimal software production	M	H
Methods integration (re-)planning	M	L
Education and training curricula	M	M
Artifact profiling	M	M
Applications range assessment	M	M
Measurements and standards	M	M
Processes/metrics introspection	M	M

more powerful discipline for converting requirements into cost-effective software-intensive systems. This is important because there are many methods, processes, models and computer-based tools that software engineers tend to over-look, and *vice versa*. The Table suggests that we look at each discipline's strengths and identify the methods, tools, processes, and techniques that explain its comparative advantage; where appropriate, these methods, models, processes, tools and techniques can be invited onto the software systems engineering team.

8 Software systems engineering

Our working premise remains that solutions are more easily found in broad disciplinary perspectives, rather than through narrow analytical lenses. The above analysis sug-gests that there will be benefits in adopting and synthe-sising the tools and techniques of systems engineering and software engineering, to yield a more powerful and adaptive approach to systems analysis, design, develop-ment, evaluation, and maintenance of software-intensive systems. For example, note that reference to systems analysis and design itself represents an expansion of the traditional role of software engineers, just as the main-tenance of software-intensive systems is an activity outside the expertise of the typical systems engineer.

In the following, we outline the new discipline at this par-ticular point in time, a snapshot of what it is, what it can do, its concerns, and how it should help prepare those who will perpetuate its application and evolution. The fol-lowing sections thus address the conceptual, operational, educational and research bases for software systems engineering.

8.1 The conceptual basis

One of the major differences between what we propose here and more conventional definitions of disciplines or fields of inquiry is its explicit commitment to practice, research *and* education. Many disciplines evolved from some key ideas, models or theorems, usually after some exotic applications, and over time developed educational

correlates. Some fields and disciplines have remained largely in academia, with relatively short, applied track records. We propose here to think about software systems engineering simultaneously as a practical, educational and research enterprise in order to enhance its relevance in all three theatres.

Fig. 6 shows the proposed conceptual basis. It organises the disciplines according to its infrastructure, enabling technologies, application modules, issues in the practice, domains, and, by implication, the educational and research activities necessary to support the evolution and application of the discipline.

8.2 The operational basis

Fig. 7 shows a proposed new life-cycle that integrates all of the above into a prescriptive agenda. It represents the dis-ciplines, analytical foci, and procedural realities (such as iteration and prototyping) that must be part of the software-intensive systems design and development process.

This life-cycle bears a resemblance to Boehm's spiral model [16] as a graphical device to represent the fact that the software systems engineer must make multiple passes through similar activities (concept development, prototyp-ing, specification, design, implementation in the next level of technology). It also can trace some heritage back to Kerola [20] and others who first observed that system development involves a set of basic activities, such as plan-ning, design, implementation, and testing, all of which are in operation (to some extent) throughout the life-cycle, being repeated with different emphases and contexts.

Looking down the time axis, the four quadrants rep-resent four major collections of system development activ-ities: goal setting, planning, design and construction. Each of these is an abstraction for a myriad of development activities, some of which span two quadrants. Depending on the position on the time axis, these activities take on different specific meanings. For example, needs analysis (labelled here as a 'goal setting' activity) at early stages of development is concerned with understanding the needs of the entire context in which a proposed system will be

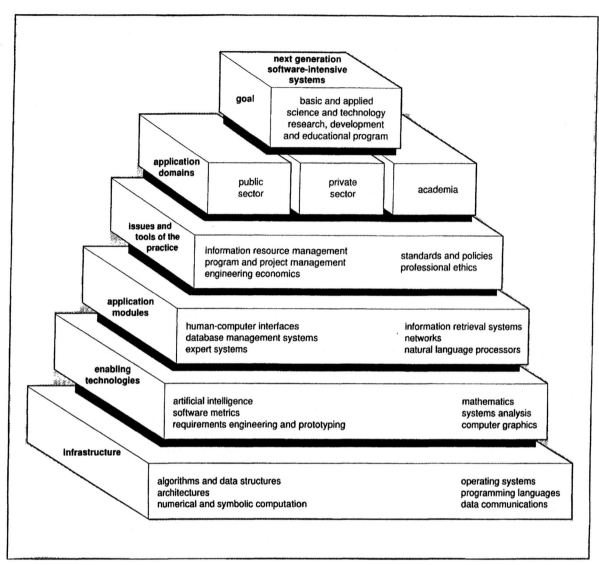

Fig. 6 The conceptual basis of software systems engineering,

embedded (thus involving potential owners, clients, users and operators of the system). At later stages of development, however, the needs analysis activities might be concerned with determining the needs of a VDT operator (thus involving psychologists, terminal operators and medical experts).

The following definitions are intended to provide a non-exclusive outline of the activities that might be found in each quadrant.

☐ *Goal setting* includes enterprise analysis, mission 'planning', needs analysis and most of the activities often associated with requirements engineering. Goal setting is front-end intensive and oriented to most aspects of the initial requirements analysis process.

☐ *Planning* includes those activities that focus on or directly affect a large amount of development work, until the next planning phase appears in the life-cycle. This includes prototyping, which provides fundamental information to help us decide how to proceed, project planning, which lays out detailed work schedules, and specification

activities, which provide the detailed 'work orders' for future work.

☐ *Design* includes those activities that devise the structures (orgnisational, hardware of all sorts, software, procedural) which, when implemented, will provide the suitably constrained functionality needed to meet the goals. We differentiate between high-level (architectural) and detailed design. Crossing into the construction realm are those activities concerned with individual components. In the case of software, this is the detailed programming activity.

☐ *Construction* activities include the various levels of testing which range from unit or component testing to acceptance or field testing. The various activities involved in measuring a system's performance and effects are included in this quadrant.

In the three-dimensional solid described by this life-cycle, different fields of expertise and different people can be seen to touch different quadrants at different levels (times). The volumes thus described are, of course, highly irregu-

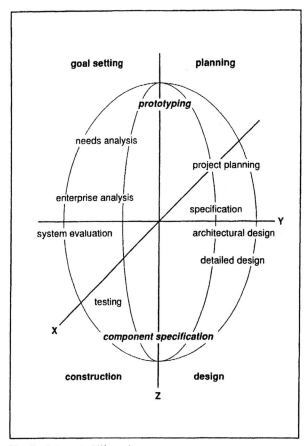

Fig. 7   Integrated life-cycle

8.3   The educational basis

The kind of educational programs necessary to sustain the discipline are today not in place. Although there are certainly institutions with broad perspectives, there are far too many institutions working well within conventional disciplinary boundaries. One of our key assumptions is that the nature of emerging software-intensive problems demands new educational programs. We believe that it will be impossible for narrowly defined disciplines to address problems that are moving more towards analytical content and away from data-oriented transactional content. Unfortunately, the nature of education and educational institutions makes change very slow.

We propose that software systems engineers should be educated using a new core program and a set of electives that crosscuts the requisite disciplines. Such a curriculum should follow the conceptual and operational bases for the field as outlined above, incorporating elements of traditional systems engineering, software engineering, behavioural, management and computer science, as well as the mathematical and engineering fundamentals necessary to those disciplines.

An essential characteristic of the curriculum is that it must prepare the student for life-long learning in and communication with other disciplines, such as management, psychology and the various traditional engineering fields. Another important aspect of the proposed curriculum is that it must be heavily experiential, focusing on the application of formal knowledge in the context of realistic development exercises.

8.4   The research basis

The research agenda should take two forms; one is a 'maintenance' agenda comprising the continuation of the fundamental research issues and questions in the discipline, and the other pushes the state-of-the-practice and the state-of-the-expectation. Fig. 8 identifies these items. The two-tier research agenda addresses the immediate and longer term futures. Like the life-cycle and the educational program, it must be flexible and adaptive to changing applications needs and emerging technology opportunities.

Fig. 8 identifies a set of research aims organised around the conceptual basis of the field presented in Fig. 7. Short-term research aims are 'maintenance' areas, and the longer term ones are part 'wish list' and part necessity. Note also that there is at least one area that appears on both lists; human–computer interaction research. There may well be others that need our immediate and continual attention.

The sort-term list includes areas such as systems and user requirements modelling, the codification of existing basic and applied knowledge, the development of quality metrics, the improvement of our evaluation and testing methods and tools, research into real-time software-intensive systems design and development, the development of computer-aided software systems engineering (CASSE) tools, and research into the promise of conceptual and algorithmic reuse etc. The longer term research goals include the development of interoperability protocols, procedures for optimal multiprocessing program-

lar. For example, psychology (in a broad sense) might come into play in the early stages of goal setting by providing an insight into the workings of a large organisation and the potential effects of a new software-intensive way of doing business; at a later stage by providing detailed parameters for VDT formats; and during operation of a system, by providing us with the methodology for evaluating the effect of a system on its clients.

Progress over time in creating, operating and modifying a software-intensive system is represented by a spiral path downward through the solid. Although such a path can represent the 'centroid' of project activity over time, it is important to remember that a complex system will involve many (perhaps thousands) of people whose activities may be spread over a large volume of the model.

Operationally, software systems engineering will encompass an egg-shaped solid centred on the Z-axis of this model. On a linear scale, this volume of activities will be centred rather high up on the Z-axis as, once a system is fully operational, the involvement decreases rapidly (except when major modifications are needed). Likewise, the extent of the activities in the X-Y plane is not regular, reaching out during certain activities to include other expertise and contracting in other places. Overall, however, the extent of activities carried out by the software systems engineer is limited at the start, expands to a maximum during design and construction of the actual system, and tapers off once the system is fully operational and modifications have either ceased or decreased to a very low level.

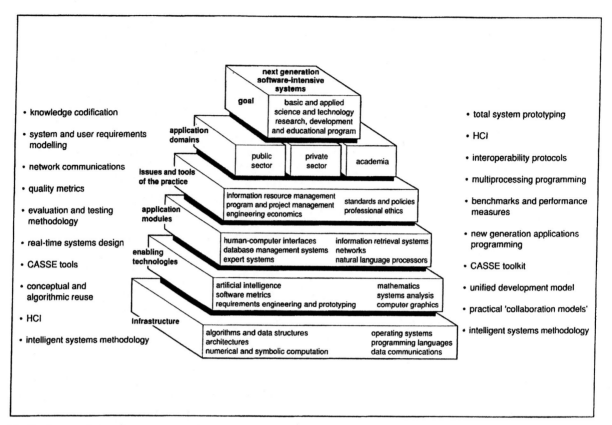

Fig. 8 A research agenda

ming, the development of a full-blow CASSE tool kit, a 'unified development model' etc.

These lists will, of course, change over time as new ideas are developed and others fall by the wayside. New hardware technology will also alter the list, as will breakthroughs in software productivity, prototyping and end-user computing.

9 Concluding remarks

We have provided an analysis of the fields of systems engineering and software engineering along several dimensions. Based on these analyses and our experience in all aspects of the fields, we have synthesised a case for a new field of software systems engineering. Although only in outline form here, we have provided the basis for conceptual, operational, educational and research activity in this new field. The simple message of this paper is that the systems problems of the coming decades will be software-intensive and they will demand results of these suggested activities.

10 Acknowledgments

Support for Dr. Andriole's research was provided by the Pennsylvania Ben Franklin Technology Center and Drexel University's College of Information Studies. Dr. Freeman's research was supported by the Virginia Center for Innovative Technology (CIT), the George Mason University Center for Software Systems Engineering and the Georgia Institute of Technology's College of Computing.

11 References

[1] PRESSMAN, R.S.: 'Software engineering: a practitioner's approach' (McGraw-Hill Book Co., New York, 1987) 2nd edn.
[2] CHESTNUT, H.: 'Systems engineering methods' (Wiley, New York, 1967)
[3] SAGE, A.P., and PALMER, J.D.: 'Software systems engineering' (John Wiley, New York, 1989)
[4] Department of Defense (DOD): 'Engineering management'. MIL-STD-499A (USAF), 1 May 1974, pp. 11–18
[5] EISNER, H.: 'Computer-aided systems engineering' (Prentice-Hall, Englewood Cliffs, New Jersey, 1988)
[6] BLANCHARD, K., and FABRYCKY, S.: 'System engineering' (Prentice-Hall, Englewood Cliffs, New Jersey, 1981)
[7] SAGE, A.P.: 'Methodology for large scale systems' (McGraw-Hill, New York, 1977)
[8] HALL, A.D.: 'Methodology for systems engineering' (Van Nostrand, Princeton, New Jersey, 1962)
[9] GOODE, H., and MACHOL, R.E.: 'Systems engineering: an introduction to the design of large scale systems' (McGraw-Hill, New York, 1957)
[10] NAUR, P., and RANDALL, B. (Eds.): 'Software engineering (report on a meeting held October 1968) NATO Science Committee, Brussels, Belgium, 1969
[11] BOEHM, B.W.: 'Software engineering', *IEEE Trans.*, 1976, C-25, (12), pp. 1226–1241
[12] MILLS, H.D.: 'Principles of software engineering', *IBM Syst. J.*, 1980, 19, (4), pp. 414–420
[13] FREEMAN, P., and VON STAA, A.: 'Towards a theory of software engineering'. Working paper, Washington DC, November 1984 (available from PAF)
[14] Defense Systems Management College (DSMC): 'Systems engineering management guide' (Washington, DC, Fort Belvoir, 1986)
[15] ROYCE, W.: 'Managing the development of large software systems'. Proc. WESCON, August 1970

[16] BOEHM, B.W.: 'A spiral model of software development', *Computer*, 1988, (5), pp. 61–72

[17] SMITH, C.: 'Analytical methods for systems engineering' a taxonomy of analytical methods'. George Mason University, School of Information Technology and Engineering, 1988

[18] KUHN, T.S.: 'The structure of scientific revolutions' (Unviersity of Chicago Press, Chicago, 1970) 2nd edn.

[19] LEHMAN, M.M., STENNING, V., and TURSKI, W.M.: 'Another look at software design methodology', *SIGSOFT Softw. Eng. Notes*, 1984, 9, (2), pp. 38–53

[20] KEROLA, P., and FREEMAN, P.A.: 'Comparison of lifecycle models'. Proc. 5th Int. Conf. on Software Engineering, IEEE Computer Society, Los Alamitos, California, 1981, pp. 90–99

[21] IIVARI, J., and KOSKELA, E.: 'The PIOCO model for IS design', *MIS Quarterly*, 1987, 11, (3)

The paper was first received on 14 April 1992 and in revised form 11 January 1993.

Stephen J. Andriole is Director, Center for Multidisciplinary Information Systems Engineering, College of Information Studies, Drexel University, Philadelphia, PA 19104, USA; Peter A. Freeman is Dean, College of Computing, Georgia Institute of Technology, Atlanta, GA 30332-0280, USA.

The Concept of Operations:
The Bridge from Operational Requirements to Technical Specifications*

Richard E. Fairley
Colorado Technical University

Richard H. Thayer
California State University, Sacramento

Abstract

This paper describes the role of a Concept of Operations (ConOps) document in specification and development of a software-intensive system. It also describes the process of developing a ConOps, its uses and benefits, who should develop it, and when it should be developed. The ConOps described in this paper is compared to other forms of operational concept documents. A detailed outline for ConOps documents is provided in an appendix to the paper.

Introduction

The goal of software engineering is to develop and modify software-intensive systems that satisfy user needs, on schedule and within budget. Accurate communication of operational requirements from those who need a software-intensive system to those who will build the system is thus the most important step in the system development process. Traditionally, this information has been communicated as follows: The developer analyzes users' needs and buyer's requirements and prepares a requirements specification that defines the developers' understanding of those needs and requirements.[1] The users and buyer review the requirements specification and attempt to verify that the developer has correctly understood their needs and requirements. A draft users' manual is sometimes written by the developer to assist users and buyer in determining whether the proposed system will operate

in a manner consistent with their needs and expectations. A prototype of the user interface may be constructed to demonstrate the developers' understanding of the desired user interface.

This traditional way of specifying software requirements introduces several problems: First, the buyer may not adequately convey the needs of the user community to the developer, perhaps because the buyer does not understand those needs. Second, the developer may not be expert in the application domain, which inhibits communication. Third, the users and buyer often find it difficult to understand the requirements produced by the developer. Fourth, the developer's requirements specification typically specifies system attributes such as functions, performance factors, design constraints, system interfaces, and quality attributes, but typically contains little or no information concerning operational characteristics of the specified system [ANSI/IEEE Std 830-1984]. This leaves the users and buyer uncertain as to whether the requirements specification describes a system that will provide the needed operational capabilities.

A draft version of the users' manual can provide some assurance that the developer understands user/buyer needs and expectations, but a draft version of the manual may not be written. If it is written, considerable time and effort have usually been spent by the time it is available for review. Major changes can require significant rework. Furthermore, it is difficult to demonstrate that the correspondences among technical specifications, users' manual, and (undocumented) operational requirements are complete and consistent.

A prototype of the user interface can be helpful, but there is a danger that demonstration of an acceptable user interface will be taken as assurance that the developer understands all of the users' operational needs. In summary, the traditional approach does not facilitate communication among users, buyer, and developer; nor does it emphasize the importance of specifying the operational requirements for the envisioned system.

---

* An ealier version of this paper appeared in *Annals of Software Engineering*, 1996.

1 Users are those who will interact with the new or modified system in the performance of their daily work activities; users include operators and maintainers. The buyer is a representative of the user community (or communities) who provides the interface between users and developer: the developer is the organization that will build (or modify) and deliver the system.

Concept analysis helps users clarify their operational needs, thereby easing the problems of communication among users, buyer, and developer. Development of a Concept of Operation document (ConOps) to record the results of concept analysis provides a bridge from user needs into the system development process. Ideally, concept analysis and development of the ConOps document are the first steps in the development process; however, (as discussed below) developing a ConOps at later stages of the system lifecycle is also cost-effective.

Subsequent sections of this paper describe the evolution of the ConOps technique, the concept analysis process, the Concept of Operations document, roles to be played by a ConOps, some guidelines on when and how to develop a ConOps, development scenarios and a process for developing the ConOps, the recommended format for a ConOps, and some issues concerning maintenance of a ConOps throughout the development process and the operational life of a software system.

History of the ConOps Approach

One of the earliest reports on formalizing the description of operational concepts for a software system is contained in a 1980 TRW report by R.J. Lano: "A Structured Approach for Operational Concept Formulation" [TRW SS-80-02]. The importance of a well-defined operational concept (for example, definition of system goals, missions, functions, components) to the success of system development is emphasized in the report. The report presented tools, techniques, and procedures for more effectively accomplishing the system engineering tasks of concept formulation, requirements analysis and definition, architecture definition, and system design.

In 1985, the Joint Logistics Commanders' Joint Regulation "Management of Computer Resources in Defense Systems" was issued. This Joint Regulation included DoD-STD-2167, which contained a Data Item Description (DID) entitled "Operational Concept Document" (OCD) [Dl-ECRS-8x25, DoD-Std-2167, 1985]. The purpose of this DID was to describe the mission of the system, its operational and support environments, and the functions and characteristics of the computer system within an overall system. The OCD DID was folded into the System/Segment Design Document [Dl-CMAN-80534, DoD-Std-2167A, 1988] in the revised version of DoD-STD-2167 [DoD-Std-2167A].

Operational concepts were moved into Section 3 of the System/Segment Design Document (SSDD), which tended to place emphasis on overall system concepts rather than software concepts. Because the OCD was no longer a stand-alone document in 2167A, many users of 2167A did sufficiently emphasize operational concepts. For software-only projects, use of the SSDD was often waived. In these cases, there was no other place within the 2167A DIDs to record operational concepts for a software-intensive system. As a result, several other government agencies, including NASA and the Federal Aviation Administration, produced their own versions of the original 2167 DID for documenting operational concepts within the 2167A framework.

Another DoD standard, DoD-Std-7935A for development of information systems, required that the functional description of the proposed information system be contained in Section 2 of that document. The Functional Description in 7935A provided little guidance on how to develop a ConOps document; furthermore, it was very specific to the information systems domain, emphasized functionality only, and allowed little flexibility for new methods and techniques of software system development.

In recognition of the importance of well-defined operational concepts to successful development of a software system, Mil-Std 498 for Software Development and Documentation, which has replaced 2167A and 7935A, includes a Data Item Description for an Operational Concept Document (OCD). The authors of this paper played a leading role in developing the draft version of the Operational Concept Document (OCD) for the Harmonization Working Group that prepared Mil-Std-498. The OCD in Mil-Std 498 is similar to the ConOps outline contained in Appendix A of this paper. IEEE Standard 1498, the commercial counterpart of Mil-Std-498 (which currently exists in draft form) incorporates an OCD similar to the one in Appendix A.

The American Institute of Aeronautics and Astronautics (AIAA) published a document titled "Operational Concept Document (OCD) Preparation Guidelines" [AIAA OCD 1992]. The AIAA OCD compares favorably with the ConOps presented in this paper; however, in the opinion of this paper's authors, the tone and language used in the AIAA OCD is biased to the developer's view of user needs rather than the users' operational view. The AIAA OCD is also biased toward embedded, real-time systems.

A major goal for the ConOps presented here is to provide a means for users of information processing systems, who are knowledgeable in their application domain but not expert in software engineering, to describe their needs and wants from their point of view; in other words, the recommended Guide is more user-oriented than existing standards and guidelines, which tend to be systems-oriented and developer-oriented.

Another difference between existing standards and the ConOps recommended in this paper is that this paper emphasizes the importance of describing both the current system's and the proposed system's characteristics, even though that may result in some redundancy in the document. The advantages of redundancy are considered to outweigh the problems.

The Concept Analysis Process

Concept analysis is the process of analyzing a problem domain and an operational environment for the purpose of specifying the characteristics of a proposed system from the users' perspective. The traditional system development process emphasizes functionality with little concern for how that functionality will be used. Concept analysis emphasizes an integrated view of a system and its operational characteristics, rather than focusing on individual functions or pieces of a system. A major goal of concept analysis is to avoid development of a system in which each individual function meets its specifications, but the system as a whole fails to meet the users' needs.

Concept analysis should be the first step taken in the overall system development process. It identifies the various classes of users and modes of operation,[2] and provides users with a mechanism for defining their needs and desires. Concept analysis is also useful to surface different users' (and user groups') needs and viewpoints, and to allow the buyer (or multiple buyers) to state their requirements for the proposed system. This process is essential to the success of the subsequent system development effort. Users have an opportunity to express their needs and desires, but they are also required to state which of those needs are essential, which are desirable, and which are optional. In addition, they must prioritize the desired and optional needs. Prioritized user needs provide the basis for establishing an incremental development process and for making trade-offs among operational needs, schedule, and budget.

Concept analysis helps to clarify and resolve vague and conflicting needs, wants, and opinions by reconciling divergent views. In the case where several user groups (or buyer groups) have conflicting needs, viewpoints, or expectations, concept analysis can aid in building consensus. In some cases, it may be determined that no single system can satisfy all of the

divergent needs and desires of multiple user groups and buyer agencies. It is better to make that determination earlier rather than later.

Concept analysis is an iterative process that should involve various people. The analysis group should include representatives from the user, buyer, and developer organizations, plus any other appropriate parties such as training and operational support. In cases where a development organization has not been selected at the time of concept analysis, the developer role may be filled by in-house development experts or consultants.

The results of concept analysis are recorded in the ConOps document, which serves as a framework to guide the analysis process and provides the foundation document for all subsequent system development activities (analysis, design, implementation, and validation). The ConOps document should say everything about the system that the users and buyer need to communicate to those who will develop the system.

The ConOps document should be repeatedly reviewed and revised until all involved parties agree on the resulting document. This iterative process helps bring to the surface many viewpoints, needs, wants, and scenarios that might otherwise be overlooked.

The Concept of Operations (ConOps) Document

The ConOps document describes the results of the conceptual analysis process. The document should contain all of the information needed to describe the users' needs, goals, expectations, operational environment, processes, and characteristics for the system under consideration. Essential elements of a ConOps include:

- A description of the current system or situation
- A description of the needs that motivate development of a new system or modification of an existing system
- Modes of operation for the proposed system
- User classes and user characteristics
- Operational features of the proposed system
- Priorities among proposed operational features
- Operational scenarios for each operational mode and class of user
- Limitations of the proposed approach
- Impact analysis for the proposed system

A detailed outline for a ConOps document containing these elements is provided in Appendix A to this paper.

---

2 Diagnostic mode, maintenance mode, degraded mode, emergency mode, and backup mode must be included, as appropriate, in the set of operational modes for a system environment, processes, and characteristics for the system under consideration.

A ConOps document should, in contrast to a requirements specifications, be written in narrative prose, using the language and terminology of the users' application domain. It should be organized to tell a story, and should make use of visual forms (diagrams, illustrations, graphs, and so forth) whenever possible. Although desirable, it is not necessary that the needs and wants expressed in a ConOps be quantified; that is, users can state their desire for "fast response" or "reliable operation." These desires are quantified during the process of mapping the ConOps to the requirements specification and during the flow-down of requirements to the system architecture. During system development, the impact of trade-offs among quantified system attributes (such as response time and reliability) must be explored within the limits of available time, money, and the state of technology.

A ConOps document should be tailored for the application domain, operational environment, and intended audience. This means that the terminology, level of abstraction, detail, technical content, and presentation format should adhere to the objectives for that particular ConOps document. The following points are worth making in this regard:

1. A ConOps document must be written in the users' language. This does not necessarily imply that it cannot use technical language, but rather that it should be written in the users' technical language if the users are experts in a technical domain. If the ConOps document is written by the buyer or developer the authors must avoid use of terminology associated with their own discipline.

2. The level of detail contained in a ConOps should be appropriate to the situation. For example, there may be instances wherein a high-level description of the current system or situation is sufficient. In other instances, a detailed description of the current system or situation may be necessary. For example, there may be no current system: A detailed statement of the situation that motivates new system development with extensively specified operational scenarios for the envisioned system may be required. Or, the new system may be a replacement for an existing system to upgrade technology while adding new capabilities. In this case, a brief description of the existing system would be appropriate, with more detail on the new capabilities to be provided. The level of detail also depends on

whether the ConOps document is for a system as a whole, or whether there will be separate ConOps documents for each system segment (for example, checkout, launch, on-orbit, and ground support elements for a spacecraft system) with an umbrella ConOps that describes operational aspects of the entire system.

3. The presentation format used in a ConOps document will vary, depending on the application of the document. In some user communities, textual documents are the tradition, while in others, storyboards are used. Examples of this difference can be seen by comparing the styles of communication in the information processing and command-and-control domains, for instance. The presentation format should be adjusted to accommodate the intended audience of the ConOps, although the use of visual forms is recommended for all audiences.

4. The comprehensive outline of a ConOps document, as presented in Appendix A, may not apply to every system or situation. If a particular paragraph of the outline does not apply to the situation under consideration, it should be marked "Not Applicable (N/A);" however, for each paragraph marked N/A, a brief justification stating why that paragraph is not applicable should be provided in place of the paragraph. "Not Applicable" should be used only when the authors of a ConOps are confident that the paragraph does not apply to the situation, and not simply because the authors don't have the required information. For example, if the authors do not know whether alternatives and trade-offs were considered (paragraph 8.3 of the ConOps outline), they should determine that fact. In the interim period, the paragraph can be marked "TBD." If they determine no alternatives or trade-offs were considered, the paragraph can be marked "not applicable." In this case, a brief justification stating why alternatives and trade-offs were not considered should be included.

To summarize, the ConOps format presented in Appendix A should be tailored to produce an efficient and cost-effective mechanism for documenting user needs and for maintaining traceability to those needs throughout the development process.

Roles for ConOps Documents

The ConOps document can fill one of several roles, or some combination thereof:

1. To communicate users' and buyer's needs/requirements to the system developers. The ConOps author might be a buyer, presenting users' views to a developer; or a user presenting the users' view to a buyer and/or a developer. In this case, the ConOps is used by the developer as the basis for subsequent development activities.

2. To communicate a developer's understanding to users and/or buyer. The developer might produce a ConOps document as an aid in communicating the technical requirements to users and buyer, or to explain a possible solution strategy to the users and/or buyer. In this case, the ConOps is reviewed by the users and buyer to determine whether the proposed approach meets their needs and expectations.

3. To communicate a buyer's understanding of user needs to a developer. In this case, the buyer would develop the ConOps, obtain user concurrence, and use the ConOps to present user needs and operational requirements to the developer.

4. To document divergent needs and differing viewpoints of various user groups and/or buyers. In this case, each user group and/or buyer might develop (or commission development of) a ConOps to document their particular needs and viewpoints. This would be done as a prelude to obtaining a consensus view (see Role 5), or to determine that no single system can satisfy all of the various users' needs and buyers' requirements.

5. To document consensus on the system's characteristics among multiple users, user groups, or multiple buyers. In this case, the ConOps provides a mechanism for documenting the consensus view obtained from divergent needs, visions, and viewpoints among different users, user groups, and buyers before further development work proceeds.

6. To provide a means of communication between system engineers and software developers. In this case, the ConOps would describe user needs and operational requirements for the overall system (hardware, software, and people) and provide a context for the role of software within the total system.

7. To provide common understanding among multiple system/software developers. In cases where multiple system development and/or software development organizations are involved, the ConOps can provide a common understanding of how the software fits into the overall system, and how each software developer's part fits into the software portion of the system. In this case, there may be multiple ConOps documents, related in a hierarchical manner that mirrors the system partitioning.

Variations on, and combinations of, these roles might be found under differing circumstances. For example, the ConOps process might play Roles 4 and 5 to obtain and document consensus among user groups and buyers prior to developer selection; the consensus ConOps document would then fill Role 1 by providing the basis for subsequent development activities by the developer.

Additional roles for the ConOps include:

8. Providing a mechanism to document a system's characteristics and the users' operational needs in a manner that can be verified by the users without requiring them to have any technical knowledge beyond what is required to perform their job functions.

9. Providing a place for users to state their desires, visions, and expectations without requiring them to provide quantified, testable specifications. For example, the users could express their need for a "highly reliable" system, and their reasons for that need, without having to produce a testable reliability requirement.

10. Providing a mechanism for users and buyer(s) to express their thoughts and concerns on possible solution strategies. In some cases, there may be design constraints that dictate particular approaches. In other cases, there may be a variety of acceptable solution strategies. The ConOps allows users and buyer(s) to record design constraints, the rationale for those constraints, and to indicate the range of acceptable solution strategies.

When Should the ConOps be Developed?

Development of a ConOps document should be the first step in the overall development process, so that it can serve as a basis for subsequent development activities.

The ConOps might be developed

1. Before the decision is made to develop a system. In this case, the ConOps document would be used to support the decision process.

2. Before the request for proposals (RFP) or in-house project authorization is issued. The ConOps would be included in the RFP package or project authorization.

3. As the first task after award of contract, so that the developer can better understand the users' needs and expectations before subsequent system development activities are started.

In cases (1) and (2), development of the ConOps document will be initiated by the users or the buyer (although the document author might be a developer; possibly the developer who will later develop the system). In case (3), development of the ConOps can be initiated by, and/or developed by, the user, buyer, or developer.

Concept analysis and preparation of a ConOps document can also be quite useful even if initiated at a later stage of the system life cycle. If, during system development, so many diverging opinions, needs, visions, and viewpoints surface that the development process cannot continue successfully, a ConOps document can provide a common vision of the system. The ConOps document for the Hubble Space Telescope System is a good example of this situation [Hubble 1983]. It was written after several attempts to develop a requirements specification; however, potential users of the space telescope could not agree on the operational requirements. The ConOps document provided the vehicle for obtaining a consensus, which in turn provided a basis for generating detailed operational requirements.

The developer who is building a system might want to develop a ConOps document, even as the requirements specifications are being generated. The developer might want the ConOps as a high-level overview and introduction to the system to serve as a guideline for the development team. Developers concerned about understanding user needs might develop a ConOps document as an aid to successfully developing a system that meets the users' needs and expectations.

A ConOps document might be developed during the operational phase of the system life cycle to support users, operators, and maintainers of the system. It might happen that potential system users do not want to use it because they do not understand the system's operational capabilities, or because they do not understand how the system would fit into their working environment. To solve these problems, the buyer or the developer might develop a ConOps document to "sell" the system to potential users.

A ConOps is also helpful to new users, operators, and maintainers who need to understand the operational characteristics of a system. The ConOps can also be used to explain the system's operational characteristics to prospective buyers who were not involved in initial system development.

If the involved parties deem it to be useful, a ConOps document can be developed at any time during the system life cycle; however, some major benefits of the document and the process of developing it are lost if it is developed after the requirements specification is baselined.

Scenarios for Developing the ConOps

Ideally, concept analysis and development of the ConOps document should be done by the users. However, depending on the purpose and timing of development, the ConOps might be developed by the users, the buyer, or the developer. Regardless of who develops the ConOps, it must reflect the views of, and be approved by, the user community.

A high degree of user involvement in concept analysis and review of the ConOps document is crucial to a successful outcome, even if concept analysis and development of the ConOps document are done by the buyer or the developer. In these cases, the buyer or developer must engage the users in the process to ensure a correct and comprehensive understanding of the current system or situation and the users' needs, visions, and expectations for the new system. One way to ensure the necessary interactions is to establish an interdisciplinary team consisting of representatives from all user groups, from the buyer(s), and from the developer(s). However, the focus must never be allowed to shift from the users' operational perspective to the buyer's or developer's perspective.

One benefit of having the users write the ConOps document is that it ensures the focus will stay on user-related issues. However, the users may not know how to develop a ConOps document or be able to realistically envision what a new system can accomplish, that is they may not know the capabilities of existing technology. To reduce the impact of these problems, qualified personnel can be brought in to assist the users in developing the ConOps document.

One benefit of having the developers write the ConOps document is that they will, in most cases, have comprehensive knowledge of available technologies, and thus may be able to propose alternative (and better) ways of solving the users' problems. Another benefit of a developer-produced ConOps is that the ConOps analysis process will provide the developer with a good understanding of the users' problems, needs, and expectations, which facilitates subsequent development activities.

An advantage of a buyer-developed ConOps is that the buyer may have a good understanding of the user community, the developer organization, the political realities of the situation, and the budgetary constraints that may exist. This knowledge can be invaluable in producing a ConOps for a system that will satisfy user needs and that can be delivered within political and budgetary constraints.

Regardless of who takes primary responsibility for producing the ConOps document, it is important that all parties (users, buyers, developers) be involved in the analysis process and that everyone contribute their particular viewpoint to development of the ConOps.

A Development Process for the ConOps

The approach described below is intended as a guideline. If the approach conflicts with what seems to be most appropriate in a specific situation, the guideline should be modified to fit that situation. For instance, there may be no current system; or the new system may be a modification of a current system; or the new system may be a total replacement for an outdated (manual or automated) system. Topics emphasized in the ConOps may be different in each situation.

1. Determine the objectives, roles, and team members for the ConOps process. This will normally be determined by the situation that motivates development of the ConOps document.

2. Tailor the recommended ConOps document format and obtain agreement on an outline for the ConOps document. This is important so that everyone understands the agreed-upon format and content areas of the document.

3. Describe the overall objectives and short-comings of the current system. Also, determine and document the overall objectives for the new or modified system. If there is no current system, describe the situation that motivates development of a new system.

4. If there is an existing system, describe the that system's scope and boundaries, and identify any external systems and the interfaces to them. Also, establish and describe in general terms the scope and boundaries for the new or modified system, and identify the major external systems and interfaces to it.

5. Describe operational policies and constraints that apply to the current system or situation and any changes to those policies and constraints for the new system.

6. Describe the features of the current system or situation. This includes the system's operational characteristics, operational environment and processes, modes of operation, user classes, and the operational support and maintenance environments.

7. State the operational policies and constraints that will apply to the new or modified system.

8. Determine the operational characteristics of the proposed system, that is, describe the characteristics the proposed system must possess to meet the users' needs and expectations.

9. Document operational scenarios for the new or modified system. Scenarios are specified by recording, in a step-by-step manner, the sequences of actions and interactions between a user and the system. The following approach can be used to develop and document operational scenarios:

   - Develop a set of scenarios that, to the extent possible, covers all modes of operation, all classes of users, and all specific operations and processes of the proposed system.

   - Walk through each scenario with the appropriate users and record information concerning normal operating states and unusual conditions that are relevant to the operation of the proposed system.

   - During the walk-throughs, establish new scenarios to cover abnormal operations such as exception handling, stress load handling, and handling of incomplete and incorrect data.

   - Establish new scenarios whenever a branch in the thread of operation is encountered. Typically, walking through the "normal" scenarios will uncover additional scenarios. Different users may also have different views of some scenarios. If these variations are significant, include them as separate scenarios.

- Repeatedly develop scenarios until all operations, and all significant variations of those operations, are covered.

- For each operational scenario, develop an associated test scenario to be used in validating the operational aspects of the delivered system in the user environment. Establish traceability between operational scenarios and test scenarios.

10. After the scenarios have been developed, validate the description of the proposed system and the operational scenarios by walking through all of the scenarios with representatives from all user groups and all classes of users for all operational modes.

11. Obtain consensus on priorities among the operational scenarios and features of the proposed system. Group the scenarios and operational features into essential, desirable, and optional categories; prioritize scenarios and features within the desirable and optional categories. Also, describe scenarios and features considered but not included in the proposed system.

12. Analyze and describe the operational and organizational impacts the proposed system will have on users, buyer(s), developers, and the support/maintenance agencies. Also, include significant impacts on these groups during system development.

13. Describe the benefits, limitations, advantages, and disadvantages of the proposed system, compared to the present system or situation.

Recommended Format of a ConOps Document

The recommended format of a ConOps document accommodates the objective of describing a proposed system from the users' point of view, in user terminology. The following format is recommended. Appendix A contains a detailed version of this outline.

1. Introduction to the ConOps document and to the system described in the document.

2. List of all documents referenced in the ConOps document.

3. Description of the current system or situation, including scope and objectives of the current system, operational policies and constraints, modes of operation, classes of users, and the support environment for the current system. If there is no existing system, describe the reasons that motivate development of a new system.

4. Nature of proposed changes and/or new features, including the justification for those changes and/or features.

5. Operational concepts for the proposed system, including scope and objectives for the proposed system, operational policies and constraints, modes of operation, classes of users, and the support environment for the proposed system.

6. Operational scenarios describing how the proposed system is to perform in its environment, relating system capabilities and functions to modes of operation, classes of users, and interactions with external systems.

7. Operational and organizational impacts on the users, buyers, developers, and the support and maintenance agencies, during system development and after system installation.

8. Alternative and trade-offs considered but not included in the new or modified system; analysis of benefits, limitations, advantages, and disadvantages of the new or modified system.

9. Notes, acronyms and abbreviations, appendices, and glossary of terms

This organization of a ConOps document provides a logical flow of information beginning with a description of the current system, transitioning through considerations of needed changes and the rationale for such changes, and leading to a description of the new or modified system. This will guide the reader through the description of the systems (both the current system or situation and the proposed system) in a simple and intuitive way.

Maintaining the ConOps

A ConOps should be a living document that is updated and maintained throughout the entire life cycle (development process and operational life) of the software product. During system development, the ConOps document must be updated to keep users informed of the operational impacts of changes in requirements, the system design, operational policies, the operational environment, and other users' needs. During the operational life of the software product, the

ConOps must be updated to reflect the evolutionary changes to the system.

It is important to maintain the ConOps document under configuration control, and to ensure that user and buyer representatives are members of the change control board for the ConOps. Placing the ConOps under configuration control will protect the document from uncontrolled changes, and through the formal process of updating and notification, help to keep all parties informed of changes. A major benefit of this approach is that users and buyers are involved in reviewing and approving the changes. This minimizes the surprise factor that can occur when a delivered system is not the same as the system users thought they agreed to at the requirements review.

The ConOps document should also be updated and maintained under configuration control throughout the operational life of the associated system. During the operational life of the system, a ConOps can aid the support, maintenance, and enhancement activities for the system in much the same way that it helped during development. Specifically, it can be used to communicate new operational needs and impacts that result in modifications, upgrades, and enhancements. Furthermore, the ConOps provides a communication tool to familiarize new personnel with the system and the application domain.

Traceability should be established and maintained among the ConOps document, the system/software requirements specifications, and the acceptance/regression test scenarios. It is important for the developer (or maintainer) to be able to demonstrate to the users, buyer, and themselves that every essential user need stated in the ConOps document, and the desirable and optional features implemented, can be traced to and from the system specifications and to and from the delivered capabilities in the final product.

Summary and Conclusions

This paper has described the evolution of the ConOps approach, the conceptual analysis process, the Concept of Operations document, roles to be played by a ConOps, some guidelines on when to develop a ConOps, development scenarios and a development process for developing the ConOps, the recommended format for a ConOps, and some issues concerning the maintenance of a ConOps throughout the development process and operational life of a software system.

As software engineers, we become so involved in the technology of software development and modification that we sometimes forget our fundamental charter: to develop and modify software-intensive systems that satisfy user needs, on time and within budget. Performing conceptual analysis and develop-

ing and maintaining a Concept of Operations document provides the bridge from users' operational requirements to technical specifications. All subsequent work products (requirements specs, design documents, source code, test plans, users' manual, training aids, and maintenance guide, for example) should flow from the ConOps. Maintaining the ConOps and the traceability of work products to the ConOps will not guarantee success; however, it can increase the probability that we will develop systems that satisfy users' needs for efficient and effective tools that help them accomplish their work activities.

Acknowledgments

The authors would like to acknowledge the support of the following individuals in preparing the ConOps Guide: Per Bjorke, Dr. Merlin Dorfman, Dr. Lisa Friendly, and Jane Radatz.

References

[AIAA OCD, 1992] AIAA Recommended Technical Practice, Operational Concept Document (OCD), Preparation Guidelines, Software Systems Technical Committee, American Institute of Aeronautics and Astronautics (AIAA), Mar. 1, 1992.

[ANSI/IEEE Std 830-1984] ANSI/IEEE Standard 830-1984: IEEE Guide for Software Requirements Specifications, The Institute of Electrical and Electronic Engineers, Inc., approved by the American National Standards Institute July 20, 1984.

[DI-CMAN-80534, DoD-Std-2167A, 1988] System/Segment Design Document (SSDD), DI-CMAN-80534, U.S. Department of Defense, Feb. 29, 1988.

[DI-ECRS-8x25, DoD-Std-2167, 1985] Operational Concept Document (OCD), DI-[ECRS-8x25] U.S. Department of Defense, June 4, 1985.

[DoD-Std-2167A, 1988] Military Standard: Defense System Software, Development, DoD-Std-2167A, U.S. Department of Defense, Feb. 29, 1988.

[DoD-Std-7935A, 1988] Functional Description (FD), DoD Automated Information Systems (AIS) Documentation Standards, DoD-Std-7935A, U.S. Department of Defense, Oct. 31, 1988, pp. 19–37.

[Hubble, 1983] Science Operations Concept, Part 1 (Final), Space Telescope Science Institute, Prepared for NASA Goddard Space Flight Center, Greenbelt, MD, May 1983.

[Lano, 1988] Lano, R.J., "A Structured Approach For Operational Concept Formulation (OCF)," TRW-SS-80-02, TRW Systems Engineering and Integration Division, Redondo Beach, Calif., Jan. 1980. Also in *Tutorial: Software Engineering Project Management*, edited by R. Thayer, Computer Society Press, Los Alamitos, Calif., 1988.

Appendix A

Outline for a Concept of Operations Document

Chapter 3

Software Engineering

1. Introduction to Chapter

Software can be considered a product of engineering just like an airplane, automobile, television, or any other object that requires a high degree of skill to turn a raw material into a usable product. Software:

- Is an entity (not a document)
- Is generally a component of a larger system (hardware/software)
- Replaces previously engineered hardware components
- Must interface with other hardware or software systems
- Must be tested before being put to use

- Is too large and complex to build without a plan (specification)
- Is expensive to build

The term *software engineering* was coined in 1967 by Professor Friedrich Bauer at a pre-conference meeting in Germany. (See the paper by Bauer in this chapter.) It was first applied as a technology in the mid-1970s and was accepted as a job title in the late 1970s. Today, most software positions (programming or engineering) are advertised as software engineering.

The purpose of software engineering was to introduce an engineering discipline to software development. It is applied to try to solve or reduce the problems of late deliveries, cost overruns, and failure to meet requirements that plagued software projects starting in the 1960s.

2. Introduction to Papers

The centerpiece of this chapter is an original paper by the well-known author and consultant, Roger Pressman. As indicated in the *Preface*, one of the problems of software engineering is the shortage of basic papers. Once something is described, practitioners and academics apparently move on to research or to the finer points of argument, abandoning the need to occasionally update the fundamentals. Dr. Pressman undertook the task of updating the basic papers on software engineering to the current state of practice. Pressman discusses technical and management aspects of software engineering. He surveys existing high-level models of the software development process (linear sequential, prototyping, incremental, evolutionary, and formal) and discusses management of people, the software project, and the software process. He discusses quality assurance and configuration management as being equally as important as technical and management issues. He reviews some of the principles and methods that form the foundation of the current practice of software engineering, and concludes with a prediction that three issues, reuse, re-engineering, and a new generation of tools, will dominate software engineering for the next ten years or so.

Pressman's most recent book is "*A Manager's Guide to Software Engineering*" (McGraw-Hill, 1993).

Paper number two credits Professor Friedrich L. Bauer with coining the phrase "software engineering." In 1967, the NATO Science Committee set about organizing a conference on the problems of building large-scale software systems. The conference was to be held in Garmisch, Germany, in 1968. At a pre-conference meeting, Professor Bauer, of Munich Technical University, proposed that the conference be called "Software Engineering" as a means of attracting attention. This one-page paper, which is the foreword from an earlier IEEE Tutorial, *Software Engineering—A European Perspective*,[1] explains the history behind the term and, as such, is included in this tutorial to give full credit to Professor Bauer.

The last paper in this chapter is a another historical perspective, the paper by Buxton entitled "Software Engineering—20 Years on and 20 Years Back." This paper provides another historical note on the origin and use of the term "software engineering." Professor Buxton is in a unique position to define the past history of software engineering as he was one of the main reporters and documentors of the second NATO software engineering conference in Rome in 1969.

1. Thayer, R. H., and A. D. McGettrick, eds., *Software Engineering—A European Perspective*, IEEE Computer Society Press, Los Alamitos, Calif., 1993.

Software Engineering

Roger S. Pressman, Ph.D.

As software engineering approaches its fourth decade, it suffers from many of the strengths and some of the frailties that are experienced by humans of the same age. The innocence and enthusiasm of its early years have been replaced by more reasonable expectations (and even a healthy cynicism) fostered by years of experience. Software engineering approaches its mid-life with many accomplishments already achieved, but with significant work yet to do.

The intent of this paper is to provide a survey of the current state of software engineering and to suggest the likely course of the aging process. Key software engineering activities are identified, issues are presented, and future directions are considered. There will be no attempt to present an in-depth discussion of specific software engineering topics. That is the job of other papers presented in this book.

1.0 Software Engineering—Layered Technology[1]

Although hundreds of authors have developed personal definitions of software engineering, a definition proposed by Fritz Bauer [1] at the seminal conference on the subject still serves as a basis for discussion:

[Software engineering is] the establishment and use of sound engineering principles in order to obtain economically software that is reliable and works efficiently on real machines.

Almost every reader will be tempted to add to this definition. It says little about the technical aspects of software quality; it does not directly address the need for customer satisfaction or timely product delivery; it omits mention of the importance of measurement and metrics; it does not state the importance of a mature process. And yet, Bauer's definition provides us with a baseline. What are the "sound engineering principles" that can be applied to computer software development? How to "economically" build software so that it is "reliable"? What is required to create computer programs that work "efficiently" on not one but many different "real machines"? These are the questions that continue to challenge software engineers.

Software engineering is a layered technology. Referring to Figure 1, any engineering approach (including software engineering) must rest on an organizational commitment to quality. Total quality management and similar philosophies foster a continuous process improvement culture, and it is this culture that ultimately leads to the development of increasingly more mature approaches to software engineering. The bedrock that supports software engineering is a quality focus.

The foundation for software engineering is the process layer. Software engineering process is the glue that holds the technology layers together and enables rational and timely development of computer software. Process defines a framework for a set of *key process areas* [2] that must be established for effective delivery of software engineering technology. The key process areas form the basis for management control of software projects, and establish the context in which technical methods are applied, deliverables (models, documents, data reports, forms, and so on) are produced, milestones are established, quality is ensured, and change is properly managed.

Software engineering methods provide the technical "how to's" for building software. Methods encompass a broad array of tasks that include: requirements analysis, design, program construction, testing, and maintenance. Software engineering methods rely on a set of basic principles that govern each area of the technology and include modeling activities, and other descriptive techniques.

Software engineering tools provide automated or semiautomated support for the process and the methods. When tools are integrated so that information created by one tool can be used by another, a system for the support of software development, called computer-aided software engineering (CASE), is established. CASE combines software, hardware, and a software engineering database (a repository containing important information about analysis, design, program construction, and testing) to create a software engineering environment that is analogous to CAD/CAE (computer-aided design/engineering) for hardware.

---

1 Portions of this paper have been adapted from *A Manager's Guide to Software Engineering* [19] and *Software Engineering: A Practitioner's Approach* (McGraw-Hill, fourth edition, 1997) and are used with permission.

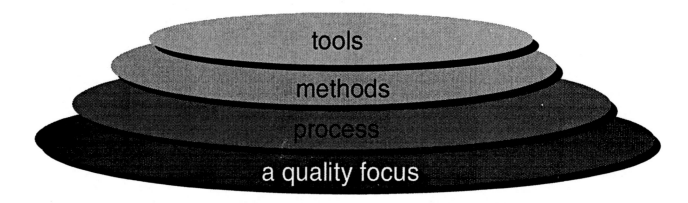

Figure 1. Software engineering layers

2.0 Software Engineering Process Models

Software engineering incorporates a development strategy that encompasses the process, methods, and tools layers described above. This strategy is often referred to as a *process model* or a *software engineering paradigm*. A process model for software engineering is chosen based on the nature of the project and application, the methods and tools to be used, and the controls and deliverables that are required. Four classes of process models have been widely discussed (and debated). A brief overview of each is presented in the sections that follow.

2.1 Linear, Sequential Models

Figure 2 illustrates the *linear sequential* model for software engineering. Sometimes called the "classic life cycle" or the "waterfall model," the linear sequential model demands a systematic, sequential approach to software development that begins at the system level and progresses through analysis, design, coding, testing, and maintenance. The linear sequential model is the oldest and the most widely used paradigm for software engineering. However, criticism of the paradigm has caused even active supporters to question its efficacy. Among the problems that are sometimes encountered when the linear sequential model is applied are:

1. Real projects rarely follow the sequential flow that the model proposes. Although the linear model can accommodate iteration, it does so indirectly. As a result, changes can cause confusion as the project team proceeds.

2. It is often difficult for the customer to state all requirements explicitly. The linear sequential model requires this and has difficulty accommodating the natural uncertainty that exists at the beginning of many projects.

3. The customer must have patience. A working version of the program(s) will not be available until late in the project time span. A major blunder, if undetected until the working program is reviewed, can be disastrous.

Figure 2. The linear, sequential paradigm

2.2 Prototyping

Often, a customer defines a set of general objectives for software, but does not identify detailed input, processing, or output requirements. In other cases, the developer may be unsure of the efficiency of an algorithm, the adaptability of an operating system, or the form that human-machine interaction should take. In these, and many other situations, a prototyping paradigm may offer the best approach.

The prototyping paradigm (Figure 3) begins with requirements gathering. Developer and customer meet and define the overall objectives for the software, identify whatever requirements are known, and outline areas where further definition is mandatory. A "quick design" then occurs. The quick design focuses on a representation of those aspects of the software that will be visible to the customer/user (for example, input approaches and output formats). The quick design leads to the construction of a prototype. The prototype is evaluated by the customer/user and is used to refine requirements for the software to be developed. Iteration occurs as the prototype is tuned to satisfy the needs of the customer, while at the same time enabling the developer to better understand what needs to be done.

Ideally, the prototype serves as a mechanism for identifying software requirements. If a working prototype is built, the developer attempts to make use of existing program fragments or applies tools (report generators, and window managers, for instance) that enable working programs to be generated quickly.

Both customers and developers like the prototyping paradigm. Users get a feel for the actual system and developers get to build something immediately. Yet, prototyping can also be problematic for the following reasons:

1. The customer sees what appears to be a working version of the software, unaware that the prototype is held together "with chewing gum and baling wire" or that in the rush to get it working we haven't considered overall software quality or long-term maintainability. When informed that the product must be rebuilt, the customer cries foul and demands that "a few fixes" be applied to make the prototype a working product. Too often, software development management relents.

2. The developer often makes implementation compromises in order to get a prototype working quickly. An inappropriate operating system or programming language may be used simply because it is available and known; an inefficient algorithm may be implemented simply to demonstrate capability. After a time, the developer may become familiar with these choices and forget all the reasons why they were inappropriate. The less-than-ideal choice has now become an integral part of the system.

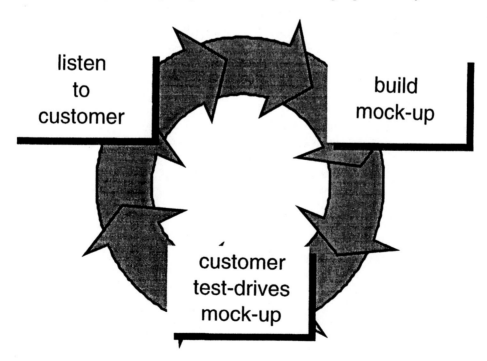

Figure 3. The prototyping paradigm

Although problems can occur, prototyping is an effective paradigm for software engineering. The key is to define the rules of the game at the beginning; that is, the customer and developer must both agree that the prototype is built to serve as a mechanism for defining requirements. It is then discarded (at least in part) and the actual software is engineered with an eye toward quality and maintainability.

When an incremental model is used, the first increment is often a *core product*. That is, basic requirements are addressed, but many supplementary features (some known, others unknown) remain undelivered. The core product is used by the customer (or undergoes detailed review). As a result of use and/or evaluation, a plan is developed for the next increment. The plan addresses the modification of the core product to better meet the needs of the customer and the delivery of additional features and functionality. This process is repeated following the delivery of each increment, until the complete product is produced.

The incremental process model, like prototyping (Section 2.2) and evolutionary approaches (Section 2.4), is iterative in nature. However, the incremental model focuses on the delivery of an operational product with each increment. Early increments are "stripped down" versions of the final product, but they do provide capability that serves the user and also provide a platform for evaluation by the user.

Incremental development is particularly useful when staffing is unavailable for a complete implementation by the business deadline that has been established for the project. Early increments can be implemented with fewer people. If the core product is well received, then additional staff (if required) can be added to implement the next increment. In addition, increments can be planned to manage technical risks. For example, a major system might require the availability of new hardware that is under development and whose delivery date is uncertain. It might be possible to plan early increments in a way that avoids the use of this hardware, thereby enabling partial functionality to be delivered to end users without inordinate delay.

2.4 Evolutionary Models

The *evolutionary* paradigm, also called the *spiral model* [3] couples the iterative nature of prototyping with the controlled and systematic aspects of the linear model. Using the evolutionary paradigm, software is developed in a series of incremental releases. During early iterations, the incremental release might be a prototype. During later iterations, increasingly more complete versions of the engineered system are produced.

Figure 4 depicts a typical evolutionary model.

Each pass around the spiral moves through six task regions:

- **customer communication**—tasks required to establish effective communication between developer and customer
- **planning**—tasks required to define resources, time lines and other project-related information
- **risk assessment**—tasks required to assess both technical and management risks
- **engineering**—tasks required to build one or more representations of the application
- **construction and release**—tasks required to construct, test, install, and provide user support (for example, documentation and training)
- **customer evaluation**—tasks required to obtain customer feedback based on evaluation of the software representations created during the engineering stage and implemented during the installation stage.

Each region is populated by a series of tasks adapted to the characteristics of the project to be undertaken.

The spiral model is a realistic approach to the development of large scale systems and software. It uses an "evolutionary" approach [4] to software engineering, enabling the developer and customer to understand and react to risks at each evolutionary level. It uses prototyping as a risk reduction mechanism, but more importantly, it enables the developer to apply the prototyping approach at any stage in the evolution of the product. It maintains the systematic stepwise approach suggested by the classic life cycle but incorporates it into an iterative framework that more realistically reflects the real world. The spiral model demands a direct consideration of technical risks at all stages of the project, and if properly applied, should reduce risks before they become problematic.

But like other paradigms, the spiral model is not a panacea. It may be difficult to convince customers (particularly in contract situations) that the evolutionary approach is controllable. It demands considerable risk assessment expertise, and relies on this expertise for success. If a major risk is not discovered, problems will undoubtedly occur. Finally, the model itself is relatively new and has not been used as widely as the linear sequential or prototyping paradigms. It will take a number of years before efficacy of this important new paradigm can be determined with absolute certainty.

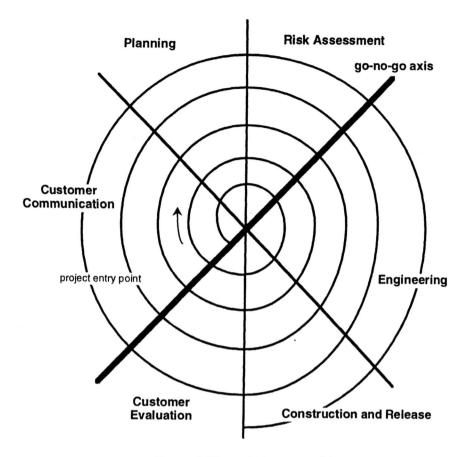

Planning

Risk Assessment

go-no-go axis

Customer
Communication

project entry point

Engineering

Customer
Evaluation

Construction and Release

Figure 4. The evolutionary model

2.5 The Formal Methods Model

The formal methods paradigm encompasses a set of activities that leads to formal mathematical specification of computer software. Formal methods enable a software engineer to specify, develop, and verify a computer-based system by applying a rigorous, mathematical notation. A variation on this approach, called cleanroom software engineering [5, 6], is currently applied by a limited number of companies.

When formal methods are used during development, they provide a mechanism for eliminating many of the problems that are difficult to overcome using other software engineering paradigms. Ambiguity, incompleteness, and inconsistency can be discovered and corrected more easily—not through ad hoc review, but through the application of mathematical analysis. When formal methods are used during design, they serve as a basis for program verification and therefore enable the software engineer to discover and correct errors that might otherwise go undetected.

Although not yet a mainstream approach, the formal methods model offers the promise of defect-free software. Yet, concern about its applicability in a business environment has been voiced:

1. The development of formal models is currently quite time-consuming and expensive.

2. Because few software developers have the necessary background to apply formal methods, extensive training is required.

3. It is difficult to use the models as a communication mechanism for technically unsophisticated customers.

These concerns notwithstanding, it is likely that the formal methods approach will gain adherents among software developers who must build safety-critical software (such as aircraft avionics and medical devices) and among developers that would suffer severe economic hardship should software errors occur.

3.0 The Management Spectrum

Effective software project management focuses on the three P's: *people, problem, and process.* The order is not arbitrary. The manager who forgets that software engineering work is an intensely human endeavor will never have success in project management. A manager who fails to encourage comprehensive customer communication early in the evolution of a project risks building an elegant solution for the wrong problem. Finally, the manager who pays little attention to the process runs the risk of inserting competent technical methods and tools into a vacuum.

3.1 People

The cultivation of motivated, highly skilled software people has been discussed since the 1960s [see 7, 8, 9]. The Software Engineering Institute has sponsored a *people-management maturity model* "to enhance the readiness of software organizations to undertake increasingly complex applications by helping to attract, grow, motivate, deploy, and retain the talent needed to improve their software development capability." [10]

The people-management maturity model defines the following key practice areas for software people: recruiting, selection, performance management, training, compensation, career development, organization, and team and culture development. Organizations that achieve high levels of maturity in the people-management area have a higher likelihood of implementing effective software engineering practices.

3.2 The Problem

Before a project can be planned, objectives and scope should be established, alternative solutions should be considered, and technical and management constraints should be identified. Without this information, it is impossible to develop reasonable cost estimates, a realistic breakdown of project tasks, or a manageable project schedule that is a meaningful indicator of progress.

The software developer and customer must meet to define project objectives and scope. In many cases, this activity occurs as part of structured customer communication process such as *joint application design* [11, 12]. Joint application design (JAD) is an activity that occurs in five phases: project definition, research, preparation, the JAD meeting, and document preparation. The intent of each phase is to develop information that helps better define the problem to be solved or the product to be built.

3.3 The Process

A software process (see discussion of process models in Section 2.0) can be characterized as shown in Figure 5. A few framework activities apply to all software projects, regardless of their size or complexity. A number of *task sets*—tasks, milestones, deliverables, and quality assurance points—enable the framework activities to be adapted to the characteristics of the software project and the requirements of the project team. Finally, umbrella activities—such as software quality assurance, software configuration management, and measurement—overlay the process model. Umbrella activities are independent of any one framework activity and occur throughout the process.

In recent years, there has been a significant emphasis on process "maturity." [2] The Software Engineering Institute (SEI) has developed a comprehensive assessment model predicated on a set of software engineering capabilities that should be present as organizations reach different levels of process maturity. To determine an organization's current state of process maturity, the SEI uses an assessment questionnaire and a five-point grading scheme. The grading scheme determines compliance with a capability maturity model [2] that defines key activities required at different levels of process maturity. The SEI approach provides a measure of the global effectiveness of a company's software engineering practices and establishes five process maturity levels that are defined in the following manner:

Level 1: Initial—The software process is characterized as ad hoc, and occasionally even chaotic. Few processes are defined, and success depends on individual effort.

Level 2: Repeatable—Basic project management processes are established to track cost, schedule, and functionality. The necessary process discipline is in place to repeat earlier successes on projects with similar applications.

Level 3: Defined—The software process for both management and engineering activities is documented, standardized, and integrated into an organization-wide software process. All projects use a documented and approved version of the organization's process for developing and maintaining software. This level includes all characteristics defined for level 2.

Level 4: Managed—Detailed measures of the software process and product quality are collected. Both the software process and products are quantitatively understood and controlled using detailed measures. This level includes all characteristics defined for level 3.

Level 5: Optimizing—Continuous process improvement is enabled by quantitative feedback from the process and from testing innovative ideas and technologies. This level includes all characteristics defined for level 4.

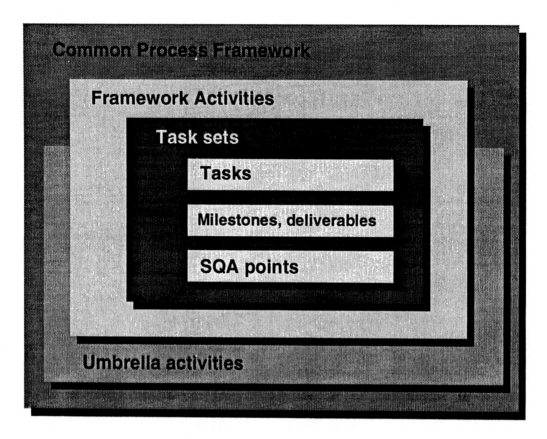

Figure 5. A common process framework

The five levels defined by the SEI are derived as a consequence of evaluating responses to the SEI assessment questionnaire that is based on the CMM. The results of the questionnaire are distilled to a single numerical grade that helps indicate an organization's process maturity.

The SEI has associated key process areas (KPAs) with each maturity level. The KPAs describe those software engineering functions (for example, software project planning and requirements management) that must be present to satisfy good practice at a particular level. Each KPA is described by identifying the following characteristics:

- *goals*—the overall objectives that the KPA must achieve

- *commitments*—requirements (imposed on the organization) that must be met to achieve the goals, provide proof of intent to comply with the goals

- *abilities*—those things that must be in place (organizationally and technically) that will enable the organization to meet the commitments

- *activities*—the specific tasks that are required to achieve the KPA function

- *methods for monitoring implementation*—the manner in which the activities are monitored as they are put into place

- *methods for verifying implementation*—the manner in which proper practice for the KPA can be verified.

Eighteen KPAs (each defined using the structure noted above) are defined across the maturity model and are mapped into different levels of process maturity.

Each KPA is defined by a set of *key practices* that contribute to satisfying its goals. The key practices are policies, procedures, and activities that must occur before a key process area has been fully instituted. The SEI defines *key indicators* as "those key practices or components of key practices that offer the greatest insight into whether the goals of a key process area have been achieved." Assessment questions are designed to probe for the existence (or lack thereof) of a key indicator.

4.0 Software Project Management

Software project management encompasses the following activities: measurement, project estimating, risk analysis, scheduling, tracking, and control. A comprehensive discussion of these topics is beyond the scope of this paper, but a brief overview of each topic will enable the reader to understand the breadth of management activities required for a mature software engineering organizations.

4.1 Measurement and Metrics

To be most effective, software metrics should be collected for both the process and the product. Process-oriented metrics [14, 15] can be collected during the process and after it has been completed. Process metrics collected during the project focus on the efficacy of quality assurance activities, change management, and project management. Process metrics collected after a project has been completed examine quality and productivity. Process measures are normalized using either lines of code or function points [13], so that data collected from many different projects can be compared and analyzed in a consistent manner. Product metrics measure technical characteristics of the software that provide an indication of software quality [15, 16, 17, 18]. Measures can be applied to models created during analysis and design activities, the source code, and testing data. The mechanics of measurement and the specific measures to be collected are beyond the scope of this paper.

4.2 Project Estimating

Scheduling and budgets are often dictated by business issues. The role of estimating within the software process often serves as a "sanity check" on the predefined deadlines and budgets that have been established by management. (Ideally, the software engineering organization should be intimately involved in establishing deadlines and budgets, but this is not a perfect or fair world.)

All software project estimation techniques require that the project have a bounded scope, and all rely on a high level functional decomposition of the project and an assessment of project difficulty and complexity. There are three broad classes of estimation techniques [19] for software projects:

- **Effort estimation techniques**. The project manager creates a matrix in which the left-hand column contains a list of major system functions derived using functional decomposition applied to project scope. The top row

contains a list of major software engineering tasks derived from the common process framework. The manager (with the assistance of technical staff) estimates the effort required to accomplish each task for each function.

- **Size-Oriented Estimation**. A list of major system functions is derived using functional decomposition applied to project scope. The "size" of each function is estimated using either lines of code (LOC) or function points (FP). Average productivity data (for instance, function points per person month) for similar functions or projects are used to generate an estimate of effort required for each function.

- **Empirical Models**. Using the results of a large population of past projects, an empirical model that relates product size (in LOC or FP) to effort is developed using a statistical technique such as regression analysis. The product size for the work to be done is estimated and the empirical model is used to generate projected effort (for example, [20]).

In addition to the above techniques, a software project manager can develop estimates by analogy. This is done by examining similar past projects then projecting effort and duration recorded for these projects to the current situation.

4.3 Risk Analysis

Almost five centuries have passed since Machiavelli said: "I think it may be true that fortune is the ruler of half our actions, but that she allows the other half to be governed by us... [fortune] is like an impetuous river... but men can make provision against it by dykes and banks." Fortune (we call it risk) is in the back of every software project manager's mind, and that is often where it stays. And as a result, risk is never adequately addressed. When bad things happen, the manager and the project team are unprepared.

In order to "make provision against it," a software project team must conduct risk analysis explicitly. Risk analysis [21, 22, 23] is actually a series of steps that enable the software team to perform risk identification, risk assessment, risk prioritization, and risk management. The goals of these activities are: (1) to identify those risks that have a high likelihood of occurrence, (2) to assess the consequence (impact) of each risk should it occur, and (3) to develop a plan for mitigating the risks when possible, monitoring factors that may indicate their arrival, and developing a set of contingency plans should they occur.

4.4 Scheduling

The process definition and project management activities that have been discussed above feed the scheduling activity. The common process framework provides a work breakdown structure for scheduling. Available human resources, coupled with effort estimates and risk analysis, provide the task interdependencies, parallelism, and time lines that are used in constructing a project schedule.

4.5 Tracking and Control

Project tracking and control is most effective when it becomes an integral part of software engineering work. A well-defined process framework should provide a set of milestones that can be used for project tracking. Control focuses on two major issues: quality and change.

To control quality, a software project team must establish effective techniques for software quality assurance, and to control change, the team should establish a software configuration management framework.

5.0 Software Quality Assurance

In his landmark book on quality, Philip Crosby [24] states:

The problem of quality management is not what people don't know about it. The problem is what they think they do know...

In this regard, quality has much in common with sex. Everybody is for it. (Under certain conditions, of course.) Everyone feels they understand it. (Even though they wouldn't want to explain it.) Everyone thinks execution is only a matter of following natural inclinations. (After all, we do get along somehow.) And, of course, most people feel that problems in these areas are caused by other people. (If only they would take the time to do things right.)

There have been many definitions of software quality proposed in the literature. For our purposes, software quality is defined as: *Conformance to explicitly stated functional and performance requirements, explicitly documented development standards, and implicit characteristics that are expected of all professionally developed software.*

There is little question that the above definition could be modified or extended. In fact, the precise definition of software quality could be debated endlessly. But the definition stated above does serve to emphasize three important points:

1. Software requirements are the foundation from which quality is assessed. Lack of conformance to requirements is lack of quality.

2. A mature software process model defines a set of development criteria that guide the manner in which software is engineered. If the criteria are not followed, lack of quality will almost surely result.

3. There is a set of implicit requirements that often go unmentioned (for example, the desire for good maintainability). If software conforms to its explicit requirements but fails to meet implicit requirements, software quality is suspect.

Almost two decades ago, McCall and Cavano [25, 26] defined a set of quality factors that were a first step toward the development of metrics for software quality. These factors assessed software from three distinct points of view: (1) product operation (using it); (2) product revision (changing it), and (3) product transition (modifying it to work in a different environment, that is., "porting" it). These factors include:

- *Correctness.* The extent to which a program satisfies its specification and fulfills the customer's mission objectives.

- *Reliability.* The extent to which a program can be expected to perform its intended function with required precision.

- *Efficiency.* The amount of computing resources and code required by a program to perform its function.

- *Integrity.* Extent to which access to software or data by unauthorized persons can be controlled.

- *Usability.* Effort require to learn, operate, prepare input, and interpret output of a program.

- *Maintainability.* Effort require to locate and fix an error in a program. [Might be better termed "correctability"].

- *Flexibility.* Effort required to modify an operational program.

- *Testability.* Effort required to test a program to insure that it performs its intended function.

- *Portability.* Effort required to transfer the program from one hardware and/or software system environment to another.

- *Reusability.* Extent to which a program [or parts of a program] can be reused in other applications—related to the packaging and scope of the functions that the program performs.

- *Interoperability.* Effort required to couple one system to another.

The intriguing thing about these factors is how little they have changed in almost 20 years. Computing technology and program architectures have undergone a sea change, but the characteristics that define high-quality software appear to be invariant. The implication: An organization that adopts factors such as those described above will build software today that will exhibit high quality well into the first few decades of the twenty-first century. More importantly, this will occur regardless of the massive changes in computing technologies that are sure to come over that period of time.

Software quality is designed into a product or system. It is not imposed after the fact. For this reason, *software quality assurance* (SQA) actually begins with the set of technical methods and tools that help the analyst to achieve a high-quality specification and the designer to develop a high-quality design.

Once a specification (or prototype) and design have been created, each must be assessed for quality. The central activity that accomplishes quality assessment is the formal technical review. The *formal technical review* (FTR)—conducted as a *walk-through* or an *inspection* [27]—is a stylized meeting conducted by technical staff with the sole purpose of uncovering quality problems. In many situations, formal technical reviews have been found to be as effective as testing in uncovering defects in software [28].

Software testing combines a multistep strategy with a series of test case design methods that help ensure effective error detection. Many software developers use software testing as a quality assurance "safety net." That is, developers assume that thorough testing will uncover most errors, thereby mitigating the need for other SQA activities. Unfortunately, testing, even when performed well, is not as effective as we might like for all classes of errors. A much better strategy is to find and correct errors (using FTRs) before getting to testing.

The degree to which formal *standards and procedures* are applied to the software engineering process varies from company to company. In many cases, standards are dictated by customers or regulatory mandate. In other situations standards are self-imposed. An assessment of compliance to standards may be conducted by software developers as part of a formal technical review, or in situations where independent verification of compliance is required, the SQA group may conduct its own audit.

A major threat to software quality comes from a seemingly benign source: changes. Every change to software has the potential for introducing error or creating side effects that propagate errors. The change control process contributes directly to software quality by formalizing requests for change, evaluating the nature of change, and controlling the impact of change. Change control is applied during software development and later, during the software maintenance phase.

Measurement is an activity that is integral to any engineering discipline. An important objective of SQA is to track software quality and assess the impact of methodological and procedural changes on improved software quality. To accomplish this, *software metrics* must be collected.

Record keeping and recording for software quality assurance provide procedures for the collection and dissemination of SQA information. The results of reviews, audits, change control, testing, and other SQA activities must become part of the historical record for a project and should be disseminated to development staff on a need-to-know basis. For example, the results of each formal technical review for a procedural design are recorded and can be placed in a "folder" that contains all technical and SQA information about a module.

6.0 Software Configuration Management

Change is inevitable when computer software is built. And change increases the level of confusion among software engineers who are working on a project. Confusion arises when changes are not analyzed before they are made, recorded before they are implemented, reported to those who should be aware that they have occurred, or controlled in a manner that will improve quality and reduce error. Babich [29] discusses this when he states:

> The art of coordinating software development to minimize... confusion is called *configuration management.* Configuration management is the art of identifying, organizing, and controlling modifications to the software being built by a programming team. The goal is to maximize productivity by minimizing mistakes.

Software configuration management (SCM) is an umbrella activity that is applied throughout the software engineering process. Because change can occur at any time, SCM activities are developed to (1) identify change, (2) control change, (3) ensure that change is being properly implemented and (4) report change to others who may have an interest.

A primary goal of software engineering is to improve the ease with which changes can be accommodated and reduce the amount of effort expended when changes must be made.

7.0 The Technical Spectrum

There was a time—some people still call it "the good old days"—when a skilled programmer created a program like an artist creates a painting: she just sat down and started. Pressman and Herron [30] draw other parallels when they write:

> At one time or another, almost everyone laments the passing of the good old days. We miss the simplicity, the personal touch, the emphasis on quality that were the trademarks of a craft. Carpenters reminisce about the days when houses were built with mahogany and oak, and beams were set without nails. Engineers still talk about an earlier era when one person did all the design (and did it right) and then went down to the shop floor and built the thing. In those days, people did good work and stood behind it.
>
> How far back do we have to travel to reach the good old days? Both carpentry and engineering have a history that is well over 2,000 years old. The disciplined way in which work is conducted, the standards that guide each task, the step by step approach that is applied, have all evolved through centuries of experience. *Software engineering* has a much shorter history.

During its short history, the creation of computer programs has evolved from an art form, to a craft, to an engineering discipline. As the evolution took place, the free-form style of the artist was replaced by the disciplined methods of an engineer. To be honest, we lose something when a transition like this is made. There's a certain freedom in art that can't be replicated in engineering. But we gain much, much more than we lose.

As the journey from art to engineering occurred, basic principles that guided our approach to software problem analysis, design and testing slowly evolved. And at the same time, methods were developed that embodied these principles and made software engineering tasks more systematic. Some of these "hot, new" methods flashed to the surface for a few years, only to disappear into oblivion, but others have stood the test of time to become part of the technology of software development.

In this section we discuss the basic principles that support the software engineering methods and provide an overview of some of the methods that have already "stood the test of time" and others that are likely to do so.

7.1 Software Engineering Methods—The Landscape

All engineering disciplines encompass four major activities: (1) the definition of the problem to be solved, (2) the design of a solution that will meet the customer's needs; (2) the construction of the solution, and (4) the testing of the implemented solution to uncover latent errors and provide an indication that customer requirements have been achieved. Software engineering offers a variety of different methods to achieve these activities. In fact, the methods landscape can be partitioned into three different regions:

- conventional software engineering methods
- object-oriented approaches
- formal methods

Each of these regions is populated by a variety of methods that have spawned their own culture, not to mention a sometimes confusing array of notation and heuristics. Luckily, all of the regions are unified by a set of overriding principles that lead to a single objective: to create high quality computer software.

Conventional software engineering methods view software as an information transform and approach each problem using an input-process-output viewpoint. Object-oriented approaches consider each problem as a set of classes and work to create a solution by implementing a set of communicating objects that are instantiated from these classes. Formal methods describe the problem in mathematical terms, enabling rigorous evaluation of completeness, consistency, and correctness.

Like competing geographical regions on the world map, the regions of the software engineering methods map do not always exist peacefully. Some inhabitants of a particular region cannot resist religious warfare. Like most religious warriors, they become consumed by dogma and often do more harm that good. The regions of the software engineering methods landscape can and should coexist peacefully, and tedious debates over which method is best seem to miss the point. Any method, if properly applied within the context of a solid set of software engineering principles, will lead to higher quality software than an undisciplined approach.

7.2 Problem Definition

A problem cannot be fully defined and bounded until it is communicated. For this reason, the first step in any software engineering project is customer communication. Techniques for customer communication [11, 12] were discussed earlier in this paper. In essence, the developer and the customer must develop an effective mechanism for defining and negotiating the basic requirements for the software project. Once this has been accomplished, requirements analysis begins. Two options are available at this stage: (1) the creation of a prototype that will assist the developer and the customer in better understanding the system to be build, and/or (2) the creation of a detailed set of analysis models that describe the data, function, and behavior for the system.

7.2.1 Analysis Principles

Today, analysis modeling can be accomplished by applying one of several different methods that populate the three regions of the software engineering methods landscape. All methods, however, conform to a set of analysis principles [31]:

1. **The data domain of the problem must be modeled.** To accomplish this, the analyst must define the data objects (entities) that are visible to the user of the software and the relationships that exist between the data objects. The content of each data object (the object's attributes) must also be defined.

2. **The functional domain of the problem must be modeled.** Software functions transform the data objects of the system and can be modeled as a hierarchy (conventional methods), as services to classes within a system (the object-oriented view), or as a succinct set of mathematical expressions (the formal view).

3. **The behavior of the system must be represented.** All computer-based systems respond to external events and change their state of operation as a consequence. Behavioral modeling indicates the externally observable states of operation of a system and how transition occurs between these states.

4. **Models of data, function, and behavior must be partitioned.** All engineering problem-solving is a process of elaboration. The problem (and the models described above) are first represented at a high level of abstraction. As problem definition progresses, detail is refined and the level of abstraction is reduced. This activity is called partitioning.

5. **The overriding trend in analysis is from essence toward implementation.** As the process of elaboration progresses, the statement of the problem moves from a representation of the essence of the solution toward implementation-specific detail. This progression leads us from analysis toward design.

7.2.2 Analysis Methods

A discussion of the notation and heuristics of even the most popular analysis methods is beyond the scope of this paper. The problem is further compounded by the three different regions of the methods landscape and the local issues specific to each. Therefore, all that we can hope to accomplish in this section is to note similarities among the different methods and regions:

- All analysis methods provide a notation for describing data objects and the relationships that exist between them.

- All analysis methods couple function and data and provide a way for understanding how function operates on data.

- All analysis methods enable an analyst to represent behavior at a system level, and in some cases, at a more localized level.

- All analysis methods support a partitioning approach that leads to increasingly more detailed (and implementation-specific models).

- All analysis methods establish a foundation from which design begins, and some provide representations that can be directly mapped into design.

For further information on analysis methods in each of the three regions noted above, the reader should review work by Yourdon [32], Booch [33], and Spivey [34].

7.3 Design

M.A. Jackson [35] once said: "The beginning of wisdom for a computer programmer [software engineer] is to recognize the difference between getting a program to work, and getting it *right*." Software design is a set of basic principles and a pyramid of modeling methods that provide the necessary framework for "getting it right."

7.3.1 Design Principles

Like analysis modeling, software design has

spawned a collection of methods that populate the conventional, object-oriented, and formal regions that were discussed earlier. Each method espouses its own notation and heuristics for accomplishing design, but all rely on a set of fundamental principles [31] that are outlined in the paragraphs that follow:

1. **Data and the algorithms that manipulate data should be created as a set of interrelated abstractions.** By creating data and procedural abstractions, the designer models software components that have characteristics leading to high quality. An abstraction is self-contained; it generally implements one well-constrained data structure or algorithm; it can be accessed using a simple interface; the details of its internal operation need not be known for it to be used effectively; it is inherently reusable.

2. **The internal design detail of data structures and algorithms should be hidden from other software components that make use of the data structures and algorithms.** Information hiding [36] suggests that modules be "characterized by design decisions that (each) hides from all others." Hiding implies that effective modularity can be achieved by defining a set of independent modules that communicate with one another only that information that is necessary to achieve software function. The use of information hiding as a design criterion for modular systems provides greatest benefits when modifications are required during testing and later, during software maintenance. Because most data and procedures are hidden from other parts of the software, inadvertent errors (and resultant side effects) introduced during modification are less likely to propagate to other locations within the software.

3. **Modules should exhibit independence.** That is, they should be loosely coupled to each other and to the external environment and should exhibit functional cohesion. Software with *effective modularity*, that is, independent modules, is easier to develop because function may be compartmentalized and interfaces are simplified (consider ramifications when development is conducted by a team). Independent modules are easier to maintain (and test) because secondary effects caused by design/code modification are limited; error

propagation is reduced; and reusable modules are possible.

4. **Algorithms should be designed using a constrained set of logical constructs.** This design approach, widely know as *structured programming* [37], was proposed to limit the procedural design of software to a small number of predictable operations. The use of the structured programming constructs (sequence, conditional, and loops) reduces program complexity and thereby enhances readability, testability, and maintainability. The use of a limited number of logical constructs also contributes to a human understanding process that psychologists call *chunking*. To understand this process, consider the way in which you are reading this page. You do not read individual letters; but rather, recognize patterns or chunks of letters that form words or phrases. The structured constructs are logical chunks that allow a reader to recognize procedural elements of a module, rather than reading the design or code line by line. Understanding is enhanced when readily recognizable logical forms are encountered.

7.3.2 The Design Pyramid

Like analysis, a discussion of even the most popular design methods is beyond the scope of this paper. Our discussion here will focus on a set of design activities that should occur regardless of the method that is used.

Software design should be accomplished by following a set of design activities as illustrated in Figure 6. *Data design* translates the data model created during analysis into data structures that meet the needs of the problem. *Architectural design* differs in intent depending upon the designer's viewpoint. Conventional design creates hierarchical software architectures, while object-oriented design views architecture as the message network that enables objects to communicate. *Interface design* creates implementation models for the human-computer interface, the external system interfaces that enable different applications to interoperate, and the internal interfaces that enable program data to be communicated among software components. Finally, *procedural design* is conducted as algorithms are created to implement the processing requirements of program components.

Like the pyramid depicted in Figure 6, design should be a stable object. Yet, many software developers do design by taking the pyramid and standing it on its point. That is, design begins with the creation of procedural detail, and as a result, interface, architectural, and data design just happen. This approach, common among people who insist upon coding the program with no explicit design activity, invariably leads to low-quality software that is difficult to test, challenging to extend, and frustrating to maintain. For a stable, high-quality product, the design approach must also be stable. The design pyramid provides the degree of stability necessary for good design.

7.4 Program Construction

The glory years of third-generation programming languages are rapidly coming to a close. Fourth-generation techniques, graphical programming methods, component-based software construction, and a variety of other approaches have already captured a significant percentage of all software construction activities, and there is little debate that their penetration will grow.

And yet, some members of the software engineering community continue to debate "the best programming language." Although entertaining, such debates are a waste of time. The problems that we continue to encounter in the creation of high-quality computer-based systems have relatively little to do with the means of construction. Rather, the challenges that face us can only be solved through better or innovative approaches to analysis and design, more comprehensive SQA techniques, and more effective and efficient testing. It is for this reason that construction is not emphasized in this paper.

7.5 Software Testing

Glen Myers [38] states three rules that can serve well as testing objectives:

1. Testing is a process of executing a program with the intent of finding an error.
2. A good test case is one that has a high probability of finding an as-yet-undiscovered error.
3. A successful test is one that uncovers an as-yet-undiscovered error.

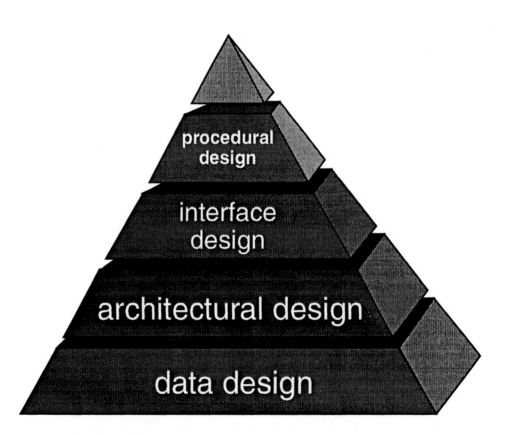

Figure 6. The design pyramid

These objectives imply a dramatic change in viewpoint. They move counter to the commonly held view that a successful test is one in which no errors are found. Our objective is to design tests that systematically uncover different classes of errors and to do so with a minimum of time and effort.

If testing is conducted successfully (according to the objective stated above), it will uncover errors in the software. As a secondary benefit, testing demonstrates that software functions appear to be working according to specification, that performance requirements appear to have been met. In addition, data collected as testing is conducted provides a good indication of software reliability and some indication of software quality as a whole. But there is one thing that testing cannot do: testing cannot show the absence of defects, it can only show that software defects are present. It is important to keep this (rather gloomy) statement in mind as testing is being conducted.

7.5.1 Strategy

A strategy for software testing integrates software test-case design techniques into a well-planned series of steps that result in the successful construction of software. It defines a template for software testing—a set of steps into which we can place specific test-case design techniques and testing methods.

A number of software testing strategies have been proposed in the literature. All provide the software developer with a template for testing, and all have the following generic characteristics:

- Testing begins at the module level and works incrementally "outward" toward the integration of the entire computer-based system.

- Different testing techniques are appropriate at different points in time.

- Testing is conducted by the developer of the software and (for large projects) an independent test group.

- Testing and debugging are different activities, but debugging must be accommodated in any testing strategy.

A strategy for software testing must accommodate low-level tests that are necessary to verify that a small source code segment has been correctly implemented, intermediate-level tests designed to uncover errors in the interfaces between modules, and high-level tests that validate major system functions against customer requirements. A strategy must provide guidance for the practitioner and a set of milestones for the manager. Because the steps of the test strategy occur at a time when deadline pressure begins to rise, progress must be measurable and problems must surface as early as possible.

7.5.2 Tactics

The design of tests for software and other engineered products can be as challenging as the initial design of the product itself. Recalling the objectives of testing, we must design tests that have the highest likelihood of finding the most errors with a minimum of time and effort.

Over the past two decades a rich variety of test-case design methods have evolved for software. These methods provide the developer with a systematic approach to testing. More importantly, methods provide a mechanism that can help to ensure the completeness of tests and provide the highest likelihood for uncovering errors in software.

Any engineered product (and most other things) can be tested in one of two ways: (1) knowing the specified function that a product has been designed to perform, tests can be conducted that demonstrate each function is fully operational; (2) knowing the internal workings of the product, tests can be conducted to ensure that "all gears mesh"; that is, internal operation performs according to specification and all internal components have been adequately exercised. The first test approach is called *black-box testing* and the second, *white-box testing* [38].

When computer software is considered, black-box testing alludes to tests that are conducted at the software interface. Although they are designed to uncover errors, black-box tests are also used to demonstrate that software functions are operational; that input is properly accepted, and output is correctly produced; that the integrity of external information (such as data files) is maintained. A black-box test examines some aspect of a system with little regard for the internal logical structure of the software.

White-box testing of software is predicated on close examination of procedural detail. Logical paths through the software are tested by providing test cases that exercise specific sets of conditions and/or loops. The status of the program may be examined at various points to determine if the expected or asserted status corresponds to the actual status.

8.0 The Road Ahead & The Three R's

Software is a child of the latter half of the twentieth century—a baby boomer. And like its human counterpart, software has accomplished much while at the same time leaving much to be accomplished. It appears that the economic and business environment of the next ten years will be dramatically different than anything that baby boomers have yet experienced.

Staff downsizing, the threat of outsourcing, and the demands of customers who won't take "slow" for an answer require significant changes in our approach to software engineering and a major reevaluation of our strategies for handling hundreds of thousands of existing systems [39].

Although many existing technologies will mature over the next decade, and new technologies will emerge, it's likely that three existing software engineering issues—I call them the three R's—will dominate the software engineering scene.

8.1 Reuse

We must build computer software faster. This simple statement is a manifestation of a business environment in which competition is vicious, product life cycles are shrinking, and time to market often defines the success of a business. The challenge of faster development is compounded by shrinking human resources and an increasing demand for improved software quality.

To meet this challenge, software must be constructed from reusable components. The concept of software reuse is not new, nor is a delineation of its major technical and management challenges [40]. Yet without reuse, there is little hope of building software in time frames that shrink from years to months.

It is likely that two regions of the methods landscape may merge as greater emphasis is placed on reuse. Object-oriented development can lead to the design and implementation of inherently reusable program components, but to meet the challenge, these components must be demonstrably defect free. It may be that formal methods will play a role in the development of components that are proven correct prior to their entry in a component library. Like integrated circuits in hardware design, these "formally" developed components can be used with a fair degree of assurance by other software designers.

If technology problems associated with reuse are overcome (and this is likely), management and cultural challenges remain. Who will have responsibility for creating reusable components? Who will manage them once they are created? Who will bear the additional costs of developing reusable components? What incentives will be provided for software engineers to use them? How will revenues be generated from reuse? What are the risks associated with creating a reuse culture? How will developers of reusable components be compensated? How will legal issues such as liability and copyright protection be addressed? These and many other questions remain to be answered. And yet, component reuse is our best hope for meeting the software challenges of the early part of the twenty-first century.

8.2 Reengineering

Almost every business relies on the day-to-day operation of an aging software plant. Major companies spend as much as 70 percent or more of their software budget on the care and feeding of legacy systems. Many of these systems were poorly designed more than decade ago and have been patched and pushed to their limits. The result is a software plant with aging, even decrepit systems that absorb increasingly large amounts of resource with little hope of abatement. The software plant must be rebuilt, and that demands a reengineering strategy.

Reengineering takes time; it costs significant amounts of money, and it absorbs resources that might be otherwise occupied on immediate concerns. For all of these reasons, reengineering is not accomplished in a few months or even a few years. Reengineering of information systems is an activity that will absorb software resources for many years.

A paradigm for reengineering includes the following steps:

- *inventory analysis*—creating a prioritized list of programs that are candidates for reengineering
- *document restructuring*—upgrading documentation to reflect the current workings of a program
- *code restructuring*—recoding selected portions of a program to reduce complexity, ready the code for future change, and improve understandability
- *data restructuring*—redesigning data structures to better accommodate current needs; redesign the algorithms that manipulate these data structures
- *reverse engineering*—examine software internals to determine how the system has been constructed
- *forward engineering*—using information obtained from reverse engineering, rebuild the application using modern software engineering practices and principles.

8.3 Retooling

To achieve the first two R's, we need a third R—a new generation of software tools. In retooling the software engineering process, we must remember the mistakes of the 1980s and early 1990s. At that time, CASE tools were inserted into a process vacuum, and failed to meet expectations. Tools for the next ten years will address all aspects of the methods landscape. But they should emphasize reuse and reengineering.

9.0 Summary

As each of us in the software business looks to the future, a small set of questions is asked and re-asked. Will we continue to struggle to produce software that meets the needs of a new breed of customers? Will generation X software professionals repeat the mistakes of the generation that preceded them? Will software remain a bottleneck in the development of new generations of computer-based products and systems? The degree to which the industry embraces software engineering and works to instantiate it into the culture of software development will have a strong bearing on the final answers to these questions. And the answers to these questions will have a strong bearing on whether we should look to the future with anticipation or trepidation.

References

[1] Naur, P. and B. Randall (eds.), *Software Engineering: A Report on a Conference Sponsored by the NATO Science Committee*, NATO, 1969.

[2] Paulk, M. et al., *Capability Maturity Model for Software*, Software Engineering Institute, Carnegie Mellon University, Pittsburgh, PA, 1993.

[3] Boehm, B., "A Spiral Model for Software Development and Enhancement," *Computer*, Vol. 21, No. 5, May 1988, pp. 61–72.

[4] Gilb, T., *Principles of Software Engineering Management*, Addison-Wesley, Reading, Mass., 1988.

[5] Mills, H.D., M. Dyer, and R. Linger, "Cleanroom Software Engineering," *IEEE Software*, Sept. 1987, pp. 19–25.

[6] Dyer, M., *The Cleanroom Approach to Quality Software Development*, Wiley, New York, N.Y., 1992.

[7] Cougar, J. and R. Zawacki, *Managing and Motivating Computer Personnel*, Wiley, New York, N.Y., 1980.

[8] DeMarco, T. and T. Lister, *Peopleware*, Dorset House, 1987.

[9] Weinberg, G., *Understanding the Professional Programmer*, Dorset House, 1988.

[10] Curtis, B., "People Management Maturity Model," *Proc. Int'l Conf. Software Eng.*, IEEE CS Press, Los Alamitos, Calif., 1989, pp. 398–399.

[11] August, J.H., *Joint Application Design*, Prentice-Hall, Englewood Cliffs, N.J., 1991.

[12] Wood, J. and D. Silver, *Joint Application Design*, Wiley, New York, N.Y., 1989.

[13] Dreger, J.B., *Function Point Analysis*, Prentice-Hall, Englewood Cliffs, N.J., 1989.

[14] Hetzel, B., *Making Software Measurement Work*, QED Publishing, 1993.

[15] Jones, C., *Applied Software Measurement*, McGraw-Hill, New York, N.Y., 1991.

[16] Fenton, N.E., *Software Metrics*, Chapman & Hall, 1991.

[17] Zuse, H., *Software Complexity*, W. deGruyer & Co., Berlin, 1990.

[18] Lorenz, M. and J. Kidd, *Object-Oriented Software Metrics*, Prentice-Hall, Englewood Cliffs, N.J., 1994.

[19] Pressman, R.S., *A Manager's Guide to Software Engineering*, McGraw-Hill, New York, N.Y., 1993.

[20] Boehm, B., *Software Engineering Economics*, Prentice-Hall, Englewood Cliffs, N.J., 1981.

[21] Charette, R., *Application Strategies for Risk Analysis*, McGraw-Hill, New York, N.Y., 1990.

[22] Jones, C., *Assessment and Control of Software Risks*, Yourdon Press, 1993.

[24] Crosby, P., *Quality is Free*, McGraw-Hill, New York, N.Y., 1979.

[25] McCall, J., P. Richards, and G. Walters, "Factors in Software Quality," three volumes, NTIS AD-A049-014, 015, 055, Nov. 1977.

[26] Cavano, J.P. and J.A. McCall, "A Framework for the Measurement of Software Quality," *Proc. ACM Software Quality Assurance Workshop*, ACM Press, New York, N.Y., 1978, pp. 133–139.

[27] Freedman, D and G. Weinberg, *The Handbook of Walkthroughs, Inspections and Technical Reviews*, Dorset House, 1990.

[28] Gilb, T. and D. Graham, *Software Inspection*, Addison-Wesley, Reading, Mass., 1993.

[29] Babich, W., *Software Configuration Management*, Addison-Wesley, Reading, Mass., 1986.

[30] Pressman, R. and S. Herron, Software Shock, Dorset House, 1991.

[31] Pressman, R., *Software Engineering: A Practitioner's Approach*, 3rd ed., McGraw-Hill, New York, N.Y., 1992.

[32] Yourdon, E., *Modern Structured Analysis*, Yourdon Press, 1989.

[33] Booch, G., *Object-Oriented Analysis & Design*, Benjamin-Cummings, 1994.

[34] Spivey, M., *The Z Notation*, Prentice-Hall, Englewood Cliffs, N.J., 1992.

[35] Jackson, M., *Principles of Program Design*, Academic Press, New York, N.Y., 1975.

[36] Parnas, D.L., "On Criteria to be used in Decomposing Systems into Modules," *Comm. ACM*, Vol. 14, No. 1, Apr. 1972, pp. 221–227.

[37] Linger, R., H. Mills, and B. Witt, *Structured Programming*, Addison-Wesley, Reading, Mass., 1979.

[38] Myers, G., *The Art of Software Testing*, Wiley, New York, N.Y., 1979.

[38] Beizer, B., *Software Testing Techniques*, 2nd ed., VanNostrand Reinhold, 1990.

[39] Pressman, R., "Software According to Nicollo Machiavelli," *IEEE Software*, Jan. 1995, pp. 101–102.

[40] Tracz, W., *Software Reuse: Emerging Technology*, IEEE CS Press, Los Alamitos, Calif., 1988.

Foreword

In the mid-1960s, there was increasing concern in scientific quarters of the Western world that the tempestuous development of computer hardware was not matched by appropriate progress in software. The software situation looked more to be turbulent. Operating systems had just been the latest rage, but they showed unexpected weaknesses. The uneasiness had been lined out in the NATO Science Committee by its US representative, Dr. I.I. Rabi, the Nobel laureate and famous, as well as influential, physicist. In 1967, the Science Committee set up the Study Group on Computer Science, with members from several countries, to analyze the situation. The German authorities nominated me for this team. The study group was given the task of "assessing the entire field of computer science," with particular elaboration on the Science Committee's consideration of "organizing a conference and, perhaps, at a later date,...setting up...an International Institute of Computer Science."

The study group, concentrating its deliberations on actions that would merit an international rather than a national effort, discussed all sorts of promising scientific projects. However, it was rather inconclusive on the relation of these themes to the critical observations mentioned above, which had guided the Science Committee. Perhaps not all members of the study group had been properly informed about the rationale of its existence. In a sudden mood of anger, I made the remark, "The whole trouble comes from the fact that there is so much tinkering with software. It is not made in a clean fabrication process," and when I found out that this remark was shocking to some of my scientific colleagues, I elaborated the idea with the provocative saying, "What we need is *software engineering*."

This remark had the effect that the expression "software engineering," which seemed to some to be a contradiction in terms, stuck in the minds of the members of the group. In the end, the study group recommended in late 1967 the holding of a Working Conference on Software Engineering, and I was made chairman. I had not only the task of organizing the meeting (which was held from October 7 to October 10, 1968, in Garmisch, Germany), but I had to set up a scientific program for a subject that was suddenly defined by my provocative remark. I enjoyed the help of my cochairmen, L. Bolliet from France, and H.J. Helms from Denmark, and in particular the invaluable support of the program committee members, A.J. Perlis and B. Randall in the sec-

tion on design, P. Naur and J.N. Buxton in the section on production, and K. Samuelson, B. Galler, and D. Gries in the section on service. Among the 50 or so participants, E.W. Dijkstra was dominant. He actually made not only cynical remarks like "the dissemination of error-loaded software is frightening" and "it is not clear that the people who manufacture software are to be blamed. I think manufacturers deserve better, more understanding users." He also said already at this early date, "Whether the correctness of a piece of software can be guaranteed or not depends greatly on the structure of the thing made," and he had very fittingly named his paper "Complexity Controlled by Hierarchical Ordering of Function and Variability," introducing a theme that followed his life the next 20 years. Some of his words have become proverbs in computing, like "testing is a very inefficient way of convincing oneself of the correctness of a program."

With the wide distribution of the reports on the Garmisch conference and on a follow-up conference in Rome, from October 27 to 31, 1969, it emerged that not only the phrase *software engineering*, but also the idea behind this, became fashionable. Chairs were created, institutes were established (although the one which the NATO Science Committee had proposed did not come about because of reluctance on the part of Great Britain to have it organized on the European continent), and a great number of conferences were held. The present volume shows clearly how much progress has been made in the intervening years.

The editors deserve particular thanks for paying so much attention to a tutorial. In choosing the material, they have tried to highlight a number of software engineering initiatives whose origin is European. In particular, the more formal approach to software engineering is evident, and they have included some material that is not readily available elsewhere. The tutorial nature of the papers is intended to offer readers an easy introduction to the topics and indeed to the attempts that have been made in recent years to provide them with the tools, both in a handcraft and intellectual sense, that allow them now to call themselves honestly *software engineers*.

Friedrich L. Bauer

Reprinted from *Software Engineering—A European Perspective*, R.H. Thayer and A.D. McGettrick, eds., p. vi.

Software Engineering—20 Years On and 20 Years Back*

J. N. Buxton

Department of Computing, Kings College, London

This paper gives a personal view of the development of software engineering, starting from the NATO conferences some 20 years ago, looking at the current situation and at possible lines of future development. Software engineering is not presented as separate from computer science but as the engineering face of the same subject. It is proposed in the paper that significant future developments will come from new localized computing paradigms in specific application domains.

20 YEARS BACK

The start of the development of software engineering as a subject in its own right, or perhaps more correctly as a new point of view on computing, is particularly associated with the NATO conferences in 1968 and 1969. The motivations behind the first of these meetings was the dawning realization that major software systems were being fuilt by groups consisting essentially of gifted amateurs. The endemic problems of the "software crisis"—software was late, over budget, and unreliable—already affected small and medium systems for well-coordinated applications and would clearly have even more serious consequences for the really big systems which were being planned.

People in the profession typically had scientific backgrounds in mathematics, the sciences, or electronics. In 1968 we had already achieved the first big breakthrough in the subject—the development of high-level programming languages—and the second was awaited. The time was ripe for the proposition which was floated by the NATO Science Committee, and by Professor Fritz Bauer of Munich, among others, that we should consider the subject as a branch of engineering; other professions built big systems of great complexity and by and large they called themselves "engineers," and perhaps we should consider whether we should do the same. Our big systems problems seemed primarily to be on the software side and the proposition was that it might well help to look at software development from the standpoint of the general principles and methods of engineering. And so, the first NATO Conference on Software Engineering was convened in Garmisch Parten-Kirchen in Bavaria.

It was an inspiring occasion. Some 50 people were invited from among the leaders in the field and from the first evening of the meeting it was clear that we shared deep concerns about the quality of software being built at the time. It was not just late and over budget; even more seriously we could see, and on that occasion we were able to share our anxieties about, the safety aspects of future systems.

The first meeting went some way to describing the problems—the next meeting was scheduled to follow after a year which was to be devoted to study of the techniques needed for its solution. We expected, of course, that a year spent in studying the application of engineering principles to software development would show us how to solve the problem. It turned out that after a year we had not solved it and the second meeting in Rome was rather an anticlimax. However, the software engineering idea was now launched: it has steadily gathered momentum over some 20 years. Some would no doubt say that it has become one of the great bandwagons of our time; however, much has been achieved and many central ideas have been developed: the need for management as well as technology, the software lifecycle, the use of toolsets, the application of quality assurance techniques, and so on.

So during some 20 years, while the business has expanded by many orders of magnitude, we have been able to keep our heads above water. We have put computers to use in most fields of human endeavor, we

Address correspondence to Professor J. N. Buxton, Department of Computing, Kings College London, Strand, London WC2R2LS, England.

*The paper is a written version of the keynote address at the International Conference on Software Engineering, Pittsburgh, May, 1989.

have demonstrated that systems of millions of lines of code taking hundreds of man-years can be built to acceptable standards, and our safety record, while not perfect, has so far apparently not been catastrophic. The early concepts of 20 years ago have been much developed: the lifecycle idea has undergone much refinement, the toolset approach has been transformed by combining unified toolsets with large project data bases, and quality control and assurance is now applied as in other engineering disciplines. We now appreciate more clearly that what we do in software development can well be seen as engineering, which must be underpinned by scientific and mathematical developments which produce laws of behavior for the materials from which we build: in other words, for computer programs.

THE PRESENT

So, where is software engineering today? In my view there is indeed a new subject of "computing" which we have to consider. It is separate from other disciplines and has features that are unique to the subject. The artifacts we build have the unique property of invisibility and furthermore, to quote David Parnas, the state space of their behavior is both large and irregular. In other words, we cannot "see" an executing program actually running; we can only observe its consequences. These frequently surprise us and in this branch of engineering we lack the existence of simple physical limits on the extent of erroneous behavior. If you build a bridge or an airplane you can see it and you can recognize the physical limitations on its behavior—this is not the case if you write a computer program.

The subject of computing has strong links and relationships to other disciplines. It is underpinned by discrete mathematics and formal logic in a way strongly analogous to the underpinning of more traditional branches of engineering by physics and continuous mathematics. We expect increasing help from relevant mathematics in determining laws of behavior for our systems and of course we rely on electronics for the provision of our hardware components. A computer is an electronic artifact and is treated as such when it is being built or when it fails; at other times we treat it as a black box and assume it runs our program perfectly.

At the heart of the subject, however, we have the study of software. We build complex multilayered programs which eventually implement applications for people—who in turn treat the software as a black box and assume it will service their application perfectly.

So, where and what is software engineering? I do not regard it as a spearate subject. Building software is perhaps the central technology in computing and much of what we call software engineering is, in my view, the face of computing which is turned toward applications. The subject of computing has three main aspects: computer science is the face turned to mathematics, from which we seek laws of behavior for programs; computer architecture is the face turned to the electronics, from which we build our computers; and software engineering is the face turned toward the users, whose applications we implement. I think the time has come to return to a unified view of our subject—software engineering is not something different from computer science or hardware design—it is a different aspect or specialty within the same general subject of computing.

20 YEARS ON

To attempt to answer the question, Where should we go next and what of the next 20 years? opens interesting areas of speculation. As software engineers, our concerns are particularly with the needs of the users and our aims are to satisfy these needs. Our techniques involve the preparation of computer programs and I propose to embark on some speculation based on a study of the levels of language inwhich these programs are written.

The traditional picture of the process of implementing an application is, in general, as follows. The user presents a problem, expressed in his own technical terminology or language, which could be that of commerce, nuclear physics, medicine or whatever, to somebody else who speaks a different language in the professional sense. This is the language of algorithms and this person devises an algorithmic solution to the specific user problem, i.e., a solution expressed in computational steps, sequences, iterations, choices. This person we call the "systems analyst" and indeed, in the historical model much used in the data processing field, this person passes the algorithms on to a "real programmer" who thinks and speaks in the codeof the basic computer hardware.

The first major advance in computing was the general introduction of higher level languages such as FORTRAN and COBOL—as in effect this eliminated from all but some specialized areas the need for the lower level of language, i.e., achine or assembly code programming. The separate roles of systems analyst and programmer have become blurred into the concept of the software engineer who indeed thinks in algorithms but expresses these directly himself in one of the fashionable languages of the day. This indeed is a breakthrough and has given us an order of magnitude advance, whether we measure it in terms of productivity, size of application we can tackle, or quality of result.

Of course we have made other detailed advances—we have refined our software engineering techniques, we have devised alternatives to algorithmic programming in functional and rule-based systems, and we have done much else. But in general terms we have not succeeded in making another general advance across the board in the subject.

In some few areas, however, there have been real successes which have brought computing to orders of magnitude more people with applications. These have been in very specific application areas, two of which spring to mind—spreadsheets and word processors. In my view, study of these successes gives us most valuable clues as to the say ahead for computing applications.

The spreadsheet provides a good example for study. The generic problem of accountancy is the presentation of a set of figures which are perhaps very complexly related but which must be coherent and consistent. The purpose is to reveal a picture of the formal state of affairs of an enterprise (so far, of course, as the accountatn thinks it wise or necessary to reveal it). The traditional working language of the accountatn is expressed in rows and columns of figures on paper together with their relationships. Now, the computer-based spreadsheet system automates the piece of paper and gives it magical extra properties which maintain consistency of the figure under the relationships between them as specified by the accountant, while he adjusts the figures. In effect, the computer program automates the generic problem rather than any specific set of accounts and so enables the accountant to express his problem of the moment and to seek solutions in his own professional language. He need know nothing, for example, of algorithms, high-level languages, or von Neuman machines, and the intermediary stages of the systems analyst and programmer have both disappeared from his view.

The same general remarks can be applied to word processing. Here what the typist sees is in effect a combination of magic correcting typewriter and filing cabinet—and again the typist need know nothing of algorithms. In both these examples there has been conspicuous success in introduction. And there are others emerging, e.g., hypertext. And historically there is much in the thesis that relates to the so-called 4GLs and, even earlier, to simulation languages in the 1960s.

Let me return to the consideration of levels of language, and summarize the argument so far. I postulated a traditional model for complete applications in which a specific user problem, expressed in the language of the domain of application, underwent a two-stage translation: first into algorithms (or some language of similar level such as functional applications or Horn logic clauses) and second down into machine code. Our first breakthrough was to automate the lower of these stages by the introduction of high-level languages, primarily algorithmic. I now postulate that the second break-

through will come in areas where we can automate the upper stage. Examples can already be found: very clearly in specific closed domains such as spreadsheets and word processors but also in more diffuse areas addressed by very high-level languages such as 4GLs and simulation generators.

Perhaps I should add a word here about object-orientedness, as this is the best known buzz word of today. I regard an object-oriented approach as a halfway house to the concept I am proposing. Objects indeed model those features of the real world readily modelable as classes of entities—that is why we invented the concept in the simulation languages of the early 1960s. However, the rules of behavior of the object are still expressed algorithmically and so an object-oriented system still embodies a general purpose language.

It is central to the argument to realize that spreadsheets and such can be used by people who do not readily think in terms of algorithms. The teaching of programming has demonstrated over many years that thinking in algorithms is a specific skill and most people have little ability in transposing problems from their own domains into algorithmic solutions. Attempts to bring the use of computers to all by teaching them programming do not work; providing a service to workers in specific domains directly in the language of that domain, however, does work and spectacularly so.

CONCLUSIONS

I come to the conclusion, therefore, that the most promising activity for the next 20 years is the search for more domains of applications in which the language used to express problems in the domain is closed, consistent, and logically based. Then we can put forward generic computer-based systems which enable users in the domain to express their problems in the language of the application and to be given solutions in their own terms. To use another buzz word of the day, I look for non-specific but localized paradigms for computing applications.

Of course this is not all that we might expect to do in the next 20 years. We can do much more in developing the underpinning technology in the intermediate levels between the user and the machine. Most of our work will still be devoted to the implementing of systems to deliver solutions to specific problems. But while we proceed with the day-to-day activities of software engineering or of the other faces of computing with which we may be concerned, wemight be wise to look out for opportunities to exploit new application domains where we can see ways to raise the "level of programming language" until it becomes the same as the professional language of that domain. Then, we will achieve another breakthrough.

Chapter 4

Software Requirements Engineering and Software Design

1.   Introduction to Chapter.

This Tutorial initially contained one chapter on requirements engineering and one chapter on design. As the papers began to accumulate, it became apparent that the topics ought to be treated together: it is not always clear when requirements engineering stops and design starts, and many of the tools and techniques are common to both disciplines. The Tutorial was therefore reorganized to cover the basics of requirements and design in one chapter and to focus on methodologies in the next.

1.1 Introduction to Software Requirements

A *software requirement* can be defined as:

- A software capability needed by the user to solve a problem or achieve an objective.

- A software capability that must be met or possessed by a system or system component to satisfy a contract, specification, standard, or other formally imposed document.

Software requirements engineering consists of the following five activities:

- *Software requirements elicitation*—The process through which the customers (buyers and/or users) and the developer (contractor) of a software system discover, review, articulate, and understand the users' needs and the constraints on the software and the development activity.

- *Software requirements analysis*—Reasoning about and analyzing the customers' and users' needs to arrive at a definition of software requirements

- *Software requirements specification*—Development of a document that clearly and precisely records each of the requirements of the software system

- *Software requirements verification*—Ensuring that the software requirements specification is in compliance with the system requirements, conforms to document standards of the requirements phase, and is an adequate basis for the architectural (preliminary) design phase

- *Software requirements management*—Planning and controlling the requirements elicitation, specification, analysis, and verification activities

This chapter concerns itself primarily with the activities of analysis and specification. Discussions of the other elements of requirements engineering can be found in other chapters in this Tutorial.

Software requirements may be categorized as follows:

- Functional requirements
- Performance requirements
- External interface requirements
- Design constraints
- Quality requirements

The last four categories are sometimes referred to as non-functional requirements or constraints.

1.2. Introduction to Software Design

Software design can be defined as the use of scientific principles, technical information, and imagination in the definition of a software system to perform specified functions with maximum economy and efficiency. Software design is also defined as the activity

of transforming a statement of what is required to be accomplished into a plan for implementing the requirements on a computer.

Others, in their attempts to separate the disciplines of requirements analysis and design, have defined analysis as being what the customer or user is interested in and design as being what the customer or user is not interested in, that is, the customer or user doesn't care about the details of how the system is implemented. A fourth view is that requirements may be implemented in more than one way, while design is the selected approach to implementation. The terms "what" and "how" are also used: requirements are "what" a system must do, and design is "how" the requirements are met.

Software design has two stages, *architectural design* and *detailed design*. *Architectural design* (sometimes called preliminary design) is the process of defining a collection of software components, their functions, and their interfaces to establish a framework for the development of a software system. *Detailed design* (sometimes called critical design) is the process of refining and expanding the software architectural design to describe the internals of the components (the algorithms, processing logic, data structures, and data definitions). Detailed design is complete when the description is sufficient for implementation, that is, coding.

2. Introduction to Papers

The first paper in this chapter, by Stuart Faulk of the US Naval Research Laboratory, is an overview of software requirements engineering. Faulk shows that "requirements problems are persistent, pervasive, and costly," and describes the difficulties that arise in the development and documentation of software requirements. He shows how a disciplined approach can help solve requirements problems. He summarizes current and emerging methods for software requirements engineering, and concludes with the observation that, while it may be impossible to do a perfect job of software requirements, a careful, systematic approach, carried out by properly trained and supported people, can contribute to a successful software development.

The second paper in this section is "Software Design: An Introduction," by David Budgen of the University of Keele, UK. Professor Budgen is the author of the recent and well-received textbook entitled "Software Design."[1]

This overview paper describes the software engineering activity of software design, terminating in a software design description (sometimes called a design specification). Budgen defines three aspects of software design:

1. *Representative* part (usually textual in form)

2. *Process* part (the procedure to be followed in developing the design model)

3. A set of *heuristics* (conveying non-procedural knowledge, such as quality attributes)

A design viewpoint as described by Budgen is an abstract description of a particular set of attributes or properties that can be used to describe design elements. They are defined as:

- *Function* viewpoint (describes what a design element does)

- *Behavioral* viewpoint (describes the transformation that occurs in response to events)

- *Structural* viewpoint (describes how elements of the solution are related)

- *Data modeling* (describes the relationships that are inherent in the design elements)

Finally Budgen delineates the changes in software design since the 1960s.

The third paper in this chapter is an original contribution by Hassan Gomaa of George Mason University, author of the recent textbook *Software Design Methods for Concurrent and Real-Time Systems.*[2] Gomaa's paper, entitled "Design Methods for Concurrent and Real Time Systems," demonstrates some of the features of software engineering as applied to designing concurrent and real-time computer-based systems. This paper discusses and compares the concepts and criteria used by software design methods for developing large-scale concurrent and real-time systems. Concurrence is addressed by task structuring while modifiability is addressed by module structuring. In addition, the behavioral aspects of a real-time system are addressed by means of finite state machines. Several real-time analysis and design tools and methods are discussed, such as DARTS, Jackson System Development, and object-oriented design.

The last paper in this section is another application-oriented paper by Robert Remington of Lockheed Martin Missiles & Space Co. Remington's paper, "Computer Human Interface Software Development Survey," familiarizes the reader with available information sources as well as recent trends in human-computer interface design, development, and evaluation. The paper describes several earlier surveys that provide the computer professional with an introduction to human-computer interface concepts, methods, and tools. It emphasizes that without good human-computer interface many systems are difficult to use and may not be used.

This paper emphasizes the need to use basic human interface design principles such as rapid prototyping techniques to obtain user feedback early and continuously throughout the design process, and systematic usability testing to validate designs.

1. Budgen, David, *Software Design*, Addison-Wesley, Publishing Company, Wokingham, England; Reading, Massachusetts, 1993

2. Gomaa, Hassan, "Software Design Methods for Concurrent and Real-Time Systems," SEI Series in Software Engineering, Addison-Wesley Publishing Company, Reading, Mass., 1993.

Software Requirements: A Tutorial

Stuart R. Faulk

"The hardest single part of building a software system is deciding precisely what to build. No other part of the conceptual work is as difficult as establishing the detailed technical requirements . . . No other part of the work so cripples the resulting system if done wrong. No other part is as difficult to rectify later."

[Brooks 87]

1. Introduction

Deciding precisely what to build and documenting the results is the goal of the requirements phase of software development. For many developers of large, complex software systems, requirements are their biggest software engineering problem. While there is considerable disagreement on how to solve the problem, few would disagree with Brooks' assessment that no other part of a development is as difficult to do well or as disastrous in result when done poorly. The purpose of this tutorial is to help the reader understand why the apparently simple notion of "deciding what to build" is so difficult in practice, where the state of the art does and does not address these difficulties, and what hope we have for doing better in the future.

This paper does not survey the literature but seeks to provide the reader with an understanding of the underlying issues. There are currently many more approaches to requirements than one can cover in a short paper. This diversity is the product of two things: different views about which of the many problems in requirements is pivotal, and different assumptions about the desirable characteristics of a solution. This paper attempts to impart a basic understanding of the requirements problem and its many facets, as well as the trade-offs involved in attempting a solution. Thus forearmed, readers can assess the claims of different requirements methods and their likely effectiveness in addressing the readers' particular needs.

We begin with basic terminology and some historical data on the requirements problem. We examine the goals of the requirements phase and the problems that can arise in attempting those goals. As in Brooks's article [Brooks 87], much of the discussion is moti-vated by the distinction between the difficulties inherent in what one is trying to accomplish (the "essential" difficulties) and those one creates through inadequate practice ("accidental" difficulties). We discuss how a disciplined software engineering process helps address many of the accidental difficulties and why the focus of such a disciplined process is on producing a written specification of the detailed technical requirements. We examine current technical approaches to requirements in terms of the specific problems each approach seeks to address. Finally, we examine technical trends and discuss where significant advances are likely to occur in the future.

2. Requirements and the Software Life Cycle

A variety of software life-cycle models have been proposed with an equal variety of terminology. Davis [Davis 88] provides a good summary. While differing in the detailed decomposition of the steps (for example, prototyping models) or in the surrounding management and control structure (for example, to manage risk), there is general agreement on the core elements of the model. Figure 1 [Davis 93] is a version of the common model that illustrates the relationship between the software development stages and the related testing and acceptance phases.

When software is created in the context of a larger hardware and software system, system requirements are defined first, followed by system design. System design includes decisions about which parts of the system requirements will be allocated to hardware and which to software. For software-only systems, the life-cycle model begins with software requirements analysis. From this point on, the role of software requirements in the development model is the same whether or not the software is part of a larger system, as shown in Figure 2 [Davis 93]. For this reason, the remainder of our discussion does not distinguish whether or not software is developed as part of a larger system. For an overview of system versus software issues, the reader is referred to Dorfman and Thayer's survey [Thayer 90].

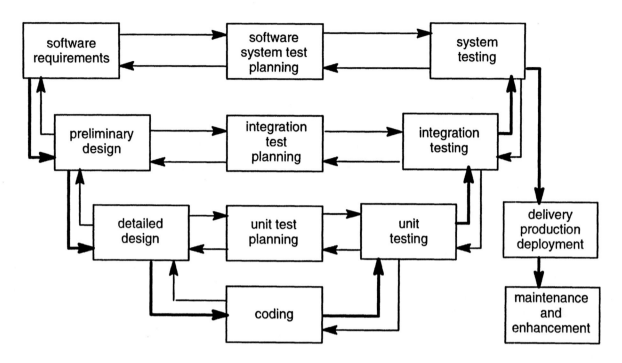

Figure 1. Software life cycle

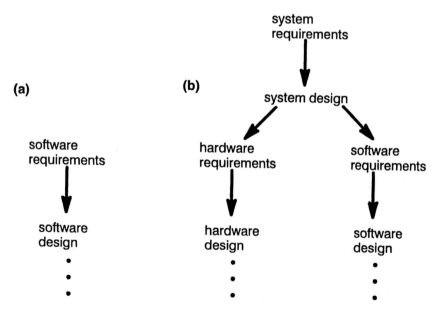

Figure 2. Development paths: (a) software, (b) systems

In a large system development, the software requirements specification may play a variety of roles:

- For customers, the requirements typically document what should be delivered and may provide the contractual basis for the development.

- For managers, it may provide the basis for scheduling and a yardstick for measuring progress.

- For the software designers, it may provide the "design-to" specification.

- For coders, it defines the range of acceptable implementations and is the final authority on the outputs that must be produced.

- For quality assurance personnel, it is the basis for validation, test planning, and verification.

The requirements may also used by such diverse groups as marketing and governmental regulators.

It is common practice (for example, see [Thayer 90]) to classify software requirements as "functional" or "nonfunctional." While definitions vary somewhat in detail, "functional" typically refers to requirements defining the acceptable mappings between system input values and corresponding output values. "Nonfunctional" then refers to all other constraints including, but not limited to, performance, dependability, maintainability, reusability, and safety.

While widely used, the classification of requirements as "functional" and "nonfunctional" is confusing in its terminology and of little help in understanding common properties of different kinds of requirements. The word "function" is one of the most overloaded in computer science, and its only rigorous meaning, that of a mathematical function, is not what is meant here. The classification of requirements as functional and non-functional offers little help in understanding common attributes of different types of requirements since it partitions classes of requirements with markedly similar qualities (for example, output values and output deadlines) while grouping others that have commonality only in what they are not (for example, output deadlines and maintainability goals).

A more useful distinction is between what can be described as "behavioral requirements" and "developmental quality attributes" with the following definitions [Clements 95]:

- *Behavioral requirements*—Behavioral requirements include any and all information necessary to determine if the runtime behavior of a given implementation is acceptable. The behavioral requirements define all constraints on the system outputs (for example, value, accuracy, timing) and resulting system state for all possible inputs and current system state. By this definition, security, safety, performance, timing, and fault tolerance are all behavioral requirements.

- *Developmental quality attributes*—Developmental quality attributes include any constraints on the attributes of the system's static construction. These include properties like testability, changeability, maintainability, and reusability.

Behavioral requirements have in common that they are properties of the runtime behavior of the system and can (at least in principle) be validated objectively by observing the behavior of the running system, independent of its method of implementation. In contrast, developmental quality attributes are properties of the system's static structures (for example, modularization) or representation. Developmental quality attributes have in common that they are functions of the development process and methods of construction. Assessment of developmental quality attributes are necessarily relativistic—for example, we do not say that a design is or is not maintainable but that one design is more maintainable than another.

3. A Big Problem

Requirements problems are persistent, pervasive, and costly. Evidence is most readily available for the large software systems developed for the US government, since the results are a matter of public record. As soon as software became a significant part of such systems, developers identified requirements as a major source of problems. For example, developers of the early Ballistic Missile Defense System noted that:

> In nearly every software project that fails to meet performance and cost goals, requirements inadequacies play a major and expensive role in project failure [Alford 79].

Nor has the problem mitigated over the intervening years. A recent study of problems in mission-critical defense systems identified requirements as a major problem source in two thirds of the systems examined [GAO 92]. This is consistent with results of a survey of large aerospace firms that identified requirements as the most critical software development problem [Faulk 92]. Likewise, studies by Lutz

[Lutz 92] identified functional and interface requirements as the major source of safety-related software errors in NASA's Voyager and Galileo spacecraft.

Results of industry studies in the 1970s described by Boehm [Boehm 81], and since replicated a number of times, showed that requirements errors are the most costly. These studies all produced the same basic result: The earlier in the development process an error occurs and the later the error is detected, the more expensive it is to correct. Moreover, the relative cost rises quickly. As shown in Figure 3, an error that costs a dollar to fix in the requirements phase may cost $100 to $200 to fix if it is not corrected until the system is fielded or in the maintenance phase.

The costs of such failures can be enormous. For example, the 1992 GAO report notes that one system, the Cheyenne Mountain Upgrade, will be delivered eight years late, exceed budget by $600 million, and have less capability than originally planned, largely due to requirements-related problems. Prior GAO reports [GAO 79] suggest that such problems are the norm rather than the exception. While data from private industry is less readily available, there is little reason to believe that the situation is significantly different.

In spite of presumed advances in software engineering methodology and tool support, the requirements problem has not diminished. This does not mean that the apparent progress in software engineering is illusory. While the features of the problem have not changed, the applications have grown significantly in capability, scale, and complexity. A reasonable conclusion is that the growing ambitiousness of our software systems has outpaced the gains in requirements technology, at least as such technology is applied in practice.

4. Why Are Requirements Hard?

It is generally agreed that the goal of the requirements phase is to establish and specify precisely what the software must do without describing how to do it. So simple seems this basic intent that it is not at all evident why it is so difficult to accomplish in practice. If what we want to accomplish is so clear, why is it so hard? To understand this, we must examine more closely the goals of the requirements phase, where errors originate, and why the nature of the task leads to some inherent difficulties.

Most authors agree in principle that requirements should specify "what" rather than "how." In other words, the goal of requirements is to understand and specify the *problem* to be solved rather than the *solution*. For example, the requirements for an automated teller system should talk about customer accounts, deposits, and withdrawals rather than the software algorithms and data structures. The most basic reason for this is that a specification in terms of the problem captures the actual requirements without overconstraining the subsequent design or implementation. Further, solutions in software terms are typically more complex, more difficult to change, and harder to understand (particularly for the customer) than a specification of the problem.

Unfortunately, distinguishing "what" from "how" itself represents a dilemma. As Davis [Davis 88], among others, points out, the distinction between what and how is necessarily a function of perspective. A specification at any chosen level of system decomposition can be viewed as describing the "what" for the next level. Thus customer needs may define the "what" and the decomposition into hardware and software the corresponding "how." Subsequently, the behavioral requirements allocated to a software component define its "what," the software design, the "how," and so on. The upshot is that requirements cannot be effectively discussed at all without prior agreement on which system one is talking about and at what level of decomposition. One must agree on what constitutes the problem space and what constitutes the solution space—the analysis and specification of requirements then properly belongs in the problem space.

Stage	Relative Repair Cost
Requirements	1–2
Design	5
Coding	10
Unit test	20
System test	50
Maintenance	200

Figure 3: Relative cost to repair a software error in different stages

In discussing requirements problems, one must also distinguish the development of large, complex systems from smaller efforts (for example, developments by a single or small team of programmers). Large system developments are multiperson efforts. They are developed by teams of tens to thousands of programmers. The programmers work in the context of an organization typically including management, systems engineering, marketing, accounting, and quality assurance. The organization itself must operate in the context of outside concerns also interested in the software product, including the customer, regulatory agencies, and suppliers.

Even where only one system is intended, large systems are inevitably multiversion as well. As the software is being developed, tested, and even fielded, it evolves. Customers understand better what they want, developers understand better what they can and cannot do within the constraints of cost and schedule, and circumstances surrounding development change. The results are changes in the software requirements and, ultimately, the software itself. In effect, several versions of a given program are produced, if only incrementally. Such unplanned changes occur in addition to the expected variations of planned improvements.

The multiperson, multiversion nature of large system development introduces problems that are both quantitatively and qualitatively different from those found in smaller developments. For example, scale introduces the need for administration and control functions with the attendant management issues that do not exist on small projects. The quantitative effects of increased complexity in communication when the number of workers rises are well documented by Brooks [Brooks 75]. In the following discussion, it is this large system development context we will assume, since that is the one in which the worst problems occur and where the most help is needed.

Given the context of multiperson, multiversion development, our basic goal of specifying what the software must do can be decomposed into the following subgoals:

1. Understand precisely what is required of the software.

2. Communicate the understanding of what is required to all of the parties involved in the development.

3. Provide a means for controlling the production to ensure that the final system satisfies the requirements (including managing the effects of changes).

It follows that the source of most requirements errors is in the failure to adequately accomplish one of these goals, that is:

1. The developers failed to understand what was required of the software by the customer, end user, or other parties with a stake in the final product.

2. The developers did not completely and precisely capture the requirements or subsequently communicate the requirements effectively to other parties involved in the development.

3. The developers did not effectively manage the effects of changing requirements or ensure the conformance of down-stream development steps including design, code, integration, test, or maintenance to the system requirements.

The end result of such failures is a software system that does not perform as desired or expected, a development that exceeds budget and schedule or, all too frequently, failure to deliver any working software at all.

4.1 Essential Difficulties

Even our more detailed goals appear straightforward; why then do so many development efforts fail to achieve them? The short answer is that the mutual satisfaction of these goals, in practice, is inherently difficult. To understand why, it is useful to reflect on some points raised by Brooks [Brooks 87] on why software engineering is hard and on the distinction he makes between essential difficulties—those inherent in the problem, and the accidental difficulties—those introduced through imperfect practice. For though requirements are inherently difficult, there is no doubt that these difficulties are many times multiplied by the inadequacies of current practice.

The following essential difficulties attend each (in some cases all) of the requirements goals:

• *Comprehension.* People do not know what they want. This does not mean that people do not have a general idea of what the software is for. Rather, they do not begin with a precise and detailed understanding of what functions belong in the software, what the output must be for every possible input, how long each operation should take, how one decision will affect another, and so on.

Indeed, unless the new system is simply a reconstruction of an old one, such a detailed understanding at the outset is unachievable. Many decisions about the system behavior will depend on other decisions yet unmade, and expectations will change as the problem (and attendant costs of alternative solutions) is better understood. Nonetheless, it is a precise and richly detailed understanding of expected behavior that is needed to create effective designs and develop correct code.

- *Communication.* Software requirements are difficult to communicate effectively. As Brooks points out, the conceptual structures of software systems are complex, arbitrary, and difficult to visualize. The large software systems we are now building are among the most complex structures ever attempted. That complexity is arbitrary in the sense that it is an artifact of people's decisions and prior construction rather than a reflection of fundamental properties (as, for example, in the case of physical laws). To make matters worse, many of the conceptual structures in software have no readily comprehensible physical analogue so they are difficult to visualize.

In practice, comprehension suffers under all of these constraints. We work best with regular, predictable structures, can comprehend only a very limited amount of information at one time, and understand large amounts of information best when we can visualize it. Thus the task of capturing and conveying software requirements is inherently difficult.

The inherent difficulty of communication is compounded by the diversity of purposes and audiences for a requirements specification. Ideally, a technical specification is written for a particular audience. The brevity and comprehensibility of the document depend on assumptions about common technical background and use of language. Such commonality typically does not hold for the many diverse groups (for example, customers, systems engineers, managers) that must use a software requirements specification.

- *Control.* Inherent difficulties attend control of software development as well. The arbitrary and invisible nature of software makes it dif-

ficult to anticipate which requirements will be met easily and which will decimate the project's budget and schedule if, indeed, they can be fulfilled at all. The low fidelity of software planning has become a cliche, yet the requirements are often the best available basis for planning or for tracking to a plan.

This situation is made incalculably worse by software's inherent malleability. Of all the problems bedeviling software managers, few evoke such passion as the difficulties of dealing with frequent and arbitrary changes to requirements. For most systems, such changes remain a fact of life even after delivery. The continuous changes make it difficult to develop stable specifications, plan effectively, or control cost and schedule. For many industrial developers, change management is the most critical problem in requirements.

- *Inseparable concerns.* In seeking solutions to the foregoing problems, we are faced with the additional difficulty that the issues cannot easily be separated and dealt with, piecemeal. For example, developers have attempted to address the problem of changing requirements by baselining and freezing requirements before design begins. This proves impractical because of the comprehension problem—the customer may not fully know what he wants until he sees it. Similarly, the diversity of purposes and audiences is often addressed by writing a different specification for each. Thus there may be a system specification, a set of requirements delivered to customer, a distinct set of technical requirements written for the internal consumption of the software developers, and so on. However, this solution vastly increases the complexity, provides an open avenue for inconsistencies, and multiplies the difficulties of managing changes.

These issues represent only a sample of the inherent dependencies between different facets of the requirements problem. The many distinct parties with an interest in a system's requirements, the many different roles the requirements play, and the interlocking nature of software's conceptual structures, all introduce dependencies between concerns and impose conflicting constraints on any potential solution.

The implications are twofold. First we are constrained in the application of our most effective strategy for dealing with complex problems—divide and conquer. If a problem is considered in isolation, the solution is likely to aggravate other difficulties. Effective solutions to most requirements difficulties must simultaneously address more than one problem. Second, developing practical solutions requires making difficult trade-offs. Where different problems have conflicting constraints, compromises must be made. Because the trade-offs result in different gains or losses to the different parties involved, effective compromises require negotiation. These issues are considered in more detail when we discuss the properties of a good requirements specification.

4.2 Accidental Difficulties

While there is no doubt that software requirements are inherently difficult to do well, there is equally no doubt that common practice unnecessarily exacerbates the difficulty. We use the term "accidental" in contrast to "essential," not to imply that the difficulties arise by chance but that they are the product of common failings in management, elicitation, specification, or use of requirements. It is these failings that are most easily addressed by improved practice.

- *Written as an afterthought.* It remains common practice that requirements documentation is developed only after the software has been written. For many projects, the temptation to rush into implementation before the requirements are adequately understood proves irresistible. This is understandable. Developers often feel like they are not really doing anything when they are not writing code; managers are concerned about schedule when there is no visible progress on the implementation. Then too, the intangible nature of the product mitigates toward early implementation. Developing the system is an obvious way to understand better what is needed and make visible the actual behavior of the product. The result is that requirements specifications are written as an afterthought (if at all). They are not created to guide the developers and testers but treated as a necessary evil to satisfy contractual demands.

Such after-the-fact documentation inevitably

violates the principle of defining what the system must do rather than the how since it is a specification of the code as written. It is produced after the fact so it is not planned or managed as an essential part of the development but is thrown together. In fact, it is not even available in time to guide implementation or manage development.

- *Confused in purpose.* Because there are so many potential audiences for a requirements specification, with different points of view, the exact purpose of the document becomes confused. An early version is used to sell the product to the customer, so it includes marketing hype extolling the product's virtues. It is the only documentation of what the system does, so it provides introductory, explanatory, and overview material. It is a contractual document, so it is intentionally imprecise to allow the developer latitude in the delivered product or the customer latitude in making no-cost changes. It is the vehicle for communicating decisions about software details to designers and coders, so it incorporates design and implementation. The result is a document in which it is unclear which statements represent real requirements and which are more properly allocated to marketing, design, or other documentation. It is a document that attempts to be everything to everyone and ultimately serves no one well.

- *Not designed to be useful.* Often, in the rush to implementation, little effort is expended on requirements. The requirements specification is not expected to be useful and, indeed, this turns out to be a self-fulfilling prophecy. Because the document is not expected to be useful, little effort is expended on designing it, writing it, checking it, or managing its creation and evolution. The most obvious result is poor organization. The specification is written in English prose and follows the author's stream of consciousness or the order of execution [Heninger 80].

The resulting document is ineffective as a technical reference. It is unclear which statements represent actual requirements. It is unclear where to put or find particular requirements. There is no effective procedure for ensuring that the specification is consistent or complete. There is no systematic way to manage requirements changes. The specification is difficult to use and difficult to maintain. It quickly becomes out of date and loses whatever usefulness it might originally have had.

- *Lacks essential properties*. Lack of forethought, confusion of purpose, or lack of careful design and execution all lead to requirements that lack properties critical to good technical specifications. The requirements, if documented at all, are redundant, inconsistent, incomplete, imprecise, and inaccurate.

Where the essential difficulties are inherent in the problem, the accidental difficulties result from a failure to gain or maintain intellectual control over what is to be built. While the presence of the essential difficulties means that there can be no "silver bullet" that will suddenly render requirements easy, we can remove at least the accidental difficulties through a well thought out, systematic, and disciplined development process. Such a disciplined process then provides a stable foundation for attacking the essential difficulties.

5. Role of a Disciplined Approach

The application of discipline in analyzing and specifying software requirements can address the accidental difficulties. While there is now general agreement on the desirable qualities of a software development approach, the field is insufficiently mature to have standardized the development process. Nonetheless, it is useful to examine the characteristics of an idealized process and its products to understand where current approaches are weak and which current trends are promising. In general, a complete requirements approach will define:

- *Process*: The (partially ordered) sequence of activities, entrance and exit criteria for each activity, which work product is produced in each activity, and what kind of people should do the work.

- *Products*: The work products to be produced and, for each product, the resources needed to produce it, the information it contains, the expected audience, and the acceptance criteria the product must satisfy.

Currently, there is little uniformity in different author's decomposition of the requirements phase or in the terminology for the activities. Davis [Davis 88] provides a good summary of the variations. Following Davis's integrated model and terminology [Davis 93],

the requirements phase consists of two conceptually distinct but overlapping activities corresponding to the first two goals for requirements enumerated previously:

1. *Problem analysis*: The goal of problem analysis is to understand precisely what problem is to be solved. It includes identifying the exact purpose of the system, who will use it, the constraints on acceptable solutions, and the possible trade-offs between conflicting constraints.

2. *Requirements specification*: The goal of requirements specification is to create a document, the Software Requirements Specification (SRS), describing exactly what is to be built. The SRS captures the results of problem analysis and characterizes the set of acceptable solutions to the problem.

In practice, the distinction between these activities is conceptual rather than temporal. Where both are needed, the developer typically switches back and forth between analysis of the problem and documentation of the results. When problems are well understood, the analysis phase may be virtually nonexistent. When the system model and documentation are standardized or based on existing specifications, the documentation paradigm may guide the analysis [Hester 81].

5.1 Problem Analysis

Problem analysis is necessarily informal in the sense that there is no effective, closed-end procedure that will guarantee success. It is an information-acquiring, -collating, and -structuring process through which one attempts to understand all the various parts of a problem and their relationships. The difficulty in developing an effective understanding of large, complex software problems has motivated considerable effort to structure and codify problem analysis.

The basic issues in problem analysis are:

- How to effectively elicit a complete set of requirements from the customer or other sources?

- How to decompose the problem into intellectually manageable pieces?

- How to organize the information so it can be understood?

- How to communicate about the problem with all the parties involved?

89

- How to resolve conflicting needs?
- How to know when to stop?

5.2 Requirements Specification

For substantial developments, the effectiveness of the requirements effort depends on how well the SRS captures the results of analysis and how useable the specification is. There is little benefit to developing a thorough understanding of the problem if that understanding is not effectively communicated to customers, designers, implementors, testers, and maintainers. The larger and more complex the system, the more important a good specification becomes. This is a direct result of the many roles the SRS plays in a multiperson, multiversion development [Parnas 86]:

1. The SRS is the primary vehicle for agreement between the developer and customer on exactly what is to be built. It is the document reviewed by the customer or his representative and often is the basis for judging fulfillment of contractual obligations.

2. The SRS records the results of problem analysis. It is the basis for determining where the requirements are complete and where additional analysis is necessary. Documenting the results of analysis allows questions about the problem to be answered only once during development.

3. The SRS defines what properties the system must have and the constraints on its design and implementation. It defines where there is, and is not, design freedom. It helps ensure that requirements decisions are made explicitly during the requirements phase, not implicitly during programming.

4. The SRS is the basis for estimating cost and schedule. It is management's primary tool for tracking development progress and ascertaining what remains to be done.

5. The SRS is the basis for test plan development. It is the tester's chief tool for determining the acceptable behavior of the software.

6. The SRS provides the standard definition of expected behavior for the system's maintainers and is used to record engineering changes.

For a disciplined software development, the SRS is the primary technical specification of the software and the primary control document. This is an inevitable result of the complexity of large systems and the need to coordinate multiperson development teams. To ensure that the right system is built, one must first understand the problem. To ensure agreement on what is to be built and the criteria for success, the results of that understanding must be recorded. The goal of a systematic requirements process is thus the development of a set of specifications that effectively communicate the results of analysis.

Requirement's accidental difficulties are addressed through the careful analysis and specification of a disciplined process. Rather than developing the specification as an afterthought, requirements are understood and specified before development begins. One knows what one is building before attempting to build it. The SRS is the primary vehicle for communicating requirements between the developers, managers, and customers, so the document is designed to be useful foro that purpose. A useful document is maintained.

6. Requirements for the Software Requirements Specification

The goals of the requirements process, the attendant difficulties, and the role of the requirements specification in a disciplined process determine the properties of a "good" requirements specification. These properties do not mandate any particular specification method but do describe the characteristics of an effective method.

In discussing the properties of a good SRS, it is useful to distinguish semantic properties from packaging properties [Faulk 92]. Semantic properties are a consequence of what the specification says (that is, its meaning or semantics). Packaging properties are a consequence of how the requirements are written—the format, organization, and presentation of the information. The semantic properties determine how effectively an SRS captures the software requirements. The packaging properties determine how useable the resulting specification is. Figure 4 illustrates the classification of properties of a good SRS.

An SRS that satisfies the semantic properties of a good specification is:

- *Complete.* The SRS defines the set of acceptable implementations. It should contain all the information needed to write software that is acceptable to the customer and no more. Any implementation that satisfies every statement in the requirements is an acceptable product. Where information is not available before development begins, areas of incompleteness must be explicitly indicated [Parnas 86].

SRS Semantic Properties	SRS Packaging Properties
Complete	Modifiable
Implementation independent	Readable
Unambiguous and consistent	Organized for reference and review
Precise	
Verifiable	

Figure 4. Classification of SRS properties

- *Implementation independent.* The SRS should be free of design and implementation decisions unless those decisions reflect actual requirements.

- *Unambiguous and consistent.* If the SRS is subject to conflicting interpretation, the different parties will not agree on what is to be built or whether the right software has been built. Every requirement should have only one possible interpretation. Similarly, no two statements of required behavior should conflict.

- *Precise.* The SRS should define exactly the required behavior. For each output, it should define the range of acceptable values for every input. The SRS should define any applicable timing constraints such as minimum and maximum acceptable delay.

- *Verifiable.* A requirement is verifiable if it is possible to determine unambiguously whether a given implementation satisfies the requirement or not. For example, a behavioral requirement is verifiable if it is possible to determine, for any given test case (that is, an input and an output), whether the output represents an acceptable behavior of the software given the input and the system state.

An SRS[1] that satisfies the packaging properties of a good specification is:

- *Modifiable.* The SRS must be organized for ease of change. Since no organization can be equally easy to change for all possible changes, the requirements analysis process must identify expected changes and the relative likelihood of their occurrence. The specification is then organized to limit the effect of likely changes.

- *Readable.* The SRS must be understandable by the parties that use it. It should clearly relate the elements of the problem space as understood by the customer to the observable behavior of the software.

- *Organized for reference and review.* The SRS is the primary technical specification of the software requirements. It is the repository for all the decisions made during analysis about what should be built. It is the document reviewed by the customer or his representatives. It is the primary arbitrator of disputes. As such, the document must be organized for quick and easy reference. It must be clear where each decision about the requirements belongs. It must be possible to answer specific questions about the requirements quickly and easily.

To address the difficulties associated with writing and using an SRS, a requirements approach must provide techniques addressing both semantic and packaging properties. It is also desirable that the conceptual structures of the approach treat the semantic and packaging properties as distinct concerns (that is, as independently as possible). This allows one to change the presentation of the SRS without changing its meaning.

In aggregate, these properties of a good SRS represent an ideal. Some of the properties may be unachievable, particularly over the short term. For example, a common complaint is that one cannot develop complete requirements before design begins because the customer does not yet fully understand what he wants or is still making changes. Further, different SRS "requirements" mitigate toward conflicting solutions. A commonly cited example is the use of English prose to express requirements. English is readily understood but notoriously ambiguous and imprecise. Conversely, formal languages are precise and unambiguous, but can be difficult to read.

Although the ideal SRS may be unachievable, possessing a common understanding of what constitutes

---

1. Reusability is also a packaging property and becomes an attribute of a good specification where reusability of requirements specifications is a goal.

an ideal SRS is important [Parnas 86] because it:

- provides a basis for standardizing an organization's processes and products,
- provides a standard against which progress can be measured, and,
- provides guidance—it helps developers understand what needs to be done next and when they are finished.

Because it is so often true that (1) requirements cannot be fully understood before at least starting to build the system, and (2) a perfect SRS cannot be produced even when the requirements are understood, some approaches advocated in the literature do not even attempt to produce a definitive SRS. For example, some authors advocate going directly from a problem model to design or from a prototype implementation to the code. While such approaches may be effective on some developments, they are inconsistent with the notion of software development as an engineering discipline. The development of technical specifications is an essential part of a controlled engineering process. This does not mean that the SRS must be entire or perfect before anything else is done but that its development is a fundamental goal of the process as a whole. That we may currently lack the ability to write good specifications in some cases does not change the fact that it is useful and necessary to try.

7. State of the Practice

Over the years, many analysis and specification techniques have evolved. The general trend has been for software engineering techniques to be applied first to coding problems (for example, complexity, ease of change), then to similar problems occurring earlier and earlier in the life cycle. Thus the concepts of structured programming led eventually to structured design and analysis. More recently, the concepts of object-oriented programming have led to object-oriented design and analysis. The following discussion characterizes the major schools of thought and provides pointers to instances of methods in each school. The general strengths and weaknesses of the various techniques are discussed relative to the requirements difficulties and the desirable qualities of analysis and specification methods.

It is characteristic of the immature state of requirements as a discipline that the more specific one gets, the less agreement there is. There is not only disagreement in terminology, approach, and the details of different methods, there is not even a commonly accepted classification scheme. The following general groupings are based on the evolution of the underlying concepts and the key distinctions that reflect paradigmatic shifts in requirements philosophy.

7.1 Functional Decomposition

Functional decomposition was originally applied to software requirements to abstract from coding details. Functional decomposition focuses on understanding and specifying what processing the software is required to do. The general strategy is to define the required behavior as a mapping from inputs to outputs. Ideally, the analysis proceeds top down, first identifying the function associated with the system as a whole. Each subsequent step decomposes the set of functions into steps or sub-functions. The result is a hierarchy of functions and the definitions of the functional interfaces. Each level of the hierarchy adds detail about the processing steps necessary to accomplish the more abstract function above. The function above controls the processing of its subfunctions. In a complete decomposition, the functional hierarchy specifies the "calls" structure of the implementation. One example of a methodology based on functional decomposition is Hamilton and Zeldin's Higher Order Software [Hamilton 76].

The advantage of functional decomposition is that the specification is written using the language and concepts of the implementors. It communicates well to the designers and coders. It is written in terms of the solution space so the transition to design and code is straightforward.

Common complaints are that functional specifications are difficult to communicate, introduce design decisions prematurely, and difficult to use or change. Because functional specifications are written in the language of implementation, people who are not software or systems experts find them difficult to understand. Since there are inevitably many possible ways of decomposing functions into subfunctions, the analyst must make decisions that are not requirements. Finally, since the processing needed in one step depends strongly on what has been done the previous step, functional decomposition results in components that are closely coupled. Understanding or changing one function requires understanding or changing all the related functions.

As software has increased in complexity and become more visible to nontechnical people, the need for methods addressing the weaknesses of functional decomposition has likewise increased.

7.2 Structured Analysis

Structured analysis was developed primarily as a

means to address the accidental difficulties attending problem analysis and, to a lesser extent, requirements specification, using functional decomposition. Following the introduction of structured programming as a means to gain intellectual control over increasingly complex programs, structured analysis evolved from functional decomposition as a means to gain intellectual control over system problems.

The basic assumption behind structured analysis is that the accidental difficulties can be addressed by a systematic approach to problem analysis using [Svoboda 90]:

- a common conceptual model for describing all problems,
- a set of procedures suggesting the general direction of analysis and an ordering on the steps,
- a set of guidelines or heuristics supporting decisions about the problem and its specification, and
- a set of criteria for evaluating the quality of the product.

While structured analysis still contains the decomposition of functions into subfunctions, the focus of the analysis shifts from the processing steps to the data being processed. The analyst views the problem as constructing a system to transform data. He analyzes the sources and destinations of the data, determines what data must be held in storage, what transformations are done on the data, and the form of the output.

Common to the structured analysis approaches is the use of data flow diagrams and data dictionaries. Data flow diagrams provide a graphic representation of the movement of data through the system (typically represented as arcs) and the transformations on the data (typically represented as nodes). The data dictionary supports the data flow diagram by providing a repository for the definitions and descriptions of each data item on the diagrams. Required processing is captured in the definitions of the transformations. Associated with each transformation node is a specification of the processing the node does to transform the incoming data items to the outgoing data items. At the most detailed level, a transformation is defined using a textual specification called a "MiniSpec." A MiniSpec may be expressed in several different ways including English prose, decision tables, or a procedure definition language (PDL).

Structured analysis approaches originally evolved for management information systems (MIS). Examples of widely used strategies include those described by DeMarco [DeMarco 78] and Gane and Sarson [Gane

79]. "Modern" structured analysis was introduced to provide more guidance in modeling systems as data flows as exemplified by Yourdon [Yourdon 89]. Structured analysis has also been adapted to support specification of embedded control systems by adding notations to capture control behavior. These variations are collectively known as structured analysis/real-time (SA/RT). Major variations of SA/RT have been described by Ward and Mellor [Ward 86] and Hatley and Pirbhai [Hatley 87]. A good summary of structured analysis concepts with extensive references is given by Svoboda [Svoboda 90].

Structured analysis extends functional decomposition with the notion that there should be a systematic (and hopefully predictable) approach to analyzing a problem, decomposing it into parts, and describing the relationships between the parts. By providing a well-defined process, structured analysis seeks to address, at least in part, the accidental difficulties that result from ad hoc approaches and the definition of requirements as an afterthought. It seeks to address problems in comprehension and communication by using a common set of conceptual structures—a graphic representation of the specification in terms of those structures—based on the assumption that a decomposition in terms of the data the system handles will be clearer and less inclined to change than one based on the functions performed.

While structured analysis techniques have continued to evolve and have been widely used, there remain a number of common criticisms. When used in problem analysis, a common complaint is that structured analysis provides insufficient guidance. Analysts have difficulty deciding which parts of the problem to model as data, which parts to model as transformations, and which parts should be aggregated. While the gross steps of the process are reasonably well defined, there is only very general guidance (in the form of heuristics) on what specific questions the analyst needs to answer next. Similarly, practitioners find it difficult to know when to stop decomposition and addition of detail. In fact, the basic structured analysis paradigm of modeling requirements as data flows and data transformations requires the analyst to make decisions about intermediate values (for example, form and content of stored data and the details of internal transformations) that are not requirements. Particularly in the hands of less experienced practitioners, data flow models tend to incorporate a variety of detail that properly belongs to design or implementation.

Many of these difficulties result from the weak constraints imposed by the conceptual model. A goal of the developers of structured analysis was to create a very general approach to modeling systems; in fact, one that could be applied equally to model human enterprises, hardware applications, software applications of different kinds, and so on. Unfortunately, such generality can be achieved only by abstracting away any semantics that are not common to all of the types of systems potentially being modeled. The conceptual model itself can provide little guidance relevant to a particular system. Since the conceptual model applies equally to requirements analysis and design analysis, its semantics provide no basis for distinguishing the two. Similarly, such models can support only very weak syntactic criteria for assessing the quality of structured analysis specifications. For example, the test for completeness and consistency in data flow diagrams is limited to determining that the transformations at each level are consistent in name and number with the data flows of the level above.

This does not mean one cannot develop data flow specifications that are easy to understand, communicate effectively with the user, or capture required behavior correctly. The large number of systems developed using structured analysis show that it is possible to do so. However, the weakness of the conceptual model means that a specification's quality depends largely on the experience, insight, and expertise of the analyst. The developer must provide the necessary discipline because the model itself is relatively unconstrained.

Finally, structured analysis provides little support for producing an SRS that meets our quality criteria. Data flow diagrams are unsuitable for capturing mathematical relations or detailed specifications of value, timing, or accuracy so the detailed behavioral specifications are typically given in English or as pseudocode segments in the MiniSpecs. These constructs provide little or no support for writing an SRS that is complete, implementation independent, unambiguous, consistent, precise, and verifiable. Further, the data flow diagrams and attendant dictionaries do not, themselves, provide support for organizing an SRS to satisfy the packaging goals of readability, ease of reference and review, or reusability. In fact, for many of the published methods, there is no explicit process step, structure, or guidance for producing an SRS, as a distinct development product, at all.

7.3 Operational Specification

The operational[2] approach focuses on addressing two of the essential requirements dilemmas. The first is that we often do not know exactly what should be built until we build it. The second is the problem inherent in moving from a particular specification of

requirements (what to build) to a design that satisfies those requirements (how to build it). The closer the requirements specification is to the design, the easier the transition, but the more likely it is that design decisions are made prematurely.

The operational approach seeks to address these problems, among others, by supporting development of executable requirements specifications. Key elements of an operational approach are: a formal specification language and an engine for executing well-formed specifications written in the language. Operational approaches may also include automated support for analyzing properties of the formal specification and for transforming the specification into an equivalent implementation. A good description of the operational approach, its rationale, and goals is given by Zave [Zave 82].

The underlying reasoning about the benefits of the operational approach is as follows:

- Making the requirements specification itself executable obviates the dilemma that one must build the system to know what to build. The developer writes the requirements specification in a formal language. The specification may then be executed to validate that the customer's needs have been captured and the right system specified (for example, one can apply scenarios and test cases). The approach is presumed to require less labor and be more cost-effective than conventional prototyping because a separate requirements specification need not be produced; the specification and the "prototype" are the same thing.

- Operational specifications allow the developer to abstract from design decisions while simplifying the transition from requirements to design and implementation. Transition to design and implementation is both simple and automatable because the behavioral requirements are already expressed in terms of computational mechanisms. During design, one makes decisions concerning efficiency, resource management, and target language realization that are abstracted from the operational specification.

For general applications, operational approaches have achieved only limited success. This is at least in part due to the failure to achieve the necessary semantic distinction between an operational computational model and conventional programming. The benefits of the approach are predicated on the assumption that the

---

2. We use the term "operational" here specifically to denote approaches based on executable specifications in the sense of Zave [Zave 82]. The term is sometimes used to contrast with axiomatic specification–that is not the meaning here.

operational model can be written in terms of the problem domain, without the need to introduce conceptual structures belonging to the solution domain. In practice, this goal has proven elusive. To achieve generality, operational languages have typically had to introduce implementation constructs. The result is not a requirements specification language but a higher-level programming language. As noted by Parnas [Parnas 85b] and Brooks [Brooks 87], the specification ends up giving the solution method rather than the problem statement. Thus, in practice, operational specifications do not meet the SRS goal of implementation independence.

The focus of operational specification is on the benefits of early simulation rather than on the properties of the specification as a reference document. Since executability requires formality, operational specifications necessarily satisfy the SRS semantic properties of being unambiguous, consistent, precise, and verifiable. The ability to validate the specification through simulation also supports completeness. However, as discussed, these properties have not been achieved in concert with implementation independence. Further, the methods discussed in the literature put little emphasis on the communication or packaging qualities of the specification, except as these qualities overlap with desirable design properties. Thus, there may be some support for modifiability but little for readability or organizing an SRS for reference and review.

7.4 Object Oriented Analysis (OOA)

There is currently considerable discussion in the literature, and little agreement, on exactly what should and should not be considered "object oriented." OOA has evolved from at least two significant sources: information modeling and object oriented design. Each has contributed to current views of OOA, and the proponents of each emphasize somewhat different sets of concepts. For the purposes of this tutorial, we are not interested in which method is by some measure "more object oriented" but in the distinct contributions of the object-oriented paradigm to analysis and specification. For an overview of OOA concepts and methods, see Balin's article [Balin 94]; Davis's book [Davis 93] includes both discussion and examples. Examples of recent approaches self-described as object oriented include work by Rumbaugh [Rumbaugh 91], Coad and Yourdon [Coad 91], Shlaer and Mellor [Shlaer 88], and Selic, Gullekson, and Ward [Selic 94].

OOA techniques differ from structured analysis in their approach to decomposing a problem into parts and in the methods for describing the relationships between the parts. In OOA, the analyst decomposes the problem into a set of interacting objects based on the entities and relationships extant in the problem domain. An object encapsulates a related set of data, processing, and state (thus, a significant distinction between object-oriented analysis and structured analysis is that OOA encapsulates both data and related processing together). Objects provide externally accessible functions, typically called services or methods. Objects may hide information about their internal structure, data, or state from other objects. Conversely, they may provide processing, data, or state information through the services defined on the object interface. Dynamic relationships between objects are captured in terms of message passing (that is, one object sends a message to invoke a service or respond to an invocation). The analyst captures static relationships in the problem domain using the concepts of aggregation and classification. Aggregation is used to capture whole/part relationships. Classification is used to capture class/instance relationships (also called "is-a" or inheritance relationships).

The structural components of OOA (for example, objects, classes, services, aggregation) support a set of analytic principles. Of these, two directly address requirements problems:

1. From information modeling comes the assumption that a problem is easiest to understand and communicate if the conceptual structures created during analysis map directly to entities and relationships in the problem domain. This principle is realized in OOA through the heuristic of representing problem domain objects and relationships of interest as OOA objects and relationships. Thus an OOA specification of a vehicle registration system might model vehicles, vehicle owners, vehicle title, and so on [Coad 90] as objects. The object paradigm is used to model both the problem and the relevant problem context.

2. From early work on modularization by Parnas [Parnas 72] and abstract data types, by way of object-oriented programming and design, come the principles of information hiding and abstraction. The principle of information hiding guides one to limit access to information on which other parts of the system should not depend. In an OO specification of requirements, this principle is applied to hide details of design and implementation. In OOA, behavior requirements are specified in terms of the data and services provided on the object interfaces; how those services are implemented is encapsulated by the object.

The principle of abstraction says that only the relevant or essential information should be presented. Abstraction is implemented in OOA by defining object interfaces that provide access only to essential data or state information encapsulated by an object (conversely hiding the incidentals).

The principles and mechanisms of OOA provide a basis for attacking the essential difficulties of comprehension, communication, and control. The principle of problem-domain modeling helps guide the analyst in distinguishing requirements (what) from design (how). Where the objects and their relationships faithfully model entities and relationships in the problem, they are understandable by the customer and other domain experts; this supports early comprehension of the requirements.

The principles of information hiding and abstraction, with the attendant object mechanisms, provide mechanisms useful for addressing the essential problems of control and communication. Objects provide the means to divide the requirements into distinct parts, abstract from details, and limit unnecessary dependencies between the parts. Object interfaces can be used to hide irrelevant detail and define abstractions providing only the essential information. This provides a basis for managing complexity and improving readability. Likewise objects provide a basis for constructing reusable requirements units of related functions and data.

The potential benefits of OOA are often diluted by the way the key principles are manifest in particular methods. While the objects and relations of OOA are intended to model essential aspects of the application domain, this goal is typically not supported by a corresponding conceptual model of the domain behavior. As for structured analysis, object-modeling mechanisms and techniques are intentionally generic rather than application specific. One result is insufficient guidance in developing appropriate object decompositions. Just as structured analysis practitioners have difficulty choosing appropriate data flows and transformations, OOA practitioners have difficulty choosing appropriate objects and relationships.

In practice, the notion that one can develop the structure of a system, or a requirements specification, based on physical structure is often found to be oversold. It is true that the elements of the physical world are usually stable (especially relative to software details) and that real-world-based models have intuitive appeal. It is not, however, the case that everything that must be captured in requirements has a physical analog. An obvious example is shared state information. Further, many real-world structures are themselves arbitrary and likely to change (for example, where two hardware functions are put on one physical platform to reduce cost). While the notion of basing requirements structure on physical structure is a useful heuristic, more is needed to develop a complete and consistent requirements specification.

A further difficulty is that the notations and semantics of OOA methods are typically based on the conceptual structures of software rather than those of the problem domain the analyst seeks to model. Symptomatic of this problem is that analysts find themselves debating about object language features and their properties rather than about the properties of the problem. An example is the use of message passing, complete with message passing protocols, where one object uses information defined in another. In the problem domain it is often irrelevant whether information is actively solicited or passively received. In fact there may be no notion of messages or transmission at all. Nonetheless one finds analysts debating about which object should initiate a request and the resulting anomaly of passive entities modeled as active. For example, to get information from a book one might request that the book "read itself" and "send" the requested information in a message. To control an aircraft the pilot might "use his hands and feet to 'send messages' to the aircraft controls which in turn send messages to the aircraft control surfaces to modify themselves" [Davis 93]. Such decisions are about OOA mechanisms or design, not about the problem domain or requirements.

A more serious complaint is that most current OOA methods inadequately address our goal of developing a good SRS. Most OOA approaches in the literature provide only informal specification mechanisms, relying on refinement of the OO model in design and implementation to add detail and precision. There is no formal basis for determining if a specification is complete, consistent, or verifiable. Further, none of the OOA techniques discussed directly address the issues of developing the SRS as a reference document. The focus of all of the cited OOA techniques is on problem analysis rather than specification. If the SRS is addressed at all, the assumption is that the principles applied to problem understanding and modeling are sufficient, when results are documented, to produce a good specification. Experience suggests otherwise. As we have discussed, there are inherent trade-offs that must be made to develop a specification that meets the needs of any particular project. Making effective trade-offs requires a disciplined and thoughtful approach to the SRS itself, not just the problem. Thus, while OOA provide the means to address packaging issues, there is typically little methodological emphasis on issues like modifiability or organization of a specification for reference and review.

7.5 Software Cost Reduction (SCR) Method

Where most of the techniques thus far discussed focus on problem analysis, the requirements work at the US Naval Research Laboratory (NRL) focused equally on issues of developing a good SRS. NRL initiated the Software Cost Reduction (SCR) project in 1978 to demonstrate the feasibility and effectiveness of advanced software engineering techniques by applying them to a real system, the Operational Flight Program (OFP) for the A-7E aircraft. To demonstrate that (then-academic) techniques such as information hiding, formal specification, abstract interfaces, and cooperating sequential processes could help make software easier to understand, maintain, and change, the SCR project set out to reengineer the A-7E OFP.

Since no existing documentation adequately captured the A-7E's software requirements, the first step was to develop an effective SRS. In this process, the SCR project identified a number of properties a good SRS should have and a set of principles for developing effective requirements documentation [Heninger 80]. The SCR approach uses formal, mathematically based specifications of acceptable system outputs to support development of a specification that is unambiguous, precise, and verifiable. It also provided techniques for checking a specification for a variety of completeness and consistency properties. The SCR approach introduced principles and techniques to support our SRS packaging goals, including the principle of separation of concerns to aid readability and support ease of change. It also includes the use of a standard structure for an SRS specification and the use of tabular specifications that improve readability, modifiability, and facilitate use of the specification for reference and review.

While other requirements approaches have stated similar objectives, the SCR project is unique in having applied software engineering principles to develop a standard SRS organization, a specification method, review method [Parnas 85a], and notations consistent with those principles. The SCR project is also unique in making publicly available a complete, model SRS of a significant system [Alspaugh 92].

A number of issues were left unresolved by the original SCR work. While the product of the requirements analysis was well documented, the underlying process and method were never fully described. Since the original effort was to reengineer an existing system, it was not clear how effective the techniques would be on a new development. Since the developers of the A-7E requirements document were researchers, it was also unclear whether industrial developers would find the rather formal method and notation useable, readable, or effective. Finally, while the A-7E

SRS organization is reasonably general, many of the specification techniques are targeted to real-time, embedded applications. As discussed in the following section, more recent work by Parnas [Parnas 91], NRL [Heitmeyer 95a,b], and others [Faulk 92] has addressed many of the open questions about the SCR approach.

8. Trends and Emerging Technology

While improved discipline will address requirement's accidental difficulties, addressing the essential difficulties requires technical advances. Significant trends, in some cases backed by industrial experience, have emerged over the past few years that offer some hope for improvement:

- *Domain specificity*: Requirements methods will provide improved analytic and specification support by being tailored to particular classes of problems. Historically, requirements approaches have been advanced as being equally useful to widely varied types of applications. For example, structured analysis methods were deemed to be based on conceptual models that were "universally applicable" (for example, [Ross 77]); similar claims have been made for object-oriented approaches.

Such generality comes at the expense of ease of use and amount of work the analyst must do for any particular application. Where the underlying models have been tailored to a particular class of applications, the properties common to the class are embedded in the model. The amount of work necessary to adapt the model to a specific instance of the class is relatively small. The more general the model, the more decisions that must be made, the more information that must be provided, and the more tailoring that must be done. This provides increased room for error and, since each analyst will approach the problem differently, makes solutions difficult to standardize. In particular, such generality precludes standardization of sufficiently rigorous models to support algorithmic analysis of properties like completeness and consistency.

Similar points have been expressed in a recent paper by Jackson [Jackson 94]. He points out that some of the characteristics separating real engineering disciplines from what is euphemistically described as "software engineering" are well-understood procedures, mathematical models, and standard designs specific to narrow classes of applications. Jackson points out the need for software methods based on the conceptual structures and mathematical models of behavior inherent in a given problem domain (for example, publication, command and control, accounting, and so on). Such common underlying constructs can provide the engineer guidance in developing the specification for a particular system.

- *Practical formalisms*: Like so many of the promising technologies in requirements, the application of formal methods is characterized by an essential dilemma. On one hand, formal specification techniques hold out the only real hope for producing specifications that are precise, unambiguous, and demonstrably complete or consistent. On the other, industrial practitioners widely view formal methods as impractical. Difficulty of use, inability to scale, readability, and cost are among the reasons cited. Thus, in spite of significant technical progress and a growing body of literature, the pace of adoption by industry has been extremely slow.

In spite of the technical and technical transfer difficulties, increased formality is necessary. Only by placing behavioral specification on a mathematical basis will we be able to acquire sufficient intellectual control to develop complex systems with any assurance that they satisfy their intended purpose and provide necessary properties like safety. The solution is better formal methods—methods that are practical given the time, cost, and personnel constraints of industrial development.

Engineering models and the training to use them are de rigueur in every other discipline that builds large, complex, or safety-critical systems. Builders of a bridge or skyscraper who did not employ proven methods or mathematical models to predict reliability and safety would be held criminally negligent in the event of failure. It is only the relative youth of the software discipline that permits us to get away with less. But, we cannot expect great progress overnight. As Jackson [Jackson 94] notes, the field is sufficiently immature that "the prerequisites for a more mathematical approach are not in place." Further, many of those practicing our craft lack the background required of licensed engineers in other disciplines [Parnas 89]. Nonetheless, sufficient work has been done to show that more formal approaches are practical and effective in industry. For an overview of formal methods and their role in practical developments, refer to Rushby's summary work [Rushby 93].

- *Improved tool support*: It remains common to walk into the office of a software develop-

ment manager and find the shelves lined with the manuals for CASE tools that are not in use. In spite of years of development and the contrary claims of vendors, many industrial developers have found the available requirements CASE tools of marginal benefit.

Typically, the fault lies not so much with the tool vendor but with the underlying method or methods the tool seeks to support. The same generality, lack of strong underlying conceptual model, and lack of formality that makes the methods weak limits the benefits of automation. Since the methods do not adequately constrain the problem space and offer little specific guidance, the corresponding tool cannot actively support the developer in making difficult decisions. Since the model and SRS are not standardized, its production eludes effective automated support. Since the underlying model is not formal, only trivial syntactic properties of the specification can be evaluated. Most such tools provide little more than a graphic interface and requirements database.

Far more is now possible. Where the model, conceptual structures, notations, and process are standardized, significant automated support becomes possible. The tool can use information about the state of the specification and the process to guide the developer in making the next step. It can use standardized templates to automate rote portions of the SRS. It can use the underlying mathematical model to determine to what extent the specification is complete and consistent. While only the potential of such tools has yet been demonstrated, there are sufficient results to project the benefits (for example, [Heitmeyer 95b], [Leveson 94]).

- *Integrated paradigms*: One of the Holy Grails of software engineering has been the integrated software development environment. Much of the frustration in applying currently available methods and tools is the lack of integration, not just in the tool interfaces, but in the underlying models and conceptual structures. Even where an approach works well for one phase of development, the same techniques are either difficult to use in the next phase or there is no clear transition path. Similarly tools are either focused on a small subset of the many tasks (for example, analysis but not documentation) or attempt to address the entire life cycle but support none of it well. The typical development employs a hodgepodge of software engineering methodologies and ad hoc techniques. Developers often build their own software to bridge the gap between CASE platforms.

In spite of a number of attempts, the production of a useful, integrated set of methods and supporting environment has proven elusive. However, it now appears that there is sufficient technology available to provide, if not a complete solution, at least the skeleton for one.

The most significant methodological trend can be described as convergent evolution. In biology, convergent evolution denotes a situation where common evolutionary pressures lead to similar characteristics (morphology) in distinct species. An analogous convergence is ongoing in requirements. As different schools of thought have come to understand and attempt to address the weaknesses and omissions in their own approaches, the solutions have become more similar. In particular, the field is moving toward a common understanding of the difficulties and common assumptions about the desired qualities of solutions. This should not be confused with the bandwagon effect that often attends real or imaginary paradigm shifts (for example, the current rush to object-oriented everything). Rather, it is the slow process of evolving common understanding and changing conventional practices.

Such trends and some preliminary results are currently observable in requirements approaches for embedded software. In the 1970s, the exigencies of national defense and aerospace applications resulted in demand for complex, mission-critical software. It became apparent early on that available requirements techniques addressed neither the complexity of the systems being built nor the stringent control, timing, and accuracy constraints of the applications. Developers responded by creating a variety of domain-specific approaches. Early work by TRW for the US Army on the Ballistic Missile Defense system produced the Software Requirements Engineering Method (SREM) [Alford 77] and supporting tools. Such software problems in the Navy led to the SCR project. Ward, Mellor, Hatley, and Pirbhai ([Ward 86], [Hatley 87]) developed extensions to structured analysis techniques targeted to real-time applications. Work on the Israeli defense applications led Harel to develop statecharts [Harel 87] and the supporting tool Statemate.

The need for high-assurance software in mission-

and safety-critical systems also led to the introduction of practical formalisms and integrated tools support. TRW developed REVS [Davis 77] and other tools as part of a complete environment supporting SREM and other phases of the life cycle. The SCR project developed specification techniques based on mathematical functions and tabular representations [Heninger 80]. These allowed a variety of consistency and completeness checks to be performed by inspection. Harel introduced a compact graphic representation of finite state machines with a well-defined formal semantics. These features were subsequently integrated in the Statemate tool that supported symbolic execution of statecharts for early customer validation and limited code generation. All of these techniques began to converge on an underlying model based on finite state automata.

More recent work has seen continuing convergence toward a common set of assumptions and similar solutions. Recently, Ward and colleagues have developed the Real-Time Object-Oriented Modeling (ROOM) method [Selic 94]. ROOM integrates concepts from operational specification, object-oriented analysis, and statecharts. It employs an object-oriented modeling approach with tool support. The tool is based on a simplified statechart semantics and supports symbolic execution and some code generation. The focus of ROOM currently remains on problem modeling and the transition to design, and execution rather than formal analysis.

Nancy Leveson and her colleagues have adapted statecharts to provide a formally based method for embedded system specification [Jaffe 91]. The approach has been specifically developed to be useable and readable by practicing engineers. It employs both the graphical syntax of statecharts and a tabular representation of functions similar to those used in the SCR approach. Its underlying formal model is intended to support formal analysis of system properties, with an emphasis on safety. The formal model also supports symbolic execution. These techniques have been applied to develop a requirements specification for parts of the Federal Aviation Administration's safety-critical Traffic Alert and Collision Avoidance System (TCAS) [Leveson 94].

Extensions to the SCR work have taken a similar direction. Parnas and Madey have extended the SCR approach to create a standard mathematical model for embedded system requirements [Parnas 91]. Heitmeyer and colleagues at NRL have extended the Parnas/Madey work by defining a corresponding formal model for the SCR approach [Heitmeyer 95b]. This formal model has been used to develop a suite of prototype tools supporting analysis of requirements properties like completeness and consistency [Heitmeyer

95a]. The NRL tools also support specification-based simulation and are being integrated with other tools to support automated analysis of application-specific properties like safety assertions. Concurrent work at the Software Productivity Consortium by Faulk and colleagues [Faulk 92] has integrated the SCR approach with object-oriented and graphic techniques and defined a complete requirements analysis process including a detailed process for developing a good SRS. These techniques have been applied effectively in development of requirements for Lockheed's avionics upgrade on the C-130J aircraft [Faulk 94]. The C-130J avionics software is a safety-critical system of approximately 100K lines of Ada code.

Other recent work attempts to increase the level of formality and the predictability of the problem analysis process and its products. For example, Potts and his colleagues are developing process models and tools to support systematic requirements elicitation that include a formal structure for describing discussions about requirements [Potts 94]. Hsia and his colleagues, among others, are investigating formal approaches to the use of scenarios in eliciting and validating requirements [Hsia 94]. Recent work by Boehm and his colleagues [Boehm 94] seeks to address the accidental difficulties engendered by adversarial software procurement processes.

While none of the works mentioned can be considered a complete solution, it is clear that (1) the work is converging toward common assumptions and solutions, (2) the approaches all provide significantly improved capability to address both accidental and essential requirements difficulties, and (3) the solutions can be effectively applied in industry.

9. Conclusions

Requirements are intrinsically hard to do well. Beyond the need for discipline, there are a host of essential difficulties that attend both the understanding of requirements and their specification. Further, many of the difficulties in requirements will not yield to technical solution alone. Addressing all of the essential difficulties requires the application of technical solutions in the context of human factors such as the ability to manage complexity or communicate to diverse audiences. A requirements approach that does not account for both technical and human concerns can have only limited success. For developers seeking new methods, the lesson is caveat emptor. If someone tells you his method makes requirements easy, keep a hand on your wallet.

Nevertheless, difficulty is not impossibility and the inability to achieve perfection is not an excuse for surrender. While all of the approaches discussed have significant weaknesses, they all contribute to the attempt to make requirements analysis and specification a controlled, systematic, and effective process. Though there is no easy path, experience confirms that the use of *any* careful and systematic approach is preferable to an ad hoc and chaotic one. Further good news is that, if the requirements are done well, chances are much improved that the rest of the development will also go well. Unfortunately, ad hoc approaches remain the norm in much of the software industry.

A final observation is that the benefits of good requirements come at a cost. Such a difficult and exacting task cannot be done properly by personnel with inadequate experience, training, or resources. Providing the time and the means to do the job right is the task of responsible management. The time to commit the best and brightest is before, not after, disaster occurs. The monumental failures of a host of ambitious developments bear witness to the folly of doing otherwise.

10. Further Reading

Those seeking more depth on requirements methodologies than this tutorial can provide should read Alan Davis' book *Software Requirements: Objects, Functions, and States* [Davis 93]. In addition to a general discussion of issues in software requirements, Davis illustrates a number of problem analysis and specification techniques with a set of common examples and provides a comprehensive annotated bibliography.

For a better understanding of software requirements in the context of systems development, the reader is referred to the book of collected papers edited by Thayer and Dorfman, *System and Software Requirements Engineering* [Thayer 90]. This tutorial work contains in one volume both original papers and reprints from many of the authors discussed above. The companion volume, *Standards, Guidelines, and Examples on System and Software Requirements Engineering* [Dorfman 90] is a compendium of international and US government standards relating to system and software requirements and provides some illustrating examples.

For enjoyable reading as well as insightful commentary on requirements problems, methods, and a host of requirements-related issues, the reader is referred to Michael Jackson's recent book, *Software Requirements and Specifications: A Lexicon of Practice, Principles, and Prejudice.* [Jackson 95]

Acknowledgments

C. Colket at SPAWAR, E. Wald at ONR and A. Pyster at the Software Productivity Consortium supported the development of this report. The quality of this paper has been much improved thanks to thoughtful reviews by Paul Clements, Connie Heitmeyer, Jim Kirby, Bruce Labaw, Richard Morrison, and David Weiss.

References

[Alford 77]   Alford, M., "A Requirements Engineering Methodology for Real-Time Processing Requirements," *IEEE Trans. Software Eng.*, Vol. 3, No. 1, Jan. 1977, pp. 60–69.

[Alford 79]   Alford, M. and J. Lawson, "Software Requirements Engineering Methodology (Development)," *RADC-TR-79-168*, U.S. Air Force Rome Air Development Center, June 1979.

[Alspaugh 92]   Alspaugh, T. et al., *Software Requirements for the A-7E Aircraft*, NRL/FR/5530-92-9194, Naval Research Laboratory, Washington, D.C., 1992.

[Balin 94]   Balin, S., "Object-Oriented Requirements Analysis," in *Encyclopedia of Software Engineering*, J. Marciniak ed., John Wiley & Sons, New York, N.Y., 1994, pp. 740–756.

[Basili 81]   Basili, V. and D. Weiss, "Evaluation of a Software Requirements Document by Analysis of Change Data," *Proc. 5th Int'l Conf. Software Eng.*, IEEE CS Press, Los Alamitos, Calif., 1981, pp. 314–323.

[Boehm 81]   Boehm, B., *Software Engineering Economics*, Prentice-Hall, Englewood Cliffs, N.J., 1981.

[Boehm 94]   Boehm, B. et al., "Software Requirements as Negotiated Win Conditions," *Proc. 1st Int'l Conf. Requirements Eng.*, IEEE CS Press, Los Alamitos, Calif., 1994, pp. 74–83.

[Brooks 75]   Brooks, F., *The Mythical Man-Month*, Addison-Wesley, Reading, Mass., 1975.

[Brooks 87]   Brooks, F., "No Silver Bullet: Essence and Accidents of Software Engineering," *Computer*, Apr. 1987, pp. 10–19.

[CECOM 89]   *Software Methodology Catalog: Second Edition*, Technical report C01-091JB-0001-01, US Army Communications-Electronics Command, Fort Monmouth, N.J., Mar. 1989.

[Clements 95]   Clements, P., private communication, May 1995.

[Coad 90]   Coad, P. and E. Yourdon, *Object Oriented Analysis*, Prentice-Hall, Englewood Cliffs, N.J., 1990.

[Davis 77]   Davis, C. and C. Vick, "The Software Development System," *IEEE Trans. Software Eng.*, Vol. 3, No. 1, Jan. 1977, pp. 69–84.

[Davis 88]   Davis, A., "A Taxonomy for the Early Stages of the Software Development Life Cycle," *J. Systems and Software*, Sept. 1988, pp. 297–311.

[Davis 93]   Davis, A., *Software Requirements (Revised): Objects, Functions, and States*, Prentice-Hall, Englewood Cliffs, N.J., 1993.

[DeMarco 78]   DeMarco, T., *Structured Analysis and System Specification*, Prentice-Hall Englewood Cliffs, N.J., 1978.

[Dorfman 90]   Dorfman, M. and R. Thayer, eds., *Standards, Guidelines, and Examples on System and Software Requirements Engineering*, IEEE CS Press, Los Alamitos, Calif., 1990.

[Faulk 92]   Faulk, S. et al., "The Core Method for Real-Time Requirements," *IEEE Software*, Vol. 9, No. 5, Sept. 1992.

[Faulk 93]   Faulk, S. et al., *Consortium Requirements Engineering Guidebook*, Version 1.0, SPC-92060-CMC, Software Productivity Consortium, Herndon, Virginia, 1993.

[Faulk 94]   Faulk, S. et al., "Experience Applying the CoRE Method to the Lockheed C-130J," *Proc. 9th Ann. Conf. Computer Assurance*, IEEE Press, Piscataway, N.J., 1994, pp. 3–8.

[GAO 79]   US General Accounting Office, *Contracting for Computer Software Development—Serious Problems Require Management Attention to Avoid Wasting Additional Millions*, Report FGMSD-80-4, November 1979.

[GAO 92]   US General Accounting Office, *Mission Critical Systems: Defense Attempting to Address Major Software Challenges*, GAO/IMTEC-93-13, December 1992.

[Gane 79]   Gane, C. and T. Sarson, *Structured Systems Analysis*, Prentice-Hall, New Jersey, 1979.

[Hamilton 76]   Hamilton, M. and S. Zeldin, "Higher Order Software-A Methodology for Defining Software," *IEEE Trans. Software Eng.*, Vol. 2, No. 1, Jan. 1976, pp. 9–32.

[Harel 87]   Harel, D., "Statecharts: a Visual Formalism for Complex Systems," *Science of Computer Programming 8*, 1987, pp. 231–274.

[Hatley 87]   Hatley, D. and I. Pirbhai, *Strategies for Real-Time Specification*, Dorset House, New York, N.Y., 1987.

[Heitmeyer 95a] Heitmeyer, C., B. Labaw, and D. Kiskis, "Consistency Checking of SCR-Style Requirements Specifications," *Proc. 2nd IEEE Int'l Symp. Requirements Eng.*, IEEE CS Press, Los Alamitos, Calif., 1995, pp. 56–63.

[Heitmeyer 95b] Heitmeyer, C., R. Jeffords, and B. Labaw, *Tools for Analyzing SCR-Style Requirements Specifications: A Formal Foundation*, NRL Technical Report NRL-7499, U.S. Naval Research Laboratory, Washington, DC, 1995.

[Heninger 80] Heninger, K., "Specifying Software Requirements for Complex Systems: New Techniques and Their Application," *IEEE Trans. Software Eng.*, Vol. 6, No. 1, Jan. 1980.

[Hester 81]   Hester, S., D. Parnas, and D. Utter, "Using Documentation as a Software Design Medium," *Bell System Technical J.*, Vol. 60, No. 8, Oct. 1981, pp. 1941–1977.

[Hsia 94]   Hsia, P. et al., "Formal Approach to Scenario Analysis," *IEEE Software*, Mar. 1994, pp. 33–41.

[Jackson 83]   Jackson, M., *System Development*, Prentice-Hall, Englewood Cliffs, N.J., 1983.

[Jackson 94]   Jackson, M., "Problems, Methods, and Specialization," *IEEE Software*, Nov. 1994, pp. 57–62.

[Jackson 95]   Jackson, M., *Software Requirements and Specifications: A Lexicon of Practice, Principles, and Prejudice*, ACM Press/Addison Wesley, Reading, Mass., 1995.

[Jaffe 91]   Jaffe, M. et al., "Software Requirements Analysis for Real-Time Process-Control Systems," *IEEE Trans. Software Eng.*, Vol. 17, No. 3, Mar. 1991, pp. 241–257.

[Leveson 94]   Leveson, N. et al., "Requirements Specification for Process-Control Systems," *IEEE Trans. Software Eng.*, Vol. 20, No. 9, Sept. 1994.

[Lutz 93]   Lutz, R., "Analyzing Software Requirements Errors in Safety-Critical Embedded Systems," *Proc. IEEE Int'l Symp. Requirements Eng.*, IEEE CS Press, Los Alamitos, Calif., 1993, pp. 126–133.

[Parnas 72]   Parnas, D., "On the Criteria to be Used in Decomposing Systems into Modules," *Comm. ACM*, Vol. 15, No. 12, Dec. 1972, pp. 1053–1058.

[Parnas 85a]   Parnas, D. and D. Weiss, "Active Design Reviews: Principles and Practices," *Proc. 8th Int'l Conf. Software Eng.*, IEEE CS Press, Los Alamitos, Calif., 1985.

[Parnas 85b]   Parnas, D. "Software Aspects of Strategic Defense Systems," *American Scientist*, Sept. 1985, pp. 432–440.

[Parnas 86]   Parnas, D. and P. Clements, "A Rational Design Process: How and Why to Fake It," *IEEE Trans. Software Eng.*, Vol. 12, No. 2, Feb. 1986, pp. 251–257.

[Parnas 89]   Parnas, D., *Education for Computing Professionals*, Technical Report 89-247, Department of Computing and Information Science, Queens University, Kingston, Ontario, 1989.

[Parnas 91]   Parnas, D. and J. Madey, *Functional Documentation for Computer Systems Engineering* (Version 2), CRL Report No. 237, McMaster University, Hamilton, Ontario, Canada, Sept. 1991.

[Potts 94]   Potts, C., K. Takahashi, and A. Anton, "Inquiry-Based Requirements Analysis," *IEEE Software*, Mar. 1994, pp. 21–32.

[Shlaer 88]   Shlaer, S. and S. Mellor, *Object-Oriented Systems Analysis: Modeling the World in Data*, Prentice-Hall, Englewood Cliffs, N.J., 1988.

[Ross 77]   Ross, D. and K. Schoman Jr., "Structured Analysis for Requirements Definitions," *IEEE Trans. Software Eng.*, Vol. 3, No. 1, Jan. 1977, pp. 6–15.

[Rumbaugh 91] Rumbaugh, M. Blaha et al, *Object-Oriented Modeling and Design*, Prentice-Hall, Englewood Cliffs, N.J., 1991.

[Rushby 93]   Rushby, J., *Formal Methods and the Certification of Critical Systems*, CSL Technical Report SRI-CSL-93-07, SRI International, Menlo Park, Calif., Nov., 1993.

[Selic 94]   Selic, B., G. Gullekson, and P. Ward, *Real-Time Object-Oriented Modeling*, John Wiley & Sons, New York, N.Y., 1994.

[Svoboda 90]   Svoboda, C., "Structured Analysis," in *Tutorial: System and Software Requirements Engineering*, R. Thayer and M. Dorfman, eds., IEEE CS Press, Los Alamitos, Calif., 1990, pp. 218–237.

[Thayer 90]   Thayer, R. and M. Dorfman, eds., *Tutorial: System and Software Requirements Engineering*, IEEE CS Press, Los Alamitos, Calif., 1990.

[Ward 86]   Ward, P. and S. Mellor, *Structured Development for Real-Time Systems*, Vols. 1, 2, and 3, Prentice-Hall, Englewood Cliffs, N.J., 1986.

[Yourdon 89]   Yourdon, E., *Modern Structured Analysis*, Yourdon Press/Prentice-Hall, Englewood Cliffs, N.J., 1989.

[Zave 82]   Zave, P., "An Operational Approach to Requirements Specification for Embedded Systems," *IEEE Trans. Software Eng.*, Vol. 8, No. 3, May 1982, pp. 250–269.

Software Design: An Introduction

David Budgen

1. The Role of Software Design

A question that should be asked (and preferably answered!) at the beginning of an overview paper such as this, is

What exactly is the purpose of design?

and the answer that we will be assuming is along the lines of

"To produce a workable (implementable) solution to a given problem."

where in our context, the eventual "solution" involves producing an artifact that will be in the form of software.

This end goal is one that we need to keep in mind in seeking to provide a concise review of some of the many factors and issues that are involved in designing software-based systems. We also need to remember the corollary to this: that the key measure of the appropriateness of any solution is that of *fitness for purpose*.

The significant characteristic of design as a problem-solving approach is that there is rarely (indeed, almost never) only one solution to a problem. So we cannot hope to identify some systematic way of finding the answer, as occurs in the physical and mathematical sciences. Instead, the designer needs to work in a creative manner to identify the properties required in the solution and then seek to devise a structure that possesses them.

This characteristic can be illustrated by a very simple example of a design task that will be familiar to many, and which is based upon that major trauma of life: moving house! When we move to a new house or apartment, we are faced with a typical design problem in deciding where our furniture is to be placed. We may also be required to assist the removal company by supplying them with an abstract description of our intentions.

There are of course many ways in which furniture can be arranged within a house or apartment. We need to decide in which room each item needs to be placed, perhaps determined chiefly by functionality, and then to decide exactly where it might go in the room. We might choose to focus our attention on getting a good balance of style in one room at the expense of another. We also need to consider the constraints imposed by the configuration of the house, so that furniture does not block doors or windows, and power outlets remain accessible.

So this simple example exhibits all of the main characteristics that are to be found in almost all design problems [1]: no single "right" solution; many factors and constraints to be balanced in choosing a solution; no one measure of "quality;" and no particular process that can ensure that we can even identify an acceptable solution!

1.1 The software design process

An important task for a designer is to formulate and develop some form of abstract design model that represents his or her ideas about a solution. Accepting that these activities that underpin the design process are creative ones, the next question that should be asked is why is it that the task of designing software seems to be even more intractable and less well understood than other forms of design? In [2], Fred Brooks has suggested that some software properties that contribute to this include:

- *The complexity of software*, with no two parts ever being quite alike, and with a process or system having many possible states during execution.

- *The problem of conformity* that arises because of the very pliable nature of software, with software designers being expected to tailor software around the needs of hardware, of existing systems, or to meet other sources of "standards."

- *The (apparent) ease of changeability*, leading to constant requirements for change from users, who fail to appreciate the true costs implied by changes.

- *The invisibility of software* so that our descriptions of design ideas lack any visual link to the form of the end product, and hence are unable to help with comprehension in the same way as usually occurs with descriptions of more physical structures.

Empirical studies of the activities involved in designing software [3, 4, 5] suggest that designers use a number of techniques to reduce the effects of at least some of these properties. These techniques include the use of abstract "mental models" of their solutions, which can then be mentally executed to simulate the final system behaviour; reusing parts of previous solutions; and making notes about future (detailed) intentions as reminders for later stages in development.

Even where designers use a particular strategy to help with developing a design model, they may still deviate from this in an opportunistic manner either:

- to *postpone* making a decision where information is not yet available; or
- to define components for which the information is ready to hand, in *anticipation* of further developments in the design.

The use of an opportunistic strategy should not be taken to imply that design decisions are being made in an *unstructured* manner. Rather, this corresponds to a situation where the designer is making use of his or her own experience and knowledge of the problem domain to help adapt their problem-solving strategy, by identifying those aspects of the solution that need to be given most attention in the early stages [6].

Where a designer lacks experience, or is unfamiliar with the type of problem being solved, then one means of acquiring the experience of others is through the use of a *software design method*. Clearly, to transfer all of the different forms of knowledge that allow the designer to use opportunistic development strategies would be difficult, and design methods are therefore limited to encouraging those forms of design practice that can be prescribed in a *procedural* manner. To do so, they provide:

1. A *representation part* consisting of a set of notations that can be used to describe a design model of the form that the method seeks to develop.

2. A *process part* that describes how the model is to be developed, expressed as a set of steps, with each step representing a transformation of the model.

3. A *set of heuristics* that provide guidance on how the process part should be modified or adapted in order to cope with particular forms of problem. These may consist of alternative procedures, or may identify useful "rules of thumb."

One important point that should be made here:

Designing software is rarely a completely *unconstrained* process. The designer not only has to produce a solution to a given problem but must also meet other customer-imposed requirements. These *constraints* may include the need to design a solution that can be implemented in a particular programming language; or one that will work within a particular environment or operating system. Constraints therefore act to limit the "solution space" that is available to the designer.

1.2 Design in the software development cycle

Constraints can affect the design process as well as the form of the product. Designing software is not an isolated and independent activity. The eventual system as implemented will be expected to meet a whole set of user needs (reminding us of the criterion of "fitness for purpose"), where these needs are likely to have been determined by some process of *requirements elicitation*. The activities of *analysis* may be used to identify the form of solution that will meet the user's needs, and the designer is then required to provide a solution that conforms to that form. But of course, the activities of all those tasks will interact, largely because each activity is likely to lead to the identification of inconsistencies between requirements and solution, as ideas about the latter develop.

In a like manner, a designer must provide a set of specifications for those who are to construct a system. These need to be as clear, complete, and unambiguous as possible, but of course it is likely that further needs for change will be identified during implementation. The designer also needs to "think ahead" in planning a solution, since few software systems are used for long without being altered and extended. So designing for "maintenance" (a term that is usually a circumlocution for "extensive further development") is another factor that may influence the form of the solution that is adopted.

1.3 Design qualities

The features of a system that may be considered as representative of our ideas of quality are apt to be dependent upon the specific relationship that we have to the system. We began by suggesting that *fitness for purpose* was a paramount need of any system, but of course, this is not an absolute measure of quality, nor one that can be measured in any direct manner. Simply doing the job correctly and within the resource constraints identified may not be enough to achieve fitness for purpose. For example, if it is anticipated that a system will be used for at least ten years, involving modification at frequent intervals, then our notions of fitness for purpose are very likely to incorporate ideas about how easily the structure of the design will accommodate the likely changes. On the other hand, if the need is for a solution that is extremely short-term, but urgent, we may place much more priority on getting a system that works than on ensuring that it can also be modified and extended.

We do not have space here for a discussion of quality factors, but a useful group to note are those that are usually referred to as the "*ilities*". The exact membership of this group may depend upon context, but the key ones are generally accepted as being *reliability, efficiency, maintainability*, and *usability*. The ilities can be considered to describe rather abstract and "top-level" properties of the eventual system, and these are not easily assessed from design information alone.

Indeed, it has generally proved to be difficult to apply any systematic form of measurement to design information. While at the level of implementation, basic code measurements (metrics) can at least be gathered by counting lexical tokens [7], the variability and the weak syntax and semantics of design notations make such an approach much less suitable for designs. More practical approaches to assessment at this level of abstraction usually involve such activities as design walk-throughs and reviews [8].

2 Describing Designs

2.1 Recording the design model: design viewpoints

In this section we examine some of the ways in which a designer's ideas about the design model can be visualised by using various forms of description.

A major need for the designer is to be able to select and use a set of abstractions that describe those properties of the design model that are relevant to the design decisions that need to be made. This is normally achieved by using a number of representation forms, where such forms can be used for:

- documenting and exploring the details of the design model;
- explaining the designer's ideas to others (including the customer, the implementors, managers, reviewers, and so forth);
- checking for consistency and completeness of the design model.

Because software design methods must rely upon constructing a design model through a fixed set of procedures, they each use an associated set of representations to describe the properties identified through following the procedures. This forms both a strength and a weakness of design methods: The representa-

tions support the procedures by helping the designer visualise those aspects of the design that are affected by the procedures; but they may also limit the designer's vision. (Indeed, the act of deviating from the procedures of a method in order to draw some other form of diagram to help highlight some issue is a good example of what was earlier termed *opportunistic* behaviour on the part of a designer.)

The representations used in software design can be grouped according to their *purpose*, since this identifies the forms of property they seek to describe. One such grouping, explored in some detail in [9] is based upon the concept of the *design viewpoint*. A design viewpoint can be regarded as being a "projection" from the design model that displays certain of the properties of the design model, as is shown schematically in Figure 1. The four viewpoints shown there are:

1. The *behavioural* viewpoint, describing the causal links between external events and system activities during program execution.

2. The *functional* viewpoint, describing what the system does.

3. The *structural* viewpoint, describing the interdependencies of the constructional components of the system, such as subprograms, modules, and packages.

4. The *data modelling* viewpoint, describing the relationships that exist between the data objects used in the system.

2.2 Design representation forms

The three principal forms of description normally used to realise the design viewpoints are text, diagrams, and mathematical expressions.

Textual descriptions
Text is of course widely used, both on its own, and in conjunction with the other two forms. We can structure it by using such forms as headings, lists (numbered, bullets), and indentation, so as to reflect the structure of the properties being described. However, text on its own does have some limitations, in particular:

- The presence of any form of structure that is implicitly contained in the information can easily be obscured if its form does not map easily onto lists and tables.
- Natural language is prone to ambiguity that can only be resolved by using long and complex sequences of text (as is amply demonstrated by any legal document!)

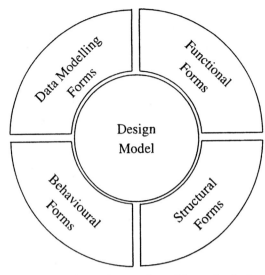

Figure 1. Design viewpoints projected from the design model.

Diagrammatical descriptions

There is a long tradition of drawing diagrams to provide abstractions in science and engineering, and even though the "invisibility" factor makes the form of these less intuitive when used to describe software, they are still very useful. Since they will form the main examples later in this section, we will not elaborate on their forms here, other than to identify the following properties as those that seem to characterise the more widely used and "successful" forms:

- *A small number of symbols.* The symbols in a diagram describe the "elements" that are modelled by that form of diagram, and the number of symbols is often in inverse pro portion to the degree of abstraction provided. Most of the widely used forms use only four or five different symbols, including circles, lines (arcs), and boxes.

- *A hierarchical structure.* The complex interactions that occur between software components together with the abstract nature of the components means that diagrams with many different symbols are often very difficult to understand. To help overcome this, many diagrammatical forms allow the use of a hierarchy of diagrams, with symbols at one level being expanded at another level with the same set of symbols, as is shown schematically in Figure 2.

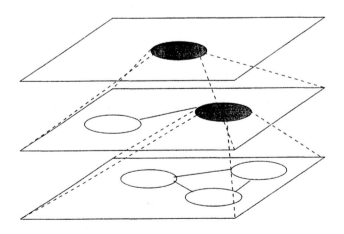

Figure 2. Use of hierarchy in representations.

107

- *Simplicity of symbol forms.* Ideally, *any* notation should be capable of being drawn using a pencil and paper only (or a whiteboard). Complicated symbols that require the support of specialised diagram drawing software can limit the ease with which designers communicate their ideas to others.

Mathematical descriptions

Mathematical notations are of course ideally suited to providing concise abstractions of ideas, and so it is hardly surprising that these have been employed in what we generally term the Formal Description Techniques, or FDTs. However, the very terse nature of mathematical descriptions, and the precision that they provide, are not necessarily compatible with the designer's need for abstraction, since they may demand early resolution of issues that the designer may wish to defer.

So far, FDTs have found their main use in specification roles, especially in providing unambiguous descriptions of requirements and descriptions of detailed design features. In both of these roles, their form makes them well suited to exploring the completeness and consistency of the specification, although less so to its development [10].

2.3 Some examples of design representations

To conclude this section we provide some simple examples of diagrammatical notations used for the four design viewpoints. This is a very small selection from the very large range of forms that have been proposed and used (for a fuller survey, see reference [9]).

Table 1 provides a summary of some widely used representations, the viewpoints that they provide, and the related design properties that they describe. (It should be noted that the conventions used in these notations do vary between different groups of users.)

The Statechart

Statecharts provide a means of modelling the behaviour of a system when viewed as a finite-state machine, [11] while providing better scope for hierarchical decomposition and composition than is generally found in behavioural representation forms.

A state is denoted by a box with rounded corners and directed arcs denote transitions. The latter are labelled with a description of the event causing the transition and, optionally, with a parenthesised condition. The hierarchy of states is shown by encapsulating state symbols.

A description of the actions of an aircraft "entity" within an air traffic control system is shown in Figure 3. Note that the short curved arc denotes the "default initial state" that is entered when an instance of the entity is added to the system. (For clarity, not all transitions have been labelled in this example.)

The Jackson Structure Diagram

This notation is very widely used under a variety of names. Its main characteristic is that it can describe the ordered structure of an "object" in terms of the three classical structuring forms of sequence, selection and iteration. For this particular example, we will show its use for modelling functional properties, although it is also used for modelling data structure and for describing time-ordered behaviour.

Table 1. Design representations and viewpoints.

Representation Form	Viewpoints	Design properties
Data-Flow Diagram (DFD)	Functional	Information flow; dependency of operations on other operations.
Entity-Relationship Diagram (ERD)	Data modelling	Static relationships between subprograms; decomposition into subprograms
Structure Chart	Structural and functional	Invocation hierarchy between subprograms; decomposition into subprograms
Structure Diagram (Jackson)	Functional, data modelling, behavioural	Algorithm forms; sequencing of data components; sequencing of actions.
Pseudocode	Functional	Algorithm forms
State Transition Diagram (STD)	Behavioural	State model describing how events cause transitions in entities.
Statechart	Behavioural	System-wide state model, including parallelism, hierarchy, and abstraction.

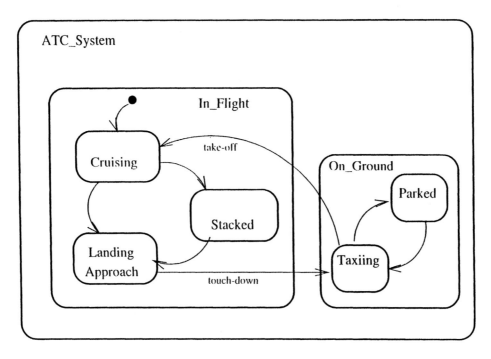

Figure 3. An example Statechart.

Figure 4 provides a simple functional description of the (British) approach to making tea. Points to note are:

- Each level is an expanded (and hence, less abstract) description of a box in the level above.
- Sequence is denoted by an ordered line of boxes, selection by a set of boxes with circles in the upper corner, and iteration by a box with an asterisk in the upper corner.
- The structuring forms should not be mixed in a group on a level. (Hence the action "put tea in the pot" forms an abstraction within a sequence, and this is then expanded separately as an iterated set of actions.)

The Structure Chart

This notation captures one aspect of constructional information, namely the invocation hierarchy that exists between subprogram units. While the tree-like form is similar to that of the Jackson Structure Diagram, the interpretation is very different, in that the elements (boxes) in a Structure Chart represent physical entities (subprograms) and the hierarchy shown is one of invocation (transfer of control) rather than of abstraction. Figure 5 shows a very simple example of

this notation. (There are different forms used to show information about parameter passing; this is just one of them.)

The structural viewpoint is concerned with the physical properties of a design, and hence it is one that may need to describe many attributes of design elements. For this reason, no one single notation can effectively project all of the relevant relationships (such as encapsulation, scope of shared information, invocation), and so an effective description of the structural viewpoint is apt to involve the use of more than a single representation.

The Entity-Relationship Diagram

The Entity-Relationship Diagram (ERD) is commonly used for modelling the details of the inter-relationships that occur between data elements in a system, although it may also perform other modelling roles [12]. Figure 6 shows a very simple example of one form of ERD containing two entities (boxes), a relationship (diamond) and the relevant attributes of the entities. Additional conventions are used to show whether the nature of a relationship is one-to-one, one-to-many or many-to-many. (In the example, the relationship is many-to-one between the entities "aircraft" and "landing stack," since one stack may contain many aircraft.)

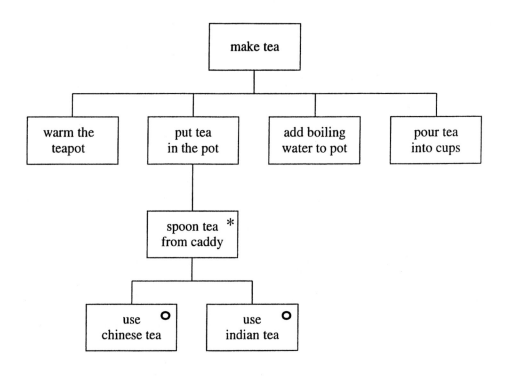

Figure 4. An example of a Jackson Structure Diagram.

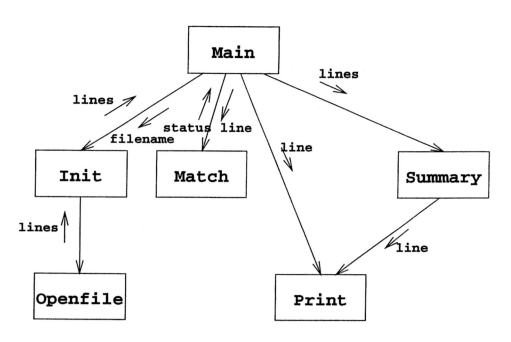

Figure 5. A simple Structure Chart.

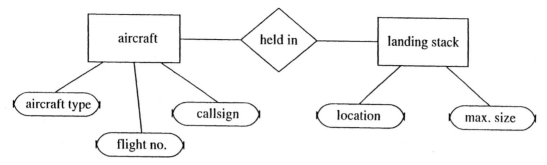

Figure 6. A simple Entity-Relationship Diagram.

3 Software Design Practices and Design Methods

Section 1.1 introduced the concept of a *software design method* as a means of transferring "knowledge" to less experienced designers. This section explores this concept a little further.

3.1 Rationale for software design methods

The use of "methods" for software design has no parallel in any other stage of software development. We do not have "testing methods" or even "programming methods." When teaching programming, we commonly provide the student with a set of "programming metaphors," together with a set of application paradigms such as trees and stacks that make use of these.

The partial analogy with programming points to one of the problems that hinders teaching about design, namely that of scale. Novice programmers can use the abstractions provided in a programming language to construct actual programs, and in the process receive feedback that can assist with revising their ideas and understanding during both compilation and execution of the programs. In contrast, novice designers have no equivalent sources of feedback to indicate where their ideas might be inconsistent, and have little or no chance of comparing an eventual implementation against the abstract design ideas. So "method knowledge" may be our only practical means for transferring experience, however inadequate this might be. (As an example, it is rather as though programmers were taught to solve all needs for iteration by using only the FOR construct.)

Other roles for software design methods include:

- Establishing common goals and styles for a *team* of developers.

- Generating "consistent" documentation that may assist with future maintenance by help-

ing the maintainers to recapture the original design model.

- Helping to make some of the features of a problem more explicit, along with their influence upon the design.

Constraints that limit their usefulness are:

- The *process part* of a method provides relatively little detailed guidance as to how a problem should be solved. It may indicate how the design model is to be developed, but not what should go into this for a given problem.

- The need to use a procedural form (do this, then do that, then...) leads to practices that conflict with the behaviour observed in experienced designers. Decisions have to be made on a method-based schedule, rather than according to the needs of the problem.

So, while at the present time software design methods probably provide the most practical means of transferring design knowledge, we cannot claim that they are particularly successful.

3.2 Design strategies

Design methods embody strategies (indeed, this is where they particularly diverge from the practices of experienced designers, since the latter are observed to adapt a strategy opportunistically in order to meet the needs of a problem). Four widely-used strategies are:

Top-down: As the name implies, this is based upon the idea of separating a large problem into smaller ones, in the hope that the latter will be easier to solve. While relatively easy to use, it has the disadvantage that important structural decisions may need to be made at an early stage, so that any subsequent need for modification may require extensive reworking of the whole design.

Compositional: As implied, this involves identifying a set of "entities" that can be modelled and which can then be assembled to create a model for the complete solution. While the earlier stages may be simple, the resultant model can become very complex.

Organisational: A strategy of this form is used where the needs of the development organisation and its management structures impose constraints upon the design process. This may require that project (and design) team members may be transferred at arbitrary times, so that the method should help with the transfer between old and new team members. A good example of this form is SSADM [13].

Template: Templates can be used in those rare cases where some general paradigm describes a reasonably large domain of problems. The classical example of this form is that of compiler design, and indeed, this is probably the only really good example.

Whatever the strategy adopted, the process part of a method is usually described as a sequence of *steps*. Each step alters the design method, either by *elaborating* the details of the model, or by *transforming* them, adding new attributes to create new viewpoint descriptions. Steps may involve many activities, and provide a set of milestones that can be used to monitor the progress of a design.

The choice of design strategy and associated method has significant implications for the resulting solution structure, or architecture. Shaw's comparative review of design forms for a car cruise-control system [14] demonstrates the wide range of solution architectures that have been produced from the use of 11 different design methods. But of course, this still leaves open the question of how to know in advance which of these is likely to be the most appropriate solution, and hence the most appropriate method! Any choice of a design method may also be further influenced by prior experience, as well as by social, political, historical, business and other nontechnical factors,

none of which can be easily quantified (or accommodated in this review).

4. Features of Some Software Design Methods

A review paper such as this cannot examine the workings of software design methods in any detail. So in this section, we briefly review the significant features of a number of well-established design methods, chosen to provide a reasonable range of examples of strategy and form. For fuller descriptions and references, see [9].

Our review starts with two first-generation design methods that provide examples of both compositional and decompositional strategies. After that, we look at two examples of second-generation methods, which typically exhibit much more complex design models.

4.1 Jackson Structured Programming (JSP)

JSP was one of the earliest design methods and provides a useful paradigm for the method-based approach to transferring and developing design knowledge. It is deliberately aimed at a very tightly constrained domain of application, and hence can be more prescriptive in its process part than is normal. In addition, it is an algorithm design method, whereas the other methods are aimed at larger systems and produce structural plans. On occasion, JSP may therefore be useful for localised design tasks within a larger system design task. JSP uses a compositional strategy.

The *representation part* of JSP is provided by the ubiquitous Jackson Structure Diagram. This is used both for modelling data structures and also for functional modelling.

The *process part* of JSP is summarised in Table 2. For each step we describe its purpose and also whether it elaborates or transforms the design model.

The heuristics of JSP are highly developed. *Readahead, back-tracking,* and *program inversion* have been widely documented and discussed. Between them, they provide a set of "adaptations" to the basic process, and they can be used to resolve some of the more commonly-encountered difficulties in applying JSP to practical problems.

Table 2. Summary of the JSP process part.

Step 1	Draw Structure Diagrams for inputs and outputs	*elaboration*
Step 2	Merge these to create the program Structure Diagram	*transformation*
Step 3	List the operations and allocate to program elements	*elaboration*
Step 4	Convert program to text	*elaboration*
Step 5	Add conditions	*elaboration*

4.2 Structured Systems Analysis and Structured Design

Like JSP, this is a relatively old method, and can be considered as an extension of the functional top-down approach to design. It consists of an "analysis" component and a "design" component. (For the purposes of this paper, the activities of analysis are considered to be integral with those of design.)

During the analysis phase (Steps 1 and 2), the designer constructs a functional model of the system (using "physical" Data-Flow Diagrams) and then uses this to develop a functional model of the solution (using "logical" DFDs). This is usually supplemented by some degree of data modelling, and some real-time variants also encourage the development of behavioural descriptions using State Transition Diagrams (STDs).

In the design phase (Steps 3 to 5), this model is gradually transformed into a structural model, based on a hierarchy of subprograms, and described by using Structure Charts. There is relatively little support for using ideas such as information hiding, or for employing any packaging concepts other than the subprogram.

The *representation part* therefore uses both DFDs and Structure Charts for the primary notations, and sometimes involves the use of ERDs and STDs.

The *process part* is summarised in Table 3, using the same format as previously.

The heuristics are far less well-defined than those of JSP. One of them is intended to help with determining which "bubble" in the DFD acts as the "central transform," while others are used to help restructure and reorganise the solution after the major Transform Analysis Step (Step 4) has generated the structural viewpoint for the design model.

As a method, this one has strong intuitive attractions, but suffers from the disadvantage of having a large and relatively disjoint transformation step.

4.3 Jackson System Development (JSD)

JSD encourages the designer to create a design model around the notion of modelling the behaviour of active "entities." In the initial stages, these entities are related to the problem, but gradually the emphasis changes to use entities that are elements of the solution.

A characteristic of second-generation design methods is that they involve constructing much more complex design models from the start, usually involving the use of more than one design viewpoint. As a result, they generally use a sequence of elaboration steps to modify the design model, rather than providing any major transformation steps.

The *representation part* of JSD makes use of *Entity-Structure Diagrams* (ESDs) to model the time-ordered behaviour of long-lived problem entities. (These diagrams use a different interpretation of the basic Jackson Structure Diagram.) The function and structure of the resulting network of interacting "processes" is then modelled using *System Specification Diagrams* (SSDs).

The *process part* can be described in terms of three stages [9,15], which can be further subdivided to form six major design activities. Table 4 provides a very basic summary of these activities, using the same format as before.

Table 3. Summary of the process part of SSA and SD.

Step 1	Develop a top-level description	*elaboration*
Step 2	Develop a model of the problem (SSA)	*elaboration*
Step 3	Subdivide into DFDs describing transactions	*elaboration*
Step 4	Transform into Structure Charts	*transformation*
Step 5	Refine and recombine into system description	*elaboration*

Table 4. Summary of the JSD process part.

1. Entity Analysis	Identify and model problem entities	*elaboration*
2. Initial Model Phase	Complete the problem model network	*elaboration*
3. Interactive Function Step	Add new solution entities	*elaboration*
4. Information Function Step	Add new solution entities	*elaboration*
5. System Timing Step	Resolve synchronisation issues	*elaboration*
6. Implementation	Physical design mappings	*elaboration*

The *heuristics* of JSD owe quite a lot to JSP, with both back-tracking and program inversion being recognisable adaptions of these ideas to a larger scale. An additional technique is that of state vector separation which can be used to increase implementational efficiency via a form of "reentrancy."

4.4 Object-Oriented Design

The topics of "what is an object?" and "how do we design with objects?" are both well beyond the scope of this paper. Some ideas about the nature of objects can be found in [16] and in [17].

It can be argued that object-oriented analysis and design techniques are still evolving (perhaps not as rapidly as was once hoped). The Fusion method [12] provides a useful example of one of the more developed uses of these ideas, and one that has brought together a number of techniques (hence its name).

The *representation part* of such methods is often a weakness, being used to document decisions at a later stage, rather than to help model the solution. Fusion seeks to make extensive use of diagrammatical forms, and especially of variations upon the Entity-Relationship Diagram.

The *process part* is described in Table 5 and includes both analysis and design activities. There are no identifiable heuristics available for such a recent method. (A fuller methodological analysis of Fusion as well as of the other methods described in this section is provided in reference [18].) A problem with object-oriented methods is that they do encourage the designer to make decisions about "structure" at a much earlier stage than "process"-oriented methods (including JSD), and hence bind the design to implementation-oriented physical issues before the details of the abstract design model have been fully worked through.

5. Conclusion

This paper has sought to review both our current understanding of how software systems are designed (and why that process is a complex one) and also how current software design methods attempt to provide frameworks to assist with this. As can be seen, even the second-generation design methods still provide only limited help with many aspects of designing a system.

We have not discussed the use of support tools. Many design support tools still provide little more than diagram editing facilities and support for version control. In particular, they tend to bind the user to a particular set of notations, and hence to a specific design process. Inevitably, this is an area of research that lags behind research into design practices.

Overall, while our understanding of how software is designed is slowly improving [19], it seems likely that this will provide an active area of research for many years to come.

References

[1] H.J. Rittel and M.M. Webber, "Planning Problems are Wicked Problems," N. Cross, ed., *Developments in Design Methodology*, Wiley, 1984, pp. 135–144.

[2] F.P. Brooks Jr., "No Silver Bullet: Essence and Accidents of Software Engineering," *Computer*, Apr. 1987, pp. 10–19.

[3] B. Adelson and E. Soloway, "The Role of Domain Experience in Software Design," *IEEE Trans. Software Eng.*, Vol. SE-11, No. 11, Nov. 1985, pp. 1351–1360.

[4] R. Guindon and B. Curtis, "Control of Cognitive Processes during Software Design: What Tools are needed?" in *Proc. CHI'88*, ACM Press, New York, N.Y., 1988, pp. 263–268.

[5] W. Visser and J.-M. Hoc, "Expert Software Design Strategies," in *Psychology of Programming*, Academic Press, New York, N.Y., 1990.

[6] B. Hayes-Roth and F. Hayes-Roth, "A Cognitive Model of Planning," *Cognitive Science*, Vol. 3, 1979, pp. 275–310.

[7] N.E. Fenton, *Software Metrics: A Rigorous Approach*, Chapman & Hall, 1991.

Table 5. The Fusion design process.

Phase	Step	Action
Analysis	1.	Develop the Object Model
Analysis	2.	Determine the System Interface
Analysis	3.	Development of the Interface Model
Analysis	4.	Check the Analysis Models
Design	5.	Develop Object Interaction Graphs
Design	6.	Develop Visibility Graphs
Design	7.	Develop Class Descriptions
Design	8.	Develop Inheritance Graphs

[8] D.L. Parnas and D.M. Weiss, "Active Design Reviews: Principles and Practices," *J. Systems & Software*, Vol. 7, 1987, pp. 259–265.

[9] D. Budgen, *Software Design,* Addison-Wesley, Wokingham, Berkshire, 1993.

[10] G. Friel and D. Budgen, "Design Transformation and Abstract Design Prototyping," *Information and Software Technology*, Vol. 33, No. 9, Nov. 1991, pp. 707–719.

[11] D. Harel, "On Visual Formalisms," *Comm. ACM*, Vol. 31, No. 5, May 1988, pp. 514–530.

[12] D. Coleman, et al., *Object-Oriented Development: The Fusion Method,* Prentice-Hall, Englewood Cliffs, N.J., 1994.

[13] E. Downs, P. Clare, and I. Coe, *SSADM: Structured Systems Analysis and Design Method: Application and Context,* Prentice-Hall, Englewood Cliffs, N.J., 2nd ed., 1992.

[14] M. Shaw, "Comparing Architectural Design Styles," *IEEE Software*, Vol. 12, No. 6, Nov. 1995, pp. 27–41.

[15] J. Cameron, *JSP & JSD: The Jackson Approach to Software Development,* 2nd ed., IEEE Computer Society Press, Los Alamitos, Calif., 1989.

[16] G. Booch, *Object-Oriented Analysis and Design,* Benjamin/Cummings, Redwood City, Calif., 1994.

[17] A. Snyder, "The Essence of Objects: Concepts and Terms," *IEEE Software*, Jan. 1993, pp. 31–42.

[18] D. Budgen, "'Design Models' from Software Design methods," *Design Studies*, Vol. 16, No. 3, July 1995, pp. 293–325.

[19] B.I. Blum, "A Taxonomy of Software Development Methods," *Comm. ACM*, Vol. 37, No. 11, Nov. 1994, pp. 82–94.

Design Methods for Concurrent and Real-Time Systems

Hassan Gomaa

Department of Information and Software Systems Engineering
George Mason University
Fairfax, Virginia 22030-4444

Abstract

This paper discusses and compares the concepts and criteria used by software design methods for developing large-scale concurrent and real-time systems. Concurrency is addressed by task structuring while modifiability is addressed by module structuring. In addition, the behavioral aspects of a real-time system are addressed by means of finite state machines. The Real-Time Structured Analysis and Design, DARTS, Jackson System Development, Naval Research Lab, and Object-Oriented Design methods are presented and compared from the perspective of how they address these concepts. Two related design methods for real-time systems, which build on the previous methods, ADARTS[SM] (Ada-based Design Approach for Real-Time Systems) and CODARTS (Concurrent Design Approach for Real-Time Systems), are also briefly described.

1. Introduction

With the massive reduction in the cost of microprocessor and semiconductor chips—and the large increase in microprocessor performance over the past few years—real-time and distributed real-time microcomputer-based systems are a very cost-effective solution to many problems. Nowadays, more and more commercial, industrial, military, medical, and consumer products are microcomputer based and either software controlled or have a crucial software component to them.

This paper presents an overview of the design of concurrent systems, as well as an important category of concurrent systems: real-time systems. The paper starts by describing three key design concepts for large-scale concurrent and real-time systems: concurrency, modularity, and finite state machines. After introducing these concepts, this paper describes and compares five software design methods for concurrent

and real-time systems that use these concepts. It then describes two related design methods for concurrent and real-time systems, ADARTS (Ada-based Design Approach for Real-Time Systems) and CODARTS (Concurrent Design Approach for Real-Time Systems), which build on these earlier methods.[1]

2. Design Concepts For Concurrent and Real-Time Systems

2.1 Concurrent Tasks

In the early days of computing, most computer systems were batch programs. Each program was sequential and ran off line. Today, with the proliferation of interactive systems and the tendency toward distributed microcomputer systems, many systems are concurrent in nature. A characteristic of a concurrent system is that it typically has many activities occurring in parallel. It is often the case that the order of incoming events is not predictable, and the events may overlap.

The concept of concurrent tasks, also frequently referred to as concurrent processes, is fundamental in the design of these systems. A concurrent system consists of many tasks that execute in parallel. The design concepts for concurrent systems are generally applicable to real-time systems and distributed applications.

A task represents the execution of a sequential program or sequential component of a concurrent program. Each task deals with one sequential thread of execution; hence no concurrency is allowed within a task. However, overall system concurrency is obtained by having multiple tasks that execute in parallel. From time to time, the tasks must communicate and synchronize their operations with each other. The concurrent tasking concept has been applied extensively in the design of operating systems, real-time systems,

---

[1] The material presented in this paper is excerpted from *Software Design Methods for Concurrent and Real-Time Systems*, by Hassan Gomaa, copyright 1993 by Addison-Wesley Publishing Company, Inc. Reprinted with permission of the publisher.

interactive systems, distributed systems, parallel systems, and in simulation applications.

Criteria for task structuring have been developed to guide a software designer in decomposing a real-time system into concurrent tasks. The main consideration in identifying tasks is the asynchronous nature of the functions within the system. The task structuring criteria were first described in the DARTS (Design Approach for Real-Time Systems) method (3,4) and later refined for the ADARTS and CODARTS methods (6).

2.2 Modularity

Modularity provides a means of decomposing a system into smaller, more manageable units with well-defined interfaces between them. However, there are many definitions of the term "module." The two definitions used in this paper are those used by the Structured Design (9,10,19) and the Naval Research Laboratory Software Cost Reduction (NRL) (11,12,13) methods. In Structured Design, a module usually means a function or procedure. In the NRL method, a module is an information hiding module (IHM) that contains the hidden information as well as the access procedures to it.

The module cohesion and coupling criteria, which originated from the work of Constantine and Myers in Structured Design (9,19), are criteria for decomposing a system into modules, where a module usually means a procedure or function. Cohesion is a criterion for identifying the strength or unity within a module. Coupling is a measure of the connectivity between modules. The goal of Structured Design is to develop a design in which the modules have strong cohesion and low coupling.

Functional cohesion, where the module performs one specific function, was considered the strongest form of cohesion (19). However, the informational cohesion criterion was added later by Myers (9) to identify information hiding modules. Data coupling is considered the lowest form of coupling (9,19), in which parameters are passed between modules. Undesirable forms of coupling include common coupling, where global data is used.

The Information Hiding principle was first proposed by Parnas (11) as a criterion for decomposing a software system into modules. The principle states that each module should hide a design decision that is considered likely to change. Each changeable decision is called the secret of the module. The reasons for applying information hiding are to provide modules that are modifiable and understandable and hence maintainable. Because information hiding modules are usually self-contained, they have a greater potential for reuse than most procedural modules.

2.3 Finite State Machines

Finite state machines address the behavioral aspects of real-time systems. They are particularly important in real-time design as real-time systems are frequently state dependent, that is, their actions depend not only on their inputs but also on what previously happened in the system.

A finite state machine may be used for modeling the behavioral aspects of a real-time system. It is a conceptual machine with a given number of states; it can be in only one of the states at any specific time. State transitions are changes in state that are caused by input events. In response to an input event, the system may transition to the same or to a different state. Furthermore, an output event may be optionally generated. Notations used to define finite state machines are the state transition diagram and the state transition table or matrix.

Finite state machine are used by several real-time design methods including Real-Time Structured Analysis, DARTS, the Naval Research Laboratory Software Cost Reduction Method, and Object-Oriented Design.

3. Survey of Software Design Methods for Concurrent and Real-Time Systems

Due to the importance of the design concepts described in the previous section, three important objectives for a design method for concurrent and real-time systems should be:

- the capability of structuring a system into concurrent tasks,
- the development of modifiable and potentially reusable software through the use of information hiding,
- definition of the behavioral aspects of a real-time system using finite state machines.

A fourth important objective for real-time systems is the ability to analyze the performance of a design to determine that it will meet its performance requirements.

3.1 Real-Time Structured Analysis and Design (RTSAD)

Real-Time Structured Analysis (RTSA) (7,18) is an extension of Structured Analysis to address the needs of real-time systems. Two variations of RTSA have been developed, the Ward/Mellor (18) and Hatley Pirbhai (7) approaches.

The first step in RTSA is to develop the system context diagram. The system context diagram defines the boundary between the system to be developed and the external environment. The context diagram shows all the inputs to the system and outputs from the system.

Next, a data flow/control flow decomposition is performed. The system is structured into functions (called transformations or processes) and the interfaces between them are defined in the form of data flows or event flows. Transformations may be data or control transformations. The system is structured as a hierarchical set of data flow/control flow diagrams that may be checked for completeness and consistency. Each leaf-node data transformation on a data flow diagram is defined by writing a minispecification (also referred to as a process specification), usually in Structured English. A data dictionary is developed that defines all data flows, event flows, and data stores.

The real-time extensions to Structured Analysis are motivated by a desire to represent more precisely the behavioral characteristics of the system being developed. With the Ward/Mellor approach (18), this is achieved primarily through the use of state transi-

tion diagrams, event flows, and integrating the state transition diagrams with data flow diagrams through the use of control transformations. Each state transition diagram shows the different states of the system (or subsystem). It also shows the input events that cause state transitions, and output events resulting from state transitions. A state transition diagram is executed by a control transformation.

After developing the specification using RTSA, the next step is to allocate transformations to processors, although little guidance is provided for this purpose. Transformations on a given processor are then structured into modules using Structured Design. Structured Design (SD) (9,10,19) uses the criteria of module coupling and cohesion in conjunction with two design strategies, Transform and Transaction Analysis, to develop a design starting from an RTSA specification. However, because SD is a program design method, the issue of structuring a system into concurrent tasks is not addressed.

An example of RTSA is given in Figures 1 and 2. Figure 1 shows a state transition diagram for the Automobile Cruise Control System (6). Figure 2 shows a data flow/control flow diagram, in which the Cruise Control control transformation executes the Cruise Control state transition diagram shown in Figure 1.

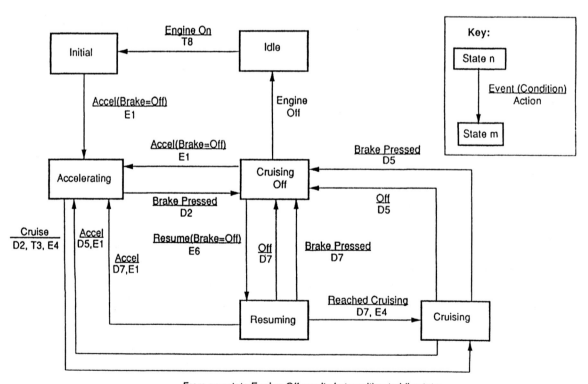

From any state, Engine Off results in transition to idle state

Figure 1. Cruise control system state transition diagram

118

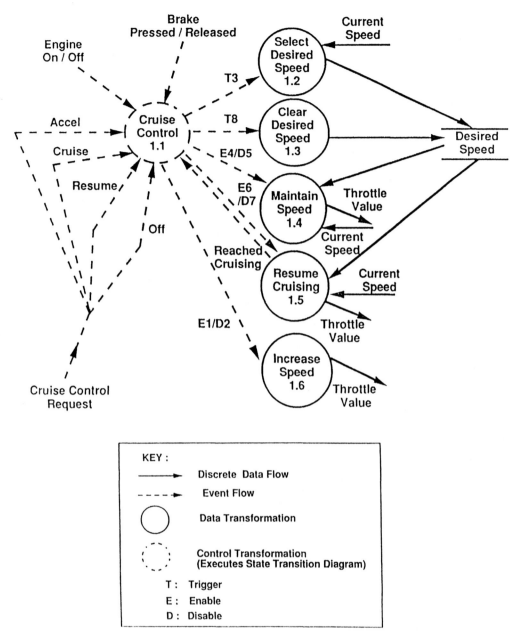

Figure 2. Data flow/control flow diagram for cruise control system

For example, if the Cruise Control control transformation receives the Accel event flow while the system is in Initial state, (and providing the brake is not pressed), the car enters Accelerating state. An action is associated with this transition, namely the data transformation Increase Speed is enabled (action E1 on Figures 1 and 2). It remains active while the vehicle is in Accelerating state, outputing to the throttle on a regular basis so that the car accelerates automatically.

An example of a structure chart for the Cruise Control System is shown in Figure 3. The main module, Perform Automobile Cruise Control, has a cyclic loop in which it determines when to call its subordinate modules. These are Get Cruise Control Input, which reads the car's input sensors, Determine Speed, to compute the current speed of the car, Control Speed, which controls the throttle when the car is under automatic control, and Display Speed.

3.2 DARTS

The DARTS (Design Approach for Real-Time Systems) design method (3,4,5) emphasizes the decomposition of a real-time system into concurrent tasks and defining the interfaces between these tasks.

119

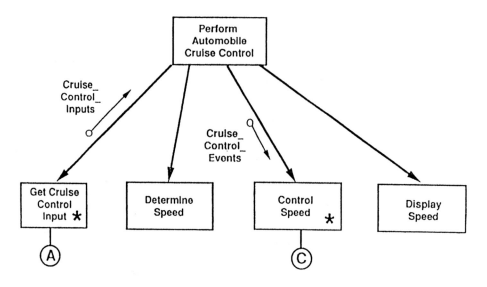

Figure 3. Structure chart for cruise control system

DARTS may be considered an extension of Real-Time Structured Analysis and Structured Design. It addresses a key limitation of Real-Time Structured Analysis and Design, that of not adequately addressing task structuring. DARTS uses a set of task structuring criteria for identifying the concurrent tasks in the system as well as a set of guidelines for defining the communication and synchronization interfaces between tasks. Each task, which represents a sequential program, is then designed using Structured Design.

After developing a system specification using Real-Time Structured Analysis, the next step in DARTS is to structure the system into concurrent tasks. The task structuring criteria assist the designer in this activity. The main consideration in identifying the tasks is the concurrent nature of the transformations within the system. In DARTS, the task structuring criteria are applied to the leaf-level data and control transformations on the hierarchical set of data flow/control flow diagrams developed using Real-Time Structured Analysis. Thus, a transformation is grouped with other transformations into a task, based on the temporal sequence in which they are executed.

A preliminary Task Architecture Diagram is drawn showing the tasks identified using the task structuring criteria. An example of a Task Architecture Diagram for the cruise control system is given in Figure 4. Several of the tasks are I/O tasks, including Monitor Cruise Control Input, which is an asynchronous device input task, and Monitor Auto Sensors, which is a periodic, temporally cohesive task that samples the brake and engine sensors. Cruise Control is a control task

that executes the cruise control state transition diagram.

In the next step, task interfaces are defined by analyzing the data flow and control flow interfaces between the tasks identified in the previous stage. Task interfaces take the form of message communication, event synchronization, or information hiding modules (IHMs). Message communication may be either loosely or tightly coupled. Event synchronization is provided in cases where no data is passed between tasks. Information hiding modules are used for hiding the contents and representation of data stores and state transition tables. Where an IHM is accessed by more than one task, the access procedures must synchronize the access to the data.

Figure 4 also shows the interfaces between tasks. Thus, the Cruise Control task receives loosely coupled cruise control messages in its message queue while it sends tightly coupled Speed Command messages to Auto Speed Control. Current Speed and Desired Speed are information hiding modules that synchronize access to the data they encapsulate.

Once the tasks and their interfaces have been defined, each task, which represents the execution of a sequential program, is designed. Using the Structured Design method, each task is structured into modules. An example of a structure chart for the Cruise Control task is given in Figure 5. The task is dormant until it receives a cruise control message. The Cruise Control state transition module encapsulates the cruise control state transition diagram, implemented as a table. The Get operation of the Current Speed IHM and the Update operation of the Desired Speed IHM are invoked from within this task.

120

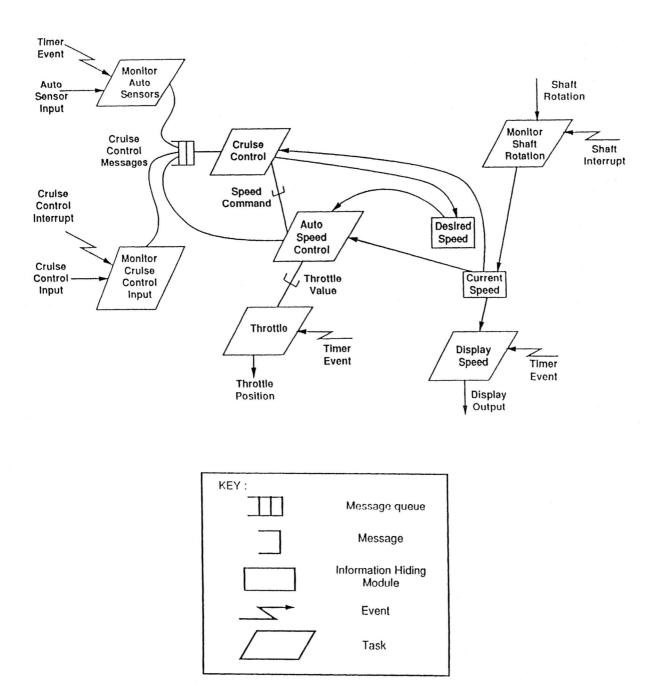

Figure 4. Task architecture diagram for cruise control system

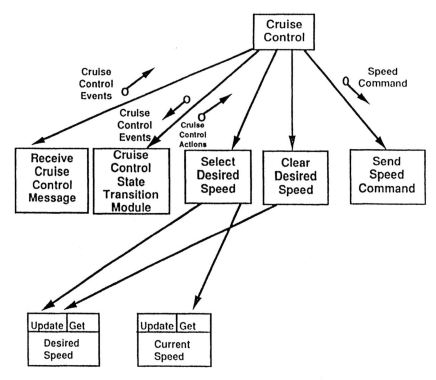

Figure 5. Structure chart for cruise control task

3.3 Jackson System Development

Concurrency is also an important theme in Jackson System Development (JSD) (8), which is a modeling approach to software design. A fundamental concept of JSD is that the design should model reality first before considering the functions of the system. The system is considered a simulation of the real world. The functions of the system are then added to this simulation.

There are three phases in JSD, the modeling, network, and implementation phases. The first phase of JSD is the Modeling Phase. A JSD design models the behavior of real-world entities over time. Each entity is mapped onto a software task (referred to as a process in JSD). During the Modeling Phase, the real-world entities are identified. The entity is defined in terms of the events (referred to as actions in JSD) it experiences. An entity structure diagram is developed in which the sequence of events experienced by the entity is explicitly shown.

Each real-world entity is modeled by means of a concurrent task called a model task. This task faithfully models the entity in the real world and has the same basic structure as the entity. Since real-world entities usually have long lives, each model task typically also has a long life.

An example of an entity structure diagram for a model task is given in Figure 6. The diagram is represented in terms of sequence, selection, and iterations of events. Figure 6 shows the structure of the Shaft model task. Shaft consists of an iteration of Shaft revolution events, one for each revolution of the shaft.

During the Network Phase, the communication between tasks is defined, function is added to model tasks, and function tasks are added. Communication between tasks is in the form of data streams of messages or by means of state vector inspections. In the first case, a producer task sends a message to a consumer, whereas in the latter case a task may read data belonging to another task. A network diagram is developed showing the communication between the model tasks.

The functions of the system are considered next. Some simple functions are added to the model tasks. Other independent functions are represented by function tasks. The network diagram is updated to show the function tasks and their communication with other function or model tasks.

An example of a network diagram is given in Figure 7. Data streams correspond to message queues between tasks and are shown as circles. In Figure 7, the Cruise Control task sends Speed Command messages to the Throttle task. A state vector corresponds to internal data maintained by a task and is shown as a diamond. Only the task that maintains its state vector can write to it, but other tasks may read from it. In Figure 7, the Shaft task maintains a state vector, Current Speed, which is read by the Cruise Control task.

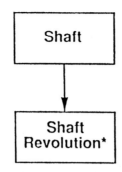

Figure 6. JSD entity structure diagram

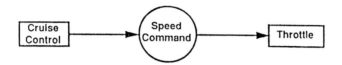

Data Stream (message) connection

State Vector Connection

Figure 7. JSD network diagrams

During the Implementation Phase, the JSD specification, consisting of potentially very large numbers of logical tasks, is mapped onto an implementation version, which is directly executable. Originally, with the emphasis on data processing, the specification was mapped onto one program using the concept of program inversion. During the implementation phase, JSD specifications can be mapped to concurrent designs, for example, Ada implementations (15).

3.4 NRL Method

The Naval Research Laboratory Software Cost Reduction Method (NRL) originated to address the perceived growing gap between software engineering principles advocated in academia and the practice of software engineering in industry and government (13). These principles formed the basis of a design method that was first applied to the development of a complex real-time system, namely the Onboard Flight Program for the US Navy's A-7E aircraft. Several principles were refined as a result of experience in applying them in this project.

The NRL method starts with a black box requirements specification. This is followed by a module-structuring phase in which modules are structured according to the information hiding criterion. The use of information hiding emphasizes that each aspect of a system that is considered likely to change, such as a system requirement, a hardware interface, or a software design decision, should be hidden in a separate information hiding module. Each module has an abstract interface that provides the external view of the module to its users.

To manage the complexity of handling large numbers of modules, the NRL method organizes information hiding modules into a tree-structured, information hiding module hierarchy and documents them in a module guide. The module hierarchy is a decomposition hierarchy. Thus only the leaf modules of the hierarchy are executable. The main categories of information hiding modules, as determined on the A7 project, are:

- *Hardware hiding modules.* These modules are categorized further into extended computer modules and device interface modules. Extended computer modules hide the characteristics of the hardware/software interface that are likely to change. Device interface modules hide the characteristics of I/O devices that are likely to change.

- *Behavior hiding modules.* These modules hide the behavior of the system as specified by the functions defined in the requirements specification. Thus changes to the requirements affect these modules.
- *Software decision modules.* These modules hide decisions made by the software designers that are likely to change.

After designing and documenting the module structure, the abstract interface specification for each leaf module in the module hierarchy is developed. This specification defines the external view of the information hiding module, including the operations provided by the module and the parameters for these operations.

The NRL method also advocates design for extension and contraction. This is achieved by means of the uses hierarchy, which is a hierarchy of operations (access procedures or functions) provided by the information hiding modules, and allows the identification of system subsets. Task structuring is considered orthogonal to module structuring (14). It is carried out later in the NRL method, and few guidelines are provided for identifying tasks.

An example of an information hiding module hierarchy for the cruise control system is given next. The module hierarchy consists of device interface modules and behavior hiding modules. There is a device interface module for each I/O device, a state transition module to hide the structure and contents of the state transition table, and data abstraction modules to encapsulate the data that needs to be stored.

Device Interface Modules
    Cruise Control Lever
    Engine Sensor
    Brake Sensor
    Drive Shaft Sensor
    Throttle Mechanism
    Display

Behavior Hiding Modules
    State Transition Module
        Cruise Control
    Data Abstraction Modules
        Desired Speed
        Current Speed

Function Driver Modules
    Speed Control

3.5 Object-Oriented Design

Object-Oriented Design (OOD), as described by Booch (1), is also based on the concept of information hiding. An object is an information hiding module that has state and is characterized by the operations it provides for other objects and the operations it uses (provided by other objects). Booch later extended his version of OOD to include classes and inheritance (2).

An informal strategy is used for identifying objects. Initially, Booch advocated identifying objects by underlining all nouns (which are candidates for objects) and verbs (candidates for operations) in the specification. However, this is not practical for large-scale systems. Booch later advocated the use of Structured Analysis as a starting point for the design, and then identifying objects from the data flow diagrams by applying a set of object structuring criteria [1], which are based on information hiding. Most recently, Booch [2] has advocated determining classes and objects directly by analyzing the problem domain and applying object structuring criteria such as those described in [17], which model objects in the problem domain using information modeling techniques.

Next, the semantics of the classes and objects are identified. This involves determining each object's interface. The operations provided by each object are determined, as well as the operations it uses from other objects. Preliminary class and object diagrams are developed.

The third step, identifying the relationships among classes and objects, is an extension of the previous step. Objects are instances of classes, and for similar objects it is necessary to determine if they belong to the same class or different classes. Static and dynamic dependencies between objects are determined; the class and object diagrams are refined. In the final step, the classes and objects are implemented. The internals of each object are developed, which involves designing the data structures and internal logic of each object.

An example of an object diagram for the cruise control system is given in Figure 8. Some objects are tangible objects that model concrete entities in the problem domain such as the engine, brake, and shaft objects. Other objects are abstract: Cruise Control is a control object that executes the Cruise Control state transition diagram, while Current Speed and Desired Speed encapsulate data that must be stored.

An example of a class diagram is shown in Figure 9, which shows how the inheritance and uses relationships are employed on the same diagram. Current

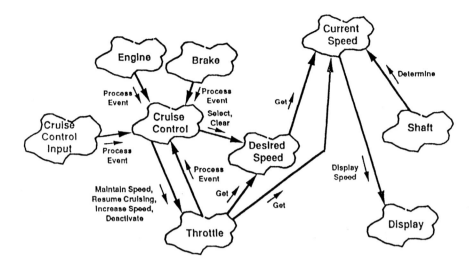

Figure 8. Example of object diagram for cruise control system

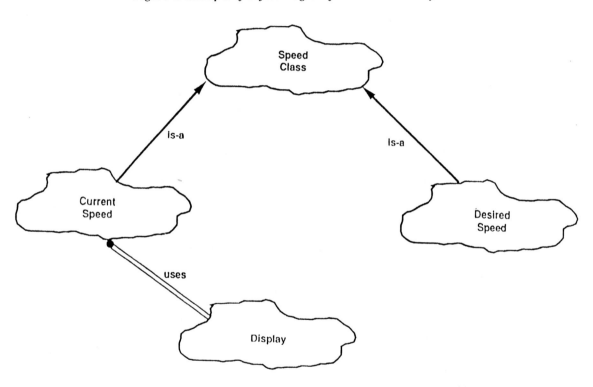

Figure 9. Example of class diagram

Speed and Desired Speed are subclasses of the Speed Class; they have the same overall structure as Speed, but they also introduce some changes through inheritance. In addition, Current Speed uses Display.

3.6 Comparison of Concurrent and Real-Time Design Methods

This section compares the design methods with respect to the objectives described in the first section.

Real-Time Structured Analysis and Design is weak in task structuring and information hiding. Structured Design does not address the issues of structuring a system into tasks. Furthermore, in its application of information hiding, Structured Design lags behind the Naval Research Lab method and Object-Oriented Design. Although Structured Design can be used for designing individual tasks, it is considered inadequate for designing real-time systems because of its weaknesses in the areas of task structuring and information hiding. However, RTSA does address the behavioral aspects of a system using state transition diagrams and tables, which have been well integrated with the functional decomposition through the use of control transformations and specifications.

DARTS addresses the weaknesses of RTSAD in the task structuring area by introducing the capability of applying the task structuring criteria and defining task interfaces. Although DARTS uses information hiding for encapsulating data stores, it does not use information hiding as extensively as NRL and OOD. Thus, it uses the Structured Design method, and not information hiding, for structuring tasks into procedural modules. DARTS addresses finite state machines as it uses RTSA as a front-end to the design method. During design, each finite state machine is mapped to a concurrent task. JSD also addresses task structuring. However, it does not support information hiding or finite state machines.

Both the NRL and OOD methods emphasize the structuring of a system into information hiding modules (objects) but place less emphasis on task structuring. Both NRL and OOD encapsulate finite state machines in information hiding modules. OOD uses the same criteria for identifying tasks (active objects) as information hiding modules (passive objects). This is contrary to the DARTS and NRL method, which both consider task structuring orthogonal to module structuring.

In conclusion, each of the methods addresses one or two of the objectives. However, none of them supports all of the objectives. Furthermore, none of the methods addresses to any great extent the performance analysis of real-time designs.

4. The ADARTS and CODARTS Design Methods

4.1 Introduction

This section describes two related methods, ADARTS (Ada-based Design Approach for Real-Time Systems and CODARTS (Concurrent Design Approach for Real-Time Systems), which build on the methods described in the previous section. Whereas ADARTS is Ada oriented, CODARTS is language independent. However, the two methods have a common approach to task and module structuring.

ADARTS and CODARTS attempt to build on the strengths of the NRL, OOD, JSD, and DARTS methods by emphasizing both information hiding module structuring and task structuring. Key features of both ADARTS and CODARTS are the principles for decomposing a real-time system into concurrent tasks and information hiding modules. To achieve the goal

of developing maintainable and reusable software components, the two methods incorporate a combination of the NRL module structuring criteria and the OOD object structuring criteria. To achieve the goal of structuring a system into concurrent tasks, they use a set of task structuring criteria that are a refinement of those originally developed for the DARTS design method.

Using the NRL method, it is often a large step from the black box requirements specification to the module hierarchy, and because of this it is sometimes difficult to identify all the modules in the system. Instead, ADARTS starts with a behavioral model developed using Real-Time Structured Analysis. CODARTS provides an alternative approach to Real-Time Structured Analysis for analyzing and modeling the system, namely Concurrent Object-Based Real-Time Analysis (COBRA), as described in the next section.

Both the task structuring criteria and the module structuring criteria are applied to the objects and/or functions of the behavioral model, which are represented by data and control transformations on the data flow/control flow diagrams. When performing task and module structuring, the behavioral model is viewed from two perspectives, dynamic and static structuring. The dynamic view is provided by the concurrent tasks, which are determined using the task structuring criteria. The static view is provided by the information hiding modules, which are determined using the module-structuring criteria. Guidelines are then provided for integrating the task and module views.

The task structuring criteria are applied first, followed by the module structuring criteria, although it is intended that applying the two sets of criteria should be an iterative exercise. The reason for applying the task-structuring criteria first is to allow an early performance analysis of the concurrent tasking design to be made, an important consideration in real-time systems.

4.2 Steps in Using ADARTS and CODARTS

1. *Develop Environmental and Behavioral Model of System.* ADARTS uses RTSA for analyzing and modeling the problem domain (18), while CODARTS uses the COBRA method (6). COBRA provides an alternative decomposition strategy to RTSA for concurrent and real-time systems. It uses the RTSA notation but addresses limitations of RTSA by providing comprehensive guidelines for performing a system decomposition. COBRA provides guidelines for developing the envi-

ronmental model based on the system context diagram. It provides structuring criteria for decomposing a system into subsystems, which may potentially be distributed. It also provides criteria for determining the objects and functions within a subsystem. Finally, it provides a behavioral approach for determining how the objects and functions within a subsystem interact with each other using event sequencing scenarios.

2. *Structure the system into distributed subsystems.* This is an optional step taken for distributed concurrent and distributed real-time applications. Thus CODARTS for Distributed Applications (CODARTS/DA) provides criteria for structuring a system into subsystems that can execute on geographically distributed nodes and communicate over a network by means of messages. CODARTS/DA builds on and substantially refines and extends the ideas from DARTS for Distributed Applications (DARTS/DA) (5).

3. *Structure the system (or subsystem) into concurrent tasks.* The concurrent tasks in the system (or subsystem of a distributed application) are determined by applying the task structuring criteria. The inter-task communication and synchronization interfaces are defined. Task structuring is applied to the whole system in the case of a nondistributed design. In the case of a distributed design, where the subsystems have already been defined, task structuring is applied to each subsystem. The performance of the concurrent tasking design is analyzed. As this step is also carried out in DARTS, an example of a task architecture diagram is given in Figure 4.

4. *Structure the system into information hiding modules.* The information hiding modules in the system are determined by applying the module structuring criteria, which are based on the NRL and OOD methods. An information hiding module hierarchy is created in which the information hiding modules are categorized. As this step is similar to the NRL method, an example of a module hierarchy is given in Section 3.4.

5. *Integrate the task and module views.* Tasks, determined using the task structuring criteria

of Step 3, and information hiding modules, determined using the module structuring criteria of Step 4, are now integrated to produce a software architecture. An example of a software architecture diagram for the Cruise Control problem is given in Figure 10. This shows the same tasks as on the task architecture diagram (Figure 4) with the information hiding modules (Section 3.4) added.

6. *Develop an Ada-based architectural design.* This step is used in ADARTS to address the Ada-specific aspects of the design. In this step, Ada support tasks are added and Ada task interfaces are defined. Additional tasks are usually required in an Ada application to address loosely coupled inter-task communication and synchronization of access to shared data (6). An example of an Ada architecture diagram is given in Figure 11, in which a Cruise Control Event buffering task replaces the Cruise Control message queue, and task entries are explicitly defined.

7. *Define component interface specifications for tasks and modules.* These represent the externally visible view of each component.

8. *Develop the software incrementally.*

5. Conclusions

This paper has described the concepts and criteria used by software design methods for developing large-scale concurrent and real-time systems. After surveying and comparing five different methods, two related software design methods for concurrent and real-time systems, ADARTS and CODARTS, which build on these methods, have been described. ADARTS and CODARTS use the task structuring criteria for identifying concurrent tasks and the information hiding module-structuring criteria for identi-fying information hiding modules. The survey, as well as the description of ADARTS and CODARTS, are covered in considerably more detail in (6). In addition, a design can be analyzed from a performance perspective by applying real-time scheduling theory (16), as described in (6).

With the proliferation of low-cost workstations and personal computers operating in a networked environment, the interest in designing concurrent and real-time systems, particularly distributed applications (6), is likely to grow rapidly in the next few years.

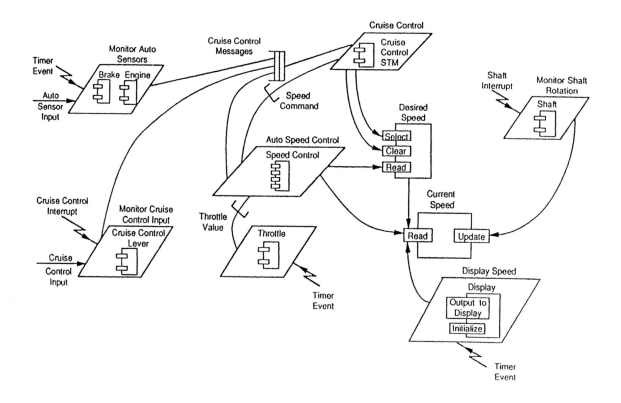

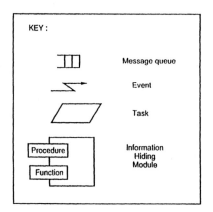

Figure 10. Cruise control system software architecture diagram

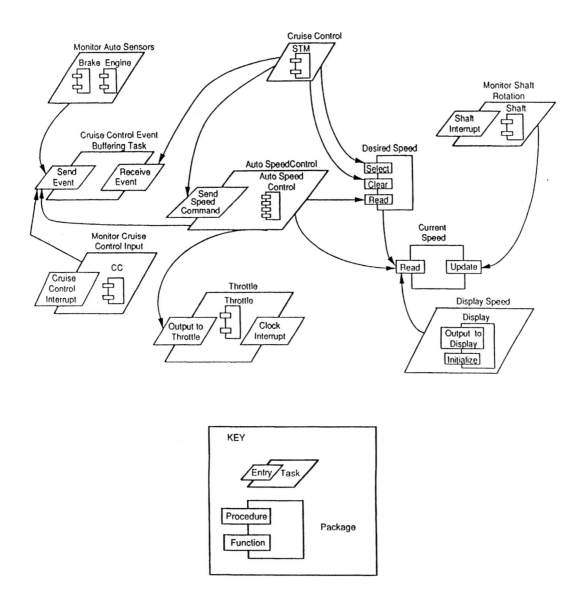

Figure 11. Cruise control system Ada architecture diagram

Acknowledgments

The author gratefully acknowledges the Software Productivity Consortium's sponsorship of the development of the ADARTS[SM] method. The author also gratefully acknowledges the contributions of Mike Cochran, Rick Kirk, and Elisa Simmons, particularly during the ADARTS validation exercise [20].

Acknowledgments are also due to David Weiss for his thoughtful comments during the formative stages of ADARTS.

References

(1) G. Booch, "Object Oriented Development," *IEEE Trans. Software Eng.*, Feb. 1986.

(2) G. Booch, *Object-Oriented Design with Applications*, Benjamin Cummings, 1991.

(3) H. Gomaa, "A Software Design Method for Real-Time Systems," *Comm. ACM*, Vol. 27, No. 9, Sept. 1984, pp. 938–949.

(4) H. Gomaa, "Software Development of Real-Time Systems," *Comm. ACM*, Vol. 29, No. 7, July 1986, pp. 657–668.

(5) H. Gomaa, "A Software Design Method for Distributed Real-Time Applications," *J. Systems and Software*, Feb. 1989.

(6) H. Gomaa, *Software Design Methods for Concurrent and Real-Time Systems*, Addison-Wesley, Reading, Mass., 1993.

(7) D. Hatley and I. Pirbhai, *Strategies for Real-Time System Specification*, Dorset House, 1988.

(8) M.A. Jackson, *System Development*, Prentice-Hall, Englewood Cliffs, N.J., 1983.

(9) G. Myers, *Composite/Structured Design*, Van Nostrand Reinhold, 1978.

(10) M. Page-Jones, *The Practical Guide to Structured Systems Design*, 2nd ed., Yourdon Press, 1988.

(11) D.L. Parnas, "On the Criteria to be Used In Decomposing Systems into Modules," *Comm. ACM*, Dec. 1972.

(12) D.L. Parnas, "Designing Software for Ease of Extension and Contraction," *IEEE Trans. Software Eng.*, Mar. 1979.

(13) D.L. Parnas, P. Clements, and D. Weiss, "The Modular Structure of Complex Systems," *Proc. 7th Int'l Conf. Software Eng.*, 1984.

(14) D.L. Parnas and S.R Faulk, "On Synchronization in Hard Real-Time Systems," *Comm. ACM*, Vol. 31, No. 3, Mar. 1988, pp. 274–287.

(15) Sanden B., *Software Systems Construction*, Prentice-Hall, Englewood Cliffs, N.J., 1994.

(16) L. Sha and J.B. Goodenough, "Real-Time Scheduling Theory and Ada," *Computer*, Vol. 23, No. 4, Apr. 1990, pp. 53–62. Also CMU/SEI-89-TR-14, Software Engineering Institute, Pittsburgh, Pa., 1989.

(17) Shlaer S. and S. Mellor, *Object Oriented Systems Analysis*, Prentice-Hall, Englewood Cliffs, N.J., 1988.

(18) P. Ward and S. Mellor, *Structured Development for Real-Time Systems*, Vols. 1 and 2, Prentice-Hall, Englewood Cliffs, N.J., 1985.

(19) E. Yourdon and L. Constantine, *Structured Design*, Prentice-Hall, Englewood Cliffs, N.J., 1979.

(20) M. Cochran and H. Gomaa, "Validating the ADARTS Software Design Method for Real-Time Systems," *Proc ACM Tri-Ada Conf.*, 1991.

Computer-Human Interface Software Development Survey

Robert J. Remington
Lockheed Martin Missiles and Space
Sunnyvale, California
CHI Rapid Prototyping and Usability Laboratory

Introduction

A young software engineer was recently assigned the responsibility to develop a graphical user interface for a modern command and control system. After pondering the assignment for a few hours he went to the project leader and asked: "Do you know if anyone has ever written a paper or report that might help me design a good user interface?"

The question, as well as the answer to the question, provides a rather persuasive case for including a chapter on computer human interface (CHI) in a software engineering tutorial.

The young software engineer's question reflects the fact that many of today's software engineering professionals have received no formal training in, and relatively little exposure to, the world of CHI software development. The answer to the young software engineer's question, if taken literally, is *no*! There is no single paper or report that, if followed religiously, will automatically lead to a good CHI design. There is no magic pill! However, there is a tremendous wealth of knowledge that can be drawn upon to help user interface developers deal with the full range of decision-making situations likely to be encountered in a typical CHI software development project.

A brief discussion of terminology might prevent some confusion as readers begin to explore the documents referenced in this survey. The term CHI will be used to refer to both the general field of *computer-human interaction*, and the *computer-human interface* (that is, the user interface that allows the person using the computer access to the facilities offered by the computer). There is no real difference between the term CHI and the term *HCI* as used in many of the technical references. People who prefer to use the name human-computer interaction, or HCI for short, tend to be making a statement that the human comes before the computer. Indeed, the human should take precedence over the computer in substantive matters such as user interface design. However, in the case of just deciding between two names, it can be argued that CHI rolls off the tongue more gracefully than HCI.

Scope and Objectives

The main objective of this chapter is to familiarize the reader with available informational sources as well as *recent* trends in CHI design, development, and evaluation. There are several earlier surveys that can provide computer science professionals with a more comprehensive introduction to CHI concepts, methods, and tools than will be offered by this brief snapshot of the current state of the CHI technology. For example, Hartson and Hix (1989) provide an extensive 92-page survey focusing on "the management of the computer science, or constructional, aspects of human-computer interface development." Similarly, Perlman (1989) provides a complete CHI course module that covers "the issues, information sources, and methods used in the design, implementation, and evaluation of user interfaces." Bass and Coutaz (1989) provide a 112-page document that introduces concepts and techniques relevant to the design and implementation of user interfaces. The present chapter should be viewed as a supplement to this excellent body of CHI knowledge, a supplement that concentrates on a few significant developments that have taken place since these earlier surveys were published.

Increased Importance of CHI

The first recent trend worth noting concerns the tremendous increase in interest being directed toward the topic of CHI by both the computer industry and user communities. There are several good reasons for the increased attention paid to CHI design and development. There is growing competitive pressure for improved user interfaces for computer software products in the marketplace. Improvement in user interface design was singled out at the 1993 Fall Comdex in Las Vegas by the software industry's leaders, including Microsoft's Bill Gates, as the biggest challenge now facing the computer industry. It is becoming more apparent to both industry and government user communities that CHI design can have a major impact on overall system performance, total life cycle costs, and user acceptance. User interface design largely determines operator performance, and how much training is required for users to reach an acceptable level of productivity. Ease-of-use and ease-of-learning have become key factors in the marketing campaigns for most consumer software products.

With the emergence of interactive graphical user interfaces (GUIs) we have seen a dramatic increase in the complexity and quantity of the CHI software component for new systems. While well-designed GUIs tend to make life more pleasant for end-users, programming them can be a very difficult, time-consuming, and error-prone process. Failure of traditional software methods and tools to deal effectively with this complex task can easily result in projects that are late and over budget, and excessive life-cycle costs of reworking poor-quality software that fails to meet user requirements. Most of the major software companies have recently experienced long delays in getting important products to the marketplace. These highly publicized failures to meet schedules and to gain user acceptance have taken a significant toll on these companies in terms of lost revenue, lost credibility, and depressed stock value.

In recent years, the development of complex software has dominated the cost of computer-based business and military application solutions, far outstripping the hardware costs. The software portion of the cost of most major computer-based systems has been estimated to run about 80 percent of the total system cost. Estimates for the CHI software component for a modern system range from 30-80 percent of the total lines of programming code. Myers and Rosson (1992) report the results of a formal survey of user interface programming. Based upon the results from 74 recent software projects it was found that an average of 48 percent of the code was devoted to the user interface portion. The average time spent on the user interface portion was 45 percent during the design phase, 50 percent during the implementation phase, and 37 percent during the maintenance phase. The most common problems reported by user interface developers included defining user requirements, writing help text, achieving consistency, learning how to use the tools, and getting acceptable graphics performance.

The increased interest in the issues and problems related to CHI software development has been accompanied by an explosion in the number of publications. Well over a thousand papers covering CHI-related topics were published in professional journals and conference proceedings in 1993 and 1994. This trend has been accompanied by an unprecedented number of books on the subject. Just a few of the new publications are referenced here. Shneiderman (1992) is a much-improved second edition of a classic CHI refer-ence work. The book by Dix et al. (1993) provides a broad coverage of the important CHI topics with an emphasis on design methods. Barfield (1993) has written a book aimed at those who are just becoming involved in CHI design, either through academic study or as practitioners. Bass and Dewan (1993) provide a collection of papers on several topics related to advanced user interface software development environments. The book by Hix and Hartson (1994) emphasizes the user interface development *process* independently of current implementation considerations. Blattner and Dannenberg (1992) focus on the issues and problems related to the recent introduction of multimedia and multimodality into user interface design. Tognazzini (1992) has written an entertaining book with many lessons for the design of graphical user interfaces, in particular the Macintosh user interface. Finally, Baecker, et al. (1994) offer a complete course in human-computer interaction with their 900-page volume that pulls together relevant materials from the research community; professional practice, and real-world applications.

CHI Design

Iterative Design Process

The simplified design-implementation-evaluation CHI development life-cycle model presented in Figure 1, from Perlman (1990), shows many of the main influences on design. They include experience with other systems, guidelines, and standards based upon human factors research, the results of evaluating previous versions, and requirements derived from task analysis. Ideally, modern CHI development tools and techniques are used to implement a prototype or the actual system based on a requirements-driven design specification. The resulting design is evaluated against system design specifications, and by means of formal usability testing of a functional prototype or working system. The actual CHI development cycle should involve several iterations of the feedback and design refinement process shown in Figure 1.

This is particularly true of complex interactive computer systems, for which the requirements cannot be fully specified at the beginning of the design cycle. For a better understanding of the iterative CHI development process and key techniques such as task analysis, rapid prototyping, and usability testing, see Bass and Coutaz (1991), Helander (1988), Nielsen (1992), and Salvendy (1987). Curtis and Hefley (1992) provide an interesting article describing the need to integrate the user interface engineering process into the overall product engineering process throughout its life cycle.

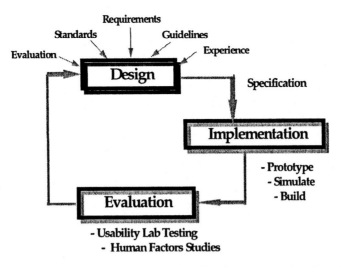

Figure 1. The design/implementation/evaluation CHI development process from Perlman (1990)

Theories, Models, and Research Foundations

With the focus of this survey on recent developments, a reader with little exposure to the field of CHI might have formed the impression that it has a short heritage of only a few years. This is definitely not the case. Human factors professionals have systematically researched the relationships between computer user interface design characteristics and user performance and acceptance since the early sixties. This research originally went under the name of *man-machine interface* research. To human factors professionals, with strong backgrounds in experimental psychology, terms such as "ease-of-use" and "ease-of-learning" have a definite meaning. For example, systematic analysis of error rates associated with alternative CHI designs has been useful in isolating inherent design characteristics highly correlated with user errors across a wide range of tasks.

The human factors approach to system design provides a conceptual model that is useful to those who are committed to designing user-oriented products. The user is viewed as an integral component of a working system. As the most important part of the system, all other components, including computer software and hardware, are adapted to match state-of-the-art knowledge regarding human capabilities, limitations, expectations, and preferences.

The Gillan and Breedin (1990) study suggests that the training and experience of the human factors specialist leads to a different way of thinking about the user interface than the way that non-human factors systems developers think. An important part of human factors training consists of developing a working knowledge of basic human capabilities (for example,

memory, attention, perception, and psycho-motor skills). It is likely that this knowledge is useful in producing user interfaces designs that do not place excessive demands on users' cognitive abilities and motor skills. It has been demonstrated that such designs lead to increased user productivity and lower error rates.

For example, Bailey (1993) found that CHI designs produced by human factors specialists allowed users to complete tasks in 60 percent of the time required for designs produced by programmers. Mismatches between CHI designs and users' capabilities and expectations have resulted in many documented cases of human errors, some of which resulted in fatal accidents. For example, Casey (1993) reports a case where a poorly designed, and inadequately tested, computer-based user interface that controlled a radiotherapy accelerator was responsible for a fatal accident involving the delivery of a lethal proton beam powered by 25 million electron volts!

Bailey (1993) presents some evidence that the iterative design methodology alone can improve designs only within a limited range. Studies by Jeffries et al. (1991) and Karat et al. (1992) indicate that successful design is the result of a combination of techniques and knowing when and how to apply them. Mayhew (1992) attempts to provide a "tool kit of design methods or principles needed by software development professionals." Borenstein (1992) offers entertaining views on most important CHI topics, including the value of CHI research. He proclaims that "the biggest danger in remaining ignorant about basic HCI research is not that you'll miss something, but that you'll hear something inaccurate and reach incorrect conclusions based on a misunderstanding of the latest research." Shneiderman's (1992) three pillars of

133

successful user interface development presented in Figure 2 illustrates the model for building user interfaces that enhance user acceptance and product success.

In the past decade, human factors researchers have been joined by other disciplines, including computer science, cognitive psychology, and graphic design. For example, the ACM Special Interest Group on Computer Human Interaction (SIG-CHI), composed mostly of human factors and computer science professionals, was formed in 1983. The CHI '94 Conference held in Boston was attended by more than 2,500 people including academic researchers and educators from various disciplines; CHI designers and developers involved in all phases of product design and development; and managers and users from major corporations. In the past few years we have seen a significant increase in research related to improving CHI design, development tools, and enabling technologies.

Marcus (1992) provides a concise survey of the strategic pursuits of leading human interface research and development centers. Over 350 representative articles and lab reviews from 63 CHI research and development centers were examined to identify research goals and their supporting technology developments. The resulting CHI research findings and technology developments have given us better theoretical models, new user interface design principles, and innovative CHI enabling technologies that will lead to more natural forms of human computer interaction.

While the topic of next-generation user interfaces is beyond the scope of this survey, several CHI researchers including Nielsen (1993), Myers (1992), Staples (1993), Baecker et al. (1994), and Blattner (1994) attempt to give us a look into the future of CHI.

CHI Guidelines, Standards and Style Guides

The use of technical reference sources in product design is a critical aspect of the engineering process. Development of CHI design guidance based upon a large body of accumulated knowledge was a lively pursuit in the mid-1980s. These early attempts to turn the wealth of information derived from empirical human factors research, associated theories and models of human information processing, and real-world experience into practical design information resulted in various CHI design *guideline* documents. The Smith and Mosier (1986) document, containing almost 1,000 guidelines for designing user interface software, is one of the more comprehensive CHI design guides. Identification and application of the particular principles and guidelines that apply to a given CHI software design project can be very difficult, but often a rewarding part of the CHI design process. These guidelines require careful and intelligent interpretation and application, which often depends on thorough analysis of the system environment, including functions and critical user tasks.

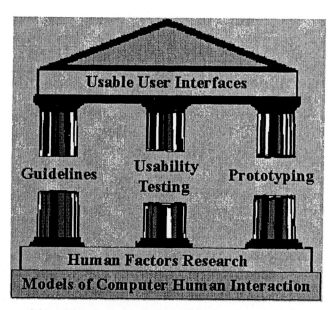

Figure 2. Three pillars of successful user interface development (design guidelines, user interface rapid prototyping, and usability laboratories for iterative testing) rest on a foundation of theories and experimental research. Shneiderman (1992)

One of the key principles of good user interface design found in all the early guidelines concerned the value of maintaining *consistency* in both the look and feel of the user interface. Consistency helps the user to develop an accurate model of the system's user environment. An accurate model fosters user acceptance and allows users to apply old skills to new applications and programs. The most direct way to achieve consistency across applications and software environments is to create CHI *standards*. The demand for standardization of fundamental aspects of the "look" and "feel" of CHI software by the user communities within business and government organizations, and software developers, has been growing in recent years.

Unfortunately, much of the recent user interface standards activities have been undertaken in the cause of the "GUI wars," and have little to do with design principles and guidelines derived from CHI research and practice. In the late 1980's a tremendous amount of effort was devoted to the creation of multiple GUIs, all aimed at preventing non-technical users from dropping into that four-letter word, Unix! The resulting proliferation of GUIs, and associated toolkits (such as Motif, OpenLook, CXI, and XUI) based upon X Window System technology, prompted a flurry of standardization activities. An early attempt at practicing safe Unix and the formation of several IEEE standards groups to deal with problems caused by too many Unix GUIs are reported by Remington (1989, 1990). By the end of 1993 OSF/Motif emerged as the victorious GUI in the Unix world.

Each of the remaining participants in the battle for the GUI market—including OSF/Motif, Macintosh, Microsoft Windows, and IBM's OS/2 Presentation Manager—have published style guides that are intended to provide precise look-and-feel user interface specifications. A comparison of the three major interface styles is presented in Figure 3. These three major GUI software platforms have several things in common, including a point-and-click direct manipulation interaction style, an object-action metaphor, and similar GUI building blocks or widgets sets (for example, pull-down menus, radio buttons, check boxes, list boxes, spin boxes, and icons). Most of the enhancements made to the Motif 2.0 release were aimed at making the Motif widget set more compatible with Microsoft Windows and IBM's OS/2 Presentation Manager. The most obvious difference between the major platforms as seen in Figure 3 is differing graphic styles. For example, notice the heavy reliance on 3D visual cues in the Motif graphic style. Other less obvious differences include a different number of mouse buttons and associated functions, different keyboard functional mappings, differences in terminology, and window management differences.

Even strict adherence to one of these user interface specifications does not necessarily result in a highly usable product. They do not provide adequate guidance in many critical aspects of CHI design. For example, the OSF Motif 2.0 Style Guide (1994) provides only a single recommendation regarding the use of color. Being told to "use color as a redundant aspect of the interface" is not much help in this problematic area of user interface design! Tognazzini (1992) notes that even with the publication of the Apple Human Interface Guidelines to help developers write Macintosh-standard user interfaces, there was an alarming growth of programs that "followed all the specifics of Apple guidelines, but were clearly not Macintosh."

There has been an increase in activity related to the production of open systems CHI standards and style guides. For example, the POSIX-sponsored IEEE P1201.2 Recommended Practice for Graphical User Interface Drivability [IEEE, 1993] specifies those elements and characteristics of all graphical user interfaces that should be consistent to permit users to transfer easily from one look and feel or application to another with minimal interference, errors, confusion, relearning, and retraining. In theory, it should be possible to define a core set of GUI elements and characteristics that support "drivability" across multiple look and feel GUIs, in the same sense that the standardization of critical automobile controls allows us to drive most makes and models without special training. Topics covered include terminology, keyboard usage, mouse or pointing device usage, menus, controls, windows, user guidance and help, and common user actions. This recommended practice does not dictate a particular software implementation or graphical style, only that the user interface meets the recommendations. The following are typical recommended practices aimed at enhancing drivability:

> *"When menu items are chosen from the keyboard, the menu item chosen should not depend upon the case (that is, shifted or unshifted, upper case, lower case, or mixed case) of character(s) entered from the keyboard."*

> *"If the system supports more than one level of undo, then the system should provide a distinct indication (for example, dim the undo control item) when no more undos are possible."*

> *"If the pointer is moved out of the active area of an armed button while SELECT [mouse button] is held down, the button should be disarmed."*

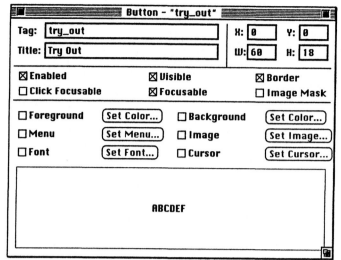

Macintosh Look-and-Feel

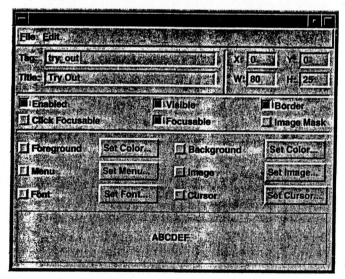

Windows Look-and-Feel

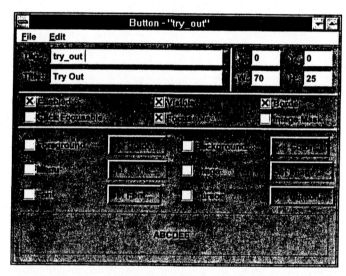

Motif Look-and-Feel

Figure 3. A comparison of the three major GUI styles

Adherence to the one-hundred-plus recommendations offered in the IEEE 1201.2 document would undoubtedly eliminate the major sources of confusion users currently experience when they transfer from one major platform to another.

Rapid Prototyping

The technique of rapid prototyping, or creating a limited, but functional, user interface to be given a "test-drive" early in the design process to gain user feedback, has proven to be a major new development in the CHI development process. Feedback resulting from the use of prototypes can be used to refine the user interface specification, leading to a user interface that is more in tune with users' expectations and capabilities. Software products with this type of user interface have a better chance of gaining wider user acceptance, and being used in a more productive fashion by the intended user population. By permitting early identification of CHI design problems, prototypes allow developers to explore solutions while they are still technically and economically feasible. It costs significantly more to rid software of errors during operation than during design. A majority of errors are not actually coding bugs, but design problems due to misunderstanding and miscommunication of user requirements. The book by Wiklund (1994) contains several detailed case studies that show "before and after" examples of improvements in GUI designs resulting from user feedback based on experience with prototypes. In some cases, cost benefits related to CHI design improvements are analyzed and reported. These include reduced customer support and service costs, reduced customer training costs, increased user productivity, and avoidance of costly delays in the product development schedule in order to fix major usability problems before going to market.

Rapid prototyping can serve an important role as an "enabling technology" by allowing designers to quickly implement and test the viability of new forms of computer human interaction. CHI designers have found that one of the main benefits of rapid prototyping is that it often provides the "breathing room" needed to experiment with optional design concepts, including innovative user interface concepts being developed at various CHI research laboratories. In the absence of a rapid prototyping approach, there is a tendency to grab onto a familiar user interface style and begin the coding process without entertaining new alternatives.

We have seen a major breakthrough in the area of CHI prototyping technology in the past few years. The products of the first-generation rapid prototyping tools consisted of user interface "look and feel" simulations driven with proprietary throw-away code. Modern CHI development tools, such as those described in the following section, have successfully evolved into tools that support both CHI rapid prototyping and software development. Now, the user interface prototype produced for early user testing becomes the actual GUI code for the delivered product. These second-generation CHI rapid development tools are available for each of the major GUI software environments including Microsoft Windows, OSF Motif, Sun's OpenLook, and Apple Macintosh.

CHI Implementation

Development Tools: Introduction

The dramatic increase in the complexity and quantity of software associated with the user interface component of modern computer systems has prompted tremendous interest in the development and application of new tools that will expedite the production of usable CHI software. The resulting outpouring of commercially available CHI software development tools is another significant trend that has occurred in the past few years. It is interesting to note that only a handful of user interface toolkits are described in the three 1989 surveys of CHI developments referenced at the beginning of this chapter. Most of these earlier proprietary toolkits have dropped by the wayside, making way for a variety of more powerful, fully supported commercial tools with established track records in dealing with large-scale and small-scale user interface development projects.

A survey of the major CHI development tools shows that they vary greatly in their capabilities with respect to their ability to allow rapid modifications, to create functional prototypes, to deal with interactive graphics, and to generate directly usable code. They also vary regarding the degree of programming skill required to use them.

Myers and Rosson (1992) provide a simplified but useful taxonomy for user interface tools ranging from the more primitive *window system and widget toolkits*, to the *Interactive Design Tools (IDTs)* and the *User Interface Management Systems (UIMS)*. Both IDTs and UIMS are generally designed to speed the development of GUIs by allowing developers to "draw," rather than hand code, significant portions of their user interfaces. They provide graphical tools that help developers to create and arrange the basic building blocks, or widgets, for a particular GUI environment such as buttons, sliders, pull-down menus, dialog boxes, scrolling lists, and other controls for applications. For example, they normally provide a palette showing the GUI building block widgets available in a given GUI toolkit, and allow the designer to interactively select, position, and size the desired widgets. Widget properties can be easily viewed and set via a special editor. Figure 4 shows the widget palette for one of the more popular Motif GUI development toolkits.

In addition to laying out the "look" of the CHI, most modern GUI development tools provide a test mode that allows developers to view and modify screens before generating and compiling various types of programming code (such as C, C++, Ada, and UIL).

For IDTs, testing of interface behavior is usually confined to demonstrating the selection of various interface objects (for example, button or menu option) without actually executing associated callback behavior (that is, what happens in the application when the user presses buttons, selects menu options, or operates a scroll bar). This is because most IDTs have no way of dynamically executing the code without first compiling it. IDT-generated sources usually require extensive editing to include the code for the callbacks.

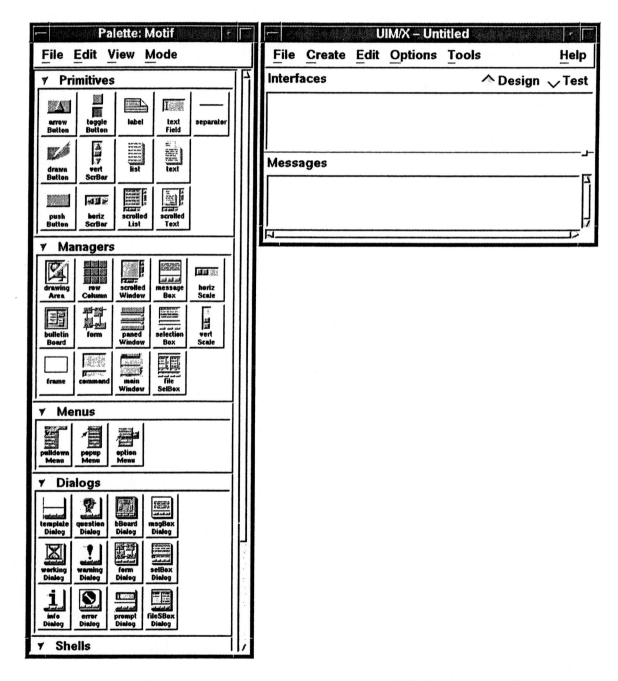

Figure 4. Widget palette for one of the more popular Motif GUI development toolkits

138

On the other hand, UIMS are generally more expensive and comprehensive tools designed to eliminate much of the hand-coding ordinarily required to (1) activate widgets, (2) feed data to be displayed by widgets, and (3) define callback functions to control the application functions. In addition to common GUI layout capabilities, they provide facilities to develop and test user interface behavior, usually with some sort of built-in interpreter. Some UIMSs separate the user interface from the application code, so the user interface is not embedded into the application code. With this separation, the CHI developer can easily create and modify the user interface without affecting the data source, permitting concurrent application development and rapid prototyping associated with early usability testing and user requirements definition.

Many of the more mature interface builders and UIMSs are now second-generation products that offer a form of visual programming. This lets developers use point-and-click and direct manipulation techniques to create a substantial portion of the CHI without writing programming code. The Myers and Rosson (1992) survey results showed that 34 percent of the systems were implemented using a toolkit, 27 percent made use of a UIMS, 14 percent used an IDT, and 26 percent used no tools. The projects using UIMSs or interface builders spent 41 percent of their time on the user interface. The study provides some good evidence that the currently available CHI software tools can be used to speed development and cut the cost of developing modern GUI-based CHIs.

Development Tools: Selection

"Horses for courses" is a simple phrase used in England to indicate that a particular approach may be best suited for a particular situation. In the CHI development tool arena, you must be knowledgeable about both the nature of the CHI development project to be undertaken (that is, the type of race course), and the relative strengths and weaknesses of the various tools that are available to do the job (the race horses). Selection of the appropriate tool(s) is often a difficult and time-consuming task. It is a task that is becoming more and more complex in the face of an increasing number of commercially available tools and the associated competing and confusing marketing claims.

First, the developer must identify the target GUI environment(s). Second, with the nature, scope, and schedule of the development project in mind, the developer must decide whether or not to use a UIMS, an IDT, or resort to programming with low-level tools such as Xlib, MacApp, or Microsoft Windows API.

There are several competing development tools for each of the major GUI environments including Motif, Open Look, Macintosh, Microsoft Windows and Windows NT, and OS/2 Presentation Manager. The requirement to develop a portable GUI to run across various Unix platforms, as well as the major non-Unix operating systems such as Microsoft Windows, OS2, and Macintosh, further complicates matters. There are, however, several tools for developing a GUI that is portable across these major platforms (for example, XVT, Neuron Data Open Interface, and Visix Galaxy).

There are often more than a dozen candidate development tools for a given CHI development project. The creation of a prioritized list of requirements, or selection criteria, is usually required to aid in the short listing process. It typically takes an experienced person three to four weeks to perform an unbiased and honest evaluation of a single CHI development tool. If schedule or budget constraints preclude a proper hands-on evaluation of how each tool handles a representative sample case, then it is often helpful to talk to other developers who have used the tool and to review evaluations reported in various professional trade journals. For example, the *IEEE Software* Tools Fair report by Forte (1992), the comparison of six GUI tools by Armstrong (1992), and a review of user interface development tools by Topper (1993) are representative of the unbiased coverage of the major GUI development tools available from professional journals. Unfortunately, the shelf life of a software tools trade study tends to be very short. New product releases about every six months tend to negate the value of earlier product comparisons related to important functional and performance capabilities.

Development Tools: Future Trends

There is still much room for improvement in CHI software tools. Current commercially available tools deal mainly with the graphical appearance and behavior of only limited parts of an application's user interface. They do not adequately support the construction of many application classes such as data visualization, command and control, and domain-specific editors. In addition, none of the commercially available GUI development tools *actively* assist developers in the design of critical and problematic areas of user interface design. For example, they do not actively assist designers in the proper use of color, font selection, screen layout, functional grouping, and selection of appropriate interaction techniques. As a result, many of the CHIs produced with today's best GUI toolkits are characterized by (1) operator fatigue due to the use of illegible fonts and color combinations, (2) operator confusion due to graphical clutter and poor screen layout, and (3) excessive operator error due to poor design and inconsistent implementation of critical interaction techniques.

Several CHI tool development projects, such as UIDE (Foley, et al. 1993), Marquise (Myers, et al., 1993), Humanoid (Szekely, et al. 1993), and CHIRP (Remington, 1994) show great promise for the future. We can expect to see many of the innovative concepts embodied in these projects (for example, intelligent design assistants and demonstrational interfaces) become commercially available the near future. The result will be development tools that exploit the strengths of both human designers and computers in the CHI design process. We can also expect to see advances in CHI development tools that closely parallel new advances in CHI enabling technologies, which will support the development of more natural forms of human-computer interaction. Figure 5 presents an example of the advances in CHI software development environments that we can expect to see as research prototypes emerge from the laboratory into commercial products.

The CHIRP Toolkit (Remington, 1994) is an integrated set of tools supporting the rapid development of CHI design and concept of operations demonstrations, and training simulations for the command and control applications domain. In addition to providing typical access to the basic building block widgets, it allows the developer to use higher-level prefabricated reusable interface modules (such as a panel of buttons and screen layout templates) application graphics libraries and interactive routines (for example, maps, globes, image and signal processing, and orbital mechanics displays). CHIRP provides an embedded Design Assistant that makes use of a CHI standards and guidelines knowledge-base to actively assist the interface designer in dealing with selected problematic aspects of CHI design.

CHI Evaluation

Usability Evaluation: Trends

In the past few years, many companies have gradually realized that it is not good business for major product usability flaws to be found by their customers after the product is released for operational use. Many of the most successful computer hardware and software companies (for instance, Apple Computers, Microsoft, Hewlett-Packard, Silicon Graphics Inc., and Intuit) attribute much of the success of their best-selling products (Macintosh personal computers, Word for Windows, LaserJet printers, SGI workstations, and Quicken Personal Financial software, respectively) to early usability testing. It is noteworthy that these were among the first companies to establish usability laboratories. The Usability Professionals Association, formed by 30 specialists at the CHI '92 Conference, now has over 1700 members and held their own conference in July 1994 with more than 350 attendees.

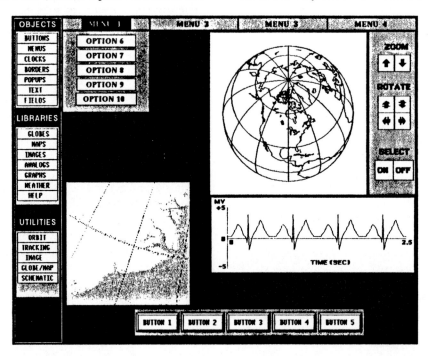

Figure 5. A developer's view of the CHIRP Toolkit (Remington, 1994)

Figure 6. A typical usability laboratory in use

Usability testing typically involves systematic observation of a sample of the potential user population performing representative tasks with an early version or prototype of the target software product in a controlled laboratory environment. Details of each user's behavior are usually captured by videotape, audio recordings, computer- logging programs, and expert observers. One-way viewing windows allow unobtrusive observation of users. Figure 6 shows a typical usability laboratory in action.

Users are encouraged to "think aloud" as they are performing a task. Quantitative behavioral measures such as the number of errors, time to complete tasks, the frequency of on-line and hard copy documentation accesses, and the number of frustration responses (for instance, pounding the table, cursing, or crying) are recorded and analyzed. Qualitative measures such as users' subjective opinions are also collected by means of post-test questionnaires and structured interviews. The results of well-designed and properly executed usability tests normally provide a clear identification of potentially serious usability problems, as well as useful insights regarding possible solutions. Highlight videos showing users working with a system can provide developers with very persuasive evidence of design flaws that detract from product usability.

For those interested in learning more about planning and conducting a usability test, analyzing data, and using the results to improve both products and processes, Dumas and Redish (1993) have written a practical guide to usability testing. Nielsen (1993) presents a more philosophical view of usability engi-

neering in general, in an attempt to "provide concrete advice and methods that can be systematically employed to ensure a high degree of usability in the final user interface." Wiklund (1994) has edited a book in which usability specialists from 17 leading companies provide informative case studies of successful usability testing programs.

Jeffries et al. (1991) provide experimental evidence regarding the strengths and weaknesses of usability testing with respect to other techniques for isolating usability problems including cognitive walkthroughs, guidelines, and heuristic evaluation. It was found that many of the most severe design flaws could only be identified with usability testing. For example, for an early version of the popular HP-VUE desktop environment, deleting your home directory made it impossible to log in at a later time. An inadvertent action of one of the usability test subjects led to the identification of this problem. None of the other methods were successful in locating this design flaw.

It is possible to develop usability metrics. Bevan and Macleod (1994) present an overview of the ESPRIT Metrics for Usability Standards in Computing (MUSiC) Project. The MUSiC project was a three-year effort to develop comprehensive and efficient techniques for usability assessment at various stages of the development life cycle. The project has resulted in development of several usability measurement methods that have been empirically tested and validated. It has also produced tools that assist in the collection of usability data. For example, the Diagnostic Recorder for Usability Measurement (DRUM) is a software tool that provides support in video control and analysis of logged data and calculation of usability metrics. The Software Usability Measurement Inventory (SUMI), developed as part of the MUSiC project measures user satisfaction and thus assesses user-perceived software quality.

Finally, based on an analysis of 11 usability studies, Nielsen and Landauer (1993) report that the detection of problems as a function of number of users tested or heuristic evaluators employed is well modeled as a Poisson process. The mathematical model resulting from this effort should prove useful in planning the amount of evaluation required to achieve desired levels of thoroughness or benefits, similar to the model developed by Dalal and Mallows (1990) to decide when to stop testing software for programming bugs.

In summary, there is no proven single technique for developing highly usable CHI software. However, an approach involving basic human factors design principles, rapid prototyping tools and techniques to obtain user feedback early and continuously throughout the entire design process, and systematic usability testing to validate designs normally results in products that are both useful and usable. Such an approach also tends to reduce the risk of serious design flaws that result in user acceptance problems and costly rework. Usability will be increasingly viewed as one of the key characteristics of software product quality. A product's software quality plan should include the critical usability characteristics that, if not met, would make the product undesirable or not needed by customers or end users. The field of CHI is currently experiencing a period of increased visibility, accelerated growth, and exciting innovation. It is important for us to continuously exploit the latest CHI design, implementation, evaluation methods, and enabling technologies to provide more usable products and systems. This is especially true today, with computer users becoming more demanding in terms of their expectations for software products that are easier to learn, less intimidating, and simply more fun to use!

References

Armstrong, J., "Six GUI Builders Face Off," *SunWorld*, Dec. 1992, pp. 67–74.

Bailey, G., "Iterative Methodology and Designer Training in Human-Computer Interface Design," *Conf. Proc. Human Factors in Computing Systems INTERCHI '93*, 1993, pp. 198–205.

Barfield, L., *The User Interface: Concepts and Design*, Addison-Wesley, Wokingham, England, 1993.

Bass, L. and Coutaz, J., "Human-Machine Interaction Considerations for Interactive Software," Software Engineering Institute Technical Report CMU/SEI-89-TR-4, Feb. 1989.

Bass, L. and Coutaz, J., *Developing Software for the User Interface*, Addison-Wesley, Reading, Mass., 1991.

Bass, L. and Dewan, P., *User Interface Software*, Wiley, New York, N.Y., 1993.

Bevan, N. and Macleod, M., "Behaviour and Information Technology" in *Usability Measurement in Context*, 1994, Vol. 13, Nos. 1 and 2, pp. 132–145.

Blattner, M., "In Our Image: Interface Design in the 1990s," *IEEE Multimedia*, Vol. 1, No. 1, 1994, pp. 25–36.

Blattner, M. and Dannenberg, L., *Multimedia Interface Design*, ACM Press, New York, N.Y., 1992.

Borenstein, N., *Programming as if People Mattered: Friendly Programs, Software Engineering, and other Noble Delusions*, Princeton University Press, Princeton, N.J., 1992.

Baecker, R., et al., *Readings in Human-Computer Interaction: Toward the Year 2000*, Morgan Kaufmann, San Mateo, Calif., 1994.

Casey, S., *Set Phaser on Stun: And Other True Tales of Design, Technology and Human Error*, Aegean Publishing Company, Santa Barbara, Calif., 1993.

Constantine, L., "More than Just a Pretty Face: Designing for Usability," *Proc. Software Development '94 Conf.*, 1994, pp. 361–369.

Corbett, M., Macleod, M. and Kelly, M., "Quantitative Usability Evaluation," *Proc. 5th Int'l Conf. Human-Computer Interaction*, 1993, pp. 313–318.

Curtis, B. and Hefley, B., "Defining a Place for Interface Engineering," *IEEE Software*, Mar. 1992, pp. 84–86.

Dalal, S. and Mallows, C., "Some Graphical Aids for Deciding When to Stop Testing Software," *IEEE J. Selected Areas Comm.*, Vol. 8, No. 2, Feb. 1990, pp. 169–175.

Dix, A., et al., *Human-Computer Interaction*, Prentice Hall, New York, N.Y., 1993.

Forte, G., "Tool Fair: Out of the Lab, Onto the Shelf." *IEEE Software*, May 1992, pp. 70–77.

Hartson, H. and Hix, D., "Human-Computer Interface Development: Concepts and Systems for Its Management." *ACM Computing Surveys*, Vol. 21. No 1, Mar. 1989.

Hix, D. and Hartson, H., *Developing User Interfaces: Ensuring Usability Through Product and Process*, John Wiley, New York, N.Y., 1994.

Helander, M. (Editor). *Handbook of Human-Computer Interaction*, North-Holland, Amsterdam, 1988.

IEEE, "Recommended Practice for Graphical User Interface Drivability," *P1201.2 Balloting Draft 2*, Sponsored by the Portable Applications Standards Committee of the IEEE Computer Society, Aug. 1993.

Jeffries, R., et al., "User Interface Evaluation in the Real World: A Comparison of Four Techniques," *CHI'91 Human Factors in Computing Systems Conf. Proc.*, ACM Press, New York, N.Y., 1991, pp. 119–124.

Karat, J. (ed.), *Taking Software Design Seriously: Practical Techniques for Human-Computer Interaction Design*, Academic Press, San Diego, Calif., 1991.

Karat, C., Campbell, R., and Fiegel, T., "Comparison of Empirical Testing and Walkthrough Methods in User Interface Evaluation," *SIGCHI'92 Human Factors in Computing Systems Proc.*, ACM Press, New York, N.Y., 1992, pp. 397–404.

Marcus, A., "A Comparison of User Interface Research and Development Centers," *Proc. Hawaii Int'l Conf. System Sciences*, Vol. 2, IEEE CS Press, Los Alamitos, Calif., 1992, pp. 741–752.

Mayhew, D., *Principles and Guidelines in Software User Interface Design*, Prentice Hall, Englewood Cliffs, N.J., 1992.

Myers, B., "Demonstrational Interfaces: A Step Beyond Direct Manipulation," *Computer*, Aug. 1992, pp. 61–73.

Myers, B. and Rosson, M., "Survey of User Interface Programming," *SIGCHI' 92: Human Factors in Computing Systems Conf. Proc.*, ACM Press, New York, N.Y., 1992.

Nielsen, J., "The Usability Engineering Life Cycle," *Computer*, Mar. 1992, pp. 12–22.

Nielsen, J., *Usability Engineering*, Academic Press, San Diego, Calif., 1993.

Nielsen, J., "Noncommand User Interfaces," *Comm. ACM*, Vol. 36, No. 4, 1993, pp. 83–99.

Nielsen, J. and Landauer, T., "A Mathematical Model of the Finding of Usability Problems," *Proc. Human Factors in Computing Systems INTERCHI '93 Conf.*, 1993, ACM Press, New York, N.Y., pp. 206–213.

Open Software Foundation, OSF/Motif Style Guide Revision 2.0, Prentice Hall, Englewood Cliffs, N.J., 1994.

Perlman. G., "User Interface Development," *Software Engineering Institute Curriculum Module*, SEI-CM-17-1.1, Nov. 1989.

Perlman, G., "Teaching User Interface Development," *IEEE Software*, Nov. 1990, pp. 85–86.

Remington, R., "X Windows: Coming to a Screen in Your Area," *Seybold's Outlook on Professional Computing*, Vol. 8, No. 5, Dec. 1989.

Remington, R., "Practicing Safe Unix on Your Dell Station with the IXI Desktop Shell," *Seybold's Outlook on Professional Computing*, Vol. 8, No. 10, May 1990.

Remington, R., "CHIRP: The Computer Human Interface Rapid Prototyping and Design Assistant Toolkit," *Proc. CHI '94: Human Factors in Computing Systems Conference Companion*, ACM Press, New York, N.Y., 1994, pp. 113–114.

Salvendy, G. (Editor), *Handbook of Human Factors*, John Wiley and Sons, New York, N.Y., 1987.

Shneiderman, B., *Designing the User Interface: Strategies for Effective Human-Computer Interaction*, Second Ed., Addison-Wesley, New York, N.Y., 1992.

Smith, S. and Mosier, J., "Guidelines for Designing User Interface Software," *Mitre Corporation Report #10090*, Bedford, Mass., 1986.

Staples, L., "Representation in Virtual Space: Visual Convention in the Graphical User Interface," *Proc. Human Factors in Computing Systems INTERCHI '93*, ACM Press, New York, N.Y., 1993, pp. 348–354.

Tognazzini, B., *Tog on Interface*, Addison-Wesley Publishing Company, Inc., 1992.

Topper, A., "Review of User Interface Development Tools." *American Programmer*, Oct. 1993.

Wiklund, M., (Editor), *Usability in Practice: How Companies Develop User-Friendly Products*, Academic Press, Cambridge, Mass, 1994.

Chapter 5

Software Development Methodologies

1. Introduction to Chapter

A *methodology*, as generally defined in software engineering and used in this Tutorial, is a set of software engineering methods, policies, procedures, rules, standards, techniques, tools, languages, and other methodologies for analyzing and specifying requirements and design. These methodologies can be used to:

- aid in determination of the software requirements and design

- represent the software requirements and design specifications prior to the beginning of either design or coding.

In order to be an acceptable methodology, a software requirements and/or design methodology must have the following attributes:

- *The methodology is documented*—the procedure for using this methodology exists in a document or users' manual

- *The methodology is repeatable*—each application of the methodology is the same

- *The methodology is teachable*—sufficient detailed procedures and examples exist that qualified people can be instructed in the methodology

SOFTWARE DEVELOPMENT METHODOLOGIES

- *The methodology is based on proven techniques*—the methodology implements proven fundamental procedures or other simpler methodologies

- *The methodology has been validated*—the methodology has been shown to work correctly on a large number of applications

- The methodology is appropriate to the problem to be solved

2. Introduction to Papers

The first paper, by Linda Northrop of the Software Engineering Institute, is an overview of object-oriented technology. This is an original paper based on her article in the 1994 *Encyclopedia of Software Engineering.* [1]

She begins with an interesting history of the object-oriented methodologies, giving credit to the original developers. In the object-oriented development model, systems are viewed as cooperative objects that encapsulate structure and behavior. She then provides a description of object-oriented programming, object-oriented design, and lastly object-oriented analysis. Although this is the reverse order from that in which these activities usually take place, the methods and tools were developed in this sequence.

She briefly describes how to transition a software development organization to object-oriented development and takes a look at possible future trends.

The second paper, by A.G. Sutcliffe, entitled "Object-Oriented Systems Development: Survey of Structured Methods," includes a description of some of the modern object-oriented analysis and design techniques, as well as a survey of the structured analysis and design methods.

Sutcliffe's paper discusses object-oriented programming and programming languages, as well as new methods of object-oriented analysis and design. The paper also defines many of the object-oriented concepts such as abstraction, encapsulation, and inheritance. Further, the paper describes some of the current object-oriented methods such as hierarchical object-oriented design (HOOD), object-oriented system design (OOSD), object-oriented system analysis (OOSA) by Schlaer and Mellor, and object-oriented analysis (OOA) by Coad and Yourdon.

The paper is particularly valuable, and is included in this chapter, because it compares object-oriented development with other methodologies such as structured analysis (developed by Yourdon and Softech in the 1970s), and the Structured System Analysis and Design Method (SSADM) used in the United Kingdom and elsewhere in Europe. The author's purpose in describing these structured methods is to determine whether or not these methods support any of the object-oriented concepts.

The third paper in this chapter, "Structured System Analysis and Design Method," by Caroline Ashworth of Scion Ltd., discusses SSADM, a popular analysis technique used in Europe and particularly in the United Kingdom. SSADM was originally developed for the government of the UK by Learmonth and Burchett Management Systems (LBMS) and has a commercial counterpart called LSDM (LBMS System Development Methodology).

SSADM is one of the better-known structured methods used in Europe. It is controlled by a UK government agency, the Central Computer and Telecommunications Agency (CCTA), which is part of HM Treasury. SSADM was introduced in 1981, and by 1987 more than 600 UK government projects were using the methodology. SSADM has the following characteristics:

- Data structure is developed at an early stage

- SSADM separates logical design from physical design

- SSADM provides three different views of the system--data structure view, data flow view, and entity life history view

- SSADM contains elements of both top-down and bottom-up approaches

- User involvement is encouraged through the use of easily understood, non-technical diagrammatic techniques supported by short, simple narrative descriptions

- Quality assurance reviews and walkthroughs are encouraged throughout the process

- SSADM forms the project documentation and is used in subsequent steps (that is, it is "self-documenting")

SSADM is similar to the structured analysis and structured design approach popular in the US, with the exception of the process known as the entities life history.

The Ashworth paper was written in 1988 and describes SSADM Version 3.x. Version 4 was released in 1990 but differed only in detail around some of the techniques, particularly in the interface area. Since then Version 4+ has been in development, with a somewhat broader scope and an emphasis on customization of the method to each individual site. No firm documentation has been developed on Version 4 or 4+, so the Ashworth paper is still the best description of SSADM available [2].

The fourth and last paper in this section is "A Review of Formal Methods" by Robert Vienneau of the Kaman Sciences Corporation. This paper is an extract from a longer report with the same title [3]. The author defines a formal method in software development as a method that provides a formal language describing a software artifact (for example, specification, design, source code) such that formal proofs are possible in principle about properties of the artifacts so expressed. Formal methods support precise and rigorous specification of those aspects of a computer system capable of being expressed in the language. Formal methods are considered to be an alternative to requirements analysis methods such as structured analysis and object-oriented analysis. The paper says that formal methods can provide more precise specifications, better communications, and higher quality and productivity.

There is a range of opinion on the proper scope of validity for formal methods with the current state of technology. The Vienneau article agrees with the Tutorial editors' views that claims of reduced errors and improved reliability through the use of formal methods are as yet unproven. This point of view is also expressed in [4]. However, there is a body of opinion that takes the more expansive view that, in critical systems such as microcode, secure systems, and perhaps safety applications, the use of formal methods to specify requirements is an important aid in detecting flaws in the requirements. This opinion is represented in [5] and [6], but even this view recognizes that the use of formal methods is expensive and there are very few applications willing to pay the cost.

1. Northrop, Linda M., "Object-Oriented Development," in *Encyclopedia of Software Engineering*, John J. Marciniak (ed.), John Wiley & Sons, Inc., New York, 1994, pp. 729–736.

2. Hall, Patrick A. V., private communication.

3. Vienneau, Robert, *A Review of Formal Methods*, Kaman Science Corporation, Utica, NY, May 26, 1993, pp. 3–15 and 27–33.

4. Fenton, Norman, Shari Lawrence Pfleeger, and Robert L. Glass, "Science and Substance: A Challenge to Software Engineers," *IEEE Software*, Vol. 11, No. 4, July 1994, pp. 86–95.

5. Gerhart, Susan, Dan Craigen, and Ted Ralston, "Experience with Formal Methods in Critical Systems," *IEEE Software*, Vol 11, No. 1, Jan. 1994, pp. 21–29.

6. Bowen, Jonathan P., and Michael G. Hinchley, "Ten Commandments of Formal Methods," *Computer*, Vol. 28, No. 4, Apr. 1995, pp. 56–63.

Object-Oriented Development

Linda M. Northrop
Software Engineering Institute

Historical Perspective

The object-oriented model for software development has become exceedingly attractive as the best answer to the increasingly complex needs of the software development community. What was first viewed by many as a research curiosity and an impractical approach to industrial strength software is now being enthusiastically embraced. Object-oriented versions of most languages have or are being developed. Numerous object-oriented methodologies have been proposed. Conferences, seminars, and courses on object-oriented topics are extremely popular. New journals and countless special issues of both academic and professional journals have been devoted to the subject. Contracts for software development that specify object-oriented techniques and languages currently have a competitive edge. Object-oriented development is to the 1990s what structured development was to the 1970s, and the object-oriented movement is still accelerating.

Concepts like "objects" and "attributes of objects" actually date back to the early 1950s when they appeared in early works in *Artificial Intelligence* (Berard, 1993). However, the real legacy of the object-oriented movement began in 1966 when Kristen Nygaard and Ole-Johan Dahl moved to higher levels of abstraction and introduced the language Simula. Simula provided encapsulation at a more abstract level than subprograms; data abstraction and classes were introduced in order to simulate a problem. During approximately this same time frame, Alan Kay was working at the University of Utah on a personal computer that he hoped would be able to support graphics and simulation. Due to both hardware and software limitations, Flex, Kay's computer venture, was unsuccessful. However, his ideas were not lost, and surfaced again when he joined Xerox at Palo Alto Research Center (PARC) in the early 1970s.

At PARC he was a member of a project that espoused the belief that computer technologies are the key to improving communication channels between people and between people and machines. The group developed Smalltalk, based upon this conviction and influenced by the class concept in Simula; the turtle ideas LOGO provided in the Pen classes; the abstract data typing in CLU; and the incremental program execution of LISP. In 1972, PARC released the first version of Smalltalk. About this time the term "object-oriented" was coined. Some people credit Alan King who is said to have used the term to characterize Smalltalk. Smalltalk is considered to be the first true object-oriented language (Goldberg, 1983), and today Smalltalk remains the quintessential object-oriented language. The goal of Smalltalk was to enable the design of software in units that are as autonomous as possible. Everything in the language is an object; that is, an instance of a class. Objects in this nascent Smalltalk world were associated with nouns. The Smalltalk effort supported a highly interactive development environment and prototyping. This original work was not publicized and was viewed with academic interest as highly experimental.

Smalltalk-80 was the culmination of a number of versions of the PARC Smalltalk and was released to the non-Xerox world in 1981. The August 1981 issue of *Byte* featured the Smalltalk efforts. On the cover of the issue was a picture of a hot air balloon leaving an isolated island that symbolized the launch of the PARC object-oriented ideas. It was time to start publicizing to the software development community. The impact was gradual at first but mounted to the current level of flurry about object-oriented techniques and products. The balloon was in fact launched and there was an effect. The early Smalltalk research in environments led to window, icon, mouse, and pull-down window environments. The Smalltalk language influenced the development in the early to mid-1980s of other object-oriented languages, most notably: Objective-C (1986), C++ (1986), Self (1987), Eiffel (1987), and Flavors (1986). The application of object orientation was broadened. Objects no longer were associated just with nouns, but also with events and processes. In 1980, Grady Booch pioneered with the concept of object-oriented design (Booch, 1982). Since then others have followed suit, and object-oriented analysis techniques have also begun to be publicized. In 1985, the first commercial object-oriented database system was introduced. The 1990s brought an ongoing investigation of object-oriented domain analysis, testing, metrics, and management. The current new frontiers in object technology are design patterns, distributed object systems, and Web-based object applications.

Motivation

Why has the object-oriented movement gained such momentum? In reality, some of its popularity probably stems from the hope that it, like so many other earlier software development innovations, will address the crying needs for greater productivity, reliability, maintainability, and manageability. However, aside from the hope that object-orientation is in fact the "silver bullet," there are many other documented arguments to motivate its adoption.

Object-oriented development adds emphasis on direct mapping of concepts in the problem domain to software units and their interfaces. Furthermore, it is felt by some that based upon recent studies in psychology, viewing the world as objects is more natural since it is closer to the way humans think. Objects are more stable than functions; what most often precipitates software change is change in required functionality, not change in the players, or objects. In addition, object-oriented development supports and encourages the software engineering practices of information hiding, data abstraction, and encapsulation. In an object, revisions are localized. Object-orientation results in software that is easily modified, extended, and maintained (Berard, 1993).

Object-orientation extends across the life cycle in that a consistent object approach is used from analysis through coding. Moreover, this pervading object approach quite naturally spawns prototypes that support rapid application development. The use of object-oriented development encourages the reuse of not only software but also design and analysis models. Furthermore, object technology facilitates interoperability; that is, the degree to which an application running on one node of a network can make use of a resource at a different node of the network. Object-oriented development also supports the concurrency, hierarchy, and complexity present in many of today's software systems. It is currently necessary to build systems—not just black-box applications. These complex systems are often hierarchically composed of different kinds of subsystems. Object-oriented development supports open systems; there is much greater flexibility to integrate software across applications. Finally, use of the object-oriented approach tends to reduce the risk of developing complex systems, primarily because system integration is diffused throughout the life cycle (Booch, 1994).

Object-Oriented Model

The object-oriented model is more than a collection of new languages. It is a new way of thinking about what it means to compute and about how infor-

mation can be structured. In the object-oriented model, systems are viewed as cooperating objects that encapsulate structure and behavior and which belong to classes that are hierarchically constructed. All functionality is achieved by messages that are passed to and from objects. The object-oriented model can be viewed as a conceptual framework with the following elements: abstraction, encapsulation, modularity, hierarchy, typing, concurrency, persistence, reusability, and extensibility.

The emergence of the object-oriented model does not mark any sort of computing revolution. Instead, object-orientation is the next step in a methodical evolution from both procedural approaches and strictly data-driven approaches. Object-orientation is the integration of procedural and data-driven approaches. New approaches to software development have been precipitated by both programming language developments and increased sophistication and breadth in the problem domains for which software systems are being designed. While in practice the analysis and design processes ideally precede implementation, it has been the language innovations that have necessitated new approaches to design and, later, analysis. Language evolution in turn has been a natural response to enhanced architecture capabilities and the ever increasingly sophisticated needs of programming systems. The impetus for object-oriented software development has followed this general trend. Figure 1 depicts the many contributing influences.

Perhaps the most significant factors are the advances in programming methodology. Over the past several decades, the support for abstraction in languages has progressed to higher levels. This abstraction progression has gone from address (machine languages), to name (assembly languages), to expression (first-generation languages, such as FORTRAN), to control (second-generation languages, such as COBOL) to procedure and function (second- and early third-generation languages, such as Pascal), to modules and data (late third-generation languages, such as Modula 2), and finally to objects (object-based and object-oriented languages). The development of Smalltalk and other object-oriented languages as discussed above necessitated the invention of new analysis and design techniques.

These new object-oriented techniques are really the culmination of the structured and database approaches. In the object-oriented approach, the smaller scale concerns of data flow-orientation, like coupling and cohesion, are very relevant. Similarly, the behavior within objects will ultimately require a function-oriented design approach. The ideas of the entity relationship (ER) approach to data modeling from the database technology are also embodied in the object-oriented model.

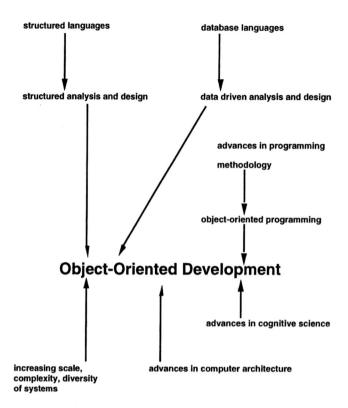

Figure 1. Influences on Object-Oriented Development

Advances in computer architecture, both in the increased capability combined with decrease in cost, and in the introduction of objects into hardware (capability systems and hardware support for operating systems concepts) have likewise affected the object-oriented movement. Object-oriented programming languages are frequently memory and MIPS intensive. They required and are now utilizing added hardware power. Philosophy and cognitive science have also influenced the advancement of the object-oriented model in their hierarchy and classification theories (Booch, 1991). And finally, the ever-increasing scale, complexity, and diversity of computer systems have helped both propel and shape object technology.

Because there are many and varied influences on object-oriented development, and because this approach has not reached maturity, there is still some diversity in thinking and terminology. All object-oriented languages are not created equal nor do they refer to the same concepts with consistent verbiage across the board. And though there is a movement toward some unification, there is no complete consensus on how to do object-oriented analysis and object-oriented design nor on the symbology to use to depict these activities. Nevertheless, object-oriented development has proven successful in many applications including: air traffic control, animation, banking, business data processing, command and control systems,

computer-aided design (CAD), computer-integrated manufacturing, databases, document preparation, expert systems, hypermedia, image recognition, mathematical analysis, music composition, operating systems, process control, robotics, space station software, telecommunications, telemetry systems, user interface design, and VLSI design. It is unquestionable that object-oriented technology has moved into the mainstream of industrial-strength software development.

Object-Oriented Programming

Concepts

Since the object-oriented programming efforts predate the other object-oriented development techniques, it is reasonable to focus first on object-oriented programming. In object-oriented programming, programs are organized as cooperating collections of objects, each of which is an instance of some class and whose classes are all members of a hierarchy of classes united via inheritance relations. Object-oriented languages are characterized by the following: object creation facility, message-passing capability, class capability, and inheritance. While these concepts can and have been used individually in other languages, they complement each other in a unique synergistic way in object-oriented languages.

Figure 2 illustrates the procedural programming model.

To achieve desired functionality, arguments are passed to a procedure and results are passed back. Object-oriented languages involve a change of perspective. As depicted in Figure 3, functionality is achieved through communication with the interface of an object. An object can be defined as an entity that encapsulates state and behavior; that is, data structures (or attributes) and operations. The state is really the information needed to be stored in order to carry out the behavior. The interface, also called the protocol, of the object is the set of messages to which it will respond.

Messaging is the way objects communicate and therefore the way that functionality is achieved. Objects respond to the receipt of messages by either performing an internal operation, also sometimes called a method or routine, or by delegating the operation to be performed by another object. All objects are instances of classes, which are sets of objects with similar characteristics, or from another viewpoint; a template from which new objects may be created. The method invoked by an object in response to a message is determined by the class of this receiver object. All objects of a given class use the same method in response to similar messages. Figure 4 shows a DOG class and objects instantiated from the dog class. All the DOG objects respond in the same way to the messages sit, bark, and roll. All DOG objects will also have the same state (data structures), though the values contained in what are typically called state variables can vary from DOG object to DOG object.

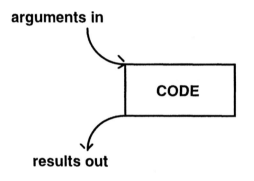

Figure 2. Procedural Model

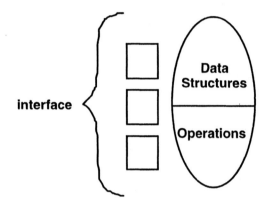

Figure 3. Object-Oriented Model

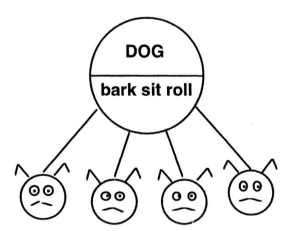

Figure 4. Instantiation of Objects From a Class

Classes can be arranged in a hierarchy. A subclass will inherit state and behavior from its superclass higher in the inheritance hierarchy structure. Inheritance can be defined as the transfer of a class' capabilities and characteristics to its subclasses. Figure 5 shows a subclass DOBERMAN of the original DOG class. An object of the DOBERMAN class will have the bark, sit, and roll behavior of the DOG class, but in addition, it will have the kill behavior particular to the DOBERMAN class. When a message is sent to an object, the search for the corresponding method begins in the class of the object and will progress up the superclass chain until such a method is found or until the chain has been exhausted (when an error would occur). In some lan-guages, it is possible for a given class to inherit from more than one superclass. This capability is called *multiple inheritance*. When dynamic binding is present, inheritance results in polymorphism. Polymorphism essentially describes the phenomenon that a given message sent to an object will be interpreted differently at execution based upon subclass determination. Figure 6 illustrates a superclass UNMEMBER with its subclasses. If the message "speak" is sent to an object, at execution time it will be determined where the appropriate speak method will be found based upon the current subclass association of the object. Thus the polymorphism means that the speak capability will vary and in fact will be determined at execution.

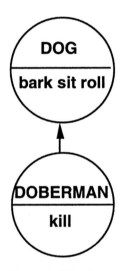

Figure 5. Inheritance

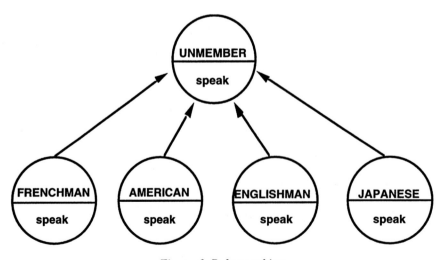

Figure 6. Polymorphism

152

Table 1. Object-Oriented Languages

Smalltalk-80
Objective C **C++** **Java**
Flavors **XLISP** **LOOPS** **CLOS**
Object Pascal **Turbo Pascal** **Eiffel** **Ada 95**

It is possible for a method to not be actually defined in the superclass but still be included in the interface and hence be inherited by subclasses. One calls such a superclass an *abstract class*. Abstract classes do not have instances and are used only to create subclasses. For example, UNMEMBER would be an abstract class if the method for the message speak was not defined in UNMEMBER. Including speak in the interface of UNMEMBER, however, would dictate that speak would be a message common to all subclasses of UNMEMBER, but the exact speak behavior would vary with each subclass. Abstract classes are used to capture commonality without determining idiosyncratic behavior.

Languages

There are essentially four branches of object-oriented languages: Smalltalk-based, C-based, LISP-based, and Pascal-based. Simula is actually the common ancestor of all of these languages. The terminology and capability of the object-oriented languages varies considerably. A sampling of popular object-oriented languages in each branch is given in Table 1. The Smalltalk-based languages include the five versions, including Smalltalk-80, developed at PARC as well as Digitalk Smalltalk and other such versions. Smalltalk-80 is considered the truest object-oriented language, although it and the others in this group do not have multiple inheritance capability.

In the C-based category are languages that are derived from C. Objective-C was developed by Brad Cox, has an extensive library, and has been used successfully to build large systems. C++ was written by Bjarne Stroustrup of AT&T Bell Labs. C's STRUCT concept is extended in C++ to provide class capability with data hiding. Polymorphism is implemented by virtual functions, which deviate from the normal C typing that is still resolved at compilation.

C++ Version 2.0 includes multiple inheritance. C++ is a popular choice in many software areas, especially those where UNIX is preferred. Similar to C and C++ but much simpler is Java, the latest object-oriented language that hit the software development scene with great fanfare in 1995. Java, developed at Sun Microsystems, in addition to being object-oriented has the capability to compile programs into binary format (applets) that can be executed on many platforms without compilation, providing embedded executable content for Web-based applications. Java is strongly typed and has multithreading and synchronization mechanisms like Ada, yet is high-performance and portable like C.

The many dialects including LOOPS, Flavors, Common LOOPS, and New Flavors, in the LISP-based branch were precipitated by knowledge representation research. Common LISP Object System (CLOS) was an effort to standardize object-oriented LISP. The Pascal-based languages include among others Object Pascal and Turbo Pascal as well as Eiffel. Object Pascal was developed by Apple and Niklaus Wirth for the Macintosh. The class library for Object Pascal is MacApp. Turbo Pascal, developed by Borland, followed the Object Pascal lead. Eiffel was released by

Bertrand Meyer of Interactive Software Engineering, Inc. in 1987. Eiffel is a full object-oriented language that has an Ada-like syntax and operates in a UNIX environment. Ada as it was originally conceived in 1983 was not object-oriented in that it did not support inheritance and polymorphism. In 1995, an object-oriented version of Ada was released. Though object-oriented, Ada 95 continues to differ from other object-oriented languages in its definition of a class in terms of types.

There are also languages that are referred to as *object-based*. A sample of object-based languages appears in Table 2. Object-based languages differ from object-oriented languages ostensibly in their lack of inheritance capability. It should be noted that while Ada 95 is object-oriented, its predecessor, Ada, is object-based.

Object-Oriented Software Engineering

Life Cycle

While the object-oriented languages are exciting developments, coding is not the primary source of problems in software development. Requirements and design problems are much more prevalent and much more costly to correct. The focus on object-oriented development techniques, therefore, should not be strictly on the programming aspects, but more appropriately on the other aspects of software engineering. The promise object-oriented methodologies hold for attacking complexity during analysis and design and accomplishing analysis and design reuse is truly significant. If it is accepted that object-oriented development is more than object-oriented coding, then a whole new approach, including life cycle, must be adopted (Booch, 1994).

The most widely accepted life cycle to date is the waterfall/structured life cycle (Lorenz, 1993). The waterfall organization came into existence to stem the ad hoc approaches that had led to the software crisis as it was first noted in the late 60s. A version of the waterfall life cycle is pictured in Figure 7.

As shown, the process is sequential; activities flow in primarily one direction. There is little provision for change and the assumption is that the system is quite clearly understood during the initial stages. Unfortunately, any software engineering effort will inherently involve a great deal of iteration, whether it is scheduled or not. Good designers have been described as practitioners who work at several levels of abstraction and detail simultaneously (Curtis, 1989). The waterfall life cycle simply does not accommodate real iteration. Likewise, prototyping, incremental builds, and program families are misfits. The waterfall/structured life cycle is also criticized for placing no emphasis on reuse and having no unifying model to integrate the phases (Korson, 1990).

The object-oriented approach begins with a model of the problem and proceeds with continuous object identification and elaboration. It is inherently iterative and inherently incremental. Figure 8 illustrates a version of the water fountain life cycle that has been used to describe the object-oriented development process (Henderson-Sellers, 1990). The fountain idea conveys that the development is inherently iterative and seamless. The same portion of the system is usually worked on a number of times with functionality being added to the evolving system with each iteration. Prototyping and feedback loops are standard. The seamlessness is accounted for in the lack of distinct boundaries during the traditional activities of analysis, design, and coding.

Table 2. Object-Based Languages

Alphard
CLU
Euclid
Gypsy
Mesa
Modula
Ada

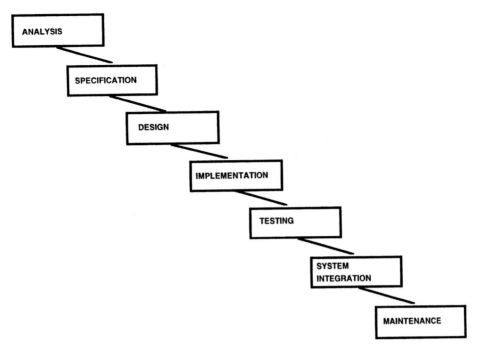

Figure 7: Waterfall Life Cycle

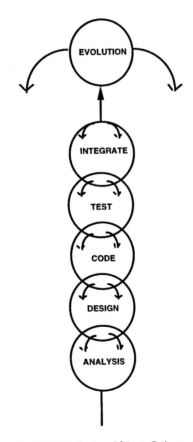

Figure 8. Water Fountain Life Cycle for Object-Oriented Software Development

The reason for removing the boundaries is that the concept of object permeates; objects and their relationships are the medium of expression for analysis, design, and implementation. There is also a switch of effort from coding to analysis and an emphasis on data structure before function. Furthermore, the iterative and seamless nature of object-oriented development makes the inclusion of reuse activities natural.

More recently a life cycle that has both a macro- and a microview has been proposed to increase the manageability of object-oriented development (Booch, 1994). The macro phases in Figure 9 are: *analysis*, to discover and identify the objects; *design*, to invent and design objects; and *implementation*, to create objects. Built into each macrophase is a microphase depicting the iteration. This life cycle suggests Boehm's Spiral Model (Boehm, 1988).

Object-Oriented Analysis (OOA) and Object-Oriented Design (OOD)

Since object-oriented technology is still relatively new, there are, as noted above, a number of approaches to Object-Oriented Analysis and Design. Most of them use graphical representations, an idea that was likely inherited from structured methodologies. Object-oriented analysis builds on previous information modeling techniques, and can be defined as a method of analysis that examines requirements from the perspective of the classes and objects found in the vocabulary of the problem domain. Analysis activities yield black-box objects that are derived from the problem domain. Scenarios are often used in object-oriented approaches to help determine necessary object behavior. A scenario is a sequence of actions that takes place in the problem domain. Frameworks have become very useful in capturing an object-oriented analysis for a given problem domain and making it reusable for related applications. Basically, a framework is a skeleton of an application or application subsystem implemented by concrete and abstract classes. In other words, a framework is a specialization hierarchy with abstract superclasses that depicts a given problem domain. One of the drawbacks of all current object-oriented analysis techniques is their universal lack of formality.

During object-oriented design, the object focus shifts to the solution domain. Object-oriented design is a method of design encompassing the process depicting both logical and physical as well as static and dynamic models of the system under design (Booch, 1994).

In both analysis and design there is a strong undercurrent of reuse. Researchers in object technology are now attempting to codify design patterns, which are a kind of reusable asset that can be applied to different domains. Basically, a design pattern is a recurring design structure or solution that when cataloged in a systematic way can be reused and can form the basis of design communication (Gamma, 1994).

OOD techniques were actually defined before OOA techniques were conceived. There is difficulty in identifying and characterizing current OOA and OOD techniques because as described above, the boundaries between analysis and design activities in the object-oriented model are fuzzy. Given that problem, the following descriptions provide an overview to some of the OOA and OOD techniques being used.

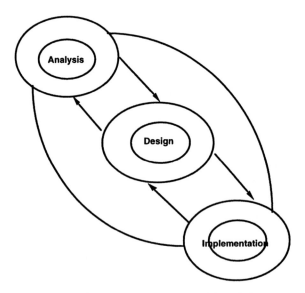

Figure 9. Iterative/Incremental Life Cyle

156

Meyer uses language as a vehicle for expressing design. His approach is really not classifiable as an OOD technique (Meyer, 1988). Booch's OOD techniques extend his previous Ada work. He advocates a "round-trip gestalt" process during which: objects are identified, semantics of the objects are identified, relationships are identified, implementation is accomplished, and iteration occurs. Originally he used class diagrams, class category diagrams, class templates, and object diagrams to record design (Booch, 1991). More recently he has taken ideas from other methods and woven them into his work. Behavior is described with Harel Statecharts in conjunction with interaction or annotated object diagrams (Booch 94).

Wirfs-Brock's OOD technique is driven by delegation of responsibilities. Class responsibility cards (CRC) are used to record classes responsible for specific functionality and collaborators with the responsible classes. The initial exploration of classes and responsibilities is followed by detailed relationship analysis and implementation of subsystems (Wirfs-Brock, 1990).

Rumbaugh et al. use three kinds of models to describe a system: the object model, which is a static structure of the objects in a system; the dynamic model, which describes the aspects of a system that change over time; and the functional model, which describes the data value transformations within a system. Object diagrams, state diagrams, and data flow diagrams are used to represent the three models, respectively (Rumbaugh, 1991).

In their OOA technique, Coad and Yourdon advocate the following steps: find classes and objects, identify structures and relationships, determine subjects, define attributes, and define services to determine a multilayer object-oriented model. The layers corresponds to the steps, namely: class and object layer, subject layer, structure layer, attribute layer, and service layer, respectively. Their OOD technique is both multilayer and multicomponent. The layers are the same as in analysis. The components include: problem domain, human interaction, task management, and data management.

Ivar Jacobson offers Objectory, an object-oriented software engineering method developed by Objective Systems in Sweden. Jacobson's method has a strong focus on a particular kind of scenario referred to as a "use-case." The use-cases become the basis for the analysis model, which gives way to the design model when the use-cases are formalized by interaction diagrams. The use-cases also drive the testing in a testing phase that Objectory makes explicit. Objectory is the most complete industrial method to date (Jacobson, 1992).

There are also other published OOA and OOD techniques as well as variations of the above that are not listed here. In recent years, as the methods have been evolving, there has been considerable convergence. In late 1995 Booch, Rumbaugh, and Jacobson joined forces and proposed the first draft of a Unified Method, which promises to add some welcome consensus and stability (Booch, 1995).

Management Issues

As organizations begin to shift to object-oriented development techniques, the management activities that support software development also necessarily have to change. A commitment to objects requires a commitment to change processes, resources, and organizational structure (Goldberg, 1995). The seamless, iterative, prototyping nature of object-oriented development eliminates traditional milestones. New milestones have to be established. Also, some of the ways in which measurements were made are less appropriate in an object-oriented context. LOC (lines of code) is definitely not helpful. Number of classes reused, inheritance depth, number of class-to-class relationships, coupling between objects, number of classes, and class size are more meaningful measurements. Most work in object-oriented metrics is relatively new, but references are beginning to surface (Lorenz, 1993).

Resource allocation needs to be reconsidered as does team organization. Smaller development teams are suggested (Booch, 1994), as is cultivation of reuse experts. Incentives should be based on reuse, not LOC. An entirely new mind set is required if reuse is to really be operative. Libraries and application frameworks have to be supported and built along with contracted application software. Long-term investment strategies are imperative as well as the processes and commitment to evolve and maintain these reuse assets.

Regarding quality assurance, typical review and testing activities are still essential, but their timing and definition must be changed. For example, a walkthrough could involve enacting a scenario of interacting objects proposed to effect some specific functionality. Testing of object-oriented systems is another area that needs to be more completely addressed. Release in terms of a steady stream of prototypes requires a flavor of configuration management that differs from that which is being used to control products generated using structured techniques.

Another management concern ought to be appropriate tool support. An object-oriented development environment is essential. Also needed are: a browser for class library, an incremental compiler, debuggers that know about class and object semantics, graphics support for design and analysis notation and reference checking, configuration management and version control tools, and a database application that functions as a class librarian. Tools are now available but need to be evaluated based upon the purpose, the organization, and the method chosen.

Estimates can also be problematic until there is object-oriented development history to substantiate proposed development estimates of resource and cost. Cost of current and future reuse must be factored into the equation. Finally, management must be aware of the risks involved in moving to an object-oriented approach. There are potential performance risks such as: cost of message passing, explosion of message passing, class encumbrance, paging behavior, dynamic allocation and destruction overhead. There are also start-up risks including: acquisition of appropriate tools, strategic and appropriate training, and development of class libraries.

Object-Oriented Transition

There are documented success stories, but there are also implicit recommendations. The transition needs to progress through levels of absorption before assimilation into a software development organization actually occurs. This transition period can take considerable time. Training is essential. Pilot projects are recommended. Combination of structured and object-oriented approaches are not recommended. There is growing evidence that success requires a total object-oriented approach for at least the following reasons: traceability improvement, reduction in significant integration problems, improvement in conceptual integrity of process and product, minimization of need for objectification and deobjectification, and maximization of the benefits of object-orientation (Berard, 1993).

Future

In summary, object-oriented development is a natural outgrowth of previous approaches and has great promise for software development in many application domains. Paraphrasing Maurice Wilkes in his landmark 29-year reprise of his 1967 ACM Turing Lecture, "Objects are the most exciting innovation in software since the 70s" (Wilkes, 1996). Object-oriented development is not, however, a panacea and has not yet reached maturity. The full potential of objects has not been realized. Yet while the future of object-oriented development cannot be defined, the predictions of the early 1990s (Winblad, 1990) are already materializing. Class libraries and application frameworks are becoming readily available in the marketplace. Transparent information access across applications and environments is conceivable. Environments in which users can communicate among applications and integrated object-oriented multimedia tool kits are emerging. It is likely that the movement will continue to gain in popularity and techniques will mature significantly as experience increases. It is also likely that object-orientation will eventually be replaced or absorbed into an approach that deals at an even higher level of abstraction. Of course these are just predictions. In the not too distant future, talk about objects will no doubt be passé, but for now there is much to generate genuine enthusiasm.

References

E.V. Berard, *Essays on Object-Oriented Software Engineering*, Vol. 1, Prentice-Hall, Inc., Englewood Cliffs, N.J., 1993.

B. Boehm, "A Spiral Model of Software Development and Enhancement," in Thayer, Richard, ed., *Software Engineering Project Management*, IEEE Computer Society Press, Los Alamitos, Calif., 1988.

G. Booch and J. Rumbaugh, "Introduction to the United Method," *OOPSLA '95 Tutorial Notes*, 1995.

G. Booch, *Object-Oriented Analysis and Design With Applications*, Addison-Wesley, Reading, Mass., 1994.

G. Booch, "Object-Oriented Design," *Ada Letters*, Vol. I, No. 3, Mar.-Apr. 1982, pp. 64–76.

G. Booch, *Object-Oriented Design with Applications*, The Benjamin/ Cummings Publishing Company, Inc., Redwood City, Calif., 1991.

T. Budd, *An Introduction to Object-Oriented Programming*, Addison-Wesley Publishing Company, Inc., New York, N.Y., 1991.

P. Coad and J. Nicola, *Object-Oriented Programming*, Prentice-Hall, Inc., Englewood Cliffs, N.J., 1993.

P. Coad and E. Yourdon, *Object-Oriented Analysis*, 2nd Ed., Prentice-Hall, Inc., Englewood Cliffs, N.J., 1991.

P. Coad and E. Yourdon, *Object-Oriented Design*, Prentice-Hall, Inc., Englewood Cliffs, N.J., 1991.

B.J. Cox, *Object-Oriented Programming: An Evolutionary Approach*, Addison-Wesley, Reading, Mass., 1986.

B. Curtis, "...But You Have to Understand. This Isn't the Way We Develop Software At Our Company," MCC Technical Report No. STP-203-89, Microelectronics and Computer Technology Corporation, Austin, Texas, 1989.

M. Fowler, "A Comparison of Object-Oriented Analysis and Design Methods," *OOPSLA '95 Tutorial Notes*, 1995.

I.E. Gamma et al., *Design Patterns*, Addison-Wesley, Reading, Mass., 1995.

A. Goldberg and P. Robson, *Smalltalk-80: The Language and Its Implementation*, Addison-Wesley, Reading, Mass., 1983.

A. Goldberg and K. Rubin, *Succeeding With Objects*, Addison-Wesley, Reading, Massachusetts, 1995.

B. Henderson-Sellers and J.M. Edwards, "The Object-Oriented Systems Life Cycle," *Comm. ACM*, Sept. 1990, pp. 143–159.

I. Jacobson et al., *Object Oriented Software Engineering*, Addison-Wesley, Reading, Mass., 1992.

T. Korson and J. McGregor, "Understanding Object-Oriented: A Unifying Paradigm," *Comm. ACM*, Sept. 1990, pp. 41–60.

M. Lorenz, *Object-Oriented Software Development*, Prentice-Hall, Inc., Englewood Cliffs, N.J., 1993.

B. Meyer, *Object-Oriented Software Construction*, Prentice-Hall, Inc., Englewood Cliffs, N.J., 1988.

D. Monarchi and G. Puhr, "A Research Typology for Object-Oriented Analysis and Design, *Comm. ACM*, Sept. 1992, pp. 35–47.

R. Pressman, *Software Engineering A Practitioner's Approach*, 3rd Ed., McGraw-Hill, Inc., New York, N.Y., 1992.

J. Rumbaugh, et al., *Object-Oriented Modeling and Design*, Prentice-Hall, Inc., Englewood Cliffs, N.J., 1991.

S. Shlaer and S.J. Mellor, *Object-Oriented Systems Analysis: Modeling the World in Data*, Yourdon Press: Prentice-Hall, Englewood Cliffs, N.J., 1988.

A.L. Winblad, S.D. Edwards, and D.R. King, *Object-Oriented Software*, Addison-Wesley Publishing Company, Inc., Reading, Mass., 1990.

R. Wirfs-Brock, B. Wilkerson, and L. Wiener, *Designing Object-Oriented Software*, Prentice-Hall, Inc., Englewood Cliffs, N.J., 1990.

M. Wilkes, "Computers Then and Now—Part 2," Invited Talk, ACM Computer Science Conference, Philadelphia, Penn., 1996.

Object-oriented systems development: survey of structured methods

A G Sutcliffe

Concepts of object-oriented system programming and system design are reviewed in the light of previous research on systems development methodologies. Key principles are identified and a selection of system development methods is then judged against these principles to determine their concordance with object-oriented design. The advantages of object-oriented system development are reviewed in the light of the study of structured system development methods.

object-oriented, object-oriented systems, structured methods, systems analysis and design

Object-oriented programming (OOP) has been the subject of several studies[1][3] that describe the principles of the object-oriented (OO) approach and their incorporation in the new generation of programming languages such as C++, Eiffel, and Smalltalk. In contrast, the object-oriented approach has received little attention in studies on system development methods. This paper aims to redress that balance and explore how OO concepts are being integrated into structured systems development methods.

Apart from the extensive interest in OOP languages, OO approaches have received some attention in office automation[4,5]. More recently, several methods have appeared claiming to be 'object-oriented' (OOSA (Object-Oriented Systems Analysis)[6], OOA (Object-Oriented Analysis)[7], and HOOD (Hierarchically Object-Oriented Design)[8]. As yet object-oriented system (OOS) development methods are not in widespread commercial practice, although interest in OO concepts continues to grow. One unanswered question is what are the essential differences between OO methods and those from the more classical 'structured camp', e.g. Structured Systems Analysis and Design Method (SSADM), Jackson System Development (JSD), and Structured Analysis/Structured Design (SA/SD). If OO methods are to become accepted, the advantages over and differences from previous methods have to be established and then the implications of migration paths from current techniques to OO methods should be made clear. This paper aims to throw some light on these questions by examining how current system development methods fit criteria for OO development.

First, OO concepts are described within the context of system development, then a selection of system development methods is reviewed.

OBJECT-ORIENTED CONCEPTS

OO development is claimed to improve software design for reliability and maintenance. Further claims are that the development process is made more efficient by reuse. The justification for these claims rests on three principles: abstraction, encapsulation, and inheritance.

Abstraction

OO approaches have been based on modelling structures in the real world. Programming languages that facilitate this modelling and support its implementation are said to create more maintainable and reliable systems with reusable program components[1].

Objects are an abstraction of parts of real-world systems and model composite units of structure and activity. Cook[3] points out that there are two roles that objects fulfil: an implementation role related to improving the maintainability of programs, and a modelling role, which addresses the problems of correct specification of system requirements. OOS development should emphasize the latter role, while supplying the necessary specifications to enhance maintainability in implementation.

Encapsulation

Encapsulation is the concept that objects should hide their internal contents from other system components to improve maintainability. By making part of the design local, objects limit the volatility of change in the system. The encapsulated parts of objects are hidden to insulate them from the effects of system modifications.

Inheritance

Objects should have generic properties, i.e., support reusability by property inheritance from superclass to subclass[3]. By organizing objects in class hierarchies, lower-level objects can receive properties from higher-level objects. This facilitates reuse of more general, higher-level objects by specialization.

Two forms of inheritance may be supported: hierarchi-

Department for Business Computing, School of Informatics, The City University, Northampton Square, London EC1V 0HB, UK

Reprinted from *Information and Software Technology*, Vol. 33, No. 6, July/Aug. 1991, A.G. Sutcliffe, "Object-Oriented Systems Development: Survey of Structured Methods," pp. 433–442, 1991, with kind permission from Elsevier Science–NL, Sara Burgerhartstraat 25; 1055 KV Amsterdam, The Netherlands.

cal, in which a child object can inherit only from its parent object, or multiple, when an object can inherit properties from several parent objects. Multiple inheritance may result in 'polymorphism', with one component having different properties in several new locations, as it is specialized in child objects.

These principles contribute to the OO model of systems, which is composed of a network of objects communicating by messages. Each object specifies both data and activity and may share properties according to a classification hierarchy. To enable comparison of methods, the basic principles of the OO approach need to be situated in a comparative framework that addresses not only OO concepts, but also more traditional models of structured methods. The ISO meta-schema (ISO TC97)[9] is taken as a starting point.

Evaluation of modelling components

The first question to resolve is what is an object, and what is the difference between objects and more traditional concepts such as entities and functions. The starting point may be taken from the entity definition given in the ISO TC97 report[9]:

Any concrete or abstract thing of interest including association among things.

The ISO report makes distinctions about entities on three levels:

- Entity instances — the actual occurrence of one example of an entity type.
- Entity type — a type defined by a set of common properties to which all instances belong.
- Entity class — all possible entity types for which a proposition holds, i.e., the set of instances for a particular entity type.

These definitions accord with the OO approach. Besides entities, the other system components recognised by the ISO report are propositions (i.e., rules), constraints, which specify the behaviour of entities, and events, which are defined as 'The fact that something has happened in either the universe of discourse, or the environment or in the information system'. Events are modelled as messages in the OO approach, i.e., messages communicate events to which objects respond. Objects record states, i.e., an unchanging reality altered by transitions from one state to another, and react to events by changing state[10]. Events are modelled as messages passed within a network of objects, and thereby controlling their behaviour[3,10]. Rules, however, are more problematic.

The ISO separation of entities representing data structures from rules specifying control does not match the OO concept because objects specify a composite of data and activity. In the ISO meta-model, entities are not considered to possess attributes, instead attributes are regarded as entities in their own right. This is contrary to OO approaches in which attributes are components of

objects. Furthermore, the ISO view of relationships does not fit the OO conceptualization of relationships between objects being either caused by events or specified in terms of a classification hierarchy.

Object orientation, therefore, shares many of the ISO concepts, but by no means all. The main point of divergence is the separation of activity and data specification, a point that re-emerges when individual methods are considered. Within the perspective of systems development, the convergence of objects and traditional concepts may be summarized as:

- Objects are close to the entity concept, i.e., something of interest defined by a collection of attributes, although objects add activity to the entity.
- Objects are a type with one or more instances of the type, essentially the same as the entity-type concept.
- Objects instances may be changed by events in the outside world or within the system and record a state resulting from change.

Objects may have more or less activity associated with them. At one extreme are data-oriented objects, which undergo no operations other than simple updates to their attributes. In contrast, a task-oriented object may possess few data items and much complex algorithmic processing. An example of the latter is a mathematical calculation in an engineering system.

Given that objects may show variable structures and properties, a useful classification is given by Booch[10], who divides objects into actors, agents, and servers. Actors are objects that perform actions which influence other objects in the system, and have similarities with tasks and procedures; servers are the recipients of an actor's activity and are related to the database entity concept; and, finally, agents are an amalgam of both characteristics. In practice, the mix of object types within a system will reflect the application, e.g., real-time systems will have more actors, whereas data retrieval systems will have more servers.

So far the components of an OO model have been contrasted with more traditional concepts. However, conceptual models are only one facet of methods. The next section develops the comparison from modelling features into an evaluation framework.

EVALUATION PROCEDURE

A meta-model of OO development is illustrated in Figure 1, summarizing the components of OO conceptual models, the principles of the approach, and the OO conceptualization of the development life-cycle. Methods should advise practitioners how to proceed as well as giving them the tools with which to analyse and design systems. Four dimensions are used in the evaluation framework:

- Conceptual modelling: the method should contain a means of modelling applications, and in the perspective of this study, the model should meet OO criteria.

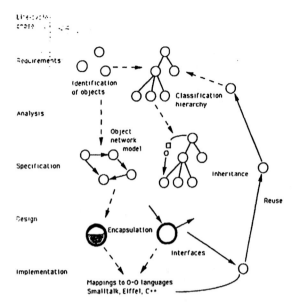

Figure 1. Summary of object-oriented meta-model

- Procedural guidance: a method should have clear steps telling the analyst how to conduct analysis, specification, and design.
- Transformations: methods should give heuristics, rules, and algorithms for changing specifications into designs. Ideally, these steps should be automatable.
- Design products: the results of specification and design should be clearly described, ideally delivering executable designs as code.

This schema was derived from previous studies[11] and shares many criteria with other evaluation frameworks[12]. Systems development methods may be classified into different groups that share some common approach or philosophical background[11]. Representative methods from different groups were selected for comparison against the following framework.

Conceptual modelling
- The data and processing control parts of a system are modelled in one unit rather than separately.
- The method produces a network system model of objects communicating by messages.
- The method explicitly models object types and instances.
- Classification of objects is supported with property inheritance.

Procedure and guidance
- The method should guide the analyst towards identifying and describing objects.
- Guidance should be available for analysis, specification, and design phases.

Transformations and products
- Design transformations should support change of OO specifications into designs implementable in OOP languages.

Table 1. Feature analysis of object-oriented methods

Method	Abstraction	Classification	Inheritance	Encapsulation	Coverage (R-A-S-D-I)
HOOD	Y	Y	Partial	Y	------
OOSD	Y	Y	Y	Y	------
OOSA	Y	Partial	-	-	-----
OOA	Y	Y	Y	-	------
ObjectOry	Y	Y	Y	Partial	-------

Key: Y = Yes.

R-A-S-D-I in coverage refers to Requirements Analysis, Analysis, Specification, Design, and Implementation. The measure of coverage is judged from the methods procedures and notations.

In the following sections, a selection of system development methods, chosen to cover diverse backgrounds from real-time to information-processing applications, is analysed to review how well they accord with OO concepts.

First, OO methods are reviewed for their support of OO principles, then traditional structured methods are surveyed in terms of their modelling perspective (data, process, or event)[12] and their potential fit to the OO approach. Selected methods are illustrated with specifications using the case study described in the Appendix. Space precludes illustration of all of the methods. Comparison of methods' specification is not the intention of this paper; instead, selected specifications are given to illuminate the differences between OO and non-OO methods.

OBJECT-ORIENTED METHODS

The claims of OO methods can now be evaluated using the OO meta-model. Each method is evaluated in terms of its fit with OO method criteria and its coverage in terms of analysis and design.

Hierarchical Object-Oriented Design (HOOD)[8]

As may be expected, this method scores well on OO properties (see Table 1). HOOD encourages modelling of objects explicitly, although there is little guidance for early analysis stages and structured analysis and design techniques are even recommended for the purpose. Objects are modelled in a hierarchical manner, with inheritance of properties between parent and child objects. There is strong emphasis on the object interface specification and encapsulation. A system network of objects communicating by messages is created with control by event messages. HOOD uses Booch's conception of actor and server objects.

HOOD supports object classes, but inheritance specification is not detailed and reuse support is not explicit. The method is better developed in the design phase and gives explicit transformations into Ada. Overall, HOOD incorporates many OO properties, but it is a real-time design method, consequently data specification and associated inheritance mechanisms receive less attention.

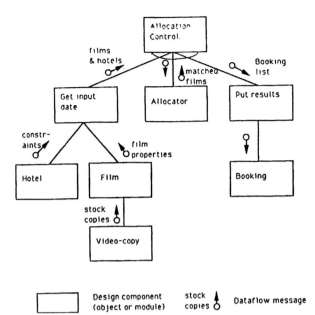

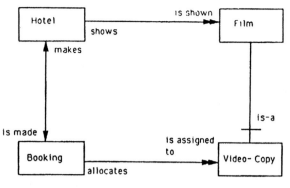

Figure 3. Object model of VI application produced by OOSA
Because OOSA takes data-modelling approach, more active objects, e.g., Clerk, Allocator, are not specified in object network. This functionality would be described in dataflow diagrams

Figure 2. Object model of VI application produced by OOSD method
OOSD design showing structure chart notation. Some design components are shared with other methods, e.g., objects Film, Hotel, Video-copy, and Booking. Other components have been added by OOSD method, e.g., Allocation control, Put results

Object-Oriented System Design (OOSD)[13]

This method assumes that an analysis phase has identified and partially specified objects. OOSD provides a detailed notation for object classes and management of inheritance. Inter-object communication is also specified in terms of event/message types. The method supplies detailed notation for interface description and encapsulation, with local data and services. Part of an OOSD specification of the case study application is given in Figure 2. The system is modelled either as a sequentially executed hierarchy using the Yourdon structure chart notation or as an asynchronous network of processes with monitors.

No analysis advice is given, so coverage of OOSD is necessarily restricted to the design phase. The notation can become overcrowded and difficult to read.

Object-Oriented Systems Analysis (OOSA)[6]

Shaler and Mellor's method is described with a case study prototyping approach. It gives many heuristics for object identification and analysis, which help initial abstraction and object modelling. OOSA owes its ancestry to the data-modelling approach and many of its recommendations are indistinguishable from entity-relationship modelling.

The method models an object relationship network with subclasses. State-transition specifications are constructed for each object and functions are modelled with dataflow diagrams. The object relationship model is illustrated in Figure 3. The method does produce a composite activity-data model, but this is achieved by attaching ment of activity to the data model, essentially merging dataflow diagrams and state-transition models with entities. The procedure for achieving this synthesis is not explicit. The main criticism of OOSA is its lack of support for inheritance. Classes are supported, but only inheritance of object properties is modelled. Inheritance of services is not considered and reuse is not explicitly supported. In addition, the method is underspecified in the design phase.

Object-Oriented Analysis (OOA)[7]

OOA covers all OO concepts, although it is an analysis method, hence coverage of design issues is weak (see Table 1). Classification and inheritance are modelled and abstraction is helped by the structure layer, which gives an overview of object groupings for large systems. Objects are a composite data activity specification. Three links between objects are supported: relationship connections, which are modelled in the familiar data model crow's feet notation, classification hierarchies, and message passing. The resulting specification can appear overcrowded, although Coad and Yourdon separate the complexity into different layers (Subject, Structure, Attribute, Service) and build the specification incrementally. An OOA specification showing the object model in the service layer is depicted in Figure 4.

The method uses hierarchical inheritance and masking rather than multiple inheritance, and specification of encapsulation and object interfaces is not as detailed as in OOSD or HOOD. Overall, however, it does meet many OO criteria.

ObjectOry[14]

This method supports OO concepts of classification, encapsulation, and inheritance. Abstraction is promoted by levels in design from higher-level system views to lower block and component levels. ObjectOry adds concepts of user-centred design 'uses cases' to the OO approach for specification of the user interfaces and tasks provided by object services. Use cases are specified

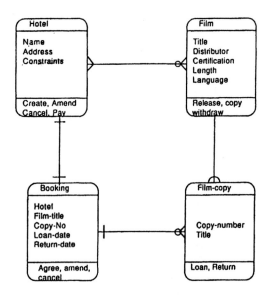

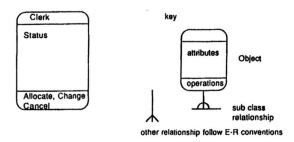

Figure 4. Object model for VI system produced by OOA method

with dataflow diagrams, and this functional specification is then mapped on to object services.

The composite data and activity definition of objects is not strongly enforced and services (described as processes) are also regarded as objects. Reuse is supported by component libraries, and design transformations to real-time languages are given (CHILL and Ada). Guidance for analysis is less comprehensive and the target applications of ObjectOry, like HOOD, appear to be real-time and engineering systems.

Summary of OO methods

The coverage of OO methods is variable and not all methods meet the necessary range of criteria. HOOD and OOSD give comprehensive design notations, but are weak on prescriptive guidance. Indeed, guidance in the analysis phase is totally absent. HOOD does fulfil most OO criteria, but does not completely support property inheritance, probably because its real-time orientation does not necessitate specification of complex data structures within objects. OOSA produces an object model with fewer components as a consequence of its data-modelling heritage, whereas OOA is more likely to identify actor as well as server objects. OOA meets many

Table 2. Summary of method specification models and approaches

Method	Functional process	Data rela-tionship	Event sequence	Coverage (R-A-S-D-I)	Application
IE	Y	Y	Y	-----------	IS
ISAC	Y	Y	N	------	IS
SASD	Y	N	Y	---------	IS
SSADM	Y	Y	Y	-----------	IS
SADT	Y	Y	N	------	IS, RT
JSD	N	Y	Y	----------IS, RT	
NIAM	Y	Y	N	--------	IS (data intensive)
Mascot	Y	N	N	--------	RT

Key: Y = Yes, N = No.
    Coverage of the life-cycle: Requirements (R), Analysis (A) Specification (S), Design (D), Implementation (I).
    Application: IS = information systems, RT = real-time.

Table 3. Summary of structured methods' object-oriented features

	Object model	Data + activity	Encapsu-lation	Types + instances	Classifi-cation
IE	Poss	N	N	Y	N
ISAC	Y	N	N	N	N
SASD	Y	N	N	N	N
SSADM	Y	N	N	Y	N
SADT	Y	N	N	N	N
JSD	Y	Y	Y	Y	N
NIAM	Poss	Poss	N	Y	Y
Mascot	Y	Y	Y	Y	N

Notes:
(1) For the object model, Poss means an object model could possibly be constructed from the data model in these methods.
(2) To score Y for the object model, methods have to specify a concurrent network of message-passing processes, however these processes may be functional or data-oriented. This can be cross-checked on column two, which records whether data and processing are modelled together in an object.

OO criteria and gives procedural advice, although its coverage of the design phase is not extensive. Consequently, no complete OO method exists, although all the issues are addressed separately in different methods.

REVIEW OF OBJECT ORIENTEDNESS OF SYSTEMS DEVELOPMENT METHODS

A summary feature analysis of the methods investigated is given in Table 2. The types of model employed by methods are categorized as functional/process (typically represented by dataflow diagrams), data relationship (entity-relationship diagrams), or event (entity life histories). The feature analysis also includes the approximate life-cycle coverage of each method. For further details of method comparisons, see Loucopoulos *et al.*[11] and Olle *et al.*[12]. A summary of the OO features is illustrated in Table 3 and described in more detail in the following sections.

Information Engineering (IE)[15]

Data modelling is an important component of IE, which encourages object modelling of the data components of a system. Functional specification uses process dependency and action diagrams, separated from data modelling, thereby discouraging common data and control specification. Cross-referencing of functions to entities is provided for and state-transition diagrams explicitly associate event-creating operations with entities, giving a partial OO specification.

Concepts of type-instance are supported; also IE encourages conceptual modelling of business processes leading towards object orientation. A data model composed of entities and relationships gives a network specification for the static part of systems, but separation during analysis of processing from data and the emphasis on functional decomposition means that IE cannot be regarded as truly object-oriented.

Information systems activity and change analysis (ISAC)[16]

This method advocates top-down functional composition of processing and data in separate specifications as activity and data diagrams. Emphasis is placed on analysis of change, and processes are viewed as transforming data, which encourages a partial OO approach. Type-instance and classification concepts are not supported. Even though a network model of processes and data structures is produced, the separation of data from system control makes ISAC more functionally oriented than object-oriented.

Structured Analysis/Structured Design (SASD)[17-19]

SASD uses top-down functional decomposition to analyse systems in terms of a network of processes connected by dataflow messages (see Figure 5). The method is based on principles of functional cohesion, which groups actions pertaining to a single goal in processing units, and coupling, which aims for low interdependence between system components. Dataflow diagrams specify the system as a network of communicating functions, which is transformed into a hierarchical design. The method does not support any OO concepts, separates data and process specification, and encourages specification of functionally based system components. More recent versions have added state-transition diagrams and bottom-up analysis driven by event identification[19]. This creates more potential for expressing OO specifications.

Structured Systems Analysis and Design Method (SSADM)[20]

SSADM is a composite method derived from structured analysis, structured design and data analysis. Process analysis is by dataflow diagramming and separated from data analysis, which employs an entity-relationship

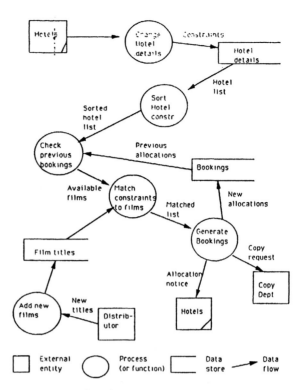

Figure 5. Dataflow diagram specification of VI application using SSA

approach. As with IE, data analysis encourages object orientation, but the separation of processing from data specification and use of top-down functional decomposition results in specification of functionally related processing structures. As a result most of the views expressed about IE also apply to SSADM. Entity life histories do associate processing events with data objects, but this is just one modelling view within the method. In version 4 of SSADM it forms a major theme within the overall specification and hence encourages OO specifications. Although SSADM does encourage data abstraction by conceptual modelling, functional modelling is also supported and hence it cannot be said to be truly object-oriented.

Structured Analysis and Design Technique (SADT)[21]

SADT uses top-down decomposition to analyse systems in successively increasing levels of detail. Specification uses network diagrams of processes connected by data flows, control messages, and mechanisms. The method does encourage modelling of real-world problems, but constructs separate activity and data models using the same box and arrow notation. More emphasis is placed on activity modelling. SADT does not support type-instance concepts, although some classification is possible in the hierarchical decomposition of data. The separation of process specification from data makes this method unsuitable for an OO approach.

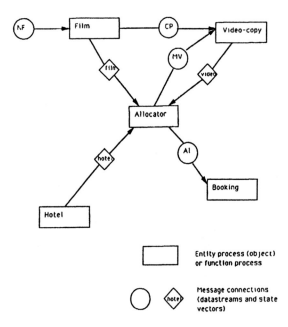

Figure 6. *System network diagram of VI system produced by JSD*

Jackson System Development (JSD)[22,23]

JSD produces system models based on networks of concurrent communicating processes, with a type-instance concept, although classification and property inheritance is not supported. System control is modelled in terms of time-ordering of actions associated with entities, and more recent versions have placed more emphasis on data analysis, resulting in an object model that combines data and operations. A JSD system specification diagram (see Figure 6) shows a network of communicating processes similar to an object model. Because of its emphasis on an entity-life-history approach, JSD has much in common with OO methods, although it does not explicitly support all OO concepts. Even though object classification is not supported, JSD does advocate alternative views on an object, called entity roles.

Nijssen's Information Analysis Method (NIAM)[24]

NIAM is a conceptual-modelling method that concentrates on data specification during the early parts of the analysis life-cycle. Based on the ANSI/SPARC schema, it supports data abstraction with conceptual modelling, thereby encouraging object orientation. Process analysis is by addition of semantic constraints to the data model and by specification of transactions for data input and output using a rule-based approach. Type-instance concepts are supported, as is classification by entity subtypes, so NIAM can be said to possess some OO properties, although it does not support inheritance. However, emphasis on constraint-based processing tightly coupled to relationship roles in the data model does detract from the OO approach.

Mascot-3[25]

Mascot advocates functional decomposition of systems, however, recent versions have introduced modular concepts of encapsulation and clearly defined interfaces for system components. Mascot system specifications consist of a network of communicating processes, and hierarchical abstraction is supported. Mascot has a type-instance concept for implementing many instances of software modules from one template 'type'. However, it does not explicitly support classification of objects, although some inheritance of communication procedures between modules is provided for by the access interface. Encapsulation is encouraged by the strongly typed interface specification of modules.

Mascot gives little guidance during early analysis, and other functional methods such as structured analysis and CORE[26] are recommended. Overall, Mascot encourages the analyst to produce a functionally oriented specification because of its imprecise early stages and emphasis on functional decomposition, although its implementation does incorporate OO features.

Summary of method evaluation

Methods using functional decomposition (e.g., SASD) encourage identification of goal-related components in systems (see Figure 5), in contrast to the OO approach (see Figures 3 and 4), which promotes system components more compatible with data models. SASD encourages specification of a hierarchy of task/procedural units that are unrelated to the objects on which the tasks act.

Although it may be argued that functions are essentially objects containing only activity, a method's viewpoint will influence modelling. An analyst trained in the functional approach will naturally identify goal-related modules using the principles of cohesion and functional decomposition[17,18]. In contrast an analyst using an OO viewpoint will identify modules that relate to a model of the real world without prejudice to processing goals. However, OO methods such as OOSD and HOOD do not encourage a specific view on object identity, so it is possible to argue that structured analysis and design modules are equivalent to actor objects in Booch's sense. Resolution of this dichotomy may depend on the fit of method and application, with real-time methods (e.g., HOOD, ObjectOry) tending towards functional, actor-type objects. For information systems, data-oriented objects may be more suitable.

Consequently for information systems, structured methods with a data-modelling heritage (e.g., IE, SSADM) are closer to the OO approach. Data modelling encourages specification of the static aspects of object structures. Unfortunately, data modelling ignores dynamic system components, and as a result these methods generally borrow functional specification for the dynamic parts of the system from methods such as structured analysis. Process specification that relies on functional decomposition will bias implementation towards functionally based structures. Another method in this group is NIAM, which emphasizes semantic data modelling, combining entities and rules in one model. In spite of this, NIAM does not explicitly attach all the system activity specified as rules to objects.

JSD views entities as being active and creates a system model explicitly based on real-world objects, combining data and control within one structure. JSD, however, does not support object classification. Instead, it advocates multiple views of an object in terms of roles that could be used to specify property sharing. Mascot cannot be regarded as truly object-oriented because it uses functional decomposition to identify modules. However, Mascot, in common with other real-time methods, does include OO concepts such as encapsulation.

In summary, current structured methods using an entity-modelling and/or entity-life-history approach have potential to evolve towards object orientation. Classification and encapsulation are supported, but separately in different methods. Inheritance is not supported, although data-oriented methods could incorporate these features, as illustrated by the evolution of OOSA and OOA.

DISCUSSION

The first part of the discussion reviews OO concepts proposed by previous studies, followed by discussion of the object orientedness of system development methods.

Object-oriented concepts

Objects are close relatives of abstract data types[27], which first brought specification of data structures and operations together. Objects, however, go beyond abstract data types, which emphasize control from a viewpoint of constraints on data structures, to encompass a wide range of system components. Booch[10] defines objects as entities characterized by their actions, essentially composite specifications of the active, processing and the static, data-related components of systems. Reviewers of OOP have also defined objects as being composite specifications of data and control/actions[1 3], combined with properties to enhance program maintenance and reusability of modules.

The importance of modelling systems that can respond to change is discussed by Maclennan[27], who points out that there is a dichotomy between valued-oriented and OO programming. The former being based on mathematics is concerned with unchanging definitions and alias values; object orientation, however, is about change and the tasks of recording and responding to it. Maclennan[27] develops this point to demonstrate that many current programming languages are value- rather than object-oriented.

While current programming languages rarely support OO principles, a new generation of languages has been developed to support object programming, some of which (e.g., C++, Smalltalk) have gained widespread acceptance. To reap the rewards of improved maintainability and reusability which these languages offer, system development methods need an OO approach, otherwise procedural specifications will continue to be implemented, failing to reap the advantages of OO design.

General conclusions

Principles of OO development have been devised to tackle problems of poor specification, the lack of maintainability, and the need for software reusability. It may be argued that use of a particular system development method will not bias implementation of OO systems and that OO designs may be derived from any specification. This view is unrealistic, as demonstrated in this study by the different specifications produced by application of OO and non-OO methods. However, data model and OO specifications show considerable convergence, suggesting a feasible migration path from structured methods such as JSD, IE, and SSADM towards further object orientation.

Functionally based development methods (e.g., Structured Analysis) are less well suited to development of OO systems. If functionally based methods are used, the designer would have to map functional components on to objects, a difficult task that may require re-specification of large parts of the system. Some attempts have tried to graft functionality on to objects in an *ad hoc* manner[28], resulting in muddled specification of objects without a clear modelling basis. More recent developments have taken the entity model as the starting point for object definitions and then used dataflow design to model services, alias functionality[6,7].

The functional bias problem arises with OO real-time methods (e.g., HOOD), which either leave the analytic phase underspecified or recommend use of methods based on functional decomposition and procedural dependency (e.g., SADT[21] and CORE[26]) as front-ends for requirements analysis and early specification stages. The OOSD method[14] builds on structured design concepts and develops a notation and design procedure for object-like modules. The method, however, does not cover requirements analysis and specification. OO analysis methods offer coverage of the early life-cycle phases[6,7], by integrating object specification with dataflow diagram specification and entity-relationship analysis, although only the Coad and Yourdon method meets all the OO modelling requirements. OO analysis does not offer good coverage in early life-cycle phases, but no design transformations are included. All of these methods have yet to be proven in practice and have little computer-aided software engineering (CASE) tool support, but they do lend support to the importance of the data model in OO concepts.

Within the current generation of structured system development methods only JSD has a truly OO approach to modelling, even though it does not support classification. However, data-modelling approaches using rules applied to data structures, as found in NIAM's semantic data model, may also provide a promising way forward. The derivation of OO specification as created by the Coad and Yourdon method demonstrates that method evolution is possible and practical. Further evidence of evolution moves may be the importance attached to entity life histories, essentially Jackson techniques, in version 4 of SSADM.

Migration to object orientation, however, will largely depend on system developers being convinced of the benefits of the approach. Thorough evaluations of OO claims for improved maintainability and reuse have not been published, if they exist at all. Object models alone are unlikely to be sufficient to promote extensive reuse as none of the OO methods contains procedures or explicit modelling techniques for reusable system development. Initial studies of this problem suggest considerable problems exist in specifying generic objects[29]. Furthermore, because much information about domains is contained in the relationships between objects and in propositional statements object models alone may be insufficient for specification of applications. OO methods may need to move in the direction of semantic data modelling e.g., TAXIS[30] and CML[31], to augment the data/activity specification of objects with richer semantics. The inter-relationship between objects and system control could also present problems for OO methods, as recognised by Nierstrasz[4]. Modelling techniques to specify inter-object communication and message-passing control will have to progress beyond concepts of client-server objects as found in HOOD.

If, to paraphrase Rentsch's[1] prediction, 'object oriented systems development will be in the 1990's what structured design was in the 1970's', system development methods will have to pay more attention to OO concepts and approaches. On the other hand, proponents of the OO approach will have to demonstrate the validity of their claims by evaluation in industrial-scale applications.

ACKNOWLEDGEMENTS

The author is grateful to colleagues at City University, Alwyn Jones and John Crinnon, for their comments and suggestions.

This work was based on research within the AMADEUS project 1229(1252), partially funded by the Esprit programme of the Commission of the European Communities.

REFERENCES

1 Rentsch, T 'Object oriented programming' *SIGPLAN Notices* Vol 17 No 9 (1982) pp 51 61
2 Cohen, A T 'Data abstraction, data encapsulation and object oriented programming' *SIGPLAN Notices* Vol 17 No 1 (1984) pp 31 35
3 Cook, S 'Languages and object oriented programming' *Soft. Eng. J.* Vol 1 No 2 (1986) pp 73–80
4 Nierstrasz, O M 'An object-oriented system' in **Tschritzis, D (ed)** *Office automation* Springer-Verlag (1985)
5 Tsichritzis, D 'Objectworld' in **Tsichritzis, D (ed)** *Office automation* Springer-Verlag (1985)
6 Shaler, S and Mellor, S J *Object oriented systems analysis* Yourdon Press (1988)
7 Coad, P and Yourdon, E *Object oriented analysis* Yourdon Press (1990)
8 Robinson, P J (ed) *The HOOD manual, issue 2.1* European Space Agency, Noordwijk, The Netherlands (1987)
9 van Griethuysen (ed) 'Concepts and terminology for the conceptual schema and the information base, computers and information processing' *ISO/TC97/SC5/WG3* International Organization for Standardization, Geneva, Switzerland (1982)
10 Booch, G 'Object oriented development' *IEEE Trans. Soft. Eng.* Vol 12 No 2 (1986) pp 211–221
11 Loucopoulos, P, Black, W J, Sutcliffe, A G and Layzell, P J 'Towards a unified view of system development methods' *Int. J. Inf. Manage.* Vol 7 No 4 (1987) pp 205 218
12 Olle, T W *et al.* *A framework for the comparative evaluation of information systems methodologies* Addison-Wesley (1989)
13 Wasserman, A, Pircher, P A and Muller, R J 'Concepts of object oriented design' *Technical report* Interactive Development Environments, San Francisco, CA, USA (1989)
14 Jacobsen, I 'Object oriented development in an industrial environment' in *Proc. OOPSLA-87* ACM Press (1987) pp 183–191
15 Macdonald, I G 'Information engineering — an improved, automatable methodology for the design of data sharing systems' in **Olle, T W, Sol, H G and Verrijn-Stuart, A A (eds)** *Information systems design methodologies: improving the practice* North-Holland (1986)
16 Lundeberg, M, Goldkuhl, G and Nilsson, A *Information systems development: a systematic approach* Prentice Hall (1981)
17 DeMarco, T *Structured analysis and system specification* Yourdon Press (1978)
18 Yourdon, E and Constantine, L *Structured design* Yourdon Press (1977)
19 Yourdon, E *Modern systems analysis* Prentice Hall (1990)
20 Longworth, P G and Nicholls, D *SSADM—Structured Systems Analysis and Design Method* NCC Publications (1986)
21 Ross, D T and Schoman, K G 'Structured analysis for requirements definition' *IEEE Trans. Soft. Eng.* Vol 3 No 1 (1977) pp 1–65
22 Jackson, M A *System development* Prentice Hall (1983)
23 Sutcliffe, A G *Jackson System Development* Prentice Hall (1988)
24 Nijssen, G M *A conceptual framework for organisational aspects of future data bases* Control Data Corporation, Brussels, Belgium (1978)
25 Simpson, H 'The Mascot method' *Soft. Eng. J.* Vol 1 No 3 (1986) pp 103–120
26 Mullery, G 'CORE — a method for controlled requirements specification' in *Proc. 4th Int. Conf. Software Engineering* IEEE (1979)
27 Maclennan, B 'Values and objects in programming languages' *SIGPLAN Notices* Vol 17 No 12 (1982) pp 75–81
28 Balin, S C 'An object oriented requirements specification method' *Commun. ACM* Vol 32 No 5 (1989) pp 608–620
29 Sutcliffe, A G 'Towards a theory of abstraction: some investigations into the object oriented paradigm' *Technical report* City University, London, UK (1991)
30 Greenspan, S J and Mylopoulos, J 'A knowledge representation approach to software engineering: the TAXIS project' in *Proc. Canadian Information Processing Society* Ontario, Canada (1983) pp 163–174
31 Jarke, M 'DAIDA: conceptual modelling and knowledge based support for information systems development process' in *Software engineering in Esprit (Techniques et Science Informatiques)* Vol 9 No 2 Dunod-AFCET (1990)

APPENDIX: CASE STUDY

A complete description of this case study can be obtained from the author. A summary is presented here.

Video International hires video tapes of films to hotels, who then transmit videos to guests via internal cable TV networks. Films are hired from distributors, who charge a rental fee based on the popularity of the film and the duration hired. Video International has contracts with hotels to supply a set number of films as specified by the hotel. Films are hired in blocks of one or more weeks and it is usual for hotels to offer guests a choice of four to five films. Hotels impose constraints on the type of film they wish to accept. Some hotels have a policy on non-violent films, some films may offend religious values, while other hotels accept films with specific running lengths. In addition, all hotels do not wish to be allocated the same film twice. Hotels may also change their film preferences from time to time.

The problem is to satisfy the demand for films from the available titles within constraints imposed by individual hotels. The hiring history of each hotel has to be examined to determine which films they have not received. Films are allocated to hotels and the appropriate number of copies are made for the demand. Video copies are delivered to hotels. Sometimes video tapes break and the copy has to be replaced. Records of the hotel video booking log have to be updated, showing which film copies have been allocated to each hotel for each week. Revenue is calculated from these logs, however, billing is not within the remit of the investigation.

Structured systems analysis and design method (SSADM)

CAROLINE M ASHWORTH

Abstract: The structured systems analysis and design method (SSADM) is the standard structured method used for computer projects in UK government departments. It is also being adopted as a standard by various other bodies. Responsibility for SSADM belongs to the Central Computer and Telecommunications Agency (CCTA), HM Treasury although support and training may be acquired through commercial organizations.

SSADM has certain underlying principles and consists of six stages which are broken down into a number of steps and tasks. Within this framework, a number of structured techniques are used and documents produced.

SSADM may be compared with methods that use some of the same techniques. Two other methods (Yourdon and Arthur Young's Information Engineering) are briefly described and some comparisons drawn with SSADM.

Keywords: systems analysis, methodologies, information systems, JSP, quality assurance.

In 1980 the UK Government initiated a lengthy procedure to select a structured method to be the standard throughout all computer projects in UK government departments. Most of the better-known structured methods were considered, but the method selected was put together specifically for the purpose by UK consultancy, Learmonth and Burchett Management Systems (LBMS). This method was seen to integrate several relatively mature structured techniques (and a newer technique) into a clear procedural framework leading from the analysis of the current system through to the physical design of the new system. After an initial hand-over period, the Central Computer and Telecommunications Agency (CCTA), HM Treasury is now the design authority. It has recently applied to register SSADM as a certification trademark.

Since its introduction in 1981, the use of SSADM has grown to the extent that in 1987 more than 600 government projects are estimated to have used or are using SSADM. SSADM has also been adopted as a standard by public utilities, local government, health authorities, foreign governments and several large

Scicon Ltd, Wavendon Tower, Wavendon, Milton Keynes, Bucks MK17 8LX, UK

private sector organizations. SSADM is now widely available outside the Government. The National Computing Centre (NCC) has a collaborative agreement with the CCTA for the development and administration of SSADM and publishes the official reference manual[1]. The method is also described in a recently published book by Downs, Clare and Coe[2].

The experience from the many government projects has been channelled back into the development of the method through several mechanisms including:

- SSADM user group
- SSADM consultants from the CCTA who support projects
- private sector organizations
- NCC

The current version in use is the third since the introduction of the method. As a result of the experience in use, together with the mechanisms for using this experience in developing and enhancing the method, SSADM can claim to be one of the most mature methods in use in the UK.

SSADM was initially designed to be used in conjunction with two other UK government standards, the Prompt project management and control methodology[3] and structured design method (SDM), a version of Jackson structured programming[4]. The method also works in the context of fourth generation technology and it is now used extensively with a variety of application generators.

BASIC PRINCIPLES

The basic principles of SSADM are shared, to a varying degree, by many of the modern structured methods of systems analysis and design. These principles underpin the whole development life cycle and should be referred to when proposing to tailor the method for specific project circumstances.

Data-driven

All application systems have an underlying, generic data structure which changes little over time, although processing requirements may change. Within SSADM, it is a central principle that this underlying data structure is developed from an early stage, checked

Reprinted from *Information and Software Technology*, Vol. 30, No. 3, Apr. 1988, C. Ashworth, "Structured System Analysis and Design Method (SSADM)," pp. 153–163, 1988, with kind permission from Elsevier Science–NL, Sara Burgerhartstraat 25; 1055 KV Amsterdam, The Netherlands.

against the processing and reporting requirements and finally built into the system's architecture.

Differentiation between logical and physical

SSADM separates logical design from physical design. A hardware/software independent logical design is produced which can be translated into an initial physical design. This helps the developers to address one problem at a time and prevents unnecessary constraints being added at too early a stage in development. This also helps communication with users who may not be computer literate but are able to validate a logical specification or design of their system.

Different views of the system

Three different views of the system are developed in analysis. These views are closely related to one another and are cross-checked for consistency and completeness. The equal weight given to these three techniques and the prescriptive procedures for checking them against one another is a strength of the SSADM approach. The views are:

- underlying structure of the system's data (the logical data structure),
- how data flows into and out of the system and is transformed within the system (data flow diagrams),
- how the system data is changed by events over time (entity life histories).

Top-down and bottom-up

SSADM contains elements of both top-down and bottom-up approaches. In the early stages of a project, top-down techniques such as data flow diagramming and logical data structuring are used. In the logical design stage bottom-up techniques such as relational data analysis are used to provide more of the detail and then reconciled with the top-down views to produce a validated logical design.

User involvement

It is considered important that end users have involvement in, and commitment to, the development of the system from an early stage. By ensuring that the specification and design match the user's requirements at each stage, the risk of producing the 'wrong' system is reduced and the possible problems can be solved before they become unmanageable.

User involvement is encouraged by the use of easily understood, non-technical diagrammatic techniques supported by short, simple narrative descriptions. Users participate in formal quality assurance reviews and informal 'walkthroughs' and should 'sign off' each stage before the developers progress to the next.

As the techniques of SSADM do not require skill in computer systems, it has been found that an ideal situation is one in which a user representative works full-time within the development team. This provides a constant supply of knowledge about the system and provides a bridge between the developers and users.

Quality assurance

The use of informal quality assurance reviews and walkthroughs is encouraged throughout the method. Formal quality assurance reviews are held at the end of each SSADM stage. The end products for the stage are scrutinized for quality, completeness, consistency and applicability by users, developers and experienced systems staff external to the project. Each stage can therefore be signed off to act as a baseline for the subsequent stage.

Self documenting

The products of each SSADM step form the project documentation and are used in subsequent steps. It becomes important that the documentation is completed at the relevant time within the project instead of being left until the project is complete, as often happens when timescales are short. This ensures that the documentation is up-to-date at all times.

OVERVIEW OF SSADM

The structured techniques fit into a framework of steps and stages, each with defined inputs and outputs. Also, there are a number of forms and documents that are specified which add information to that held within the diagrams. Thus, SSADM consists of three features of equal importance:

- structure of the method,
- structured techniques and their interrelationship,
- documents and forms produced.

Structure of the method

Figure 1 shows the stages of an SSADM project. Each stage is broken down into a number of steps which define inputs, outputs and tasks to be performed. The products of each step and the interfaces between steps are clearly defined in the SSADM documentation[1].

The structure of the method illustrates several features of the SSADM approach. First, the current system, in its current implementation, is studied to gain an understanding of the environment of the new system. This view of the current system is used to build the specification of the required system. However, the required system is not constrained by the way in which the current system is implemented. The specification of requirements is detailed to the extent that detailed technical options can be formulated. The detailed design is completed at the logical level before implementation issues are addressed. Finally, the logical design is converted into physical design by the

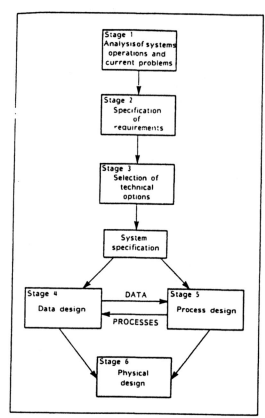

Figure 1. Stages of SSADM

application of simple (first cut) rules. The resulting design is tuned using the technique of physical design control before implementation. The breakdown of each stage into constituent steps is shown at annex A at the end of this paper.

Stage one: Analysis system operation and current problems

The current system is investigated for several reasons, for example, the analysts learn the terminology and function of the users' environment. The data required by the system can be investigated. The current system provides the users with a good introduction to the techniques and the boundaries of the investigation can be clearly set.

The second reason illustrates one of the principles of SSADM that the underlying structure of the data of a system will not change much over time. Even though the introduction of a new computer system may change the functions (a computer system can increase what can be tackled by users), the underlying data required to perform the functions will not change much. If there is no current system, for example where there is a new law that requires support, this stage consists of initiating the project and beginning to document the new requirements.

Stage two: Specification of requirements

In order that the new system will not be constrained by the current implementation, there are a number of steps within this stage to gradually lead the analysts away from the current system towards a fresh view of the requirements.

First, the current system view built up in stage one is redrawn to extract what the system does without any indication of how this is achieved. The resulting picture is the logical view of the current system. This allows the analyst to concentrate on what functions are performed in the current system and to make decisions about what must be included in the new system.

The current system is surpassed by the business system options (BSOs) which are completed next. The BSOs express the requirements in a number of different ways to reflect the different ways in which the system might be organized. These are not implementation decisions, although they may constrain the way the system is implemented. Instead, this is a way of taking a fresh view of what the system is required to do and how the business can be organized to make the best use of the system. Based upon the selected business system option, a detailed specification of the required system is built up and checked extensively.

Stage three: Selection of technical options

At this stage, if the purchase of new computer equipment is required, the development team have enough information to compile the different implementation options for the system. Each option costed out and the benefits weighed against the costs to help the user choose the final solution. This might form the basis for competitive tendering for the final system hardware.

Stage four: Logical data design

This stage builds up the logical data design so that all the required data will be included. It applies a relational analysis technique to groups of data items in the system to act as a cross-check on the data definition built up in stage two. The final data design is checked against the logical processes, developed in stage five, to ensure that all the data needed by the processes is present in the data design.

Stage five: Logical process design

The definition developed in stage two is expanded to a low level of detail so that the implementor can be given the detail necessary to build the system. This processing definition is checked against the data definitions derived in stage four.

Stage six: Physical design

The complete logical design, both data and processing, is converted into a design that will run on the target environment. The initial physical design is tuned on paper before being implemented so that it will meet the performance requirements of the system. In this stage, much of the documentation required during the system implementation is produced. The implementation of the system takes place, traditionally, after this stage when the detailed program specifications are used as the basis for program design and coding, possibly using a program design method such as Jackson structured programming[4].

Structured techniques

The techniques of SSADM give standards for how each step and task is to be performed. The rules of the syntax and notation of each technique are supplemented with guidelines on how it should be applied in a particular step. The diagrammatic techniques of SSADM are data flow diagrams, logical data structuring, entity life histories and logical dialogue design. In addition, there are techniques and procedures that are not diagrammatic including:

- relational data analysis (TNF)
- first cut rules
- physical design control
- quality assurance reviewing
- project estimating

The SSADM reference material gives clear guidelines on each of the techniques and, more importantly, shows how they are interrelated and can be used to cross-check one another. The principal diagrammatic techniques and procedures are described in more detail below.

a. Logical data structure (LDS)

This is a method for describing what information should be held by the system. The approach used in SSADM is similar to entity modelling in other methods. A diagram is produced showing the entities and their relationships, this is further documented by a set of entity description forms detailing their data contents.

A logical data structure (LDS) is produced for the current system. This is extended to meet the requirements of the new system, resulting in a required system LDS. This LDS becomes the composite logical data design (CLDD) by comparison with the results of relational data analysis. The CLDD is used as the basis for the physical data design.

The major conventions of LDSs are summarized in Figure 2. These conventions are the same for the CLDD.

An entity can be thought of as either a 'thing' of significance to the system about which information will be held or a group of related data items that can be uniquely identified by a key. Which view predominates is influenced by the way in which the logical data structures are built up within SSADM; the former view is adopted when starting the whole process in Stage one and gradually the latter view is adopted so that by the time the composite logical data design is completed, the structure is thought of as 'system data'.

A relationship is a logical association between two entities. Within SSADM, only one-to-many relationships are permitted (one-to-one relationships are resolved by merging the entities and many-to-many relationships are resolved by inserting a 'link' entity). The 'crow's foot' indicates the 'many' end of the relationship. The relationships are validated by checking the assertions that, for example, an instance of 'overdrawn status' is related to many instances of 'customer' and that an instance of 'customer' will always be related to one, and only one, instance of 'overdrawn status'. If it is possible that 'customer' could exist without 'overdrawn status', then this relationship becomes optional, indicated by a small circle on the relationship. In Figure 2 the exclusive notation for relationships is illustrated, showing that instances of the two relationships to 'personal customer' and 'company' will never exist concurrently for the same 'bank account' entity.

b. Data flow diagrams (DFDs)

A data flow diagram[5,10] is a diagrammatic representation of the information flows within a system, showing how information enters and leaves the system; what changes the information; and where information is stored. Data flow diagrams are an important technique of systems analysis as a means of *boundary definition*. The diagrams clearly show the boundaries and scope of the system being represented. They also *check the completeness of analysis*. The construction of the diagrams, and their cross-comparison with the other major SSADM techniques, help ensure that all information flows, stores of information and activities within the system have been considered. DFDs denote the major functional areas of the system, and therefore the programs or program suites required. They may be

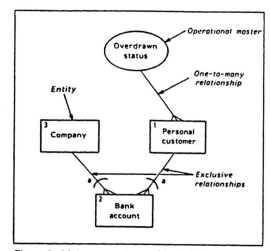

Figure 2. Major conventions of logical data structures

173

used to represent a physical system or a logical abstraction of a system.

In SSADM four sets of data flow diagrams are developed. First, the current physical. The current system is modelled in its present implementation. Second, the logical. The purely logical representation of the current system is extracted from the current physical DFDs. Third, the business system options. Several proposed designs are developed, each satisfying the requirements of the new system. Each of these is expressed as an overview, known as a business system option. Fourth, using the selected business system option and the logical data flow diagrams, a full set of data flow diagrams representing the new system is developed. The relationship between the different sets of data flow diagrams is represnted in Figure 3. The conventions of DFDs are illustrated in Figure 4.

External entities are sources or recipients of data, processes transform the data within the system and data stores are repositories of information. Data stores are closely related to entities on the logical data structure.

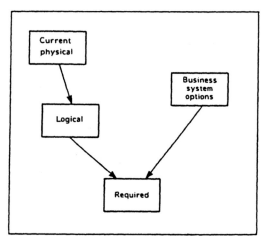

Figure 3. Data flow diagrams in SSADM

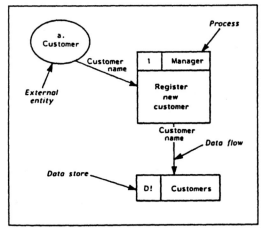

Figure 4. Conventions of data flow diagrams

Each process can be decomposed into a lower level data flow diagram, successively adding detail through each level.

c. Entity life histories (ELHs)

These are models of how the system's data is changed over time by events acting on entities. For each entity the sequence, selection and iteration of events affecting it are shown using a notation derived from Jackson[4].

An event is whatever triggers a process to update system data. As it would be too complicated to model the entire set of events for a whole system at once, the effects of the events upon each entity from the logical data structure are modelled. These individual views of the event sequences are drawn together in an entity/event matrix (ELH matrix) and process outlines. The major conventions of the entity life history technique are shown in Figure 5. The state indicators are a re-expression of the structure of the entity life history and may be used in validation in the implemented system.

d. Logical dialogue outlines

Logical dialogue outlines were introduced in version three of SSADM to allow developers to specify requirements for man-machine dialogues at an early stage in the development. The prototyping of dialogues using a screen painter, or similar rapid development software, to demonstrate the man-machine interface to users is obviously more effective in the specification of user requirements for dialogues, so dialogue outlines are designed to be used generally where prototyping

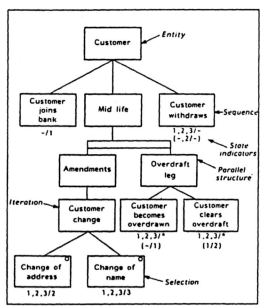

Figure 5. Major conventions of the entity life history technique

facilities are not available. A logical dialogue outline is produced for each non-trivial online event or enquiry identified during analysis. Thus, this technique is used towards the end of requirements definition in stage two. The data items flowing across the man-machine boundary are detailed, the sequence of logical 'screens' and an overview of the processing done to satisfy the dialogue are modelled using a flow-chart style notation. It is also possible to add the requirements for the time taken at each stage of the dialogue, points at which users will be required to make decisions, an indication of some messages that might be used and a cross-reference to operations on process outlines. An extract from a simple logical dialogue outline is shown in Figure 6. It is possible to create 'levels' by reflecting the context of one or more logical dialogue outlines on a higher-level outline called a logical dialogue control.

e. Relational data analysis (TNF)

Relational data analysis, based upon Codd's aproach[6], is used in the logical design stage of SSADM (Stage four) where it complements the logical data structuring done during requirements analysis. The merging of the two techniques results in the composite logical data design (CLDD) which is the basis for the physical database or file design.

Any collection of data items that have been defined without direct reference to the logical data structure can be used as an input to relational data analysis or normalization. Commonly, the input/output descriptions or screen definitions are used as inputs to this technique.

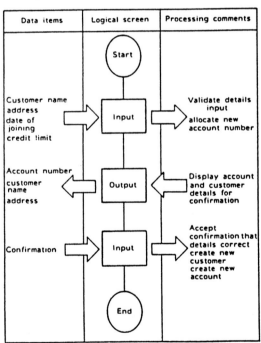

Figure 6. Example logical dialogue outline

Normalization consists of a progression from the original, unnormalized, data through several refinements (normal forms) until the data items are arranged to eliminate any repeating items or duplication. The results of performing this analysis on several different groups of data items are merged or optimized to give sets of data items that should correspond to the entities on the logical data structure. At this point, the logical data structure is merged with the results of the normalization.

The process of relational data analysis ensures that all data items required by the system are included in the system's data structure. Also, it is a good way to ensure that the data is fully understood. Although the rules of normalization appear to be mechanical, to apply them effectively the underlying relationships between data items must be well understood.

f. First cut rules and physical design control

The conversion of the logical process and data design into a workable physical design takes place in two phases. First, simple rules are applied which roughly convert the logical design into a corresponding design for the target environment. This design might work, but would probably not be efficient or exploit the features of the particular hardware or software that will be used. Therefore, the 'first cut' design is tuned using a process called physical design control. This consists of successively calculating the time taken to execute certain critical transactions, modifying the design slightly and recalculating until the performance objectives (defined in stage three) are met.

g. Quality assurance reviewing

SSADM places emphasis on holding formal quality assurance reviews at the end of each stage. It is important to ensure that the products from each stage are technically correct and that they meet the objectives of the users. The work for the second stage of SSADM has its foundations in the work done in the first stage. This principle applies throughout the project: each stage builds on the work done in the previous stage. There is a high risk that all subsequent work will be poor if the foundations are poor.

A formal sign-off by a group consisting principally of users emphasizes the joint responsibility for the project of both the users and the project team. This ensures the ongoing active interest of the users in the project and avoids the situation commonly encountered in systems analysis and design where communication between the project team and the users is minimal during the development phase leading to the implemented system not meeting the users' requirements.

Products from each stage should be reviewed by a team comprising responsible users who will have the authority to authorize the continuation of the project and at least one person with a good understanding of SSADM who will be referred to here as the 'technical reviewer'. This should be done on a formal basis to force the correction of errors identified by the reviewers before work is allowed to proceed to the subsequent stages.

The following procedures are an example of how quality assurance reviewing is undertaken within SSADM.

Before the review

All participants receive an invitation to the review meeting one week in advance of the meeting, together with a copy of all the documents they will be required to review. If any of the reviewers is unfamiliar with the conventions of the diagrams, then the analysts might arrange to explain the aspects of the diagrams that are relevant to a reviewer. This can be done on a one-to-one basis but can be achieved more efficiently when a number of people are involved. This is done by organizing a presentation to state the purpose and basic conventions of the diagrams with a more general discussion about quality assurance review procedures.

The review meeting

The actual review would not be more than one to two hours long. The chairman is either a user who has been closely involved with the project or the project team manager. The meeting should not attempt to solve the difficulties that might arise but should highlight errors for subsequent resolution away from the meeting. An analyst from the project team walks through the documentation being reviewed and invites comments from the reviewers. A list of errors is compiled by the chairman and agreed by the meeting. The reviewers may decide that the documentation contains no errors and meets its objectives in which case will sign the stage off at this meeting. More commonly, there will be a number of non-critical errors detected in which case the documentation may be signed off provided that certain follow-up action is taken and subsequently agreed by the reviewers out of the meeting. If there are numerous errors and the reviewers are not confident that the project team has met the objectives of the stage, then a date for another quality assurance review is set and the documentation failed.

After the review

Any necessary corrections are made to the documentation within a week of the review and circulated to the members of the review team. If the errors are only minor, the reviewers may sign it off individually. If the errors are more severe, the documentation is reviewed a second time at another review meeting.

The resources required to hold a quality assurance review are significant and should not be underestimated when the project plan is being prepared. At least three elapsed weeks should be allowed for each formal review and one to two weeks for informal reviews. It is a temptation to cut this time when project timescales are tight. But compared to the weeks or months that might be wasted later in the project on trying to sort out compounded errors arising from poor quality assurance, it is time well spent.

h. Project estimating

Project estimating guidelines have been developed from experience and may be made available to project managers. They are based upon the techniques, steps and stages of SSADM. Certain factors will make timescales longer or shorter, for example the number of user areas and the complexity of the project. The estimating guidelines are applied after an initial data flow diagram and logical data structure have been drawn. The number of processes and entities on these initial diagrams give an indication of the number of diagrams that will be completed throughout the project. The results of the estimating guidelines are refined throughout the project. The estimates produced at the beginning of a project will not be accurate but will give some idea of the order of magnitude of a project.

Documents and forms

Documentation standards define how the products of this development activity should be presented. The forms are either supporting detail of the techniques or additional non-diagrammatic information. In the former category are entity descriptions and elementary function descriptions; in the latter category are the problems/requirements list and function catalogues.

In addition to forms, there are several working documents, principally matrices, which are used to help the start-up to some of the techniques. An entity matrix is used to identify relationships between entities as an initial step in the logical data structuring techniques and an entity-event (ELH) matrix is used as a basis for entity life histories.

One of the most central documents in the analysis stages of SSADM is the problem/requirement list. It is used as a checklist of all the factors that must be accounted for in the new system and can be used to measure the success of a project by checking that all the problems and requirements have a corresponding solution.

It is tempting for the analyst to accept a user requirement written by the users without any additional analysis work. Experience has shown that a statement of requirements produced by users will often include detail such as 'I need a terminal linked to a central mainframe' rather than 'I need my data to be up-to-date at all times and I will need to be able to access the data during the hours of nine to five'. It is the analyst's responsibility to make sure that the requirements and problems are stated in logical terms. It is important to have this logical statement of requirements so that the final solution does not become constrained. It must be left to the systems analyst/designer to specify the best solution to fit the users requirements not allowing the user's preconceptions to be carried through to an ill-judged implementation.

The problem/requirement list is initiated in stage one, the survey of the current system. During the analysis of requirements, the problem/requirement list is expanded to include design constraints and requirements for the system auditing, controls and security.

AUTOMATED SUPPORT FOR SSADM

One of the principle features required of the method chosen to become SSADM was that it was designed to be supported by automated support tools. A simple database tool was introduced by the CCTA soon after the introduction of the method to act as a prototype for future support tools. From experience of the use of this tool together with other tools, such as CAD and word-processing software, it was possible to define the desirable features of a software tool to support SSADM. Some of these features are summarized here, in no particular sequence:

- automatic production of documentation,
- assistance in creating and amending SSADM diagrams,
- enforcement of diagram syntax,
- enforcement and help with the rules of the method,
- consistency and completeness checking,
- traceability of specification through to logical and physical design,
- automatic generation of elements of the design,
- presentation of the information in different formats and combinations,
- integration of diagram information with data dictionary information.

There are several software tools to support SSADM and there is a growing number of other tools that can be used to support aspects of SSADM. These other tools are either designed to support other similar methods or are tailorable to a number of different methods including SSADM. They provide varying support to such techniques as data flow diagramming, entity modelling, functional decomposition, relational data analysis, action diagramming and database design. Some provide generation of database definitions and program code. These tools are generally single user, running on IBM PC/AT or compatible hardware, although some multiuser tools are becoming available.

TRENDS IN DEVELOPMENT

Developments in the area of SSADM are driven principally by user experience (ease of use) and the need for automation. Advanced state-of-the-art ideas must also always be considered to ensure better techniques are not ignored. The whole method must remain consistent through any changes made and, being a government standard method, fit in with other standards that have been set.

User experience

Some SSADM projects often develop their own interpretation of the ways in which techniques can be used successfully in their particular environment. Occasionally, these local practices can have wider applicability and developers of SSADM have been keen to introduce well-tried new ideas that have been shown to be beneficial in practice. As well as developing new practices, projects have introduced new forms or pointed out gaps in the method where inadequacies have become apparent.

It is important to take this type of experience into account because it is wasteful for different projects to start again from the beginning when an improvement is required. The benefits of standardization should not be diluted by too many local variants.

An example of a development introduced as a result of user experience is the logical dialogue design element of SSADM. Several different projects perceived a need to be able to model human-computer interactions in the analysis stage of the method and were inventing their own approaches. The experiences gained as a result of this were integrated into SSADM after several pilot uses of the techniques in projects.

The need for automation

It is generally considered to be a fact that methods will become more automated as the technology of software tools increases. The trend towards automation will determine the competitiveness of methods in the future. Methods will be determined by the tools available to support them. Eventually, the method and tool will become synonymous and the manual structured methods will fall into disuse. This means that the development of SSADM must always take into account whether particular ideas will be readily automated or whether they will make automation more difficult. This consideration is often in direct opposition to the wish to enhance the usability of the manual method as it stands currently. If a technique has strict rules of syntax associated with it, the manual use of it will seem arduous; however, a software tool needs to have a large number of such rules defined in order to give the best possible support for the technique.

As a move towards automation, the CCTA commissioned a detailed entity model of SSADM. The production of this model meant that many definitions had to be made tighter and rules had to take the place of guidelines.

COMPARISON WITH OTHER METHODS

SSADM is most readily compared with other methods that employ data flow diagrams as a major technique of analysis and design. These include the Yourdon method[7] and Arthur Young's information engineering method[8]. A brief overview of these methods and a comparison with SSADM follow.

Yourdon method

The Yourdon method is based upon the approach of DeMarco[5]. Data flow diagrams are used to build a number of models of the system required. A logical (essential) view of the required system is developed supported by an entity-relationship diagram, a data dictionary and process descriptions. An implementation-dependent view (implementation model) is developed from the logical diagram by assigning processes to processors and showing how the system will be organized. The data flow diagrams are developed down to a low level of detail. The bottom-level processes that constitute a program or module are drawn together into a program structure which becomes the program design. In addition, certain extensions have been added to the basic notation to cope with realtime control aspects of systems. A controlling process which enables, disables and triggers the transformation processes may be represented by state transition diagrams which form the basis for design. The entity-relationship diagrams are used as the basis for database design.

The main different between the Yourdon method and SSADM is that there is no structure of steps, stages and deliverables and detailed task lists defined in the Yourdon method. A sequence is implied by the way in which each model is developed but it is left to the developer to build project management and review procedures around the techniques.

Another difference is in the approach to process design. In the Yourdon method, the design is derived through successive decomposition of the data flow diagrams. Each bottom-level process is described by a detailed process description or mini-spec. In SSADM, the data flow diagrams are used mostly in the requirements specification; the process definition is taken through to design using the events identified from entity life histories: each event is expanded by a process outline which is subsequently converted into a program specification.

SSADM emphasizes the fact that three different views of the system are developed and compared in analysis whereas the principal technique that is used throughout the Yourdon method is data flow diagramming. The entity-relationship diagram developed in the Yourdon method is not given as much emphasis as the data flow diagrams. The Yourdon data dictionary is defined in terms of the contents of data flows and data stores whereas in SSADM the data is defined with reference to the logical data structure.

Arthur Young information engineering method (AY-IEM)

Arthur Young information engineering method (AY-IEM)[8] is based upon the concepts described by James Martin[9]. Within this basic framework, Arthur Young have developed a detailed method which requires the use of their software tool, information engineering workbench (IEW), to implement the concepts fully.

The method consists of a number of steps and stages leading from strategy to construction. Emphasis is placed upon the data model as the foundation for good system design. The data model developed is similar to the logical data structure of SSADM. Data flow diagrams are fully integrated with the data model. The data flow diagrams are also cross-referenced to a function decomposition diagram which effectively summarizes the hierarchy of processes within the data flow diagrams. The detail of processing is defined in terms of action diagrams.

Both AY information engineering and SSADM contain steps and stages. SSADM has detailed task lists with define inputs, outputs and activities whereas AY information engineering concentrates upon stressing the aims and objectives of each step and stage, leaving more freedom to choose the most appropriate way of achieving the objectives. Information engineering concentrates more upon providing a set of techniques and tools, together with a project framework and allowing the developer to decide upon the best way of combining them to meet the objectives. This means that there are no specified inputs and outputs of steps and no forms to fill in. The central database, or encyclopoedia, of the tools contains all the necessary information to support the developer.

Other differences between the two methods include the fact that SSADM uses a third view in analysis provided by the entity life history technique and information engineering has action diagrams and structure charts to define the structure of the processes.

CONCLUSION

SSADM has been used in a large number of projects principally in the area of government data processing systems. Several of the larger projects are now live and their implementation was considered to be a success. Experience shows that the method has improved the quality of systems analysis and design. The role of a central group in introducing, promoting, controlling and supporting SSADM has been a major contributor in ensuring its success.

References

1 Longworth, G and Nichols, D *The SSADM Manual* National Computer Centre, Manchester, UK (1987)
2 Downs, Clare and Coe *Structured Systems Analysis and Design Method – Application and Context* Prentice-Hall, (1988)
3 Yeates, D *Systems Project Management* Pitman Publishing Ltd, London, UK (1986)
4 Jackson, M A *Principles of Program Design* Academic Press, London, UK (1975)

5 **DeMarco, T** *Structured Analysis and System Specification* Prentice-Hall, Englewood Cliffs, NJ, USA (1979)

6 **Codd, E R** 'A relational model of data for large shared data banks' *Commun. ACM* Vol 13 No 6 (June 1970) pp 377–387

7 *Yourdon Method*, Yourdon Europe, 15–17 Ridgmount Street London WC1 7BH, UK

8 *Arthur Young Information Engineering Method*, Arthur Young, Rolls House, 7 Rolls Buildings, Fetter Lane, London EC4A 1NH, UK

9 **Martin, J** 'Information Engineering' Savant Research Studies, 2 New Street, Carnforth, Lancs LA5 9BX, UK (1986)

10 **Gane, C and Sarson, T** *Structured Systems Analysis: Tools and Techniques* Prentice-Hall Englewood Cliffs, NJ, USA (1979)

□

Annex A

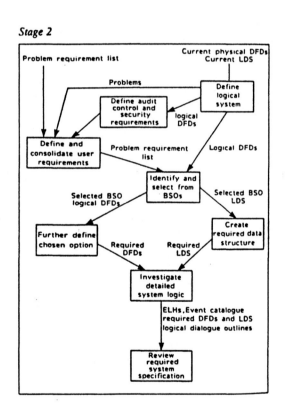

Stage 1

Stage 2

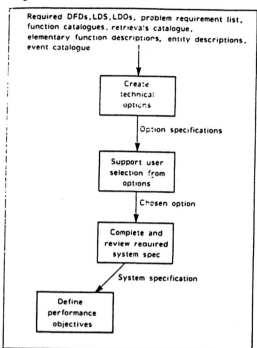

Required DFDs, LDS, LDOs, problem requirement list, function catalogues, retrievals catalogue, elementary function descriptions, entity descriptions, event catalogue

Create technical options

Option specifications

Support user selection from options

Chosen option

Complete and review required system spec

System specification

Define performance objectives

Stage 6

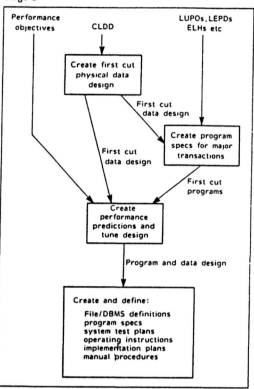

Performance objectives

CLDD

LUPOs, LEPDs ELHs etc

Create first cut physical data design

First cut data design

First cut data design

Create program specs for major transactions

First cut programs

Create performance predictions and tune design

Program and data design

Create and define:

File/DBMS definitions
program specs
system test plans
operating instructions
implementation plans
manual procedures

Stage 4 *Stage 5*

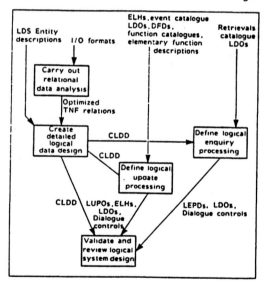

LDS Entity descriptions

I/O formats

ELHs, event catalogue LDOs, DFDs, function catalogues, elementary function descriptions

Retrievals catalogue LDOs

Carry out relational data analysis

Optimized TNF relations

Create detailed logical data design

CLDD

Define logical enquiry processing

CLDD

Define logical update processing

CLDD LUPOs, ELHs, LDOs, Dialogue controls

LEPDs, LDOs, Dialogue controls

Validate and review logical system design

180

A Review of Formal Methods

Prepared for:
Rome Laboratory
RL/C3C
Griffiss AFB, NY 13441-5700

Prepared by:
Robert Vienneau
Kaman Sciences Corporation
258 Genesee Street
Utica, New York 13502-4627

Introduction

The seventies witnessed the structured programming revolution. After much debate, software engineers became convinced that better programs result from following certain precepts in program design. Recent imperative programming languages provide constructs supporting structured programming. Achieving this consensus did not end debate over programming methodology. Quite the contrary, a period of continuous change began, with views on the best methods of software development mutating frequently. Top-down development, modular decomposition, data abstraction, and, most recently, object oriented design are some of the jargon terms that have arisen to describe new concepts for developing large software systems. Both researchers and practitioners have found it difficult to keep up with this onslaught of new methodologies.

There is a set of core ideas that lies at the base of these changes. Formal methods have provided a unifying philosophy and central foundation upon which these methodologies have been built. Those who understand this underlying philosophy can more easily adopt these and other programming techniques. This report provides the needed understanding of formal methods to guide a software manager in evaluating claims related to new methodologies. It also provides an overview for the software engineer and a guide to the literature. Ample examples are provided to fully convey the flavor of using formal methods.

The underlying philosophy for formal methods has not changed in over two decades. Nevertheless, this approach is a revolutionary paradigm shift from conventional notions about computer programming. Many software engineers have adopted the new methodologies that grew out of this work without understanding or even being aware of the root concepts.

The traditional notion of programming looks at the software engineer's task as the development of code to instruct a physically existing machine to compute a desired result. Existing computers possess many idiosyncrasies reflecting hardware engineering concerns. Likewise user interfaces and the desired function can be expected to introduce additional complexities. In the traditional view of programming, these details can be expected to appear in a design, or even a specification, at all levels of abstraction. The engineer's job is seen as the introduction of more details and tricks to get the utmost in speed and performance out of computers. Since software development is therefore a "cut and fit" process, such complex systems can be expected to be full of bugs. A careful testing process is seen as the means of detecting and removing these bugs.

The mindset behind formal methods is directly opposite to the traditional view. It is the job of the hardware engineer, language designer, and compiler writer to provide a machine for executing code, not the reverse:

> Originally I viewed it as the function of the abstract machine to provide a truthful picture of the physical reality. Later, however, I learned to consider the abstract machine as the 'true' one, because that is the only one we can "think" it is the physical machine's purpose to supply "a working model," a (hopefully!) sufficiently accurate physical simulation of the true, abstract machine...It used to be the program's purpose to instruct our computers; it became the computer's purpose to execute our programs. [Dijkstra 76]

The software engineer's task is to produce several models or descriptions of a system for an abstract machine, with accompanying proofs that models at lower levels of abstraction correctly implement higher-level models. Only this design process can ensure high levels of quality, not testing. Edsger Dijkstra has asserted that testing can demonstrate the presence of faults, not their absence. Since software engineers must be able to read and reason about designs, implementation details must be prevented from influencing the expression of designs as long as possible. A separation of concerns exists here, and if microefficiency concerns are allowed to dominate, produced code will reflect a design that cannot be convincingly demonstrated correct by anyone.

The contrast between these views is controversial (for example, see the discussion engendered in the ACM Forum by [DeMillo 79], [Fetzer 88], [Dijkstra 89], or [Gries 91]). Advocates of formal methods argue that many have adopted structured programming and top-down development without really understanding the underlying formalism [Mills 86]. A concern with formal methods can produce more rigorous specifications, even if they are expressed in English [Meyer 85]. Designs and code will be easier to reason about, even if fully formal proofs are never constructed. Critics focus on the difficulties in scaling up to large systems, the impracticalities of formalizing many inherently complex aspects of systems (for example, user interactions and error-checking code), and the radical retraining needed for the large population of already existing software engineers.

This report's purpose is not to advocate one or another position on formal methods. Rather, it overviews the technical basis for formal methods, while critically noting weaknesses. Polemics are avoided, but enough information is reviewed to allow the reader to form an informed judgment on formal methods. Formal methods are beginning to see more widespread industrial use, especially in Europe. Their use is characteristic of organizations with a Defined (Level 3) process or better, as specified in the process maturity framework developed by the Software Engineering Institute [Humphrey 88]. Formal methods have the potential of engendering further revolutionary changes in practice and have provided the underlying basis of past changes. These reasons make it imperative that software managers and engineers be aware of the increasingly widespread debate over formal methods.

Definition and Overview of Formal Methods

Wide and narrow definitions of formal methods can be found in the literature. For example, Nancy Leveson states:

A broad view of formal methods includes all applications of (primarily) discrete mathematics to software engineering problems. This application usually involves modeling and analysis where the models and analysis procedures are derived from or defined by an underlying mathematically- precise foundation. [Leveson 90]

A more narrow definition, however, better conveys the change in practice recommended by advocates of formal methods. The definition offered here is based on that in [Wing 90], and has two essential components. First, formal methods involve the essential use of a formal language. A formal language is a set of strings over some well-defined alphabet. Rules are given for distinguishing those strings, defined over the alphabet, that belong to the language from strings that do not.

Second, formal methods in software support formal reasoning about formulae in the language. These methods of reasoning are exemplified by formal proofs. A proof begins with a set of axioms, which are to be taken as statements postulated to be true. Inference rules state that if certain formulas, known as premises, are derivable from the axioms, then another formula, known as the consequent, is also derivable. A set of inference rules must be given in each formal method. A proof consists of a sequence of well-defined formulae in the language in which each formula is either an axiom or derivable by an inference rule from previous formulae in the sequence. The last axiom in the sequence is said to be proven. The following definition summarizes the above discussion:

A formal method in software development is a method that provides a formal language for describing a software artifact (for instance, specifications, designs, or source code) such that formal proofs are possible, in principle, about properties of the artifact so expressed.

Often, the property proven is that an implementation is functionally correct, that is, it fulfills its specification. Thus, either the formal language associated with a method permits a system to be described by at least two levels of abstraction or two languages are provided for describing a specification and its implementation. The method provides tools with which an implementation can be proven to satisfy a specification. To be practically useful, the method should also provide heuristics and guidelines for developing elegant specifications and for developing implementations and proofs in parallel.

The concept of formalism in formal methods is borrowed from certain trends in 19th and 20th century mathematics. The development of consistent non-Euclidean geometries, in which supposedly parallel lines may intersect, led mathematicians to question their methods of proof and to search for more rigorous foundations. Eventually, these foundations came to be seen as describing numbers, sets, and logic. Leading mathematicians in this movement included Karl Weierstrass, Gottlob Frege, Giuseppe Peano, and David Hilbert. By the turn of the century, a foundation seemed to be in place, but certain strange examples and antinomies caused mathematicians to question the security of their foundations and even their own intuition on fundamental matters. A mechanical method of manipulating symbols was thus invented to investigate these questions. Due to fundamental discoveries of Kurt Godel, Thoralf Skolem, and Leopold Lowenheim, the results of using this method were ambiguous. Nevertheless, the axiomatic method became widely used in advanced mathematics, especially after impetus was added to this tendency by an extremely influential group of French mathematicians writing around World War II under the pseudonym of Nicholas Bourbaki [Kline 80].

Formal methods are merely an adoption of the axiomatic method, as developed by these trends in mathematics, for software engineering. In fact, Edsger Dijkstra has suggested, somewhat tongue-in-cheek, that computer science be renamed Very Large Scale Application of Logic (VLSAL) [Dijkstra 89]. Mastery of formal methods in software requires an understanding of this mathematics background. Mathematical topics of interest include formal logic, both the propositional calculus and predicate logic, set theory, formal languages, and automata such as finite state machines. The full flavor of the relevant mathematics cannot be conveyed here.

Use of Formal Methods

How are the mathematics of formal languages applied in software development? What engineering issues have been addressed by their application? Formal methods are of global concern in software engineering. They are directly applicable during the requirements, design, and coding phases and have important consequences for testing and maintenance. They have influenced the development and standardization of many programming languages, the programmer's most basic tool. They are important in ongoing research that may change standard practice, particularly in the areas of specifications and design methodology. They are entwined with lifecycle models that

may provide an alternative to the waterfall model, namely rapid prototyping, the Cleanroom variant on the spiral model, and "transformational" paradigms.

What Can be Formally Specified

Formal methods support precise and rigorous specifications of those aspects of a computer system capable of being expressed in the language. Since defining what a system should do and understanding the implications of these decisions are the most troublesome problems in software engineering, this use of formal methods has major benefits. In fact, practitioners of formal methods frequently use formal methods solely for recording precise specifications, not for formal verifications ([Hall 90] and [Place 90]).

Some of the most well-known formal methods consist of or include specification languages for recording a system's functionality. These methods include:

- Z (pronounced "Zed")
- Communicating Sequential Processes (CSP)
- Vienna Development Method (VDM)
- Larch
- Formal Development Methodology (FDM).

Formal methods can be used to specify aspects of a system other than functionality. The emphasis of this report is on functionality since such techniques are currently the most well-known, developed, and of general interest. Software safety and security are other areas where formal methods are sometimes applied in practice. The benefits of proving that unsafe states will not arise, or that security will not be violated, can justify the cost of complete formal verifications of the relevant portions of a software system. Formal methods can deal with many other areas of concern to software engineers but, other than in research organizations, have not been much used for dealing with issues unrelated to functionality, safety, and security. Areas in which researchers are exploring formal methods include fault tolerance, response time, space efficiency, reliability, human factors, and software structure dependencies [Wing 90].

Formal methods can include graphical languages. Data Flow Diagrams (DFDs) are the most well-known graphical technique for specifying the function of a system. DFDs can be considered a semi-formal method, and researchers have explored techniques for treating DFDs in a completely formal manner. Petri nets provide another well-known graphical technique, often used in distributed systems [Peterson 77]. Petri nets are a fully formal technique. Finally, finite state machines are often presented in tabular form. This does not decrease the formalism in the use of finite state machines. So the definition of formal methods provided earlier is quite encompassing.

Software engineers produce models and define the properties of systems at several levels of abstraction. Formal methods can be employed at each level. A specification should describe what a system should do, but not how it is done. More details are provided in designs, with the source code providing the most detailed model. For example, Abstract Data Types (ADTs) frequently are employed at intermediate levels of abstraction. ADTs, being mathematical entities, are perfect candidates for formal treatment and are often so treated in the literature.

Formal methods are not confined to the software components of large systems. System engineers frequently use formal methods. Hardware engineers also use formal methods, such as VHSIC Hardware Description Language (VHDL) descriptions, to model integrated circuits before fabricating them.

Reasoning about a Formal Description

Once a formal description of a system has been produced, what can be done with it? Usable formal methods provide a variety of techniques for reasoning about specifications and drawing implications. The completeness and consistency of a specification can be explored. Does a description imply a system should be in several states simultaneously? Do all legal inputs yield one and only one output? What surprising results, perhaps unintended, can be produced by a system? Formal methods provide reasoning techniques to explore these questions.

Do lower level descriptions of a system properly implement higher level descriptions? Formal methods support formal verification, the construction of formal proofs that an implementation satisfies a specification. The possibility of constructing such formal proofs was historically the principle driver in the development of formal methods. Prominent technology for formal verification includes Edsger Dijkstra's "weakest precondition" calculus ([Dijkstra 76] and [Gries 81]) and Harlan Mills' "functional correctness" approach [Linger 79].

Tools and Methodology

Developments in supporting tools and methodologies have accompanied the development of technology for formalizing software products. The basic idea is that the ultimate end-product of development is not solely a working system. Of equal importance are specifications and proofs that the program meets its specification. A proof is very hard to develop after the fact. Consequently, proofs and programs should be developed in parallel, with close interconnections in the development history. Since programs must be proven correct, only those constructions that can be clearly understood should be used. This is the primary motivation that many early partisans had for advocating structured programming.

A challenge is to apply these ideas on large scale projects. Formal specifications seem to scale up much easier than formal verifications. Nevertheless, ideas relating to formal verifications are applicable to projects of any size, particularly if the level of formality is allowed to vary. David Gries recommends a design methodology incorporating certain heuristics that support more reliable and provable designs [Gries 81]. Harlan Mills has spent considerable effort developing the Cleanroom approach, a lifecycle in which formal methods, inspections, and reliability modeling and certification are integrated in a social process for producing software ([Mills 87] and [Dyer 92]).

Formal methods have also inspired the development of many tools. These tools may bring formal methods into more widespread practice, although interestingly enough, many advocates of formal methods are not strong believers in tools. An obvious example of such tools are program provers. Some tools animate specifications, thereby converting a formal specification into an executable prototype of a system. Other tools derive programs from specifications through various automated transformations. Under some approaches a program is found as a solution to an equation in a formal language. Transformational implementation suggests a future in which many software systems are developed without programmers, or at least with more automation, higher productivity, and less labor ([Agresti 86] and [KBSE 92]).

In some sense, no programmer can avoid formal methods, for every programming language is, by definition, a formal language. Ever since Algol 60 was introduced, standards defining programming languages have used a formal notation for defining language syntax, namely Backus-Naur Form (BNF). Usually, standards do not formally define the semantics of programming languages, although, in principle, they could. The convention of using natural language descriptions for defining language semantics is due to not having yet developed settled techniques for defining all constructs included in large languages. Nevertheless, formal methods have resulted in one widely agreed criterion for evaluating language features: how simply can one formally reason about a program with a proposed new feature? The formal specification of language semantics is a lively area of research. In particular, formal methods have always been an interest of the Ada community, even before standardization ([London 77], [McGettrick 82] and [Preston 88]).

Limitations of Formal Methods

Given the applicability of formal methods throughout the lifecycle, and their pervasive possibilities for almost all areas of software engineering, why are they not more widely visible? Part of the problem is educational. Revolutions are not made by conversion, but by the old guard passing away. More recent university graduates tend to be more willing to experiment with formal methods.

On the other hand, the only barrier to the widespread transition of this technology is not lack of knowledge on the part of practitioners. Formal methods do suffer from certain limitations. Some of these limitations are inherent and will never be overcome. Other restrictions, with research and practice, will be removed as formal methods are transitioned into wider use.

The Requirements Problem

The inherent limitations in formal methods are neatly summarized in the oft-repeated aphorism, "You cannot go from the informal to the formal by formal means." In particular, formal methods can prove that an implementation satisfies a formal specification, but they cannot prove that a formal specification captures a user's intuitive informal understanding of a system. In other words, formal methods can be used to verify a system, but not to validate a system. The distinction is that validation shows that a product will satisfy its operational mission, while verification shows that each step in the development satisfies the requirements imposed by previous steps [Boehm 81].

The extent of this limitation should not be underemphasized. One influential field study, [Curtis 88], found that the three most important problems in software development are:

- The thin spread of application domain knowledge
- Changes in and conflicts between requirements
- Communication and coordination problems.

Successful projects were often successful because of the role of one or two key exceptional designers. These designers had a deep understanding of the applications domain and could map the applications requirements to computer science concerns. These findings suggest the reduction of informal application knowledge to a rigorous specification is a key problem area in the development of large systems.

Empirical evidence does suggest, however, that formal methods can make a contribution to the problem of adequately capturing requirements. The discipline of producing a formal specification can result in fewer specification errors. Furthermore, implementors without an exceptional designer's knowledge of the application area commit less errors when implementing a formal specification than when relying on hazy knowledge of the application [Goel 91]. These benefits may exist even when the final specification is expressed in English, not a formal language [Meyer 85]. A specification acts as a "contract" between a user and a developer. The specification describes the system to be delivered. Using specifications written in a formal language to complement natural language descriptions can make this contract more precise. Finally, developers of automated programming environments, which use formal methods, have developed tools to interactively capture a user's informal understanding and thereby develop a formal specification [Zeroual 91].

Still, formal methods can never replace deep application knowledge on the part of the requirements engineer, whether at the system or the software level. The application knowledge of the exceptional designer is not limited to one discipline. For example, an avionics application might require knowledge of flight control, navigation, signal processing, and electronic countermeasures. Whether those drawing on interdisciplinary knowledge in developing specifications come to regard formal methods as just another discipline making their life more complicated, or an approach that allows them to simply, concisely, and accurately record their findings, will only be known with experience and experimentation.

Physical Implementations

The second major gap between the abstractions of formal methods and concrete reality lies in the nature of any actual physically existing computer. Formal methods can verify that an implementation satisfies a specification when run on an idealized abstract machine, but not when run on any physical machine.

Some of the differences between typical idealized machines and physical machines are necessary for humanly-readable correctness proofs. For instance, an abstract machine might be assumed to have an infinite memory, while every actual machine has some upper limit. Similarly, physical machines cannot implement real numbers, as axiomatically described by mathematicians, while proofs are most simply constructed assuming the existence of mathematically precise reals. No reason in principle exists why formal methods cannot incorporate these limitations. The proofs will be much messier and less elegant, and they will be limited to a particular machine.

A limitation in principle, however, does exist here. Formal proofs can show with certainty, subject to mistakes in calculation, that given certain assumptions, a program is a correct implementation of a specification. What cannot be formally shown is that those assumptions are correct descriptions of an actual physical system. A compiler may not correctly implement a language as specified. So a proof of a program in that language will fail to guarantee the execution behavior of the program under that compiler. The compiler may be formally verified, but this only moves the problem to a lower level of abstraction. Memory chips and gates may have bugs. No matter how thoroughly an application is formally verified, at some point one must accept that an actual physical system satisfies the axioms used in a proof. Explanations must come to an end sometime.

Both critics [Fetzer 88] and developers ([Dijkstra 76] and [Linger 79]) of formal methods are quite aware of this limitation, although the critics do not always seem to be aware of the developers' explicit statements on this point. This limitation does not mean formal methods are pointless. Formal proofs explicitly isolate those locations where an error may occur. Errors may arise in providing a machine that implements the abstract machine, with sufficient accuracy and efficiency, upon which proofs are based. Given this implementation, a proof vastly increases confidence in a program [Merrill 83].

Although no prominent advocate of formal methods recommends testing be avoided entirely, it is unclear what role testing can play in increasing confidence in the areas not addressed by formal methods. The areas addressed by testing and formal methods may overlap, depending on the specific methodologies employed. From an abstract point of view, the question of what knowledge or rational belief can be provided by testing is the riddle of the rational basis for induction. How can an observation that some objects of a given type have a certain property ever convince anyone that all objects of that type have the property? Why should a demonstration that a program produces the correct outputs for some inputs ever lead to a belief that the program is likely to produce the correct output for all inputs? If a compiler correctly processes certain programs, as defined by a syntactical and semantic standard, why should one conclude that any semantic axiom in the standard can be relied upon for a formal proof of the correctness of a program not used in testing the compiler? Over two centuries ago, the British philosopher David Hume put related questions at the center of his epistemology.

Two centuries of debate have not reached a consensus on induction. Still, human beings are inclined to draw these conclusions. Software developers exhibit the same inclination in testing computer programs. Formal methods will never entirely supplant testing, nor do advocates intend them to do so. In principle, a gap always exists between physical reality and what can be formally verified. With more widespread use of formal methods, however, the role of testing will change.

Implementation Issues

The gaps between users' intentions and formal specifications and between physical implementations and abstract proofs create inherent limitations to formal methods, no matter how much they may be developed in the future. There are also a host of pragmatic concerns that reflect the current state of the technology.

The introduction of a new technology into a large-scale software organization is not a simple thing, particularly a technology as potentially revolutionary as formal methods. Decisions must be made about whether the technology should be completely or partially adopted. Appropriate accompanying tools need to be acquired. Current personnel need to be retrained, and new personnel may need to be hired. Existing practices need to be modified, perhaps drastically. All of these issues arise with formal methods. Optimal decisions depend on the organization and the techniques for implementing formal methods. Several schemes exist, with various levels of feasibility and impact.

The question arises, however, whether formal methods are yet suitable for full-scale implementation. They are most well-developed for addressing issues of functionality, safety, and security, but even for these mature methods, serious questions exist about their ability to scale up to large applications. In much academic work, a proof of a hundred lines of code was seen as an accomplishment. The applicability of such methods to a commercial or military system, which can be over a million lines of code, is seriously in doubt. This issue of scaling can be a deciding factor in the choice of a method. Harlan Mills claims his program function approach applies easier on large systems than Dijkstra's competing predicate calculus method [Mills 86]. Likewise, the languages considered in academic work tend to be extremely simplified compared to real-world programming languages.

One frequently adopted scheme for using formal methods on real-world projects is to select a small subset of components for formal treatment, thus finessing the scalability problem. These components might be selected under criteria of safety, security, or criticality. Components particularly amenable to formal proof might be specifically selected. In this way, the high cost of formal methods is avoided for the entire project, but only incurred where project requirements justify it. Under this scheme, the issue of scaling is avoided, for formal methods are never applied on a large scale.

Decisions about tool acquisition and integration need to be carefully considered. Advocates of formal methods argue that they should be integrated into the design process. One does not develop a specification and an implementation and then attempt to prove the implementation satisfies the specification. Rather, one designs the implementation and proof in parallel, with continual interaction. Sometimes discussion about automated verifiers suggests that the former approach, not the latter, provides an implementation model ([DeMillo 79] and [Merrill 83]). Selective implementation of formal methods on small portions of large projects may make this integration difficult to obtain.

Another approach can have much more global impacts. Perhaps the entire waterfall lifecycle should be scrapped. An alternate approach is to develop formal specifications at the beginning of the lifecycle and then automatically derive the source code for the system. Maintenance, enhancements, and modifications will be performed on the specifications, with this derivation process being repeated. Programmers are replaced by an intelligent set of integrated tools, or at least given very strong guidance by these tools. Knowledge about formal methods then becomes embodied in the tools, with Artificial Intelligence techniques being used to direct the use of formal methods. This revolutionary programmerless methodology is not here yet, but it is providing the inspiration for many tool developers. For example, this vision is close to that of Rome Laboratory's Knowledge-Based Software Engineering project [KBSE 92].

A third alternative is to partially introduce formal methods by introducing them throughout an organization or project, but allowing a variable level of formality. In this sense, informal verification is an argument meant to suggest that details can be filled in to provide a completely formal proof. The most well-known example of this alternative is the Cleanroom methodology, developed by Harlan Mills [Mills 87]. Given varying levels of formality, tools are much less useful under this approach. The Cleanroom methodology involves much more than formal methods, but they are completely integrated into the methodology. Other technologies involved include the spiral lifecycle, software reliability modeling, a specific testing approach, reliability certification, inspections, and statistical process control. Thus, although this approach allows partial experimentation with formal methods, it still requires drastic changes in most organizations.

No matter to what extent an organization decides to adopt formal methods, if at all, training and education issues arise. Most programmers have either not been exposed to the needed mathematical background, or do not use it in their day-to-day practice. Even those who thoroughly understand the mathematics may have never realized its applicability to software development. Set theory is generally taught in courses in pure mathematics, not computer programming. Even discrete mathematics, a standard course whose place in the university curriculum owes much to the impetus of computer science professional societies, is often not tied to software applications. Education in formal methods should not be confined to degreed university programs for undergraduates newly entering the field. Means need to be found, such as seminars and extension courses, for retraining an existing workforce. Perhaps this educational problem is the biggest hurdle to the widespread transition of formal methods.

Specification Methods

Formal methods were originally developed to support verifications, but higher interest currently exists in specification methods. Several methods and languages can be used for specifying the functionality of computer systems. No single language, of those now available, is equally appropriate for all methods, application domains, and aspects of a system. Thus, users of formal specification techniques need to understand the strength and weaknesses of different methods and languages before deciding on which to adopt. This section briefly describes characteristics of different methods now available.

The distinction between a specification method and a language is fundamental. A method states what a specification must say. A language determines in detail how the concepts in a specification can be expressed [Lamport 89]. Some languages support more than one method, while most methods can be used in several specification languages. Some methods are more easily used with certain languages.

Semantic Domains

A formal specification language contains an alphabet of symbols and grammatical rules that define well-formed formulae. These rules characterize a language's "syntactic domain." The syntax of a language shows how the symbols in the language are put together to form meaningless formulae. Neither the nature of the objects symbolized nor the meanings of the relationships between them are characterized by the syntax of a language.

Meanings, or interpretations of formulae, are specified by the semantics of a language. A set of objects, known as the language's "semantic domain," can provide a model of a language. The semantics are given by exact rules which state what objects satisfy a specification. For example, Cartesian Geometry shows how theorems in Euclidean Geometry can be modeled by algebraic expressions. A language can have several models, but some will seem more natural than others.

A specification is a set of formulae in a formal language. The objects in the language's semantic domain that satisfy a given specification can be nonunique. Several objects may be equivalent as far as a particular specification is concerned. Because of this nonuniqueness, the specification is at a higher level of abstraction than the objects in the semantic domain. The specification language permits abstraction from details that distinguish different implementations, while preserving essential properties. Different specification methods defined over the same semantic domain allow for specifying different aspects of specified objects. These concepts can be defined more precisely using mathematics. The advantage of this mathematics is that it provides tools for formal reasoning about specifications. Specifications can then be examined for completeness and consistency.

Specification languages can be classified by their semantic domains. Three major classes of semantic domains exist [Wing 90]:

- Abstract Data Type specification languages
- Process specification languages
- Programming languages.

ADT specification languages can be used to specify algebras. An ADT 'defines the formal properties of a data type without defining implementation features' [Vienneau 91]. Z, the Vienna Development Method, and Larch are examples of ADT specification languages. Process specification languages specify state sequences, event sequences, streams, partial orders, and state machines. C.A.R. Hoare's Communicating Sequential Processes (CSP) is the most well-known process specification language.

Programming languages provide an obvious example of languages with multiple models. Predicate transformers provide one model, functions provide another model, and the executable machine instructions that are generated by compiling a program provide a third model. Formal methods are useful in programming because programs can be viewed both as a set of commands for physical machines and as abstract mathematical objects as provided by these alternative models.

Operational and Definitional Methods

The distinction between operational and definitional methods provides another important dimension for classifying formal methods [Avizienis 90]. Operational methods have also been described as constructive or model-oriented [Wing 90]. In an operational method, a specification describes a system directly by providing a model of the system. The behavior of this model defines the desired behavior of the system. Typically, a model will use abstract mathematical structures, such as relations, functions, sets, and sequences. An early example of a model-based method is the specification approach associated with Harlan Mills' functional correctness approach. In this approach, a computer program is defined by a function from a space of inputs to a space of outputs. In effect, a model-oriented specification is a program written in a very high-level language. It may actually be executed by a suitable prototyping tool.

Definitional methods are also described as property-oriented [Wing 90] or declarative [Place 90]. A specification provides a minimum set of conditions that a system must satisfy. Any system that satisfies these conditions is functionally correct, but the specification does not provide a mechanical model showing how to determine the output of the system from the inputs. Two classes of definitional methods exist, algebraic and axiomatic. In algebraic methods, the properties defining a program are restricted to equations in certain algebras. Abstract Data Types are often specified by algebraic methods. Other types of axioms can be used in axiomatic methods. Often these axioms will be expressed in the predicate calculus. Edsger Dijkstra's method of specifying a program's function by preconditions and postconditions is an early example of an axiomatic method.

Use of Specification Methods

Different specification methods are more advantageous for some purposes than others. In general, formal methods provide for more precise specifications. Misunderstandings and bugs can be discovered earlier in the lifecycle. Since the earlier a fault is detected, the cheaper it can be removed; formal specification methods can dramatically improve both productivity and quality. Cost savings can only be achieved if formal methods are used appropriately. How to best use them in a specific environment can only be determined through experimentation.

Formal specifications should not be presented without a restatement of the specification in a natural language. In particular, customers should be presented with the English version, not a formal specification. Very few sponsors of a software development project will be inclined to read a specification whose presentation is entirely in a formal language.

Whether an ADT or process specification language should be adopted depends on the details of the project and the skills of the analysts. Choosing between operational and definitional methods also depends on project-specific details and experience. Generally, programmers are initially more comfortable with operational methods since they are closer to programming. Operational specifications may lead to over-specification. They tend to be larger than definitional specifications. Their complexity thus tends to be greater, and relationships among operations tend to be harder to discern.

Definitional specifications are generally harder to construct. The appropriate axioms to specify are usually not trivial. Consistency and completeness may be difficult to establish. Usually completeness is more problematic than consistency. Intuition will tend to prevent the specification of inconsistent axioms. Whether some axioms are redundant, or more are needed, is less readily apparent. Automated tools are useful for guidance in answering these questions [Guttag 77].

Conclusions

This report has briefly surveyed various formal methods and the conceptual basis of these techniques. Formal methods can provide:

- More precise specifications
- Better internal communication
- An ability to verify designs before executing them during test
- Higher quality and productivity.

These benefits will come with costs associated with training and use. Hard and fast rules do not exist on how to properly vary the level of formalism on a project or on how to transition the use of formal methods into an organization. Their enthusiastic use certainly depends on the organization's members perceiving a need that formal methods can fill. No change is likely to be achievable in an organization that is satisfied with its current practice.

Even if formal methods are not integrated into an organization's process, they can still have positive benefits. Consider a group whose members have been educated in the use of formal methods, but are not encouraged to use formal methods on the job. These programmers will know that programs can be developed to be fault-free from the first execution. They will have a different attitude to both design and testing, as contrasted to programmers who have not been so exposed to formal methods. They will be able to draw on a powerful set of intellectual tools when needed. They will be able to use formal methods on a personal basis and, to a limited extent, to communicate among one another. If management provides the appropriate milieu, this group can be expected to foster high quality attitudes with consequent increases in both productivity and quality.

To get their full advantages, formal methods should be incorporated into a software organization's standard procedures. Software development is a social process, and the techniques employed need to support that process. How to fully fit formal methods into the lifecycle is not fully understood. Perhaps there is no universal answer, but only solutions that vary from organization to organization.

The Cleanroom as a Lifecycle with Integrated Use of Formal Methods

Harlan Mills has developed the Cleanroom methodology [Mills 87], which is one approach for integrating formal methods into the lifecycle. The Cleanroom approach combines formal methods and structured programming with Statistical Process Control (SPC), the spiral lifecycle and incremental releases, inspections, and software reliability modeling. It fosters attitudes, such as emphasizing defect prevention over defect removal, that are asociated with high quality products in non-software fields.

Cleanroom development begins with the requirements phase. Ideally, specifications should be developed in a formal language, although the Cleanroom approach allows the level of formality to vary. The Cleanroom lifecycle uses incremental releases to support SPC. Cleanroom-developed specifications include:

- Explicit identification of functionality to be included in successive releases
- Failure definitions, including levels of severity
- The target reliability as a probability of failure-free operation
- The operational profile for each increment, that is, the probability distribution of user inputs to the system
- The reliability model that will be applied in system test to demonstrate reliability.

The design and coding phases of Cleanroom development are distinctive. Analysts must develop proofs of correctness along with designs and codes. These proofs use functional correctness techniques and are meant to be human-readable. They serve a social role and are not intended to be automatically checked by automated verification tools. Inspections are emphasized for reviewing designs, proofs, and code. The design process is intended to prevent the introduction of defects. In keeping with this philosophy, the Cleanroom methodology includes no unit or integration test phase. In fact, coders are actually forbidden to compile their programs. Cleanroom development takes its name from just this aspect of the methodology. Testing is completely separated from the design process, and analysts are not permitted to adopt the attitude that quality can be tested in. Instead, they must produce readable programs which can be convincingly shown correct by proof.

Testing does play a very important role in Cleanroom development. It serves to verify that reliability goals are being attained. Given this orientation, testing is organized differently than in traditional methods. Unit and integration testing do not exist. Functional methods, not structural testing methods, are employed. Furthermore, the testing process is deliberately designed to meet the assumptions of the chosen software reliability model. Test cases are statistically chosen from the specified operational profile. Although faults are removed when detected, the testing group's responsibility is not to improve the product to meet acceptable failure-rate goals. Rather, the testing group exists to perform reliability measurement and certification.

When testing fails to demonstrate the desired reliability goal is met, the design process is altered. The level of formality may be increased, or more inspections may be planned. Testing and incremental builds are combined to provide feedback into the development process under a Statistical Process Control philosophy as tailored for software. Formal methods are embodied in an institutional structure designed to foster a "right the first time" approach. The Cleanroom methodology draws upon evolving concepts of the best practice in software, including formal methods. The Cleanroom approach is beginning to generate interest and experimentation in organizations unassociated with Harlan Mills and International Business Machines [Selby 87].

Technologies Supported by Formal Methods

Researchers are drawing on formal methods in developing tools and techniques that may not be state-of-the-practice for several years. Lifecycle paradigms that rely on automatically transforming specifications to executable code are necessarily formal. Many software development tools, whether standalone or integrated into a common environment, draw on formal methods. Consequently, as software development becomes more tool intensive, formal methods will be more heavily used. Inasmuch as these formal methods are embodied in the tools, tool users may not be fully aware of the embedded formalism. Tool users who are trained in formal methods will be able to wield some of these tools more effectively. Formal methods, through their use in tools, have the promise of being able to transform the software development lifecycle from a labor-intensive error-prone process to a capital-intensive high quality process.

Emerging technologies that are increasingly widespread today also draw on formal methods. A knowledge of formal methods is needed to completely understand these popular technologies and to use them most effectively. These technologies include:

- Rapid prototyping
- Object Oriented Design (OOD)
- Structured programming
- Formal inspections.

Rapid prototyping depends on the ability to quickly construct prototypes of a system to explore their ability to satisfy user needs. Using executable specifications to describe a system at a high level is a typical approach. The tool that compiles the specification fills in the details. Specifications constructed under a rapid prototyping methodology, if executable, are by definition in a formal language. Often the languages used in prototyping tools involve the same set theoretical and logical concepts used in formal specification methods not intended for prototyping.

OOD is another increasingly well-known technology that is based on formal methods. Abstract Data Types provide a powerful basis for many classes in Object Oriented systems. Furthermore, at least one pure object oriented language, Eiffel, has assertions, preconditions, postconditions, and loop invariants built into the language to a certain extent. Simple boolean expressions are checked during execution of an Eiffel program, but not all assertions, such as those with existential and universal quantifiers, can be expressed in the language [Meyer 88]. Thus, formal methods can be usefully combined with object oriented techniques.

The connection between formal methods and structured programming is very close. Structured programming is a set of heuristics for producing high quality code. Only a limited set of constructs should be used. Programs should be developed in a top-down fashion. The historical source for these heuristics lies in formal methods. Programs developed with these precepts will be capable of being rigorously proven correct. Consequently, they will also be capable of being understood intuitively and nonrigorously. Structured programming cannot be completely understood without understanding the rigorous mathematical techniques associated with formal methods. Adopting formal methods is a natural progression for software development teams who employ structured programming techniques.

Inspections throughout the lifecycle have been shown to increase both productivity and quality. A rigorous methodology has been defined for inspections [Fagan 76]. Those participating in inspections play specified roles: moderator, author, coder, tester, and so on. Inspections should be organized to include representatives from specified departments (for example, Quality Assurance) within a software organization. Fault data is collected during inspections and analyzed to ensure the development process is under control. Inspections rely on the ability of individuals to reason about software products and to convince others of the correctness of their reasoning. Training in formal methods provides inspection team members with a powerful language to communicate their trains of reasoning. Formal and semi-formal verifications can lead to more effective inspections. The Cleanroom methodology demonstrates the potential synergy between formal methods and inspections.

Summary

Formal methods promise to yield benefits in quality and productivity. They provide an exciting paradigm for understanding software and its development, as well as a set of techniques for use by software engineers. Over the last 20 years, researchers have drawn on formal methods to develop certain software technologies that are currently becoming increasingly popular and are dramatically altering software development and maintenance. Further revolutionary advances based on formal methods are highly likely considering research currently in the pipeline.

Many organizations have experience with the use of formal methods on a small scale. Formal methods are typically used in organizations attaining a Level 3 rating and above on the Software Engineering Institute's process maturity framework. Increasingly, recently trained software engineers have had some exposure to formal methods. Nevertheless, their full scale use and transition is not fully understood. An organization that can figure out how to effectively integrate formal methods into their current process will be able to gain a competitive advantage.

References

[Agresti 86] W.W. Agresti, *New Paradigms for Software Development*, IEEE Computer Society Press, Los Alamitos, Calif., 1986.

[Aho 86] A.V. Aho, R. Sethi, and J.D. Ullman, *Compilers: Principles, Techniques, and Tools*, Addison-Wesley, Reading, Mass., 1986.

[Avizienis 90] A. Avizienis and C.-S. Wu, "A Comparative Assessment of Formal Specification Techniques," *Proc. 5th Ann. Knowledge-Based Software Assistant Conf.*, 1990.

[Baber 91] R.L. Baber, *Error-Free Software: Know-how and Know-why of Program Correctness*, John Wiley & Sons, New York, N.Y., 1991.

[Backus 78] J. Backus, "Can Programming Be Liberated from the von Neumann Style? A Functional Style and Its Algebra of Programs," *Comm. ACM*, Vol. 21, No. 8, Aug. 1978.

[Boehm 81] B.W. Boehm, *Software Engineering Economics*, Prentice-Hall, Inc., Englewood Cliffs, N.J., 1981.

[Curtis 88] B. Curtis, H. Krasner, and N. Iscoe, "A Field Study of the Software Design Process for Large Systems," *Comm. ACM*, Vol. 31, No. 11, Nov.1988.

[DeMillo 79] R. DeMillo, R. Lipton, and A. Perlis, "Social Processes and Proofs of Theorems and Programs," *Comm. ACM*, Vol. 22, No. 5, May 1979.

[DeRemer 76] F. DeRemer and H.H. Kron, "Programming-in-the-Large Versus Programming-in-the-Small," *IEEE Trans. Software Eng.*, Vol. SE-2, No. 2, June 1976, pp. 312–327.

[Dijkstra 76] E.W. Dijkstra, *A Discipline of Programming*, Prentice Hall, Englewood Cliffs, N.J., 1976.

[Dijkstra 89] E.W. Dijkstra, "On the Cruelty of Really Teaching Computer Science," *Comm. ACM*, Vol. 32, No. 12, Dec. 1989.

[Dyer 92] M. Dyer, *The Cleanroom Approach to Quality Software Development*, John Wiley & Sons, New York, N.Y., 1992.

[Fagan 76] M.E. Fagan, "Design and Code Inspections to Reduce Errors in Program Development," *IBM Systems J.*, Vol. 15, No. 3, 1976.

[Fetzer 88] J.H. Fetzer, "Program Verification: The Very Idea," *Comm. ACM*, Vol. 31, No. 9, Sept. 1988.

[Goel 91] A.L. Goel and S.N. Sahoo, "Formal Specifications and Reliability: An Experimental Study," *Proc. Int'l Symp. Software Reliability Eng.* IEEE Computer Society Press, Los Alamitos, Calif., 1991, pp. 139–142.

[Gries 81] D. Gries, *The Science of Programming*, Spring-Verlag, New York, N.Y., 1981.

[Gries 91] D. Gries, "On Teaching and Calculation," *Comm. ACM*, Vol. 34, No. 3, Mar. 1991.

[Guttag 77] J. Guttag, "Abstract Data Types and the Development of Data Structures," *Comm. ACM*, Vol. 20, No. 6, June 1977.

[Hall 90] A. Hall, "Seven Myths of Formal Methods," *IEEE Software*, Vol. 7, No. 5, Sept. 1990, pp. 11–19.

[Hoare 85] C.A.R. Hoare, *Communicating Sequential Processes*, Prentice-Hall International, 1985.

[Hoare 87] C.A.R. Hoare, "Laws of Programming," *Comm. ACM*, Vol. 30, No. 8, Aug. 1987.

[Humphrey 88] W.S. Humphrey, "Characterizing the Software Process: A Maturity Framework," *IEEE Software*, Vol. 5, No. 2, Mar. 1988, pp. 73–79.

[KBSE 92] *Proc. 7th Knowledge-Based Software Eng. Conf.*, 1992.

[Kline 80] M. Kline, *Mathematics: The Loss of Certainty*, Oxford University Press, 1980.

[Lamport 89] L. Lamport, "A Simple Approach to Specifying Concurrent Systems," *Comm. ACM*, Vol. 32, No. 1, Jan. 1989.

[Leveson 90] N.G. Leveson, "Guest Editor's Introduction: Formal Methods in Software Engineering," *IEEE Trans. Software Eng.*, Vol. 16, No. 9, Sept. 1990, pp. 929–931.

[Linger 79] R.C. Linger, H.D. Mills, and B.I. Witt, *Structured Programming: Theory and Practice*, Addison-Wesley Publishing Company, Reading, Mass., 1979.

[London 77] R.L. London, "Remarks on the Impact of Program Verification on Language Design," in *Design and Implementation of Programming Languages*, Springer-Verlag, New York, N.Y., 1977.

[Lyons 77] J. Lyons, *Noam Chomsky*, Penguin Books, Revised Edition 1977.

[McGettrick 82] Andrew D. McGettrick, *Program Verification using Ada*, Cambridge University Press, 1982.

[Merrill 83] G. Merrill, "Proofs, Program Correctness, and Software Engineering," *SIGPLAN Notices*, Vol. 18, No. 12, Dec. 1983.

[Meyer 85] B. Meyer, "On Formalism in Specifications," *IEEE Software*, Vol. 2, No. 1, Jan. 1985, pp. 6–26.

[Meyer 88] B. Meyer, *Object-Oriented Software Construction*, Prentice-Hall, Englewood Cliffs, N.J., 1988.

[Mills 86] H.D. Mills, "Structured Programming: Retrospect and Prospect," *IEEE Software*, Vol. 3, No. 6, Nov. 1986, pp. 58–66.

[Mills 87] H.D. Mills, Michael Dyer, and Richard C. Linger, "Cleanroom Software Engineering," *IEEE Software*, Vol. 4, No. 5, Sept. 1987, pp. 19–25.

[Peterson 77] J.L. Peterson, "Petri Nets," *Computing Surveys*, Vol. 9, No. 3, Sept. 1977.

[Place 90] P.R.H. Place, W. Wood, and M. Tudball, *Survey of Formal Specification Techniques for Reactive Systems*, Software Engineering Institute, CMU/SEI-90-TR-5, May 1990.

[Preston 88] D. Preston, K. Nyberg, and R. Mathis, "An Investigation into the Compatibility of Ada and Formal Verification Technology," *Proc. 6th Nat'l Conf. Ada Technology*, 1988.

[Selby 87] R.W. Selby, V.R. Basili, and F.T. Baker, "Cleanroom Software Development: An Empirical Evaluation," *IEEE Trans. Software Eng.*, Vol. SE-13, No. 9, Sept. 1987, pp. 1027–1037.

[Spivey 88] J.M. Spivey, *Understanding Z: A Specification Language and its Formal Semantics*, Cambridge University Press, 1988.

[Stolyar 70] A.A. Stolyar, *Introduction to Elementary Mathematical Logic*, Dover Publications, 1970.

[Suppes 72] P. Suppes, *Axiomatic Set Theory*, Dover Publications, 1972.

[Terwilliger 92] R.B. Terwilliger, "Simulating the Gries/Dijkstra Design Process," *Proc. 7th Knowledge-Based Software Eng. Conf.*, IEEE Computer Society Press, Los Alamitos, Calif., 1992, pp. 144–153.

[Vienneau 91] R. Vienneau, *An Overview of Object Oriented Design*, Data & Analysis Center for Software, Apr. 30, 1991.

[Wing 90] J.M. Wing, "A Specifier's Introduction to Formal Methods," *Computer*, Vol. 23, No. 9, Sept. 1990, pp. 8–24.

[Zeroual 91] K. Zeroual, "KBRAS: A Knowledge-Based Requirements Acquisition System," *Proc. 6th Ann. Knowledge-Based Software Eng. Conf.*, IEEE Computer Society Press, Los Alamitos, Calif., 1991, pp. 38–47.

Chapter 6

Coding

1. Introduction to Chapter

This chapter is deemed essential by the Tutorial editors in order to complete the classic life cycle model of a software development, that is, requirements, design, implementation and testing. Coding, along with unit testing, is in the implementation phase of a software development. The coding aspect of software engineering is considered very important in the final product but is a relatively mature discipline and as such receives less discussion than the other phases. However, the editors have selected two papers that are appropriate for this Tutorial. The first describes the history and possible future of structured programming; the second covers the application of programming languages to software engineering.

The editors selected the term "coding" over the term "programming" as more appropriate to a discussion of the activities in relationship to software engineering. The term "programming" is not well defined and could include such activities as analysis, design, coding and testing—many of the activities we include in software engineering. Coding, on the other hand, is more precisely defined as translating a low-level (or detailed-level) software design into a language capable of operating a computing machine.

CODING

2. Introduction to Papers

The first paper, by Harlan Mills, entitled "Structured Programming: Retrospect and Prospect," is from one of the tutorials that periodically appear in the IEEE publication *IEEE Software*. This paper discusses the origin of the term "structured programming," which first appeared in Edsger Dijkstra's 1969 article "Structured Programming" [1]. The paper also looks at the impact of structured programming on software development, as well as some of the earlier experiences such as the classic New York Times project for which Mills was the project manager. Structured programming is a corollary to Dijkstra's proposal to prohibit the unconditional "goto." [2] Mills brings up the concept of cleanroom software development and discusses how it relates to the structured programming approach.

Harlan Mills was one of the true pioneers of software engineering in both academic and industrial settings. He was a major contributor to the state of the art and the state of the practice for more than 30 years. His recent death saddened his many friends and deprives the profession of one of its most prolific contributors.

The second and last paper in this chapter is based upon a chapter in a book, *Software Engineering: A Programming Approach* [3]. The book's authors, Doug Bell, Ian Morrey, and John Pugh, revised and updated the chapter for this Tutorial. The paper discusses the features that a good programming language should have from the viewpoint of software engineering, that is, the features that assist the software development process.

The authors divide the discussion into "programming in the small" and "programming in the large." Programming in the small concerns itself with those language features that support the programming of modules or small programs. These features include simplicity, clarity, and the language's syntax and facilities for control and data abstraction. Programming in the large is concerned with those features that support programs that are made up of many components. These features include facilities for separately compiling individually developed modules, features for controlling the interaction between components, and support tools associated with the language.

There is tendency to interpret programming in the small as "coding" and programming in the large as "software engineering." The authors of this paper avoid that interpretation and describe how programming in the small also applies to software engineering.

1. Dijkstra, Edsger W., "Structured Programming," in *Software Engineering Techniques*, J.N. Buxton and B. Randell, eds., NATO Science Committee, Rome, 1969, pp. 88–93.

2. Dijkstra, E., "GOTO Statement Considered Harmful," *Comm. ACM*, Vol. 11, No. 3, Mar. 1968.

3. Bell, Doug, Ian Morrey, and John Pugh, *Software Engineering: A Programming Approach,* Prentice Hall International, Englewood Cliffs, N.J., 1987.

Structured Programming: Retrospect and Prospect

Harlan D. Mills, IBM Corp.

Structured programming has changed how programs are written since its introduction two decades ago. However, it still has a lot of potential for more change.

Edsger W. Dijkstra's 1969 "Structured Programming" article[1] precipitated a decade of intense focus on programming techniques that has fundamentally altered human expectations and achievements in software development.

Before this decade of intense focus, programming was regarded as a private, puzzle-solving activity of writing computer instructions to work as a program. After this decade, programming could be regarded as a public, mathematics-based activity of restructuring specifications into programs.

Before, the challenge was in getting programs to run at all, and then in getting them further debugged to do the right things. After, programs could be expected to both run and do the right things with little or no debugging. Before, it was com-

mon wisdom that no sizable program could be error-free. After, many sizable programs have run a year or more with no errors detected.

Impact of structured programming. These expectations and achievements are not universal because of the inertia of industrial practices. But they are well-enough established to herald fundamental change in software development.

Even though Dijkstra's original argument for structured programming centered on shortening correctness proofs by simplifying control logic, many people still regard program verification as academic until automatic verification systems can be made fast and flexible enough for practical use.

By contrast, there is empirical evidence[2] to support Dijkstra's argument that infor-

Introducing the fundamental concepts series

A group of leading software engineers met in Columbia, Maryland, in September 1982 to provide recommendations for advancing the software engineering field. The participants were concerned about the rapid changes in the software development environment and about the field's ability to effectively deal with the changes.

The result was a report issued six months later and printed in the January 1985 issue of *IEEE Software* ("Software Engineering: The Future of a Profession" by John Musa) and in the April 1983 *ACM Software Engineering Notes* ("Stimulating Software Engineering Progress — A Report of the Software Engineering Planning Group").

The group's members were members of the IEEE Technical Committee on Software Engineering's executive board, the ACM Special Interest Group on Software Engineering's executive committee, and the IEEE Technical Committee on VLSI.

In the area of software engineering technology creation, the highest priority recommendation was to "commission a 'best

idea' monograph series. In each monograph, an idea from two to four years ago, adjudged a 'best idea' by a panel of experts, would be explored from the standpoint of how it was conceived, how it has matured over the years, and how it has been applied. A key objective here is to both stimulate further development and application of the idea and encourage creation of new ideas from the divergent views of the subject."

Another way to state the objectives of the series is to (1) explain the genesis and development of the research idea so it will help other researchers in the field and (2) transfer the idea to the practicing software engineer.

After the report was published in this magazine, an editorial board was created to implement the series. John Musa, then chairman of the IEEE Technical Committee on Software Engineering, and Bill Riddle, then chairman of ACM SIGSE, appointed the following board members:

- Bruce Barnes, of the National Science Foundation,
- Meir Lehman, of Imperial College, as adviser,

KEVIN REAGAN

mal, human verification can be reliable enough to replace traditional program debugging before system testing. In fact, structured programming that includes human verification can be used as the basis for software development under statistical quality control.[3]

It seems that the limitations of human fallibility in software development have been greatly exaggerated. Structured programming has reduced much of the unnecessary complexity of programming

---

- Peter Neumann, of SRI International (and no longer with the board),
- Norman Schneidewind, of the Naval Postgraduate School, as editor-in-chief, and
- Marv Zelkowitz, of the University of Maryland.

Rather than produce a monograph series, the board decided that *IEEE Software* would be a better medium for the series, since it reaches a large readership. Furthermore, the magazine's editor-in-chief, Bruce Shriver of IBM, strongly supported the series' objectives.

I am delighted that Harlan Mills, an IBM fellow, agreed to write the first article, "Structured Programming: Retrospect and Prospect," in this series. I am also grateful for Bruce Shriver's enthusiastic support and for agreeing to publish the series in *IEEE Software*. Future articles in this series will appear in this magazine. I also thank the *IEEE Software* reviewers for the excellent job they did of refereeing Mills's article.

In presenting this series, the editorial board is not advocat-

ing the idea of this or any article published. Rather, our purpose is to be an agent for the transfer of technology to the software engineering community. We believe it is the readers who should evaluate the significance to software engineering of the ideas we present.

The board is very interested in your opinions on this article and on the general concept of the series. Do you think it is a good idea? Has the article helped you to better understand the origins, concepts, and application of structured programming? What topics would you like covered? Please send your thoughts and opinions to Norman Schneidewind, Naval Postgraduate School, Dept. AS, Code 54Ss, Monterey, CA 93943.

Norman Schneidewind

Norman Schneidewind
Series Editor-in-Chief

and can increase human expectations and achievements accordingly.

Early controversies. Dijkstra's article proposed restricting program control logic to three forms — sequence, selection, and iteration — which in languages such as Algol and PL/I left no need for the goto instruction. Until then, the goto statement had seemingly been the foundation of stored-program computing. The ability to branch arbitrarily, based on the state of data, was at the heart of programming ingenuity and creativity. The selection and iteration statements had conditional branching built in implicitly, but they seemed a pale imitation of the possibilities inherent in the goto.

As a result, Dijkstra's proposal to prohibit the goto was greeted with controversy: "You must be kidding!" In response to complex problems, programs were being produced with complex control structures — figurative bowls of spaghetti, in which simple sequence, selection, and iteration statements seemed entirely inadequate to express the required logic. No wonder the general practitioners were skeptical: "Simple problems, maybe. Complex problems, not a chance!"

In fact, Dijkstra's proposal was far broader than the restriction of control structures. In "Notes on Structured Programming"[4] (published in 1972 but privately circulated in 1970 or before), he discussed a comprehensive programming process that anticipated stepwise refinement, top-down development, and program verification.

However, Dijkstra's proposal could, indeed, be shown to be theoretically sound by previous results from Corrado Boehm and Giuseppe Jacopini[5] who had showed that the control logic of any flowchartable program — any bowl of spaghetti — could be expressed without gotos, using sequence, selection, and iteration statements.

So the combination of these three basic statements turned out to be more powerful than expected, as powerful as any flowchartable program. That was a big surprise to rank and file programmers.

Even so, Dijkstra's proposal was still greeted with controversy: "It can't be practical." How could the complex bowls of spaghetti written at that time otherwise be explained? Formal debates were held at conferences about practicality, originality, creativity, and other emotional issues in programming, which produced more heat than light.

Early industrial experience

The *New York Times* project. An early published result in the use of structured programming in a sizable project helped calibrate the practicality issue. F. Terry Baker reported on a two-year project carried out by IBM for the *New York Times*, delivered in mid-1971, that used structured programming to build a system of some 85,000 lines of code.[6] Structured programming worked!

The project used several new techniques simultaneously: chief-programmer team organization, top-down development by stepwise refinement, hierarchical modularity, and functional verification of programs. All were enabled by structured programming.

The *New York Times* system was an on-line storage and retrieval system for news-

---

Unlike a spaghetti program, a structured program defines a natural hierarchy among its instructions.

---

paper reference material accessed through more than a hundred terminals — an advanced project in its day. The *Times* system met impressive performance goals — in fact, it achieved throughputs expected in an IBM 360/Model 50 using an interim hardware configuration of a Model 40. The IBM team also achieved an impressive level of productivity — a comprehensive internal study concluded that productivity, compared to other projects of similar size and complexity, was a factor of five better.

In this case, since the *New York Times* had little experience in operating and maintaining a complex, on-line system, IBM agreed to maintain the system for the newspaper over the first year of operation. As a result, the exact operational experience of the system was also known and published by Baker.[7]

The reliability of the system was also a pleasant surprise. In a time when on-line software systems typically crashed several times a day, the *Times* software system crashed only once that year.

The number of changes required, for any reason, was 25 during that year, most of them in a data editing subsystem that was conceived and added to the system after the start of the project. Of these,

about a third were external specification changes, a third were definite errors, and a third interpretable either way.

The rate of definite errors was only 0.1 per thousand lines of code. The highest quality system of its complexity and size produced to that time by IBM, the *Times* project had a major effect on IBM software development practices.

The structure theorem and its top-down corollary. Even though structured programming has been shown to be possible and practical, there is still a long way to go to achieve widespread use and benefits in a large organization. In such cases, education and increased expectations are more effective than exhortations, beginning with the management itself.

The results of Boehm and Jacopini were especially valuable to management when recast into a so-called structure theorem,[8] which established the existence of a structured program for any problem that permitted a flowchartable solution.

As an illustration, hardware engineering management implicitly uses and benefits from the discipline of Boolean algebra and logic, for example, in the result that any combinational circuit can be designed with Not, And, and Or building blocks. If an engineer were to insist that these building blocks were not enough, his credibility as an engineer would be questioned.

The structure theorem permits management by exception in program design standards. A programmer cannot claim the problem is too difficult to be solved with a structured program. To claim that a structured program would be too inefficient, a program must be produced as proof. Usually, by the time a structured program is produced, the problem is understood much better than before, and a good solution has been found. In certain cases, the final solution may not be structured — but it should be well-documented and verified as an exceptional case.

The lines of text in a structured program can be written in any order. The history of which lines were written first and how they were assembled into the final structured program are immaterial to its execution. However, because of human abilities and fallibilities, the order in which lines of a structured program are written can greatly affect the correctness and completeness of the program.

For example, lines to open a file should be written before lines to read and write the file. This lets the condition of the file be checked when coding a file read or write statement.

The key management benefit from top-down programming was described in the top-down corollary[8] to the structure theorem. The lines of a structured program can be written chronologically so that every line can be verified by reference only to lines already written, and not to lines yet to be written.

Unlike a spaghetti program, a structured program defines a natural hierarchy among its instructions, which are repeatedly nested into larger and larger parts of the program by sequence, selection, and iteration structures. Each part defines a sub-hierarchy executed independently of its surroundings in the hierarchy. Any such part can be called a program stub and given a name — but, even more importantly, it can be described in a specification that has no control properties, only the effect of the program stub on the program's data.

The concept of top-down programming, described in 1971,[9] uses this hierarchy of a structured program and uses program stubs and their specifications to decompose program design into a hierarchy of smaller, independent design problems. Niklaus Wirth discussed a similar concept of stepwise refinement at the same time.[10]

Using the top-down corollary. The top-down corollary was counterintuitive in the early 1970's because programming was widely regarded as a synthesis process of assembling instructions into a program rather than as an analytic process of restructuring specifications into a program. Furthermore, the time sequence in which lines of text were to be written was counter to common programming practice.

For example, the corollary required that the JCL (job-control language) be written first, the LEL (linkage-editor language) next, and ordinary programs in programming languages last. The custom then was to write them in just the reverse order. Further, the hard inner loops, usually worked out first, had to be written last under the top-down corollary. In fact, the top-down corollary forced the realization that the linkage editor is better regarded as a language processor than a utility program.

It is easy to misunderstand the top-down corollary. It does not claim that the thinking should be done top-down. Its benefit is in the later phases of program design, after the bottom-up thinking and perhaps some trial coding has been accomplished. Then, knowing where the top-down development is going, the lines of the structured

program can be checked one by one as they are produced, with no need to write later lines to make them correct. In large designs, the top-down process should look ahead several levels in the hierarchy, but not necessarily to the bottom.

The *New York Times* team used both the structure theorem and its top-down corollary. While the proof of the structure theorem (based on that of Boehm and Jacopini) seemed more difficult to understand, the team felt the application of the top-down corollary was more challenging in program design, but correspondingly more rewarding in results.

For example, with no special effort or prestated objectives, about half of the *Times* modules turned out to be correct after their first clean compile. Other techniques contributed to this result, including chief-programmer team organization, highly visible program development library

---

Dijkstra's proposal to prohibit the goto was greeted with controversy: "You must be kidding!"

---

procedures, and intensive program reading. However, these techniques were permitted to a great extent by top-down structured programming, particularly in the ability to defer and delegate design tasks through specifications of program stubs.

NASA's Skylab project. In 1971-74, a much larger but less publicized project demonstrated similar benefits of top-down structured programming in software development by IBM for the NASA Skylab space laboratory's system. In comparison, the NASA Apollo system (which carried men to the Moon several times) had been developed in 1968-71, starting before structured programming was proposed publicly.

While the *New York Times* project involved a small team (originally four but enlarged to 11) over two years, Apollo and Skylab each involved some 400 programmers over consecutive three years of development. In each system, the software was divided into two major parts, of similar complexity: (1) a simulation system for flight controller and astronaut training and (2) a mission system for spacecraft control during flight.

In fact, these subsystems are mirror

images in many ways. For example, the simulation system estimates spacecraft behavior from a rocket engine burn called for by an astronaut in training, while the mission system will observe spacecraft behavior from a rocket engine burn called for by an astronaut in flight.

Although less spectacular than Apollo, the Skylab project of manned space study of near-Earth space was in many ways more challenging. The software for the Skylab simulation system was about double the size of Apollo's, and the complexity was even greater.

The Skylab software project was initiated shortly after the original proposals for structured programming, and a major opportunity for methodology comparison arose. The Skylab mission system was developed by the same successful methods used for both subsystems in Apollo. But the Skylab simulation system was developed with the then-new method of top-down structured programming under the initiative of Sam E. James.

The Skylab results were decisive. In Apollo, the productivity of the programmers in both simulation and mission systems was very similar, as to be expected. The Skylab mission system was developed with about the same productivity and integration difficulty as experienced on both Apollo subsystems.

But the Skylab simulation system, using top-down structured programming, showed a productivity increase by a factor of three and a dramatic reduction in integration difficulty.

Perhaps most revealing was the use of computer time during integration. In most projects of the day, computer time would increase significantly during integration to deal with unexpected systems problems. In the Skylab simulation system, computer time stayed level throughout integration.

Language problems. By this time (the mid-1970's), there was not much debate about the practicality of structured programming. Doubtless, some diehards were not convinced, but the public arguments disappeared.

Even so, only the Algol-related languages permitted direct structured programming with sequence, selection and iteration statements in the languages. Assembly languages, Fortran, and Cobol were conspicuous problems for structured programming.

One approach with these languages is to design in structured forms, then hand-translate to the source language in a final coding step. Another approach is to create a language preprocessor to permit final coding in an extended language to be mechanically translated to the source language. Both approaches have drawbacks.

The first approach requires more discipline and dedication than many programming groups can muster. It is tempting to use language features that are counter to structured programming.

The second approach imposes a discipline, but the programs actually compiled in the target language will be the result of mechanical translation themselves, with artificial labels and variables that make reading difficult. The preprocessing step can also be cumbersome and expensive, so the temptation in debugging is to alter the mechanically generated target code directly, much like patching assembly programs, with subsequent loss of intellectual control.

As a result of these two poor choices of approach, much programming in assembly languages, Fortran, and Cobol has been slow to benefit from structured programming.

Paradoxically, assembly language programming is probably the easiest to adapt to structured programming through the use of macroassemblers. For example, the Skylab simulation and mission systems were both programmed in assembly language, with the simulation system using structured programming through a macroassembler.

Both Fortran and Cobol have had their language definitions modified to permit direct structured programming, but the bulk of programming in both languages — even today — probably does not benefit fully from structured programming.

Current theory and practice

Mathematical correctness of structured programs. With the debate over and the doubters underground, what was left to learn about structured programming? It turned out that there was a great deal to learn, much of it anticipated by Dijkstra in his first article.[1]

The principal early discussions about structured programming in industry focused on the absence of gotos, the theoretical power of programs with restricted control logic, and the syntactic and typographic aspects of structured programs (indentation conventions and pretty printing, stepwise refinement a page at a time).

These syntactic and typographic aspects permitted programmers to read each other's programs daily, permitted them to conduct structured walk-throughs and program inspections, and permitted managers to understand the progress of software development as a process of stepwise refinement that allowed progressively more accurate estimates of project completion.

When a project was claimed to be 90-percent done with solid top-down structured programming, it would take only 10 percent more effort to complete it (instead of possibly another 90 percent!).

However, Dijkstra's first article on structured programming did not mention syntax, typography, readability, stepwise refinement, or top-down development. Instead, his main argument for structured programming was to shorten the mathe-

---

The ideas of structured programming, mathematical correctness, and high-level languages are mutually independent.

---

matical proofs of correctness of programs! That may seem a strange argument when almost no one then (and few now) bothered to prove their programs correct anyway. But it was an inspired piece of prophecy that is still unfolding.

The popularizations of structured programming have emphasized its syntactic and superficial aspects because they are easiest to explain. But that is only half the story — and less than half the benefit — because there is a remarkable synergy between structured programming and the mathematical correctness of programs. And there have been many disappointments for people and organizations who have taken the structured-programming-made-easy approach without mathematical rigor.

Two reasons that Dijkstra's argument about the size of proofs of correctness for structured programs seems to be inspired prophecy are

• The proof of program's correctness is a singularly appropriate definition for its necessary and sufficient documentation. No gratuitous or unnecessary ideas are needed and the proof is sufficient evidence that the program satisfies its specification.

• The size of a correctness proof seems at least a partial measure of the complexity of a program. For example, a long pro-

gram with few branches may be simpler to prove than a shorter one with many loops — and it may be less complex, as well. Or, tricky use of variables and operations may reduce the number of branches but will make the proof longer.

However, unless programmers understand what proofs of correctness are, these insights will not be realized. That was the motivation of the article "How to Write Correct Programs and Know It."[9] Then, whether structured programs are proved correct or not, this understanding will implicitly reduce complexity and permit better documentation.

In fact, Dijkstra's argument shows that the mathematical correctness of programs was an independent and prior idea to structured programming (even anticipated by writings of von Neumann and Turing). Yet it was strange and unknown to most programmers at the time. It is curious, although the earliest computers were motivated and justified by the solution of numerical problems of mathematics (such as computing ballistic tables), that the programming of such computers was not widely viewed as a mathematical activity.

Indeed, when it was discovered that computers could be used in business data processing, dealing with mostly character data and elementary arithmetic, the relation between programming and mathematics seemed even more tenuous.

As the Skylab project showed, structured programming is also independent of high-level languages. As treated syntactically and superficially, structured programming may have seemed dependent on high-level languages. But this is not true. Of course, high-level languages have improved programmer productivity as well, but that is a separate matter.

The ideas of structured programming, mathematical correctness, and high-level languages are mutually independent.

Program functions and correctness. A terminating program can be regarded as a rule for a mathematical function that converts an initial state of data into a final state, whether the problem being solved is considered mathematical or not.

For example, a payroll program defines a mathematical function just as a matrix inversion program does. Even nonterminating programs, such as operating systems and communication systems, can be expressed as a single nonterminating loop that executes terminating subprograms endlessly.

The function defined by any such terminating program is simply a set of ordered pairs: the initial and final states of data that can arise in its execution. That matrix inversion seems more mathematical than payroll processing is a human cultural illusion, an illusion not known to or shared by computers.

Since programs define mathematical functions, which thereby abstract out all details of execution — including even which language or which computer is used — it is possible to discuss the correctness of a program with respect to its specification as a purely mathematical question. Such a specification is a relation. If the specification admits no ambiguity of the correct final state for a given initial state, the specification will be a function.

For example, a square root specification that requires an answer correct to eight decimal places (so any more places can be arbitrary) is a relation. But a sort specification permits only one final ordering of any initial set of values, and is thus a function.

A program will be correct with respect to a specification if and only if, for every initial value permissible by the specification, the program will produce a final value that corresponds to that initial value in the specification.

A little notation will be helpful. Let function f be defined by program P, and relation r be a specification (r is possibly a function). Then program P is correct with respect to relation r if and only if a certain correctness equation between f and r holds, as follows: domain($f \cap r$) = domain(r).

To see this, note that $f \cap r$ consists of just those pairs of r correctly computed by P, so domain($f \cap r$) consists of all initial values for which P computes correct final values. But domain(r) is just the set of initial values for which r specifies acceptable final values, so it should equal domain($f \cap r$).

Such an equation applies equally to a payroll program or a matrix inversion program. Both can be mathematically correct, regardless of human interpretations of whether the computation is mathematical or not.

To picture this correctness equation, we can diagram f and r in a Venn diagram with projections of these sets of ordered pairs into their domain sets (see Figure 1). The correctness equation requires that the two domain sets D($f \cap r$) and D(r) must coincide.

Mathematical correctness proofs. In principle, a direct way to prove the mathematical correctness of a program is clear.

Start with a program P and the specification r. Determine from P its function f and whether the correctness equation between f and r holds.

In practice, given a spaghetti program, such a proof may be impractical — even impossible — because of the program's complexity. But a structured program with the same function f will be simpler to prove correct because of the discipline on its control structure. In retrospect, the reason lies in an algebra of functions that can be associated with structured programming.

It is easy to see in principle why a program is a rule for a function. For any initial state from which the program terminates normally (does not abort or loop endlessly), a unique final state is determined. But unlike classical mathematical function rules (such as given by polynomial expressions, trigonometric expressions, and the like), the function rules determined by programs can be quite arbitrary and complex. The final state, even though unique, may not be easily described because of complex dependencies among individual instructions.

For a spaghetti program, the only reasonable way to think of the program as a rule for a function is to imagine it being executed with actual data — by mental simulation. For small programs, a limited generic simulation may be possible (for example, "for negative values the program is executed in this section").

But for a structured program, there is a much more powerful way to think of it: as a function rule that uses simpler functions. For example, any sequence, selection, or iteration defines a rule for a function that uses the functions of its constituent parts.

Algebra of part functions. The remarkable thing about building these functions from the nested parts of a structured program is that the rules for constructing them are very simple and regular. They are simply described as operations in a certain algebra of functions.

The rules for individual instructions depend on the programming language. For example, the rule for an assignment statement $x := y + z$ is that the final state is exactly the same as the initial state except that the value attached to identifier x is changed to the value attached to identifier y plus the value attached to identifier z.

The rule for sequence is function composition. For example, if statements $s1, s2$ have functions $f1, f2$, the function for the sequence $s1; s2$ will be the composition $f1 \bigcirc f2 = \{<x,y>\} : y = f2(f1(x))\}$.

It is important to note that the rules at each level use the functions at the next lower level, and not the rules at the next lower level. That is, a specific program part determines the rule of a function, but the rule itself is not used at higher levels. This means that any program part can be safely changed at will to another with the same function, even though it represents a different rule.

For example, the program parts $x := y$ and If $x \neq y$ Then $x := y$ define different rules for the same function and can be exchanged at will.

Axiomatic and functional verification. There is a curious paradox today between university and industry. While program correctness proofs are widely taught in universities for toy programs, most academics not deeply involved in the subject

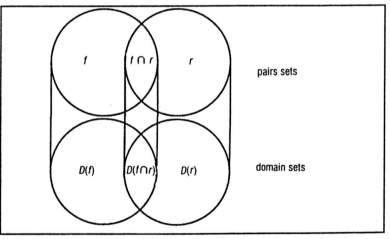

Figure 1. Correctness equation diagram with projections of the ordered pair sets into their domain sets.

regard program correctness as academic. Their motivation is cultural: "You'd never want to do this in practice, but it is good for you to know how to do it."

On the other hand, the IBM Software Engineering Institute curriculum is centered on the idea of program correctness exactly because it is not academic. Rather, it provides a practical method of reasoning about large programs that leads to much improved quality and productivity in software development.

There is also a simple answer to this paradox. Academics primarily teach a form of program correctness, called axiomatic verification, applied directly to toy programs, while the IBM Software Engineering Institute teaches a different form called functional verification in a way intended to scale up to large programs.

Axiomatic verification proves correctness by reasoning about the effect of programs on data. This reasoning takes the form of predicates on data at various places in the program that are invariant during execution. The relations between these predicates are given by axioms of the programming language (hence the name), and the entry/exit predicates together define the program function in an alternative form. Tony Hoare has given a beautiful explanation for this reasoning as a form of natural deduction, now called Hoare logic.[11]

Functional verification is based on function theory from the outset. For example, a simple assignment statement $x := y + z$ defines a function that can be denoted by $[x := y + z]$ and then used as a function in the algebra of structured-program part functions. In practice, functional verification is harder to teach but easier to scale up to large programs because of the presence of algebraic structure in an explicit form.

The most critical difference in practice between axiomatic and functional verification arises in the treatment of loops. In axiomatic verification, a loop invariant must be invented for every loop. In functional verification, during stepwise refinement, no such loop invariants are required because they are already embodied in the loop specification function or relation.[8]

Axiomatic verification can be explained directly in terms of program variables and the effects of statements on them, concretely in any given programming language. But when programs get large, the number of program variables get large, too — while the number of functions remains just one. The variable-free theory scales up

to a more complex function rather than to many more variables.

Such a function may be defined in two lines of mathematical notation or a hundred pages of English. But its mathematical form is the same: a set of ordered pairs. There are many more opportunities for ambiguity and fallibility in a hundred pages of English, but increased individual fallibility can be countered by checks and balances of well-managed teams, rather than abandoning the methodology.

As a result, the functional verification of a top-level design of a 100,000 lines has the same form as for a low-level design of 10 lines: There is one function rule to be verified by using a small number of functions at the next level. The function defines a

---

Eliminate the use of arrays in structured programs, and use instead data abstractions without arbitrary access.

---

mapping from initial states to final states. These states will eventually be represented as collections of values of variables, but can be reasoned about as abstract objects directly in high-level design.

While most of this reasoning is in the natural language of the application, its rules are defined by the algebra of functions, which is mathematically well-defined and can be commonly understood among designers and inspectors. There is considerable evidence that this informal kind of reasoning in mathematical forms can be effective and reliable in large software systems (exceeding a million lines) that are designed and developed top-down with very little design backtracking.[12]

There is yet another way to describe the reasoning required to prove the correctness of structured programs. The predicates in program variables of axiomatic verification admit an algebra of predicates whose operations are called predicate transformers in a classic book by Edsger Dijkstra,[13] and followed in a beautiful elaboration by David Gries.[14]

Looking to the future

Data-structured programming. The objective of reducing the size of formal correctness proofs can be reapplied to structured programs with a surprising and

constructive result. In carrying out proofs of structured programs, the algebraic operations on the functions involved are the same at every level, but the functions become more complex in the upper parts of the hierarchy.

Two features in the data of the program have a large effect on the size of formal proofs: (1) The sheer number of program variables that define the data and (2) assignments to arrays.

Arrays represent arbitrary access to data just as gotos represent arbitrary access to instructions. The cost of this access shows up directly in the length and complexity of proofs that involve array assignments. For example, an array assignment, say $x[i] := y[j + k]$ refers to three previous assignments to i, j, and k. The values of i or $j + k$ may be out of range, and certainly must be accounted for if in range. Furthermore, array x will be altered at location i, and this fact must be accounted for the next time x is accessed again for the same value of i (which may be the value of another variable m).

Dijkstra's treatment of arrays[13] is very illuminating evidence of their complexity. Gries has also given the predicate transformers for array assignments,[14] which are much more complex than for simple assignments.

Happily, there is a way to address both of these proof expanders in one stroke: eliminate the use of arrays in structured programs, and use instead data abstractions without arbitrary access. Three simple such abstractions come to mind immediately: sets, stacks, and queues — the latter two data structures with LIFO and FIFO access disciplines. No pointers are required to assign data to or from stacks or queues, so fewer variables are involved in such assignments.

Furthermore, the proofs involving assignments to sets, stacks, and queues are much shorter than proofs involving arrays. It takes a good deal more thinking to design programs without arrays, just as it takes more thinking to do without gotos. But the resulting designs are better thought out, easier to prove, and have more function per instruction than array programs.

For example, the array-to-array assignment $x[i] := y[j + k]$ is but one of four instructions needed to move an item of data from y to x (assignments required for x, i, j, and k).

On the other hand, a stack to queue assignment, such as $back(x) := top(y)$ moves the top of stack y to the back of queue x with no previous assignments. Of course it takes more planning to have the right item at the top of stack y when it is needed for the back of queue x.

This discipline for data access, using stacks and queues instead of arrays, has been used in developing a complex language processing system of some 35,000 lines.[2] Independent estimates of its size indicates a factor of up to five more function per instruction than would be expected with array designs.

The design was fully verified, going to system test without the benefit of program debugging of any kind. System testing revealed errors of mathematical fallibility in the program at a rate of 2.5 per thousand instructions, all easily found and fixed. The kernel of the system (some 20,000 instructions) has been operating for two years since its system test with no errors detected.

Functional verification instead of unit debugging. The functional verification of structured programs permits the production of high-quality software without unit debugging. Just as gotos and arrays have seemed necessary, so unit debugging has also seemed necessary. However, practical experience with functional verification has demonstrated that software can be developed without debugging by the developers with some very beneficial results.

This latent ability in programmers using functional verification has a surprising synergy with statistical testing at the system level — that is, testing software against user-representative, statistically-generated input.[3] Statistical testing has not been used much as a development technique — and indeed for good reason in dealing with software that requires considerable defect removal just to make it work at all, let alone work reliably. However, statistical testing of functionally verified structured programs is indeed effective.

Cleanroom software development. The combined discipline of no unit debugging and statistical testing is called cleanroom software development. The term "cleanroom" refers to the emphasis on defect prevention instead of defect removal, as used in hardware fabrication, but applied now to the design process rather than the manufacturing process.

In fact, cleanroom software development permits the development of software under statistical quality control by iterating incremental development and testing. Early increments can be tested statistically for scientific estimates of their quality and for management feedback into the development process for later increments to achieve prescribed levels of quality.

At first glance, no unit debugging in software development seems strange, because unit debugging appears to be such an easy way to remove most of the defects that might be in the software. However, unit debugging is a good way to inadvertently trade simple blunders for deep system errors through the tunnel vision of debugging. And the very prospect of unit testing invites a dependence on debugging that undermines concentration and discipline otherwise possible.

More positively, eliminating unit testing and debugging leads to several benefits:

• more serious attention to design and verification as an integrated personal activity by each programmer,

---

> *The latent ability of people in new technologies is a source of continual amazement to experts.*

• more serious attention to design and verification inspection by programming teams,

• preserving the design hypothesis for statistical testing and control (debugging compromises the design),

• selecting qualified personnel by their ability to produce satisfactory programs without unit debugging, and

• high morale of qualified personnel.

On the other hand, user-representative, statistical testing of software never before debugged provides several benefits:

• valid scientific estimates of the software's reliability and the rate of its growth in reliability when errors are discovered and fixed during system testing,

• forced recognition by programmers of the entire specification input space and program design by specification decomposition (instead of getting a main line running then adding exception logic later), and

• the most effective way to increase the reliability of software through testing and fixing.

The evidence is that industrial programming teams can produce software with unprecedented quality. Instead of coding in 50 errors per thousand lines of code and removing 90 percent by debugging to leave five errors per thousand lines, programmers using functional verification can produce code that has never been executed

with less than five errors per thousand lines and remove nearly all of them in statistical system testing.

Furthermore, the errors found after functional verification are qualitatively different than errors left from debugging. The functional verification errors are due to mathematical fallibility and appear as simple blunders in code — blunders that statistical tests can effectively uncover.

Limits of human performance. The latent ability of people in new technologies is a source of continual amazement to experts. For example, 70 years ago, experts could confidently predict that production automobiles would one day go 70 miles an hour. But how many experts would have predicted that 70-year-old grandmothers would be driving them?!

Thirty years ago, experts were predicting that computers would be world chess champions, but not predicting much for programmers except more trial and error in writing the programs that would make chess champions out of the computers. As usual, it was easy to overestimate the future abilities of machines and underestimate the future abilities of people. Computers are not chess champions yet, but programmers are exceeding all expectations in logical precision.

From the beginning of computer programming, it has been axiomatic that errors are necessary in programs because people are fallible. That is indisputable, but is not very useful without quantification. Although it is the fashion to measure errors per thousand lines of code, a better measure is errors released per person-year of software development effort.

Such a measure compensates for the differences in complexity of programs — high complexity programs have more errors per thousand lines of code but also require more effort per thousand lines of code. It normalizes out complexity differences and has the further advantage of relating errors to effort rather than product, which is more fundamental.

For example, the *New York Times* released error rate was about one error per person-year of effort. That was considered an impossible goal before that time, but it is consistently bettered by advanced programming teams today.

An even better result was achieved by Paul Friday in the 1980 census software system for the distributed control of the national census data collection and communications network. The real-time software contained some 25,000 lines, developed with structured programming and functional verification, and ran throughout the production of the census (almost a year) with no errors detected.

Friday was awarded a gold medal, the highest award of the Commerce Department (which manages the Census Bureau), for this achievement. Industrial software experts, looking at the function provided, regard the 25,000 lines as very economical, indeed. (It seems to be characteristic of high-quality, functionally verified software to have more function per line than is usual.)

At 2500 lines of code per person-year for software of moderate complexity, and one error per 10 person-years of effort, the result is one expected error for a 25,000-line software system. Conversely, a 25,000-line software system should prove to be error-free with appreciable probability.

These achievements already exist. With data structured programming, functional verification and cleanroom software development (and good management), we can expect another factor of 10 improvement in this dimension of performance in the next decade.

Structured programming has reduced much of the unnecessary complexity of programming and can increase human expectations and achievements accordingly. Even so, there is much yet to be done. It is not enough to teach university students how to verify the correctness of toy programs without teaching them how to scale up their reasoning to large and realistic programs. A new undergraduate textbook[15] seeks to address this issue.

Better software development tools are needed to reduce human fallibility. An interactive debugger is an outstanding example of what is not needed — it encourages trial-and-error hacking rather than systematic design, and also hides marginal people barely qualified for precision programming. A proof organizer and checker is a more promising direction.

It is not enough for industrial management to count lines of code to measure productivity any more than they count words spoken per day by salesmen. Better management understandings are needed for evaluating programming performance, as are increased investment in both education and tools for true productivity and quality.

But the principal challenge for management is to organize and focus well-educated software engineers in effective teams. The limitations of human fallibility, while indisputable, have been greatly exaggerated, especially with the checks and balances of well-organized teams. ☐

Acknowledgments

I appreciate the early help of the Fundamental Concepts in Software Engineering Series' editorial board, especially its editor-in-chief, Norman Schneidewind, in materially shaping this article. Key technical suggestions and improvements, due to David Gries and *IEEE Software*'s referees, are appreciated very much.

References

1. Edsger W. Dijkstra, "Structured Programming," in *Software Engineering Techniques*, J.N. Buxton and B. Randell, eds., NATO Science Committee, Rome, 1969, pp. 88-93.
2. Harlan D. Mills and Richard C. Linger, "Data Structured Programming: Program Design without Arrays and Pointers," *IEEE Trans. Software Eng.*, Vol. SE-12, No. 2, Feb. 1986, pp. 192-197.
3. Paul A. Currit, Michael Dyer, and Harlan D. Mills, "Certifying the Reliability of Software," *IEEE Trans. Software Eng.*, Vol. SE-12, No. 1, Jan. 1986, pp. 3-11.
4. O.J. Dahl, Edsger W. Dijkstra, and C.A.R. Hoare, *Structured Programming*, Academic Press, New York, 1972.
5. Corrado Boehm and Giuseppe Jacopini, "Flow Diagrams, Turing Machines, and Languages with Only Two Formation Rules," *Comm. ACM*, Vol. 9, No. 5, May 1966, pp. 366-371.
6. F. Terry Baker, "Chief-Programmer Team Management of Production Programming," *IBM Systems J.*, Vol. 1, No. 1, 1972, pp. 56-73.
7. F. Terry Baker, "System Quality Through Structured Programming," *AFIPS Conf. Proc. FJCC, Part 1*, 1972, pp. 339-343.
8. Richard C. Linger, Harlan D. Mills, and Bernard I. Witt, *Structured Programming: Theory and Practice*, Addison-Wesley, Reading, Mass., 1979.
9. Harlan D. Mills, *Software Productivity*, Little, Brown, and Co., Boston, 1983.
10. Niklaus Wirth, "Program Development by Stepwise Refinement," *Comm. ACM*, Vol. 14, No. 4, April 1971, pp. 221-227.
11. C.A.R. Hoare, "An Axiomatic Basis for Computer Programming," *Comm. ACM*, Vol. 12, No. 10, Oct. 1969, pp. 576-583.
12. Anthony J. Jordano, "DSM Software Architecture and Development," *IBM Technical Directions*, Vol. 10, No. 3, 1984, pp. 17-28.
13. Edsger W. Dijkstra, *A Discipline of Programming*, Prentice-Hall, Englewood Cliffs, N.J., 1976.
14. David Gries, *The Science of Programming*, Springer-Verlag, New York, 1981.
15. Harlan D. Mills et al., *Principles of Computer Programming: A Mathematical Approach*, Allyn and Bacon, Rockleigh, N.J., 1987.

The Programming Language

Doug Bell

School of Computing and Management Science
Sheffield Hallam University
Hallamshire Business Park
Sheffield S11 8HB, UK,

Ian Morrey

School of Computing and Management Science
Sheffield Hallam University
Hallamshire Business Park
Sheffield S11 8HB, UK

John Pugh

School of Computer Science
Carleton University
Ottawa, Canada

1. Introduction

Everyone involved in programming has their favourite programming language, or language feature they would like to have available. This paper does not present a survey of programming languages, nor is it an attempt to recommend one language over another. Rather, we wish to discuss the features that a good programming language should have from the viewpoint of the software engineer. We limit our discussion to 'traditional' procedural languages such as Fortran, Cobol, Pascal, C, and Ada. The main thrust will be a discussion of the features a language should provide to assist the software development process. That is, what features encourage the development of software that is reliable, maintainable, and efficient?

It is important to realise that programming languages are very difficult animals to evaluate and compare. For example, although it is often claimed that language X is a general-purpose language, in practice languages tend to be used within particular communities. Thus, Cobol is often the preferred language of the data processing community; Fortran, the language of the scientist and engineer; C, the language of the systems programmer; and Ada, the language for developing real-time or embedded computer systems. Cobol is not equipped for applications requiring complex numerical computation, just as the data description facilities in Fortran are poor and ill-suited to data processing applications.

Programming languages are classified in many ways, for example, "high-level" or "low-level." A high-level language such as Cobol, Fortran, or Ada, is said to be problem-oriented and to reduce software production and maintenance costs. A low-level language such as assembler is said to be machine-oriented and to allow programmers complete control over the efficiency of their programs. Between high- and low-level languages, another class, the systems implementation language or high-level assembler, has emerged. Languages such as C attempt to bind into a single language the expressive power of a high-level language and the ultimate control that only a language that provides access at the register and primitive machine instruction level can provide. Languages may also be classified using other concepts such as whether they are block-structured or not, whether they are weakly or strongly typed, and whether they are compiled or interpreted.

The selection of a programming language for a particular project will be influenced by many factors not directly related to the programming language itself. For example, many organisations have a substantial investment in a particular programming language. Over a period of time, hundreds of thousands of lines of code may have been developed, and the programming staff will have built up considerable expertise with the language. In such a situation, there is often considerable resistance to change even if a "superior" language is available. There are other factors that can influence programming language selection. The software developer may be bound by a contract that actually specifies the implementation language. Decisions by the U.S. government to support Cobol and, more recently, Ada, considerably influenced the acceptance of those languages. Support from suppliers of major software components, such as language compilers and database management systems, will influence language selection for many developers. If an apparent bug appears in a compiler, for example, they need to know that they can pick up the telephone and get the supplier to help them. Similarly, the availability of software tools such as language-sensitive editors, debugging systems and project management tools may favour one programming language over another. The development of language-based programming environments that combine the programming language with an extensive set of development tools, such as UNIX (for C) and the Ada Programming Support Environment (APSE) will be an increasing influence on language selection.

Although the factors discussed above may influence the choice of programming language for a particular project, it is still most important to define what characteristics we expect from a programming language for software engineering. It is useful to divide the discussion into those features required to support *programming in the small* and those required to support *programming in the large*. By programming in the small, we mean those features of the language required to support the coding of individual program modules or small programs. In this category, we include the simplicity, clarity, and orthogonality of the language, the language syntax, and facilities for control and data abstraction. By programming in the large, we mean those features of the language that support the development of large programs. Here, we define a "large" program as one whose size or complexity dictates that it be developed by a number of programmers and which consists of a collection of individually developed program modules. In this category we include facilities for the separate compilation of program modules, features for controlling the interaction between program modules, high-level functional and data abstraction tools, and programming environments or support tools associated with the language.

2. Programming in the Small

2.1 Simplicity, Clarity, and Orthogonality

An important current school of thought argues that the only way to ensure that programmers will consistently produce reliable programs is to make the programming language simple. For programmers to become truly proficient in a language, the language must be small and simple enough that it can be understood in its entirety. The programmer can then use the language with confidence, probably without recourse to a language manual.

Cobol and PL/1 are examples of languages that are large and unwieldy. The ANSI standard for Cobol is 3 cm thick. By contrast, somewhat unfairly, the Pascal standard is 3 mm thick. What are the problems of large languages? Because they contain so many features, some are seldom used and, consequently, rarely fully understood. Also, since language features must not only be understood independently but also in terms of their interaction with each other, the larger the number of features, the more complex it will be to understand their interactions.

Although smaller, simpler languages are clearly desirable, the software engineer of the near future will have to wrestle with existing large, complex languages. For example, to meet the requirements laid down by its sponsors, the U.S. Department of Defense, the programming language Ada is a large and complex language requiring a three hundred page reference manual to describe it.

The clarity of a language is also an important factor. In recent years, there has been a marked and welcome trend to design languages for the programmers who program in them rather than for the machines the programs are to run on. Many older languages incorporate features that reflect the instruction sets of the computers they were originally designed to be executed on. The language designers of the sixties were motivated to prove that high-level languages could generate efficient code. Although we will be forever grateful to them for succeeding in proving this point, they introduced features into languages, such as Cobol and Fortran, that are clumsy and error-prone from the programmers' viewpoint. Moreover, even though the languages have subsequently been enhanced with features reflecting modern programming ideas, the original features still remain.

A programming language is the tool that programmers use to communicate their intentions. It should therefore be a language that accords with what people find natural, unambiguous, and meaningful—in other words, clear. Perhaps language designers are not the best judges of the clarity of a new language feature. A better approach to testing a language feature may be to set up controlled experiments in which subjects are asked to answer questions about fragments of program code. This experimental psychology approach is gaining some acceptance and some results are discussed later in the section on control abstractions. A programmer can only write reliable programs if he or she understands precisely what every language construct does. The quality of the language definition and supporting documentation are critical. Ambiguity or vagueness in the language definition erodes a programmer's confidence in the language. It should not be necessary to have to write a program fragment to confirm the semantics of some language feature.

Programming languages should also display a high degree of orthogonality. This means that it should be possible to combine language features freely; special cases and restrictions should not be prevalent. Although more orthogonal than many other languages, Pascal displays a lack of orthogonality in a number of areas. For example, it is entirely reasonable for a programmer to infer that values of all scalar types can be both read and written. In Pascal this is generally true, with the exception that booleans may be written but not read, and that enumerated types may not be read or written. Similarly, one would expect that functions would be able to return values of any type, rather than be restricted to returning values of only scalar types. A lack of orthogonality in a language has an unsettling effect on programmers; they no longer have the confidence to make generalizations and inferences about the language.

It is no easy matter to design a language that is simple, clear, and orthogonal. Indeed, in some cases these goals would seem to be incompatible with one another. A language designer could, for the sake of orthogonality, allow combinations of features that are not very useful. Simplicity would be sacrificed for increased orthogonality! While we await the simple, clear, orthogonal programming language of the future, these concepts remain good measures with which the software engineer can evaluate the programming languages of today.

2.2 Language Syntax

The syntax of a programming language should be consistent, natural, and promote the readability of programs. Syntactic flaws in a language can have a serious effect on program development. For example, studies have shown that syntax errors due to the misuse of semi-colons are ten times more likely to occur in a language using the semi-colon as a separator than in a language using it as a terminator. Another syntactic flaw found in languages is the use of BEGIN .. END pairs or bracketing conventions for grouping statements together. Omitting an END or closing bracket is a very common programming error. The use of explicit keywords, such as END IF and END WHILE, leads to fewer errors and more readily under-standable programs. Programs are also easier to maintain.

The static, physical layout of a program should reflect as far as is possible the dynamic algorithm that the program describes. There are a number of syntactic concepts to help achieve this goal. The ability to freely format a program allows the programmer the freedom to use techniques such as indentation and blank lines to highlight the structure and improve the readability of a program. Older languages such as Fortran and Cobol imposed a fixed formatting style on the programmer. Components of statements were constrained to lie within certain columns on each input source line. These constraints are not intuitive to the programmer; rather, they date back to the time when programs were normally presented to the computer in the form of decks of 80-column punched cards. A program statement was normally expected to be contained on a single card.

The readability of a program can also be improved by the use of *meaningful identifiers* to name program objects. Limitations on the length of names, as found in early versions of BASIC (2 characters) and Fortran (6 characters), force the programmer to use unnatural, cryptic, and error-prone abbreviations. These restrictions were dictated by the need for efficient programming language compilers. Arguably, programming languages should be designed to be convenient for the programmer rather than the compiler and the ability to use meaningful names, irrespective of their length, enhances the self-documenting properties of a program.

Another factor that affects the readability of a program is the consistency of language syntax. For example, operators should not have different meanings in different contexts. The operator '=' should not double as both the assignment operator and the equality operator. Similarly, it should not be possible for the meaning of language keywords to change under programmer control. The keyword IF, for example, should be used solely for expressing conditional statements. If the programmer is able to define an array with the identifier IF, the time required to read and understand the program will be increased as we must now examine the context in which the identifier IF is used to determine its meaning.

2.3 Control Abstractions

A programming language for software engineering must provide a small but powerful set of control structures to describe the flow of execution within a program unit. In the late sixties and seventies there was considerable debate as to what control structures were required. The advocates of structured programming have largely won the day and there is now a reasonable consensus of opinion as to what kind of primitive control structures are essential. A language must provide primitives for the three basic structured programming constructs: sequence, selection, and repetition. There are, however, considerable variations both in the syntax and the semantics of the control structures found in modern programming languages. Early programming languages, such as Fortran, did not provide a rich set of control structures. The programmer used a set of low-level control structures, such as the unconditional branch or GOTO statement and the logical IF to express the control flow within a program. These low-level control structures provide the programmer with too much freedom to construct poorly structured programs. In particular, uncontrolled use of the GOTO statement for controlling program flow leads to programs that are hard to read and unreliable.

There is now general agreement that higher level control abstractions must be provided and should consist of:

- *Sequence*—to group together a related set of program statements
- *Selection*—to select whether a group of statements should be executed or not based on the value of some condition.
- *Repetition*—to repeatedly execute a group of statements.

This basic set of primitives fits in well with the top-down philosophy of program design; each primitive has a single entry point and a single exit point. These primitives are realized in similar ways in most programming languages. For brevity, we will look in detail only at representative examples from common programming languages.

2.3.1 Selection

Ada provides two basic selection constructs; the first, the IF statement, provides one or two-way selection and the second, the CASE statement, provides a convenient multi-way selection structure. When evaluating the conditional statements in a programming language, the following factors must be considered.

- Does the language use explicit closing symbols, such as END IF, thus avoiding the 'dangling else' problem?
- Nested conditional statements can quite easily become unreadable. Does the language provide any help? For example, the readability of "chained" IF statements can be improved by the introduction of an ELSIF

clause. In particular, this eliminates the need for multiple ENDIF's to close a series of nested IF's.

- The expressiveness of the case statement is impaired if the type of the case selector is restricted. It should not have to be an integer.
- Similarly, it should be easy to specify multiple alternative case choices (for example, 1 | 5 | 7 meaning 1 or 5 or 7) and a range of values as a case choice (for example, Monday .. Friday or 1 .. 99).
- The reliability of the case statement is enhanced if the case choices must specify actions for **ALL** the possible values of the case selector. If not, the semantics should, at least, clearly state what will happen if the case expression evaluates to an unspecified choice. The ability to specify an action for all unspecified choices through a WHEN OTHERS or similar clause is optimal.

It would be natural to think that there would no longer be any controversy over language structures for selection. The IF-THEN-ELSE is apparently well-established. However, the lack of symmetry in the **IF** statement has been criticised. While it is clear that the THEN part is carried out if the condition is true, the ELSE part is instead tagged on at the end to cater for all other situations. Experimental evidence suggests that significantly fewer bugs will result if the programmer is required to restate the condition (in its negative form) prior to the ELSE as shown below:

```
IF condition THEN
    statement_1
NOT condition ELSE
    statement_2
ENDIF
```

2.3.2 Repetition

Control structures for repetition traditionally fall into two classes: loop structures where the number of iterations is fixed, and those where the number of iterations is controlled by the evaluation of some condition. The usefulness and reliability of the FOR statement for fixed length iterations can be affected by a number of issues:

- The type of the loop control variable should not be limited to integers. Any ordinal type should be allowed. However, reals should not be allowed. For example, how many iterations are specified by the following:

```
FOR X := 0.0 TO 1.0 STEP 0.33 DO
```

It is not at all obvious, and things are made worse by the fact, that computers represent real values only approximately. (Note how disallowing the use of reals as loop control variables conflicts with the aim of orthogonality).

- The semantics of the FOR is greatly affected by the answers to the following questions. When and how many times are the initial expression, final expression, and step expressions evaluated? Can any of these expressions be modified within the loop? What is of concern here is whether or not it is clear how many iterations of the loop will be performed. If the expressions can be modified and the expressions are recomputed on each iteration, then there is a distinct possibility of producing an infinite loop.

- Similar problems arise if the loop control variable can be modified within the loop. A conservative but safe approach similar to that taken by Pascal (which precludes assignment into the loop control variable) is preferred.

- The scope of the loop control variable is best limited to the FOR statement. If it is not, then what should its value be on exit from the loop, or should it be undefined?

Condition controlled loops are far simpler in form. Almost all modern languages provide a leading decision repetition structure (WHILE .. DO) and some, for convenience, also provide a trailing decision form (REPEAT .. UNTIL). The WHILE form continues to iterate while a condition evaluates to true. Since the test appears at the head of the form, the WHILE performs zero or many iterations of the loop body. The REPEAT, on the other hand, iterates until a condition is true. The test appears following the body of the loop ensuring that the REPEAT performs at least one iteration.

The WHILE and REPEAT structures are satisfactory for the vast majority of iterations we wish to specify. For the most part, loops that terminate at either their beginning or end are sufficient. However, there are situations, notably when encountering some exceptional condition, where it is appropriate to be able to branch out of a repetition structure at an arbitrary point within the loop. Often it is necessary to break out of a series of nested loops rather than a single loop. In many languages, the programmer is limited to two options. The terminating conditions of each loop can be modified to accommodate the "exceptional" exit and IF statements can be used within the loop to transfer control to the end of the

loop should the exceptional condition occur. This solution is clumsy at best and considerably decreases the readability of the code. A second, and arguably better, solution is to use the much-maligned GOTO statement to branch directly out of the loops. Ideally however, since there is a recognised need for *N and a half* times loops, the language should provide a controlled way of exiting from one or more loops. Ada provides such a facility where an orderly EXIT may be made but only to the statement following the loop(s).

2.4 Data Types and Strong Typing

A significant part of the software engineer's task is concerned with how to model, within a program, objects from some problem domain. Programming, after all, is largely the manipulation of data. In the words of Niklaus Wirth, the designer of Pascal, Algorithms + Data Structures = Programs. The data description and manipulation facilities of a programming language should therefore allow the programmer to represent 'real-world' objects easily and faithfully. In recent years, increasing attention has been given to the problem of providing improved data abstraction facilities for programmers. Discussion has largely centered around the concept of a data type, the advantages of strongly typed languages, and language features to support abstract data types. The latter is an issue best considered in the context of 'programming in the large' and will therefore be discussed later.

A data type is a set of data objects and a set of operations applicable to all objects of that type. Almost all languages can be thought of as supporting this concept to some extent. Many languages require the programmer to explicitly define the type (for example, integer or character) of all objects to be used in a program and, to some extent or another, depending on the individual language, this information prescribes the operations that can be applied to the objects. Thus, we could state, for example, that Fortran, Cobol, C, Pascal, and Ada are all typed languages. However, only Pascal (mostly) and Ada would be considered strongly typed languages.

A language is said to be *strongly typed* if it can be determined at compile-time whether or not each operation performed on an object is consistent with the type of that object. Operations inconsistent with the type of an object are considered illegal. A strongly typed language therefore forces the programmer to consider more closely how objects are to be defined and used within a program. The additional information provided to the compiler by the programmer allows the compiler to perform automatic type-checking operations and discover type inconsistencies. Studies have shown that programs written in strongly typed languages are clearer, more reliable, and more portable. Strong typing necessarily places some restrictions on what a programmer may do with data objects. However, this apparent decrease in flexibility is more than compensated for by the increased security and reliability of the ensuing programs. Languages such as Lisp, APL, and POP-2 allow a variable to change its type at run-time. This is known as *dynamic typing* as opposed to the *static typing* found in languages where the type of an object is permanently fixed.

Where dynamic typing is employed, type checking must occur at run-time rather than compile-time. Dynamic typing provides additional freedom and flexibility but at a cost. More discipline is required on the part of the programmer so that the freedom provided by dynamic typing is not abused. That freedom is often very useful, even necessary, in some applications—for example, problem-solving programs that use sophisticated artificial intelligence techniques for searching complex data structures would be very difficult to write in languages without dynamic typing.

What issues need to be considered when evaluating the data type facilities provided by a programming language? We suggest the following list:

- Does the language provide an adequate set of primitive data types?

- Can these primitives be combined in useful ways to form aggregate or structured data types?

- Does the language allow the programmer to define new data types? How well do such new data types integrate with the rest of the language?

- To what extent does the language support the notion of strong typing?

- When are data types considered equivalent?

- Are type conversions handled in a safe and secure manner?

- Is it possible for the programmer to circumvent automatic type checking operations?

2.4.1 Primitive Data Types

Programmers are accustomed to having a rudimentary set of primitive data types available. We have come to expect that the primitive types, *Boolean*, *Character*, *Integer*, and *Real*, together with a supporting cast of operations (relational, arithmetic etc.) will be provided. For each type, it should be possible to clearly define the form of the literals or constants that make up the type. For example , the constants *true* and *false* make up the set of constants for the type *Boolean*.

Similarly, we should be able to define the operations for each type. For the type *Boolean*, these might include the operations =, <>, NOT, AND, and OR. For certain application domains, advanced computation facilities such as extended precision real numbers or long integers might be essential. The ability to specify the range of integers and reals and the precision to which reals are represented reduces the dependence on the physical characteristics, such as the word size, of a particular machine and thus increases the portability of programs. Types should only be associated with objects through explicit declarations. Implicit declarations, such as those allowed in Fortran, where, by default, undeclared variables beginning with the letters "I" through "N" are considered to be of type integer, should be avoided. The use of such conventions encourages the use of cryptic names.

The *Pointer* data type is provided by modern languages such as Pascal and Ada but not by older languages such as Fortran and Cobol. Pointers provide the programmer with the ability to refer to a data object indirectly. We can manipulate the object 'pointed' to or referenced by the pointer. Pointers are particularly useful in situations where the size of a data aggregate cannot be predicted in advance or where the structure of the aggregates are dynamically varying. Recursive data structures, such as lists and trees, are more easily described using pointers. Similarly, operations such as deleting an element from a linked list or inserting a new element into a balanced binary tree are more easily accomplished using pointers. Although such data types can be implemented using arrays, the mapping is less clear and certainly less flexible.

The use of pointers is not without pitfalls. The pointer is often mentioned in the same sentence as the infamous GOTO as a potential source for obtuse and error-prone code. A number of issues should be considered when evaluating a language's implementation of pointers.

- Since the same data object may be referenced through more than one pointer variable, care must be taken not to create 'dangling references'. That is, a pointer that references a location that is no longer in use. Does the language provide any assistance in reducing the opportunities for such errors?

- The security of pointers is enhanced in languages, such as Ada and Pascal, that require the programmer to bind a pointer variable to reference only objects of a particular type. Programs written in languages, such as C, that allow pointers to dynamically reference different types of object are often awkward to debug.

- What provisions, for example, scoping mechanisms, explicit programmer action, or garbage collection procedures, does the language provide for the reclamation of space that is no longer referenced by any pointer variable?

The readability, reliability, and data abstraction capabilities of a language are enhanced considerably if the programmer can extend the primitive data types provided as standard by the language. The ability to define user-defined types separates the languages Pascal and Ada from their predecessors. In addition to defining completely new types, it is also useful to be able to define types that are subranges of existing types. In a strongly typed language the compiler can automatically generate code to perform run-time checks to ensure that this will always be so. In a weakly typed language, the responsibility for adding such code falls on the programmer.

2.4.2 Structured Data Types

Composite data types allow the programmer to model structured data objects. The most common aggregate data abstraction provided by programming languages is the *array*; a collection of homogeneous elements that may be referenced through their positions within the collection. Arrays are characterised by the type of their elements and by the index or subscript range or ranges that specify the size, number of dimensions, and how individual elements of the array may be referenced. Individual elements of an array can be referenced by specifying the array name and an expression for each subscript. The implementation of arrays in programming languages raises the following considerations for the programmer.

- What restrictions are placed on the element type? For complete freedom of expression, there should be no restrictions. Similarly, the index type should be any valid subrange of any ordinal type.
- At what time must the size of an array be known? The utility of arrays in a programming language is governed by the time (compile-time or run-time) at which the size of the array must be known.
- What aggregate operations may be applied to arrays? For example, it is very convenient to be able to carry out array assignment between compatible arrays.

- Are convenient methods available for the initialisation of arrays?

The time at which a size must be bound to an array has important implications on how the array may be used. In Pascal, the size of an array must be defined statically. The size and subscript ranges are required to be known at compile-time. This has the advantage of allowing the compiler to generate code to automatically check for out of range subscripts. However, the disadvantage of this simple scheme is that, to allow the program to accommodate data sets of differing sizes, we often wish to delay determining the size of the array until run-time. A further problem exists in Pascal in that formal array parameters to procedures must also specify their size statically. This makes it impossible to write a general routine to manipulate an arbitrary-sized matrix. Rather, a specific routine must be defined for each particular size of matrix. This is very inconvenient and inefficient; many implementations of Pascal now include a feature (conformant arrays) to deal with this very problem. However, less restrictive approaches are to be found. Ada, for example, allows the specification of array types in which the subscript ranges are not fixed at compile-time.

Data objects in problem domains are not always simply collections of homogeneous objects. Rather, they are often collections of heterogeneous objects. Although such collections can be represented using arrays, most programming languages, but notably not Fortran, provide a *record* data aggregate. *Records* (or structures) are generalisations of arrays where the elements (or fields) may be of different types and where individual components are referenced by (field) name rather than by position. Each component of a record may be of any type including aggregate types such as arrays and records. Similarly, the element type of an array might be a record type.

Programming languages that provide data abstractions such as arrays and records and allow them to be combined orthogonally in this fashion allow a wide range of real data objects to be modelled in a natural fashion. This is not true of all languages; for example, Fortran. Components of records are selected by naming the required field rather than by providing a numeric subscript.

Sometimes, records whose structure is not completely fixed can be useful. Such records normally contain a special field, known as the tag field, the value of which determines the structure of the record. Records with varying structures are known as *variant records* or, since the record type can be thought of as a union of several subtypes based on some discriminating tag field, as *discriminated unions*. In Pascal, the

210

implementation of variant records is very insecure. Pascal allows programmers to assign into the tag field of a variant record variable at any time. This logically indicates a dynamic change in the structure of the record. As a consequence no run-time checks are performed and the onus is on the programmer to write defensive code to ensure no illegal references to variant fields are made. Furthermore, Pascal allows the tag field to be omitted.

Variant records are one reason why Pascal is not considered as strongly typed as Ada. Ada adopts a safer approach, restricting the programmer to specify the tag field when a record variable is created and disallowing subsequent changes to the value of the tag field.

2.4.3 Strong versus Weak Typing

The debate as to whether strongly typed languages are preferable to weakly typed languages closely mirrors the earlier debate among programming language afficionados about the virtues of the GOTO statement. The pro-GOTO group argued that the construct was required and its absence would restrict programmers. The anti-GOTO group contended that indiscriminate use of the construct encouraged the production of "spaghetti-like" code. The result has been a compromise; the use of the GOTO is restricted to cases where it is clearly the most convenient control structure to use.

The anti-strongly typed languages group similarly argue that some classes of programs are very difficult, if not impossible, to write in strongly typed languages. The pro-strongly typed languages group argue that the increased reliability and security outweigh these disadvantages. We believe that a similar compromise will be struck; strong typing will be generally seen as most desirable but languages will provide well-defined escape mechanisms to circumvent type checking for those instances where it is truly required.

What programmer flexibility is lost in a strongly typed language? Weakly typed languages such as Fortran and C provide little compile-time type-checking support. However, they do provide the ability to view the representation of an object as different types. For example, using the EQUIVALENCE statement in Fortran, a programmer is able to subvert typing. This language feature is dangerous; programs using it will be unclear and not be portable. Variant records in Pascal can be used in a similar, underhand fashion to circumvent type-checking operations.

To a small number of systems programming applications, the ability to circumvent typing to gain access to the underlying physical representation of data is essential. How should this be provided in a language that is strongly typed? The best solution seems to be to force the programmer to state *explicitly* in the code that he or she wishes to violate the type checking operations of the language. This approach is taken by Ada where an object may be reinterpreted as being of a different type only by using the UNCHECKED_CONVERSION facility.

The question of conversion between types is inextricably linked with the strength of typing in a language. Fortran, being weakly typed, performs many conversions (or coercions) implicitly during the evaluation of arithmetic expressions. These implicit conversions may result in a loss of information and can be dangerous to the programmer. Fortran allows mixed mode arithmetic and freely converts reals to integers on assignment. Pascal and strongly typed languages perform implicit conversions **only** when there will be no accompanying loss of information. Thus, an assignment of an integer to a real variable will result in implicit conversion of the integer to a real. However, an attempt to assign a real value to an integer variable will result in a type incompatibility error. Such an assignment must be carried out using an explicit conversion function. That is, the programmer is forced by the language to explicitly consider the loss of information implied by the use of the conversion function.

2.5 Procedural Abstraction

Procedural or algorithmic abstraction is one of the most powerful tools in the programmer's arsenal. When designing a program, we abstract *what* should be done before we specify *how* it should be done. Program designs evolve as layers of abstractions; each layer specifying more detail than the layer above. Procedural abstractions in programming languages, such as procedures and functions, allow the layered design of a program to be accurately reflected in the modular structure of the program text. Even in relatively small programs, the ability to factor a program into small, functional modules is essential; factoring increases the readability and maintainability of programs. What does the software engineer require from a language in terms of support for procedural abstraction? We suggest the following list of requirements.

- An adequate set of primitives for defining procedural abstractions, including support for recursion.
- Safe and efficient mechanisms for controlling communication between program units.
- Simple, clearly defined mechanisms for controlling access to data objects defined within program units.

211

The basic procedural abstraction primitives provided in programming languages are *procedures* and *functions*. Procedures can be thought of as extending the statements of the language while functions can be thought of as extending the operators of the language. When a procedure is called, it achieves its effect by modifying the environment of the program unit that called it. Optimally, this effect is communicated to the calling program unit in a controlled fashion by the modification of the parameters passed to the procedure. Functions, like their mathematical counterparts, may return only a single value and must therefore be embedded within expressions.

The power of procedural abstraction is that it allows the programmer to consider the procedure or function as an independent entity performing a well-described task largely independent of the rest of the program. It is critical that the interface between program units be small and well defined if we are to achieve independence between units. Procedures should only accept and return information through their parameters. Functions should accept but not return information through their parameters. A single result should be returned as the result of invoking a function.

Unfortunately, programming languages do not enforce even these simple, logical rules. It is largely the responsibility of the programmer to ensure that procedures and functions do not have side effects. The programming language itself does not prevent programmers from directly accessing and modifying data objects defined outside of the local environment of the procedure or function. Many abstractions, particularly those that manipulate recursive data structures such as lists, graphs, and trees, are more concisely described recursively. Amongst widely used languages, Cobol and Fortran do not support recursion directly.

2.5.1 Parameter Passing Mechanisms

Programmers require three basic modes of interaction through parameters:

- *Input Parameters* to allow a procedure or function *read-only* access to an actual parameter. The actual parameter is purely an input parameter; the procedure or function should not be able to modify the value of the actual parameter.

- *Output Parameters* to allow a procedure *write-only* access to an actual parameter. The actual parameter is purely an output parameter; the procedure should not be able to read the value of the actual parameter.

- *Input-Output Parameters* to allow a procedure *read-write* access to an actual parame-

ter. The value of the actual parameter may be modified by the procedure.

Note that, by definition, Output and Input-Output parameters should not be supplied to functions. Most programming languages, including Fortran and Pascal, do not automatically enforce this restriction. Again, the onus is on the programmer not to write functions with side-effects. These same languages also, unfortunately, restrict the type of result that may be returned from functions to scalar types only. Ada only allows Input variables to functions but side effects may still occur through modification of non-local variables.

A number of parameter-passing schemes are employed in programming languages but no language provides a completely safe and secure parameter-passing mechanism. Fortran employs only a single parameter passing mode; *call by reference*. This mode equates to Input-Output parameters. Thus, undesirably, all actual parameters in Fortran may potentially be changed by any subroutine or function. The programmer is responsible for ensuring the safe implementation of Input and Output parameters. Using call by reference, the location of the actual parameter is bound to the formal parameter. The formal and actual parameter names are thus *aliases*; modification of the formal parameter automatically modifies the actual parameter. This method is particularly appropriate for passing large, aggregate data structures as parameters as no copying of the values of the parameters will be carried out.

Pascal uses both call by reference (*VAR* parameters) and *call by value*. Call by reference is used for both Input-Output and Output parameters while call by value provides a more secure implementation of Input parameters. When parameters are passed by value, a copy of the value of the actual parameter is passed to the formal parameter, which acts as a variable local to the procedure; modification of the formal parameter therefore does not modify the value of the actual parameter. This method is inefficient for passing large, aggregate data structures, as copies must be made. In such situations, it is commonplace to pass the data structure by reference even if the parameter should not be modified by the procedure.

Call by value-result is often used as an alternative to call by reference for Input-Output parameters. It avoids the use of aliases at the expense of copying. Parameters passed by value-result are initially treated as in call by value; a copy of the value of the actual parameter is passed to the formal parameter that again acts as a local variable. Manipulation of the formal parameter does not immediately affect the actual parameter. On exit from the procedure, the final value of the formal is assigned into the actual parameter.

Call by result may be used as an alternative to call by reference for Output parameters. Parameters passed by value are treated exactly as those passed by value-result except that no initial value is assigned to the local formal parameter.

The parameter-passing mechanisms used in Ada (*in*, *out*, and *in out*) are described in a similar fashion to the input, output, and input-output parameters described above and would therefore seem to be ideal. However, Ada does not specify whether they are to be implemented using sharing or copying. Though beneficial to the language implementor, since the space requirements of the parameter can be used to determine whether sharing or copying should be used, this decision can be troublesome to the programmer. In the presence of aliases, call by value-result and call by reference may return different results.

2.5.2 Scoping Mechanisms and Information Hiding

It should not be necessary for the programmer to know the implementation details of a procedure or a function in order to use it. In particular, the programmer should not need to consider the names used within the procedure or function. Large programs use thousands of names; the names used within a procedure should not influence the choice of names outside it. Similarly, objects used within the procedure, other than output or input-output parameters, should have no effect outside the procedure. When programs are developed by more than one programmer these issues become critical. Programmers must be able to develop routines independently of each other. The software engineer requires that a language support the concept of *information hiding*; concealing information that is not required. Advanced language features for the support of information hiding will be discussed in the next section. We limit discussion here to the control of access to data objects through scoping.

Programming languages use the concept of *scope* to control the visibility of names. The scope of a name in a program is the part of the program in which the name may be referenced. Support for scoping varies from language to language. BASIC provides no scoping and all names may therefore be referenced anywhere in a program. That is, all variables are *global*. This severely limits the usefulness of the language for the development of large programs.

The unit of scope in Fortran is the subroutine or function. Since subroutines and functions may not be nested, the scope of a name is the subroutine or function in which it is implicitly or explicitly declared. That is, all names are *local* to the program unit in which they are declared. There are no global names although the same effect may be achieved through the use of shared COMMON blocks.

Algol, Pascal, and Ada are known as *block-structured* languages. They use the more sophisticated concept of nested program blocks to control the scope of names. The scope of a name is the block (program, procedure, or function) in which it is declared. The multi-level scoping control offered by block-structured languages is of great assistance to the software engineer. Names may be re-used within the same program safely. More importantly, some information hiding is now possible.

3. Programming In The Large

The programming of very large, complex software projects, or programming in the large, introduces many new problems for the software engineer. First, what are the characteristics of such software systems? The size of the code is an obvious factor. Large systems consist of tens of thousands of lines of source code; systems with hundreds of thousands of lines are not uncommon. Projects of this size must be developed by teams of programmers; for very large projects the programming team may consist of hundreds of programmers. Such systems are implemented over a long period of time and when completed are expected to undergo continual maintenance and enhancement over an extended lifetime. Many of the problems associated with such large projects are logistical, caused by the sheer size of the task and the number of personnel involved. Methodologies for managing such projects have been developed and clearly many software tools, other than the programming language being used, are required to assist and control the development of such large systems. A recent trend has been to integrate these software tools with a particular programming language to form an integrated software development environment. An example of this is the Ada Programming Support Environment (APSE). In this section, we concentrate on support for programming in the large at the programming language level.

What support can we expect from a programming language? The programmer's chief tool in managing complexity is abstraction. Abstraction allows the programmer to keep a problem intellectually manageable. The programming language must therefore provide mechanisms that can be used to encapsulate the most common abstractions used by programmers: functional (or procedural) abstraction and data abstraction. The simplest mechanism, provided by nearly all programming languages, is the procedure: a program unit that allows the encapsulation of a functional abstraction. Programming in the large requires that higher level abstraction primitives than the procedure be provided.

The use of abstractions promotes modularity, which itself encourages the production of reusable code, and promotes the notion of information hiding. Modularity and module independence are essential in an environment where individual modules will most often be developed by different programmers. The programming language can support development in multi-programmer environments by providing mechanisms for hiding from a user irrelevant details concerning the implementation of a module.

Additionally, the interface between modules must be carefully controlled. It is essential to eliminate the possibility that the implementation of one module may affect another module in some unanticipated manner. This is also important when a system is being maintained or enhanced in some way. It must be possible to localise the effect of some system enhancement or error fix to specific modules of the system; side effects of changes should not propagate throughout the complete system.

Clearly, many of these issues are as much system design issues as they are programming language issues. No programming language will solve the problems of a poor system design. On the other hand, the implementation of a good system design can be hampered if the implementation language is of limited expressive power. If modules are to be developed independently, the programming language must also provide facilities for the independent compilation of program modules. In addition, the language should provide strong type-checking across module boundaries to ensure the consistency of calls to externally defined modules.

3.1 Functional and Data Abstraction

Functional abstraction is the traditional abstraction tool of the programmer. Programming methodologies such as top-down, stepwise refinement rely totally on functional abstraction. In programming language terms, such abstractions can be thought of as extending the operations provided by the language and appear within programs in the form of procedures and functions. In recent years, increasing attention has been paid to the notion of data abstraction. Many program design decisions involve:

- selecting an internal representation for some set of data objects from the problem domain.
- defining the operations to be performed on those objects.

In programming language terms, this can be thought of as extending the built-in primitive data types provided by a language with new *abstract data types*. The two abstraction mechanisms are comple-

mentary and are often used in concert with one another. Functional abstraction is often used to describe the implementation of the operations on abstract data types.

What do we require in terms of programming language support for data abstraction? An abstract data type consists of a set of objects and a set of operations that can be applied to those objects. The power of an abstraction mechanism is that it permits understanding of the essential ideas whilst suppressing irrelevant details. Thus, programming languages should support the concept of information hiding; that is, users should be provided with sufficient information to use the data type but nothing more. The most common way of achieving this is to separate out the specification of the data type from its implementation and to implement protection (scoping) mechanisms to ensure the privacy of information that should not be accessible to users. Users of a data type should be provided with a specification of the effect of each of the operations provided and a description of how to use each operation. They should not be required to know the representation of the data type nor be able to access it other than indirectly through an operation provided by the type. In summary, programming language support for abstraction should include:

- high-level encapsulation mechanisms for both functional and data abstraction.
- a clear separation between the specification (the users' view) of an abstraction and its implementation (the implementor's view).
- protection mechanisms to prevent user access to private information.
- support for the reusable program modules, that is, provision of library facilities and simple mechanisms for importing library modules into user programs.

3.1.1 Abstraction in Pascal

Pascal provides support for functional abstraction at the level of the procedure or function. There are no standard mechanisms to encapsulate collections of procedures although many non-standard extensions exist. Programming language support for abstract data types is variable; many programming languages, including Pascal, only provide support for what might be termed *transparent* data types: data types whose representation may be directly accessed by the programmer. That is, the representation is visible, not hidden. Pascal provides little support for data abstraction. There is no way of encapsulating a data type into a single program module. The data type and the application program are inextricably mixed. There is no clear mapping between the logical data type specified by the designer and the physical modules of the program. The lack of an encapsulation mechanism and the strict ordering (CONST, TYPE, VAR ..) of declarations enforced by Pascal poses almost insurmountable organisation problems in programs that require the use of multiple data types.

3.1.2 Abstraction in Ada

Ada provides far greater support for programming in the large than Pascal. Ada provides encapsulation mechanisms at the subprogram and package level. A package can encapsulate simply a collection of related procedures or can be used to encapsulate an abstract data type. A package consists of two parts; a specification and a body (or implementation). Each of these parts may be separately compiled. The specification can be used by the programmer to describe to users how to use the package and to determine what components of the package are to be visible to the user. The package body contains the implementation of all procedures belonging to the package and is not normally seen by users of the package. Thus, Ada satisfies our requirements for a high-level encapsulation mechanism and for a clear separation between the specification of an abstraction and its implementation.

Logically, details of the representation of the type should be in the package body rather than the specification. Unfortunately, Ada requires that details of the representation be provided in the specification. This enables the specification and body of the package to be compiled separately. However, the representation of the type is declared as private and described in the private part of the specification and is thus automatically protected from access by users of the type.

Unlike in Pascal, it is not possible for the Ada programmer to directly reference the representation of the type. Indeed, the representation of the type could be altered by the implementor without impacting on users of the type. Ada promotes reusable software by viewing packages as resources that should normally reside in a library from where they may be imported into any program, and it is the responsibility of the Ada programmer to explicitly state the dependency relationships between modules.

3.1.3 Generics—An advanced abstraction mechanism

The strong typing philosophy of programming languages such as Pascal and Ada can have a detrimental effect on programming efficiency. For example, suppose we defined a stack of integers as an abstract data type with the normal stack operations of Push and Pop, and so forth. If we subsequently needed another stack type, but one in which the elements were booleans rather than integers, then clearly the specification and implementation would be identical apart from the different stack element types. In Pascal, our only recourse would be to duplicate the stack data type; Push and Pop operations and a different representation would have to be provided for each of the two stack types. A more powerful stack abstraction is required that allows the stack element type to be parameterised.

The generic facility found in Ada and other languages provides a partial answer to this problem. Generics allow programmers to define templates (or patterns) for packages and procedures. These templates may then be used to instantiate actual packages and procedures with different parameters. Notwithstanding generics, statically typed programming languages restrict programmer flexibility in dealing with abstract data types. For example, in a statically typed language such as Ada all packages must be instantiated at compile-time. It is not possible, for example, to create stacks whose element types are determined dynamically or where the elements in the stack may not all be of the same type.

3.2 Separate Compilation

A programming language is ill-suited for the development of large, complex programs if it does not provide facilities for the separate compilation of program modules. Large programs must necessarily be developed by teams of programmers; individual programmers must be able to work independently and at the same time access programs written by other members of the team. Programming language support is required for the integration of routines that have been developed separately. Additional support in this area is often provided by environmental tools such as linkers, cross-reference generators, file librarians, and source code control systems. What support should the programming language itself provide? We suggest the following:

- independent compilation of program modules.
- easy access to libraries of precompiled software.
- the ability to integrate routines written in different languages.
- strong type checking across module boundaries.
- the ability to avoid the unnecessary recompilation of pre-compiled modules.

One of the foremost reasons for the continued popularity of Fortran is the tremendous resource of reusable software available to scientists and engineers through the readily accessible libraries of scientific and engineering subroutines. Fortran provides independent compilation of modules at the subroutine level and easy access to library routines but performs no run-time checking of calls to external routines. It is the responsibility of the programmer to check that the correct number and type of parameters are used in the calling program.

Standard Pascal provides no support for separate compilation. All modules must be integrated into a single, large program that is then compiled. In order to support the development of large programs, many implementations support language extensions that provide at least independent compilation, access to libraries, and the ability to integrate assembly language routines into Pascal programs. The major disadvantage of this approach is that programs using these non-standard extensions are no longer immediately portable.

Ada provides far greater support for separate compilation than Pascal or Fortran. Both subprograms and packages may be compiled as separate modules with strong type checking across module boundaries to ensure that they are used in accordance with their specifications. The specification and implementation of a package may be compiled in two separate parts. This has a number of advantages for the software engineer. The strong type checking ensures that all specifications stay in line with their implementations. Also, it means that once the specification for a package has been compiled, modules that use that package may also be compiled (even before the implementation of the package has been completed).

4. Summary

In this paper we have surveyed the characteristics that a programming language should have from the viewpoint of the software engineer. In summary, the following issues have been considered fundamentally important.

A programming language should:

- be well matched to the application area of the proposed project
- be clear and simple, and display a high degree of orthogonality
- have a syntax that is consistent and natural, and that promotes the readability of programs
- provide a small but powerful set of control abstractions
- provide an adequate set of primitive data abstractions
- support strong typing
- provide support for scoping and information hiding
- provide high-level support for functional and data abstraction
- provide a clear separation of the specification and the implementation of program modules
- support separate compilation

While software engineers, language designers and programmers might argue about the inclusion of particular items on the above list (or may suggest other issues that have been excluded), it is apparent that the features of an implementation language can have a profound effect on the success or failure of a project. Moreover, the programming task should not be isolated from its wider software engineering context.

5. Bibliography

Watt, D.A. *Programming Language Concepts and Paradigms*, Prentice Hall, Englewood Cliffs, N.J., 1990.

Meyer, B. *Introduction to the Theory of Programming Languages*, Prentice Hall, Englewood Cliffs, N.J., 1990.

Bell, D., Morrey, I. and Pugh, J. *Software Engineering—A Programming Approach*, Prentice Hall, Englewood Cliffs, N.J., 1992.

Booch, G. and Bryan, D. *Software Engineering with Ada*, Addison-Wesley, Reading, Mass., 1994.

Chapter 7

Software Validation, Verification, and Testing

1. Introduction to Chapter

In the past, testing was considered to be a separate phase of the software life cycle that followed coding. Two developments have caused this idea to be reconsidered. First, the linear sequential view of the life cycle is now only one of many possible approaches, so the activities that precede or follow another activity cannot always be stated completely and in advance. Second, the activity of ensuring that software is correct is no longer considered to take place only after the code has been written—it takes place throughout the software development process.

This second viewpoint has led to the concept of validation and verification (V&V) as a unified approach to identifying and resolving software problems and high-risk issues early in the software cycle [1]. V&V can also be defined as a software system engineering process employing a rigorous methodology for evaluating the correctness and quality of the software product through the software lifecycle [2]. However, in some contexts, validation and verification retain separate, independent definitions:

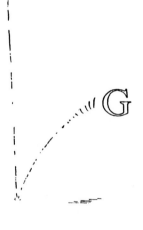

- *Verification and Validation* (V&V)—the process of determining whether the requirements for a system or component are complete and correct, the products of each development phase fulfill the requirements or conditions imposed by the previous phase, and the final system or component complies with specified requirements [3].

- *Verification*—the process of determining whether or not the products of a given phase of the software development cycle fulfill the requirements established for them at the end of the previous phase. Verification answers the question, "Are we building the system right?"

- *Validation*—the determination of the correctness of the final program or software produced from a development project with respect to the user's needs and requirements. Validation answers the question, "Are we building the right system?" [1]

Readers interested in a more extensive treatment of software verification and validation than can be provided in this Tutorial are referred to a recent publication by Robert O. Lewis [4].

This Tutorial takes the viewpoint that testing is integral to a program of ensuring the correctness of the software product, so the topics of V&V and testing are treated together in this chapter.

2. Introduction to Papers

The first paper on software verification and validation is a revision and updating of the US National Institute of Standards and Technology (NIST) Special Publication 500-165. Both the NIST publication and the new paper were written by Roger Fujii and Dolores Wallace. This paper describes software V&V and its objectives and recommended tasks, and provides guidance for selecting techniques to perform the task. It explains the differences between V&V and quality assurance, and how development, quality assurance, V&V, and other software engineering practitioners can use V&V techniques to produce quality software.

The second article, an original paper by Frank Ackerman, describes software inspections, undoubtedly one of the best tools available to the software engineering practitioner to assure a quality software system. Software inspections were developed and described by Michael Fagan [5], who worked for IBM in the 1970s. Essentially, software inspections are a form of peer review (like walkthroughs), which use the ability of individuals, not under pressure, willing to discuss freely the work being done to find errors in a software artifact.

Ackerman's paper provides a description of an inspection, the steps that the team must go through to ensure a quality inspection, a description of the people involved in a software inspection, and the benefits and results of a good software inspection. Ackerman also shows that properly applied software inspections are cost-effective through early detection of software errors.

The third paper in this chapter is an original paper by John Marciniak on the subject of reviews and audits. This paper is an update to Marciniak's article of the same title in the *Encyclopedia of Software Engineering* [6]. In addition to writing that article, Marciniak edited the entire encyclopedia. In this paper, Marciniak describes a review as a process during which a work product or a set of work products is presented to project personnel, managers, users, customers, and/or interested parties for consent or approval. Types of reviews include audits, peer reviews, design reviews, formal qualification reviews, requirements reviews and test reviews. A definition is provided for each of these review types.

Marciniak also defines two categories of reviews: formal reviews, which are required by contract commitment, and informal reviews, which, although not contractually required, are held because of their perceived benefits. He also integrates reviews, audits, walkthroughs, and inspections into the software development life cycle and shows when a given review might be held as well as the impact this review has on the life cycle and its products. He does not describe the activities of an inspection, only those of a walkthrough.

The fourth paper, on traceability, was written for this Tutorial by James Palmer of George Mason University. Palmer defines traceability and a number of other related terms. He notes that traceability should be established among requirements, design, code, test, and implementation. He then describes the state of the practice, and the benefits of establishing and maintaining traceability during system development. He notes that, even with tool support, establishment of traceability is a labor-intensive process, because it is necessary to read and understand the system documents (requirements, design, test plans, and so forth) in order to define those elements that trace to each other.

Palmer describes an ideal process for establishing traceability and explains why the actual process used in practice is different. He states that it is difficult or impossible to establish the "return on investment" of traceability, because, while the cost is easy to determine, the benefit is in errors or rework avoided and in reducing the risk of building an unsatisfactory product. He describes the current state of tool support for traceability. Most tools require the user to establish traceability; the tools then manage the resulting database and provide information conveniently. Some tools, however, provide semi-automated approaches that assist the user in establishing traceability. Palmer concludes with a summary of current research and a projection of future tools and technology for traceability.

The final paper in this chapter is "A Review of Software Testing," by David Coward of Bristol Polytechnic in the UK. The paper was taken from an earlier IEEE Tutorial, *Software Engineering: A European Perspective*. The author acknowledges that, until software can be built perfectly, there will be some need for software testing. The principal objective of testing, according to Coward, is to gain confidence in the software.

Coward divides testing into two categories, functional and non-functional. Functional testing addresses whether the program produces the correct output. Non-functional testing addresses such elements as quality, design constraints, and interface specifications.

The author describes and recommends several testing strategies, for example:

- *Functional versus structural testing— Functional testing* requires you to derive test data from the functions (requirements) of a system. *Structural testing* requires you to derive test data from the structure (design) of the system, and includes program proving, symbolic execution, and anomaly analysis. The terms "black box" and "white box," respectively, are also used to describe these two forms of testing.

- *Static versus dynamic analysis—Static analysis* involves measuring the system under test when it is not running. *Dynamic analysis* requires that the software be executed and relies on instrumenting the program to measure internal data and logic states as well as outputs.

Coward emphasizes the need to separate software developers from software testers in order to ensure that the software is given a rigorous test. The author provides a very good bibliography of testing references at the end of his paper.

1. Boehm, B.W., "Verifying and Validating Software Requirements and Design Specifications," *IEEE Software*, Vol. 1, No. 1, Jan. 1984, pp. 75–88.

2. *IEEE Standards for Verification and Validation Plans Seminar*, The Institute of Electrical and Electronics Engineers, Inc., Piscataway, NJ, 1987.

3. IEEE Standard 610.12, *IEEE Standard Glossary of Software Engineering Terminology*, The Institute of Electrical and Electronics Engineers, Inc., Piscataway, NJ, 1993.

4. Lewis, Robert O., Independent Verification & Validation: A Life Cycle Engineering Process for Quality Software, Wiley and Sons, New York, 1992.

5. Fagan, M.E., "Design and Code Inspections to Reduce Errors in Program Development," *IBM Systems J.*, Vol. 15, No. 3, 1976, pp. 182–211.

6. Marciniak, John J., Editor-in-Chief, *Encyclopedia of Software Engineering*, 2 vols., John Wiley, New York, 1994.

Software Verification and Validation (V&V)

Roger U. Fujii

Logicon, Incorporated
222 West Sixth Street
San Pedro, CA 90733-0471

Dolores R. Wallace

National Computer Systems Laboratory
National Institute of Standards and Technology
Gaithersburg, MD 20899

Abstract

Software engineering standards tie together to provide a strong framework for ensuring quality computer systems. Standards for software verification and validation (V&V), a systems engineering approach to ensure quality software, support the requirements of standards for project management and quality assurance. When used together, they contribute to safe, secure, reliable, and maintainable computer systems.

This report describes software V&V, its objectives, recommended tasks, and guidance for selecting techniques to perform the tasks. It explains differences between V&V and quality assurance, and how development, quality assurance, V&V, and other software engineering practitioners can use V&V techniques to produce quality software. While two studies of V&V's cost-effectiveness have different conclusions, an analysis of the parameters of those studies suggests that the benefits of V&V outweigh the costs associated with it.

This report describes six existing software engineering standards for software verification and validation. A description is provided on which standards contain guidance for scoping the V&V effort, planning the V&V effort, and managing the V&V effort.

1. Introduction

The purpose of this paper is to provide a brief introduction to Software Verification and Validation (V&V). Traditionally, software V&V is defined as a systems engineering methodology to ensure that quality (that is, emphasizing correctness, reliability, and usability) is built into the software during development. The analysis and test activities performed by V&V evaluate and assess the software products and development processes during each software life cycle phase in parallel with, not after the completion of, the development effort. This evaluation and assessment provides early identification of errors, assessment of software performance, compliance with requirements, identification of program risks, and assessment of the quality of development processes and products. Because software is becoming an integral part of linking the system together, V&V ensures that the examined software performs correctly within the system context (that is, system performance, system stimuli and operating environment, user features across the system, among others).

Software V&V is complementary to and supportive of quality assurance, project management, systems engineering, and development. V&V utilizes unique V&V techniques in addition to well-proven techniques used by these other complementary development functional groups. V&V uses these techniques to (1) unravel the details of the software product or process; (2) examine each individual detail piece to determine its correctness; and (3) determine completeness, correctness, and other quality attributes when the pieces are viewed as a whole from an unbiased persepective. Figure 1 illustrates how V&V activities supports the other functional groups (that is, development, systems engineering, and quality assurance) of the development effort.

By examining the software in detail and assessing the detailed pieces against the total system requirements, software V&V attacks two of the major contributors to software failures: (1) incorrect or missing requirements (lack of understanding the problem to be solved by software); and (2) poor organization in software architecture and failure to plan effectively (managing information complexity). Our modern software paradigms and techniques can assist in deal-

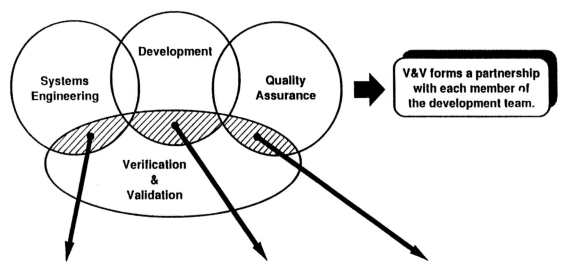

Figure 1. Relationship of V&V to the development team

ing with these causes of primary software failures, and software V&V in particular is a powerful technique to address these types of failures.

In the remainder of the paper, the primary V&V techniques used in life cycle phase will be described. A section of the paper will describe a selction of standards on software V&V that are representative of the currect standards used by United States Federal agencies, industries, and academia.

2. Overview Of Software Verification and Validation

In 1961, a software error caused the destruction of a Mariner payload on board a radio-controlled Atlas booster. The Atlas guidance software had used incorrect radar data to compute navigation and steering commands. The cause was a simple programming error of misusing a hyphen on previous data rather than on the corrected, extrapolated data.

This simple but expensive error led the Air Force to require independent review of the guidance equations and software implementation of all future mission-critical space launches. This need to ensure software quality and to have high confidence in the correct performance of the system gave birth to the methodology of software verification and validation. At a time when missile guidance theories and computer technologies were still in their infancy and many

unknowns were yet to be solved, software V&V proved highly successful in providing the independent assessment of the proposed technical solution's correctness. Through early identification and correction of errors, V&V also succeeded in developing higher confidence in the system. Program managers made better decisions because they now had the technical insight and advanced notice of risk-prone areas to make informed decisions. Since then, software V&V has become a powerful risk management tool.

As these and other benefits of V&V became apparent in improved software quality, including safety and security, complex information systems outside the Department of Defense began using the V&V methodology. Today, the methodology has proliferated throughout the Department of Defense (DOD) services, the Federal Aviation Administration, and the National Aeronautics and Space Administration, as well as medical and nuclear power industries. The history of the growth of V&V is shown in Figure 2; some agencies, like the Food and Drug Administration, are presently deciding how to incorporate V&V requirements into their policies and procedures regarding medical devices.

In many cases, V&V is governed by standards establishing software development, project management, and software quality assurance requirements. Government and industry began to develop V&V standards because managers needed a specification of

INITIAL RELEASE	STANDARD/REGULATION
AFR 122-9/-10 1970	"Design Certification Program for Nuclear Weapon System Software and Firmware" for Air Force nuclear weapon systems software (mandatory)
AFR 800-14 1975	"Acquisition Management: Acquisition and Support Procedures for Computer Resources in Systems" for acquisition of major Air Force embedded computer systems
MIL-STD-1679 1978	"Software Development" for Navy systems
JCMPO INST 8020.1 1981	"Safety Studies, Reviews, and Evaluation Involving Nuclear Weapon Systems" for Navy nuclear cruise missile weapon systems software (mandatory)
ANSI/IEEE - ANS 7.4.3.2 1982	"Application Criteria for Programmable Digital Computer Systems in Safety Systems of Nuclear Power Generating Stations" for Nuclear power generation embedded software
FIPSPUB101 1983	"Guideline for Lifecycle Validation, Verification, and Testing of Computer Software" for general guidance to computer software industry
DoD-STD-2167A and 2168 1985-1988	"Defense System Software Development; Quality Program" for development of DoD mission critical computer system software
ANSI/IEEE-STD 1012 1986	"Standard for Software Verification and Validation Plans" for any software development
NASA SMAP GUIDEBOOKS 1986	"Software Verification and Validation for Project Managers" for software intensive systems for NASA
FIPSPUB132 1987	"Guideline for Software Verification and Validation Plans" for uniform and minimum requirements of V&V; adopts ANSI/IEEE 1012
ANS/ANS 10.4 1987	"Guidelines for V&V of Scientific and Engineering Computer Programs for the Nuclear Industry" for scientific and engineering programs (R&D) for nuclear power industry
ARMY REG 50-4 1986	"Software Studies and Reviews of Nuclear Weapon Systems" for Army nuclear weapon system software
AFSCP 800-5 1988	"Software Independent Verification and Validation" for Air Force systems with potential to cause death, system loss, more than $550K damage to equipment, or severe illness/injury
FAA STD 0-26 (DRAFT) ----	"National Aerospace System Software Development" for national airspace system-advanced automation system
FDA XXX ----	"Reviewer Guidance for Computer Controlled Medical Devices" for computer controlled medical devices.

4/89-0035-SMV-6480

Figure 2. History of V&V standards

this methodology for contract procurements and for monitoring the technical performance of V&V efforts.

2.1. Objectives of V&V

Software V&V comprehensively analyzes and tests software during all stages of its development and maintenance in parallel with the development process to

- determine that it performs its intended functions correctly,
- ensure that it performs no unintended functions, and
- measure and assess the quality and reliability of software.

As a systems engineering discipline, software V&V also assesses, analyzes, and tests the software on how it interfaces with, influences the performance of, or reacts to stimuli from the system elements. These systems elements include the following:

- hardware including all hardware directly or indirectly influenced by the software,
- users that interface with the software or other system components,
- external software linked to the system,
- and system environment (such as stimuli, inputs, operating conditions).

222

A software error needs the system elements to be present for the error to cause an effect. Software performing correctly in one set of conditions or system environment could fail under different system stimuli. Therefore, in order to determine software correctness, software V&V must always consider the system when performing V&V analysis and testing. When performed in parallel with software development, V&V yields several benefits:

- uncovers high risk errors early, giving the design team time to evolve a comprehensive solution rather than forcing them into a make-shift fix to accommodate software deadlines.

- evaluates the correctness of products against system and software requirements.

- provides management with in-depth technical visibility into the quality and progress of the development effort that is continuous and comprehensive, not just at major review milestones (which may occur infrequently).

- provides the user an incremental preview of system performance, with the chance to make early adjustments.

- provides decision criteria for whether or not to proceed to the next development phase.

2.2 Responsibilities of V&V Versus Other Groups

While the techniques of V&V may be applied by anyone involved in software development and maintenance, a comprehensive V&V effort is often administered by a specific group. Similarly, a project may have developers who are from the end-user organization or who may be contractors or subcontractors. Other groups may be quality assurance, configuration management, and data management. The organizational structure of a project depends on many characteristics (for example, size, complexity, purpose of the software, corporate culture, project standards, contractual requirements). Often these groups are separate, but in many instances, especially for small projects, the structure is not as diverse. On these projects, the functions described in this section must still be performed but may be distributed differently.

A functional view demonstrates how V&V and other groups complement their software quality responsibilities. The software development group builds the software product to satisfy the established quality and performance requirements. The group relies on its quality assurance group, systems engineering, requirements analysts, designers, program-

mers, testers, data and configuration management specialists, documentation specialists, and others.

The quality assurance group verifies that the development process and products conform to established standards and procedures. Via reviews, audits, inspections, and walk-throughs, it acts as a formal check and balance to monitor and evaluate software as it is being built. The software systems engineering group ensures that the software product satisfies system requirements and objectives. It uses techniques such as simulations to gain reasonable assurance that system requirements are satisfied.

The configuration and data management groups monitor and control the software program versions and data during its development, using such techniques as formal audits, change control records, traceability of requirements, and sign-off records. The user group must provide assurance that the software product satisfies user requirements and operational needs. Typically, it uses techniques such as formal design reviews and acceptance testing.

Like software systems engineering, the V&V group is responsible for verifying that the software product at each life cycle phase satisfies software quality attributes and that the software product at each phase satisfies the requirements of the previous phase. In addition, V&V is responsible for validating that the software satisfies overall system requirements and objectives. The activities are directed at the software, but V&V must consider how the software interacts with the rest of the system, including hardware, users, other software, and with other external systems. V&V maintains its own configuration and data management functions on programs, data, and documentation received from the development organization to assure V&V discrepancy reports are against controlled documents and to repeat V&V tests against controlled software releases. V&V responsibilities may vary for different projects; some examples are provided in Section 2.3.

V&V documentation, evaluation, and testing are different from those conducted by other groups. The quality assurance group reviews documents for compliance to standards. V&V performs a check on the technical correctness of the document contents. V&V may perform in-depth evaluation by such activities as rederiving the algorithms from basic principles, computing timing data to verify response time requirements, and developing control flow diagrams to identify missing and erroneous requirements. V&V may suggest, if appropriate, alternative approaches. V&V testing is usually separate from the development group's testing. In some cases, V&V may use development test plans and results and supplement them with additional tests.

2.3 Organizing a V&V Effort

A major influence on the responsibilities of V&V, and its relationship to other groups, is to whom V&V reports. Four methods of organizing a V&V effort are described: independent; embedded in the development system engineering group; embedded in the development quality assurance group; and embedded in the user group.

The traditional approach is that the V&V group is independent of the development group and is called *independent V&V* or IV&V. As IV&V, the V&V group reports directly to the system program manager, often the acquisition organization, who manages the separate development and IV&V teams. In this relationship, the V&V organization establishes formal procedures for receiving software releases and documentation from the development team. V&V sends all evaluation reports and discrepancy reports to both the program manager and development group. To maintain an unbiased technical viewpoint, V&V may selectively use results or procedures from the quality assurance or systems engineering groups.

The V&V tasks are oriented toward engineering analysis (for example, algorithm analysis, control/data flow analysis) and comprehensive testing (such as simulation). The objective is to develop an independent assessment of the software quality and to determine whether the software satisfies critical system requirements. Advantages of this approach are detailed analysis and test of software requirements; an independent determination of how well the software performs; and early detection of high-risk software and system errors. Disadvantages are higher cost to the project and additional development interfaces.

When the V&V group is embedded in development's systems engineering group, the V&V tasks are to review the group's engineering analyses (for instance, algorithm development, sizing/timing) and testing (like test evaluation or review of the adequacy of the development test planning document). In some instances, the V&V organization may be the independent test team for the systems engineering group, sharing some test data generated by the systems engineering group. V&V's results are reviewed and monitored by the systems engineering and quality assurance groups. An independent V&V group reporting to the systems engineering group is another alternative. Advantages to using systems engineering personnel in the V&V tasks are minimum cost impact to the project; no system learning for the staff; and no additional development interfaces. A disadvantage is the loss of engineering analysis objectivity.

When the V&V group is embedded in the development's quality assurance group, its tasks take on a monitoring, auditing, and reviewing content (for example, audit performance, audit support, test witnessing, walk-through support, documentation review). In these tasks, the V&V group is part of quality assurance and maintains its relationship to systems engineering and other development groups in the same manner as quality assurance. The main advantages of embedding V&V as part of quality assurance are low cost to the project and bringing V&V analysis capabilities into reviews, audits, and inspections. A disadvantage is the loss of an independent software systems analysis and test capability.

When the V&V group is embedded in the user group, its tasks are an extension of the users' responsibilities. The tasks consist of configuration management support of development products, support of formal reviews, user documentation evaluation, test witnessing, test evaluation of the development test planning documents, and user testing support (for example, user acceptance testing and installation and checkout testing).

As an extension of the user group, the V&V group would receive formal software product deliverables and provide comments and data to the development project management that distributes the information to its own development team. An advantage of this approach is the strong systems engineering and user perspective that can be brought to bear on the software product during development. Main disadvantages are loss of detailed analysis and test of incremental software products (since these typically are not formal deliverables) and error detection and feedback to the development team constrained by the frequency of formal product deliverables. If the user group has an IV&V group reporting to it, then the disadvantages can be overcome. However, in this instance, the project incurs the disadvantage of having an additional development interface.

2.4 Applying V&V to a Software Life Cycle

The minimum recommended V&V tasks that are required by the ANSI/IEEE Standard for Software Verification and Validation Plans (SVVP) [1] for the development phases are shown in Figure 3. They are considered effective and applicable to all types of software applications. Tailoring V&V for a specific project is accomplished by adding tasks to the minimum set or, when appropriate, deleting V&V tasks. Figures 4a and 4b list additional V&V tasks in the life cycle phase where they most likely can be applied, and considerations that one might use to assign the tasks to V&V. The SVVP standard requires V&V management tasks spanning the entire software life cycle and V&V tasks for operations and maintenance.

PHASE	TASKS	KEY ISSUES
Concept	Concept-documentation evaluation	Satisfy user needs; constraints of interfacing systems
Requirements Definition	Traceability analysis	Trace of requirements to concept
	Requirements validation	Correctness, consistency, completeness, accuracy, readability, and testability; satisfaction of system requirements
	Interface analysis	Hardware, software, and operator interfaces
	Begin planning for V&V system testing	Compliance with functional requirements; performance at interfaces; adequacy of user documentation; performance at boundaries
	Begin planning for V&V acceptance testing	Compliance with acceptance requirements
Design	Traceability analysis	Trace of design to requirements
	Design evaluation	Correctness; design quality
	Interface analysis	Correctness; data items across interface
	Begin planning for V&V component testing	Compliance to design; timing and accuracy; performance at boundaries
	Begin planning for V&V integration testing	Compliance with functional requirements; timing and accuracy; performance at stress limits
Implementation	Traceability analysis	Trace of source code to design
	Code evaluation	Correctness; code quality
	Interface analysis	Correctness; data/control access across interfaces
	Component test execution	Component integrity
Test	V&V integration-test execution	Correctness of subsystem elements; subsystem interface requirements
	V&V system-test execution	Entire system at limits and user stress conditions
	V&V acceptance-test execution	Performance with operational scenarios
Installation and Checkout	Installation-configuration audit	Operations with site dependencies; adequacy of installation procedure
	V&V final report generation	Disposition of all errors; summary of V&V results

4/89-0036-SMV-6480

Figure 3. Minimum set of recommended V&V tasks

TECHNIQUE/TOOLS (column headings)

Walkthroughs · Tracing · Timing · Test Support Facilities · Test Drivers · Test Data Generator · Test Coverage Analyzer · Symbolic Execution · Structural Testing · Specification Base · Software Monitors · Sizing · Simulations · Roundoff Analysis · Requirements Parsing · Regression Testing · Physical Units Testing · Peer Review · PDL Processor · Mutation Analysis · Metrics · Interface Checker · Interactive Test Aids · Inspections · Functional Testing · Formal Verification · Formal Review · Execution Time Estimator · Design Compliance Analyzer · Data Flow Analyzer · Data Base Analyzer · Cross Reference Generator · Criticality Analysis · Control Flow Analyzer · Comparator · Code Auditor · Cause Effect Graphing · Assertion Processing · Assertion Generation · Analytic Modeling · Algorithm Analysis

V&V ISSUES (row headings)

Acceptance Tests · Accuracy · Algorithm Efficiency · Assertion Violations · Bottlenecks · Boundary Test Cases · Branch & Path Identification · Branch Testing · Call Structure Of Modules · Checklist (Reqmts, Design, Code) · Code Reading · Component Tests · Consistency In Computation · Data Characteristics · Design Evaluation · Design To Code Correlation · Dynamic Testing Of Assertions · Error Propagation · Environment Interaction · Evaluation Of Program Paths · Execution Monitoring · Execution Sampling · Execution Support · Expected Vs Actual Results · Feasibility · File Sequence Error · Formal Specification Evaluation · Global Information Flow · Go-No-Go Decisions · Hierarchical Interrelationship Of Modules · Information Flow Consistency · Inspections · Integration Tests

2/88-0118-MSW-6360

Figure 4a. Cross-reference of V&V issues to V&V techniques/tools (part 1)

226

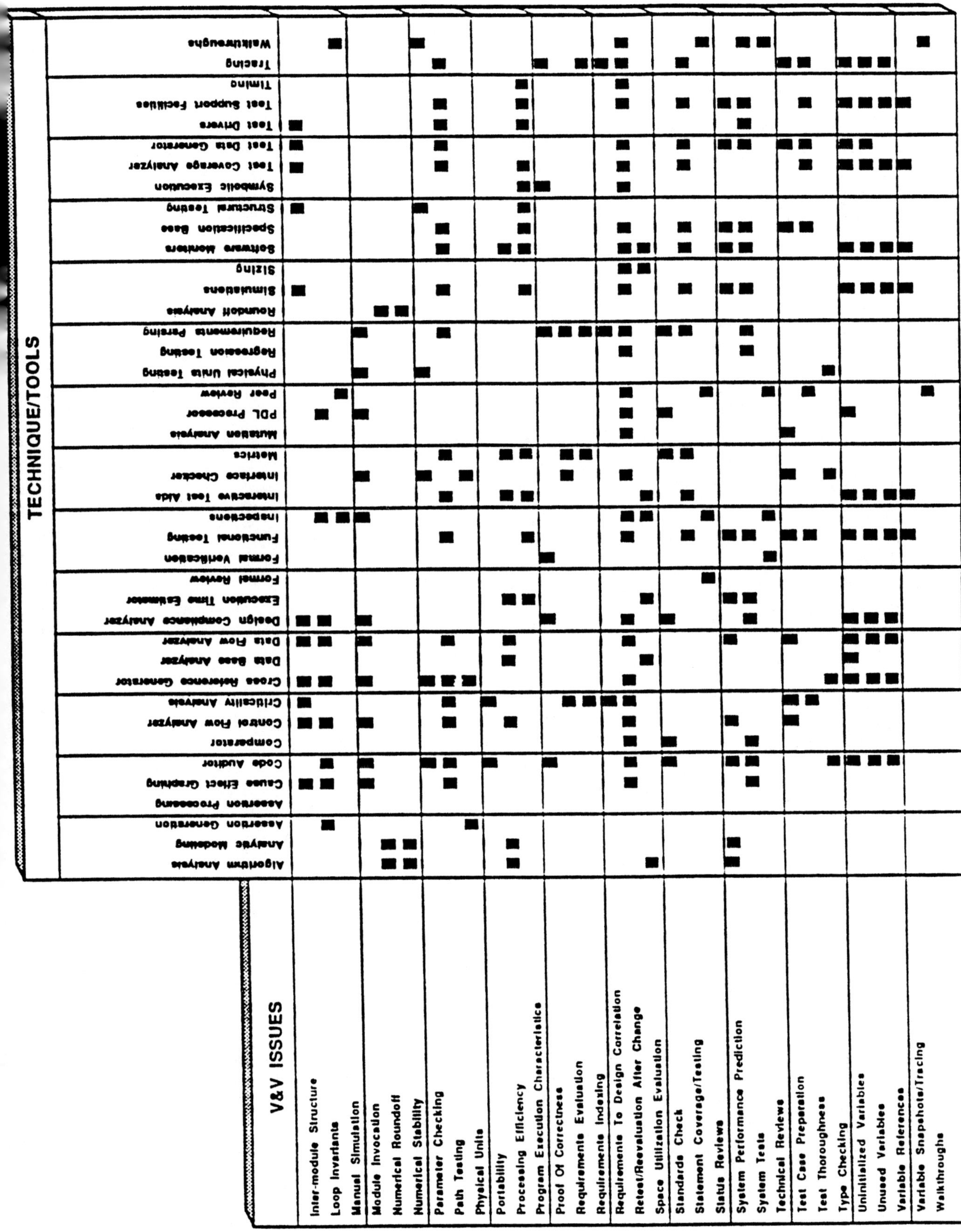

Figure 4b. Cross-reference of V&V issues to V&V techniques/tools (part 2).

These V&V tasks can be applied to different life cycle models simply by mapping traditional phases to the new model. Examples include variations of the traditional waterfall, Boehm's spiral development [2], rapid prototyping, or evolutionary development models [3]. The V&V tasks are fully consistent with the ANSI/IEEE standard for software life cycle processes [4]. The SVVP standard specifies minimum input and output requirements for each V&V task; a V&V task may not begin without specific inputs, and is not completed until specific outputs are completed.

2.4.1 Management of V&V

Management tasks for V&V span the entire life cycle. These tasks are to plan the V&V process; coordinate and interpret performance and quality of the V&V effort; report discrepancies promptly to the user or development group; identify early problem trends and focus V&V activities on them; provide a technical evaluation of the software performance and quality at each major software program review (so a determination can be made of whether the software product has satisfied its requirements well enough to proceed to the next phase); and assess the full impact of proposed software changes. The output of the V&V activities consists of the Software Verification and Validation Plan (SVVP), task reports, phase summary reports, final report, and discrepancy report.

Major steps in developing the V&V plan are as follows:

- Define the quality and performance objectives (for example, verify conformance to specifications, verify compliance with safety and security objectives, assess efficiency and quality of software, and assess performance across the full operating environment).

- Characterize the types of problems anticipated in the system and define how they would show up in the software.

- Select the V&V analysis and testing techniques to effectively detect the system and software problems.

The plan may include a tool acquisition and development plan and a personnel training plan. The SVVP is a living document, constantly being revised as knowledge accumulates about the characteristics of the system, the software, and the problem areas in the software.

An important V&V management activity is to monitor the V&V technical progress and quality of results. At each V&V phase, planned V&V activities are reviewed and new tasks are added to focus on the critical performance/quality functions of the software and its system. The monitoring activity conducts formal reviews of V&V discrepancy reports and technical evaluation results to provide a check of their correctness and accuracy. V&V studies (reference) have shown that responding to discrepancy reports and V&V evaluation reports consumes the largest portion of a development group's interface time with the V&V group.

Boehm and Papaccio [5] report that the Pareto analysis, that is, 20 percent of the problems cause 80 percent of the rework costs, applies to software; they recommend that V&V "focus on identifying and eliminating the specific high-risk problems to be encountered by a software project." Part of the V&V management activities is to define and use methods to address these problems of rework and risk management. One method of providing early delivery of information is to have the development team deliver incremental documents (for example, draft portions) and "software builds" to V&V. A software build represents a basic program skeleton containing portions of the full software capabilities. Each successive build integrates additional functions into the skeleton, permitting early software deliveries to V&V in an orderly development process. Based on discrepancy or progress reports, software program management can make the technical and management decisions to refocus the V&V and development team onto the program's specific problem areas of the software.

Criticality analysis, a method to locate and reduce high-risk problems, is performed at the beginning of a project. It identifies the functions and modules that are required to implement critical program functions or quality requirements (such as safety and security). The steps of the analysis are:

- Develop a block diagram or control-flow diagram of the system and its software. Each block or control flow box represents a system or software function (module).

- Trace each critical function or quality requirement through the block or control flow diagram.

- Classify all traced software functions (modules) as critical to either the proper execution of critical software functions or the quality requirements.

- Focus additional analysis on these traced software functions (modules).

- Repeat criticality analysis for each life cycle phase to observe whether the implementation details shift the emphasis of the criticality.

The criticality analysis may be used along with the cross-reference matrix of Figure 4 to identify V&V techniques to address high-risk concerns.

2.4.2 Concept Definition Evaluation

In this phase, the principal V&V task is to evaluate the concept documentation to determine whether the defined concept satisfies user needs and project objectives (for example, statement of need, project initiation memo) in terms of system performance requirements, feasibility (for example, overestimation of hardware capabilities), completeness, and accuracy. The evaluation also identifies major constraints of interfacing systems and constraints/limitations of the proposed approach and assesses the allocation of system functions to hardware and software, where appropriate. The evaluation assesses the criticality of each software item defined in the concept.

Most of the techniques in the cross-reference matrix of Figure 4 are described in a publication from the National Institute of Standards and Technology (formerly the National Bureau of Standards), the National Bureau of Standards Special Publication 500-93, "Software Validation, Verification, and Testing Technique and Tool Reference Guide" [6]. In Figure 4, the techniques are mapped against specific V&V issues [7] which they address.

While the use of the cross-reference matrix for selecting V&V techniques and tools is applicable to all phases, its use is illustrated in this report only for examining how concept feasibility is determined. Of several techniques for determining feasibility of a software concept and architecture, those most commonly used are requirements parsing, analytic modeling, and simulation. These give the V&V analyst a way to parse the desired performance requirements from other concept data; analytically model the desired performance; and, by creating a simulation of the proposed operating environment, execute test data to determine whether the resulting performance matches the desired performance. Criticality analysis is especially useful during concept definition to identify the critical functions and their distribution within the system architecture. Test data generation defines the performance limits of the proposed system concept; the predicted performance can be verified by using the simulation to execute the test scenario.

2.4.3 Requirements Analysis

Poorly specified software requirements (for example, incorrect, incomplete, ambiguous, or not testable) contribute to software cost overruns and problems with reliability due to incorrect or misinterpreted requirements or functional specifications. Software often encounters problems in the mainte-nance phase because general requirements (such as maintainability, quality, and reusability) were not accounted for during the original development. The problem of outdated requirements is intensified by the very complexity of the problems being solved (which causes uncertainty in the intended system performance requirements) and by continual changes in requirements to incorporate new technologies. V&V tasks verify the completeness of all the requirements.

The most commonly used V&V tasks for requirements analysis are control flow analysis, data flow analysis, algorithm analysis, and simulation. Control and data flow analysis are most applicable for real-time and data-driven systems. These flow analyses transform logic and data requirements text into graphic flows that are easier to analyze than the text. PERT, state transition, and transaction diagrams are examples of control flow diagrams. Algorithm analysis involves rederivation of equations or evaluation of the suitability of specific numerical techniques. Simulation is used to evaluate the interactions of large, complex systems with many hardware, user, and other interfacing software components.

Another activity in which V&V plays an important role is test management. V&V looks at all testing for the software system and ensures that comprehensive testing is planned. V&V test planning begins in the requirements phase and spans almost the full range of life cycle phases. Test planning activities encompass four separate types of testing—component, integration, system, and acceptance testing. The planning activities result in documentation for each test type consisting of a test plan, test design, test case, and test procedure documents.

Component testing verifies the design and implementation of software units or modules. Integration testing verifies functional requirements as the software components are integrated, directing attention to internal software interfaces and external hardware and operator interfaces. System testing validates the entire software program against system requirements and software performance objectives. V&V system tests validate that the software executes correctly in a simulated system environment. They do not duplicate or replace the user and development team's responsibilities of testing the entire system requirements (for example, those pertaining to hardware, software, and users).

Acceptance testing validates the software against V&V acceptance criteria, defining how the software should perform with other completed software and hardware. One of the distinctions between V&V system and acceptance testing is that the former uses a laboratory environment in which some system features are simulated or performed by nonoperational hardware or software, and the latter uses an operational environment with final configurations of other system hardware and software. V&V acceptance testing usually consists of tests to demonstrate that the software will execute as predicted by V&V system testing in the operational environment. Full acceptance testing is the responsibility of the user and the development systems engineering group.

2.4.4 Design Evaluation

The minimum set of design phase V&V tasks—traceability, interface analysis, and design evaluation—assures that (1) requirements are not misrepresented or incompletely implemented, (2) unintended requirements are not designed into the solution by oversight or indirect inferences, and (3) requirements are not left out of the design. Design errors can be introduced by implementation constraints relating to timing, data structures, memory space, and accuracy, even though the basic design satisfies the functional requirements.

The most commonly used V&V tasks are algorithm analysis, database analysis, timing/sizing analysis, and simulation. In this phase, algorithm analysis examines the correctness of the equations or numerical techniques as in the requirements analysis phase, but also examines truncation and round-off effects, numerical precision of word storage and variables (for example, single- versus extended-precision arithmetic), and data-typing influences. Database analysis is particularly useful for programs that store program logic in data parameters. A logic analysis of these data values is required to determine the effect these parameters have on program control. Timing/sizing analysis is useful for real-time programs having response time requirements and constrained memory execution space requirements.

2.4.5 Implementation (Code) Evaluation

Clerical and syntactical errors have been greatly reduced through use of structured programming and reuse of code, adoption of programming standards and style guides, availability of more capable computer languages, better compiler diagnostics and automated support, and, finally, more knowledgeable programmers. Nevertheless, problems still occur in translating design into code and can be detected with some V&V analyses.

Commonly used V&V tasks are control flow analysis, database analysis, regression analysis, and sizing/timing analysis. For large code developments, control flow diagrams showing the hierarchy of main routines and their subfunctions are useful in understanding the flow of program control. Database analy-

sis is performed on programs with significant data storage to ensure that common data and variable regions are used consistently between all call routines; data integrity is enforced and no data or variable can be accidentally overwritten by overflowing data tables; and data typing and use are consistent throughout all program elements.

Regression analysis is used to reevaluate requirements and design issues whenever any significant code change is made. This technique ensures project awareness of the original system requirements. Sizing/timing analysis is done during incremental code development and compared against predicted values. Significant deviations between actual and predicted values is a possible indication of problems or the need for additional examination.

Another area of concern to V&V is the ability of compilers to generate object code that is functionally equivalent to the source code, that is, reliance on the correctness of the language compiler to make data-dependent decisions about abstract, programmer-coded information. For critical applications, this problem is solved by validating the compiler or by validating that the object code produced by the compiler is functionally equivalent to the source.

Other tasks indicated in Figure 4 for code evaluation are walk-throughs, code inspections, and audits. These tasks occur in interactive meetings attended by a team that usually includes at least one member from the development group. Other members may belong to the development group or to other groups involved in software development. The duration of these meetings is usually no more than a few hours in which code is examined on a line-by-line basis.

In these dynamic sessions, it may be difficult to examine the code thoroughly for control logic, data flow, database errors, sizing, timing and other features that may require considerable manual or automated effort. Advance preparation for these activities may be necessary and includes additional V&V tasks shown in Figure 4. The results of these tasks provide appropriate engineering information for discussion at meetings where code is evaluated. Regardless of who conducts or participates in walk-throughs and inspections, V&V analyses may be used to support these meetings.

2.4.6 Testing

As already described, V&V test planning is a major portion of V&V test activities and spans several phases. A comprehensive test management approach to testing recognizes the differences in objectives and strategies of different types of testing. Effective testing requires a comprehensive understanding of the system. Such understanding develops from systematically analyzing the software's concept, requirements, design, and code. By knowing internal software details, V&V testing is effective at probing for errors and weaknesses that reveal hidden faults. This is considered structural, or white-box, testing. It often finds errors for which some functional, or black-box, test cases can produce the correct output despite internal errors.

Functional test cases execute part or all of the system to validate that the user requirement is satisfied; these test cases cannot always detect internal errors that will occur under special circumstances. Another V&V test technique is to develop test cases that violate software requirements. This approach is effective at uncovering basic design assumption errors and unusual operational use errors. In general, the process of V&V test planning is as effective in detecting errors as test executions.

The most commonly used optional tasks are regression analysis and test, simulation, and user document evaluation. User document evaluation is performed for systems having an important operator interface. For these systems, V&V reviews the user documentation to verify that the operating instructions are consistent with the operating characteristics of the software. The system diagnostic messages and operator recovery procedures are examined to ensure their accuracy and correctness with the software operations.

2.4.7 Installation and Checkout Activities

During installation and checkout, V&V validates that the software operates correctly with the operational hardware system and with other software, as specified in the interface specifications. V&V may verify the correctness and adequacy of the installation procedures and certify that the verified and validated software is the same as the executable code delivered for installation. There may be several installation sites with site-dependent parameters. V&V verifies that the program has been accurately tailored for these parameters and that the configuration of the delivered product is the correct one for each installation.

Optional V&V tasks most commonly used in this phase are regression analysis and test, simulation, and test certification. Any changes occurring from installation and test are reviewed using regression analysis and test to verify that our basic requirement and design assumptions affecting other areas of the program have not been violated. Simulation is used to test operator procedures and to help isolate any installation problems. Test certification, especially in critical software systems, is used to demonstrate that the delivered software product is identical to the software product subjected to V&V.

2.4.8 Operations and Maintenance Evaluation and Test

For each software change made in the operations and maintenance phase, all life cycle phase V&V activities of Figure 3 are considered and possibly repeated to ensure that nothing is overlooked. V&V activities are added or deleted to address the type of software change made. In many cases, an examination of the proposed software change shows that V&V needs to repeat its activities on only a small portion of the software. Also, some V&V activities such as concept documentation evaluation require little or no effort to verify a small change. Small changes can have subtle but significant side effects in a software program.

If V&V is not done in the normal software development phase, then the V&V in the maintenance phase must consider performing a selected set of V&V activities for earlier life cycle phases. Some of the activities may include generating requirements or design information from source code, a process known as reverse engineering. While costly and time-consuming, it is necessary when the need exists for a rigorous V&V effort.

2.5 Effectiveness of V&V

The effectiveness of V&V varies with project size and complexity, and V&V staff experience. Two study results are provided as follows:

Radatz's 1981 study [8] for Rome Air Development Center reported V&V effectiveness results for four large IV&V projects ranging from 90K to 176K lines of code. The projects were real-time command and control, missile tracking, and avionics programs and a time-critical batch trajectory computation program. The projects varied from 2.5 to 4 years to develop. Two projects started V&V at the requirements phase, one at the code phase, and one at testing. The V&V organization used a staff of 5 to 12 persons per project.

In 1982, McGarry [9] reported on three small projects at the Software Engineering Laboratory (SEL) at NASA Goddard Space Flight Center. Three flight dynamics projects ranging in size from 10K to 50K lines of code were selected. V&V was involved in requirements and design verification, separate system testing, and validation of consistency from start to finish. The V&V effort lasted 18 months and used a staff averaging 1.1, peaking at 3, persons.

Based on these studies, some positive effects of V&V on a software project include:

Radatz Study	McGarry Study
• Errors were detected early in the development—50 percent to 89 percent detected before development testing began. • Large number of discrepancies were reported (total 1,259) on average of over 300 per program.	• Rates of uncovering errors early in the development cycle were better.
• V&V found an average 5.5 errors per thousand lines of code.	• V&V found 2.3 errors per thousand lines of code.
• Over 85 percent of the errors affected reliability and maintainability.	• Reliability of the software was no different from other SEL projects.
• Effect on programmer productivity was very positive—total savings per error of 1.3 to 6.1 hours.	• Productivity of the development teams was the lowest of any SEL project (due to the V&V interface).
• The largest savings amounted to 92–180 percent of V&V costs.	• Cost rate to fix all discovered errors was no less than in any other SEL project.

• Better quality (for example, complete, consistent, readable, testable) and more stable requirements.

• More rigorous development planning, at least to interface with the V&V organization.

• Better adherence by the development organization to programming language and development standards and configuration management practices.

• Early error detection and reduced false starts.

• Better schedule compliance and progress monitoring.

• Greater project management visibility into interim technical quality and progress.

• Better criteria and results for decision-making at formal reviews and audits.

Some negative effects of V&V on a software development project include:

• Additional project cost of V&V (10–30 percent).

• Additional interface involving the development team, user, and V&V organization (for example, attendance at V&V status meeting, anomaly resolution meeting).

• Lower development staff productivity if programmers and engineers spend time explaining the system to V&V analysts and resolving invalid anomaly reports.

Some steps can be taken to minimize the negative effects and to maximize the positive effects of V&V. To recover much of the V&V costs, V&V is started early in the software requirements phase. The interface activities for documentation, data, and software deliveries between developer and V&V groups should be considered as an inherently necessary step required to evaluate intermediate development products. This is a necessary by-product of doing what's right in the beginning.

To offset unnecessary costs, V&V must organize its activities to focus on critical areas of the software so that it uncovers critical errors for the development group and thereby results in significant cost savings to the development process. To do this, V&V must use its criticality analysis to identify critical areas and it must scrutinize each discrepancy before release to ensure that no false or inaccurate information is released to prevent the development group from wasting time on inaccurate or trivial reports.

To eliminate the need to have development personnel train the V&V staff, it is imperative that V&V select personnel who are experienced and knowledgeable about the software and its engineering application. When V&V engineers and computer scientists reconstruct the specific details and idiosyncracies of the software as a method of reconfirming the correctness of engineering and programming assumptions, they often find subtle errors. They gain detailed insight into the development process and an ability to spot critical errors early. The cost of the development interface is minimal, and at times nonexistent, when the V&V assessment is independent.

3. Standards and Guidelines For Planning and Managing V&V

The documents in Figure 5 establish guidelines for planning and managing a V&V effort. Their activities produce information that satisfies the life cycle requirements of standards governing projects. They have the following features:

PROCEDURE	AFSC 800-5	ANS 10.4	FIPSPUB 132	FIPSPUB 101	ANSI/IEEE STD 1012	JPL
SCOPE THE V&V EFFORT						
Criticalty Assessment	■					
Organization	■	■				
Costing	■					
PLAN THE V&V EFFORT						
Planning Preparation		■	■	■	■	
Objectives		■	■	■	■	■
General Task Selection	■	■	■	■	■	■
Minimum, Required			■		■	
Optional			■		■	
Recommendations for Criticality Levels	■			■		
Test Management			■		■	
Test Types			■	■		■
Objectives			■			
Documentation			■			
Coverage		■	■	■	■	■
Planning	■	■	■	■	■	
Planning V&V for Maintenance		■	■	■	■	
MANAGE THE V&V EFFORT						
V&V Management Tasks			■		■	
Reporting		■	■		■	

4/89-0040-SMV-6480

Figure 5. Planning V&V with guidance from V&V documents

- Require V&V to determine how well evolving and final software products comply with their requirements.
- Permit users to select specific techniques to satisfy their application needs.
- Identify a broad spectrum of V&V analysis and test activities.

Brief descriptions of each document follow:

The NIST issued the Federal Information Processing Standards Publication "Guideline for Lifecycle Validation, Verification and Testing," in 1983 [10]. This document was followed in 1987 with the "Guideline for Software Verification and Validation Plans," [11] which adopted the ANSI/IEEE standard for V&V planning [1]. Reference to the guideline, FIPSPUB132, includes reference to the ANSI/IEEE specifications.

FIPSPUB101 permits performance of V&V activities by developers, the same organization, or some independent group [10]. FIPSPUB132 /IEEE1012 does not require independence; it does require the SVVP to "define the relationship of V&V to other efforts such as development, quality assurance, configuration or data management, or end user" [1,11]. Internal and external lines of communication to V&V must be defined; V&V could occur independently or within one of the other efforts.

233

The Air Force pamphlet, "AFSC /AFLCP 800-5 Software Independent Verification and Validation," [12] is concerned only with software IV&V. It describes V&V activities typically performed by an independent V&V group separate from the developer's quality assurance group required by DOD-STD-2167A Standard, "Defense System Software Development" [13]. The AF pamphlet provides the criteria for selecting an independent V&V group.

The V&V activities of "Guidelines for the Verification and Validation of Scientific and Engineering Computer Programs for the Nuclear Industry," ANS 10.4, [14] may be performed by the program developer, as a task separate from development, or by an IV&V agent. The guideline contains an example of a division of V&V responsibilities.

The "Independent Verification and Validation of Computer Software: Methodology" from the Jet Propulsion Laboratory (JPL) [15] states that V&V activities should be performed independently of the development organization to ensure effectiveness and integrity of the V&V effort. The document allows flexibility in selecting the extent of the detailed V&V effort it describes.

4. Summary

Software V&V is a proven systems engineering discipline for generating correct and quality software. In addition to early error detection and correction benefits, software V&V has become a powerful risk management tool by providing the detailed technical insight into the "true" performance of the software. All software V&V is performed with a system perspective to ensure that the software is solving the "right problem."

Acknowledgments

The following people have provided substantive guidance to the authors through their reviews of this report: Dr. William Bryan, Grumman Data Systems; Fletcher Buckley, General Electric Company; Taz Daughtrey, Babcock and Wilcox; Dr. Herbert Hecht, SoHar, Incorporated; Tom Kurihara, Department of Defense; Dr. Jerome Mersky, Logicon, Incorporated; George Tice, Mentor Graphics Corporation; Dr. Richard Thayer, California State University–Sacramento, and Dr. N. Pat Wilburn, Columbia Software.

References

[1] ANSI/IEEE Std.1012-1986, "Standard for Software Verification and Validation Plans," IEEE, Inc., New York, NY, Nov. 1986.

[2] Boehm, B.W., "A Spiral Model of Software Development and Enhancement," *Computer*, May 1988, pp. 61–72.

[3] Davis, A.M., E.H. Bersoff, and E.R. Comer, "A Strategy for Comparing Alternative Software Development Life Cycle Models," *IEEE Trans. Software Eng.*, Vol. 14, No. 10, Oct. 1988, pp. 1453-1461.

[4] ANSI/IEEE 1074-1991, "Standard for Software Life Cycle Processes," IEEE, Inc., New York, NY.

[5] Boehm, B.W., and P.N. Papaccio, "Understanding and Controlling Software Costs," *IEEE Trans. Software Eng.*, Oct. 1988.

[6] Powell, P.B., "Software Validation, Verification and Testing Technique and Tool Reference Guide," *National Bureau of Standards Special Publication 500-93*, National Institute of Standards and Technology, Gaithersburg, MD 20899, 1982.

[7] Adrion, W.R., M.A. Branstad, and J.C. Cherniavsky, "Validation, Verification, and Testing of Computer Software," *ACM Computing Surveys*, Vol. 14, No. 2, June 1982.

[8] Radatz, J.W., "Analysis of IV&V Data," RADC-TR-81-145, Logicon, Inc., Rome Air Development Center, Griffiss AFB, NY, June 1981.

[9] McGarry, F., and G. Page, "Performance Evaluation of an Independent Software Verification and Integration Process," NASA Goddard, Greenbelt, MD, SEL 81-110, September 1982.

[10] "Guideline for Lifecycle Validation, Verification and Testing of Computer Software," FIPSPUB101, National Institute of Standards and Technology, Gaithersburg, MD 20899, 1983.

[11] "Guideline for Software Verification and Validation Plans," FIPSPUB132, National Institute of Standards and Technology, Gaithersburg, MD 20899, 1987.

[12] AFSC/AFLCP 800-5 Air Force Systems Command and Air Force Logistics Command Software Independent Verification and Validation, Washington, DC, 22 May 1988.

[13] DoD-Std-2167A Military Standard Defense System Software Development, AMSC No. 4327, Department of Defense, Washington, DC, Feb. 29, 1988.

[14] ANSI/ANS-10.4-1987, "Guidelines for the Verification and Validation of Scientific and Engineering Computer Programs for the Nuclear Industry," American Nuclear Society, La Grange Park, IL 1987.

[15] Blosiu, J.O., "Independent Verification and Validation of Computer Software: Methodology," National Aeronautics and Space Administration, Jet Propulsion Laboratory, Pasadena, Calif., JPL D-576, Feb. 9, 1983.

Software Inspections and the Cost Effective Production of Reliable Software

A. Frank Ackerman*

Institute for Zero Defect Software
San Jose, California

Software inspections were first defined for IBM by M. E. Fagan in 1976 [FGN76]. Since that time they have been used within IBM [DBN81] and other organizations [PEL82]. An IEEE software engineering standard covering inspections was approved in 1988 [IEEE88]. This paper describes software inspections as they were used in a large telecommunications R&D organization, and the technology transfer program that was used for their effective implementation. It also describes the placement of software inspections within the overall development process, and discusses their use in conjunction with other verification and validation techniques.

1. Introduction

The routine production of software products of high reliability produced within budget and on schedule continues to be an elusive goal. The root cause of the difficulty is that although software development can be conceptualized as an industrial process [FGN76], most of the individual steps of this process must be performed by individual "intellectual artisans." The scope of an artisan's work is inherently difficult to bound, the techniques employed can not be specified precisely, and the quality of the resulting products is variable. By contrast, in a well-organized industrial process, each individual operation is clearly delineated, the techniques employed are clearly defined, and the whole process can be managed in such a way that it predictably produces products of specified quality. Software inspections, as defined in this paper, were first employed by M.E. Fagan in 1974 at the IBM Corporation as a method for reducing variability in the quality of individual operations in a software development process. Inspections also facilitated tighter, more rational process control [FGN76].

This paper is based on the results of a software engineering technology transfer program to implement software inspections at a large telecommunications R&D organization. Used for more than two years on a wide variety of applications, the program trained more than 2,400 software developers and managers in 40 different projects. The current evaluation of such programs is that software inspections can indeed produce the quality and productivity benefits claimed by M.E. Fagan, but that the implementation of software inspections within a development organization is a challenging task. This task requires not only a sound understanding of software development technology, but also a keen appreciation of the behavior and motivation of individual developers and the organizational culture in which these individuals work.

Sections 2, 3, and 4 of this paper describes software inspections and how they can be used to improve the industrial production of software products. Section 5 discusses the relationship of software inspections to other verification tasks. Section 6 describes a method for implementing software inspections within development organizations.

2. Software Inspections Overview

Software inspections are designed to address the three major tasks of process management: planning, measurement, and control. For software development, the corresponding tasks are (1) the definition of a software development process as a clearly defined series of individual operations, (2) the collection of quantitative quality data at different points in the process, and (3) the use of this data for improving the process.

The individual operations within a complete development process can be delineated by specifying explicit exit criteria to be met by the work products produced by each operation. The process can then be "thought of as a continuous process during which sequential sets of exit criteria are satisfied, the last set in the entire series requiring a well-defined end product" [FGN76]. For example, the exit criteria for the completion of module coding might be: compilation with no faults, no warnings from a portability checker, and no violations from a standards checker.

* This paper is adapted from an earlier paper, "Software Inspections and the Industrial Production of Software," by the author, Priscilla J. Fowler, and Robert G. Ebenau, which appeared in *Software Validation*, H.I. Hausen, ed., Elsevier, Amsterdam, 1984, pp. 13–40.

DATE:				UNIT:			
MODERATOR:				TYPE:			
INSPECTORS:				AMOUNT:			

DISPOSITION:
OVERVIEW: ESTIMATED REWORK COMPLETION:
PREPARATION: ESTIMATED REWORK EFFORT:
MEETING: ACTUAL REWORK EFFORT:

	DEFECTS THIS OPERATION				DEFECTS IN PRIOR OPERATION			
	M	W	E	TOTAL	DOCU-MENT	ERROR TYPE	ERROR CLASS	MR/STR NUMBER
IF: INTERFACE								
DA: DATA								
LO: LOGIC								
IO: INPUT/OUTPUT								
PF: PERFORMANCE								
FN: FUNCTIONALITY								
HF: HUMAN FACTORS								
ST: STANDARDS								
DC: DOCUMENTATION								
SN: SYNTAX								
TE: TEST ENVIRONMENT								
TC: TEST COVERAGE								
OT: OTHER								
	TOTAL							

M = MISSING   W = WRONG   E = EXTRA

Figure 1. Software inspection data

The operations which make up a particular development process, and the exit criteria which define their completion, are dependent on the particular application, the development techniques being used, and the culture of the organization. The only essential requirements are that the criteria be explicit, unambiguous, and verifiable.

One of the mechanisms used to collect quantitative quality data at defined points in the development process is a software inspection. A software inspection is a group review process that is used to detect and correct defects in a software work product. It is a formal, technical activity that is performed by the work product author and a small peer group on a limited amount of material. It produces a formal, quantitative report on the resources expended and the results achieved.

Software inspections are often compared to walk-throughs [YRD78] and indeed there are many similarities. But there are major differences in focus and intent. Walk-throughs are generally considered to be a developer technique that can be used by individuals to improve the quality of their work. Inspections, on the other hand, are intended to be a process management

tool that will not only improve the quality of individual work products, but will also produce data that can be used for rational, quantitative decision-making. Thus, within each development process, software inspections must be formally and rigorously defined and they must be executed according to specification. More details on software inspections are provided in the next section.

An example of the data collected for an individual software inspection is shown in Figure 1.[1] The use of these data for process control is illustrated in Figure 2. In Figure 2, inspection data is shown as being used in three different ways: feed-back, feed-forward, and feed-into. For example, a series of design inspections might reveal an unexpectedly high percentage of data definition defects that could indicate a need for better

---

[1] Figure 1 uses the term "defects" rather than "errors," which is the term used by Fagan [FGN76]. The reason for this change of terminology is to be consistent with IEEE Std 729-1983, *IEEE Standard Glossary of Software Engineering Terminology*. All the terms used in this paper are consistent with this standard unless otherwise noted.

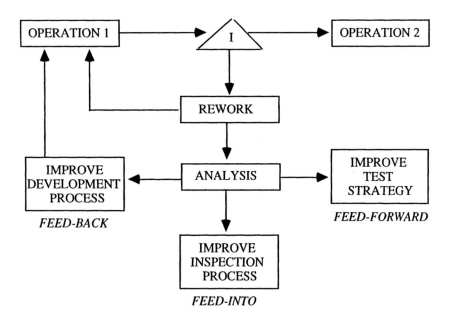

Figure 2. The use of inspection data

control of documentation for data layouts, that is, a need for a process adjustment to assure higher quality in subsequent work products. Information feed-forward can provide intelligence on treatment adjustments for individual work products. For example, a work product that was found to have an unusually high percentage of logic defects could be subjected to more rigorous testing.

The third use of inspection data (feed-into) can provide effectiveness and quality data about the inspection operations themselves. (For example, Are work products being examined carefully? are inspectors sufficiently prepared? and so on.) The collection and analysis of inspection data in conjunction with other process measures, such as reports on quality and productivity from testing operations, allows individual inspection operations to be adjusted for overall effectiveness. Thus, used properly, software inspections are self-regulating. They have repeatedly proven to be an effective method for improving both quality and productivity.

In his paper, Fagan reports on the effectiveness of software inspections applied to the development of a moderately complex component of a large operating system [FGN76]. Software inspections were held on detail designs, on cleanly compiled code, and at the completion of unit test. The result was a 23 percent productivity improvement and a 38 percent quality improvement, when compared with the development of a similar component that used walk-throughs.

In a trial of software inspections on a time-sharing system component upgrade at a large telecommunications R&D organization, software inspections were held on 1,482 noncommentary lines of source code after clean compile and some unit testing. The results were that 32 failures were detected by inspections with a total documented expenditure of 116 staff hours. The product (which altogether contained 8,940 lines of old, new, and changed code) was then subjected to system test, which detected 21 failures with an estimated expenditure of 162 staff hours.

3. Software Inspection Specifics

The Software Inspection Process. Each software inspection is itself a five or six-step process that is carried out by a designated moderator, by the author of the work product being inspected, and by at least one other peer inspector. The six steps are:

- Planning
- Overview
- Preparation
- Meeting
- Rework
- Follow-up

237

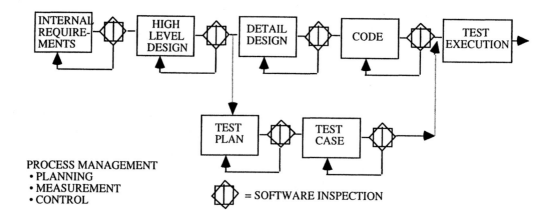

Figure 3. Software development process

Planning for an inspection begins when an author's work product meets the entry criteria established for this type of inspection. The first step is to select a moderator—a peer developer responsible for carrying out the inspection. A moderator may be selected by the author or a first-line manager from among a pool of qualified developers, or may be selected from an independent group with overall responsibility for the conduct of inspections for that organization. Since the moderator has overall responsibility for the inspection, including the final decision on the work product's disposition at the end of the inspection, it is important that he or she be as objective as possible. One way to ensure this is to specify that the moderator not be a member of a group that has direct production responsibility for the work product being inspected.

The moderator's first task is to meet with the author and to verify that the work product to be inspected meets the entry criteria for this type of inspection. When the work product meets these criteria, the next step is to decide whether or not to hold an overview, to select the other inspectors, and to schedule the overview and the meeting.

A software inspection overview is a presentation that is made to provide inspectors with any background information they may need in order to properly inspect the author's work product. Typically, an overview is given by an author, and it often covers material pertinent to a number of inspections. For example, for the time-sharing system component cited above, a single overview of the whole system was held for all prospective inspectors before beginning any of the individual inspections.

Another use of an overview is to provide a tutorial session on a specialized design or implementation technique that is used in the work product to be inspected, for example, a specialized enqueue and dequeue technique for synchronizing independent processes. The purpose of the overview is educational; the only inspection data collected during this step are the author's preparation time and the time the author and the inspectors spend at the overview presentation.

Preparation for a software inspection is an individual activity. The author prepares by collecting all the material required for this inspection and by completing an Inspection Profile Form (see Form 1 at the end of this paper). The other inspectors prepare by studying the work product to be inspected and by completing an Inspection Preparation Log (see Form 2). The purpose of individual preparation is to develop an understanding of the work product and to note places where this understanding is incomplete, or where the work product appears to have defects. Obvious defects are noted during this step, but detailed analysis and classification of defects is deferred to the inspection meeting.

The inspection meeting is conducted by the moderator. There is an established agenda that consists of:

- Introduction
- Establishing preparedness
- Examining the material and recording defects
- Reviewing defect list
- Determining disposition
- Debriefing.

During the introduction, the moderator introduces the inspectors and the material to be examined and states the purpose of the meeting. Preparedness is established by having each inspector report his or her preparation time as entered on the Inspection Preparation Log. The moderator sums these times for entry on the Inspection Management Report (see Form 3). If the moderator feels that preparation has been insufficient for an effective meeting, he or she may postpone the meeting.

Examining the material and recording defects are the major activities of an inspection meeting. At the meeting, one of the inspectors takes the role of reader and paces the group through the material by paraphrasing each "line" or section of the material aloud for the group. As the reader proceeds through the material in what he or she has selected as the most effective sequence for defect detection, the inspectors (including the reader) interrupt with questions and concerns. Each of these is either handled immediately or tabled. Whenever the group agrees, or the moderator rules, that a defect has been detected, the recorder for that inspection notes the location, description, class, and type on the Inspection Defect List (Form 4). (The role of recorder can be assumed by the moderator or any other inspector other than the author.)

After the reading and recording of defects, the moderator has the recorder review the Defect List to make sure that all defects have been recorded and correctly classified. After this is done, the inspectors determine the disposition of the material: "meets," "rework," or "re-inspect." The disposition of "meets" is given when the work product as inspected meets the exit criteria (or needs only trivial corrections) required for that type of inspection. The disposition of "re-inspect" is given when rework will change the work product in a substantial way.

Since an inspection meeting is to determine and record defects in a peer's work product, there is always the potential that interpersonal tension will develop during the meeting. An experienced moderator will note this and after the meeting initiate a suitable "debriefing exercise" to give these tensions opportunity for safe release. The debriefing exercise that we teach in our inspections training classes simply gives each participant an opportunity to briefly share his or her experience of the meeting in a supportive atmosphere.

Our experience with the interpersonal aspect of inspections is that problems in this area can be significant when inspections are initially introduced in a project, but they tend to disappear as inspections become a routine procedure. The two-day workshop we give to all inspectors considers the interpersonal problems associated with the use of inspections throughout the course and the final lecture deals with this area exclusively. Given this training, our experience is that most groups are able to handle any initial start-up problems without undue difficulty.

From the above description, it may appear that an inspection meeting is a formidable affair. It is not. The formality of the agenda, the assigned rules, the specified defect classification, and the limited purpose of the meeting all serve to create an effective meeting in which all the participants know what is to be done, and how to do it. With a modicum of training (described in a subsequent section), a synergistic team effort develops during the meeting that produces a result superior to the sum of what could be accomplished by isolated individual efforts. The meeting often develops the spirit of a detective drama because each participant's remarks provide clues in a vigorous effort to detect defects.

Inspection rework is performed by the author. It consists simply of correcting the defects noted in the Inspection Defect List.

The follow-up step is the responsibility of the moderator. It consists of verifying the corrections made during rework and completing the Inspection Management Report and the Inspection Defect Summary Report (Form 5).

Figure 4 gives a schematic of the overall process. Rework, and/or Follow-up may be skipped if the disposition is "meets."

Software Inspection Roles. Routine, effective, and hassle-free execution of an inspection process is facilitated by recognizing the specific inspection roles mentioned above. The following table provides a brief summary of the roles in an inspection.

Author	the producer (or current owner) of the subject work product
Moderator	an inspector responsible for organizing, executing, and reporting a software inspection
Reader	an inspector who guides the examination of the work product at the meeting Recorder an inspector who enters all the defects found during the meeting on the Inspection Defect List (Form 4)
Inspector	a member of an inspection team other than the author. Often chosen to represent a specific development role: designer, tester, technical writer, for example

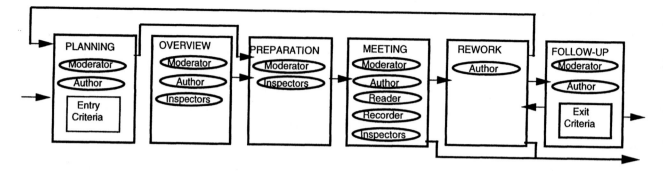

Figure 4. Software inspection process

In Figure 4 each role is associated with the step in which it participates.

Software Inspections As A Process Control Tool. As described in the previous section, the use of software inspections as a process control tool requires that they be employed at specified points throughout the development process. Figure 3 provides an example of a development process with software inspections being applied to internal requirements, high-level design, detail design, coding, test plans, and test cases. Within a development process each of these inspections is defined by specifying:

- Entry criteria
- Exit criteria
- Recommended participants
- Defect classifications
- Defect detection strategies.

Entry criteria are the pro-form conditions that a work product must meet before it is considered ready for inspection. These generally include the development operation exit criteria that would apply if an inspection were not specified for that operation, but they also include requirements for an effective inspection. For example, the entry criteria for a code inspection would require a clean compile, but it would also specify that the material to be inspected have visible line numbers and that the pertinent requirements, design, and change information be included as part of the inspection package.

Exit criteria are the completion conditions for an inspection. Typically, these are the correction of all detected defects and the documentation of any uncorrected defects in the project problem-tracking system.

Since a software inspection is a cooperative process that relies on group synergy, the selection of participants is an important issue. At inspections held early in the development process, for example, at

requirements or high-level design, both the user and system test viewpoints should be represented, as well as that of the developers responsible for implementation. The representation of all of these points of view will sometimes require inspection teams as large as seven or eight. At inspections held later in the development process, for example, code inspections, teams of three or four developers concerned only with detail design, coding, and unit test are effective [BCK81].

Strategies for detecting defects depend on the type of inspection, the kind of material, and the defect categories. In Fagan's implementations [FGN76], the inspectors are provided with checklists keyed to the defect types. In our implementations we have stressed "understanding" during preparation rather than defect detection. So a checklist organized by defect type is not appropriate. What we are now tending to provide are "preparation guidelines" that are keyed to the organization of the material being inspected. For example, for high-level designs it is important to verify that the functionality being specified in the design is in one-to-one correspondence with the requirements. Hence a high-level design preparation guideline might provide useful questions to be asked of each part of each subprogram and module design to check for this correspondence.

As described in the previous section, defect counts are used as process control data. Thus, the precise classification of defects is an essential part of the specification of each type of inspection. For software inspections, a defect is defined to be noncompliance with a product specification or document standard. Thus, as shown in Figure 1, defects are categorized by type and class. The classes, as defined by Fagan, are M="missing", E="extra," and W="wrong" [FGN76]. "Missing" is used for material that is called for in the specification or the standard, but is absent. "Extra" is used for material that exceeds the specification or the standard. "Wrong" is used for material that should be present, and is present, but contains a flaw.

Defect-type classifications depend on the nature of the material being inspected and on the specific development process. It should be possible to classify any defect easily and unambiguously during an inspection meeting. Furthermore, the resulting defect counts, when taken over time, should yield useful process control information. The thirteen defect types listed in Figure 1 form a generic set that has been used as a starting point with many different development projects. The appropriate types for each kind of inspection are selected from these thirteen and given definitions that apply to a particular inspection for a given project. An example of this kind of tailoring is given in Figure 5. An example of the kind of material inspected for these particular defects is given in Figure 6.

Other Aspects of the Use of Software Inspections. My experience with the implementation of software inspections in many development organizations is that the introduction of this technique often provides additional benefits beyond the measurable improvements in productivity and quality. One of the motivations in establishing software inspections as a standard part of a development process is that the use of inspections makes a frequently opaque operation more visible. Unlike a number of other software engineering techniques, software inspections are adaptable enough to be effective with primitive methodologies.

Every software project must produce code, and it is always possible to define an initial set of useful error types and detection strategies for a code inspection. Hence, about the only project for which inspections cannot be applied to at least the code is a project where the individual code modules are very large (greater than 500 lines) and are so badly structured that they cannot be partitioned. In my experience I have found that the use of the basic notions of structured programming is widespread so the occurrence of large, unstructured modules is rare.

When it is clear to the developers that their management supports their use of inspections as a technique for making improvements in quality and productivity, the experience of performing code inspections leads rapidly into consideration of other software engineering techniques. In many projects the precision of the inspection process points out the usefulness of a separate requirements document, and this in turn can lead to a better understanding of the usefulness of design documentation. Furthermore, when some of these other techniques are implemented, the data collected by inspections can be used to quantify the quality improvements achieved by these techniques.

Performance (PF)
- There is a plausible argument that the component will not meet the performance objectives stated in the requirements.

Data (DA)
- Missing or extra item in an Input, Output, or Update section.
- Incorrect or missing data type in an Input, Output, or Update section.

Interface (IF)
- Missing or extra routine call in a Processing section.
- An incorrect Invocation section.

Functionality (FN)
- In a Processing section a step is missing, extra, or erroneous.
- In a Processing section logical conditions are missing, extra, or erroneous.

Documentation (DC)
- The content of a Description section is. incomplete or misleading.
- The description of a data item is ambiguous.
- A processing step is not clearly described.

Standard (ST)
- An applicable standard in the Project Standards Manual is violated.

Syntax (SN)
- A defect in grammar, punctuation, or spelling.

Other (OT)
- A defect that does not fall under any of the types given above.

Figure 5. Example of High-Level Design Inspection Defect Types

SUBPROGRAM: prcl

TITLE: Print in columns

DESCRIPTION: This subprogram formats an input file into a columnized output file.

INPUTS:

-l	optional length command
-k	optional number of columns
-w	optional page width command
filename	input file

UPDATES: N/A

OUTPUTS:

Formatted output	listed to standard output file
Error message	to standard error file
Status	process status code

PROCESSING:

1. Formats input file into **k** columns per page on standard output.
2. If error detected sends error message to standard error file.
3. Return status code of 0 for normal exit or 1 for error exit.

INVOCATION: Called form the shell using the following format:
  prcl [-**l**integer] [-**k**integer] [-**w**integer] filename

Figure 6. Example of High-Level Design Specification

The process of inspecting all the work products produced by a given development operation exposes the development group as a whole to both good and bad examples. The inspection both develops and enforces group norms for quality workmanship. Participating in inspections thus eliminates much of the ambiguity about what is expected of each developer. Participating in inspections also spreads detail technical information around. This is especially important in projects where much of the essential information isn't formally written down. Finally, although project management is strongly warned against formally using detailed inspection data for personnel evaluation, the process does provide individuals with an objective means for dynamically assessing the quality of their work. For example, if I know the overall project defect rate for detail designs, I can use that information to motivate improvements in my own work, while also realizing that the inspection process will correct my mistakes before they become public.[2]

4. Software Inspections Data and Process Control

The collection and analysis of data is the essential feature that sets software inspections apart from other peer review techniques, for example, walk-throughs as described by Yourdon [YRD78].

The first use of inspection data is made by the first-line manager. The inspection disposition of "meets," "rework," or "reinspect," and the estimated effort and dates for rework provide essential process scheduling information. If the amount of rework is extensive, and scheduling constraints are tight, the manager may need to negotiate a reduction in the amount of functionality to be delivered. Some of the defects can then be documented with trouble reports so that they can be addressed during the next development cycle, and the rework limited to the corrections that can be made without impacting the scheduled delivery to the next operation.

---

[2] At the completion of one trial of inspections at IBM [IBM77], a study was made of individual defect rates. During the course of the

project defect rates decreased for all the developers. The software inspection process has the potential for enhancing professional growth and increasing job satisfaction.

The next use of inspection data is made by the developers or verifiers who receive the work product at later stages in the process. The Inspection Defect Summary Report[3] is essentially an "intelligence" report on the state of the work product at the time it was inspected. Although these defects are normally corrected during the rework step, the data nonetheless points to potential weak spots in the product.

The data on the amount of material inspected, the amount of inspector preparation, and the speed with which the material was examined during the meeting can be used by a quality assurance function to assess the effectiveness of an inspection. In a study performed by F.O. Buck at IBM [BCK81], it was found that inspection preparation and examination rates during the meeting were significant predictors of an effective inspection. For example, during the course of one development project inspection teams that inspected design and code at, or less than, the recommended rate found more than 100 percent more defects per thousand lines of code than did teams that exceeded this recommended rate. Furthermore, for a series of 106 inspections held as part of an inspection training effort, it was found that unless a team prepared for the recommended amount of time, it would, on the average, inspect faster, (less effectively) than the recommended rate.

The determination of recommended inspection and preparation rates is a quality assurance responsibility. The optimal rate depends on the type of material and the application. For code the initial recommendation is to plan for a rate of 100 lines of code per hour. This recommendation is derived from the study by Buck [BCK81] and has been substantiated in experience. For straightforward application code, some of our projects are reporting higher rates. On the other hand, for inspections of performance sensitive microcode, one project reported a rate of 40 lines of code per hour. Within each project, the reported rates should be scrutinized by quality assurance by studying the number and kinds of defects uncovered at different rates for similar workproducts.

The above are all examples of the immediate use of data from individual inspections. When inspection data are accumulated over time, summarized, and used in conjunction with other process data, rational, real-time control of a software development process becomes a possibility. For example, one of the standard inspection reports is the normalized distribution of the types of defects detected at each inspection point during designated time periods (Figure 7).

When a report such as this shows that a particular process is experiencing higher than normal defect percentages during initial development increments, it may be possible to remedy the problem and improve the quality of subsequent workproducts. For example, the sample report in Figure 7 shows that about one in every four defects is a documentation problem, an unexpectedly high percentage for this type of inspection. Perhaps the documentation standards for this work product are confusing; perhaps some of the developers need additional training in the application of these standards. At any rate, the inspection report has indicated the need for further investigation and remedy.

By comparing the defect detection and correction efficiencies between different inspection points and testing points, project management can make informed decisions for optimizing a development process overall. For example, in [DBN81], J.A. Dobbins and R.D. Buck report that an analysis of inspection data in their organization led to a shift in emphasis from code inspections to design inspections. They also report that an analysis of test reports led to the realization that an additional interface inspection needed to be added to their development process.

5. Software Inspections and Other Verification Techniques

As discussed above, software inspections are a process control tool, and are thus designed to work in cooperation with any other technique employed during a development process. In particular, the above discussion assumes that a development process employing software inspections will also employ testing,[4] reviews, and audits. Proof-of-correctness techniques are currently not widely used for the industrial production of software, but as argued by R.A. De Millo, et al., [DML79] a proof is a social process, not a formal one, and hence the use of proof techniques is also compatible with the use of software inspections.

---

[3] The Inspection Defect List (Form 4) is private to the inspection team. It is only used during the meeting to collect raw data and during follow-up. The data contained on the Defect List is summarized by the moderator on the Inspection Defect Summary Report (Form 5).

---

[4] "Testing" refers to the process of exercising or evaluating a system or system component by automated (not manual) means to verify that it satisfies specified requirements or to identify differences between expected and actual results.

Defect Type	Defect Category Missing	Wrong	Extra	Total Defect	Defect %
IF (Interface)	5	17	1	23	6.6
DA (Data)	3	21	1	25	7.2
LO (Logic)	32	40	14	77	24.8
IO (Input/Output)	7	9	3	19	5.5
PF (Performance)	0				
FN (Functionality)	5	7	2	14	4.0
HF (Human Factors)	3	2	5	10	2.9
ST (Standards)	25	24	3	52	14.9
DC (Documentation)	37	51	10	92	28.1
SN (Syntax)	4	9	1	14	4.0
TE (Test Environment)	0				
TC (Test Coverage)	0				
OT (Other)	2	5		7	2.0
	123	185	40	348	100.0

Figure 7. Software Inspection Summary Report. (Simulated Data)

Testing and software inspections both have the same purpose, that is, to discover defects [MRS79]. Within a given software development process, they play complementary and supporting roles. The first thing to note in discussing the relationship of software inspections and testing is that software inspections may be employed early in the development process while testing, since it requires executable units of code, cannot complete until these units have been specified, designed, and compiled. Since the cost of detecting and correcting defects in a software product rises exponentially as one proceeds through the development process [BHM76], the use of inspections as an adjunct to testing can often result in cost savings. To fully understand the relationship between inspections and testing, it is necessary to distinguish the different kinds of testing that are performed in the course of developing a software product. Below we discuss the relationship between unit testing, system testing, and software inspections.

In unit testing, an individual unit of program production (a function, or a collection of functions) is subjected to detailed testing to discover if there are any input combinations that will cause the unit to behave in an unexpected manner, or to produce incorrect results. Since it is practically impossible to test all input combinations, the art of unit testing is that of specifying a limited set of inputs that will most likely reveal defects. One of the concepts used for the specification of such input sets is that of code coverage, for example, that all statements be executed or all branches be executed. In practice, it is extremely difficult to specify input sets that give 100 percent branch coverage; but detailed design and code inspections are a line-by-line examination of designs and code, and

hence provide 100 percent coverage because all branches are considered. For processes where data is being collected on the relative effort and effectiveness of unit testing and software inspections, rational judgments can be made on which to use, or how they should be combined.

For system testing, the situation is different because this operation exercises many units (including the entire system) and thus provides an opportunity for defect detection beyond the scope of the inspection of individual units. However, there is still a use for inspections in this area. For example, in one case cited above [DBN81], the detection of a large number of interface defects during a test operation led to the creation of a special interface inspection to detect and correct these defects prior to this testing operation. The overall result was an improvement in productivity. The reason for this is that one inspection may find a number of errors that are then corrected all at once, while testing tends to find and correct defects one by one.

A further use of software inspections in relation to testing is in the use of test plan and test case inspections [LRS75]. The purpose of these inspections is to improve the effectiveness of the test operation by improving the defect detection potential of the tests. An application of test plan and test case inspections at IBM reported that the number of test cases was increased by 30 percent, but that the overall result was an 85 percent improvement in test productivity [EBN81].

By definition, software inspections are a small peer group process whose purpose is the detection and correction of defects. When development work products must be examined by larger groups, or by management, software inspections do not apply. Nor do they apply when the purpose of the examination is other than defect detection, for example, the consideration of architectural or design alternatives. Each of these cases calls for procedures specifically designed to achieve the desired objectives.

The proper design and execution of various kinds of review procedures is beyond the scope of this paper, but we can make some suggestions on the use of reviews in relationship to inspections. Where it is the case that the purpose of a manual examination of a work product is strictly to detect and correct defects, then inspections have been shown to be superior to other review procedures [FGN76], and in addition, they provide data for process management. Of course, in order to detect defects in a work product there must be a clear understanding of the product specifications and document standards.

Often the use of a special review procedure will be dictated by considerations other than verification, and the question then arises as to whether the review subsumes the defect detection and correction function of an inspection, or whether an inspection should be held in addition to the review. In general, the answer to this question is that if it appears that an inspection might be of benefit, then the inspection can be implemented and the resulting inspection data can then decide the question.

Audits by definition[5] involve an agent external to the process being examined. Except for special cases, for example, the auditing of financial software by outside auditors, auditing of software development work products is not an efficient verification technique because it involves the duplication of technical expertise within an auditing function.

Procedural audits are another matter. In the case of software inspections, it is assumed that a quality assurance function has responsibility for auditing inspection procedures to ensure (1) that the procedures are being performed as specified, and (2) that the procedures, when faithfully executed, are producing the intended results in quality and productivity. In this application of audits, inspection reports become input to the audit operation.

Where formal verification techniques, such as Dijkstra's discipline of programming [DJK76], are being utilized as part of the design and implementation operations, software inspections are a natural choice for a peer examination technique. Where automatic verifiers are used in a development process, the situa-

tion is similar to that in which a compiler is employed. The compiler is assumed to operate correctly, and the problem is that of saying the right things in the higher level language. Software inspections can be applied to the verification of correctness conditions just as they are to compiler input.

Walk-throughs, as described in [IEEE88], are often compared to inspections. The essential differences between inspections and walk-throughs are: (1) walk-throughs are not a formally documented and implemented development process, (2) walk-throughs do not create quality records that can be used for process improvement, (3) walk-throughs do not create quality records that provide evidence that detected defects have been corrected and the corrections verified.

Terminology is not the issue here. A software development work product verification process that does not have the three characteristics just listed does not satisfy the requirements of ISO 9001; more is required. Furthermore, a process that can be managed and relied on throughout the life of an organization is needed. Walk-throughs, as the term is used here, do not meet these requirements.

6. A Software Inspection Implementation Program

The Development and Training Environment. Installing software inspections as an effective technique in a development organization can be a difficult job since it involves changing the behavior of a whole organization. The required behavior changes are not large, but they must be coordinated between the developers, first-level management, project management, and software quality assurance. In addition, for long-running projects, the changes must be planned and executed within existing scheduling constraints.

This section describes a comprehensive inspections implementation program that was carried out in the early eighties at a large telecommunications R&D organization. Similar programs have since been used in many other organizations for the successful installation of effective inspection processes.

In the subject organization each project was an independent organizational entity. The management of each project had the responsibility for choosing the appropriate means of achieving project objectives, and a wide variety of approaches were employed. The approach that was selected depended largely on the past experience of the managers and senior developers. Tools, techniques, and procedures were borrowed freely between projects, but generally they were tailored, or reimplemented to fit the project's perception of its needs.

---

[5] IEEE-Std-729, op cit, gives two definitions. The first is "an independent review for the purpose of assessing compliance."

Within the subject organization, the systems training department had the responsibility for providing software engineering training in subject matter that was applicable to a number of different projects. For example, it provided training in the use of the Unix operating system, the C language, microprocessor application design, data communications, and so on.

Within the systems training department, the system development technology group had responsibility for developing and delivering training in software engineering methodologies that could be utilized by a variety of application areas regardless of the specific implementation techniques being utilized. Figure 8 shows the subject matter covered by this group's curriculum.

During the course of developing the software inspections program within this curriculum, it became apparent that if this training program wanted to use actual, effective implementations of software inspections on individual projects as its measure of success, it would have to take a novel approach. The approach that was developed was called *consultative training*

and became the group's primary method of software engineering technology transfer. Consultative training utilized a project-oriented view of the subject matter of software engineering, as shown in Figure 9 [EMR83].

Software Inspection Program Design Concepts. For software inspections, the application of the consultative training concept resulted in the following program design concepts:

- The software inspections program was focused on entire software projects, as opposed to traditional training focused on individual developers. Within Bell Laboratories, individual software projects normally correspond with a single organizational element, for example, a group or a department, and hence this approach allowed us to work in concert with project management as well as the developers. It also allowed us to schedule the various implementation steps at the project's convenience.

THE SOFTWARE ENGINEERING CURRICULUM

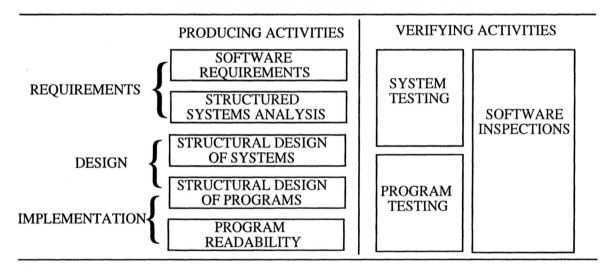

Figure 8. Our original software engineering curriculum

246

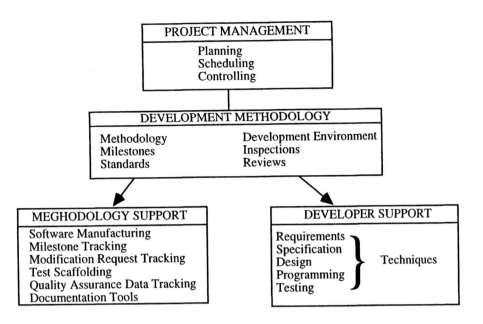

Figure 9. Project-Oriented View of Software Engineering

- Within each project, our major concern was with motivating and training developers and first-line managers. We obtained the support of upper management and coordinated the program with them, but we avoided a top-down approach. Our assumption was that effective behavioral change cannot be dictated from above.[6]

- We employed formal classroom training as a major part of our program, but we also provided direct consulting. We assisted projects in selecting the appropriate inspection points within their existing methodology, and we helped specify the entry and exit criteria, defect types and detection strategies, and the recommended participants. As part of this effort we supplied each project with first drafts of a Project Inspection Manual that contained our initial suggestions for the specification of each type of inspection the project would use. This manual also contained inspection data collection forms tailored to the project's needs.

- We entered into an ongoing relationship with each client project and provided whatever as-

sistance was appropriate when problems arose. In particular, we performed evaluation and review activities to determine whether the project was in fact following its procedures, whether these procedures were in fact producing the desired results, and whether the overall perception of the developers and first-line managers was that inspections were making a positive contribution to their project.

- In order to make our formal classroom training directly applicable to an individual project, we separated the teaching and exercise material into two classes: (1) that which taught principles and techniques generic to any application of software inspections, and (2) that which considered aspects that could be specialized for a particular project. This meant, for example, that we could apply the project's own definitions of defect types and detection strategies against class exercise material developed from actual project work products.

- Wherever possible, software inspections were introduced into a project on a trial basis. A trial allowed a shakedown of the software inspection procedures in the project environment, and also allowed the project to directly experience the benefits of inspections before making a full-scale commitment.

---

[6] This is no longer an assumption. In the few instances where we violated this principle, we were emphatically taught its general validity.

Software Inspections Program Implementation. To implement the concepts just discussed above we designed the six-step program shown in Figure 10. This formal approach to the delivery of this program allowed us to keep track of each project's progress through its implementation plan. It also helped us manage and allocate our own resources among the constantly changing needs of our clients, and it at times provided a structure for charging for our services. This six-step program also served to make clear to each project what its responsibilities were during each step of the program. Each of these six steps is described below.

1. *Software Inspections Overview.* The overview was a presentation to managers and key developers on a project. It introduced the software inspections technique, discussed how it would be carried out, what the expected benefits would be, what the costs would be, and what project resources would be required for implementation. At the conclusion of this presentation, the project decided whether or not it wished to proceed with a software inspections implementation program at that time and, if it did, who on the project would have responsibility for initiating the effort.

2. *Needs-Assessment.* The needs-assessment activity consisted of meeting with the project members who were assigned to initiate the program, and one or two members of the software inspection program staff. Project members first presented an overview of the project, including the nature of the application, project resources and schedules, and the development environment. Project members and the software inspections program staff then determined training requirements and schedules, project development phase demarcations with appropriate software inspection types, and a schedule and participants for the trial use of software inspections. The trial period was designed to correspond to some part of the project's development cycle so that any defect data from the project's normal quality assurance procedures could be used later in evaluating the use of software inspections on that project. A software inspections coordinator, who would have responsibility for the project's inspection program, and who interfaced with the inspection program staff was designated by project management.

3. *Implementation Support.* The classroom training on inspections was most effective when there was sufficient time in the project's inspection implementation schedule to prepare (1) an initial draft of the project's software inspections manual and (2) practice inspection material based on an actual project work product. These materials were produced through a joint effort between the software inspections staff and the project's software inspections coordinator. This effort supplemented the inspections staff's understanding of inspections in general with essential information about the project's specific environment. The inspections staff involvement in turn overcame the project's lack of expertise and, more subtly, provided an outside impetus toward completing work that was not directly related to the immediate development schedule. The inspections staff involvement also provided the coordinator with psychological support—the coordinator, after all, must deal directly with his or her colleagues' resistance to changes in project procedures.

COURSE/ACTIVITY	AUDIENCE	PURPOSE	LENGTH
1. Software Inspections Overview	Project Management Key Developers	To provide decision base	½ Day class
2. Software Inspections Needs Assessment	Project Management Key Developers	To plan project use of process	½–1 Day consulting
3. Implementation	Inspections Coordinator	Design and document project process	1–2 Days support
4. Software Inspections Workshop	Project Development Groups	To provide developer training	2 Day class
5. Software Inspections Management Seminar	Project Management	To provide management training	½ Day class
6. Software Inspections Review and Evaluation	Project Management Key Developers	To "tune" the process	Interview as needed

Figure 10. The Bell Labs Software Inspections Program

4. *Developer Workshop.* The developer workshop taught the steps needed to prepare for, participate in, and lead an inspection. A major section of the workshop was a full-scale practice inspection that inspected the project material especially prepared for this purpose, and that utilized draft copies of the project's inspections manual. This exercise thus not only provided the developers with experience in the inspection technique generally, but it also gave them a chance to trial the specific procedures that would be used on their project, and a chance to offer their own suggestions for improving these procedures. The workshop concluded with a discussion of project implementation considerations by the software inspections coordinator who worked with the training staff to tailor the program to the project.

5. *Management Seminar.* In the initial implementation period of inspections on a project, the inspections staff sought to maximize the involvement of the developers on whom the success of the technique ultimately depended and to minimize involvement by management. Once inspections began to take hold, however, there was a need to provide management with additional information. In fact, project management ultimately has a key role to play in a successful project implementation of inspections. This role was discussed with the developers in the workshop, and skepticism about whether or not management will play its role properly was blunted by the inspections staff's commitment to bring the developers' concerns directly to the management. For small projects, this could be handled informally; for large projects, a half-day seminar was used for this purpose.

6. *Evaluation and Review.* At the conclusion of a trial, and at appropriate intervals thereafter, a project should review its software inspection procedures to determine what changes, if any, should be made in its procedures. In this step, the software inspections program staff evaluated the project's inspection process using project inspection data, direct observation of inspection meetings, and formal interviews with participating developers and their first-level managers. The collected data was then evaluated and presented, along with recommendations for improvements, to the project's software inspections coordinator and to interested developers and managers.

The results of this program were positive. Of the 42 projects that participated in the program by the middle of 1984, 25 were using inspections as an established part of their development process, 4 were trailing inspections, and 5 had training scheduled. The remaining 8 projects did not immediately continue the program for a variety of reasons: one project did not follow the training with the necessary implementation resources, in another the supervisor sabotaged the process by attending inspection meetings, and so on. The review and evaluation step described above was completed for 6 projects.

Data for one completed evaluation was obtained from a series of 40 interviews with developers and project management, from inspection records, and by direct observation. The results were that:

- inspections were being consistently used;
- the developers and managers were enthusiastic and supportive of the inspection process; and
- more than 90 percent of those interviewed felt that inspections increased product quality and enhanced developer growth, with a majority perceiving no delay in production schedules as a result of using inspections.

These results have been corroborated by other studies and by less formal project evaluations. The bottom line is that this approach to the implementation of software inspections is effective. However, there were still some problems:

Timing and Initial Implementation. The least effective software inspection is the code inspection since it can find errors only after the completion of requirements, design, and coding. Yet one large project chose to restrict the initial application of inspections to code because they had just implemented a new methodology that contained detailed procedures for design reviews. Had we been able to start our work with this project a few months sooner, most likely we would have been able to convince them to use design inspections rather than reviews. Our philosophy has been to work with whatever opportunities have presented themselves to us and to let the effectiveness of the inspection technique speak for itself over the long haul

Data Collection and Analysis. Most projects agree in theory with the need to collect and analyze data on the effectiveness of the inspection process. They understand the potential benefits from having the data: immediate and well-documented results from software inspection meetings; indication of troublesome areas in system implementation in time for preventive measures, such as redesign or more thorough testing; and measures of the costs of the inspection process versus other defect detection and correction methods. However, few projects as yet are willing to invest in other than the most minimal of data collection and analysis efforts. Fear of misuse of the information is one problem. Another is limited staff for doing the work involved. One answer is more mechanized support for data collection and analysis, and then more specific procedures for how to use the results.

Management Support. Management support is key to the success of any new technique. If a sustained commitment to spending the resources required is not maintained, failure is certain, and much effort will be wasted. A well-defined trial use of software inspections helps give management a good measure of the benefits and costs of using software inspections in their particular projects.

Continued success is possible, however, only when management uses inspections in a way that is consistent with other project objectives and with developer expectations. One failure we experienced was the direct result of the management's lack of proper support and encouragement for developers in implementing this process.

7. Conclusions

Software inspections have been shown [FGN76] [IBM77] [PEL82] [MCK81] [EBN81a] to be an efficient and effective method for improving project productivity and product quality in a wide variety of industrial software development environments. Software inspections can be effectively employed together with testing, product reviews, procedural audits, and formal verification techniques. The successful installation of software inspections within ongoing projects is complex, but well-conceived and supported programs have been successful in numerous development organizations.

References

[ACK82] Ackerman, A.F., Ackerman, A.S., and Ebenau, R.G., "A Software Inspections Training Program," *Proc. COMPSAC 82* IEEE Computer Society Press, Los Alamitos, Calif., 1982, pp. 443–444.

[BCK81] Buck, F.O., "Indicators of Quality Inspection," IBM Technical Report TR21.802, Systems Communications Division, Kingston, N.Y., 1981.

[BHM76] Boehm, B.W., "Software Engineering," *IEEE Trans. Computers*, Dec. 1976, pp. 1,226–1,241.

[DML79] DeMillo, R.A., Lipton, R.J., and Perles, A.J., "Social Processes and Proofs of Theories and Programs," *Comm. ACM*, Vol. 22, No. 5, 1979, pp. 271–280.

[DBN81] Dobbins, J.A. and Buck, R.D., "Software Quality in the 80's," *Proc. Trends and Applications Symp.*, IEEE Computer Society Press, Los Alamitos, Calif., 1981, pp. 31–37.

[DJK76] Dijkstra, E.W., *A Discipline of Programming*, Prentice-Hall, Englewood Cliffs, N.J., 1976.

[EBN81] Ebenau, R.G., Private communication

[EBN81a] Ebenau, R.G., "Inspecting For Software Quality," *Proc. 2nd Nat'l Symp. EDP Quality Assurance*, 1981, DPMA Education Foundation, produced by U. S. Professional Development Institute, Inc., 12611 Davon Drive, Silver Spring, Md. 20904

[EMR83] Emerson, T.J., et al., "Training For Software Engineering Technology Transfer," *Workshop on Software Engineering Technology*, IEEE Computer Society Press, Los Alamitos, Calif., 1983, pp. 34–41.

[FGN76] Fagan, M.E., "Design and Code Inspections to Reduce Errors in Program Development," *IBM System J.*, Vol. 15, No. 3, 1976.

[IBM77] "Inspections in Application Development—Introduction and Implementation Guidelines," IBM publication GC20-2000, July 1977, IBM Technical Publications, Department 824, 1133 Westchester Avenue, White Plains, N.Y. 10604

[IEEE88] IEEE, ANSI/IEEE Std 1028-1988, Standard for Software Reviews and Audits.

[LRS75] Larson, R.R., "Test Plan and Test Case Inspection Specifications," Technical Report TR21.586, April 4, 1975, IBM Corporation, Kingston, N.Y.

[MCK81] McCormick, K.K., "The Results of Using a Structured Methodology, Software Inspections, and a New Hardware/Software Configuration on Application Systems," *Proc. 2nd National Symp. EDP Quality Assurance*, 1981, DPMA Education Foundation, produced by US Professional Development Institute, Inc., 12611 Davan Drive, Silver Spring, MD 20904.

[MRS79] Myers, G.J., *The Art of Software Testing*, John Wiley & Sons, New York, N.Y., 1979.

[PEL81] Peele, R., "Design Code Inspection Pilot Project Evaluation," *Proc. 2nd Nat'l Symp. EDP Quality Assurance*, DPMA Education Foundation, produced by US Professional Development Institute, Inc. 12611 Davan Drive, Silver Spring, MD 20904.

[PEL82] Peele, R., "Code Inspections at First Union Corporation," *Proc. COMPSAC 82*, IEEE Computer Society Press, Los Alamitos, Calif., 1982, pp. 445–446.

[YRD78] Yourdon, E., *Structured Walkthroughs*, Yourdon, Inc., 1978.

INSPECTION PROFILE

System: _____ Release: _____ Increment: _____ Date: _____

Unit: _____

Inspection type:

☐ Internal Requirements   ☐ Detail Design   ☐ Test Plan

☐ High Level Design   ☐ Code   ☐ Test Cases

Size of material: _____ (unit) _____

Is this a re-inspection: ☐ No   ☐ Yes

Summary of open items: _____

_____

_____

_____

Other comments: _____

_____

_____

_____

Prepared by: _____

Form 1: Sample software inspection profile form

INSPECTION PREPARATION LOG

System:_____ Release:_____ Increment:_____ Date:_____

Unit:_____

Inspector:_____ Room:_____ Phone:_____

Role: ☐ Author ☐ Moderator ☐ Peer Inspector

Overview attendance: ☐ No ☐ Yes

Date received Inspection Package: _____

	date:	time:
Preparation Log:	_____	_____
	_____	_____
	_____	_____
	_____	_____

Total Preparation: _____

hours

CONCERNS

Location	Description
_____	_____
	_____
	_____
_____	_____
	_____
	_____
_____	_____
	_____
	_____
_____	_____
	_____

Form 2: Sample inspection preparation log

INSPECTION MANAGEMENT REPORT

System:_____ Release: _____ Increment:___ Inspection date: _____

Unit:_____

Moderator:_____ Room:_____ Phone:_____

Inspection type:

☐ Internal Requirements ☐ Detail Design ☐ Test Plan

☐ High Level Design   ☐ Code   ☐ Test Cases

Overview held: ☐ No   ☐ Yes   Overview duration: _____

Number attending: _____

Number of inspection meetings:_____ Total meeting duration:_____

Total number of inspectors:_____ Total preparation time:_____

Module disposition: ☐ meets ☐ follow-up ☐ re-inspect

Estimated rework effort:_____ (days)

Rework to be completed by:_____

Actual rework effort:_____

Re-inspection scheduled for:__'_____

Other inspectors:

_____   _____

_____   _____

_____   _____

_____   _____

Moderator certification:_____ Date: _____

Additional comments:_____

_____

_____

_____

_____

Form 3: Sample software inspection management report

INSPECTION DEFECT LIST

System:_____ Release:_____ Increment:_____ Date:_____

Unit:_____

Moderator:_____ Room:_____ Phone:_____

Inspection type:

☐ Internal Requirements ☐ Detail Design ☐ Test Plan

☐ High Level Design ☐ Code ☐ Test Cases

			Defect	
Document:	Location:	Defect Description:	Type:	Class:
____	____	_____	___	___
____	____	_____	___	___
____	____	_____	___	___
____	____	_____	___	___
____	____	_____	___	___
____	____	_____	___	___
____	____	_____	___	___
____	____	_____	___	___
____	____	_____	___	___
____	____	_____	___	___
____	____	_____	___	___
____	____	_____	___	___
____	____	_____	___	___
____	____	_____	___	___
____	____	_____	___	___
____	____	_____	___	___
____	____	_____	___	___

Error type: IF=Interface DA=Data LO=Logic IO=Input/Output PF=Performanc HF=Human factors ST=Standards
　　　　　DC=Documentation SN=Syntax OT=Other
Error class: M=Missing W=Wrong E=Extra
Error stage: RQ=Requirements HL=High Level Design DD=Detail Design CD=Code TP=Test Plan TC=Test Case

Form 4: Sample software inspection defect list

Page____of____

INSPECTION SUMMARY

System: _____ Release: _____ Increment: _____ Inspection Date: _____

Unit: _____

Moderator: _____ Room: _____ Phone: _____

Inspection type:
- ☐ Internal Requirements   ☐ Detail Design   ☐ Test Plan
- ☐ High Level Design   ☐ Code   ☐ Test Cases

Error		DEFECTS THIS OPERATION			
		M	W	E	Total
IF:	Interface				
DA:	Data				
LO:	Logic				
IO:	Input/Output				
PF:	Performanc				
HF:	Human factors				
ST:	Standards				
DC:	Documentation				
SN:	Syntax				
TE:	Test Environment				
TC:	Test Coverage				
OT:	Other				
			Total		

DEFECT IN PRIOR OPERATIONS			
Defect Stage	Defect Type	Defect Class	MR Number

Major Errors This Stage:
Requirement=IF+PF+HF
High Level Design=IF+DA+LO+IO+PF+HF
Detail Design=IF+DA+LO+IO+PF
Code=IF+DA+LO+IO+PF
Test Plan=TE+TC
Test Case=TE+TC

MAJOR DEFECT THIS OPERATION	
Defect Type	Total
Total	

Form 5: Sample software inspections summary form

255

Reviews and Audits

John J. Marciniak
Kaman Sciences Corporation

Reviews and audits are valuable tools used in software development projects, as well as in systems development. The distinction between software management and systems management, as well as software engineering and systems engineering, is becoming blurred as "systems" development involves an increasing integration of these disciplines. One example is in reengineering projects where the trade-off between new software development is intrinsically related to the development or use of new hardware. The economics of reengineering projects dictate the acquisition approach and the degree of hardware and software development. The types of reviews discussed apply equally to the total system environment; however, their genesis is in software development. Some of these review types will vary in area of application while others such as the Formal Inspection, are more pertinent to the practice of software development.

Reviews come in different forms and names. Some of these are: formal reviews, inspections, audits, and walk-throughs. In each of these categories, the terms have different connotation and meaning. For example, general management reviews include project reviews and management oversight. Irrespective of the use or purpose, the form of the review is most important. Thus, one has to distinguish between the review as a practice and its use in practice.

The most common characteristics that distinguish review forms are: purpose, scope, and method. It is the purpose of this article to introduce these forms, explain the basic differences between them, and provide insight in how they are applied in software development practice. In general the purpose and scope of the review will determine the method used and the degree of formality applied. In Table 1 we depict these general characteristics.

The scope of a review may range from the entire project to a review of the design, or a single document such as the users' guide. In general, the scope of a review does not appreciably affect the review procedure, only the impact that it has on the level and area of application. The purpose of a review may range from an audit or inspection of a specific product, to an assessment or completion of a development milestone. For example, to determine the adequacy of a design specification, an inspection may be used. To determine the status of the progress of development at various milestones such as the completion of software design, management reviews or walk-throughs may be used. The method may vary from free form, or informal, to a specific methodology such as formal inspections. A free-form, or less formal procedure, may be used in technical interchange meeting (TIMs), while a formal inspection may be applied to assess the status of a specific product at the various points in its development.

Definitions

According to the *IEEE Standard Glossary of Software Engineering Terminology* (IEEE, 1990a), a review is

> A process or meeting during which a work product, or a set of work products, is presented to project personnel, managers, users, customers, or other interested parties for comment or approval. Types include code review, design review, formal qualification review, requirements review, and test readiness review.

This is the most general form and, as we shall see, is focused and customized depending on the specific purpose of the review.

Reviews are further classified according to formality. A formal review is typically one that is required by a contract commitment that is usually invoked through the application of a standard such as military standard 498 (MIL-STD-498), which are often more prevalent in government acquisition projects. The implication is that it is a contractual milestone witnessed by the customer or acquirer of the system, and normally denotes the completion of certain activities such as detailed design or system testing and results in a development or formal baseline for continued development of the software system.

Table 1. Review Characteristics

Type	Scope	Purpose	Method
Reviews	Usually broad	Project progress assessment of milestone completion	Ad hoc
Walk-throughs	Fairly narrow	Assess specific development products	Static analysis of products
Inspections	Narrow	Assess specific development products	Noninteractive, fairly procedural
Audits	Narrow to broad	Check processes and products of development	Formal, mechanical and procedure

In another perspective, Freedman and Weinberg use the following criteria to classify a formal review: (Freedman, 1990a)

1. A written report on the status of the product reviewed—a report that is available to everyone involved in the project, including management;

2. Active and open participation of everyone in the review group, following some traditions, customs, and written rules as to how such a review is to be conducted;

3. Full responsibility of all participants for the quality of the review—that is, for the quality of the information in the written report.

One can see that, from this description, the criteria shifts to certain responsibilities for the review participants as opposed to the contract vehicle.

As we see, there are different views as to the formality of the review. In contradistinction, informal reviews are those that are held which are not contractually required, or less formal from the perspective of Freedman and Weinberg, such as technical interchange meetings. The procedures applied for both formality types are similar, the principal difference being the rigor applied in the conduct of the review, for example, formal management of minutes.

There are other types of review classifications. For example, there are internal management reviews. (Marciniak, 1990) These may be periodic reviews of the project by senior management within the developing organization to assess progress or special reviews based on specific issues such as the impact of the development on other market areas. In the latter, management uses the review to provide general awareness of the direction of the project in order to take advantage of the resulting product in other market areas or to avoid conflict with other company projects.

Another major classification of reviews is the peer review. Peer reviews are usually walk-throughs, inspections, and round-robin reviews (Freedman, 1990b). The common characteristic of a peer review is

that it is conducted by peers. A walk-through is normally a peer review; however, in many cases it is conducted with participants who are nonpeers. These reviews are normally confined to a single product such as a segment of the design, or a code unit, or component. The definitions of these reviews follows.

A Walk-through is

A static analysis technique in which a designer or programmer leads members of the development team and other interested parties through a segment of documentation or code, and the participants ask questions and make comments about possible errors, violation of development standards, and other problems. (IEEE, 1990b)

Walk-throughs are sometimes referred to as structured walk-throughs (not to be confused with formal inspections, see below); however, according to Freedman and Weinberg they are one and the same (Freedman, 1990c). A walk-through is probably the most common review technique in a software project, and the method will vary based on individual implementation.

A special form of a walk-through is the Formal Inspection. The Formal Inspection was developed at IBM (Fagan, 1976) and is often referred to simply as Fagan Inspections. A principal distinguishing factor between a walk-through and a formal inspection is that the formal inspection is led by a moderator independent of the person responsible for the product, while the walk-through is led by a reader or presenter who may be the developer of the product.

In a formal inspection the collection of anomalies is carefully structured to capture statistical evidence of the effort. A formal inspection should not be confused with an inspection. The choice of the term is perhaps unfortunate as the formal inspection is a type of walk-through rather than an inspection. Hollocker discusses the procedures used for Formal Inspections; however, chooses to use the words "Software Inspection." (Hollocker, 1990)

Inspection

An inspection is

A static analysis technique that relies on visual examination of development products to detect errors, violations of developing standards, and other problems. Types include code inspection; design inspections. (IEEE, 1990c)

Freedman and Weinberg define inspection as "a method of rapidly evaluating material by confining attention to a few selected aspects, one at a time" (Freedman, 1990d). The inspection is carried out in an noninteractive manner, usually by a party that is detached from the developer.

The difference between inspections and audits is not obvious, and perhaps the difference is not pertinent. The differences are stated in Evans (Evans, 1987a).

An inspection normally has a narrow focus evaluating only a segment of the project environment. The inspection structure is very rigid and the evaluation criteria are predetermined based on a model of acceptability.

An audit may also have a narrow focus, but, in most cases, is use to evaluate the broader aspects of the project environment. Besides checking individual segments of the project infrastructure against plans, audits may evaluate the interrelationships between segments of the infrastructure. When assessing the implementation attributes, audits tend to be more "freewheeling" allowing the auditor to pursue paths not necessarily included in the initial audit.

Another view put forth in Evans, focuses on interaction (Evans 1987b). An audit is normally more interactive in that the auditor communicates with the project staff. In an inspection, the inspector uses a rigid set of guidelines or a checklist to assess the degree of compliance with the checklist or guidelines. In either event, the important thing is to focus on the purpose of the procedure, then apply the mechanism that is more appropriate for the project.

Audits

An audit is much like an inspection; however, as indicated above, it tends to be of a broader nature and involve interactions with the project staff.

In the general form an audit is

An independent examination of a work product or set of work products to assess compliance with specifications, standards, contractual agreements, or other criteria. (IEEE, 1990d)

The IEEE defines two specific forms of audits, the Functional Configuration Audit (FCA) and the Physical Configuration Audit (PCA).

A functional configuration audit (FCA) is

An audit conducted to verify that the development of a configuration item has been completed satisfactorily, that the item has achieved the performance and functional characteristics specified in the functional or allocated configuration identification, and that its operational and support documents are complete and satisfactory. (IEEE, 1990e)

A physical configuration audit (PCA) is

An audit conducted to verify that a configuration item, as built, conforms to the technical documentation that defined it. (IEEE, 1990f)

These two audits are formal audits because they are required by the contractual instruments that govern the development project. If there were no contractual instrument, the eventual user would still conduct a form of the above to verify the product. A simple example is buying an automobile. When the automobile is ordered, a spec sheet or contract is normally filled out calling for items such as fog lights and radios. A functional audit would verify that the radio performs, for example, that it plays the bands specified, while a physical audit would verify that the type of radio ordered is the one that is actually delivered with the automobile.

There are other types of audits that are conducted during the development process. For example, there are quality assurance audits that audit a particular process of development such as the conduct of reviews and walk-throughs. There are configuration management audits that audit the processes of configuration management. The distinguishing factor in these types of audits is that they are carried out by the function with that specific responsibility. For example, a software quality assurance (SQF) audit is carried out by the software quality assurance function, and it is based on SQA plans and procedures.

Application in the life cycle

Reviews, audits, walk-throughs, and inspections are used to provide assessment of the progress, processes used, and products of the project. The program management plan, or software development plan, will normally specify the types of reviews used and the methods that are applied in their use. Certain reviews, as mentioned above, will be dictated by contract requirements, usually through the use of development standards such as IEEE Std 1498 (IEEE, 19XX). In Figure 1 we show a typical waterfall life cycle with examples of system development reviews and audits.

There are three parts to a review: the planning phase, the review conduct, and the post review phase. All are important to any successful review. The elimination or neglect of any of the phases will jeopardize a successful review.

In the planning phase, the actions generally include stating the purpose of the review, arranging for participants, ensuring that review materials are provided for their inspection well prior to the conduct of the review, making physical arrangements for the location and support required, and preparing an agenda. During the conduct of the review, it is important to follow the agenda in a disciplined manner. Generally speaking, the purpose of the review conduct is not to fix problems that are identified, but, to identify them and assign action for their resolution. Reviews can very easily get contentious so it is important to ensure that a moderator or review leader maintains control of the proceedings. A recorder or scribe has to be assigned to transcribe the proceedings into recorded form for the purpose of preparing a record of the review and a postreview action list. The postreview period can be flexible depending on the actions required. These are normally followed to completion by management and reported on at the next review. It is possible that another review may be required if the review results are unsatisfactory. Naturally, this could result in some project impact, usually of schedule and cost.

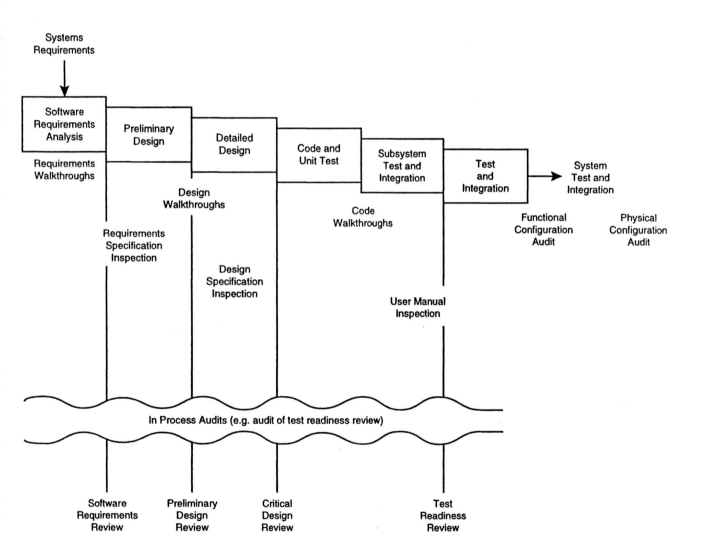

Figure 1. Reviews in the software life cycle

Management Reviews

Objective. A management review is a formal management-team evaluation of a project-level plan or a project's status relative to such a plan. The review team communicates progress, coordinates the decision making within their span of control, and provides recommendations for:

- Making activities progress according to plan, based on an evaluation of product development status
- Changing project direction or identifying the need for alternative planning
- Maintaining global control of the project through adequate allocation of resources

Moreover, to further tailor this review process for an individual project milestone, specific objectives are to be identified in a "Statement of Objectives" made available before the review meeting. The management review concept can be applied to new development or to maintenance activities. It can also be useful in managing process improvement projects.

People and Their Agendas. Roles for the management review include:

- Leader
- Reporter
- Team member

The review leader is responsible for the administrative tasks pertaining to the review, for assuring that the review is conducted in an order manner, and for issuing any minutes or reports. The reporter is responsible for having the project status and all supporting documentation available for distribution before the meeting. This individual is also responsible for documenting the findings, decisions, and recommendations of the review team.

When to Hold a Management Review. Typically, the project planning documents (for example, Software Quality Assurance Plan, Software Development Plan, or Software Verification and Validation Plan) establish the need for conducting specific management reviews. As stated in these plans, a management review can be initiated by the completion of a project phase or specific software deliverable (for example, a planning document, a requirements specification, or a design document). Moreover, management reviews not required by plan may occur, as needed, to deal with any unscheduled events or contingencies.

A selected review leader establishes or confirms a statement of objectives for the meeting and verifies that any appropriate software deliverables and any other documents or reports available are sufficiently complete to support the review objectives. In addition to any applicable reference material supplied by project management, or requested by the review leader, these would include:

- A Statement of Objectives for the management review and its agenda
- Current project schedule, resource, and cost data
- Pertinent reports (for example, managerial review reports, technical review reports, or audit reports) from other reviews and/or audits already completed
- Software deliverable status or current disposition

Procedures. The review leader, having identified the team, schedules facilities for the meeting and distributes any materials needed by the review team for advanced preparation (for example, statement of objectives, agenda, or presentation requirements). In addition, the review leader might consider requesting that a project representative conduct an overview session for the review team. This overview can occur as part of the examination meeting or as a separate meeting. The management review process is considered complete when all issues identified in the review "Statement of Objectives" have been addressed and the management review report has been issued. Project management typically tracks any action items through to resolution. If a re-review is required, it would provide confirmation of action item completion.

Output. The Management Review Report identifies:

- The project being reviewed and the team that participated in that review
- Inputs to the review
- Review objectives
- Action item ownership, status, and tracking responsibility
- Project status and a list of issues that must be addressed for the project to meet its milestone
- Recommendations regarding any further reviews and audits, and a list of additional information and data that must be obtained before they can be executed

The Walk-through

Objective. The walk-through process has much in common with both the general technical review process and the inspection process. It, too, is used to evaluate a specific software element and provide evidence that the software element satisfies its specifications and conforms to applicable standards. Its statement of objectives includes software element specific objectives. They also exist in the form of a checklist that varies with the product being presented. Objectives typically do not pertain to any additional constraints on the walk-through process.

Distinctions from other review processes, however, are established by unique objectives. The following always appear in the Statement of Objectives for the application of the walk-through process:

- Detect, identify, and describe software element defects
- Examine alternatives and stylistic issues
- Provide a mechanism that enables the authors to collect valuable feedback on their work, yet allows them to retain the decision-making authority for any changes

People and Their Agendas. Roles for the walk-through are similar to those for other review processes, with one important distinction. The leader responsible for conducting a specific walk-through, handling the administrative tasks pertaining to the walk-through, and ensuring that the walk-through is conducted in an orderly manner is usually the author.

The scribe is responsible for writing down all comments made during the walk-through that pertain to errors found, questions of style, omissions, contradictions, suggestions for improvement, or alternative approaches.

Each team member is responsible for reviewing any input material prior to the walk-through and participating during the walk-through to ensure that it meets its objective. Roles may be shared among the walk-through members.

When to Hold the Walk-through Meeting. The need for conducting walk-throughs, as with all product reviews, can be established either by local practice or in planning documents. Completion of a specific software element can trigger the walkthrough for the element. Additional walk-throughs can be conducted during development of the software element at the request of the author or management from various functional areas. A walk-through is conducted when the author indicates readiness.

Procedures. *Planning.* During the planning process phase the author:

- Identifies the walk-through team
- Schedules the meeting and selects the meeting place
- Distributes all necessary input materials to the participants, allowing for adequate preparation time

Overview. An overview presentation is made by the author as part of the walk-through meeting. Before that meeting, however, individual preparation is still required.

Preparation. During the preparation phase participants review the input material that was distributed to them and prepare a list of questions and issues to be brought up during the walk-through.

Examination. During the walk-through meeting:

- The author makes an overview presentation of the software element
- The author "walks through" the specific software element so that members of the walk-through team may ask questions or raise issues about the software element, and/or make notes documenting their concerns
- The scribe writes down comments and decisions for inclusion in the walk-through report

At the completion of the walk-through, the team may recommend a follow-up walk-through that follows the same process and would, at a minimum, cover areas changed by the author. The walk-through process is complete when the entire software element has been walked through in detail and all deficiencies, omissions, efficiency issues, and suggestions for improvement have been noted. The walk-through report is issued, as required by local standards.

Output. The walk-through report contains:

- Identification of the walk-through team
- Identification of the software element(s) being examined
- The statement of objectives that were to be handled during this walk-through meeting
- A list of the noted deficiencies, omissions, contradictions, and suggestions for improvement

- Any recommendations made by the walk-through team on how to dispose of deficiencies and unresolved issues. If follow-up walk-throughs are suggested, that should be mentioned in the report as well

Formal Inspections

Objective. A formal inspection, as stated earlier, is a variant of the procedure used for a structured walk-through. The differences are described in the following procedure and contrasted with the above procedures for a walk-through.

The objective of the formal inspection is to detect defects in the product being inspected by comparison with a checklist that typifies the types of defects that are common to the type of product being inspected. These are recorded and a statistical report is prepared so that evidential data is compiled. These data are used: to compare the product at this stage of development with later stages; compile a basis for statistical measure of the product; and to build an experience base to be used for other products in the same or similar projects.

People and Their Agendas. The roles in a formal inspection include a moderator, participants or inspectors, the preparer or developer of the product, and a recorder. The moderator is normally a peer who is selected for his/her technical expertise with the type of material. This person should be someone who is from outside the project. The participants are peers of the preparer and normally from the project staff to ensure that they are familiar with the project from a technical point of view.

Procedures. Prior to the inspection, the moderator makes arrangements for the inspection based on similar procedures used for a walk-through. The materials to be inspected, the checklists to be used, and the facilities where the inspection is to be located are all planning functions that need to be accomplished. The moderator controls the inspection process by walking through the code or design in a step-by-step manner. The peers comment on the product and these are recorded by the recorder.

It is important to identify the checklist that will be used and ensure that the recorder understands his/her duties with respect to recording the results. The checklist, which is the basis for the inspection, is composed of the common types of defects that are found in the product. For example, in a code inspection the following types of defects may be listed in the checklist (Vliet, 1993):

1. wrongful use of data: uninitialized variables, array index out of bounds, dangling pointers, and so forth;

2. faults in declarations, such as the use of undeclared variables, or the declaration of the same name in nested blocks;

3. faults in computations; division by zero, overflow, wrong use of variables of different types in one and the same expression, faults caused by an erroneous conception of operator priorities, etc.;

4. faults in relational expressions, such as using an incorrect operator, or an erroneous conception of priorities of Boolean operators;

5. faults in control flow, such as infinite loops, or a loop that gets executed n+1 or n-1 times rather than n;

6. faults in interfaces, such as an incorrect number of parameters, parameters of the wrong type, or an inconsistent use of global variables.

When to Hold the Formal Inspection Meeting. Inspections are regularly scheduled in accordance with project plans based on the status of a product. For example, periodic inspections of the product could be conducted at the preliminary design, detailed design, and implementation or code completion.

Output. The result of the inspection is a list of the defects that are found. Defects may be categorized according to severity. The defects are corrected after the inspection and the results are checked by the moderator. A reinspection may be called for if the product is deemed unsatisfactory to proceed.

Audits

Objective. Audits, performed in accordance with documented plans and procedures, provide an independent confirmation that product development and process execution adhere to standards, guidelines, specifications, and procedures. Audit personnel use objective audit criteria (for example, contracts and plans; standards, practices and conventions: or requirements and specifications) to evaluate:

- Software elements
- The processes for producing them
- Projects
- Entire quality programs

People and Their Agendas. It is the responsibility of the audit team leader to organize and direct the audit and to coordinate the preparation and issuance of the audit report. The audit team leader is ultimately responsible for the proper conduct of the audit and its reports, and makes sure that the audit team is prepared.

The entity initiating the audit is responsible for authorizing the audit. Management of the auditing organization assumes responsibility for the audit and the allocation of the necessary resources to perform the audit.

Those whose products and processes are being audited provide all relevant materials and resources and correct or resolve deficiencies cited by the audit team.

When to Audit. The need for an audit is established by one of the following events:

- A special project milestone, calendar date, or other criterion has been met and, as part of its charter, the auditing organization is to respond by initiating an audit.

- A special project milestone has been reached. The audit is initiated per earlier plans (for example, the Software Quality Assurance Plan, or Software Development Plan). This includes planned milestones for controlling supplier development.

- External parties (for example, regulatory agencies or end users) require an audit at a specific calendar date or project milestone. This may be in fulfillment of a contract requirement or as a prerequisite to contractual agreement.

- A local organizational element(s)(for example, project management, functional management, systems engineering, or internal quality assurance/control) has requested the audit, establishing a clear and specific need.

Perhaps the most important inputs required to assure the success of the audit are the purpose and scope of the audit. Observations and evaluations performed as part of the audit require objective audit criteria, such as contracts requirements, plans, specifications, procedures, guidelines, and standards. The software elements and processes to be audited need to be made accessible, as do any pertinent histories. Background information about the organization responsible for the products and processes being audited (for example, organization charts) are critical for both planning and execution of the audit.

Procedures. The auditing organization develops and documents an audit plan for each audit. This plan should, in addition to restating the audit scope, identify the:

- Project processes to be examined (provided as input) and the time frame for audit team observations

- Software to be examined (provided as input) and their availability where sampling is used, a statistically valid sampling methodology is used to establish selection criteria and sample use

- Reporting requirements (that is, results report, and, optionally, the recommendations report with their general format and distribution defined), whether recommendations are required or excluded should be explicitly stated

- Required follow-up activities

- Activities, elements, and procedures necessary to meet the scope of the audit

- Objective Audit Criteria that provide the basis for determining compliance (provided as input)

- Audit Procedures and Checklists

- Audit Personnel requirements (for example, number, skills, experience, and responsibilities)

- Organizations involved in the audit (for example, the organization whose products and processes are being audited)

- Date, time, place, agenda, and intended audience of "overview" session (optional)

The audit team leader prepares an audit team having the necessary background and (when allowed) notifies the involved organizations, giving them a reasonable amount of advance warning before the audit is performed. The notification should be written to include audit scope, the identification processes and products to be audited, and the auditors' identity.

An optional overview meeting with the audited organization is recommended to "kick off" the examination phase of the audit. The overview meeting, led by the audit team leader, provides:

- Overview of existing agents (for example, audit scope, plan and related contracts)

- Overview of production and processes being audited

- Overview of the audit process, its objectives, and outputs
- Expected contributions of the audited organization to the audit process (that is, the number of people to be interviewed, meeting facilities, et cetera)
- Specific audit schedule

The following preparations are required by the audit team:

- Understand the organization: It is essential to identify functions and activities performed by the audited organization and to identify functional responsibility
- Understand the products and processes: It is a prerequisite for the team to learn about the products and processes being audited through readings and briefings
- Understand the Objective Audit Criteria: It is important that the audit team become familiar with the objective and criteria to be used in the audit
- Prepare for the audit report: It is important to choose the administrative reporting mechanism that will be used throughout the audit to develop the report that follows the layout identified in the audit plan
- Detail the audit plan: Choose appropriate methods for each step in the audit program

In addition, the audit team leader makes the necessary arrangements for:

- Team orientation and training
- Facilities for audit interviews
- Materials, documents, and tools required by the audit procedures
- The software elements to be audited (for example, documents, computer files, personnel to be interviewed)
- Scheduling interviews

Elements that have been selected for audit are evaluated against the Objective Audit Criteria. Evidence is examined to the depth necessary to determine if these elements comply with specified criteria.

An audit is considered complete when:

- Each element(s) within the scope of the audit has been examined

- Findings have been presented to the audited organization
- Response to draft findings have been received and evaluated
- Final findings have been formally presented to the audited organization and initiating entity
- The audit report has been prepared and submitted to recipients designated in the audit plan
- The recommendation report, if required by plan, has been prepared and submitted to recipients designated in the audit plan
- All of the auditing organization's follow-up actions included in the scope (or contract) of the audit have been performed.

Output. Following a standard framework for audit reports, the draft and final audit reports contain:

- Audit Identification: Report title, audited organization, auditing organization, and date of the audit
- Scope: Scope of the audit, including an enumeration of the standards, specifications, practices, and procedures constituting the Objective Audit Criteria against which the audit of the software elements and processes were conducted
- Conclusions: A summary and interpretation of the audit findings, including the key items of nonconformance
- Synopsis: A listing of all the audited software elements and processes, and associated findings
- Follow-up: The type and timing of audit follow-up activities

Additionally, when stipulated by the audit plan, recommendations are provided to the audited organization, or the entity that initiated the audit. Recommendations are reported separately from results.

Comments and issues raised by the audited organization must be resolved. The final audit report should then be prepared, approved, and issued by the audit team leader to the organizations specified in the audit plan.

Inspections

Inspections are limited forms of an audit. The procedures for conducting an inspection are similar to an audit except that they are limited due to the focus of the inspection.

Future directions

As previously mentioned, the use of reviews and audits in the software development business is becoming more blurred because of the concentration on a systems perspective. Thus, we will see more emphasis on systems engineering. This will not change the mechanisms or practices that are used. They will be applied, however, in more of a systems management and engineering context. Thus, the use of specific review procedures will be more broadly applied in the development or acquisition of the system.

One trend that we currently see is the use of more interactive techniques. A walk-through is an interactive procedure. The moderator or inspector, participants, recorder—all communicate as the product is being "walked through". As systems development becomes more dynamic, as we already see in Web development, electronic techniques will enhance this procedure. It is possible to have an on-line review conducted across geographic distances. It is even possible to make dynamic changes to products as the capability to do so advances (for example, in the development of a home page as an element of Web site development). If a product such as a document is being reviewed, changes to it can be accomplished in real time. This will place more emphasis on the rigor or formality required of the process to properly control and account for changes. Configuration management will take on a real-time (and more dramatic) meaning in this environment.

Another trend that is quite possible is the more prevalent use of formal inspections. It has already been demonstrated that this technique has great benefit to the development of software. As software engineering progresses in maturity, there will be more emphasis on the attainment of specific attributes of the product. We should be able to relate the attainment software quality factors such as reliability, usability, and complexity described by the work of McCall and Bowen directly to the product (Vincent, 1988). Thus, the coupling or relationship of these factors to the product will be a more measured one. This will afford the quantifiable prediction of quality, and control of the product in order to meet these predictions. The implication is that checklists, based on experiential data associated with the attainment of specific quality attributes, will be more widely used.

Summary

The different types of reviews used in a software development process range from informal technical reviews to formal reviews such as the FCA. The types and number of reviews are largely determined by the complexity and size of the project. In a project that is internal to an organization, reviews tend to be more informal compared to a project that is under contract. Normally, the number and types of reviews will be detailed in management plans with specific methods left to a procedures and standards handbook.

Although there are different reasons for conducting reviews, the principal purpose is to assess the progress or integrity of a process or product. Reviews are also important for gathering data. The systematic collection of data is essential for assessing the process in order to support process improvement programs as well as developing experiential data for applying to new projects. These data can support the prediction of various activities such as the quality of products through comparisons of previous data collected on prior projects.

Thus, reviews of all sorts provide a basic performance and assessment technique that bridges the individual project, and even the organization. They are the essential performance technique in software development practice.

Portions of this article have been excised from Software Reviews and Audits, Charles Hollocker, John Wiley & Sons, New York, N.Y., 1990.

References

M. Evans and J. Marciniak, *Software Quality Assurance and Management*, John Wiley & Sons, New York, N.Y., 1987a, p. 115; 1987b, p. 229.

Michael Fagan, "Design and Code Inspection to Reduce Errors in Program Development," *IBM Systems J.*, Vol. 15, No. 3, 1976.

Daniel P. Freedman and Gerald M. Weinberg, *Walk-throughs, Inspections, and Technical Reviews*, Dorset House, New York, N.Y., Third Ed., 1990a, pp. 10–11; 1990b, p. 232; 1990c, p. 232; 1990d, p. 239.

Charles Hollocker, *Software Reviews and Audits*, John Wiley & Sons, New York, N.Y., 1990, pp. 44–48.

IEEE Std 610.12-1990, *Standard Glossary of Software Engineering Terminology*, IEEE, New York, N.Y., 1990a, p. 64;. 1990b, p. 81; 1990c, p. 40; 1990d, p. 11; 1990e, p. 35; 1990f, p. 55.

IEEE Std 1498, IEEE, New York, N.Y.

John J. Marciniak and Donald J. Reifer, *Software Acquisition Management*, John Wiley & Sons, New York, N.Y., 1990, p. 26.

Mil-Std-498, "Software Development and Documentation," Department of Defense, 1994.

J. Vincent, A. Waters, and J. Sinclair, *Software Quality Assurance*, Prentice-Hall, Englewood Cliffs, N.J., Vol. 1, 1988, pp. 11–28.

Traceability

James D. Palmer

*Professor Emeritus, George Mason University
and Software Consultant
860 Cashew Way
Fremont, CA 94536*

Abstract

Traceability gives essential assistance in understanding the relationships that exist within and across software requirements, design, and implementation and is critical to the development process by providing a means of ascertaining how and why system development products satisfy stakeholder requirements, especially for large complex systems. Traceability provides a path to the validation and verification of stakeholder requirements to assure these needs are met by the delivered system, as well as information on testing procedures, performance measures, non-functional characteristics, and behavioral aspects for the delivered system. Both syntactic and semantic information are needed to successfully implement tracing. It is not enough to know the form; it is also necessary to know the substance of the entities to be traced.

However, traceability is often misunderstood, frequently misapplied, and seldom performed correctly. There are many challenges to achieving traceability, particularly the absence of automated techniques to assist in the identification of linkages from requirements to design, or test, or operation needed to trace entities within and across the system development process. One of the particular challenges to providing traceability to and from system level requirements is that it becomes necessary to utilize both the constructs of language semantics as well as syntax.

Traceability is introduced, and its place in a development process, coupled with the values and pitfalls are covered. The essentials of traceability are examined together with how to implement tracing within a development life cycle for large complex systems. Working definitions and related terms are provided to assure common understanding of the terminology and application of tracing in system and software development. A review of contemporary approaches to implement tracing with an overview of several of the Computer Supported Software (or System) Engineering (CASE) tools that purport to support tracing are given and future trends are examined.

Introduction

Successful system development depends on the ability to satisfy stakeholder needs and requirements and to reflect these in the delivered system. Requirements, design, and implementation that are complete, correct, consistent, and error free, play a major role in ensuring that the delivered system meets stakeholder needs. Critical keys to this are understanding and tracing the relationships that exist amongst system requirements, design, code, test, and implementation. Large-scale complex systems are initiated by stakeholder determination that a need exists that is not met by existing systems. From this beginning, system level requirements are developed to broadly outline the desired capabilities, which, in turn, are investigated to ascertain feasibility and practicality and examine trade-offs. Once the feasibility and practicality of the desired system have been determined to be necessary and sufficient to launch a new system (or significant modification of an existing or legacy system), design is completed and systems are constructed, tested, and fielded. It is essential to maintain traceability from the system requirements to operation and maintenance to assure that the delivered system meets the stated organizational needs of the stakeholder.

System Life Cycle for Traceability Management

Generally, a system or process development life cycle is followed to produce the desired system. There are many life cycle models [1], and one of the simplest is the system development or waterfall life cycle model depicted in Figure 1. It also serves as the basis for most life cycle models in use today, such as the spiral model, the evolutionary model, and the prototyping model. Within any system development life cycle, requirements must be traced both forward and backward to assure that the correct system is being designed and produced, and that the correct design and production approaches are used.

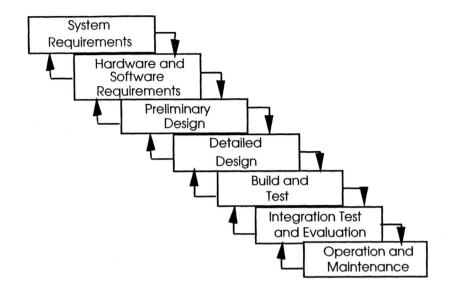

Figure 1. Typical system and software development life cycle

In the life cycle model of Figure 1, system requirements, usually prepared in natural language, are provided by the stakeholder to the developer. These system requirements, if they exist at all, may be poorly written and only vaguely define stakeholder desires for the new system. This may impact the ability to construct a system that will satisfy the stakeholder. From these system requirements, hardware and software requirements and specifications are prepared. Requirement and specification development are followed by preliminary design; detailed design; construction of the system including hardware and software; system integration, testing and evaluation; and finally installation including operation and maintenance.

These life cycle activities require documentation of needs and outcomes. Each must trace forward to the subsequent activity and backward to the preceding one. Clearly, traceability, both forward and backward, is essential to verify that the requirements of one phase translate to outcomes of that phase which become the requirements for the next phase, and so on through the development activity. Traceability is equally essential to validate that system requirements are satisfied during operation.

Need for Traceability

Traceability is essential to verification and validation and is needed to better understand the processes used to develop the system and the products that result. It is needed for quick access to information, information abstraction, and to provide visualization into the techniques used for system development. Traceability is needed for change control, develop-

ment process control, and risk control. Tracing provides insights to non-behavioral components such as quality, consistency, completeness, impact analysis, system evolution, and process improvement. It is equally important to have the capability to trace a requirement or design or code module to its origin, as well as test. Stakeholders recognize the value of properly tracing within and across the entities of a system through risk management insights, appropriate integration tests, and the delivery of a project that meets the needs statements of the requirements. [2]

Traceability supports assessment of under- or over designs; investigation of high-level behavior impact on detailed specifications, as well as non-functional requirements such as performance and quality factors. Moreover, traceability supports conflict detection by making it feasible to examine linkages within and across selected entities and by providing visibility into the entire system. Through tracing, there is the assurance that decisions made later in the system development life cycle are consistent with earlier decisions. Test cases check that coverage for code and integration testing and for requirements validation is provided. Traceability provides the basis for the development of an audit trail for the entire project by establishing the links within and across system entities, functions, behavior, and performance, for example.

While there is widespread acceptance of the necessity to trace, there is considerable controversy as to the ultimate need, purpose, and cost of tracing from requirements to delivered product. The controversy arises primarily because of the lack of automated approaches to implement the process and the concomitant time and effort that must be applied with any of the presently available support tools. Developers simply do not see the benefits that may accrue to the final product when traceability is fully implemented compared to the time and effort required.

Problems and Issues Concerning Traceability

Difficulties related to tracing generally revolve around the necessity to manually add trace elements to requirements documents and subsequent work products from software development. Since these products have little or no direct consequence to the development team, assignment of trace elements generally has a low priority. The benefits of traceability are not seen until much later in the development life cycle, usually during validation testing and system installation and operation, and then primarily by integration testers and stakeholders rather than developers. Additionally, traceability is often misunderstood, frequently misapplied, and seldom performed correctly.

Issues and concerns emanate from the complexity of a project itself that must be confronted when implementing traceability. Each discipline, such as avionics, communications, navigation, security, or safety, may have languages, methods, and tools peculiar to the discipline. This results in a lack of ability to trace across disciplines, which, in turn, may lead to errors in traceability matrices used to provide linkages within and across disciplines. Some of the issues that need to be addressed by the stakeholder and developer at the time of system development include how to apportion projects by discipline, the type and nature of information that should be traced across different disciplines, and the types of tools that can be used to provide consistent and correct traceability across disciplines. Establishing threads across disciplines is also difficult due to language, method, and tool peculiarities.

Currently, there is no single modeling method or language sufficiently rich to represent all aspects of a large complex system and still be understandable to those involved. In tracing information across different disciplines and toolsets, and to provide threads across these, essential system properties and the classification schemes used are needed. Such properties and schemas do not usually exist. Thus, for verification and validation, traceability must always focus on a common denominator; the approved system requirements. Finally, internal consistency of the baseline documentation may not be adequate to support tracing. This latter is usually a significant problem in the modification of legacy systems.

Definition of Terms

There are many terms that describe, delineate, or relate to traceability. Some of these correlate to the "how and why" for traceability, while others connect to the outcomes or "what" of traceability. In general, the basic meaning of the terms is first that provided by Webster's New Collegiate Dictionary [3], while the last meaning is given in the context of systems and software engineering, as an example of usage.

Allocation: The act of distributing; allotment or apportionment; as to assign or apportion functions to specific modules.

Audit: A formal checking of records, to determine that what was stated was accomplished; to examine and verify; as to confirm a stated capability is met in the software product.

Behavior: The way in which a system acts, especially in response to a stimulus; stimulus-response mechanisms; as activity or change in reliability across sub-systems.

Bottom-up: A design philosophy or policy that dictates the form and partitioning of the system from the basic functions that the system is to perform and moving up to the top level requirements; as a design policy that provides basic modules followed by top-level constructs.

Classification: A group of entities ranked together as possessing common characteristics or quality; the act of grouping or segregating into classes which have systematic relationships; a systematic grouping of entities based upon some definite scheme; as to classify requirements according to organizational or performance characteristics.

Flowdown: To move or circulate from upper to lower levels; as to trace a requirement from a top level to designs to code to test.

Function: The characteristic action or the normal or special action of a system; one aspect of a system is so related to another that there is a correspondence from one to the other when an action is taken; as an algorithm to provide the equations of motion.

Hierarchy: A series of objects or items divided or classified in ranks or orders; as in a type of structure in which each element or block has a level number (1= highest), and each element is associated with one or more elements at the next higher level and lower levels; as a single high level requirement decomposes to lower level requirements and to design and code.

Impact Analysis: Separation into constituent parts to examine or distinguish contact of one on another, a communicating force; as to focus on software changes and the traceable consequences; relating software requirements to design components.

Policy: Management or procedure based primarily on material interest; as a settled course or level to be followed for system security.

Requirement: A requisite condition; a required quality; to demand; to claim as by right or authority; to exact; as to demand system performance by the stakeholder.

Thread: To connect; as to pass a thread through; string together; as to link behaviors of a system together.

Top-down: A design philosophy or policy that dictates the form and partitioning of the system from the top-level requirements perspective to the lower level design components; as in a design policy for all activities from high-level requirements to design and code.

Top-level requirement: A requisite condition leveled by the stakeholder; as a system level requirement for security.

Traceability: The course or path followed; to follow or track down; to follow or study out in detail or step by step, especially by going backward over evidence (as to trace requirements from design); to discover or uncover by investigation; as to trace to the source; as to follow requirements from the top level to design and code and back; or as to identify and document the allocation/flowdown path (downward) and derivation path (upward) of requirements into the hierarchy. The Department of Defense (DoD) defines traceability in the Standard for Defense System Software Development DoD-Std-2167A to be a demonstration of completeness, necessity, and consistency. Specifically, DoD- Std -21267A defines traceability as: "(1) the document in question contains or implements all applicable stipulations of the predecessor document, (2) a given term, acronym, or abbreviation means the same thing in all documents, (3) a given item or concept is referred to by the same name or description in the documents, (4) all material in the successor document has

its basis in the predecessor document, that is, no untraceable material has been introduced, and (5) the two documents do not contradict one another."

Traceability Management: To control and direct; guide; administer; give direction to accomplish an end; as to control and direct tracing from top level through to design and code.

Tree: A diagrammatic representation that indicates branching from an original stem; as software components derived from a higher level entity to more discrete lower level entities.

State of the Practice of Traceability

Traceability management applies to the entire development life cycle from project initiation through operation and maintenance as shown in Figure 2. It is presently feasible to manage tracing using a combination of manual and automated assistance, thus providing some assurance that the development of a system meets the needs as provided by the stakeholder. An essential element of successful traceability management, provided by currently available CASE tools, is the ability to provide links from requirements forward to designs, code, test, and implementation, and backward from any of these activities to requirements once these links have been manually entered into the CASE tool.

Techniques currently in use to establish and maintain traceability from requirements through designs, code, test, and operation begin with manual identification of linkages. These linkages may be subsequently supported by document managers, a database, or CASE tools specifically designed for requirements traceability management.

Contemporary Traceability Practices

Traceability has traditionally been accomplished by manually assigning and linking unique identifiers; that is, a sentence or paragraph (or other partition) requirement is assigned a particular alpha-numeric reference. This information is subsequently managed in a word processor or database, often through use of a CASE tool. Even with the use of a CASE tool, the initial identification of trace entities and linkages must be accomplished manually. By establishing a unique identification system and following this scheme throughout the life of the project, it is possible to trace these specific entities both forward and backward from

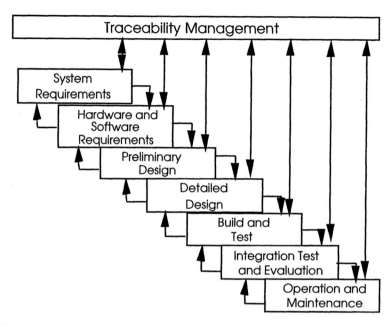

Figure 2. Traceability management across the system development life cycle

requirements to product. This unique identity may be linked within and across documents using manually derived traceability tables to assure full traceability over all aspects of the project.

A typical output of tracing is a traceability matrix that links high-level requirements to each and every other requirement or specification of the system. A typical traceability table for a large complex system is shown in Table 1. In this table, individual requirements in the Systems Requirements Document (SRD) have been manually linked to more detailed system requirements in the Systems Specification which in turn have been manually linked to particular specifications in the System Segments.

Other matrices or tables may provide more details such as cryptic messages, partial text, critical values, or the entire text. The system represented in the traceability table is configured as in Figure 3. The SRD represents stakeholder input, the SS represents the initial interpretation of these high level requirements by developers, and the segment specifi-

cations provide more detailed information to design. The Interface Control Document (ICD) provides linkages for all messages that occur within and across segments.

In most system development programs, there is the added expectation of continuous change in the system as requirements are added, modified, and deleted. Thus, the management of an ever-changing requirements base becomes a very important traceability function, as tracing provides a review of how the system requirements flowdown to lower levels and how lower level requirements are derived from higher levels. These traces may or may not contain information as to why the system is to be partitioned in a particular manner. As new requirements are added or existing ones are updated, deleted, or modified, the management process continues to provide traceability and impact analysis to assure that each of the changes is properly included in the system development process. This provides the major verification and validation procedure to assure stakeholder needs are met.

Table 1. Traceability matrix for multi-segment system

SRD	SS	Segment 1	Segment 2	Segment 3	ICD
3.1.2.1	3.3.4.5 3.3.4.6	3.2.2.5.6 3.2.2.5.7 3.4.5.6.2	3.5.3.2		3.1.4.6.7 3.1.4.6.8 3.1.4.6.9
3.4.3.1	3.6.7.2 3.8.4.3	3.5.2.5.1	3.7.4.3.1 3.7.4.3.2	3.6.4.5.2	3.3.2.4.5 3.3.2.4.7

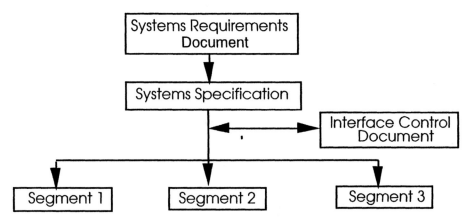

Figure 3. Typical requirements classification schema for a large complex system

Traceability is especially critical for the operation and maintenance phase. This is when significant stakeholder changes may be made and change impacts and impact analyses must be performed. Such changes are difficult to trace; however, without tracing it is nearly impossible to ascertain the extent of the full impact of additions, deletions, or modifications to the system.

An Ideal Process for Traceability

To understand what must be traced, we need a defined process for developing system architectural views, classification schemes, as well as processes for specifying and verifying the products to be constructed. This is generally provided by the stakeholder in consort with the developer. The development of these views is necessary to partition the project for design and construction.

An ideal traceability process consists of the steps of identification, architecture selection, classification, allocation, and flowdown as depicted in Figure 4. The process begins with the identification of requirements at the system level, specification of system architecture, and selection of classification schema. Following this, allocations are made in accordance with the selected schema. Following allocation, the requirements flow down to design, code, and test. This top-down approach has proven most effective in the management of traceability for large scale complex projects.

However, this approach is basically a manual activity that requires significant investment of time and effort on the part of skilled personnel. The outcomes represent a system hierarchy along the lines of the classification structure used for the architectural allocations. It is also necessary to provide threads through the various behavioral and non-behavioral aspects of the project to complete the traceability process. These thread paths are manually assigned using approaches such as entity-relation-attribute diagrams. For example, tests are threaded back to requirements through code and design.

Once the system hierarchy, the architecture, and classification schema have been defined, identified system requirements are assigned to the top-level block of the hierarchy. At this time, they are added to the traceability database for storage, retrieval, and reuse. After appropriate analyses, these requirements are decomposed and flow down into more detailed requirements for each of the lower level blocks to which the requirement was allocated, as was shown in the example of Figure 3. The higher level requirements are sometimes referred to as parents and the lower level ones as children. Change notification should be rigorously traced to determine the impact of such activities on changes in cost, schedule, and feasibility of system design and implementation, on tests that must be conducted, and on support software and hardware.

Actual Practice for Implementing Traceability

In actual practice, tracing is a labor intensive and aggravating task. Domain experts follow a process to decompose the system that is similar to that depicted in Figure 3. Once appropriate systems architectures are identified, a classification schema or schemas for purposes of allocation of requirements to system specific architectures is prepared and requirements are assigned to specific units. As examples of the types of classification schemes used, one may be centered on functional aspects of the project; such as navigation, communications, or threat assessment; another may concentrate on performance and security; while yet another may be focused on stakeholder organization. It is not feasible to enumerate, a priori- , all the ways in which the project may need to be partitioned and

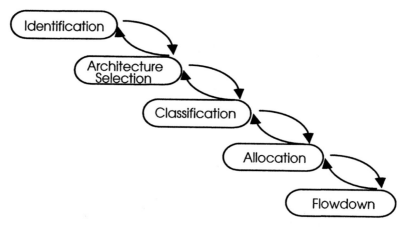

Figure 4. The ideal traceability process

viewed; thus, traceability becomes a continuous process as perspectives change and as requirements change. To validate these various views, there is only one common basis from which to form trace linkages, the system requirements.

The next step, after receipt of the requirements documents and delineation of the system architecture, is to determine the nature of the tracing to be accomplished. Several options are feasible; these include working with statements that contain "shall," "will," "should," "would," or similar verbs; or with entire paragraphs; or the total set of statements provided by the stakeholder. The strongest selection is "shall" statements, which may be the only contractually acceptable designation for a requirement. This is followed by the development of classification schemes according to function, data object, behavior, organization, or other approaches. Once the option(s) has been selected, the requirements are parsed according to the option and assigned a unique identity. For example, if "shall" has been selected as the option, sentences with "shall" as a verb are collected and are identified sequentially, while also retaining the original identification system provided by the stakeholder. This new identification system is maintained throughout the life of the project.

Syntactic and semantic information are both necessary to perform tracing. Language semantics are needed to assure the trace is related to the meaning or context of the requirement or set of requirements, while syntax is necessary to trace to a specific word or phrase, without regard to meaning or context. Integration of both constructs is required to provide for full traceability from natural language statements to the other steps as shown in Figure 2. Manual verification of outcomes is required to assure compliance with the intent and purpose of the tracing activity.

Next comes allocation according to the classification scheme. This likewise is a manual task, even with

automated assistance from one of the available CASE tools, as most of these tools require the operator to physically establish the links from one entity to another for traceability. All linkages must be designated and maintained and traceability matrices are generated from these outcomes. If a CASE tool has been used that supports generation of traceability matrices, these are created automatically; otherwise, these matrices must be manually prepared. These steps are depicted graphically in Figure 5. These results are usually stored in a traceability database. The traceability linkages are subsequently designated and maintained across the entire development project from design to code to test to operation and maintenance.

Return on Investment for Traceability

It is not feasible to measure the return on investment (ROI) for traceability. Although most of the costs associated with implementation can be documented, the benefits are quite difficult to ascertain unless comparative case studies are conducted. Costs of implementation include the investment of time and effort of domain experts to provide system architectural perspectives and classification schema, the initial cost of acquiring CASE tools to manage requirements traceability, and the expended costs of training and maintenance in the use of such tools. Due to the manual approaches required to establish architectural perspectives, classification schema, allocation, linkage, and system maintenance, fixing costs, while manageable, is a difficult task. These costs may be either estimated or accounted for with some degree of accuracy. This may be done for an ongoing project or by estimating the time, effort, capitalization costs, and expended costs involved.

The benefits are largely intangible and are related to the avoided costs associated with rework and possible failure of the product to satisfy stakeholders. To

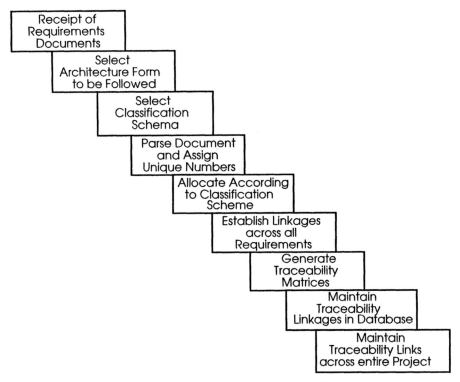

Figure 5. Steps to accomplish traceability

estimate the benefits, it would be necessary to prepare various scenarios, simulate the outcomes due to failure of various aspects of the development process, and estimate the value of avoiding these failures. Risk factors must also be taken into consideration in calculation of the potential benefits, including the potential that the project will not meet stakeholder needs. Assessing benefits without comparative analyses is generally not possible. Generating this information is considered to be unfeasible due to the costs of running such experiments and the need to develop realistic scenarios that may or may not ever be replicated in actual practice.

Current Traceability Tools

Typical of the currently available automated (or semi-automated) assistance approaches to traceability are those that provide for traceability through a variety of syntactic language components: hypertext linking, unique identifiers, syntactical similarity coefficients, or combinations of these. In hypertext linking, the "hotword" or word/phrase to be linked to other requirements is manually identified and entered into the hypertext tool. Links are automatically made and maintained by the tool to provide forward and reverse traceability for the word selection. In the unique identifier approach, an identifier is assigned that remains with the individual requirement throughout the life of

the project. To assure traceability, this unique identifier provides a "fan-out" capability within a hierarchical structure such that one system level ("A" level) requirement may be the parent to many "B" level requirements which, in turn, may be the parents for great numbers of "C" level requirements, as depicted in Table 1. Use of syntactic similarity coefficients ascertains whether or not a pre-defined set of words of a given requirement are found in another requirement. When the degree of similarity is above a pre-defined threshold, the two requirements in question are said to trace.

There are problems with each of these approaches. They do not consider the semantics or context in which the tracing is to occur. Hypertext linking finds the search text without regard to the placement in the text and without regard to the way in which the words are used. Use of a unique identifier provides access only to those requirements so identified with no perspective as to meaning or context. Syntactic similarity coefficient traceability is like hypertext linking in that it is indiscriminate as to the meaning and context of the requirement to be traced.

Commercially available requirements tools utilize straightforward traceability links that must be manually developed to relate requirements to other requirements and to design, code, and implementation. Current methods for implementing traceability with these commercial tools generally involve the manual provision of links within and across documents and then automated management of these documents. Traceability links are used to establish the one-to-one, one-to many, many-to-one, or many-to-many relationships that may exist, as may be seen from Table 1. As noted previously, linkages are not automatically established by tools during the development process, but must be manually generated. From this point, automated assistance is provided by the tool to manage traceability.

At present, there are no standards available to support tools for traceability, which has led to the development and use of a large number of commercial tools, each with differing methods, as well as proprietary tools developed by certain industries because it is considered to be a competitive advantage for most large complex projects. A number of commercially available tools have been developed to support traceability and a number of general CASE tools provide support to traceability management, especially from requirements forward to design, code, test, and operation. One of the common activities for all tools is manual development of architectural perspectives and classification schemas. Another common feature is the need to manually establish the initial linkages within and across all traceable entities. Once the initial linkages have been established, these tools effectively and efficiently manage a traceability database or word processor document.

Common Tool Characteristics

There are some common tool characteristics that are deemed to be minimal to provide support for traceability. The tool must be well understood by and be responsive to users and match the characteristics of the development environment used by the developers. Tools must also accept and utilize the data that is provided in the form provided. In addition, the tool must be flexible, capable of operation in an automated assistance mode to support various activities and services; such as active and passive data checking; batch as well as on-line processing; addition, deletion, and modification of a requirement; customization to specific domain applications; dynamic database structure for change management; and a tailorable user interface. Traceability tools will never be fully automated, as human decision making is essential to the establishment of classification schema and system architecture designation. Human interaction and decision making is both desirable and necessary to maximize the interaction of the stakeholder/developer in the development of the project.

Commercial CASE Tools for Traceability

Some commercially available tools have been developed for traceability link information expressed by a single discipline within a single phase, while others have been developed specifically to link requirements to other activities within the development life cycle. Cadre TeamWork for Real-Time Structured Analysis (CADRE) is a tool that operates on a single discipline within a single phase. Tools that link information from multiple disciplines and phases include: Requirements Traceability Manager (RTM) (Marconi Corporation) [4], SLATE (TD Technologies) [5], and DOORS (Zycad Corporation) [6]. These tools use an entity-relation-attribute-like schema to capture information on a system database, either relational or object-oriented, enable formation of queries about traceable entities, and for report generation. RTM uses a relational database structure to capture information and provide management, while DOORS provides an object-oriented database for management of information. SLATE follows a multi-user, client-server, object-oriented approach that provides dynamic representation of the system as it evolves.

Another method used by commercial tool vendors is the hypertext approach. In this approach, keywords or phrases are identified as being indicative of traces. These are linked through hypertext throughout the document or set of documents that comprise the requirements. An example of a tool that uses this approach is Document Director [7].

Some general-purpose analysis tools are also used for tracing. Some of the more robust tool sets include: Requirements Driven Design (RDD-100 by Ascent Logic) [8], which is used to document system conceptual models and Foresight [9], which is utilized to maintain a data dictionary and document system simulation.

Other tools and techniques that support requirements traceability include Software Requirements Methodology (SREM); Problem Statement Language/Problem Statement Analyzer (PSL/PSA); N2 charts; Requirement Networks (R-Nets); and ARTS (a database management system for requirements). Not all of the CASE tools support requirements traceability; however; most do support some form of requirements management.

Future Trends and Conclusions

The future in traceability support lies in the development of the capability to deal directly with requirements in natural language, the ability to provide auto-mated assistance to allocation of requirements to various architectural and classification systems, and the ability to manage these. From this automated assistance, it becomes feasible to provide for and manage a traceable baseline for the entire system.

The following issues are being addressed in ongoing research programs:

- automated allocation of entities to architectures and classifications
- traceability that is independent of methods used to develop architectures and classifications
- tracing product attributes from requirements to the lowest levels

Several research programs are working on the problems associated with natural language; the two addressing traceability are from George Mason University and Trident Systems. The Center for Software Systems Engineering at George Mason University has developed and applied an automated assistance approach to the problems of allocation of entities to architectures and classification called the Automated Integrated Requirements Engineering System (AIRES) [10]. Trident Systems intends to develop a CASE tool called RECAP (Requirements Capture) which is intended to manage natural language requirements [11].

AIRES provides an assessment framework and techniques for integrated application of both semantic and syntactic rules for effective, efficient, and comprehensive identification of traceable and non-traceable requirements in large complex multiple-segment systems. The framework provides for the categorization of requirements in classification structures through the application of a diverse combination of rules and procedures, each of which applies unique combinations of both semantic and syntactic classification rules and tables for the categorization of requirements. These serve as the basic building blocks of the assessment framework and may be applied either singly or in combinations. AIRES supports automated development of linkages that may be transferred electronically to commercially available traceability tools such as RTM for management of a requirements database and report generation. AIRES is presently available in prototype form and has been utilized in support of several large complex system development for traceability support [12].

RECAP, presently a conceptual design, is intended to provide a set of interfaces that permit the operator to manipulate natural language requirements. RECAP

proposes to combine the information management and extraction capabilities of information retrieval system approaches with knowledge-base rules. It also intends to provide sequential and string search access to any portion of the document set. Quick access to information is proposed through keywords, sentence identifiers, or rule-based queries. The user will be required to provide information for resolution of ambiguity, mistakes in statements, and addition of missing items. RECAP is intended to aid the user in making these decisions. [11].

Information linked by these tracing tools is not dependent upon a model or discipline. It is possible to link entities as needed; for example, it may be desirable to link the estimated footprint, weight, and power usage of a piece of computer equipment (stored in a hardware modeling tool) to the estimated throughput and memory requirements for a piece of software (stored in a software modeling tool). To efficiently use these tracing tools, it is necessary to automatically transfer the information captured to CASE tools used downstream in the development life cycle. This is accomplished by tracing system definitions, system development processes, and interrelationships across system units.

While tracing from origination to final product is a difficult and arduous, manually intensive task at the present time, advances in technology should soon be commercially available to assist in automated allocation and classification procedures. These advances will make the traceability task much more reasonable, feasible, and supportable for large complex system developments due to the automated assistance provided for allocation and classification, the most labor intensive aspects of tracing. In each of the approaches, the CASE tool provides automated assistance to tracing, but requires human operator inputs only for decision-making activities. These tools represent a significant advance over the present state of the practice for traceability.

References

[1] Sage, Andrew P. and Palmer, James D., *Software Systems Engineering*, John Wiley and Sons, New York, N.Y., 1990.

[2] White, Stephanie, "Tracing Product and Process Information when developing Complex Systems," *CSESAW '94*, 1994, pp. 45–50, NSWCDD/MP-94/122.

[3] *Webster's New Collegiate Dictionary*, Sixth Ed., G.&C. Merriam Co., Springfield, Mass., 1951.

[4] "RTM-Requirements & Traceability Management, Practical Workbook," GEC-Marconi Limited, Oct., 1993.

[5] Nallon, John, "Implementation of NSWC Requirements Traceability Models," *CSESAW*, 1994, pp. 15–22, NSWCDD/MP-94/122.

[6] Rundley, Nancy and Miller, William D., "DOORS to the Digitized Battlefield: Managing Requirements Discovery and Traceability," *CSESAW*, 1994, pp. 23–28.

[7] "Document Director-The Requirements Tool," B.G. Jackson Associates, 17629 E. Camino Real, Suite 720, Houston, Tex., 77058, 1989.

[8] "RDD-100-Release Notes Release 3.0.2.1, Oct., 1992," Requirements Driven Design, Ascent Logic Corporation, 180 Rose Orchard Way, #200, San Jose, Calif., 95134, 1992.

[9] Vertal, Michael D., "Extending IDEF: Improving Complex Systems with Executable Modeling," *Proc. 1994 Ann. Conf. for Business Re-engineering*, IDEF Users Group, Richmond, VA, May, 1994.

[10] Palmer, James D. and Evans Richard P., "An Integrated Semantic and Syntactic Framework for Requirements Traceability: Experience with System Level Requirements for a Large Complex Multi-Segment Project," *CSESAW*, 1994, pp. 9–14, NSWCDD/MP-94/122.

[11] Hugue, Michelle, Casey, Michael, Wood, Glenn, and Edwards, Edward, "RECAP: A REquirements CAPture Tool for Large Complex Systems," *CSESAW*, 1994, pp. 39–44, NSWCDD/MP-94/122.

[12] Palmer, James D. and Evans Richard P., "Software Risk Management: Requirements-Based Risk Metrics," *Proc. IEEE 1994 Int'l Conf. SMC*, IEEE Press, Piscataway, N.J., 1994.

A review of software testing

P DAVID COWARD

Abstract: Despite advances in formal methods of specification and improved software creation tools, there is no guarantee that the software produced meets its functional requirements. There is a need for some form of software testing. The paper introduces the aims of software testing. This is followed by a description of static and dynamic analysis, and, functional and structural testing strategies. These ideas are used to provide a taxonomy of testing techniques. Each technique is briefly described.

Keywords: software development, software testing, formal methods

Before software is handed over for use, both the commissioner and the developer want the software to be correct. Unfortunately, what is meant by 'correct' is not clear. It is often taken to mean that the program matches the specification. However, the specification itself may not be correct. Correctness is then concerned with whether the software meets user requirements. Whatever the definition of correctness there is always the need to test a system.

Testing is one of the many activities that comprise the larger complex task of software development. The need for testing arises out of an inability to guarantee that earlier tasks in the software project have been performed adequately, and attempts to assess how well these tasks have been performed.

There is no agreed definition of testing. The term is often used to describe techniques of checking software by executing it with data. A wider meaning will be adopted in this paper: testing includes *any* technique of checking software, such as symbolic execution and program proving as well as the execution of test cases with data. Checking, implies that a comparison is undertaken. The comparison is made between the output from the test and an expected output derived by the tester. The expected output is based on the specification and is derived by hand.

Two terms often associated with testing are *verification* and *validation*. Verification refers to ensuring correctness from phase to phase of the software development cycle. Validation involves checking the software against the requirements. These strategies have been termed *horizontal* and *vertical* checks. Sometimes, verification is associated with formal proofs of correctness, while validation is concerned

Department of Computer Studies, Bristol Polytechnic, Coldharbour Lane, Frenchay, Bristol BS16 1QY, UK

with executing the software with test data. This paper avoids these terms and instead refers only to *testing* and *checking*, both terms being used synonymously.

Testing may be subdivided into two categories: *functional* and *nonfunctional*.

Functional testing addresses itself to whether the program produces the correct output. It may be employed when testing a new program or when testing a program that has been modified. *Regression testing* is the name given to the functional testing that follows modification. Primarily, regression testing is undertaken to determine whether the correction has altered the functions of the software that were intended to remain unchanged. There is a need for the automatic handling of regression testing. Fischer[1] describes software for determining which tests need to be rerun following a modification.

Implementing the functions required by the customer will not necessarily satisfy *all* the requirements placed upon a software system. Additional requirements, which are the subject of nonfunctional testing, involve checking that the software:

- satisfies legal obligations,
- performs within specified response times,
- is written to a particular house style,
- meets documentation standards.

The scope of this paper is limited to addressing the testing of the commissioner's functional requirements. The literature is not united about the aims of software testing. The variety of aims seem to fall into one of two camps:

- testing is concerned with finding faults in the software,
- testing is concerned with demonstrating that there are no faults in the software.

These may be viewed as an individual's attitude towards testing which may have an impact on how testing is conducted. Aiming to find faults is a destructive process, whereas aiming to demonstrate that there are no faults is constructive. Adopting the latter strategy may cause the tester to be gentle with the software, thus, giving rise to the risk of missing inherent faults. The destructive stance is perhaps more likely to uncover faults because it is more probing. Weinberg[2] suggests that programmers regard the software they produce as an extension of their ego. To be destructive in testing is therefore difficult. NASA long ago established teams of software validators separate from the software creators[3] a practice which is

Reprinted from *Information and Software Technology*, Vol. 30, No. 3, Apr. 1988, P. David Coward, "A Review of Software Testing," pp. 189–198, 1988, with kind permission from Elsevier Science–NL, Sara Burgerhartstraat 25; 1055 KV Amsterdam, The Netherlands.

now widespread in large software development organizations.

There are a large number of questions about testing. How much testing should be undertaken? When should we have confidence in the software? When a fault is discovered, should we be pleased that it has been found, or dismayed that it existed? Does the discovery of a fault lead us to suspect that there are likely to be more faults? At what stage can we feel confident that all, or realistically most, of the faults have been discovered? In short, what is it that we are doing when we test software? To what extent is testing concerned with quality assurance?

Perhaps testing is about both finding faults *and* demonstrating their absence. The aim is to demonstrate the absence of faults. This is achieved by setting out to find them. These views are reconciled by establishing the notion of the 'thoroughness of testing'. Where testing has been thorough, faults found and corrected, retested with equal thoroughness, then one has established confidence in the software. If, on the other hand, there is no feel for the thoroughness of the test one has no means of establishing confidence in the results of the testing. Much work has been done to establish test metrics to assess the thoroughness of a set of tests and to develop techniques that facilitate thorough testing.

Testing strategies

There are many widely differing testing techniques. But, for all the apparent diversity they cluster or separate according to their underlying principles. There are two prominent strategy dimensions: function/structural and static/dynamic. A solely functional strategy uses only the requirements defined in the specification as the basis for testing; whereas a structural strategy is based on the detailed design. A dynamic approach executes the software and assesses the performance, while a static approach analyses the software without recourse to its execution.

Functional versus structural testing

A testing strategy may be based upon one of two starting points: either the specification or the software is used as the basis for testing. Starting from the specification the required functions are identified. The software is then tested to assess whether they are provided. This is known as *functional testing*. If the strategy is based on deriving test data from the structure of a system this is known as *structural testing*. Functions which are included in the software, but not required; for example, functions which relate to the access of data in a database but which are not specifically asked for by a user, are more likely to be identified by adopting a structural testing strategy in preference to a functional testing strategy.

Functional testing

Functional testing involves two main steps. First, identify the functions which the software is expected to perform. Second, create test data which will check whether these functions are performed by the software. No consideration is given to *how* the program performs these functions.

There have been significant moves towards more systematic elicitation and expression of functional requirements[4-7]. These may be expected to lead to a more systematic approach to functional testing. Rules can be constructed for the direct identification of function and data from systematic design documentation. These rules do not take account of likely fault classes. Weyuker and Ostrand[8] have suggested that the next step in the development of functional testing, is a method of formal documentation which includes a description of faults associated with each part of the design as well as the design features themselves.

Howden[9] suggests this method be taken further. He claims that it is not sufficient to identify classes of faults for parts of the design. Isolation of particular properties of each function should take place. Each property will have certain fault classes associated with it. There are many classifications of faults. One detailed classification is given by Chan[10] and is a refinement of Van Tassel's[11] classification. Chan's classification consists of 13 groups which are subdivided to produce a total of 47 categories.

Functional testing has been termed a black box approach as it treats the program as a box with its contents hidden from view. Testers submit test cases to the program based on their understanding of the intended function of the program. An important component of functional testing is an *oracle*.

An oracle is someone who can state precisely what the outcome of a program execution will be for a particular test case. Such an oracle does not always exist and, at best, only imprecise expectations are available[12]. Simulation software provides a powerful illustration of the problem of determining an oracle. No precise expectation can be determined, the most precise expectation of output that can be provided is a range of plausible values.

Structural testing

The opposite to the black box approach is the white box aproach. Here testing is based upon the detailed design rather than on the functions required of the program, hence the name structural testing.

While functional testing requires the execution of the program with test data, there are two possible scenarios for structural testing. The first scenario, and the one most commonly encountered, is to execute the program with test cases. Second, and less common, is where the functions of the program are compared with the required functions for congruence. The second of these approaches is characterized by symbolic execution and program proving.

Structural testing involving the execution of a program may require the execution of a single path through the program, or it may involve a particular level of coverage such as 100% of all statements have been executed. The notion of a minimally-thorough test has occupied researchers over the years, i.e. they have been trying to discover what is the minimum amount of testing that is required to ensure a degree of reliability. Some of these are shown below:

- All statements in the programs should be executed at least once[13].
- All branches in the program should be executed at least once[13].
- All linear code sequence and jumps (LCSAJs) in the program should be executed at least once[14]. An LCSAJ is a sequence of code ending with a transfer of control out of the linear code sequence.

Probably the most thorough set of test metrics has been specified by Miller[15] who listed 13 structure-based metrics for judging test thoroughness. Obviously, the best test is an exhaustive one where all possible paths through the program are tested. However, there are two obstacles to this goal which account for the existence of the above measures.

The first obstacle is the large number of possible paths. The number of paths is determined by the numbers of conditions and loops in the program. All combinations of the conditions must be considered and this causes a rapidly increasing number of combinations as the number of conditions increases. This is known as the combinatorial explosion of testing. Loops add to the combinatorial explosion and give rise to an excessively large number of paths. This is most acute when the number of iterations is not fixed but determined by input variables.

The second obstacle is the number of infeasible paths. An infeasible path is one which cannot be executed due to the contradiction of some of the predicates at conditional statements. Most developers, when asked, would be surprised at the existence of infeasible code in a system. However, such code can be quite extensive, for example, in a recent study of a sample of programs, which involve examining 1000 shortest paths, only 18 were found to be feasible[16].

As an example of path infeasibility consider the following block of code.

```
1   Begin
2       Readln (a);
3       If a>15
4       then
5           b:=b+1
6       else
7           c:=c+1;
8       if a<10
9       then
10      d:=d+1
11  end;
```

There are four paths through this block as follows:

Path 1   lines   1,2,3,4,5,8,11.

Path 2   1,2,3,6,7,8,9,10,11.

Path 3   1,2,3,6,7,8,11.

Path 4   1,2,3,4,5,8,9,10,11.

Path 1 can be executed so long as the value of *a* is greater than 15 after the execution of line 2.

Path 2 can be executed so long as the value of *a* is less than 10 after the execution of line 2.

Path 3 can be executed so long as the value of *a* lies in the range 10 to 15 inclusive after the execution of line 2.

Path 4 cannot be executed regardless of the value of *a* because *a* cannot be both greater than 15 and less than 10 simultaneously. Hence this path is infeasible.

Even trivial programs contain a large number of paths. Where a program contains a loop which may be executed a variable number of times the number of paths increases dramatically. A path exists for each of the following circumstances: where the loop is not executed, where the loop is executed once, where the loop is executed twice etc.

The number of paths is dependent on the value of the variable controlling the loop. This poses a problem for a structural testing strategy. How many of the variable-controlled-loop-derived paths should be covered? Miller and Paige[17] sought to tackle this problem by introducing the notion of a level-i path and have employed testing metrics which utilize this notion.

A further difficulty in achieving 100% for any metric of testing coverage is the presence of island code. This is a series of lines of code, following a transfer of control or program termination, and which is not the destination of a transfer of control from elsewhere in the program. An example of island code is a procedure that is not invoked. Island code should not exist. It is caused by an error in the invocation of a required procedure, or the failure to delete redundant code following maintenance.

Static versus *dynamic analysis*

A testing technique that does not involve the execution of the software with data is known as *static analysis*. This includes program proving, symbolic execution and anomaly analysis. Program proving involves rigorously specifying constraints on the input and output data sets for a software component such as a procedure using mathematics. The code that implements the procedure is then proved mathematically to meet its specification. Symbolic execution is a technique which executes a software system, with symbolic values for variables being used rather than the normal numerical or string values. Anomaly analysis searches the program source for anomalous features such as island code.

Dynamic analysis requires that the software be executed. It relies on the use of probes inserted into a program [18, 19]. These are program statements which make calls to analysis routines that record the frequency of execution of elements of the program. As a result the tester is able to ascertain information such as the frequency that certain branches or statements are executed and also any areas of code that have not been exercised by the test.

Dynamic analysis can act as a bridge between functional and structural testing. Initially functional testing may dictate the set of test cases. The execution of these test cases may then be monitored by dynamic analysis. The program can then be examined structurally to determine test cases which will exercise the code left idle by the previous test. This dual approach results in the program being tested for the function required and the whole of the program being exercised. The latter feature ensures that the program does not perform any function that is not required.

Taxonomy of testing techniques

It is only over the last 15 years that testing techniques have achieved importance. Consequently, there is no generally accepted testing technique taxonomy. The degree to which the techniques employ a static *versus* dynamic analysis or a functional *versus* structural strategy provides one possible basis for a simple classification of testing techniques. The following grid outlines one classification. The techniques in the grid are described later in the paper. Domain testing, described later in this section, has been included under both structural and functional strategies.

Table 1. Simple classification of testing techniques

	Structural	Functiona
Static	Symbolic execution Program proving Anomaly analysis	
Dynamic	Computation testing Domain testing Automatic path-based test data generation Mutation analysis	Random testing Domain testing Cause-effect graphing Adaptive perturbation testing

Static-structural

No execution of the software is undertaken. Assessment is made of the soundness of the software by criteria other than its run-time behaviour. The features assessed vary with the technique. For example, anomaly analysis checks for peculiar features such as the existence of island code. On the other hand, program proving, aims to demonstrate congruence between the specification and the software.

Symbolic execution

Symbolic execution, sometimes referred to as symbolic evaluation, does not execute a program in the traditional sense of the word. The traditional notion of execution requires that a selection of paths through the program is exercised by a set of test cases. In symbolic execution actual data values are replaced by symbolic values. A program executed using inputs consisting of actual data values results in the output of a series of actual values. Symbolic execution on the other hand produces a set of expressions, one expression per output variable. Symbolic evaluation occupies a middle ground of testing between testing data and program proving. There are a number of symbolic execution systems[20–23].

The most common approach to symbolic execution is to perform an analysis of the program, resulting in the creation of a flow-graph. This is a directed graph which contains decision points and the assignments associated with each branch. By traversing the flow-graph from an entry point along a particular path a list of assignment statements and branch predicates is produced.

The resulting path is represented by a series of input variables, condition predicates and assignment statements. The execution part of the approach takes place by following the path from top to bottom. During this path traverse each input variable is given a symbol in place of an actual value. Thereafter, each assignment statement is evaluated so that it is expressed in terms of symbolic values of input variables and constants.

Consider paths 1–11 through the program in Figure 1. The symbolic values of the variables and the path condition at each branch are given in the right hand columns for the evaluation of this path.

At the end of the symbolic execution of a path the output variable will be represented by expressions in terms of symbolic values of input variables and constants. The output expressions will be subject to constraints. A list of these constraints is provided by the set of symbolic representations of each condition predicate along the path. Analysis of these constraints may indicate that the path is not executable due to a contradiction. This infeasibility problem is encountered by all forms of path testing.

A major difficulty for symbolic execution is the handling of loops (or iterations). Should the loops be symbolically evaluated once, twice, a hundred times or not at all? Some symbolic executors take a pragmatic approach. For each loop three paths are constructed, each path containing one of the following: no execution of the loop, a single execution of the loop and two executions of the loop.

		Path Condition	a	b	c	d
1	Begin	–	–	–	–	–
2	Read a, b, c, d	–	a	b	c	d
3	a := a+b	–	a+b	b	c	d
4	IF a>c	a+b<=c	a+b	b	c	d
5	THEN d := d+1					
6	ENDIF	a+b<=c	a+b	b	c	d
7	IF b=d	a+b<=c AND b<>d	a+b	b	c	d
8	THEN WRITE ('Success', a, d)					
9	ELSE WRITE ('Fail', a, d)	a+b<=c AND b<>d	a+b	b	c	d
10	ENDIF	a+b<=c AND b<>d	a+b	b	c	d
11	END	a+b<=c AND b<>d	a+b	b	c	d

Figure 1. Program fragment and symbolic values for a path

Partition analysis

Partition analysis uses symbolic execution to identify subdomains of the input data domain. Symbolic execution is performed on both the software and the specification. The path conditions are used to produce the subdomains, such that each subdomain is treated identically by both the program and the specification. Where a part of the input domain cannot be allocated to such a subdomain then either a structural or functional (program or specification) fault has been discovered. In the system described by Richardson[24] the specification is expressed in a manner close to program code. This is impractical. Specifications need to be written at a higher level of abstraction if this technique is to prove useful.

Program proving

The most widely reported approach to program proving is the 'inductive assertion verification' method developed by Floyd[25]. In this method assertions are placed at the beginning and end of selected procedures. Each assertion describes the function of the procedure mathematically. A procedure is said to be correct (with respect to its input and output assertions) if the truth of its input assertion upon procedure entry ensures the truth of its output assertion upon procedure exit[26].

There are many similarities between program proving and symbolic execution. Neither technique executes with actual data and both examine the source code. Program proving aims to be more rigorous in its approach. The main distinction between program proving and symbolic execution is in the area of loop handling. Program proving adopts a theoretical approach in contrast to symbolic execution. An attempt is made to produce a proof that accounts for all possible iterations of the loop. Some symbolic execution systems make the assumption that if the loop is correct when not executed, when executed just once and when executed twice. then it will be correct for any number of iterations.

Program proving is carried out as the following steps:

- Construct a program.
- Examine the program and insert mathematical assertions at the beginning and end of all procedures blocks.
- Determine whether the code between each pair of start and end assertions will achieve the end assertion given the start assertion.
- If the code achieves the end assertions then the block has been proved correct.

If the code fails to achieve the end assertion then mistakes have been made in either the program or the proof. The proof and the program should be checked to determine which of these possibilities has occurred and appropriate corrections made.

DeMillo et al[27] describe how theorems and proofs can never be conceived as 'correct' but rather, only 'acceptable' to a given community. This acceptability is achieved by their being examined by a wide audience who can find no fault in the proof. Confidence in the proof increases as the number of readers, finding no faults, increases. This approach has clear parallels with the confidence placed in software. The wider the audience that has used the software and found no fault the more confidence is invested in the software.

When a program has been proved correct, in the sense that it has been demonstrated that the end assertions will be achieved given the initial assertions, then the program has achieved partial correctness. To achieve total correctness it must also be shown that the block will terminate, in other words the loops will terminate[28].

Anomaly analysis

The first level of anomaly analysis is performed by the compiler to determine whether the program adheres to the language syntax. This first level of analysis is not usually considered testing. Testing is usually deemed to commence when a syntactically correct program is produced.

The second level of anomaly analysis searches for anomalies that are not outlawed by the programming language. Examples of such systems which carry out such an analysis are Dave[29], Faces[30] and Toolpack[31]. Anomalies which can be discovered by these systems include:

- The existence of (island code) unexecutable code,
- Problems concerning array bounds,
- Failure to initialize variables,
- Labels and variables which are unused,
- Jumps into and out of loops.

Some systems will even detect high complexity and departure from programming standards.

Discovery of these classes of problem is dependent on the analysis of the code. The first phase of anomaly analysis is to produce a flow-graph. This representation of the software can now be easily scanned to identify anomalies. Determining infeasible paths is not within the bounds of anomaly analysis.

Some features of anomaly analysis have been grouped under the title of *data flow analysis*. Here, emphasis is placed on a careful analysis of the flow of data. Software may be viewed as flow of data from input to output. Input values contribute to intermediate values which, in turn, determine the output values. 'It is the ordered use of data implicit in this process that is the central objective of study in data flow analysis'[32] The anomalies detected by data flow analysis are:

- Assigning values to a variable which is not used later in the program,
- Using a variable (in an expression or condition) which has not previously been assigned a value,
- (Re)assigning a variable without making use of a previously assigned value.

Data flow anomalies may arise from mistakes such as misspelling, confusion of variable names and incorrect parameter passing. The existence of a data flow anomaly is not evidence of a fault, it merely indicates the possibility of a fault. Software that contains data flow anomalies may be less likely to satisfy the functional requirements than software which does not contain them.

The role of data flow analysis is one of a program critic drawing attention to peculiar uses of variables. These peculiarities must be checked against the programmer's intentions and, if in disagreement, the program should be corrected.

Dynamic-functional

This class of technique executes test cases. No consideration is given to the detailed design of the software. Cause-effect graphing creates test cases from the rules contained in the specification. Alternatively, test cases may be generated randomly. Domain testing creates test cases based on a decomposition of the required functions. Adaptive testing attempts to create further, more effective, test cases by modifying previous test cases. In all the approaches there is the need for an oracle to pronounce on the correctness of the output.

Domain testing

This is the least well defined of the dynamic-functional approaches. Test cases are created based on an informal classification of the requirements into domains. Either data or function may provide the basis for the domain partitioning. The test cases are executed and compared against the expectation to determine whether faults have been detected.

Random testing

Random testing produces data without reference to the code or the specification. The main software tool required is a random number generator. Duran and Ntafos[33,34] describe how estimates of the operational reliability of the software can be derived from the results of random testing.

Potentially, there are some problems for random testing. The most significant is that it may seem that there is no guarantee to complete coverage of the program. For example, when a constraint on a path is an equality e.g. $A=B+5$ the likelihood of satisfying this constraint by random generation seems low. Alternatively, if complete coverage is achieved then it is likely to have generated a large number of test cases. The checking of the output from the execution would require an impractical level of human effort.

Intuitively, random testing would appear to be of little practical value. Some recent studies have attempted to counter this view by randomly testing instrumented programs[33–35]. Ince and Hekmatpour record that an average branch coverage of 93% was achieved for a small set of randomly generated test cases. The key to this approach is to examine only a small subset of

the test results. The subset is chosen to give a high branch coverage.

Adaptive perturbation testing

This technique is based on assessing the effectiveness of a set of test cases. The effectiveness measure is used to generate further test cases with the aim of increasing the effectiveness. Both Cooper[36] and Andrews[37] describe systems which undertake this automatically.

The cornerstone of the technique is the use of executable assertions which the software developer inserts into the software. An assertion is a statement about the reasonableness of values of variables. The aim is to maximize the number of assertion violations. An initial set of test cases are provided by the tester. These are executed and the assertion violations recorded. Each test case is now considered in turn. The single input parameter of the test case that contributes least to the assertion violation count is identified. Optimization routines are then used to find the best value to replace the discarded value such that the number of assertion violations is maximized. The test case is said to have undergone *perturbation*. This is repeated for each test case. The perturbed set of test cases are executed and the cycle is repeated until the number of violated assertions can be increased no further.

Cause-effect graphing

The strength of cause-effect graphing lies in its power to explore input combinations. The graph is a combinatorial logic network, rather like a circuit, making use of only the Boolean logical operators AND, OR and NOT. Myers[38] describes a series of steps for determining cases using cause-effect graphs as follows:

- Divide the specification into workable pieces. A workable piece might be the specification for an individual transaction. This step is necessary because a cause-effect graph for a whole system would be too unwieldy for practical use.
- Identify causes and effects. A cause is an input stimulus, e.g. a command typed in at a terminal, an effect is an output response.
- Construct a graph to link the causes and effects in a way that represents the semantics of the specification. This is the *cause-effect graph*.
- Annotate the graph to show impossible effects and impossible combinations of causes.
- Convert the graph into a limited-entry decision table. Conditions represent the causes, actions represent the effects and rules (columns) represent the test cases.

In a simple case, say with three conditions, one may be tempted to feel that the cause-effect graph is an unnecessary intermediate representation. However, Myers illustrates the creation of test cases for a specification containing 18 causes. To progress immediately to the decision table would have given 262 potential test cases. The purpose of the cause-effect graph is to identify a small number of useful test cases.

Dynamic-structural

Here the software is executed with test cases. Creation of the test cases is generally based upon an analysis of the software.

Domain and computation testing

Domain and computation testing are strategies for selecting test cases. They use the structure of the program and select paths which are used to identify domains. The assignment statements on the paths are used to consider the computations on the path. These approaches also make use of the ideas of symbolic execution.

A *path computation* is the set of algebraic expressions, one for each output variable, in terms of input variables and constants for a particular path. A *path condition* is the conjunction of constraint on the path. A path domain is the set of input values that satisfy the path condition. An empty path domain means that the path is infeasible and cannot be executed.

The class of error that results when a case follows the wrong path due to a fault in a conditional statement is termed a *domain error*. The class of error that results when a case correctly follows a path which contains faults in an assignment statement is termed a computation error.

Domain testing is based on the observation that points close to, yet satisfying boundary conditions are most sensitive to domain errors[39]. The domain testing strategy selects test data on and near the boundaries of each path domain[8, 40].

Computation testing strategies focus on the detection of computation errors. Test data for which the path is sensitive to computation errors are selected by analysing the symbolic representation of the path computation[39]. Clarke and Richardson[24] list a set of guidelines for selecting test data for arithmetic and data manipulation computations.

Automatic test data generation

Use is made of automatic generation of test data when the program is to be executed and the aim is to achieve a particular level of courage indicated by a coverage metric.

It has been suggested that test data can be generated from a syntactic description of the test data expressed in, say, BNF[41]. This may seem novel as it is not usual to prepare such a syntactic description of the data, but it is a technique familiar to compiler writers[42, 43]. In the case of compilers a carefully prepared data description: that of the programming language, is available. The principle may be transferable to test data generation in general.

Many automatic test data generators have used the approach of path identification and symbolic execution to aid the data generation process, for example, CASEGEN[23] and the FORTRAN testbed[44]. The system of predicates produced for a path is part-way to generating test data. If the path predicates cannot be solved due to a contradiction, then the path is infeasible. Any solution of these predicates will provide a series of data values for the input variables so providing a test case.

Repeated use of the path generation and predicate solving parts of such a system may produce a set of test cases in which one has confidence of high coverage of the program. The initial path generation will provide the highest coverage. Subsequent attempts to find feasible paths which incorporate remaining uncovered statements, branches and LCSAJs will prove increasingly difficult, some impossibly difficult.

A path-based approach which does not use symbolic execution is incorporated in the SMOTL system[45]. The system has a novel approach to minimizing the number of paths required to achieve full branch coverage.

A program that has been tested with a high coverage may still not meet its specification. This may be due to the omission in the program of one of the functions defined in the specification. Data that is generated from the specification would prove useful in determining such omissions. To achieve this automatically requires a rigorous means of specification. The increasing use of formal specification methods may provide the necessary foundations on which to build automated functional test data generators.

Mutation analysis

Mutation analysis is not concerned with creating test data, nor of demonstrating that the program is correct. It is concerned with the quality of a set of test data[46, 47]. Other forms of testing use the test data to test the program. Mutation analysis uses the program to test the test data.

High quality test data will harshly exercise a program thoroughly. To provide a measure of how well the program has been exercised mutation analysis creates many, almost identical, programs. One change is made per mutant program. Each mutant program and the original program are then executed with the same set of test data. The output from the original program is then compared with the output from each mutant program in turn. If the outputs are different then that particular mutant is of little interest as the test data has discovered that there is a difference between the programs. This mutant is now *dead* and disregarded. A mutant which produced output that matches with the original is interesting. The change has not been detected by the test data, and the mutant is said to be *live*.

Once the output from all the mutants has been examined, a ratio of dead to live mutants will be available. A high proportion of live mutants indicates a poor set of test data. A further set of test data must be devised and the process repeated until the number of live mutants is small, indicating that the program has been well tested.

A difficulty for mutation analysis occurs when a mutant program is an equivalent program to the original program. Although the mutant is textually different from the original it will always produce the same results as the original program. Mutation analysis will record this as a live mutant even though no test data can be devised to kill it. The difficulty lies in the fact that determining the state of equivalence is, in general, unsolvable and hence cannot be taken into account when assessing the ratio of live to killed mutants.

Mutation analysis relies on the notion that if the test data discovers the single change that has been made to produce the mutant program then the test data will discover more major faults in the program. Thus, if the test data has not discovered any major faults, and a high proportion of the mutants have been killed, then the program is likely to be sound.

Summary

The principal objective of software testing is to gain confidence in the software. This necessitates the discovery of both errors of omission and commission. Confidence arises from thorough testing. There are many testing techniques which aim to help achieve thorough testing.

Testing techniques can be assessed according to where along the two main testing strategy dimensions they fall. The first dimension, the functional-structural dimension, assesses the extent to which the function description in the specification, as opposed to the detailed design of the software, is used as a basis for testing. The second dimension, the static-dynamic dimension, considers the degree to which the technique executes the software and assesses its run-time behaviour, as opposed to inferring its run-time behaviour from an examination of the software. These two dimensions can be used to produce four categories of testing technique:

- static-functional
- static-structural
- dynamic-functional
- dynamic-structural

As with all classifications this one is problematic at the boundaries. Some techniques appear to belong equally well in two categories.

The aims of testing techniques range from: demonstrating correctness for all input classes (e.g. program proving), to, showing that for a particular set of test cases no faults were discovered (e.g. random testing). Debate continues as to whether correctness can be proved for life-size software and about what can be inferred when a set of test cases finds no errors. A major question facing dynamic testing techniques is whether the execution of a single case demonstrates anything more than that the software works for that particular case. This has led to work on the identifica-

tion of domains leading to the assertion that a text case represents a particular domain of possible test cases.

Many of the structural techniques rely on the generation of paths through the software. These techniques are hampered by the lack of a sensible path generation strategy. There is no clear notion of what constitutes a *revealing* path worthy of investigation, as opposed to a *concealing* path which tells the tester very little.

Testers often utilize their experience of classes of faults associated with particular functions and data types to create additional test cases. To date there is no formal way of taking account of these heuristics.

Symbolic execution looks to be a promising technique. Yet, few full symbolic execution systems currently exist[48]. Of the experimental systems that have been developed none address commercial data processing software written in languages such as COBOL.

Whenever a program is executed with data values, or symbolically evaluated, the success of the testing lies in the ability to recognize that errors have occurred. Who is responsible for deeming an output correct? The notion of an oracle is used to overcome this difficulty. Whoever commissions the software is deemed capable of assessing whether the results are correct. This may be satisfactory in many situations such as commercial data processing software. However, there are instances when this is not a solution. For example, software to undertake calculations in theoretical physics may be developed precisely because the calculations could not be undertaken by hand.

One of the few pieces of empirical data on testing techniques is provided in a study by Howden[49]. The study tested six programs of various types using several different testing techniques. The results are encouraging for the use of symbolically evaluated expressions for output variables. Out of a total of 28 errors five were discovered where it would be 'possible for the incorrect variable to take on the values of the correct variable during testing on actual data, thus hiding the presence of the error.' The paper concluded that the testing strategy most likely to produce reliable software was one that made use of a variety of techniques. Over the last few years effort has been directed at construction of integrated, multitechnique software development environments.

Formal proofs, dynamic testing techniques and symbolic execution used together look likely to provide a powerful testing environment. What is necessary now is an attempt to overcome the division that has arisen between the formalists and the structuralists. The level of mathematics required by many approaches to program proving is elementary in comparison with the abilities necessary to produce the software itself. On the other hand, the formalists must resist the temptation to proclaim that their approach is not just necessary but that it is also sufficient. For the production of correct software the wider the range of testing techniques used the better the software is likely to be.

References

1 Fischer, K F 'A test case selection method for the validation of software maintenance modification' *Proc. COMPSAC 1977*, pp 421–426 (1977)

2 Weinberg, G M *The Psychology of Computer Programming* Van Nostrand Reinhold (1971)

3 Spector, A and Gifford, D 'Case study: the space shuttle primary computer system' *Commun. ACM* Vol 27 No 9 (1984) pp 874–900

4 DeMarco, T *Structured Analysis and System Specification*, Yourden Press (1981)

5 Hayes, I *Specification Case Studies* Prentice-Hall International (1987)

6 Jackson, M *Principles of Program Design*, Academic Press (1975)

7 Jones, C B *Systematic Software Development using VDM* Prentice-Hall International (1986)

8 Weyuker, F J and Ostrand, T J 'Theories of program testing and the application of revealing subdomains' (IEEE) *Trans. Software Eng.* Vol 6 No 3 (1980) pp 236–246

9 Howden, W E 'Errors, design properties and functional program tests' *Computer Program Testing* (Eds Chandrasekaran, B and Radicchi, S) North-Holland, (1981)

10 Chan, J *Program debugging methodology* M Phil Thesis, Leicester Polytechnic (1979)

11 Van Tassel, D *Program Style, Design, Efficiency, Debugging and Testing* Prentice-Hall (1978)

12 Weyuker, E J 'On testing non-testable programs' *The Comput. J.* Vol 25 No 4 (1982) pp 465–470

13 Miller, J C and Maloney, C J Systematic mistake analysis of digital computer programs, *Commun. ACM* pp 58–63 Vol 6 (1963)

14 Woodward, M R, Hedley, D and Hennell, M A 'Experience with path analysis and testing of programs' (IEEE) *Trans. Software Eng.* Vol 6 No 6 (1980) pp 278–285

15 Miller, E F 'Software quality assurance' *Presentation* London, UK (14–15 May 1984)

16 Hedley, D and Hennell, M A 'The cause and effects of infeasible paths in computer programs' *Proc. Eight Int. Conf. Software Eng.* (1985)

17 Miller, E F and Paige, M R Automatic generation of software tescases, *Proc. Eurocomp Conf.* pp 1–12 (1974)

18 Knuth, D E and Stevenson, F R 'Optimal measurement points for program frequency count' *BIT* Vol 13 (1973)

19 Paige, M R and Benson, J P 'The use of software probes in testing FORTRAN programs' *Computer* pp 40–47 (July 1974)

20 Boyer, R S, Elpas, B and Levit, K N 'SELECT – a formal system for testing and debugging programs by symbolic execution' *Proc. Int. Conf. Reliable Software* pp 234–244 (1975)

21 Clarke, L A 'A system to generate test data and symbolically execute programs' (IEEE) *Trans. Software Eng.* Vol 2 No 3 (1976) pp 215–222

22 King, J C Symbolic execution and program testing, *Commun. ACM* Vol 19 No 7 (1976) pp 385–394

23 Ramamoothy, C V, Ho, S F and Chen, W J 'On the automated generation of program test data' (IEEE) *Trans. Software Eng.* Vol 2 No 4 (1976) pp 293–300

24 Richardson, D J and Clarke L A 'A partition analysis method to increase program reliability' *Proc. Fifth Int. Conf. Software Eng.* pp 244–253 (1981)

25 Floyd, R W 'Assigning meaning to programs' *Proc. of the Symposia in Applied Mathematics* Vol 19 pp 19–32 (1967)

26 Hantler, S L and King, J C 'An introduction to proving the correctness of programs' *Computing Surveys* Vol 18 No 3 (1976) pp 331–353

27 Demillo, R A, Lipton, R J and Perlis, A J 'Social processes and proofs of theorems and programs' *Commun. ACM* Vol 22 No 5 (1979) pp 271–280

28 Elpas, B, Levitt, K N, Waldinger, R J and Wakemann, A 'An assessment of techniques for proving program correctness' *Computing Surveys* Vol 4 No 2 (1972) pp 97–147

29 Osterweil, L J and Fosdick, L D 'Some experience with DAVE- a FORTRAN program analyser' *Proc. AFIPS Conf.* pp 909–915 (1976)

30 Ramamoorthy, C V and Ho, S F 'FORTRAN automatic code evaluation system' *Rep. M-466* Electron. Resl Lab, University California, Berkeley, CA, USA (August 1974)

31 Osterweil, L J 'TOOLPACK – An experimental software development environment research project (IEEE) *Trans. Software Eng.* Vol 9 No 6 (1983) pp 673–685

32 Fosdik, L D and Osterwell, L J 'Data flow analysis in software reliability' *Computing Surveys* Vol 8 No 3 (1976) pp 305–330

33 Duran, J W and Ntafos, S C 'A report on random testing' *Proc. Fifth Int. Conf. Software Eng.* pp 179–183 (1981)

34 Duran, J W and Ntafos, S C 'An evaluation of random testing' (IEEE) *Trans. Software Eng.* Vol 10 No 4 (1984) pp 438–444

35 Ince, D C and Hekmatpour, S 'An evaluation of some black-box testing methods' *Technical report No 84/7* Computer Discipline, Faculty of Mathematics, Open University, Milton Keynes,UK (1984)

36 Cooper, D W 'Adaptive testing' *Proc. Second Int. Conf. Software Eng.* pp 223–226 (1976)

37 Andrews, D and Benson, J P 'An automated program testing methodology and its implementation' *Proc. Fifth Int. Conf. Software Eng.* pp 254–261 (1981)

38 Myers, G J *The Art of Software Testing* John Wiley (1979)

39 Clarke, L A and Richardson, D J 'The application of error-sensitive testing strategies to debugging' *ACM SIGplan Notices* Vol 18 No 8 (1983) pp 45–52

40 White, L J and Cohen, E I 'A domain strategy for computer program testing' (IEEE) *Trans. Software Eng.* Vol 6 No 3 (1980) pp 247–257

41 **Ince, D C** The automatic generation of test data, *The Comput. J.* Vol 30 No 1 (1987) pp 63–69

42 **Bazzichi, F and Spadafora, I** 'An automatic generator for compiler testing' (IEEE) *Trans. Software Eng.* Vol 8 No 4 (1982) pp 343–353

43 **Payne, A J** 'A formalized technique for expressing compiler exercisers', *SIGplan Notices* Vol 13 No 1 (1978) pp 59–69

44 **Hedley, D** *Automatic test data generation and related topics* PhD Thesis, Liverpool University (1981)

45 **Bicevskis, J, Borzovs, J, Straujums, U, Zarins, A and Miller, E F** 'SMOTL – a system to construct samples for data processing program debugging' (IEEE) *Trans. Software Eng.* Vol 5 No 1 (1979) pp 60–66

46 **Budd, T A and Lipton, R J** 'Mutation analysis of decision table programs' *Proc. Conf. Information Science and Systems* pp 346–349 (1978)

47 **Budd, T A, Demillo, R A, Lipton, R J and Sayward, F G** 'Theoretical and empirical studies on using program mutation to test the functional correctness of programs' *Proc. ACM Symp. Principles of Prog. Lang.* pp 220–222 (1980)

48 **Coward, P D** 'Symbolic execution systems – a review' *The Software Eng. J.* (To appear)

49 **Howden, W** 'An evaluation of the effectiveness of symbolic testing' *Software Pract. Exper.* Vol 8 (1978) pp 381–397 ☐

Chapter 8

Software Maintenance

1. Introduction to Chapter

1.1 Overview of Software Maintenance

Conventional wisdom says that software maintenance represents from 40 to 70 percent of the total cost of a software system. The major reason that so much money is spent on software maintenance is that maintenance is a term often used to describe many things that are not really "maintenance" but might be categorized as software development, for example, correcting a delivered software system that was not specified, designed, programmed, or tested correctly in the first place. It is not unheard of for developers to say during testing, "...let's fix this problem during the maintenance phase, after the system is delivered." Often, developers and customers agree that enhancements or changes that are identified during development will not be implemented until the maintenance phase, so as not to delay delivery of the originally specified capabilities.

1.2 Categories of Software Maintenance

The term *maintenance* may be used to refer to enhancements made to improve software performance, maintainability, or understandability, as well as to fix mistakes.

Software maintenance includes changes that result from new or changing requirements. Maintenance may involve activities designed to make the system easier to understand and to work with, such as restructuring or redocumenting the software system. Optimization of code to make it run faster or use storage more efficiently might be included. These types of maintenance are called *perfective maintenance* and account for some 60 to 70 percent of the overall maintenance effort.

Other modifications are made to a system to satisfy or accommodate changes in the processing environment. These are required changes and are not normally under the control of the software maintainer. These changes may include changes to rules, laws, and regu-

SOFTWARE MAINTEN

DIGERNESS 91

lations that affect the system, as well as changes to enable the software to run on new hardware. This type of maintenance is called *adaptive maintenance.*

And, lastly, error correction that is required to keep the system operational is called *corrective maintenance.* Corrective maintenance is usually a reactive process to failures in the software system.

2. Introduction to Paper

This chapter consists of only one paper. Prof. Keith Bennett, a leading authority on software maintenance in the UK, wrote the paper specifically for this Tutorial. Prof. Bennett defines and describes the maintenance process and points out that as software development has matured more funds are now spent on the maintenance of many software systems than was spent on their development.

Maintenance terminology is defined. To the conventionally defined types of maintenance (perfective, adaptive, and corrective), Bennett has added a new category, preventive maintenance.

Professor Bennett describes software maintenance from the points of view of:

- Management and the organization

- Process models

- Technical issues

The paper discusses why software maintenance is such a major problem. Management may or may not look favorably on software maintenance activities. In one regard, maintenance can be looked at as a drain on resources; on the opposite side, maintenance is required to keep a product competitive. Therefore, software maintenance activities need to be justified in terms of "return on investment."

The author looks at the IEEE Standard for Software Maintenance [1] as one of the best maintenance processes. He describes the activities of software maintenance and the quality control over each activity.

Prof. Bennett points out that the technology required for software maintenance is similar to that needed for new development. He discusses the need for configuration management, traceability, impact analysis, metrics, and CASE tools.

Next Bennett discusses legacy systems, typically large, old, much-modified software systems that are expensive and difficult to maintain but would also be very expensive to replace with new systems. He discusses options other than continued maintenance or replacement, including re-engineering and reverse engineering. Finally research topics in software maintenance are discussed, and the vehicles for maintenance technology (conferences, journals, organizations, and research programs) are presented.

1. IEEE Std 1912-1992, *Standard for Software Maintenance*, The Institute of Electrical and Electronics Engineers, Inc., Piscataway, NJ, 1993.

Software Maintenance: A Tutorial

Keith H. Bennett

Computer Science Department
University of Durham
Durham, UK
tel: +44 91 374 4596
fax: +44 91 374 2560
Email: keith.bennett@durham.ac.uk

1. Objectives for the Reader

The objectives of this tutorial are:

- to explain what is meant by software maintenance.
- to show how software maintenance fits into other software engineering activities
- to explain the relationship between software maintenance and the organization
- to explain the best practice in software maintenance in terms of a process model
- to describe important maintenance technology such as impact analysis
- to explain what is meant by a legacy system and describe how reverse engineering and other techniques may be used to support legacy systems.

2. Overview of Tutorial

This tutorial starts with a short introduction to the field of software engineering, thereby providing the context for the constituent field of software maintenance. It focuses on solutions, not problems, but an appreciation of the problems in software maintenance is important. The solutions are categorized in a three layer model: organizational issues; process issues; and technical issues.

Our presentation of organizational solutions to maintenance concentrates on software as an asset whose value needs to be sustained.

We explain the process of software maintenance by describing the IEEE standard for the maintenance process. Although this is only a draft standard at present, it provides a very sensible approach which is applicable to many organizations.

Technical issues are explained by concentrating on techniques of particular importance to maintenance.

For example, configuration management and version control are as important for initial development as for maintenance, so these are not addressed. In contrast, coping with the ripple (domino) effect is only found during maintenance, and it is one of the crucial technical problems to be solved. We describe solutions to this.

By this stage the tutorial will have presented the typical iterative maintenance process that is used, at various levels of sophistication, in many organizations. However, the software may become so difficult and expensive to maintain that special, often drastic action is needed. The software is then called a "legacy system," and the particular problems of and solutions to coping with legacy code are described.

The tutorial is completed by considering some fruitful research directions for the field.

3. The Software Engineering Field

Software maintenance is concerned with modifying software once it is delivered to a customer. By that definition it forms a sub-area of the wider field of Software Engineering [IEEE91], which is defined as:

> the application of the systematic, disciplined, quantifiable approach to the development, operation and maintenance of software; that is the application of engineering to software.

It is helpful to understand trends and objectives of the wider field in order to explain the detailed problems and solutions concerned with maintenance. McDermid's definition in the Software Engineer's Reference book embodies the spirit of the engineering approach. He states that [MCDER 91]:

> software engineering is; the science and art of specifying, designing, implementing and evolving—with economy, time limits and elegance—programs, documentation and operat-

ing procedures whereby computers can be made useful to man.

Software Engineering is still a very young discipline and the term itself was only invented in 1968. Modern computing is only some 45 years old; yet within that time we have gained the ability to solve very difficult and large problems. Often these huge projects consume thousands of person-years or more of design. The rapid increase in the size of the systems which we tackle, from 100 line programs 45 years ago to multi-million line systems now, presents many problems of dealing with *scale*, so it is not surprising that evolving such systems to meet continually changing user needs is difficult.

Much progress has been made over the past decade in improving our ability to construct high quality software which does meet users' needs. Is it feasible to extrapolate these trends? Baber (BABE 91) has identified three possible futures for software engineering:

(a) Failures of software systems are common, due to limited technical competence and developers. This is largely an extrapolation of the present situation.

(b) The use of computer systems is limited to those application in which there is a minimal risk to the public. There is wide spread scepticism about the safety of software based systems. There may be legislation covering the use of software in safety critical and safety related systems.

(c) The professional competence and qualifications of software designers are developed to such a high level that even very challenging demands can be met reliably and safely. In this vision of the future, software systems would be delivered on time, fully meet their requirements, and be applicable in safety critical systems.

In case (a), software development is seen primarily as a craft activity. Option (b) is unrealistic; software is too important to be restricted in this way. Hence there is considerable interest within the software engineering field in addressing the issues raised by (c). In this tutorial, we feel (c) defines the goal of software maintenance and addresses *evolving* systems.

A root problem for many software systems, which also causes some of the most difficult problems for software maintenance, is complexity. Sometimes this arises because a system is migrated from hardware to software in order to gain the additional functionality

found in software. Complexity should be a result of implementing an inherently complex application (for example in a tax calculation package, which is deterministic but non-linear; or automation of the UK Immigration Act, which is complex and ambiguous). The main tools to control complexity are modular design and building systems as separated layers of abstraction that separate concerns. Nevertheless, the combination of scale and application complexity mean that it is infeasible for one person alone to understand the complete software system.

4. Software Maintenance

Once software has been initially produced, it then passes into the *maintenance* phase. The IEEE definition of software maintenance is as follows [IEEE91]:

software maintenance is the process of modifying the software system or component after delivery to correct faults, improve performance or other attributes, or adapt to a change in environment.

Some organizations use the term software maintenance to refer only to the implementation of very small changes (for example, less than one day), and the term software development to refer to all other modifications and enhancements. However, to avoid confusion, we shall continue to use the IEEE standard definition.

Software maintenance, although part of software engineering, is by itself of major economic importance. A number of surveys over the last 15 years have shown that for most software, software maintenance occupies anything between 40 and 90 percent of total life cycle costs. (see [FOST93] for a review of such surveys) A number of surveys have also tried to compute the total software maintenance costs in the UK and in the US. While these figures need to be treated with a certain amount of caution, it seems clear that a huge amount of money is being spent on software maintenance.

The inability to undertake maintenance quickly, safely, and cheaply means that for many organizations, a substantial *applications backlog* occurs. The Management Information Services Department is unable to make changes at the rate required by marketing or business needs. End-users become frustrated and often adopt PC solutions in order to short circuit the problems. They may then find that a process of rapid prototyping and end-user computing provides them (at least in the short term) with quicker and easier solutions than those supplied by the Management Information Systems Department.

In the early decades of computing, software maintenance comprised a relatively small part of the software life cycle; the major activity was writing new programs for new applications. In the late 1960s and 1970s, management began to realize that old software does not simply die, and at that point the software maintenance started to be recognized as a significant activity. An anecdote about the early days of electronic data processing in banks illustrates this point. In the 1950s, a large US bank was about to take the major step of employing its very first full-time programmer. Management raised the issue of what would happen to this person once the programs had been written. The same bank now has several buildings full of data processing staff.

In the 1980s, it was becoming evident that old architectures were severely constraining new design. In another example from the US banking system, existing banks had difficulty modifying their software in order to introduce automatic teller machines. In contrast, new banks writing software from scratch found this relatively easy. It has also been reported in the UK that at least two mergers of financial organizations were unable to go ahead due to the problems of integrating software from two different organizations.

In the 1990s, a large part of the business needs of many organization has now been implemented so that business change is represented by evolutionary change to the software, not revolutionary change, and that most so-called development is actually enhancement and evolution.

5. Types of Software Maintenance

Leintz and Swanson [LEIN78][LEIN80] undertook a survey which categorized maintenance into four different categories.

(1) *Perfective maintenance*; changes required as a result of user requests (also known as *evolutive* maintenance)

(2) *Adaptive maintenance*; changes needed as a consequence of operated system, hardware, or DBMS changes

(3) *Corrective maintenance*; the identification and removal of faults in the software

(4) *Preventative maintenance*; changes made to software to make it more maintainable

The above categorization is very useful in helping management to understand some of the basic costs of maintenance. However, it will be seen from Section 9 that the processes for the four types are very similar, and there is little advantage in distinguishing them

when designing best practice maintenance processes.

It seems clear from a number of surveys that the majority of software maintenance is concerned with evolution deriving from user requested changes.

The important requirement of software maintenance for the client is that changes are accomplished quickly and cost effectively. The reliability of the software should at worst not be degraded by the changes. Additionally, the maintainability of the system should not degrade, otherwise future changes will be progressively more expensive to carry out. This phenomenon was recognized by Lehman, and expressed in terms of his well known laws of evolution [LEHE80][LEHE84]. The first law of continuing change states that *a program that is used in a real world environment necessarily must change or become progressively less useful in that environment.*

This argues that software evolution is not an undesirable attribute and essentially it is only useful software that evolves. Lehman's second law of increasing complexity states that *as an evolving program changes, its structure tends to become more complex. Extra resources must be devoted to preserving the semantics and simplifying the structure.* This law argues that things will become much worse unless we do something about it. The problem for most software is that nothing has been done about it, so changes are increasingly more expensive and difficult. Ultimately, maintenance may become too expensive and almost infeasible: the software then becomes known as a *legacy system* (see section 11). Nevertheless, it may be of essential importance to the organization.

6. Problems of Software Maintenance

Many technical and managerial problems occur when changing software quickly, reliably, and cheaply. For example, user changes are often described in terms of the *behavior* of the software system and must be interpreted as changes to the source code. When a change is made to the code, there may be substantial consequential changes, not only in the code itself, but within documentation, design, and test suites, (this is termed the *domino*, or *ripple effect*). Many systems under maintenance are very large, and solutions which work for laboratory scale pilots will not scale up to industrial sized software. Indeed it may be said that any program which is small enough to fit into a textbook or to be understood by one person does not have maintenance problems.

There is much in common between best practice in software engineering in general, and software maintenance in particular. Software maintenance problems essentially fall into three categories:

(a) *Alignment with organizational objectives.* Initial software development is usually project based with a defined timescale, and budget. The main emphasis is to deliver on time and within budget to meet user needs. In contrast, software maintenance often has the objective of extending the life of a software system for as long as possible. In addition, it may be driven by the need to meet user demand for software updates and enhancements. In both cases, return on investment is much less clear, so that the view at senior management level is often of a major activity consuming large resources with no clear quantifiable benefit for the organization.

(b) *Process issues.* At the process level, there are many activities in common with software development. For example, configuration management is a crucial activity in both. However, software maintenance requires a number of additional activities not found in initial development. Initial requests for changes are usually made to a "help desk" (often part of a larger end-user support unit), which must assess the change (as many change requests derive from misunderstanding of documentation) and, if it is viable, then pass it to a technical group who can assess the cost of making the change. Impact analysis on both the software and the organization, and the associated need for system comprehension, are crucial issues. Further down the life cycle, it is important to be able to perform regression tests on the software so that the new changes do not introduce errors into the parts of the software that were not altered.

(c) *Technical issues.* There are a number of technical challenges to software maintenance. As noted above, the ability to construct software that it is easy to comprehend is a major issue [ROBS91]. A number of studies have shown that the majority of time spent in maintaining software is actually consumed in this activity. Similarly, testing in a cost effective way provides major challenges. Despite the emergence of methods based on discrete mathematics (for example, to prove that an implementation meets its specification), most current software is tested rather than verified, and the cost of repeating a full test suite on a major piece of software can be very large in terms of money and time. It will be better to select a sub-set of tests that only stressed those parts of the system that had been changed, together with the regression tests. The technology to do this is still not available, despite much useful progress. As an example, it is useful to consider a major billing package for an industrial organization. The change of the taxation rate in such a system should be a simple matter; after all, generations of students are taught to place such constants at the head of the program so only a one line edit is needed. However, for a major multi-national company dealing with taxation rates in several countries with complex and different rules for tax calculations (that is, complex business rules), the change of the taxation rate may involve a huge expense.

Other problems are related to the lower status of software maintenance compared with software development. In the manufacture of a consumer durable, the majority of the cost lies in production, and it is well understood that design faults can be hugely expensive. In contrast, the construction of software is automatic, and development represents almost all the initial cost. Hence in conditions of financial stringency, it is tempting to cut costs by cutting back design. This can have a very serious effect on the costs of subsequent maintenance.

One of the problems for management is assessing a software product to determine how easy it is to change. This leaves little incentive for initial development projects to construct software that is easy to evolve. Indeed, lucrative maintenance contracts may follow a software system where shortcuts have been taken during its development [WALT94].

We have so far stressed the *problems* of software maintenance in order to differentiate it from software engineering in general. However, much is known about best practice in software maintenance, and there are excellent case studies, such as the US Space Shuttle on-board flight control software system, which demonstrate that software can be evolved carefully and with improving reliability. The remainder of this paper is focused on solutions rather than problems. The great majority of software in use today is neither geriatric nor state of the art, and the tutorial addresses this type of software. It describes a top-down approach to successful maintenance, addressing:

(a) Software Maintenance and the organization
(b) Process models
(c) Technical Issues

In particular, we shall focus on the new proposed IEEE standard for software maintenance process, which illustrates the improving maturity of the field.

7. Organizational Aspects of Maintenance

In 1987, Colter (COLT87) stated that the major problem of software maintenance was not technical, but managerial. Software maintenance organizations were failing to relate their work to the needs of the business, and therefore it should not be a surprise that the field suffered from low investment and poor status, compared to initial development which was seen as a revenue and profit generator.

Initial software development is product-oriented; the aim is to deliver an artifact within budget and timescale. In contrast, software maintenance is much closer to a *service*. In many Japanese organizations, for example, (BENN94), software maintenance is seen at senior management level primarily as a means of ensuring continued satisfaction with the software; it is closely related to quality. The customer expects the software to continue to evolve to meet his or her changing needs, and the vendor must respond quickly and effectively or lose business. In Japan, it is also possible in certain circumstances to include software as an asset on the balance sheet. These combine to ensure that software maintenance has a high profile with senior management in Japan.

Like any other activity, software maintenance requires financial investment. We have already seen that within senior management, maintenance may be regarded simply as a drain on resources, or distant to core activities, and it becomes a prime candidate for funding reduction and even elimination. Software maintenance thus needs to be expressed in terms of return on investment. In many organizations undertaking maintenance for other internal divisions, the service is rarely charged out as a revenue-generating activity from a profit center. In the UK defense sector, there has been a major change in practice in charging for maintenance. Until recently, work would be charged to Government on the time taken to do the work plus a profit margin. Currently, competitive tendering (procurement) is used for specific work packages.

Recently there has been a trend for software maintenance to be *outsourced*; in other words, a company will contract out its software maintenance to another which specializes in this field. Companies in India and China are becoming increasingly competitive in this market. This is sometimes done for peripheral software, as the company is unwilling to release the software used in its core business. An outsourcing company will typically spend a number of months assessing the software before it will accept a contract. Increasingly, *service level agreements* between the maintenance organization (whether internal or external) and the customer are being used as a contractual mechanism for defining the maintenance service that will be provided. The UK Central Computer and Telecommunications Agency has produced a series of guidelines on good practice in this area, in the form of the Information Technology Infrastructure Library (ITIL93).

When new software is passed over to the customer, payment for subsequent maintenance must be determined. At this stage, primary concerns are typically:

- repair of errors on delivery
- changes to reflect an ambiguous specification

Increasingly, the former is being met by some form of warranty to bring software in line with other goods (although much commodity software is still ringed with disclaimers). Hence, the vendor pays. The latter is much more difficult to resolve and addresses much more than the functional specification. For example, if the software is not delivered in a highly maintainable form, there will be major cost implications for the purchaser.

Recently, Foster [FOST93] proposed an interesting investment cost model which regards software as a corporate asset which can justify financial support and sustain its value. Foster uses his model to determine the optimum release strategy for a major software system. This is hence a business model, allowing an organization the ability to calculate return on investment in software by methods comparable with investment in other kinds of assets. Foster remarks that many papers on software maintenance recognize that it is a little understood area, but it consumes vast amounts of money. With such large expenditure, even small technical advances must be worth many times that cost. The software maintenance manager, however, has to justify investment into an area which does not directly generate income. Foster's approach allows a manager to derive a model for assessing the financial implications of the proposed change of activity, thereby providing the means to calculate both cost and benefit. By expressing the result in terms of return on investment, the change can be ranked against competing demands for funding.

Some work has been undertaken in applying predictive cost modeling to software maintenance, based on the COCOMO techniques. The results of such work remain to be seen.

The AMES project [HATH94, BOLD94, BOLD95] is addressing the development of methods and tools to aid application management, where application management is defined as:

the contracted responsibility for the management and execution of all activities related to the maintenance of existing applications.

Its focus is on the formalization of many of the issues raised in this section, and in particular, customer-supplier relations. It is developing a maturity model to support the assessment in a quantitative and systematic way of this relationship.

8. Process Models

Process management [IEEE91] is defined as:

> the direction, control and coordination of work performed to develop a product or perform a service.

This definition therefore encompasses software maintenance and includes quality, line management, technical, and executive processes. A mature engineering discipline is characterized by mature well-understood processes, so it is understandable that modeling software maintenance, and integrating it with software development, is an area of active concern [MCDER91]. A software process model may be defined [DOWS85] as:

> a purely descriptive representation of the software process, representing the attributes of a range of particular software processes and being sufficiently specific to allow reasoning about them.

The foundation of good practice is a mature process, and the Software Engineering Institute at Carnegie-Mellon University has pioneered the development of a scale by which process maturity may be measured. A questionnaire approach is used to assess the maturity of an organization and also provides a metric for process improvement. More recently, the BOOTSTRAP project has provided an alternative maturity model from a European perspective.

A recent IEEE draft standard for software maintenance [IEEE94] promotes the establishment of better understood processes and is described in the next section. It reflects the difference between maintenance and initial development processes, and, although it is only a draft, it represents many of the elements of good practice in software maintenance. The model is based on an iterative approach of accepting a stream of change requests (and error reports), implementing the changes, and, after testing, forming new software releases. This model is widely used in industry, in small to medium-sized projects, and for in-house support. It comprises four key stages:

- **Help desk**: the problem is received, a preliminary analysis undertaken, and if the problem is sensible, it is accepted.
- **Analysis**: a managerial and technical analysis of the problem is undertaken to investigate and cost alternative solutions.
- **Implementation**: the chosen solution is implemented and tested.
- **Release:** the change (along with others) is released to the customer.

Most best practice models (for instance, that of Hinley [HINL92]) incorporate this approach, though it is often refined into much more detailed stages (as in the IEEE model described in the next section). Wider aspects of the software maintenance process, in the form of applications management, are addressed in [HATH94].

9. IEEE Standard for Software Maintenance

9.1 Overview of the standard

This new proposed standard describes the process for managing and executing software maintenance activities. Almost all the standard is relevant for software maintenance. The focus of the standard is in a seven stage activity model of software maintenance, which incorporates the following *stages*:

> Problem Identification
> Analysis
> Design
> Implementation
> System Test
> Acceptance Test
> Delivery

Each of the seven activities has five associated attributes; these are:

> Input life cycle products
> Output life cycle products
> Activity definition
> Control
> Metrics

A number of these, particularly in the early stages of the maintenance process, are already addressed by existing IEEE standards.

As an example, we consider the second activity in the process model, the *analysis phase*. This phase accepts as its input a validated problem report, together with any initial resource estimates and other repository information, plus project and system documentation if available. The process is seen as having two substantial components. First of all, feasibility analysis is undertaken which assesses the impact of the modification, investigates alternative solutions, assesses short and long term costs, and computes the benefit value of making the change. Once a particular approach has been selected, then the second stage of detailed analysis is undertaken. This determines firm requirements of the modification, identifies the software involved, and requires a test strategy and an implementation plan to be produced.

In practice, this is one of the most difficult stages of software maintenance. The change may effect many aspects of the software, including not only documentation, test suites, and so on, but also the environment and even the hardware. The standard insists that all affected components shall be identified and brought in to the scope of the change.

The standard also requires that at this stage a test strategy is derived comprising at least three levels of test, including unit testing, integration testing, and user-orientated functional acceptance tests. It is also required to supply regression test requirements associated with each of these levels of test.

9.2 Structure of the standard

The standard also establishes quality control for each of the seven phases. For example, for the analysis phase, the following controls are required as a minimum:

1. Retrieve the current version of project and systems documentation from the configuration control function of the organization

2. Review the proposed changes and an engineering analysis to assess the technical and economic feasibility and to assess correctness

3. Consider the integration of the proposed change within the existing software

4. Verify that all appropriate analysis and project documentation is updated and properly controlled

5. Verify that the testing organization is providing a strategy for testing the changes and that the change schedule can support the proposed test strategy

6. Review the resource estimates and schedules and verification of their accuracy

7. Undertake a technical review to select the problem reports and proposed enhancements

to be implemented and released. The list of changes shall be documented

Finally, at the end of the analysis phase, a risk analysis is required to be performed. Any initial resource estimate will be revised, and a decision that includes the customer is made on whether to proceed onto the next phase.

The phase deliverables are also specified, again as a minimum as follows:

1. Feasibility report for problem reports
2. Detailed analysis report
3. Updated requirements
4. Preliminary modification list
5. Development, integration and acceptance test strategy
6. Implementation plan

The contents of the analysis report is further specified in greater detail by the proposed standard.

The proposed standard suggests the following metrics are taken during the analysis phase:

Requirement changes
Documentation area rates
Effort per function area
Elapsed time
Error rates generated, by priority and type.

The proposed standard also includes appendices which provide guidelines on maintenance practice. These are not part of the standard itself, but are included as useful information. For example, in terms of our analysis stage, the appendix provides a short commentary on the provision of change on impact analysis. A further appendix addresses supporting maintenance technology, particularly re-engineering and reverse engineering. A brief description of these processes is also given.

9.3 Assessment of the Proposed Standard

The standard represents a welcome step forward in establishing a process standard for software maintenance. A strength of the approach is that it is based on existing IEEE standards from other areas in software engineering. It accommodates practical necessities, such as the need to undertake emergency repairs.

On the other hand, it is clearly oriented towards classic concepts of software development and maintenance. It does not cover issues such as rapid application development and end-user computing, nor does it address executive level issues in the process model nor establish boundaries for the scope of the model.

The process model corresponds approximately to level two in the SEI five level model. The SEI model is forming the basis of the SPICE process assessment standards initiative.

Organizations may well be interested in increasing the maturity of their software engineering processes. Neither the proposed IEEE standard nor the SEI model give direct help in process improvement. Further details of this may be found in [HINL92]. Additionally, there is still little evidence in practice that improving software process maturity actually benefits organizations, and the whole edifice is based on the assumption that the success of the product is determined by the process. That this is not necessarily true is demonstrated by the success of certain commodity software.

It is useful to note that the International Standards Organization [ISO90] have published a draft standard for a process model to assess the quality (including maintainability) of software. Many technical problems in measurement remain unsolved, however.

10. Technical Aspects of Software Maintenance

10.1 Technical issues

Much of the technology required for software maintenance is similar to that needed for initial development, but with minor changes. For example, configuration management and version control are indispensable for both. Information relating to development and maintenance will be kept in a repository. For maintenance, the repository will be used to hold frequently occurring queries handled by the help desk. Metrics data for product and process will be similar. CASE tools, supporting graphical representation of software, are widely used in development and maintenance. These topics are described in other Chapters, and here we concentrate on issues of specific importance to maintenance.

In our description of the IEEE standard process model we identified the need for impact analysis. This is a characteristic of software maintenance that is not needed in initial software development. We shall present further details of this technique as an example of the technology needed to support software maintenance.

In the above process model, it was necessary to determine the cost of making a change to meet a software change request. In this section we examine how impact analysis can help this activity. To amplify the analysis needed, the user-expressed problem must first

of all be translated into software terms to allow the maintenance team to decide if the problem is viable for further work or if it should be rejected. It then must be localized; this step determines the origin of the anomaly by identifying the primary components to the system which must be altered to meet the new requirement.

Next, the above step may suggest several solutions, all of which are viable. Each of these must be investigated, primarily using impact analysis. The aim is to determine all changes which are consequence to the primary change. It must be applied to all software components, not just code. At the end of impact analysis, we are in the position to make a decision on the best implementation route or to make no change. Weiss [WEIS 89] has shown, for three NASA projects, the primary source of maintenance changes deriving from user problem reports:

Requirements Phase	19 percent
Design Phase	52 percent
Coding Phase	7 percent

He noted that 34 percent of changes affected only one component and 26 percent affected two components.

10.2 The Problem

One of the major difficulties of software maintenance which encourages maintainers to be cautious is that a change made at one place in the system may have a ripple effect elsewhere, so consequence changes must be made. In order to carry out a consistent change, maintainers must investigate all such ripple effects, such as the impact of the change assessed and changes possibly made in all affected contexts. Yau [YAU87] defines this as:

ripple effect propagation is a phenomenon by which changes made to a software component along the software life cycle (specification, design, code, or test phase) have a tendency to be felt in other components.

As a very simple example, a maintainer may wish to remove a redundant variable X. It is obviously necessary to also remove all applied occurrences of X, but for most high level languages the compiler can detect and report undeclared variables. This is hence a very simple example of an impact which can be determined by *static analysis*. In many cases, ripple effects cannot determine statically, and dynamic analysis must be used. For example, an assignment to an element of an array, followed by the use of a subscripted variable, may or may not represent a ripple effect depending on the particular elements accessed. In large programs containing pointers aliases, for instance, the problem is much harder. We shall define the problem of impact analysis [WILD93] as:

the task for assessing the effects for making the set of changes to a software system.

The starting point for impact analysis is an explicit set of primary software objects which the maintainer intends to modify. He or she has determined the set by relating the change request to objects such as variables, assignments, goals, an so on. The purpose of impact analysis is ensuring that the change has been correctly and consistently bounded. The impact analysis stage identifies a set of further objects impacted by changes in the primary sector. This process is repeated until no further candidate objects can be identified.

10.3 Traceability

In general, we require traceability of information between various software artifacts in order to assess impact in software components. Traceability is defined [IEEE91] as:

Traceability is a degree to which a relationship can be established between two or more products of the development process, especially products having a predecessor successor or master subordinate relationship to one another.

Informally, traceability provides us with semantic links which we can then use to perform impact analysis. The links may relate similar components such as design documents or they may link between different types such as a specification to code.

Some types of traceability links are very hard to determine. For example, even a minor alteration of the source code may have performance implications which causes a real time system to fail to meet a specification. It is not surprising that the majority of work in impact analysis has been undertaken at the code level, as this is the most tractable. Wilde [WILD89] provides a good review of code level impact analysis techniques.

Many modern programming languages are based on using static analysis to detect or stop ripple effect. The use of modules with opaque types, for example, can prevent at compile time several unpleasant types of ripple effect. Many existing software systems are unfortunately written in older languages, using programming styles (such as global aliased variables) which make the potential for ripple effects much greater, and their detection much harder.

More recently, Munro and Turver [TURV94] have described an approach which has placed impact analysis within the overall software maintenance process. The major advance is that documentation is included within the objects analyzed; documentation is modeled using a ripple propagation graph and it is this representation that is used for analysis. The approach has the advantage that it may be set in the early stages of analysis to assess costs without reference to the source code.

Work has also been undertaken recently to establish traceability links between HOOD design documents [FILL94] in order to support impact analysis of the design level.

In a major research project at Durham, formal semantic preserving transformations are being used to derive executable code from formal specifications and in reverse engineering to derive specifications from existing code. The ultimate objective is to undertake maintenance at the specification level rather than the code level, and generate executable code automatically or semi-automatically. The transformation technique supports the derivation of the formal traceability link between the two representations, and research is underway to explore this as a means of enhancing ripple effect across wider sections of the life cycle (see WARD93, WARD94, WARD94a, YOUN94, BENN95, BENN95b for more details).

11. Legacy Systems

11.1 Legacy problems

There is no standard definition of a legacy system; but many in industry will recognize the problem. A legacy system is typically very old, and has been heavily modified over the years to meet continually evolving needs. It is also very large, so that a team is needed to support it; although none of the original members of the software development team may still be around. It will be based on old technology, and be written in out-of-date languages such as Assembler. Documentation will not be available and testing new releases is a major difficulty. Often the system is supporting very large quantities of live data.

Such systems are surely a candidate for immediate replacement. The problem is that the software is often at the core of the business and replacing it would be a huge expense. While less than ideal, the software works and continues to do useful things.

An example of a legacy system is the billing software for a telecommunications company. The software was developed many years ago when the company was owned by the Government, and the basic service sold was restricted to a telephone connection to each premises. The system is the main mechanism for generating revenue and it supports a huge on-line database of paying customers.

Over the years the software has been maintained to reflect the changing telecommunications business: from government to private ownership; from simple call charging to wide ranging and complex (and competitive) services; from single country to international organizations with highly complex VAT (value added tax) systems. The system now comprises several million lines of source code.

While the process of maintenance to meet continually evolving customer needs is becoming better understood, and more closely linked with software engineering in general, dealing with legacy software is still very hard. It has been estimated that there are 70 billion lines of COBOL in existence that are still doing useful work. Much of the useful software being written today will end up as legacy software in 20 years time. Software which is 40 years old is being used in mission critical applications.

It is easy to argue that the industry should never have ended up in the position of relying on such software. It is unclear whether steps are being taken to avoid the problem for modern software. There seems to be a hope that technology such as object-oriented design will solve the problems for future generations, though there is as yet little positive evidence.

In this section, we shall analyze why it might be useful not just to discard the legacy system and start again. In the subsequent section, we shall present solutions to dealing with legacy systems.

11.2 Analysis of legacy systems

In some cases, discarding the software and starting again may be the courageous, although expensive, solution following analysis of the business need and direction and the state of the software. Often the starting point is taking an inventory of the software, as this may be unknown. As a result of analysis, the following solutions for the legacy system may be considered:

- carry on as now, possibly subcontracting the maintenance.
- replace software with a package.
- re-implement from scratch.
- discard software and discontinue.

- freeze maintenance and phase in new system.
- encapsulate the old system and call as a server to the new.
- reverse engineer the legacy system and develop a new software suite.

In the literature, case studies addressing these types of approaches are becoming available. The interest of this tutorial is focused on reverse engineering, as it appears to be the most fruitful approach. Increasing interest is being shown in encapsulation as a way of drawing a boundary round the legacy system. The new system is then evolved so that it progressively takes over functionality from the old, until the latter becomes redundant. Currently, few successful studies have been published, but it is consistent with the move to distributed open systems based on client-server architectures.

11.3 Reverse Engineering

Chikofsky and Cross [CHIK90] have defined several terms in this field which are now generally accepted. Reverse engineering is:

the process of analyzing a subject system to identify the system's components and their inter-relationships, and to create representations of the system in another form or at higher levels of abstraction.

It can be seen that reverse engineering is *passive*; it does not change the system, or result in a new one, though it may add new representations to it. For example, a simple reverse engineering tool may produce call graphs and control flow graphs from source code. These are both higher level abstractions, though in neither case is the original source code changed. Two important types of reverse engineering are redocumentation, which is:

the creation or revision of a semantically equivalent representation within the same relative abstraction layer;

and design recovery, which:

involves identifying meaningful higher level abstractions beyond those obtained directly by examining the system itself.

The main motivation is to provide help in program comprehension; most maintainers have little choice but to work with source codes in the absence of any documentation. Concepts such as procedure structures and control flow are important mechanisms by which the maintainer understands the system, so tools have been constructed to provide representations to help the process.

If good documentation existed (including architectural, design, and test suite documentation) reverse engineering would be unnecessary. However, the types of documentation needed for maintenance are probably different than those produced during typical initial development. As an example, most large systems are too big for one person to maintain; yet the maintainer rarely needs to see a functional decomposition or object structure; he or she is trying to correlate external behavior within internal descriptions. In these circumstances, *slicing* offers help: slicing is a static analysis technique in which only those source code statements which can affect a nominated variable are displayed.

Pragmatically, many maintainers cover lineprinter listings with notes and stick-on pieces of paper. In an attempt to simulate this, Foster and Munro [FOST87] and Younger [YOUN93] have built tools to implement a hypertext form of documentation which is managed incrementally by the maintainer who is able to attach "notes" to the source code. An advantage of this approach is that it does not attempt to redocument the whole system; documentation is provided by the maintainer, in the form preferred, only for the "hotspots." Those parts of the code which are stable, and are never studied by the maintainer (often large parts), do not have to be redocumented, thereby saving money.

For a description of a reverse engineering method, see [EDWA95].

11.4 Program comprehension

Program comprehension is a topic in its own right and has stimulated an annual IEEE workshop. Documentation is also an active area; see for example Knuth's WEB [KNUT84], and also Gilmore [GILM90] for details of issues concerned with psychology. In [YOUN93], there is a useful list of criteria for software maintenance documentation:

- integrated source code, via traceability links
- integrated call graphs, control graphs, etc.
- integration of existing documentation (if any)
- incremental documentation
- informal update by maintainer.
- quality assurance on the documentation.
- configuration management and version control of all representations.

- information hiding to allow abstraction
- team use.

It may be decided that active change of the legacy system is needed. Restructuring is:

the transformation from one representation to another at the same relative level of abstraction, while preserving the system's external behavior.

Lehman's second law argues that such remedial action is essential in a system which is undergoing maintenance; otherwise, the maintainability will degrade and the cost of maintenance correspondingly increases. Examples include:

- control flow restructuring to remove "spaghetti" code.
- converting monolithic code to use parameterized procedures.
- identifying modules and abstract data types.
- removing dead code and redundant variables.
- simplifying aliased/common and global variables

Finally, Re-engineering is:

the examination and alteration of the subject system to reconstitute it in a new form, and the subsequent implementation of the new form.

Re-engineering is the most radical (and expensive) form of alteration. It is not likely to be motivated simply by wanting more maintainable software. For example, owners of on-line systems produced in the 1960s and 1970s would like to replace the existing character based input/output with a modern graphical user interface. This is usually very difficult to achieve, so it may be necessary to undertake substantial redesign.

11.5 Reverse and re-engineering

In [BENN93], a list of 26 decision criteria for considering reverse engineering is presented. In abbreviated form, these are:

Management criteria

- enforcing product and process standards (such as the IEEE draft standard introduced above)

- permit better maintenance management
- legal contesting of reverse engineering legislation
- better audit trails

Quality criteria

- simplification of complex software
- facilitating detection of errors
- removing side effects
- improve code quality
- undertaking major design repair correction
- production of up-to-date documentation
- preparing full test suites
- improving performance
- bringing into line with practices elsewhere in the company
- financial auditing
- facilitate quality audits (such as ISO9000)

Technical criteria

- to allow major changes to be made
- to discover the underlying business model
- to discover the design, and requirements specification
- to port the system
- to establish a reuse library
- to introduce technical innovation such as fault tolerance or graphic interfaces
- to reflect evolving maintenance processes
- to record many different types of high level representations
- to update tool support
- disaster recovery

It is useful to amplify two of the above points. Firstly, many legacy systems represent years of accumulated experience, and this experience may now no longer be represented anywhere else. Systems analysis cannot start with humans and hope to introduce automation; the initial point is the software which contains the business rules.

Secondly, it is not obvious that a legacy system, which has been modified over many years, does actually have a high level, coherent representation. Is it simply the original system plus the aggregation of many accumulated changes? The evidence is not so pessimistic. The current system reflects a model of current reality, and it is that model we are trying to discover.

11.6 Techniques

Work on simplifying control flow and data flow graphs has been undertaken for many years. A very early result showed that any control graph (for instance, using unstructured goto's) can be restructured into a semantically equivalent form using sequences, if-then-else-if conditionals, and loops, although this may cause flag variables to be introduced. A good review of this type of approach can be found in the Redo Compendium [ZUYL93]. This work is generally mature, and commercial tools exist for extracting, displaying, and manipulating graphical representations of source code. In [WARD93], an approach using formal transformations is described which is intended to support the human maintainer, rather than act as a fully automated tool. This work shows that much better simplification is achievable, such as the conversion of monolithic code with aliased variables to well-structured code using parameterized procedures.

Much research in reverse engineering, especially in the USA, has been based on the program plan or cliché approach, pioneered by Rich and Waters [RICH90]. This is based on the recognition that many programs use a relatively small number of generic design ideas, which tend to be used over and over again. Reverse engineering should then attempt to find such plans in existing source code by matching from a set of patterns in a library. This would appear to have had some modest success, but there are many open issues. For example, how should patterns be represented? How generic are they? And how good is the matching process? This approach shares many of the problems of libraries of reusable components.

Most researchers aim to make their approach source language independent, so that different languages may be handled by adding front ends. Thus, design of intermediate languages is an important issue. In [ZUYL93], an approach called UNIFORM is described.

Ward [WARD93] uses a formally defined wide spectrum language WSL as the heart of his system. A wide spectrum language is used as the representational format because only one language is then needed for both low and high levels of abstractions and intermediary points. The approach has been shown to work for large (80K line) assembler programs and also for very challenging benchmark cases such as the Schorr-Waite graph-marking algorithm.

Further details are given in [BULL92] and [BULL94]. ([BULL94] also contains a useful review of other transformation systems).

Cimitile and his colleagues have done research on producing tools and methods for discovering abstract data types in existing code [CANF94]. Sneed [SNEE91, as well asNYAR95, SNEE93], has presented his experience in reverse engineering large commercial COBOL systems using partial tool support.

It is encouraging to observe that most new promising approaches to reverse engineering address two basic properties of legacy systems:

- they are very large, and "toy" solutions are not applicable

- they must be taken as they are, not how the engineer would like them to be. Often this means "on-off" solutions.

12. Research Questions

Although software maintenance tends to be regarded in academic circles as of minor importance, it is of major commercial and industrial significance. It is useful to end the tutorial with a brief review of promising trends.

There are many interesting research problems to be solved which can lead to important commercial benefits. There are also some grand challenges which lie at the heart of software engineering.

How do we change software quickly, reliably, and safely? In safety critical systems for example, enormous effort is expended in producing and validating software. If we wish to make a minor change to the software, do we have to repeat the entire validation or can we make the cost of the change proportionally in some way to its size? There are several well publicized cases where very minor changes to important software has caused major crashes and failures in service. A connected problem lies in the measurement of how easily new software can be changed. Without this, it is difficult to purchase software knowing that a reduced purchase price may mean enormous maintenance costs later on. Almost certainly, solution to this problem will involve addressing process issues as well as attributes of the product itself. This is a major problem for Computer Science. A new approach is described in [SMIT95].

In practice, much existing software has evolved in ad-hoc ways and has suffered the fate predicted by Lehman's laws. Despite its often central role of many organizations, such legacy systems provide a major headache. Management and technical solutions are needed to address the problems of legacy systems; otherwise, we shall be unable to move forward and introduce new technology because of our commitments and dependence on old technology.

It is often thought that the move to end-user computing, open systems, and client service systems will remove this problem. In practice, it may well make it considerably worse. A system which is comprised of many components, from many different sources by horizontal and vertical integration, and possibly across a widely distributed network, poses major problems when any of those components change. For further details of this issue, see [BENN94b].

13. Professional support

Over the last 10 years, professional activity in software maintenance has increased considerably. The annual International Conference on Software Maintenance, sponsored by the IEEE, represents the major venue which brings academics and practitioners together to discuss and present the latest results and experiences. Also relevant is the IEEE workshop on program comprehension. The proceedings of both conferences are published by the IEEE Computer Society Press.

In Europe, the main annual event is the annual European workshop on Software maintenance, organized in Durham. This is mainly aimed at practitioners, and again the proceedings are published.

The *Journal of Software Maintenance — Practice & Experience*, which appears bi-monthly, acts as a journal of record for significant research and practice advances in the field.

Finally, aspects of software maintenance are increasingly being taught in University courses, and PhD graduates are starting to appear who have undertaken research in the field.

14. Conclusions

We have described a three level approach to considering software maintenance in terms of the impact on the organization, on the process, and on technology supporting that process. This has provided a framework in which to consider maintenance. Much progress has been made in all three areas and we have described briefly recent work on the establishment of a standard maintenance process model. The adoption of such models, along with formal process assessment and improvement, will do much to improve the best practice and average practice in the software maintenance.

We have also described a major problem that distinguishes software maintenance: coping with legacy systems. We have presented several practical techniques for addressing such systems.

Thus we have presented software maintenance not as a problem but as a solution. However, there are still major research issues of strategic industrial importance to be solved. We have defined these as, firstly, to learn how to evolve software quickly and cheaply; and secondly, how to deal with large legacy systems. When a modern technology such as object-oriented systems claim to improve the situation, the claim is based largely on hope with little evidence of actual improvement. Such technology may introduce new maintenance problems (see for example [SMIT92, TURN93, TURN95] for new testing methods associated with object oriented programs). As usual, there are no magic bullets, and the Japanese principle of *Kaizen*—the progressive and incremental improvement of practices—is likely to be more successful.

Acknowledgments

Much of the work at Durham in Software Maintenance has been supported by SERC (now EPSRC) and DTI funding, together with major grants from IBM and British Telecom. I am grateful to colleagues at Durham for discussions which lead to ideas presented in this paper, in particular to Martin Ward and Malcolm Munro. A number of key ideas have arisen from discussions with Pierrick Fillon. Thanks are due to Cornelia Boldyreff for reading drafts of this paper.

References

BABE91 Baber R.L., "Epilogue: Future Developments," in *Software Engineer's Reference Book*, ed. McDermid, Butterworth-Heinemann, 1991.

BENN93 Bennett, K.H., "An Overview of Maintenance and Reverse Engineering," in *The REDO Compendium*, ed. van Zuylen, Wiley, 1993.

BENN94 Bennett, K.H., "Software Maintenance in Japan." Report published under the auspices of the U.K. Department of Trade and Industry, Sept. 1994. Available from the Computer Science Department, University of Durham, South Road, Durham, DH1 3LE, UK.

BENN94b Bennett, K.H., "Theory and Practice of Middle-out Programming to Support Program Understanding," *Proc IEEE Conf. Program Comprehension*, IEEE Computer Society Press, Los Alamitos, Calif., 1994, pp. 168–175.

BENN95 Bennett, K.-H. and Ward, M.P. "Formal Methods for Legacy Systems," *J. Software Maintenance: Research and Practice*, Vol. 7, No. 3, May-June 1995, pp. 203–219.

BENN95b Bennett, K.H. and Yang, H., "Acquisition of ERA Models from Data Intensive Code," *Proc IEEE Int'l Conf. Software Maintenance*, IEEE Computer Society Press, Los Alamitos, Calif., 1995, pp. 116–123.

BOLD94 Boldyreff C., Burd E., and Hather R., "An Evaluation of the State of the Art for Application Management," *Proc. Int'l Conf. Software Maintenance*, IEEE Computer Society Press, Los Alamitos, Calif., 1994, pp. 161–169.

BOLD95 Boldyreff, C., Burd E., Hather R.M., Mortimer R.E., Munro M., and Younger E.J., "The AMES Approach to Application Understanding: A Case Study," *Proc. Int'l Conf. Software Maintenance*, IEEE Computer Society Press, Los Alamitos, Calif, 1995, pp. 182-191.

BULL94 Bull, T., "Software Maintenance by Program Transformation in a Wide Spectrum Language, PhD. thesis, Department of Computer Science, University of Durham. 1994.

BULL92 Bull, T.M., Bennett, K.H., and Yang, H., "A Transformation System for Maintenance—Turning Theory into Practice," *Proc. IEEE Conf. Software Maintenance*, IEEE Computer Society Press, Los Alamitos, Calif., 1992, pp. 146–155.

CANF94 Canfora, G., Cimitile, A., and Munro, M., "RE2: Reverse Engineering and Reuse Re-engineering," *J. Software Maintenance: Research & Practice*, Vol. 6, No. 2, Mar.-Apr. 1994, pp. 53–72.

COLT87 Colter, M., "The Business of Software Maintenance," *Proc. 1st Workshop Software Maintenance*, University of Durham, Durham, 1987. Available from the Computer Science Department (see BENN94).

DOWS85 Dowson M. and Wilden J.C., "A Brief Report on the International Workshop on the Software Process and Software Environment," *ACM Software Engineering Notes*, Vol. 10, 1985, pp. 19–23.

EDWA95 Edwards, H.M., Munro M., and West, R., "The RECAST Method for Reverse Engineering," Information Systems Engineering Library, CCTA, HMSO, ISBN:1 85 554705 8, 1995.

FILL94 Fillon P., "An Approach to Impact Analysis in Software Maintenance," MSc. Thesis, University of Durham, 1994.

FOST87 Foster, J. and Munro, M., "A Documentation Method Based on Cross-Referencing," *Proc. IEEE Conf. Software Maintenance*, IEEE Computer Society Press, Los Alamitos, Calif., 1987.

FOST93 Foster, J., "Cost Factors in Software Maintenance," PhD thesis, Computer Science Department, University of Durham, 1993.

GILM90 Gilmore, D., "Expert Programming Knowledge: A Strategic Approach," in *Psychology of Programming*, Hoc, J.M., Green, T.R.G., Samurcay, R., and Gilmore, D.J., Ed., Academic Press, New York, N.Y., 1990.

HATH94 Hather, R, Burd, L., and Boldyreff, C., "A Method for Application Management Maturity Assessment," *Proc. Centre for Software Reliability Conference*, 1994 (to be published).

HINL92 Hinley, D.S. and Bennett K.H., "Developing a Model to Manage the Software Maintenance Process," *Proc. Conf. Software Maintenance,* IEEE Computer Society Press, Los Alamitos, Calif, 1992, pp. 174–182.

IEEE91 IEEE Std. 610.12-1990, *IEEE Standard Glossary of Software Engineering Terminology*, IEEE, 1991, New York.

IEEE94 *IEEE Standard for Software Maintenance* (unapproved draft). IEEE ref. P1219, IEEE, 1994, New York.

ISO90 "Information Technology—Software Product Evaluation—Quality Characteristics and Guidlelines for Their Use," International Standards Organization ISO/IEC JTC1 Draft International Standard 9126.

ITIL93 Central Computer & Telecommunications Agency, "The IT Infrastructure Library," CCTA, Gildengate House, Upper Green Lane, Norwich, NR3 1DW.

KNUT84 Knuth, D.E., "Literate Programming," *Comp. J.*, Vol. 27, No. 2, 1984, pp. 97–111.

LEHE80 Lehman, M.M., "Programs, Lifecycles and the Laws of Software Evolution," *Proc. IEEE*, Vol. 19, 1980, pp. 1060–1076.

LEHE84 Lehman, M.M., "Program Evolution," *Information Processing Management*, Vol. 20, 1984, pp. 19–36.

LEIN78 Lientz, B., Swanson, E.B., and Tompkins, G.E., "Characteristics of Applications Software Maintenance" *Comm. ACM*, Vol. 21, 1978, pp. 466–471.

LEIN80 Leintz, B. and Swanson, E.B., *Software Maintenance Management*, Addison-Wesley, Reading, Mass., 1980.

McDER91 SERB McDermid J., ed., *Software Enginering Reference Book*, Butterworth-Heinemann, 1991.

LEVE93 Leveson N.G. and Turner C.S., "An Investigation of the Therac-25 Accidents," *Computer*, Vol. 26, No. 7, July 1993, pp. 18–41.

NYAR95 Nyary E. and Sneed H., "Software Maintenance Offloading at the Union Bank of Switzerland," *Proc IEEE Int'l Conf. Software Maintenance,* IEEE Computer Society Press, Los Alamitos, Calif., 1995, pp. 98–108.

RICH90 Rich, C. and Waters, R.C., *The Programmer's Apprentice*, Addison-Wesley, Reading, Mass., 1990.

ROBS91 Robson, D.J. et al., "Approaches to Program Comprehension," *J. Systems Software*, Vol. 14, No. 1, 1991.

SMIT92 Smith M.D. and Robson D.J., "A Framework for Testing Object-Oriented Programs," *J. Object-Oriented Programming*, Vol. 5, No. 3, June 1992, pp. 45–53.

SMIT95 Smith S.R., Bennett K.H., and Boldyreff C., "Is Maintenance Ready for Evolution?" *Proc. IEEE Int'l Conference Software Maintenance*, IEEE Computer Society Press, Los Alamitos, Calif., 1995, pp. 367–372.

SNEE91 Sneed H., "Economics of Software Re-engineering," *J. Software Maintenance: Research and Practice*, Vol. 3, No. 3, Sept. 1991, pp. 163–182.

SNEE93 Sneed H. and Nyary E., "Downsizing Large Application Programs," *Proc. IEEE Int'l Conf. Software Maintenance,* IEEE Computer Society Press, Los Alamitos, Calif., 1993, pp. 110–119.

TURN93 Turner C.D. and Robson D.J., "The State-based Testing of Object-Oriented Programs," Proc. *IEEE Conf. Software Maintenance*, IEEE Computer Society Press, Los Alamitos, Calif., 1993, pp. 302–310.

TURN95 Turner C.D. and Robson D.J., "A State-Based Approach to the Testing of Class-Based Programs," *Software—Concepts and Tools*, Vol 16, No. 3, 1995, pp. 106-112.

TURV94 Turver R.J. and Munro M., "An Early Impact Analysis technique for Software Maintenance, *J. Software Maintenance: Research and Practice*, Vol. 6, No. 1, Jan. 1994, pp. 35–52.

WALT94 Walton D.S., "Maintainability Metrics," *Proc. Centre for Software Reliability Conf.*, Dublin, 1994. Available from Centre for Software Reliability, City University, London, UK.

WARD93 Ward M.P., "Abstracting a Specification from Code," *J. Software Maintenance: Practice and Experience*, Vol. 5, No. 2, June 1993, pp. 101–122.

WARD94 Ward M.P., "Reverse Engineering through Formal Transformation," *Computer J.*, Vol. 37, No 9, 1994.

WARD94a Ward M.P., "Language Oriented Programming," *Software—Concepts and Tools*, Vol. 15, 1994, pp. 147–161.

WEIS89 Weiss D.M., "Evaluating Software Development by Analysis of Change," PhD dissertation, Univ. of Maryland, USA.

WILD93 Wilde N., "Software Impact Analysis: Processes and Issues," Durham University Technical Report 7/93, 1993.

YAU87 Yau S.S. and Liu S., "Some Approaches to Logical Ripple Effect Analysis," Technical Report, SERC, USA, 1987.

YOUN93 Younger, E., "Documentation," in *The REDO Compendium*, van Zuylen, ed., Wiley, 1993.

YOUN94 Younger E. and Ward M.P., "Inverse Engineering a Simple Real Time Program," *J. Software Maintenance: Research and Practice*, Vol. 6, 1994, pp. 197–234.

ZUYL90 van Zuylen, H., ed., *The REDO Compendium*, Wiley, 1993.

Chapter 9

Software Quality and Quality Assurance

1. Introduction to Chapter

Software quality assurance (SQA), unlike verification and validation, is primarily concerned with assuring the quality of the software development process rather than the quality of the product. Quality assurance includes development standards and the methods and procedures used in ensuring that the standards are complied with. IEEE Standard 610.12-1990 [1] provides two definitions for software quality assurance:

- A planned and systematic pattern of all actions necessary to provide adequate confidence that an item or product conforms to established technical requirements
- A set of activities designed to evaluate the process by which products are developed or manufactured

SQA cannot be properly implemented without the use of *standards*. Standards are accepted procedures for describing a process or product. Standards exist in order that there be a common understanding of how something should be developed or what attributes it should possess at delivery.

Software standards are primarily (but not entirely) documentation standards. Proper documentation of software products (such as requirements specifications, project plans, code, and test procedures) is a very critical part of software engineering. Software is invisible; documentation makes it visible. Product visibility makes it possible to track progress against the project's plans.

Often included with quality assurance in the category of process assurance is software configuration management. *Configuration management* (CM) is a discipline for applying technical and administrative direction and surveillance in order to [1]:

SOFTWARE QUALITY AND QUALITY ASSURANCE

DIGERNESS 91

305

- Identify and document the functional and physical characteristics of a configuration item
- Control characteristics of those items
- Record and report change processing and implementation status
- Verify compliance with specified requirements

Configuration management is also the mechanism for maintaining the various baselines. The elements of configuration management are (adapted from IEEE Standard 610.12-1990 [2]:

- *Configuration Item*—Any aggregation of a hardware/software system, or any of its portions, that satisfies an end-use function and is designated by the customer or developer for configuration management.

- *Configuration identification*—The process of designating the hardware/software configuration items in a system and recording their characteristics.

- *Configuration control*—The process of evaluating, approving or disapproving, and coordinating changes to hardware/software configuration items after formal establishment of their configuration identification.

- *Configuration status accounting*—The recording and reporting of the information that is needed to manage a hardware/software configuration effectively, including a listing of the approved configuration identification, the status of proposed changes to configuration, and the implementation status of approved changes.

- *Configuration auditing*—The process of verifying that all required hardware/software configuration items have been produced, that the current version agrees with specified requirements, that the technical documentation completely and accurately describes the configuration items, and that all change requests have been resolved.

- *Configuration control board* (CCB)—The authority responsible for evaluating and approving or disapproving proposed engineering changes to the hardware/software configuration that are under formal configuration control, and ensuring implementation of the approved changes.

- *Software development library*—A software library containing computer-readable and

human-readable information relevant to a software development effort.

CM is sometimes grouped into formal CM and informal CM.

Formal configuration management (also called external CM or baseline CM) is used to manage the configuration between the customer/user and the developer. CM is also frequently used to maintain the configuration after delivery during the maintenance and operations phase of the life cycle. The configuration control board is the agency responsible for managing the configuration.

Informal configuration management (also called internal CM or developmental CM) is used for maintaining configuration control for products under development, such as plans, specifications, versions, test procedures and test results, and deliverable (but not yet delivered) documents. The project manager acts as the CCB and an individual called the product support librarian provides the accounting and auditing.

2. Overview of Papers

The first paper in this chapter is an original article by Patricia Hurst of Fastrak Training, Inc. Hurst reviews the history of software quality assurance (SQA) and its role in software development. She provides a number of reasons for developers to practice good SQA, ranging from a moral obligation to develop a high-quality product to the pressures of competition. She surveys current world-wide initiatives in software quality improvement and provides two definitions, one comparatively narrow and one broad, of SQA.

Next Hurst describes those SQA functions carried out across an entire development organization as well as on a particular project. Finally she reviews how a software developer would organize and carry out the SQA functions. She also notes that an effective program of software quality assurance has proven to be cost-effective in many environments.

The next paper dates from 1984 but is still the best overview of software configuration management (SCM). Ed Bersoff defines configuration management as the discipline of identifying the configuration of a system at discrete points in time for the purpose of systematically controlling changes to the configuration and maintaining the integrity and traceability of the configuration throughout the system life cycle. Configuration management keeps track of the various artifacts developed during the lifetime of a software project through identifying, controlling, auditing, and status accounting of the various software development products.

Bersoff reminds us that controlling code is *not*

enough; the documentation that enables us to use and operate the code must also be controlled. This paper also provides a lengthy description of the program support library (PSL). Bersoff discusses the major problems involved in deciding how to properly manage the software configuration: too much control is cumbersome; too little control invites disaster.

The third paper in this chapter is entitled "Evaluating Software Engineering Standards" and was written by Shari Lawrence Pfleeger, Norm Fenton, and Stella Page of the Center for Software Reliability at the University of London. While not specifically a tutorial paper as described in the Preface, this paper does provide a definition of standards and an overview of the types of standards, their presumed benefits, and a comparison of the characteristics of software standards with those in other fields of specialization. The paper then reports on a study of the effectiveness of standards in industrial practice. The study revealed that in many cases it was impossible to determine whether or not the standards were being followed (because compliance was not testable); that in cases where compliance was testable, management was not aware that compliance was less than complete; and that software standards, far more than those in other fields, apply to the process of development rather than to the final product. The authors also conclude that progress is needed in defining, collecting, and analyzing software metrics before the effectiveness of standards can be judged adequately—an excellent lead-in to the metrics articles in Chapter 12 of this Tutorial.

The authors note that the body of software standards is large and growing: as of the date of the article there were over 250 software engineering standards worldwide, and the IEEE computer society typically completes several new standards or revisions per year. At the time of this writing, the US Department of Defense is in the midst of a major initiative to reduce the use of standards and specifications that are peculiar to the military environment, and to use commercial standards, especially process standards, wherever possible. Thus, the highly dynamic nature of the body of software standards can be expected to continue.

To provide a benchmark on the status of standards as of the date of this Tutorial, one of the editors (Richard Thayer) has surveyed and listed the software standards currently available worldwide. This survey is included as an Appendix to the Tutorial.

The last paper in the chapter was written by John Musa and William Everett of AT&T Bell Laboratories. It introduces a discipline that the authors call *software reliability engineering*. The authors include a number of activities, taking place during all phases of the life cycle, as part of software-reliability engineering, for example:

- Defining the quality factors (reliability and others) that the software should attain
- Helping determine the architecture and process to meet the reliability goal
- Predicting reliability from the product and process
- Measuring the reliability during testing
- Managing reliability during operations and maintenance
- Using measured reliability to improve the development process

Musa and Everett distinguish between *failures* (behavior of the software that does not meet requirements) and *faults* (the defects in the code that cause the failures). They note that failures can be measured by execution time or by calendar time, and that all faults are not equally likely to cause failures—faults in software functions that are used more frequently by the end user will cause more failures than faults in less-used functions. It should also be noted that not all failures are equal: failures in critical functions may be of more consequence to the users.

By orienting the test program toward critical functions and portions of the program executed most frequently, it is possible to leverage testing to eliminate a higher percentage of the failures that will occur in operations and that will be of greatest consequence to the users.

Finally, the authors define areas where research may bring about further improvement in the discipline of software-reliability engineering. They rate reliability prediction as the most important research area. Estimation of the number of faults in the software at the start of testing (based on errors found in earlier phases) and estimating failure intensity during unit testing are also promising areas.

1. IEEE Standard 610.12-1990, *IEEE Standard Glossary of Software Engineering Terminology*, The Institute of Electrical and Electronics Engineers, Inc., Piscataway, NJ, 1990.

2. IEEE Standard 610.12-1990, *IEEE Standard Glossary of Software Engineering Terminology*, The Institute of Electrical and Electronics Engineers, Inc., Piscataway, NJ, 1990.

Software Quality Assurance: A Survey of an Emerging View

Patricia W. Hurst

Fastrak Training, Inc.

Columbia, MD

Abstract

Since the mid 1980s, the term "quality assurance" has assumed increasing importance in the software development industry. The once accepted practice of relying on back-end testing to assure quality is fading with the recognition that quality must be addressed from conception, through development, and throughout the maintenance activities. Quality programs are being organized and implemented by many organizations using the Capability Maturity Model developed by the Software Engineering Institute for guidance. This survey article provides a historical perspective and rationale for quality assurance, discusses U. S. and international initiatives to improve quality, defines an emerging view of quality assurance as a subset of a broader Quality Management concern, defines the functions required for a Quality Management program, and presents an organizational structure to support these functions.

INTRODUCTION

Since the mid 1980s, the term "quality assurance" has assumed increasing importance in the software development industry. It is being recognized that quality must be addressed throughout the software life cycle in order to supply software products which meet the needs of our society and its consumers. The once accepted practice of relying on back-end testing of the product to assure quality is fading with the recognition that quality must be addressed from conception, through development, and throughout the maintenance activities.

This recognition has not been sudden, but has emerged over the decades since software was first produced in the 1940s. This emergence has occurred as many software products and systems have repeatedly failed to meet expectations in terms of costs, schedules, functionality, and corrective maintenance. These failed expectations have continued in spite of numerous improvements in platforms, operating systems, languages, development methodologies, computer-aided software engineering (CASE) tools, and management practices. The industry has diligently searched for a "silver bullet" to eliminate the nightmares experienced by developers. However, the community is learning, as has virtually every other area of engineering, that advances in quality and productivity do not occur simply through new technologies. Rather, improvement requires attention to the processes used to develop and maintain software products.

This survey article provides a historical perspective and rationale for quality assurance, discusses U. S. and international initiatives to improve quality, defines an emerging view of quality assurance as a subset of a broader Quality Management concern, defines the functions required for a Quality Management program, and presents an organizational structure to support these functions.

BACKGROUND

From a historical perspective, the early years through the 1960s can be viewed as the functional era of software engineering, the 1970s as the schedule era, and the 1980s as the cost era [5]. In the late 1960s, the focus began to shift from the singular issue of "what functions should the software perform," to the broader recognition that software was expensive, of insufficient quality, hard to schedule, and difficult to manage. Thus, the focus in the 1970s was placed on planning and controlling of software projects. Life-cycle models which defined development phases were introduced and project planning and tracking procedures emerged. In the 1980s, information technology spread through every facet of our institutions and became available to individuals as well. Driven by competition, issues of productivity became more significant and various models used for estimating costs were developed by organizations in industry and academia. In the mid 1980s, quality issues emerged and have subsequently increased in importance. The decade of the 1990s is already being characterized as the "quality era" [34]. As society's dependence on software increases and technology provides for expanding functionality, the demand for quality intensifies. For vendors of software to compete in the marketplace at home and abroad, quality is becoming more of a necessity. In this decade, quality has become a key issue in how software is conceived, developed and maintained for the broad and diverse customer base.

With this focus on quality, the software industry is recognizing that producing quality products requires a concern for not only quality of product but quality of process as well. In a 1987 article, "No Silver Bullet" [8], Brooks argued that the difficulties of software development are inevitable for they arise not from accident, but from software's inescapable essence — the complexity of interlocking constructs. Indeed, for 25 years, software engineers have sought methods which they hoped would provide a technological "fix" for the software crisis. Although small improvement can be made by the use of specific methods, there is little empirical evidence to support the hypothesis that such fixes can radically improve the way we develop software systems [21]. While attention to quality issues may not slay the dragon of software complexity and satisfy Brook's yardstick for a technological breakthrough of a tenfold improvement in quality or productivity, or both, there is growing evidence that it can provide a significant step in that direction. Several companies [11, 16, 17, 28, 54, 56] have reported increases in quality and productivity by focusing on improving the quality of their development processes.

RATIONALE

There are many reasons for wanting to improve software processes and quality. These include a moral obligation, customer satisfaction, cost effectiveness, predictability, application demand, and international competition.

Moral obligation. The increasing reliance on software in life-critical systems morally obligates the producers to provide products that are reliable in performing their needed functions and can be counted on to do no harm. The realities of software fragility are evident in critical systems that we build. As examples [36], a Patriot missile timing error may have contributed to the deaths of 28 soldiers in Dhahran during the Gulf War and software has been suspect in the Therac-25 radiation-therapy machine which has been implicated in at least two deaths.

Customer satisfaction. From the customer's view, quality is conformance to expectations and requirements. Customers today often have multiple sources from which to select products or services; they are increasingly demanding more assurances that their expectations will be met.

Cost effectiveness. With the increase in size and complexity of software systems, the costs have correspondingly increased. With the decrease in hardware costs over the years, the cost of labor has become a major contributor to development costs. Improved development processes are needed to make more efficient use of personnel resources.

Predictability. The need for better predictability of costs, schedules and product quality is driven by customer demands and cost concerns. For example, a Federal Aviation Administration (FAA) project to develop new workstation software for air-traffic controllers was reported in 1994 to be bug-infested and running five years late accompanied by $1 billion over budget [23]. A 1994 survey by IBM's Consulting Group [23] of leading companies that developed large distributed systems showed that 55% of the projects cost more than expected, 68% overran their schedules and 88% had to be substantially redesigned.

Application demand. The demands for software continue to increase in terms of size, complexity, and new domains. Modern, windows-based commercial products average 100,000 lines of code (LOC) [33]. Operating and data-base management systems often exceed one million LOC and complex telephone switching systems are up to 10 million LOC [37]. Because hardware capabilities rapidly advance, an order of magnitude growth in system size every decade is expected for many industries. Such growth in system size is stressing our cultural tradition founded in the prowess of the individual programmer.

International competition. The 21st century will be very competitive for software vendors in the global marketplace. Software is a labor intensive activity. Third world countries, with low wage earners, looking to "leap frog" into the technological age have discovered that software can be key to a competitive strategy for their future. Past practices that enabled U. S. software producers to achieve supremacy will not suffice and bold steps are needed to ensure that our software industry will not fall to foreign competition. Other industries such as automotive, steel, and consumer

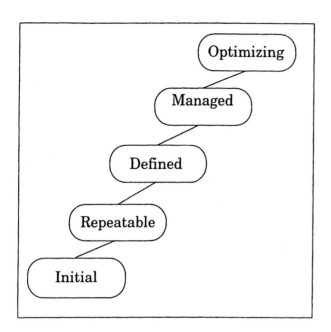

Figure 1. SEI Capability Maturity Model

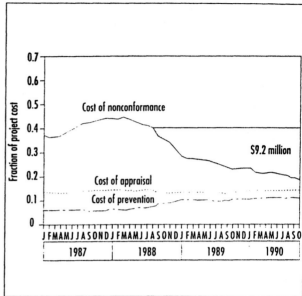

Figure 2. Raytheon's Savings Due to Rework

electronics faced the same challenge and in their hesitation to change, lost marketshare. The challenge for the software industry will be to provide customer satisfaction at a competitive price.

QUALITY IMPROVEMENT INITIATIVES

A movement to improve software development emerged in the mid 1980s. Shortcomings in managing development and maintenance processes were recognized as prime inhibitors of growth in software productivity and quality. This movement focused on the underlying foundation of development efforts — a foundation composed of people, tasks, tools, methods, and a well-defined and documented process. Several initiatives to provide the needed foundation have been undertaken.

Software Engineering Institute. In November 1986, the Software Engineering Institute (SEI) began developing a process-maturity framework that would help developers improve their software process. This work has evolved into the Capability Maturity Model (CMM) Version 1.1 [44] which presents recommended practices in a number of key process areas that have been shown to enhance the software development and maintenance capability of an organization. The CMM provides a rating scale composed of five maturity levels as shown in Figure 1. It is based on the principles of incremental and continuous process improvement espoused by Walter Shewart, W. Edwards Deming, Joseph Juran, and Philip Crosby.

Many organizations in the U. S. are using the SEI model as a catalyst for change. For example, the Air Force has mandated that all of its software development organizations must reach Level 3 of the CMM by 1998 [23]. A similar directive has been issued by the Navy and NASA is considering such a policy [23]. Industry organizations using the CMM include large and small companies.

Improvement efforts have shown that the return on investment is high and published results demonstrate this cost effectiveness. Results from a two-year effort to progress to Level 3 at the Software Engineering Division of Hughes Aircraft [28] indicate a $2 million per year savings. Intangible benefits cited include increased pride in work, quality of work life, and in general, fewer problems. Raytheon achieved similar results over a three-year improvement effort that took the Equipment Division from a Level 2 to a Level 3 [17]. Their analysis, as shown in Figure 2, indicates that $9.2 million was saved by reducing rework on a base of nearly $115 million in development costs. During the past several years, Computer Sciences Corporation has experienced about a 20% annual increase in productivity and quality [11]. This is a result of applying the SEI approach as well as other ongoing improvement activities. Procase Corporation, a smaller company which is a producer of CASE tools, progressed from a Level 1 to a Level 2 over an 18-month period [54]. The company is now shipping releases close to a 6-month cycle compared with a previous 30-month cycle.

The CMM represents a broad consensus of the software community on best practices and is providing guidance for many organizational software process-improvement efforts.

ISO 9000-3. Another method for assessing the ability of an organization to produce software with predictability and quality is *ISO 9000-3, Guidelines for the Application of ISO 9001 to the Development, Supply, and Maintenance of Software*, which is part of the ISO 9000 series of standards published by the International Standards Organization (ISO) [2]. These standards describe the requirements for various types of companies and organizations doing business in the European Community.

BOOTSTRAP. BOOTSTRAP [35], a project under the auspices of the European Strategic Programme for Research in Information Technology (ESPRIT), applied the SEI model to the European software industry. Although the CMM maturity levels are still recognizable, the assessment methodology yields more detailed capability profiles of organizations and projects. As of 1993, 90 projects in 37 organizations had been assessed with results showing that 73% of the organizations were at Level 1 with the remainder at Level 2.

SPICE. In 1993, the International Standards Group for Software Engineering sponsored the Software Process Improvement and Capability dEtermination (SPICE) project which has been endorsed by the international community [18]. Its objective is to develop an international standard for software process assessment by building on the best features of existing software assessment methods such as the SEI model.

Other Models. Other improvement models have been developed and used by large companies, such as Hewlett-Packard's Software Quality and Productivity Analysis (SQPA) [25]. Models have also been developed as an adjunct to consulting services, such as those offered by R. S. Pressman & Associates, Inc., Howard Rubin & Associates, and Capers Jones through Software Productivity Research, Inc.

QUALITY ASSURANCE DEFINITION

Over a decade ago, Buckley [9] stated, "You can wander into any bar in town and get into a fight over quality assurance." This is still true. There are various definitions of quality assurance and related concepts. Definitions provided by the IEEE [32] and by the CMM [44] are as follows:

IEEE Definition 1. A planned and systematic pattern of all actions necessary to provide adequate confidence that an item or product conforms to established technical requirements.

IEEE Definition 2. A set of activities designed to evaluate the process by which products are developed or manufactured.

CMM Definition of Purpose. The purpose of quality assurance is to provide management with appropriate visibility into the process being used by the software project and of the products being built.

The first IEEE definition is very broad in scope and includes plans and subsequent actions taken by a project's development personnel as well as by others in organizational support roles. Such plans address areas such as project planning and tracking, development process models, deliverable and in-process documentation, reviews and audits, requirements management, configuration management, verification and validation procedures, and training. The *IEEE Standard for Software Quality Assurance Plans* [31] provides the contents of such a comprehensive plan.

The second IEEE definition of quality assurance and the CMM definition of its purpose are similar and narrower in scope. The key phrases are "to evaluate" and to provide "appropriate visibility into" the process being used to develop the software products. These definitions imply an oversight function concerned with assuring that defined processes are in place for the development and support activities required to produce a quality product and with assuring that these processes are being complied with.

To bridge this chasm between the broad and the narrow definitions, terms such as "Quality Management" and "Quality Program" are being used to encompass the broad spectrum of quality-oriented activities while the term "Quality Assurance" is applied to the oversight function. The terms are in a state of evolution and are being influenced by the increasing popularity of the CMM among developer organizations.

In the remainder of this paper, the terms Quality Management (QM) and Quality Assurance (QA) will be used in conformance with this emerging new view.

QUALITY MANAGEMENT FUNCTIONS

Quality Management is concerned with quality-related activities across the spectrum of a software development organization. Since consistency is needed

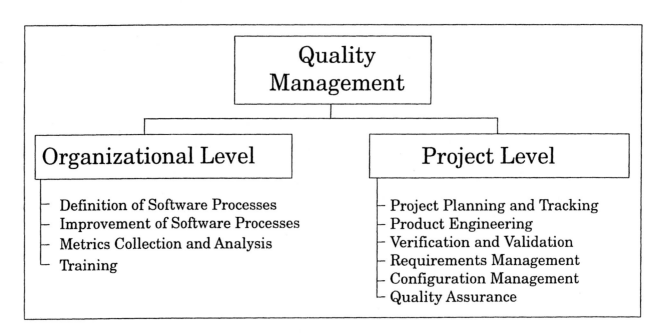

Figure 3. Primary Quality Management Functions

both for reliable prediction of schedules, costs, and product quality and for improvement over time, a primary goal is to provide for consistency across a multitude of individual software projects. This applies to the various processes and methodologies used by the various projects. Thus, QM must address quality functions at two levels, the organizational and the project levels. The organizational-level functions include those necessary to define and support the processes and methodologies which will be used by individual projects within the organization. The project-level functions include those necessary to carry out the defined processes, using the defined methodologies, for a specific project. The primary functions addressed by QM are shown in Figure 3.

Organizational Level Functions

Primary functions at the organizational level include definition and improvement of software development processes, metrics collection and analysis, and training.

Definition of Software Development Processes. This function is to define and document the processes which development projects will follow. These processes encompass the activities, procedures, documentation, and standards required to carry out the QM functions shown at the project level.

Software process models are at the heart of improving the way software is developed and thus the quality of the resultant products. While a life-cycle model, such as the waterfall, spiral, or evolutionary, defines the

high-level activities for the development effort, a process model is a more detailed decomposition and is usually displayed as a network of activities.

A software process model defines the various development activities which must be performed. For each activity, the model defines information or documents which must be available for the activity to occur, work-products that are produced, standards that must be met, methodologies and tools that must be used, verification and validation procedures that will be applied, configuration management activities that will be applied, and quality assurance activities that will be applied. Thus, a process model integrates the various quality management activities appropriate for a project.

Automated support is available for modeling and enacting a defined process. These tools aid in ensuring that the personnel participating on a project follow the defined process. A description of several tools is given in [52]. Examples include Process Weaver from Cap Gemini, InConcert from Xsoft Inc., and Process Engineer from Learmonth & Burchett Management Systems.

Procedures and standards apply to various products during a project's life. Document templates are typically developed for deliverable and non-deliverable work-products such as the project plan, the requirement specifications, user and operator manuals, various design documents, and test plans. Documents which contains descriptions of the processes and procedures

312

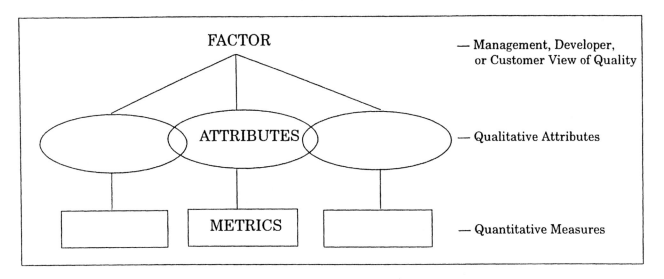

Figure 4. Software Metrics Framework

to be followed on individual projects, such as for configuration management, verification and validation, and quality assurance activities, are also required. Coding standards include expectations and restrictions on items such as descriptive comments, programming languages, control structures, data structures, naming conventions, source-code size, and operating system interfaces.

Defined processes are used, perhaps with tailoring, by individuals on specific projects to guide them in performing their work according to expectations.

Improvement of Software Development Processes. Improving development processes requires evaluating the current processes being used and products produced, identifying areas that are weak, and modifying the defined processes in these areas. It also includes follow-up evaluation to ensure that the modifications are indeed improving productivity and/or product quality.

Metrics Collection and Analysis. Software metrics play an important role in evaluating and improving the development processes and the software products. Such improvement results in increased productivity and quality, and reduced cycle time, all of which improve a company's competitiveness. Although there are a number of successful metrics programs in industry [16, 24, 25, 38. 48, 59], only about 25% of application development organizations have a formal metrics program [59]. Implementation of metrics is a complex issue as indicated in a survey by Howard Rubin & Associates, as mentioned in [39], that reported two out of three measurement efforts either failed or were discontinued after two years.

An example of a successful metrics program is found within Motorola. Their six sigma program has a quality goal of no more than 3.4 defects per million lines of code. One Motorola Division achieved a 50X reduction in released-software defect density within 3.5 years [16].

An example of a small software group that has benefited from a measurement program is from Eastman Kodak Company [56]. Since 1990, the group has measured the time spent in different work phases on development and maintenance projects. Distribution trends have been used to set quantitative improvement goals, identify opportunities that can increase productivity, and develop heuristics to assist with estimating new projects. The focus has been on improving up-front activities such as requirements analysis, instituting design and code inspections, and formalizing software quality assurance practices. A notable result has been a reduction in the corrective maintenance effort from 13.5% to a steady state of less than 2%.

Metrics can be classified into two broad categories — process metrics and product metrics. Process metrics can be used to improve the development and maintenance processes. Examples include defects associated with testing and inspections, defect containment efficiency, and labor consumed. Product metrics can be used to improve the software and its associated products. Examples include complexity of the design, the size of the source code, and the usability of the documentation produced.

A popular approach to defining product metrics is through a hierarchical framework [51, 53]. A three-level framework is shown in Figure 4. The first level

313

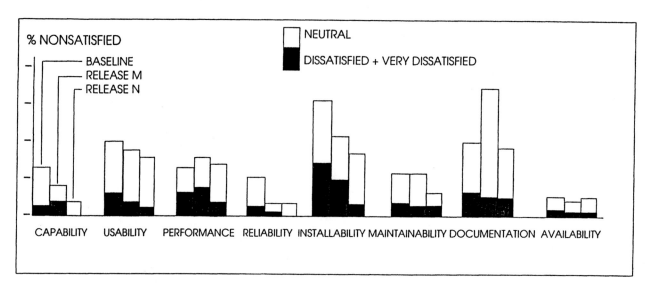

Figure 5. Monitoring Software Quality in Terms of Customer Satisfaction

establishes high-level quality factors; the second identifies the software attributes which define the factor; and the third identifies the metrics which can be used to measure the degree of presence of each attribute, and thus the quality factor. For example, the quality factor "maintainability" may be decomposed into three attributes: consistency, simplicity and modularity; the attribute simplicity may be decomposed into metrics describing the LOC and the maximum loop-nesting level for a module. The framework can be used for individual modules or for a system to enforce standards and to measure deviations from quality goals. Commonly accepted quality factors include correctness, reliability, efficiency, integrity, usability, maintainability, testability, flexibility, portability, reusability, and interoperability [46]. The concept of a metrics framework is supported by several commercial packages such as Logiscope marketed by Verilog, Inc.

Another example of quality factors, with focus on customer satisfaction/dissatisfaction, is found in the CUPRIMDA model used by IBM's AS/400 Division as part of a corporate strategy of market-driven quality (MDQ) [34]. CUPRIMDA is an acronym for eight quality factors as shown in Figure 5. Each factor is defined through a set of metrics and used to measure products across different releases and against benchmarked competitors. This information is used to improve the process and as a result, the product, in areas contributing to low customer satisfaction.

In a similar way of measuring customer satisfaction, the Hewlett-Packard Company focuses on FURPS (functionality, usability, reliability, performance, and supportability) [24, 25]. Similar dimensions of quality

are used by other companies.

A useful approach for developing a set of metrics is provided by the "goal/question/metric" paradigm [3, 4]. It is well described by Grady [25]: "The basic principle behind the paradigm is that each organization or project has a set of goals. For each goal there is a set of questions that you might ask to help you understand whether you are achieving your goal. Many of these questions have answers that can be measured. To the extent that the questions are a complete set, and to the extent the metric data satisfactorily answers the questions, you can measure whether you are meeting goals." The relationships among goals, questions, and metrics are shown in Figure 6. This approach was used in brainstorming sessions by the Hewlett-Packard's Software Metrics Council as an initial step in defining a set of software maintenance metrics [25]. As such, the "metrics" were not precisely defined but provided a platform for further discussion, feedback and refinement. An example follows:

Goal: Minimize Engineering Effort and Schedule

Question: Where are the resources going and where are the worst rework loops in the process?

Metrics: Engineering months by product/component/activity.

Increasingly, a metrics program is being viewed by industry and government organizations as a powerful tool for improving the quality of products and processes in software development. The IEEE has developed standards for productivity metrics [30] and software

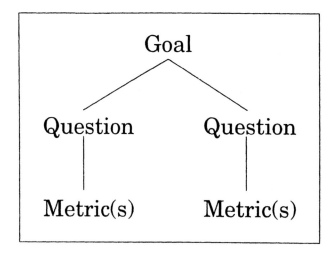

Figure 6. Goal/Question/Metric Paradigm

quality metrics [29]. The Department of Defense (DoD) is developing a software-metrics database which is to become a national repository for all DoD organizations, on both in-house and contracted projects, and for others who choose to contribute [40]. An Air Force policy requires software-intensive programs, whether embedded, command and control, or management information systems, to have a metrics program which collects the core attributes of size, effort, schedule, quality and rework [40].

Metrics programs are well supported by vendor tools. Software Productivity Research provides Checkpoint for estimating staffing and quality levels. Industry baselines for productivity and quality measures are provided through products such as SLIM from Quantitative Software Management and several from Howard Rubin & Associates. McCabe & Associates provides a toolset to support the analysis of software structure.

A comprehensive metrics training program is provided through METKIT, a product produced by an ESPRIT project [1]. The industrial package consists of 18 modules, a computer-aided instruction system, and a textbook [21].

Training. For a viable quality program, the organization needs to provide for training of personnel in their processes, standards, and metrics program. Management, technical and support staff who are to be involved in the project-level activities should be included.

Project Level Functions

The primary functions at the project level are implementations of the defined processes established by the organization as standards to be followed by all software projects within the organization. These functions include project planning and tracking, product engineering, verification and validation, requirements management, configuration management, and quality assurance.

Project Planning and Tracking. Project planning is performed at the beginning of a project and includes defining the work to be performed, estimating resources required, and producing a schedule. The planning process itself adheres to the process defined at the organization level and the resultant plan should incorporate processes defined for the other project-level functions described below. Tailoring of the defined processes may be necessary for a specific project and is performed during the planning phase. The project tracking functions involve assessing the status of the work and work-products as the project progresses, evaluating adherence to the plan, and taking action to correct any deviation.

Product Engineering. Product engineering involves following the defined software process model, with the appropriate methods and tools, to develop the software and associated products. Activities defined by product engineering include requirements analysis, design, implementation, and testing.

Verification and Validation (V&V). V&V is "the process of determining whether the requirements for a system or component are complete and correct, the products of each development phase fulfill the requirements or conditions imposed by the previous phase, and the final system or component complies with specified requirements" [32]. This process should be integrated into the software process model and includes "gate-keeping" activities at each process step to ensure freedom from defects and compliance with standards and requirements. Example activities include producing traceability matrices, holding technical reviews and inspections, and performing unit, integration and system testing. Reviews and inspections are particularly important V&V activities.

The idea of software reviews has been around almost as long as software. Babbage and von Neumann regularly asked colleagues to examine their programs [22]. By the 1970s, various review methods had emerged and were called walkthroughs, structured walkthroughs, and code inspections. Petroski, in his text *To Engineer is Human* [47] states that "it is the essence of modern engineering not only to be able to check one's own work, but also to have one's work checked and to be able to check the work of others." The value of reviews is based on the fact that the cost of fixing a defect rises dramatically the later it is found in the development cycle. Reviews of requirements, design, and code allow early detection of defects and thus, lower costs.

Over the years, many companies have reported their experiences with inspections [19, 50, 58]. At Bell-Northern Research, code inspections uncovered approximately 80% of all defects on an ultralarge project of 2.5 million lines of code [50].

Requirements Management (RM). Software requirements are essential for proper planning of software development activities. Requirements management includes ensuring that requirements are well defined, agreed to by appropriate parties, used for project planning, and modified according to a defined procedure. The modification procedure must ensure that later changes are incorporated properly and that project plans are updated accordingly. If appropriate, the requirements may be placed under the full rigor of formal configuration management.

Configuration Management (CM). The purpose of CM [44] is to "establish and maintain the integrity of the products of the software project throughout the project's software life cycle." This involves identifying the software work products — called configuration items — to be placed under CM control and providing the technical and administrative procedures required to ensure that approved baselined versions exist at specific points during the project, that changes are incorporated in a defined manner, and that the status of configurations items are accounted for. Examples of work products that may be designated as configuration items include the project plan, the requirements, the architectural design, the source code, and the user manual.

CM has been addressed by many organizations [41]. About 80% of organizations examined in one survey have well-developed mechanisms for controlling changes to requirements, design, and code. There are a number of automated tools, which support elements of CM, especially for source code. Examples include Digital Equipment Corporation's VMS, Softool Corporation's CCC, and Expertware Inc.'s CMVision. However, many CM tools were developed on mainframe machines and few fully support the needs required in distributed client-server environments [10].

Quality Assurance. QA, as noted previously, is an oversight function providing assurance that all processes defined in the project plan are followed. Thus, QA ensures that all product engineering, V&V, RM and CM activities are carried out as planned and that work products conform to standards. QA also assures that the project plan itself was developed according to defined procedures and meets the standards for the organization. QA functions are performed through a series of reviews, audits, and consultations.

QA reviews ensure documented processes are followed and that planned activities such as project reviews and inspections are held. QA personnel may attend technical and management reviews and may attend work-product inspections. Their presence, however, is not as a technical contributor with responsibility for detecting technical-content errors. Their presence is to observe that the meeting processes are being implemented as planned and to note deviations. For example, they may note that the moderator of a code inspection did not distribute materials in advance and that the inspectors are not prepared. They may also evaluate effectiveness of the meeting procedures and make recommendations for change. QA personnel may perform reviews to ensure proper records, status-accounting reports, and other physical documents are present and are being used as planned. For example, QA may periodically review the project manager's records to ensure that monthly reports, inspection meeting reports, and testing reports are being produced, distributed and saved according to procedures. QA may also review CM records to ensure that monthly reports are being produced, distributed and saved according to procedures.

QA may audit a variety of work products for which standards have been established. This includes auditing of deliverable work-products such as code and manuals prior to delivery. Similar to attending reviews, their purpose is not to detect technical-content errors but to ensure that all items are present, that all standards are complied with, and that all activities, such as completion of test-traceability matrices, have been completed prior to delivery. QA may also review non-deliverable work-products, such as design documents and test plans, for standards compliance.

QA personnel provide consulting services throughout the project life from initial planning through final product delivery. This includes advising the project management on implementing and tailoring the organizational processes and standards as well as advising on corrective actions required to eliminate discrepancies detected during reviews and audits.

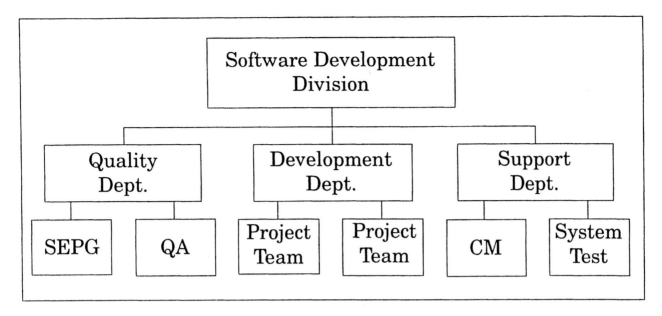

Figure 7. Organizational Structure Supporting Quality Management Activities

An important part of the QA function is reporting to project management and to senior management regarding the status of project adherence to defined processes as described in the project plan. Noncompliance issues that cannot be resolved within the software project are addressed by senior management.

The QM functions defined at the organizational and project levels provide a comprehensive set of well-integrated processes needed for prediction and control of project costs and schedule and of product quality.

QUALITY MANAGEMENT ORGANIZATION

The organization of personnel and other resources required to carry out the development and QM functions is a critical element of success in implementing a quality program. The organizational structure used to define roles and responsibilities of personnel can vary depending on the resources, skills, and culture inherent in the organization itself. The structure presented in this section is a composite based on the author's experience as an instructor and consultant for organizations seeking to institute a QM program, and thus, is intended as a representative structure. The structure is shown in Figure 7. Some alternatives are described in the text.

Software Engineering Process Group (SEPG). The SEPG is responsible for capturing, documenting, maintaining and disseminating the organization's software process activities. The SEI's CMM requires

an SEPG, or similar group, for Level 3 [44]. In the context of this paper, the SEPG performs the functions defined at the organizational level, which include definition and improvement of software development processes, metrics collection and analysis, and training.

Many software development organizations are in the early stage of implementing QM functions with primary focus on definining the various processes required. As such, the SEPG may not be considered a permanent organizational entity with traditional line management as shown, but instead may report to a "Steering Committee" composed of managers who will implement the defined procedures on software projects. The Steering Committee would include the division and department managers and the project team, QA, CM, and Test managers. In this early stage, "working groups" are created to define and document a specific process(es) which will become the organizational standard. For example, a requirements working group would be responsible for defining and documenting the process to be followed by individual projects for requirements management. The working groups report to the SEPG. The SEPG and the working groups are typically staffed with software development personnel on a part- or full-time basis.

Quality Assurance (QA). The QA group is responsible for assuring defined processes are followed by those organizational entities carrying out the project-level QM function. Thus, the QA group performs those QA functions defined at the project level which include reviews, audits, and consultations.

The QA organization is staffed with personnel who have in-depth knowledge of the processes for which they are providing oversight; thus, experience in software engineering is a desirable pre-requisite. The organization may have part- or full-time staff positions and may rotate software engineers into QA positions for a period of time.

Project Team. The project team includes the software project manager and software engineers who develop the software and related products. This group performs all project-level QM functions except for QA functions. The project manager is responsible for project planning and tracking and software engineers are responsible for product engineering, verification and validation (other than system testing), and requirements management.

Configuration Management (CM). The CM group performs the configuration management activities for all projects in the organization. It is not uncommon in small development organizations, however, for the project team to perform these functions for a specific project.

System Test. The system test group is responsible for the independent V&V activity of testing the complete system prior to delivery. It is not uncommon in small development organizations, however, for the project team to perform these functions for a project.

SUMMARY

The future prospects for improvement in software quality appear promising. Quality Management programs are being organized and implemented by many development organizations using the Capability Maturity Model developed by the Software Engineering Institute for guidance. Quality Assurance as an entity of Quality Management is emerging as an important oversight function to ensure that documented processes are being followed and that they are effective. Organizations such as Hughes Aircraft, Motorola, Raytheon, and IBM have shown that improvements in quality and productivity go hand-in-hand in the field of software development, as has been shown in other industries such as manufacturing. The technologies needed for improvement are defined and available to organizations through methodologies and supporting tools. Quality initiatives by industry and by government agencies provide strong incentives for a change in culture from the ad-hoc development processes of the past decades to a more defined structure for the future. Only through a focus on quality issues can the U. S. software industry maintain its supremacy and meet the challenges of the competitive 21st century.

REFERENCES

1. Ashley, Nicholas, "METKIT: Training in How to Use Measurement as a Software Management Tool," *Software Quality Journal*, 3, 1994, pp. 129-136.
2. Bamford, Robert and Deibler, William, "Comparing, Contrasting ISO 9001 and the SEI Capability Maturity Model," *IEEE Computer*, October 1993, pp. 68-70.
3. Basili, V. R. and Weiss, D. M., "A Methodology for Collecting Valid Software Engineering Data," *IEEE Transactions on Software Engineering*, Vol. SE-10, No. 6, November 1984.
4. Basili, V. R. and Rombach, H. D., "Tailoring the Software Process to Project Goals and Environments," *IEEE Proceedings of the Ninth International Conference on Software Engineering*, Monterey, CA, April 1987.
5. Basili, V.R. and Musa, J. D., "The Future Engineering of Software: A Management Perspective," *IEEE Computer*, Vol. 24, No. 9, September 1991, pp. 90-96.
6. Basili, Victor *et al*, "Technology Transfer at Motorola," *IEEE Software*, March 1994, pp. 70-76.
7. Brooks, F. P., *The Mythical Man-Month*, Addison-Wesley, 1975.
8. Brooks, Fred, "No Silver Bullet: Essence and Accidents of Software Engineering," *IEEE Computer*, April 1987.
9. Buckley, Fletcher J., "Software Quality Assurance," *IEEE Transactions on Software Engineering*, January 1984, pp. 36-41.
10. Buckley, Fletcher J., "Implementing a Software Configuration Management Environment," *IEEE Computer*, February 1994, pp. 56-61.
11. Card, David, "The SEI Software Process Improvement Approach: A Case Study," *Software Engineering Strategies*, November/December 1993, pp. 7-14.
12. Crosby, P. B., *Quality is Free: The Art of Making Quality Certain*, McGraw-Hill, 1979.
13. Crosby, Philip, *Quality Without Tears*, McGraw-Hill, 1984.
14. Curtis, B. and Paulk, M., "Creating a Software Process Improvement Program," *Information and Software Technology*, June/July, 1993, pp. 381-386.
15. Cusumano, Michael, *Japan's Software Factories: A Challenge to U. S. Management*, M.I.T. Press, 1991.
16. Daskalantonakis, Michael, "A Practical View of Software Measurement and Implementation Experiences within Motorola, *IEEE Transactions on Software Engineering*, November 1992, pp. 998-1010.
17. Dion, Raymond, "Elements of a Process-Improvement Program," *IEEE Software*, July 1992, pp. 83-85.
18. Dorling, A., "SPICE: Software Process Improvement and Capability dEtermination," *Information and Software Technology*, June/July 1993, pp. 404-406.
19. Ebenau, Robert G., "Predictive Quality Control with Software Inspections," *CrossTalk*, June 1994, pp. 9-16.
20. Fenton, Norman, *Software Metrics: A Rigorous Approach*, Chapman & Hall, 1991.
21. Fenton, Norman, "How Effective Are Software Engineering Methods?" *The Journal of Systems and Software*, 22, 1993, pp. 141-146.
22. Freedman, D. P. and Weinberg, G. M., "Reviews, Walkthroughs, and Inspections," *IEEE Transactions on Software Engineering*, January 1984.

23. Gibbs, W. Wayt, "Software's Chronic Crisis," *Scientific American*, September 1994, pp. 86-95.
24. Grady, R. B. and Caswell, D. L., *Software Metrics: Establishing a Company-wide Program*, Prentice-Hall, 1986.
25. Grady, Robert B., *Practical Software Metrics for Project Management and Process Improvement*, Prentice-Hall, 1992.
26. Hausler, P. A., Linger, R. C., and Trammell, C. J., "Adopting Cleanroom Software Engineering With a Phased Approach," *IBM Systems Journal*, Vol. 33, No. 1, 1994, pp. 89-109.
27. Humphrey, Watts, *Managing the Software Process*, Addison-Wesley, 1989.
28. Humphrey, W., Snyder, T. and Willis, R., "Software Process Improvement at Hughes Aircraft," *IEEE Software*, July 1991.
29. *IEEE Standard for a Software Quality Metrics Methodology*, IEEE Std 1061-1992, IEEE, 1992.
30. *IEEE Standard for Software Productivity Metrics*, IEEE Std 1045-1992, IEEE, 1992.
31. *IEEE Standard for Software Quality Assurance Plans*, IEEE 730-1989, IEEE, 1989.
32. *IEEE Standard Glossary of Software Engineering Terminology*, Std 610.12-1990, IEEE, 1990.
33. Jones, Capers, "Determining Software Schedules," *IEEE Computer*, February 1995, pp. 73-75.
34. Kan, S. H., Basili, V. R., and Shapiro, L. N., "Software Quality: An Overview from the Perspective of Total Quality Management," *IBM Systems Journal*, Vol. 33, No. 1, 1994, pp. 4-19.
35. Kuvaja, Pase and Bicego, Adriana, "BOOTSTRAP — a European Assessment Methodology", *Software Quality Journal*, 3, 1994, 99 117-127.
36. Lutz, Michael, "Complex Software: Unsafe at any Level," *IEEE Software*, November 1994, pp. 110-111.
37. Marciniak, John J., Editor-in-Chief, "Quality Assurance", *Encyclopedia of Software Engineering*, Volume 2, John Wiley & Sons, 1994, pp. 941-958.
38. McGarry, F. E., "Results of 15 Years of Measurement in the SEL," *Proceedings: Fifteenth Annual Software Engineering Workshop*, NASA/Goddard Space Flight Center, November, 1990.
39. Miluk, G. "Cultural Barriers to Software Measurement," *Proceedings: First International Conference on Applications of Software Measurement*, November 1990.
40. Mosemann, Lloyd K., "Predictability", *Crosstalk*, August 1994, pp. 2-6.
41. Oliver, Paul, "Using a Process Assessment to Improve Software Quality," *Software Engineering Strategies*, March/April, 1993, pp. 14-20.
42. Over, James, "Motivation for Process-Driven Development," *Crosstalk*, January 1993, pp. 17-24.
43. Parnas, E. W. and Weiss, D. M., "Active Design Reviews: Principles and Practices," *Proceedings of ICSE '85* (London, England, Aug. 28-30), IEEE Computer Society, 1985, pp. 132-136.
44. Paulk, Mark C. *et al.*, *Capability Maturity Model for Software, Version 1.1*, CMU/SEI-93-TR-24, Software Engineering Institute, 1993.
45. Paulk, Mark *et al.*, "Capability Maturity Model, Version 1.1," *IEEE Software*, July 1993, pp. 18-26.
46. Perry, William, "Quality Concerns in Software Development," *Information Systems Management*, Spring 1992, pp. 48-52.
47. Petroski, Henry, *To Engineer is Human*, St. Martin's Press, 1985.
48. Pfleeger, S. L., Fitzgerald, J. C., and Porter, A., "The CONTEL Software Metrics Program," *Proceeding: First International Conference on Applications of Software Measurement*, November, 1990.
49. Pressman, Roger, "Assessing Software Engineering Practices for Successful Technology Transition," *Software Engineering Strategies*, 1992, pp. 6-14.
50. Russell, Glen W., "Experience with Inspections in Ultralarge-Scale Developments," *IEEE Software*, January 1991, pp. 25-30.
51. Schulmeyer, G. Gordon and McManus, James I., *Handbook of Software Quality Assurance*, Van Nostrand Reinhold, 1987.
52. Sharon, David and Bell, Rodney, "Tools that Bind: Creating Integrated Environments," *IEEE Software*, March 1995, pp. 76-85.
53. *Specification of the Software Quality Attributes, Vol. 1, 2, and 3*, RADC-TR-85-37, Rome Laboratories, 1985.
54. Sudlow, Bill, "Moving from Chaos to SEI Level 2", *Software Development*, December 1994, pp. 37-40.
55. *The Project Management Body of Knowledge* (Draft), Project Management Institute, August 1994.
56. Weigers, Karl, "Lessons from Software Work Effort Metrics," *Software Development*, October 1994, pp. 37-47.
57. Weinberg, Gerald and Freedman Daniel, *Handbook of Walkthoroughs, Inspections, and Technical Reviews*, Third Ed., Dorset House, 1990.
58. Weller, Edward F., "Lessons from Three Years of Inspection Data," *IEEE Software*, September 1993, pp. 38-45.
59. Yourdon, Ed, "Software Metrics," *Application Development Strategies*, Vol. VI, No. 11, November 1994, pp. 1-16.

ABOUT THE AUTHOR

PATRICIA W. HURST is a senior lecturer/instructor with Fastrak Training, Inc. in Columbia, MD. Her seminars and workshops include software engineering topics such as quality assurance, project management, process modeling and risk management. She is the author of *Software Quality Assurance: Control, Metrics and Testing*, a course published by Technology Exchange Company, Reading, MA. She is past Editor and Publisher of *Deadline Newsletter*, a bimothly publication of abstracts from leading journals and other publications of interest to the software-engineering community.

Elements of Software Configuration Management

EDWARD H. BERSOFF, SENIOR MEMBER, IEEE

Abstract—Software configuration management (SCM) is one of the disciplines of the 1980's which grew in response to the many failures of the software industry throughout the 1970's. Over the last ten years, computers have been applied to the solution of so many complex problems that our ability to manage these applications has all too frequently failed. This has resulted in the development of a series of "new" disciplines intended to help control the software process.

This paper will focus on the discipline of SCM by first placing it in its proper context with respect to the rest of the software development process, as well as to the goals of that process. It will examine the constituent components of SCM, dwelling at some length on one of those components, configuration control. It will conclude with a look at what the 1980's might have in store.

Index Terms—Configuration management, management, product assurance, software.

INTRODUCTION

SOFTWARE configuration management (SCM) is one of the disciplines of the 1980's which grew in response to the many failures of our industry throughout the 1970's. Over the last ten years, computers have been applied to the solution of so many complex problems that our ability to manage these applications in the "traditional" way has all too frequently failed. Of course, tradition in the software business began only 30 years ago or less, but even new habits are difficult to break. In the 1970's we learned the hard way that the tasks involved in managing a software project were not linearly dependent on the number of lines of code produced. The relationship was, in fact, highly exponential. As the decade closed, we looked back on our failures [1], [2] trying to understand what went wrong and how we could correct it. We began to dissect the software development process [3], [4] and to define techniques by which it could be effectively managed [5]-[8]. This self-examination by some of the most talented and experienced members of the software community led to the development of a series of "new" disciplines intended to help control the software process.

While this paper will focus on the particular discipline of SCM, we will first place it in its proper context with respect to the rest of the software development process, as well as to the goals of that process. We will examine the constituent components of SCM, dwelling at some length on one of those components, configuration control. Once we have woven our way through all the trees, we will once again stand back and take a brief look at the forest and see what the 1980's might have in store.

Manuscript received April 15, 1982; revised December 1, 1982 and October 18, 1983.
The author is with BTG, Inc., 1945 Gallows Rd., Vienna, VA 22180.

SCM IN CONTEXT

It has been said that if you do not know where you are going, any road will get you there. In order to properly understand the role that SCM plays in the software development process, we must first understand what the goal of that process is, i.e., where we are going. For now, and perhaps for some time to come, software developers are people, people who respond to the needs of another set of people creating computer programs designed to satisfy those needs. These computer programs are the tangible output of a thought process—the conversion of a thought process into a product. The goal of the software developer is, or should be, the construction of a product which closely matches the real needs of the set of people for whom the software is developed. We call this goal the achievement of "product integrity." More formally stated, product integrity (depicted in Fig. 1) is defined to be the intrinsic set of attributes that characterize a product [9]:

- that fulfills user functional needs;
- that can easily and completely be traced through its life cycle;
- that meets specified performance criteria;
- whose cost expectations are met;
- whose delivery expectations are met.

The above definition is pragmatically based. It demands that product integrity be a measure of the satisfaction of the real needs and expectations of the software user. It places the burden for achieving the software goal, product integrity, squarely on the shoulders of the developer, for it is he alone who is in control of the development process. While, as we shall see, the user can establish safeguards and checkpoints to gain visibility into the development process, the prime responsibility for software success is the developer's. So our goal is now clear; we want to build software which exhibits all the characteristics of product integrity. Let us make sure that we all understand, however, what this thing called software really is. We have learned in recent times that equating the terms "software" and "computer programs" improperly restricts our view of software. Software is much more. A definition which can be used to focus the discussion in this paper is that software is information that is:

- structured with logical and functional properties;
- created and maintained in various forms and representations during the life cycle;
- tailored for machine processing in its fully developed state.

So by our definition, software is not simply a set of computer programs, but includes the documentation required to define, develop, and maintain these programs. While this notion is not very new, it still frequently escapes the software

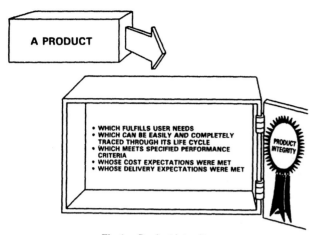

Fig. 1. Product integrity.

development manager who assumes that controlling a software product is the same as controlling computer code.

Now that we more fully appreciate what we are after, i.e., to build a software product with integrity, let us look at the one road which might get us there. We have, until now, used the term "developer" to characterize the organizational unit responsible for converting the software idea into a software product. But developers are, in reality, a complex set of interacting organizational entities. When undertaking a software project, most developers structure themselves into three basic discipline sets which include:

- project management,
- development, and
- product assurance.

Project management disciplines are both inwardly and outwardly directed. They support general management's need to see what is going on in a project and to ensure that the parent or host organization consistently develops products with integrity. At the same time, these disciplines look inside a project in support of the assignment, allocation, and control of all project resources. In that capacity, project management determines the relative allocation of resources to the set of development and product assurance disciplines. It is management's prerogative to specify the extent to which a given discipline will be applied to a given project. Historically, management has often been handicapped when it came to deciding how much of the product assurance disciplines were required. This was a result of both inexperience and organizational immaturity.

The development disciplines represent those traditionally applied to a software project. They include:

- analysis,
- design,
- engineering,
- production (coding),
- test (unit/subsystem),
- installation,
- documentation,
- training, and
- maintenance.

In the broadest sense, these are the disciplines required to take a system concept from its beginning through the development life cycle. It takes a well-structured, rigorous technical approach to system development, along with the right mix of development disciplines to attain product integrity, especially for software. The concept of an ordered, procedurally disciplined approach to system development is fundamental to product integrity. Such an approach provides successive development plateaus, each of which is an identifiable measure of progress which forms a part of the total foundation supporting the final product. Going sequentially from one baseline (plateau) to another with high probability of success, necessitates the use of the right development disciplines at precisely the right time.

The product assurance disciplines which are used by project management to gain visibility into the development process include:

- configuration management,
- quality assurance,
- validation and verification, and
- test and evaluation.

Proper employment of these product assurance disciplines by the project manager is basic to the success of a project since they provide the technical checks and balances over the product being developed. Fig. 2 represents the relationship among the management, development, and product assurance disciplines. Let us look at each of the product assurance disciplines briefly, in turn, before we explore the details of SCM.

Configuration management (CM) is the discipline of identifying the configuration of a system at discrete points in time for the purpose of systematically controlling changes to the configuration and maintaining the integrity and traceability of the configuration throughout the system life cycle. Software configuration management (SCM) is simply configuration management tailored to systems, or portions of systems, that are comprised predominantly of software. Thus, SCM does not differ substantially from the CM of hardware-oriented systems, which is generally well understood and effectively practiced. However, attempts to implement SCM have often failed because the particulars of SCM do not follow by direct analogy from the particulars of hardware CM and because SCM is a less mature discipline than that of hardware CM. We will return to this subject shortly.

Quality assurance (QA) as a discipline is commonly invoked throughout government and industry organizations with reasonable standardization when applied to systems comprised only of hardware. But there is enormous variation in thinking and practice when the QA discipline is invoked for a software development or for a system containing software components. QA has a long history, and much like CM, it has been largely developed and practiced on hardware projects. It is therefore mature, in that sense, as a discipline. Like CM, however, it is relatively immature when applied to software development. We define QA as consisting of the procedures, techniques, and tools applied by professionals to insure that a product meets or exceeds prespecified standards during a product's development cycle; and without specific prescribed standards, QA entails insuring that a product meets or

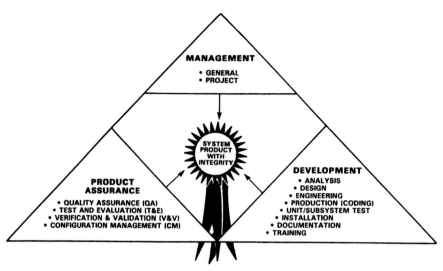

Fig. 2. The discipline triangle.

exceeds a minimum industrial and/or commercially acceptable level of excellence.

The QA discipline has not been uniformly treated, practiced or invoked relative to software development. First, very few organizations have software design and development standards that compare in any way with hardware standards for detail and completeness. Second, it takes a high level of software expertise to assess whether a software product meets prescribed standards. Third, few buyer organizations have provided for or have developed the capability to impose and then monitor software QA endeavors on seller organizations. Finally, few organizations have been concerned over precisely defining the difference between QA and other product assurance disciplines, CM often being subservient to QA or vice versa in a given development organization. Our definition of software given earlier suggests still another reason for the software QA discipline being in the same state as SCM so far as its universal application within the user, buyer, and seller communities. Software, as a form of information, cannot be standardized; only structures for defining/documenting software can be standardized. It follows that software development techniques can only be meaningfully standardized in relation to information structures, not information content.

The third of the four product assurance disciplines is validation and verification (V&V). Unlike CM and QA, V&V has come into being expressly for the purpose of coping with software and its development. Unlike QA, which prinicipally deals with the problem of a product's adherence to pre-established standards, V&V deals with the issue of how well software fulfills functional and performance requirements and the assurance that specified requirements are indeed stated and interpreted correctly. The verification part of V&V assures that a product meets its prescribed goals as defined through baseline documentation. That is, verification is a discipline imposed to ascertain that a product is what it was intended to be relative to its preceding baseline. The validation part of V&V, by contrast, is levied as a discipline to assure that a product not only meets the objectives specified through baseline documentation, but in addition, does the right job.

Stated another way, the validation discipline is invoked to insure that the end-user gets the right product. A buyer or seller may have misinterpreted user requirements or, perhaps, requirements have changed, or the user gets to know more about what he needs, or early specifications of requirements were wrong or incomplete or in a state of flux. The validation process serves to assure that such problems do not persist among the user, buyer, and seller. To enhance objectivity, it is often desirable to have an independent organization, from outside the developing organization, perform the V&V function.

The fourth of the product assurance disciplines is test and evaluation (T&E), perhaps the discipline most understood, and yet paradoxically, least practiced with uniformity. T&E is defined as the discipline imposed outside the development project organization to independently assess whether a product fulfills objectives. T&E does this through the execution of a set of test plans and procedures. Specifically in support of the end user, T&E entails evaluating product performance in a live or near-live environment. Frequently, particularly within the miliatry arena, T&E is a major undertaking involving one or more systems which are to operate together, but which have been individually developed and accepted as stand-alone items. Some organizations formally turn over T&E responsibility to a group outside the development project organization after the product reaches a certain stage of development, their philosophy being that developers cannot be objective to the point of fully testing/evaluating what they have produced.

The definitions given for CM, QA, V&V, and T&E suggest some overlap in required skills and functions to be performed in order to invoke these disciplines collectively for product assurance purposes. Depending on many factors, the actual overlap may be significant or little. In fact, there are those who would argue that V&V and T&E are but subset functions of QA. But the contesting argument is that V&V and T&E have come into being as separate disciplines because conventional QA methods and techniques have failed to do an adequate job with respect to providing product assurance, particularly for computer-centered systems with software components. Management must be concerned with minimizing the application of excessive and redundant resources to address the overlap of these disciplines. What is important is that all the functions defined above are performed, not what they are called or who carries them out.

THE ELEMENTS OF SCM

When the need for the discipline of configuration management finally achieved widespread recognition within the software engineering community, the question arose as to how closely the software CM discipline ought to parallel the extant hardware practice of configuration management. Early SCM authors and practitioners [10] wisely chose the path of commonality with the hardware world, at least at the highest level. Of course, hardware engineering is different from software engineering, but broad similarities do exist and terms applied to one segment of the engineering community can easily be applied to another, even if the specific meanings of those terms differ significantly in detail. For that reason, the elements of SCM were chosen to be the same as those for hardware CM. As for hardware, the four components of SCM are:

- identification,
- control,
- auditing, and
- status accounting.

Let us examine each one in turn.

Software Configuration Identification: Effective management of the development of a system requires careful definition of its baseline components; changes to these components also need to be defined since these changes, together with the baselines, specify the system evolution. A system baseline is like a snapshot of the aggregate of system components as they exist at a given point in time; updates to this baseline are like frames in a movie strip of the system life cycle. The role of software configuration identification in the SCM process is to provide labels for these snapshots and the movie strip.

A baseline can be characterized by two labels. One label identifies the baseline itself, while the second label identifies an update to a particular baseline. An update to a baseline represents a baseline plus a set of changes that have been incorporated into it. Each of the baselines established during a software system's life cycle controls subsequent system development. At the time it is first established a software baseline embodies the actual software in its most recent state. When changes are made to the most recently established baseline, then, from the viewpoint of the software configuration manager, this baseline and these changes embody the actual software in its most recent state (although, from the viewpoint of the software developer, the actual software may be in a more advanced state).

The most elementary entity in the software configuration identification labeling mechanism is the software configuration item (SCI). Viewed from an SCM perspective, a software baseline appears as a set of SCI's. The SCI's within a baseline are related to one another via a tree-like hierarchy. As the software system evolves through its life cycle, the number of

branches in this hierarchy generally increases; the first baseline may consist of no more than one SCI. The lowest level SCI's in the tree hierarchy may still be under development and not yet under SCM control. These entities are termed design objects or computer program components (see Fig. 3). Each baseline and each member in the associated family of updates will exist in one or more forms, such as a design document, source code on a disk, or executing object code.

In performing the identification function, the software configuration manager is, in effect, taking snapshots of the SCI's. Each baseline and its associated updates collectively represents the evolution of the software during each of its life cycle stages. These stages are staggered with respect to one another. Thus, the collection of life cycle stages looks like a collection of staggered and overlapping sequences of snapshots of SCI trees. Let us now imagine that this collection of snapshot sequences is threaded, in chronological order, onto a strip of movie film as in Fig. 4. Let us further imagine that the strip of movie film is run through a projector. Then we would see a history of the evolution of the software. Consequently, the identification of baselines and updates provides an explicit documentation trail linking all stages of the software life cycle. With the aid of this documentation trail, the software developer can assess the integrity of his product, and the software buyer can assess the integrity of the product he is paying for.

Software Configuration Control: The evolution of a software system is, in the language of SCM, the development of baselines and the incorporation of a series of changes into the baselines. In addition to these changes that explicitly affect existing baselines, there are changes that occur during early stages of the system life cycle that may affect baselines that do not yet exist. For example, some time before software coding begins (i.e., some time prior to the establishment of a design baseline), a contract may be modified to include a software warranty provision such as: system downtime due to software failures shall not exceed 30 minutes per day. This warranty provision will generally affect subsequent baselines but in a manner that cannot be explicitly determined *a priori*. One role of software configuration control is to provide the administrative mechanism for precipitating, preparing, evaluating, and approving or disapproving all change proposals throughout the system life cycle.

We have said that software, for configuration management purposes, is a collection of SCI's that are related to one another in a well-defined way. In early baselines and their associated updates, SCI's are specification documents (one or more volumes of text for each baseline or associated update); in later baselines and their associated updates, each SCI may manifest itself in any or all of the various software representations. Software configuration control focuses on managing changes to SCI's (existing or to be developed) in all of their representations. This process involves three basic ingredients.

1) Documentation (such as administrative forms and supporting technical and administrative material) for formally precipitating and defining a proposed change to a software system.

2) An organizational body for formally evaluating and

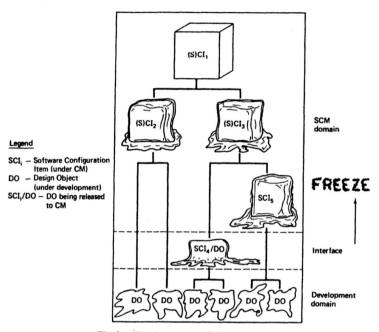

Fig. 3. The development/SCM interface.

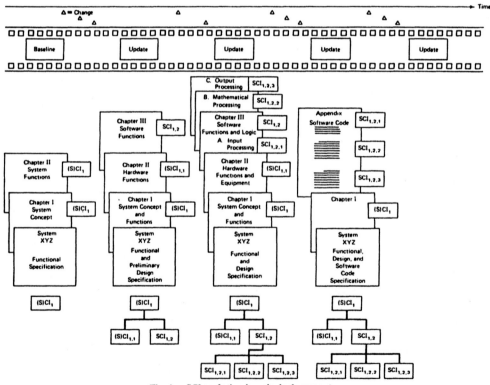

Fig. 4. SCI evolution in a single document.

approving or disapproving a proposed change to a software system (the Configuration Control Board).

3) *Procedures for controlling changes to a software system.* The Engineering Change Proposal (ECP), a major control document, contains information such as a description of the proposed change, identification of the originating organization, rationale for the change, identification of affected baselines and SCI's (if appropriate), and specification of cost and schedule impacts. ECP's are reviewed and coordinated by the CCB, which is typically a body representing all organizational units which have a vested interest in proposed changes.

Fig. 5 depicts the software configuration control process.

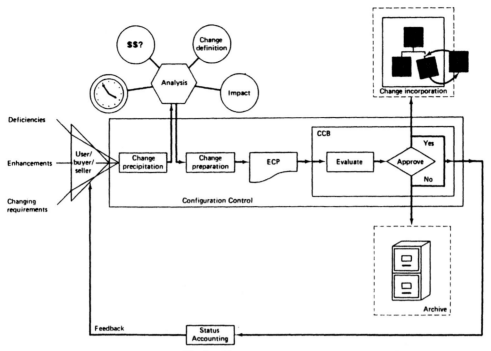

Fig. 5. The control process.

As the figure suggests, change incorporation is not an SCM function, but monitoring the change implementation process resulting in change incorporation is. Fig. 5 also emphasizes that the analysis that may be required to prepare an ECP is also outside the SCM purview. Note also from the figure how ECP's not approved by the CCB are not simply discarded but are archived for possible future reference.

Many automated tools support the control process. The major ones aid in controlling software change once the coding stage has been reached, and are generically referred to as program support libraries (PSL's). The level of support provided by PSL's, however, varies greatly. As a minimum, a PSL should provide a centralized and readily available repository for authoritative versions of each component of a software system. It should contain the data necessary for the orderly development and control of each SCI. Automation of other functions, such as library access control, software and document version maintenance, change recording, and document reconstruction, greatly enhance both the control and maintenance processes. These capabilities are currently available in systems such as SOFTOOL's change and configuration control environment (CCC).

A PSL supports a developmental approach in which project personnel work on a common visible product rather than on independent components. In those PSL's which include access controls, project personnel can be separately assigned read/write access to each software document/component, from programs to lines of code. Thus, all project personnel are assured ready access to the critical interface information necessary for effective software development. At the same time, modifications to various software components, whether sanctioned baselines or modules under development, can be closely controlled.

Under the PSL concept, the programmer operates under a well-defined set of parameters and exercises a narrower span of detailed control. This minimizes the need for explicit communication between analysts and programmers and makes the inclusion of new project personnel less traumatic since interface requirements are well documented. It also minimizes the preparation effort for technical audits.

Responsibility for maintenance of the PSL data varies depending on the level of automation provided. For those systems which provide only a repository for data, a secretary/librarian is usually responsible for maintaining the notebooks which will contain the data developed and used by project personnel and for maintenance of the PSL archives. More advanced PSL systems provide real time, on-line access to data and programs and automatically create the records necessary to fully trace the history of the development. In either case the PSL provides standardization of project recordkeeping, ensures that system documentation corresponds to the current system configuration, and guarantees the existence of adequate documentation of previous versions.

A PSL should support three main activities: code development, software management, and configuration control. Support to the development process includes support to design, coding, testing, documentation, and program maintenance along with associated database schema and subschema. A PSL provides this support through:

- storage and maintenance of software documentation and code,
- support to program compilation/testing,
- support for the generation of program/system documentation.

Support to the management of the software development process involves the storage and output of programming data such as:

- collection and automatic reporting of management data related to program development,

325

- control over the integrity and security of the data in the PSL,
- separation of the clerical activity related to the programming process.

PSL's provide support to the configuration control process through:

- access and change authorization control for all data in the library,
- control of software code releases,
- automatic program and document reconstruction,
- automatic change tracking and reporting,
- assurance of the consistency between documentation, code, and listings.

A PSL has four major components: internal libraries in machine-readable form, external libraries in hardcopy form, computer procedures, and office procedures. The components of a PSL system are interlocked to establish an exact correspondence between the internal units of code and external versions (such as listings) of the developing systems. This continuous correspondence is the characteristic of a PSL that guarantees ongoing visibility and identification of the developing system.

Different PSL implementations exist for various system environments with the specifics of the implementation dependent upon the hardware, software, user, and operating environment. The fundamental correspondence between the internal and external libraries in each environment, however, is established by the PSL librarian and computer procedures. The office procedures are specified in a project CM Plan so that the format of the external libraries is standard across software projects, and internal and external libraries are easily maintainable.

Newer PSL systems minimize the need for both office and computer procedures through the implementation of extensive management functionality. This functionality provides significant flexibility in controlling the access to data and allocating change authority, while providing a variety of status reporting capabilities. The availability of management information, such as a list of all the software structures changed to solve a particular Software Trouble Report or the details on the latest changes to a particular software document, provides a means for the control function to effectively operate without burdening the development team with cumbersome procedures and administrative paperwork. Current efforts in PSL refinement/development are aimed at linking support of the development environment with that of the configuration control environment. The goal of such systems is to provide an integrated environment where control and management information is generated automatically as a part of a fully supported design and development process.

Software Configuration Auditing: Software configuration auditing provides the mechanism for determining the degree to which the current state of the software system mirrors the software system pictured in baseline and requirements documentation. It also provides the mechanism for formally establishing a baseline. A baseline in its formative stages (for example, a draft specification document that appears prior to the existence of the functional baseline) is referred to as a "to-be-established" baseline; the final state of the auditing process conducted on a to-be-established baseline is a sanctioned baseline. The same may be said about baseline updates.

Software configuration auditing serves two purposes, configuration verification and configuration validation. Verification ensures that what is intended for each software configuration item as specified in one baseline or update is actually achieved in the succeeding baseline or update; validation ensures that the SCI configuration solves the right problem (i.e., that customer needs are satisfied). Software configuration auditing is applied to each baseline (and corresponding update) in its to-be-established state. An auditing process common to all baselines is the determination that an SCI structure exists and that its contents are based on all available information.

Software auditing is intended to increase software visibility and to establish traceability throughout the life cycle of the software product. Of course, this visibility and traceability are not achieved without cost. Software auditing costs time and money. But the judicious investment of time and money, particularly in the early stages of a project, pays dividends in the latter stages. These dividends include the avoidance of costly retrofits resulting from problems such as the sudden appearance of new requirements and the discovery of major design flaws. Conversely, failing to perform auditing, or constraining it to the later stages of the software life cycle, can jeopardize successful software development. Often in such cases, by the time discrepancies are discovered (if they are), the software cannot be easily or economically modified to rectify the discrepancies. The result is often a dissatisfied customer, large cost overruns, slipped schedules, or cancelled projects.

Software auditing makes visible to management the current status of the software in the life cycle product audited. It also reveals whether the project requirements are being satisfied and whether the intent of the preceding baseline has been fulfilled. With this visibility, project management can evaluate the integrity of the software product being developed, resolve issues that may have been raised by the audit, and correct defects in the development process. The visibility afforded by the software audit also provides a basis for the establishment of the audited life cycle product as a new baseline.

Software auditing provides traceability between a software life cycle product and the requirements for that product. Thus, as life cycle products are audited and baselines established, every requirement is traced successively from baseline to baseline. Disconnects are also made visible during the establishment of traceability. These disconnects include requirements not satisfied in the audited product and extraneous features observed in the product (i.e., features for which no stated requirement exists).

With the different point of view made possible by the visibility and traceability achieved in the software audit, management can make better decisions and exercise more incisive control over the software development process. The result of a software audit may be the establishment of a baseline, the redirection of project tasking, or an adjustment of applied project resources.

The responsibility for a successful software development project is shared by the buyer, seller, and user. Software auditing uniquely benefits each of these project participants. Appropriate auditing by each party provides checks and

326

balances over the development effort. The scope and depth of the audits undertaken by the three parties may vary greatly. However, the purposes of these differing forms of software audit remain the same: to provide visibility and to establish traceability of the software life cycle products. An excellent overview of the software audit process, from which some of the above discussion has been extracted, appears in [11].

Software Configuration Status Accounting: A decision to make a change is generally followed by a time delay before the change is actually made, and changes to baselines generally occur over a protracted period of time before they are incorporated into baselines as updates. A mechanism is therefore needed for maintaining a record of how the system has evolved and where the system is at any time relative to what appears in published baseline documentation and written agreements. Software configuration status accounting provides this mechanism. Status accounting is the administrative tracking and reporting of all software items formally identified and controlled. It also involves the maintenance of records to support software configuration auditing. Thus, software configuration status accounting records the activity associated with the other three SCM functions and therefore provides the means by which the history of the software system life cycle can be traced.

Although administrative in nature, status accounting is a function that increases in complexity as the system life cycle progresses because of the multiple software representations that emerge with later baselines. This complexity generally results in large amounts of data to be recorded and reported. In particular, the scope of software configuration status accounting encompasses the recording and reporting of:

1) the time at which each representation of a baseline and update came into being;

2) the time at which each software configuration item came into being;

3) descriptive information about each SCI;

4) engineering change proposal status (approved, disapproved, awaiting action);

5) descriptive information about each ECP;

6) change status;

7) descriptive information about each change;

8) status of technical and administrative documentation associated with a baseline or update (such as a plan prescribing tests to be performed on a baseline for updating purposes);

9) deficiencies in a to-be-established baseline uncovered during a configuration audit.

Software configuration status accounting, because of its large data input and output requirements, is generally supported in part by automated processes such as the PSL described earlier. Data are collected and organized for input to a computer and reports giving the status of entities are compiled and generated by the computer.

THE MANAGEMENT DILEMMA

As we mentioned at the beginning of this paper, SCM and many of the other product assurance disciplines grew up in the 1970's in response to software failure. The new disciplines were designed to achieve visibility into the software engineering process and thereby exercise some measure of control over that process. Students of mathematical control theory are taught early in their studies a simple example of the control process. Consider being confronted with a cup of hot coffee, filled to the top, which you are expected to carry from the kitchen counter to the kitchen table. It is easily verified that if you watch the cup as you carry it, you are likely to spill more coffee than if you were to keep your head turned away from the cup. The problem with looking at the cup is one of overcompensation. As you observe slight deviations from the straight-and-level, you adjust, but often you adjust too much. To compensate for that overadjustment, you tend to overadjust again, with the result being hot coffee on your floor.

This little diversion from our main topic of SCM has an obvious moral. There is a fundamental propensity on the part of the practitioners of the product assurance disciplines to overadjust, to overcompensate for the failures of the development disciplines. There is one sure way to eliminate failure completely from the software development process, and that is to stop it completely. The software project manager must learn how to apply his resources intelligently. He must achieve visibility and control, but he must not so encumber the developer so as to bring progress to a virtual halt. The product assurers have a virtuous perspective. They strive for perfection and point out when and where perfection has not been achieved. We seem to have a binary attitude about software; it is either correct or it is not. That is perhaps true, but we cannot expect anyone to deliver perfect software in any reasonable time period or for a reasonable sum of money. What we need to develop is software that is good enough. Some of the controls that we have placed on the developer have the deleterious effect of increasing costs and expanding schedules rather than shrinking them.

The dilemma to management is real. We must have the visibility and control that the product assurance disciplines have the capacity to provide. But we must be careful not to overcompensate and overcontrol. This is the fine line which will distinguish the successful software managers of the 1980's from the rest of the software engineering community.

ACKNOWLEDGMENT

The author wishes to acknowledge the contribution of B. J. Gregor to the preparation and critique of the final manuscript.

REFERENCES

[1] "Contracting for computer software development—Serious problems require management attention to avoid wasting additional millions," General Accounting Office, Rep. FGMSD 80-4, Nov. 9, 1979.

[2] D. M. Weiss, "The MUDD report: A case study of Navy software development practices," Naval Res. Lab., Rep. 7909, May 21, 1975.

[3] B. W. Boehm, "Software engineering," *IEEE Trans. Comput.*, vol. C-25, pp. 1226–1241, Dec. 1976.

[4] *Proc. IEEE* (Special Issue on Software Engineering), vol. 68, Sept. 1980.

[5] E. Bersoff, V. Henderson, and S. Siegel, "Attaining software product integrity," *Tutorial: Software Configuration Management,* W. Bryan, C. Chadbourne, and S. Siegel, Eds., Los Alamitos, CA, IEEE Comput. Soc., Cat. EHO-169-3, 1981.

[6] B. W. Boehm *et al., Characteristics of Software Quality, TRW Series of Software Technology,* vol. 1. New York: North-Holland, 1978.

[7] T. A. Thayer, *et al., Software Reliability, TRW Series of Software Technology,* vol. 2. New York: North-Holland, 1978.

[8]   D. J. Reifer, Ed., *Tutorial: Automated Tools for Software Eng.*, Los Alamitos, CA, IEEE Comput. Soc., Cat. EHO-169-3, 1979.

[9]   E. Bersoff, V. Henderson, and S. Siegel, *Software Configuration Management*.   Englewood Cliffs, NJ: Prentice-Hall, 1980.

[10] ——, "Software configuration management: A tutorial," *Computer*, vol. 12, pp. 6–14, Jan. 1979.

[11] W. Bryan, S. Siegel, and G. Whiteleather, "Auditing throughout the software life cycle: A primer," *Computer*, vol. 15, pp. 56–67, Mar. 1982.

[12] "Software configuration management," Naval Elec. Syst. Command, Software Management Guidebooks, vol. 2, undated.

Evaluating Software Engineering Standards

Shari Lawrence Pfleeger, Norman Fenton, and Stella Page
Centre for Software Reliability

oftware engineering standards abound; since 1976, the Software Engineering Standards Committee of the IEEE Computer Society has developed 19 standards in areas such as terminology, documentation, testing, verification and validation, reviews, and audits.[1] In 1992 alone, standards were completed for productivity and quality metrics, software maintenance, and CASE (computer-aided software engineering) tool selection. If we include work of the major national standards bodies throughout the world, there are in fact more than 250 software engineering standards. The existence of these standards raises some important questions. How do we know which practices to standardize? Since many of our projects produce less-than-desirable products, are the standards not working, or being ignored? Perhaps the answer is that standards have codified approaches whose effectiveness has not been rigorously and scientifically demonstrated. Rather, we have too often relied on anecdote, "gut feeling," the opinions of experts, or even flawed research, rather than on careful, rigorous software engineering experimentation.

This article reports on the results of the Smartie project (Standards and Methods Assessment Using Rigorous Techniques in Industrial Environments), a collaborative effort to propose a widely applicable procedure for the objective assessment of standards used in software development. We hope that, for a given environment and application area, Smartie will enable the identification of standards whose use is most likely to lead to improvements in some aspect of software development processes and products. In this article, we describe how we verified the practicality of the Smartie framework by testing it with corporate partners.

Suppose your organization is considering the implementation of a standard. Smartie should help you to answer the following questions:

- What are the potential benefits of using the standard?
- Can we measure objectively the extent of any benefits that may result from its use?
- What are the related costs necessary to implement the standard?
- Do the costs exceed the benefits?

Given the more than 250 software engineering standards, why do we sometimes still produce less than desirable products? Are the standards not working, or being ignored?

Reprinted from *IEEE Software*, Vol. 11, No. 5, Sept. 1994, pp. 71–79.

To that end, we present Smartie in three parts. First, we analyze what typical standards look like, both in software engineering and in other engineering disciplines. Next, we discuss how to evaluate a standard for its applicability and objectivity. Finally, we describe the results of a major industrial case study involving the reliability and maintainability of almost two million lines of code.

Software engineering standards

Standards organizations have developed standards for standards, including a definition of what a standard is. For example, the British Standards Institute defines a standard as

> A technical specification or other document available to the public, drawn up with the cooperation and consensus or general approval of all interests affected by it, based on the consolidated results of science, technology and experience, aimed at the promotion of optimum community benefits.[2]

Do software engineering standards satisfy this definition? Not quite. Our standards are technical specifications available to the public, but they are not always drawn up with the consensus or general approval of all interests affected by them. For example, airline passengers were not consulted when standards were set for building the A320's fly-by-wire software, nor were electricity consumers polled when software standards for nuclear power stations were considered. Of course, the same could be said for other standards; for example, parents may not have been involved in the writing of safety standards for pushchairs (strollers). Nevertheless, the intention of a standard is to reflect the needs of the users or consumers as well as the practices of the builders. More importantly, our standards are not based on the consolidated results of science, technology, and experience.[3] Programming languages are declared to be corporate or even national standards without case studies and experiments to demonstrate the costs and benefits of using them. Techniques such as cleanroom, formal specification, or object-oriented design are mandated before we determine under what circumstances they are most beneficial. Even when scientific analysis and evaluation

exist, our standards rarely reference them. So even though our standards are laudably aimed at promoting community benefits, we do not insist on having those benefits demonstrated clearly and scientifically before the standard is published. Moreover, there is rarely a set of objective criteria that we can use to evaluate the proposed technique or process.

Thus, as Smartie researchers, we sought solutions to some of the problems with software engineering standards. We began our investigation by posing three simple questions that we wanted Smartie to help us answer:

- On a given project, what standards are used?
- To what extent is a particular standard followed?
- If a standard is being used, is it effective? That is, is it making a difference in quality or productivity?

What is a standard — and what does it mean for software engineering?

Often, a standard's size and complexity make it difficult to determine whether a particular organization is compliant. If partial compliance is allowed, measurement of the degree of compliance is difficult, if not impossible — consider, for example, the ISO 9000 series and the 14 major activities it promotes.[4] The Smartie project suggests that large standards be considered as a set of smaller "ministandards." A ministandard is a standard with a cohesive, content-related set of requirements. In the remaining discussion, the term *standard* refers to a ministandard.

What is a good standard?

We reviewed dozens of software engineering standards, including international, national, corporate, and organizational standards, to see what we could learn. For each standard, we wanted to know

- How good is the standard?
- What is affected by the standard?
- How can we determine compliance with the standard?
- What is the basis for the standard?

"Goodness" of the standard was difficult to determine, as it involved at least three distinct aspects. First, we wanted to know whether and how we can tell if the standard is being complied with. That is, a standard is not a good standard if there is no way of telling whether a particular organization, process, or piece of code complies with the standard. There are many examples of such "bad" standards. For instance, some testing standards require that all statements be tested "thoroughly"; without a clear definition of "thoroughly," we cannot determine compliance. Second, a standard is good only in terms of the success criteria set for it. In other words, we wanted to know what attributes of the final product (such as reliability or maintainability) are supposed to be improved by using the standard. And finally, we wanted to know the cost of applying the standard. After all, if compliance with the standard is so costly as to make its use impractical, or practical only in certain situations, then cost contributes to "goodness."

We developed a scheme to evaluate the degree of objectivity inherent in assessing compliance. We can classify each requirement being evaluated into one of four categories: reference only, subjective, partially objective, and completely objective. A reference-only requirement declares that something will happen, but there is no way to determine compliance; for example, "Unit testing shall be carried out." A subjective requirement is one in which only a subjective measure of conformance is possible; for example, "Unit testing shall be carried out effectively." A subjective requirement is an improvement over a reference-only requirement, but it is subject to the differing opinions of experts. A partially objective requirement involves a measure of conformance that is somewhat objective but still requires a degree of subjectivity; for example, "Unit testing shall be carried out so that all statements and the most probable paths are tested." An objective requirement is the most desirable kind, as conformance to it can be determined completely objectively; for example, "Unit testing shall be carried out so that all statements are tested."

Clearly, our goal as a profession should be to produce standards with require-

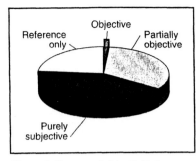

Figure 1. Degree of objectivity in software engineering standards' requirements.

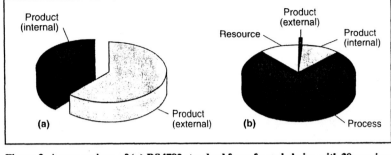

Figure 2. A comparison of (a) BS4792 standard for safe pushchairs, with 29 requirements, and (b) DEF STD 00-55 for safe software, with 115 requirements, shows that software standards place more emphasis on process than on the final product.

ments that are as objective as possible. However, as Figure 1 illustrates, the Smartie review of the requirements in software engineering standards indicates that we are a long way from reaching that goal.

To what do our standards apply?

To continue our investigation, Smartie researchers reviewed software engineering standards to determine what aspect of software development is affected by each standard. We considered four distinct categories of requirements in the standards: process, internal product, external product, and resources. Internal product requirements refer to such items as the code itself, while external product requirements refer to what the user experiences, such as reliability. For examples of these categories, we turn to the British Defence Standard DEF STD 00-55 (interim),[5] issued by the Ministry of Defence (second revision in 1992) for the procurement of safety-critical software in defense equipment. Some are internal product requirements:

- Each module should have a single entry and exit.
- The code should be indented to show its structure.

Others are process requirements:

- The Design Team shall validate the Software Specification against Software Requirements by animation of the formal specification.

while some are resource requirements:

- All tools and support software . . . shall have sufficient safety integrity.
- The Design Authority shall demonstrate . . . that the seniority, authority, qualifications and experience of the staff to be employed on the project are satisfactory for the tasks assigned to them.

Typical of many software standards, DEF STD 00-55 has a mixture of all four types of requirements.

Are software standards like other standards?

Standardization has made life easier in many disciplines. Because of standard voltage and plugs, an electrical appliance from Germany will work properly in Italy. A liter of petrol in one country is the same as a liter in another, thanks to standard measurement. These standards, products of other engineering disciplines, offer lessons that we can learn as software engineers. So the next step in the Smartie process was to examine other engineering standards to see how they differ from those in software engineering. In particular, we asked

- Is the mix of product, process, and resource roughly the same?
- Is the mix of objective and nonobjective compliance evaluation roughly the same?

The answer to both questions is a resounding no. To show just how different software engineering standards are, Figure 2 compares the British standard for pushchair safety with DEF STD 00-55, a

software safety standard.

The figure shows what is true generally: Software engineering standards are heavy on process and light on product, while other engineering standards are the reverse. That is, software engineering standards reflect the implicit assumption that using certain techniques and processes, in concert with "good" tools and people, will necessarily result in a good product. Other engineering disciplines have far less faith in the process; they insist on evaluating the final product in their standards.

Another major difference between our standards and those of other engineering disciplines is in the method of compliance assessment. Most other disciplines include in their standards a description of the method to be used to assess compliance; we do not. In other words, other engineers insist that the proof of the pudding is in the eating: Their standards describe how the eating is to be done, and what the pudding should taste like, look like, and feel like. By contrast, software engineers prescribe the recipe, the utensils, and the cooking techniques, and then assume that the pudding will taste good. If our current standards are not effective, it may be because we need more objective standards and a more balanced mix of process, product, and resource requirements

The proof of the pudding: Case studies

The Smartie framework includes far more than we can describe here — for example, guidelines for evaluating the experiments and case studies on which the standards are based. We address all of these issues in Smartie technical reports, available from the Centre for Software Reliability. For the remainder of this article, we focus on an aspect of Smartie that distinguishes it from other research on standards: its practicality. Because Smartie includes industrial partners, we have evaluated the effectiveness of Smartie itself by applying it to real-life situations. We present here two examples of the Smartie "reality check": (1) applying the framework to written standards for a major company and (2) evaluating the use of standards to meet specified goals.

Both examples involve Company X, a large, nationwide company whose services depend on software. The company is interested in using standards to enhance its software's reliability and maintainability. In the first example, we examine some of the company's programming standards to see if they can be improved. In the second example, we recommend changes to the way data is collected and analyzed, so that management can make better decisions about reliability and maintainability.

Reality check 1: How good are the written standards? We applied the Smartie techniques to a ministandard for using Cobol. The Cobol standard is part of a larger set of mandated standards, called programming guidelines, in the company's system development manual.

Using the guidelines reputedly "facilitate[s] the production of clear, efficient and maintainable Cobol programs." The guidelines were based on expert opinion, not on experiments and case studies demonstrating their effectiveness in comparison with not following the guidelines. This document is clearly designed as a standard rather than a set of guidelines, since "enforceability of the standards is MANDATORY," with "any divergence" being "permanently recorded."

We focused on the layout and naming conventions, items clearly intended to make the code easier to maintain. Layout requirements such as the following can be measured in a completely objective fashion:

- Each statement should be terminated by a full stop.
- Only one verb should appear on any one line.
- Each sentence should commence in

column 12 and on a new line, second and subsequent lines being neatly indented and aligned vertically .... Exceptions are ELSE which will start in the same column as its associated IF and which will appear on a line of its own.

Each line either conforms or does not, and the proportion of lines conforming to all layout requirements represents overall compliance with the standard.

On the other hand, measuring conformance to some naming conventions can be difficult, because such measurements are subjective, as is the case with

- Names must be meaningful.

The Smartie approach recommends that the standard be rewritten to make it

---

The Smartie framework has guidelines for evaluating the case studies on which the standards are based.

---

more objective. For example, improvements might include

- Names must be English or scientific words which themselves appear as identifiable concepts in the specification document(s).
- Abbreviations of names must be consistent.
- Hyphens must be used to separate component parts of names.

Conformance measures can then use the proportion of names that conform to the standard. Analysis of the commenting requirements also led to recommendations that would improve the degree of objectivity in measuring conformance.

Reality check 2: Do the standards address the goals? Company X collects reliability and maintainability data for many of its systems. The company made available to Smartie all of its data relating to a large system essential to its business.

Initiated in November 1987, the system had had 27 releases by the end of 1992. The 1.7 million lines of code for this system involve two programming languages: Cobol (both batch Cobol and CICS Cobol) and Natural (a 4GL). Less than a third of the code is Natural; recent growth (15.2 percent from 1991 to 1992) has been entirely in Cobol. Three corporate and organizational goals are addressed by measuring this system: (1) monitoring and improving product reliability, (2) monitoring and improving product maintainability, and (3) improving the overall development process. The first goal requires information about actual operational failures, while the second requires data on discovering and fixing faults. The third goal, process improvement, is at a higher level than the other two, so Smartie researchers focused primarily on reliability and maintainability as characteristics of process improvement.

The system runs continuously. Users report problems to a help desk whose staff determines whether the problem is a user error or a failure of the system to do something properly. Thus, all the data supplied to Smartie related to software failures rather than to documentation failures. The Smartie team received a complete set of failure information for 1991-92, so the discussion in this section refers to all 481 software failures recorded and fixed during that period. We reviewed the data to see how data collection and analysis standards addressed the overall goal of improving system reliability and maintainability. In many cases, we recommended a simple change that should yield additional, critical information in the future. The remainder of this section describes our findings.

A number is assigned to each "fault" report. We distinguish a fault (what the developer sees) from a failure (what the user sees).[6] Here we use "fault" in quotation marks, since failures are labeled as faults. A typical data point is identified by a "fault" number, the week it was reported, the system area and fault type, the week the underlying cause was fixed and tested, and the actual number of hours to repair the problem (that is, the time from when the maintenance group decides to clear the "fault" until the time when the fix is tested and integrated with the rest of the system). Smartie researchers analyzed this data and made several recommendations about how to improve data collection and analysis to

Existing closure report	Revised closure report
Fault ID: F752	Fault ID: F752
Reported: 18/6/92	Reported: 18/6/92
Definition: Logically deleted work done records appear on enquiries	Definition: Logically deleted work done records appear on enquiries
Description: Causes misleading information to users. Amend Additional Work Performed RDVIPG2A to ignore work done records with flag-amend = 1 or 2	Effect: Misleading information to users
	Cause: Omission of appropriate flag variables for work done records
	Change: Amend Additional Work Performed RDVIPG2A to ignore work done records with flag-amend = 1 or 2

Figure 3. Examples of an existing closure report and a proposed revision.

get a better picture of system maintainability. Nevertheless, the depth of data collection practiced at Company X is to be applauded. In particular, the distinction between hours-to-repair and time between problem-open ("week in") and problem-close ("week out") is a critical one that is not usually made in maintenance organizations.

The maintenance group designated 28 system areas to which underlying faults could be traced. Each system area name referred to a particular function of the system rather than to the system architecture. There was no documented mapping of programs or modules to system areas. A typical system area involved 80 programs, with each program consisting of 1,000 lines of code. The fault type indicated one of 11, many of which were overlapping. In other words, the classes of faults were not orthogonal, so it was possible to find more than one fault class appropriate for a given fault. In addition, there was no direct, recorded link between "fault" and program in most cases. Nor was there information about program size or complexity.

Given this situation, we made two types of recommendations. First, we examined the existing data and suggested simple changes to clarify and separate issues. Second, we extracted additional information by hand from many of the programs. We used the new data to demonstrate that enhanced data collection could provide valuable management information not obtainable with the current forms and data.

Issue 1: Faults versus failures. Because the cause of a problem (that is, a fault) is not always distinguished from the evidence to the user of that problem (that

is, a failure), it is difficult to assess a system's reliability or the degree of user satisfaction. Furthermore, with no mapping from faults to failures, we cannot tell which particular parts or aspects of the system are responsible for most of the problems users are encountering.

• *Recommendation:* Define fault and failure, and make sure the maintenance staff understands the difference between the two. Then, consider failure reports separate from fault reports. For example, a design problem discovered during a design review would be described in a fault report; a problem in function discovered by a user would be described in a failure report.

Issue 2: Mapping from program to system area. Use of system areas to describe faults is helpful, but a mapping is needed from program name to system area. The current information does not reveal whether code in one system area leads to problems in another system area. The batch reporting and integration into the system of problem repairs compounds this difficulty because there is then no recorded link from program to fault. This information must have existed at some point in the maintenance process in order for the problem to be fixed; capturing it at the time of discovery is much more efficient than trying to elicit it well after the fact (and possibly incorrectly).

• *Recommendation:* Separate the system into well-defined system areas and provide a listing that maps each code module to a system area. Then, as problems are reported, indicate the system area affected. Finally, when the cause of the problem is identified, document the

names of the program modules that caused the problem.

Issue 3: Ambiguity and informality inherent in the incident closure reports. The description of each problem reflects the creativity of the recorder rather than standard aspects of the problem. This lack of uniformity makes it impossible to amalgamate the reports and examine overall trends.

• *Recommendation:* The problem description should include the manifestation, effect, and cause of the problem, as shown in Figure 3. Such data would permit traceability and trend analysis.

Issue 4: Fault classification scheme. Because the scheme contains nonorthogonal categories, it is difficult for the maintainer to decide in which category a particular fault belongs. For this reason, some of the classifications may be arbitrary, resulting in a misleading picture when the faults are aggregated and tracked.

• *Recommendation:* Redefine fault categories so that there is no ambiguity or overlap between categories.

Issue 5: Unrecoverable data. By unrecoverable, we mean that the information we need does not exist in some documented form in the organization. For example, most of the problem report forms related a large collection of faults to a large collection of programs that were changed as a result. What appears to be unrecoverable is the exact mapping of program changes to a particular fault. On the other hand, some information was recoverable, but with great difficulty. For example, we re-created size information

Table 1. Recoverable (documented) data versus nonrecoverable (undocumented) data.

Recoverable	Nonrecoverable
Size information for each module Static/complexity information for each module Mapping of faults to programs Severity categories	Operational usage per system (needed for reliability assessment) Success/failure of fixes (needed to assess effectiveness of maintenance process) Number of repeated failures (needed for reliability assessment)

manually from different parts of the data set supplied to us, and we could have related problem severity to problem cause if we had had enough time.

• *Recommendation:* The data in Table 1 would be useful if it were explicit and available to the analysts.

Figures 4 through 8 show what we can learn from the existing data; Figures 9 through 11 (page 78) show how much more we can learn using the additional data.

Since we have neither mean-time-between-failure data nor operational usage information, we cannot depict reliability directly. As an approximation, we examined the trend in the number of "faults" received per week. Figure 4 shows that there is great variability in the number of "faults" per week, suggesting that there is no general improvement in system reliability.

The chart in Figure 5 contrasts the "faults" received with the "faults" addressed and resolved ("actioned") in a given week. Notice that there is wide variation in the proportion of "faults" that are actioned each week. In spite of the lack-of-improvement trend, this chart provides managers with useful information; they can use it to begin an investigation into which "faults" are handled first and why.

Examining the number of "faults" per system area is also useful, and we display the breakdown in Figure 6. However, there is not enough information to know why particular system areas generate more "faults" than others. Without information such as size, complexity, and operational usage, we can draw no definitive conclusions. Similarly, an analysis of "faults" by fault type revealed that data and program faults dominated user, query, and other faults. However, the fault types are not orthogonal, so again there is little that we can conclude.

Figures 7 and 8 show, respectively,

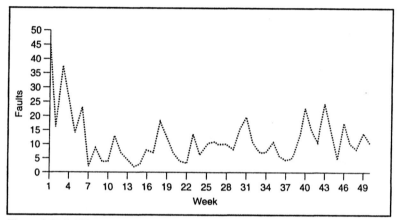

Figure 4. Reliability trend charting the number of faults received per week.

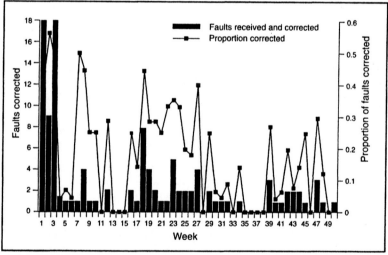

Figure 5. Charting the faults received and acted upon in the same week helps show how Company X deals with software failures.

mean time to repair fault by system area and by fault type. This information highlights interesting variations, but our conclusions are still limited because of missing information about size.

The previous charts contain only the information supplied to us explicitly by Company X. The following charts reflect additional information that was recovered manually. As you can see, this re-

334

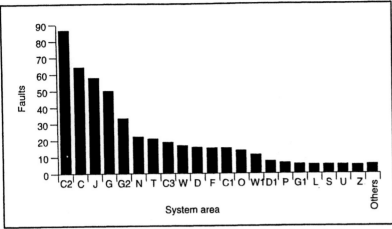

Figure 6. Plotting the number of faults per system area helps isolate fault-prone system areas.

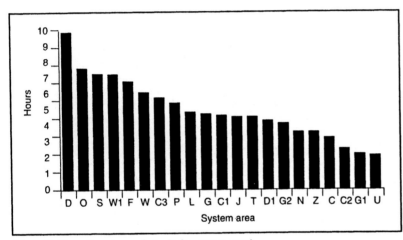

Figure 7. Mean time to repair fault (by system area).

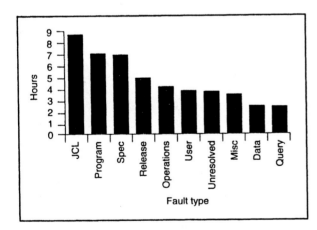

Figure 8. Mean time to repair fault (by fault type).

examined. Recall that Figures 4, 5, and 6 revealed limited information about the distribution of "faults" in the overall system. However, by adding size data, the resulting graph in Figure 10 shows the startling result that C2 — one of the smallest system areas (with only 4,000 lines of code) — has the largest number of "faults." If the fault rates are graphed by system area, as in Figure 11, it is easy to see that C2 dominates the chart. In fact, Figure 11 shows that, compared with published industry figures, each system area except C2 is of very high quality; C2, however, is much worse than the industry average. Without size measurement, this important information would not be visible. Consequently, we recommended that the capture of size information be made standard practice at Company X.

These charts represent examples of our analysis. In each case, improvements to standards for measurement and collection are suggested in light of the organizational goals. Our recommendations reflect the need to make more explicit a small degree of additional information that can result in a very large degree of additional management insight. The current amount of information allows a manager to determine the status of the system; the additional data would yield explanatory information that would allow managers to be proactive rather than reactive during maintenance.

Lessons learned in case studies

The Company X case study was one of several intended to validate the Smartie methodology, not only in terms of finding missing pieces in the methodology, but also by testing the practicality of Smartie for use in an industrial environment (the other case studies are not complete as of this writing). The first and most serious lesson learned in performing the case studies involved the lack of control. Because each investigation was retrospective, we could not

- require measurement of key productivity and quality variables,
- require uniformity or repetition of measurement,
- choose the project, team, or staff characteristics that might have eliminated confounding effects,

covered information enriches the management decisions that can be made on the basis of the charts.

By manually investigating the (poorly documented) link between individual programs and system areas, we examined the relationships among size, language, and system area. Figure 9 shows the variation between CICS Cobol and Natural in each of the main system areas

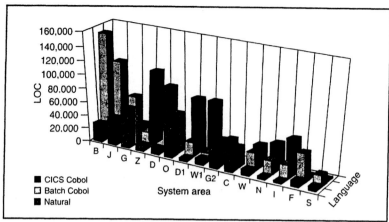

Figure 9. System structure showing system areas with more than 25,000 lines of code and types of programming languages.

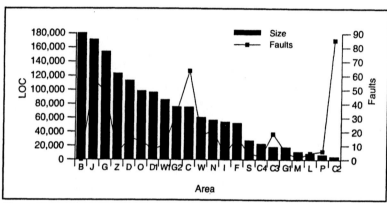

Figure 10. System area size versus number of faults.

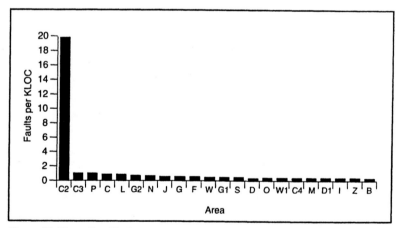

Figure 11. Normalized fault rates.

- choose or rewrite standards so that they were easy to apply and assess,
- choose the type of standard, or

- establish a baseline condition or environment against which to measure change.

The last point is the most crucial. Without a baseline, we cannot describe with confidence the effects of using (or not using) the standards. As a consequence, a great deal of expert (but nevertheless highly subjective) judgment was necessary in assessing the results of the case studies. It is also clear that a consistent level of control must be maintained throughout the period of the case study. There were many events, organizational and managerial as well as technical, that affected the outcome of the case study, and about which we had no input or control. In particular, lack of control led to incomplete or inconsistent data. For example, a single problem report usually included several problems related only by the time period in which the problems occurred. Or the description of a single type of problem varied from report to report, depending on the documentation style of the maintainer and the time available to write the description. With such inconsistency, it is impossible to aggregate the problem reports or fault information in a meaningful way; it is also impossible to evaluate the root causes of problems and relate them to the use of standards. Indeed, the very lack of standards in data collection and reporting inhibits us from doing a thorough analysis.

A final difficulty with our assessment derives from the lack of information about cost. Although we have Company X data on the time required to fix a problem, the company did not keep careful records on the cost of implementation or maintenance at a level that allows us to understand the cost implications of standards use. That is, even if we can show that using standards is beneficial for product quality, we cannot assess the trade-offs between the increase in quality and the cost of achieving that quality. Without such information, managers in a production environment would be loath to adopt standards, even if the standards were certifiably effective according to the Smartie (or any other) methodology.

We learned a great deal from reviewing standards and administering case studies. The first and most startling result of our work is that many standards are not really standards at all. Many "standards" are reference or subjective requirements, suggesting that they are really guidelines (since degree of compliance cannot be evaluated). Organizations with such standards should revisit their goals and revise the standards to address the goals in a more objective way.

We also found wide variety in conformance from one employee to another as well as from one module to another. In one of our case studies, management assured us that all modules were 100 percent compliant with the company's own structured programming standards, since it was mandatory company practice. Our review revealed that only 58 percent of the modules complied with the standards, even though the standards were clearly stated and could be objectively evaluated.

A related issue is that of identifying the portion of the project affected by the standard and then examining conformance only within that portion. That is, some standards apply only to certain types of modules, so notions of conformance must be adjusted to consider only that part of the system that is subject to the standard in the first place. For example, if a standard applies only to interface modules, then 50 percent compliance should mean that only 50 percent of the interface modules comply, not that 50 percent of the system is comprised of interface modules and that all of them comply.

More generally, we found that we have a lot to learn from standards in other engineering disciplines. Our standards lack objective assessment criteria, involve more process than product, and are not always based on rigorous experimental results.

Thus, we recommend that software engineering standards be reviewed and revised. The resulting standards should be cohesive collections of requirements to which conformance can be established objectively. Moreover, there should be a clearly stated benefit to each standard and a reference to the set of experiments or case studies demonstrating that benefit. Finally, software engineering standards should be better balanced, with more product requirements in relation to process and resource requirements. With standards expressed in this way, managers can use project objectives to guide standards' intention and implementation.

The Smartie recommendations and framework are practical and effective in identifying problems with standards and in making clear the kinds of changes that are needed. Our case studies have demonstrated that small, simple changes to standards writing, and especially to data collection standards, can improve significantly the quality of information about what is going on in a system and with a project. In particular, these simple changes can move the project from assessment to understanding. ∎

Acknowledgments

We gratefully acknowledge the assistance of other participants in the SERC/DTI-funded Smartie project: Colum Devine, Jennifer Thornton, Katie Perrin, Derek Jaques, Danny McComish, Eric Trodd, Bev Littlewood, and Peter Mellor.

References

1. *IEEE Software Engineering Technical Committee Newsletter*, Vol. 11, No. 3, Jan. 1993, p. 4.

2. British Standards Institute, *British Standards Guide: A Standard for Standards*, London, 1981.

3. N. Fenton, S.L. Pfleeger, and R.L. Glass, "Science and Substance: A Challenge to Software Engineers," *IEEE Software*, Vol. 11, No. 4, July 1994, pp. 86-95.

4. International Standards Organization, *ISO 9000: Quality Management and Quality Assurance Standards — Guidelines for Selection and Use*, 1987 (with ISO 9001 - 9004).

5. Ministry of Defence Directorate of Standardization, *Interim Defence Standard 00-55: The Procurement of Safety-Critical Software in Defence Equipment, Parts 1-2*, Glasgow, Scotland, 1992.

6. P. Mellor, "Failures, Faults, and Changes in Dependability Measurement," *J. Information and Software Technology*, Vol. 34, No. 10, Oct. 1992, pp. 640-654.

Software-Reliability Engineering: Technology for the 1990s

John D. Musa and *William W. Everett*, AT&T Bell Laboratories

Software engineering is about to reach a new stage — the reliability stage — that stresses customers' operational needs. Software-reliability engineering will make this stage possible.

Where will software engineering head in the 1990s? Not an easy question to answer, but a look at its history and recent evolution may offer some clues. Software engineering has evolved through several stages during its history, each adding a new expectation on the part of users:

• In the initial *functional* stage, functions that had been done manually were automated. The return on investment in automation was so large that *providing* the automated functions was all that mattered.

• The *schedule* stage followed. By this point, users' consciousness had been raised about the financial effects of having important operational capabilities delivered earlier rather than later. The need to introduce new systems and features on an orderly basis had become evident. Users were painfully aware of operational disruptions caused by late deliveries. Schedule-estimation and -management technology used for hardware systems was coupled with data and experience gained from software development and applied.

• The *cost* stage reflected the widespread use of personal computers, where price was a particularly important factor. Technology for estimating software productivity and cost and for engineering and managing it to some degree — however imperfect — was developed.

• We are now seeing the start of the fourth stage — *reliability* — which is based on engineering the level of reliability to be provided for a software-based system. It derives from the increasingly absolute operational dependence of most users on their information systems and the concomitant heavily increasing costs of failure. This stage must respond to the need to consider reliability as one of a set of factors (principally functionality, delivery date, cost, and reliability) that customers view as comprising quality. It must contend with the reality — not always fully recognized by users — that for any stage of tech-

Reprinted from *IEEE Software*, Vol. 7, No. 4, Nov. 1990, pp. 36–43.

nology, improving one of the quality factors may adversely affect one of the others.

In response to this challenge, a substantial technology — software-reliability engineering — has been developed[1] and is already seeing practical use.[2] Trends indicate that it will be extensively applied and perfected in the 1990s.

What is it?

Software-reliability engineering is the applied science of predicting, measuring, and managing the reliability of software-based systems to maximize customer satisfaction. Reliability is the probability of failure-free operation for a specified period. Software-reliability engineering helps a product gain a competitive edge by satisfying customer needs more precisely and thus more efficiently.

Software-reliability engineering includes such activities as
- helping select the mix of principal quality factors (reliability, cost, and availability date of new features) that maximize customer satisfaction,
- establishing an operational (frequency of use) profile for the system's functions,
- guiding selection of product architecture and efficient design of the development process to meet the reliability objective,
- predicting reliability from the characteristics of both the product and the development process or estimating it from failure data in test, based on models and expected use,
- managing the development process to meet the reliability objective,
- measuring reliability in operation,
- managing the effects of software modification on customer operation with reliability measures,
- using reliability measures to guide development process improvement, and
- using reliability measures to guide software acquisition.

Software-reliability engineering works in concert with fault-tolerance, fault-avoidance, and fault-removal technologies, as well as with failure-modes and -effects analysis and fault-tree analysis. It should be applied in parallel with hardware-reliability engineering, since customers are interested in the reliability of the whole *system*.[3]

Why is it important?

The intense international competition in almost all industries that developed in the late 1980s and that will probably in-

---

There appears to be a strong correlation between interest in adopting reliability-engineering technology and the competitiveness of the organization or project concerned.

---

crease in this decade has made software-reliability engineering an important technology for the 1990s. The sharply dropping costs of transportation and, particularly, communication, the rapidly increasing competitiveness of the Pacific Rim countries, the ascent of the European Economic Community, and the entry of the Communist bloc into the world economy all indicate the likely continued strength of this trend.

The fact that the world economy has evolved from being labor-intensive to capital-intensive (with the Industrial Revolution) and now to information-intensive to meet this competition makes high-quality information processing critical to the viability of every institution. Thus, customers of software suppliers have become very

demanding in their requirements. Fierce competition has sprung up between suppliers for their business.

It is no longer possible to tolerate one-dimensional conservatism when engineering quality factors. If you err on the safe side and build unneeded reliability into products, a competitor will offer your customers the reliability they do need at a lower price or with faster delivery or some combination of both. You must understand and deal with the real interactive multidimensionality of customer needs and make trade-offs. Above all, you must precisely specify, measure, and control the key quality factors.

We have observed an interesting phenomenon: There appears to be a strong correlation between interest in adopting reliability-engineering technology and the competitiveness of the organization or project concerned.

The arguments for achieving quality in software products are persuasive. A study[4] of factors influencing long-term return on investment showed that the top third of companies in customer-perceived quality averaged a return of 29 percent; the bottom third, 14 percent. Increased demand for quality also increases the importance of precisely measuring how well your competitors are doing in providing quality to the market.

It is also becoming increasingly important that the right level of reliability be achieved the first time around. In the past, without customer-oriented measures to guide us, we often approached reliability incrementally. We guessed what the customer wanted, provided an approximation to it, awaited the customer's dissatisfactions, and then tried to ameliorate them.

But the costs of operational disruption and recovery that the customer encounters due to failures have increased and are increasing relative to other costs. With

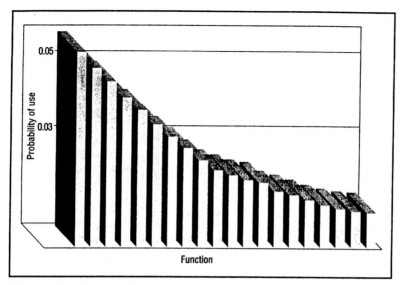

Figure 1. Operational profile.

such pressures, loss of confidence in a software supplier can be rapid. This trend argues for greatly increased and quantified communication between supplier and customer — from the start.

Thus, the application and perfection of sofware reliability engineering is rapidly growing in importance. It provides a measurement dimension of quality that has until recently been lacking, with very detrimental results.

Basic concepts

To understand software-reliability engineering, you must start with some important definitions:

• A software *failure* is some behavior of the executing program that does not meet the customer's operational requirements.

• A software *fault* is a defect in the code that may cause a failure.

For example, if a command entered at a workstation does not result in the requisite display appearing, you have a failure. The cause of that failure may be a fault consisting of an incorrect argument in a calling statement to a subroutine.

Failures are customer-oriented; faults are developer-oriented.

New thinking in software-reliability engineering lets you combine functionality and reliability into one generic reliability figure, if desired. System requirements are interpreted both in terms of functions explicitly included in a product and in terms of those that the customer needs but that are not included in the product. If a function is lacking, the product is charged with a failure each time the customer needs the absent function. Thus a

low level of functionality will result in a low level of reliability.

Of course, some objective basis for "needs" must be established, such as an analysis of the customer's operation or the union of all features of competitive products. Otherwise, the needs list could become an open-ended list of unrealistic wishes.

There are two alternative ways of expressing the software-reliability concept, which are related by a simple formula[1]:

• *Software reliability* proper is the probability of failure-free operation for a specified time duration.

• The other expression is *failure intensity*, the number of failures experienced per time period. Time is *execution time*: the actual time the processor is executing the program. As an example, a program with a reliability of 0.92 would operate without failure for 10 hours of execution with a probability of 0.92. Alternatively, you could say that the failure intensity is eight failures per thousand hours of execution.

Varying operational effects of failures can be handled by classifying failures by *severity*, usually measured by threat to human life or by economic impact. You can determine a reliability or failure intensity for each severity class, or you can combine the classes through appropriate weighting to yield a loss function like dollars per hour of operation.

Fault measures, often expressed as *fault density* or faults per thousand executable source lines, are generally not useful to customers. Although they can help developers probe the development process to try to understand the factors that influ-

ence it, you must relate them to measures like failure intensity and reliability if — as is proper — measures of customer satisfaction are to be the ultimate arbiters.

Another important concept is the *operational profile*. It is the set of the functions the software can perform with their probabilities of occurrence. Figure 1 shows a sample operational profile. The profile expresses how the customer uses or expects to use the software.[1,5]

Setting improvement goals. Companies' software-improvement goals have usually not been set from the customer's perspective. However, percentage-improvement goals stated in terms of the customer-oriented failure intensity (failures per thousand CPU hours) rather than the developer-oriented fault density (faults per thousand source lines) are both better in meeting the customer's needs and *much easier* to achieve.

Improving failure intensity is easier because you can take advantage of an operational profile that is usually nonuniform and concentrate your quality-improvement efforts on the functions used most frequently.

A simple example illustrates this point. For the same amount of testing, the failure intensity is proportional to the number of faults introduced into the code during development.[1] Let the proportionality factor be k. Assume that a system performs only two functions: function A 90 percent of the time and function B 10 percent. Suppose that the software contains 100 faults, with 50 associated with each function.

Improving the fault density by 10 times means that you must improve development over the entire program so that 90 fewer faults are introduced.

The current failure intensity is $0.9(50)k + 0.1(50)k$, or $50k$. If you concentrate your development efforts on the most frequently used function so it has no faults, the new failure intensity will be $0.1(50)k$, or $5k$.

You have reduced the failure intensity by a factor of 10 through improvements in development involving only a factor-of-two reduction in the number of faults (50 faults). A similar but more extended analysis could also take account of failure severity.

Reliability models. Models play an important role in relating reliability to the factors that affect it. To both represent the failure process accurately and have maximum usefulness, reliability models need two components:

• The *execution-time* component relates failures to execution time, properties of the software being developed, properties of the development environment, and properties of the operating environment. Failure intensity can decrease, remain fixed, or increase with execution time. The last behavior is not of practical interest. Decreasing failure intensity, shown in Figure 2, is common during system test because the removal of faults reduces the rate at which failures occur. Constant failure intensity usually occurs for systems released to the field, when systems are ordinarily stable and no fault removal occurs.

• The *calendar-time* component relates the passage of calendar time to execution time. During test, it is based on the fact that resources like testers, debuggers, and computer time are limited and that these resources, each at a different time, control the ratio between calendar time and execution time. During field operation, the relationship is simpler and depends only on how the computer is used.

Life cycle

You apply software-reliability engineering in each phase of the life cycle: definition, design and implementation, validation, and operation and maintenance.[6] The definition phase focuses on developing a requirements specification for a product that can profitably meet some set of needs for some group of customers. System and software engineers develop product designs from the product requirements, and software engineers implement them in code in the design and implementation phase. Test teams, usually independent of the design and implementation teams, operate the product in the validation phase to see if it meets the requirements. In the operation and maintenance phase, the product is delivered to and used by the customer. The maintenance staff responds to customer requests for new features and to reported problems by developing and delivering software changes.

Definition phase. Good product definition is essential for success in the marketplace. The primary output of the definition phase is a product-requirements specification. The product's failure-intensity objective should be explicitly included.

The first step in setting the failure-intensity objective is to work with the customer to define what a failure is from the customer's perspective. Next, you categorize failures by *severity*, or the effect they have on the customer. Determine the customer's tolerance to failures of different severities and willingness to pay for reduced failure intensities in each failure-severity category.

Looking at the customer's experiences with past and existing products will help both of you determine the value of reliability. A larger market reduces the per-unit cost of reliability, making higher reliability more feasible.

Another consideration is assessing the reliability of competitors' products. You must also determine the effects of meeting the failure-intensity objective on delivery date.

You can then use the information developed in each of these steps to establish failure-intensity objectives, trading off product reliability, cost, and delivery date.

Customers generally view the foregoing communication very favorably. It greatly improves the match between product characteristics and customer needs, and it generally increases the customer's trust in the supplier.

Now, you need two other items:

• The operational profile, since the product's reliability may depend on how the product will be used.

• Estimates relating calendar time to execution time, so that failure-intensity objectives expressed in terms of calendar time (the form customers can relate to) can be translated into failure-intensity objectives expressed in terms of execution time (the form relevant to software).

So you can readily determine failure intensity in testing and in the field, you should consider building automatic failure identification and reporting into the system.

Two questions often asked about applying models during the definition phase are:

• How accurate are the reliability predic-

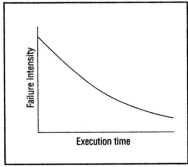

Figure 2. General appearance of the software-reliability model's execution-time component.

tions made at this time?

• Is the effort to model reliability at this point worth it?

There is not enough information to give a definitive answer to the first question today, although there are some indications that the accuracy may be within a factor of three or four. Accuracy is likely to be determined and to improve as the field progresses and appropriate data is collected.

As to the second question, the effort would probably not be worth it if the modeling were carried no further than just predicting software reliability. However, the modeling should continue into the design and implementation, validation, and operation and maintenance phases. Particularly during the validation and the operation and maintenance phases, you can use modeling with collected data to track whether reliability objectives are being met. Also, you can use the results to refine the prediction process for the future.

The real utility of modeling becomes evident in this cycle of model, measure, and refine. Furthermore, applying models during the definition phase forces project teams to focus very early on reliability issues and baseline assumptions about the product's reliability *before* development begins.

Design and implementation phase. The first goal of the design and implementation phase is to turn the requirements specification into design specifications for the product and the development pro-

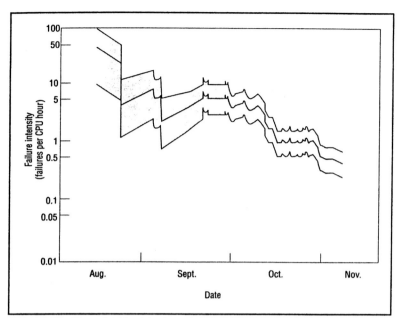

Figure 3. Tracking reliability status in system test. The center curve indicates the most likely value of failure intensity. The shaded area represents the interval within which the true failure intensity lies with 75-percent confidence. The *y* axis is logarithmic so the data can fit the graph.

cess. Then the process is implemented.

An early activity of this phase is allocating the system-reliability objective among the components. In some cases, you may want to consider different architectural options. You should analyze whether you can attain the reliability objective with the proposed design.

It will usually be necessary to identify critical functions for which failure may cause catastrophic effects. You should then identify the modules whose satisfactory operation is essential to the functions, using techniques like failure-modes and -effects analysis and fault-tree analysis. You can then single out the critical modules for special fault-avoidance or fault-removal activities. You may also use fault-tolerance techniques like periodic auditing of key variables during program execution and recovery blocks.

The design of the development process consists of determining the development activities to be performed with their associated time and resource requirements. Usually, more than one plan can meet the product requirements, but some plans are faster, less expensive, or more reliable than others.

The software-reliability-engineering part of the development-process design involves examining the controllable and uncontrollable factors that influence reliability. Controllable factors include such

things as use or nonuse of design inspections, thoroughness of design inspections, and time and resources devoted to system test. Uncontrollable (or perhaps minimally controllable) factors are usually related to the product or the work environment; for example, program size, volatility of requirements, and average experience of staff.

You use the uncontrollable factors to predict the failure intensity that would occur without any attempt to influence it. You then choose suitable values of the controllable factors to achieve the failure-intensity objective desired within acceptable cost and schedule limits. Techniques now exist to predict the effects of some of the factors, and appropriate studies should be able to determine the effects of the others. The relationships between the factors and reliability must be expressed in simple terms that software engineers can intuitively understand. Otherwise, they are not likely to apply them.

You should construct a reliability time line to indicate goals for how reliability should improve as you progress through the life cycle from design through inspection to coding to unit test to system test to release. You use this time line to evaluate progress. If progress is not satisfactory, several actions are possible:

• Reallocate project resources (for example, from test team to debugging team

or from low-usage to high-usage functions).

• Redesign the development process (for example, lengthening the system-test phase).

• Redesign subsystems that have low reliability.

• Respecify the requirements in negotiation with the customers (they might accept lower reliability for on-time delivery).

Reliability can't be directly measured in the design and coding stages. However, there is a good chance that indirect methods will be developed based on trends in finding design errors and later trends in discovering code faults by inspection or self-checking.

Syntactic faults are usually found by compilers or perhaps editors, so you should concentrate on *semantic* faults to predict reliability. In unit test, we anticipate that methods will be developed to estimate reliability from failure trends.

Another important activity is to certify the reliability of both acquired software and reused software (not only application software but also system software like operating-system and communication-interface software). You should establish the reliability of such components through testing with the operational profile expected for the new product.

The operational profile can help increase productivity and reduce cost during the design and implementation phase by helping guide where you should focus design resources.

Verification activities like inspections, unit test, and subsystem test are commonly conducted during the design and implementation phase. You can apply inspections to both design and code.

Validation phase. The primary thrust of validation is to certify that the product meets customer requirements and is suitable for customer use. Product validation for software generally includes system tests and field trials.

Software-reliability measurements are particularly useful in combination with reliability testing (also called longevity or stability testing). During reliability testing, you generally execute functions with relative frequencies that match what is specified in the operational profile. When fail-

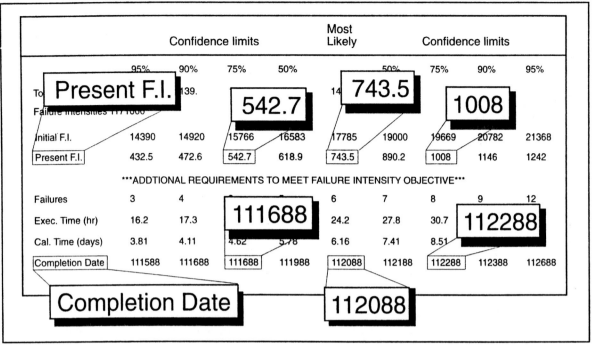

	Confidence limits				Most Likely		Confidence limits		
	95%	90%	75%	50%	50%		75%	90%	95%
Failure intensities	139.		**542.7**		**743.5**	14	**1008**		
Initial F.I.	14390	14920	15766	16583	17785	19000	19669	20782	21368
Present F.I.	432.5	472.6	542.7	618.9	743.5	890.2	1008	1146	1242

ADDTIONAL REQUIREMENTS TO MEET FAILURE INTENSITY OBJECTIVE

Failures	3	4	**111688**		6	7	8	9	12
Exec. Time (hr)	16.2	17.3			24.2	27.8	30.7	**112288**	
Cal. Time (days)	3.81	4.11	4.62	5.78	6.16	7.41	8.51		
Completion Date	111588	111688	111688	111988	112088	112188	112288	112388	112688

Present F.I.

Completion Date   **112088**

Figure 4. Sample printout from Reltools. The present failure intensity lets you determine whether the failure-intensity objective has been met. Key quantities are called out here for emphasis.

ures are experienced, developers start a correction process to identify and remove the faults causing them.

You may use multiple operational profiles, each relating to a different application with its associated market segment.

We expect it will be possible in the future to test using strategies with function-occurrence frequencies that depart from the operational profile. You would compensate for this departure from the profile by adjusting the measured failure intensities.

To obtain the desired reliability quantities, you first record failures and the corresponding execution times (from the start of test). Then you run a software-reliability-estimation program like Reltools (available from the authors), which uses statistical techniques to estimate the parameters of the software-reliability model's execution-time component, based on the recorded failure data. Applying the execution-time component with the estimated parameters, it determines such useful quantities as current failure intensity and the remaining execution time needed to meet the failure-intensity objective. It also uses the calendar-time component to estimate remaining calendar time needed for testing to achieve the failure-intensity objective.[7]

Managers and engineers can track reli-

ability status during system test, as Figure 3 shows. The plot shows real project data. The downward trend is clear despite real-world perturbations due to statistical noise and departures of the project from underlying model assumptions. The actual improvement in failure intensity is about 70 to 1, a fact deemphasized by the need to use a logarithmic scale to fit the curves on the chart.

Problems are highlighted when the downward trend does not progress as expected, which alerts you before the problem gets too severe. Cray Research is one company that applies reliability tracking for this purpose as standard practice in its compiler development.

Figure 4 shows a sample printout produced by Reltools. The way it presents current failure intensity lets you determine whether the failure-intensity objective has been met. You can use this as a criterion for release, so you are confident that customer needs are met before shipping. There have been several demonstrations of the value of software reliability as a release criterion, including applications at AT&T[8] and Hewlett-Packard.[9] Cray Research[10] uses such a release criterion as standard practice.

Operation and maintenance phase. The primary thrust of the operation and main-

tenance phase is to move the product into the customers' day-to-day operations, support customers in their use of the product, develop new features needed by customers, and fix faults in the software that affect the customers' use of the product.

For those organizations that have operational responsibility for software products, reliability measurement can help monitor the operating software's reliability. You can use the results to determine if there is any degradation in reliability over time (for example, degradation caused by the introduction of additional faults when software fixes are installed). Software-reliability measurement can help you time the addition of new software features so reliability is not reduced below a tolerable level for the user.

Field-support engineers can use operational software-reliability measures to compare the customer's perceived level of reliability to the reliability measured by the supplier at release. Several factors could cause these measures to differ: different definitions of "failure," different operational profiles, or different versions of the software. Determining which factors contribute to the differences and feeding information back to the appropriate people is an important task.

You can also apply software-reliability engineering to maintenance. One prime example is using the frequency and severity of failures to rank the order for repairing underlying faults. In addition to other considerations, users usually consider failures in old functions more severe than those in new functions because their operations are likely to be more heavily affected by the old functions they depend on.

You can also use software-reliability-engineering methods to size the maintenance staff needed to repair faults reported from field sites. You can use the methods to estimate PROM production rates for firmware. Also, you can use them to estimate warranty costs. A potential use is to determine the optimum mix of fault-removal and new-feature activities in releases.

Process improvement. The most important activity that you can conduct near the end of the life cycle is a *root-cause analysis* of faults. Such an analysis determines when and how the faults are introduced and what changes should be made to the development process to reduce the number introduced in the future.

Also, if you have used a new technique, tool, or other "improvement" to the software-engineering process, you should try to evaluate its effect on reliability. This implies a comparison with another situation in which all product and process variables are held constant except the one whose effect is being checked. That can be difficult across projects, so it may be more feasible to test the "improvement" across subsystems of the same project.

Research opportunities

The applications of software-reliability engineering described here have in most cases been based on existing capabilities, which in some instances have already been used on a pilot basis. However, some depend on extensions requiring studies, usually based on actual project data. The structure of this research appears reasonably clear, and in many cases it is well under way. There is of course some risk that all the extensions might not come to fruition.

Predicting reliability. The largest and most significant area of potential advance is the prediction of reliability before pro-

gram execution from characteristics of the software product and the development process. Initial work[1] indicates that failure intensity is related to the number of faults remaining in the software at the start of system test, the size of the program in object instructions, the average processing speed of the computer running the software, and the fault-exposure ratio. The fault-exposure ratio represents the proportion of time that a hypothetical encounter of a fault, based on processing speed and program size, would result in failure.

Some evidence indicates that the fault-exposure ratio may be a constant. This needs to be verified over a range of projects. If not constant, it may vary with a few factors like some measures of program "branchiness" and "loopiness." These relationships would need to be developed.

The number of faults remaining at the start of system test is clearly related to program size. You can approximate it by the number of faults detected in system test and operation, provided the operating period totaled over all installations is large and the rate of detection of faults is approaching zero.

Studies indicate that it depends (to a lesser degree) on the number of specification changes, thoroughness of design documentation, average programmer skill level, percent of reviews accomplished, and percent of code read. It is possible that adding more factors would further improve such predictions; finding out requires a study of multiple projects.

The selection of appropriate factors might be aided by insight gained from root-cause analysis of why faults get introduced. Our experience indicates that the factors are most likely related to characteristics of the development process rather than the product itself.

Interestingly, complexity other than that due to size seems to average out for programs above the module level. Thus, it is not an operative factor. This fact appears to support the conjecture that the fault-exposure ratio may be constant.

Estimating before test. An area of challenge is to find a way to estimate the number of remaining faults based on patterns of data taken on design errors detected in

design inspections and coding faults detected in desk-checking or code walk-throughs.

This estimate of remaining faults is needed to estimate software reliability before test for comparison with a reliability time line. One possibility would be to apply an analog of software-reliability-modeling and -estimation procedures to the values of inspection or walkthrough execution times at which you experience the design errors or code faults.

Estimating during test. Work is needed to develop ways of applying software-reliability theory to estimating failure intensity during unit test. There are two problems to deal with:

• the small sample sizes of failures and
• efficiently determining the operational profiles for units from the system's operational profile.

Estimating reliability from failure data in system test works fairly well, but improvements could be made in reducing estimation bias for both parameters and predicted quantities. Adaptive prediction, which feeds back the prediction results to improve the model, is showing considerable promise.

Other opportunities. Current work on developing algorithms to compensate for testing with run profiles that are different from the operational profile may open up a substantially expanded range of application for sofwtare-reliability engineering.

As software-reliability engineering is used on more and more projects, special problems may turn up, as is the case with any new technology. These offer excellent opportunities for those who can closely couple research and practice and communicate their results.

Software-reliability engineering, although not yet completely developed, is a discipline that is advancing at a rapid pace. Its benefits are clear. It is being practically applied in industry. And research is proceeding to answer many of the problems that have been raised. It is likely to advance further in the near future. This will put the practice of software engineering on a more quantitative basis. ❖

Acknowledgments

The authors are grateful to Frank Ackerman, Jack Adams, Bob Brownlie, Mary Donnelly, Anthony Iannino, Tom Riedl, Sheldon Robinson, and the other authors in this special issue for their helpful reviews.

References

1. J.D. Musa, A. Iannino, and K. Okumoto, *Software Reliability: Measurement, Prediction, Application*, McGraw-Hill, New York, 1987.

2. J.D. Musa, "Tools for Measuring Software Reliability," *IEEE Spectrum*, Feb. 1989, pp. 39-42.

3. L. Bernstein and C.M. Yuhas, "Taking the Right Measure of System Performance," *Computerworld*, July 30, 1984, pp. ID-1–ID-4.

4. R.D. Buzzell and B.T. Gale, *The PIMS Principles: Linking Strategy to Performance*, The Free Press, New York, 1987, p. 109.

5. W.K. Ehrlich, J.P. Stampfel, and J.R. Wu, "Application of Software-Reliability Modeling to Product Quality and Test Process," *Proc. 12th Int'l Conf. Software Eng.*, CS Press, Los Alamitos, Calif., pp. 108-116.

6. W.W. Everett, "Software-Reliability Measurement," *IEEE J. Selected Areas in Comm.*, Feb. 1990, pp. 247-252.

7. J.D. Musa and A.F. Ackerman, "Quantifying Software Validation: When to Stop Testing?" *IEEE Software*, May 1989, pp. 19-27.

8. P. Harrington, "Applying Customer-Oriented Quality Metrics," IEEE Software, Nov. 1989, pp. 71, 74.

9. H.D. Drake and D.E. Wolting, "Reliability Theory Applied to Software Testing," *Hewlett-Packard J.*, April 1987, pp. 35-39.

10. K.C. Zinnel, "Using Software-Reliability Growth Models to Guide Release Decisions," *Proc. IEEE Subcommittee Software-Reliability Eng.*, 1990, available from the authors.

Chapter 10

Software Project Management

1. Introduction to Chapter

Management can be defined as all the activities and tasks undertaken by one or more persons for the purpose of planning and controlling the activities of others in order to achieve an objective or complete an activity that could not be achieved by the others acting independently [1]. The classic management model as portrayed by well-known authors in the field of management [2], [3], [4], [5], [6] contains the following components:

Planning
Organizing
Staffing
Directing
Controlling

Project management is defined as a system of procedures, practices, technologies, and know-how that provides the planning, organizing, staffing, directing, and controlling necessary to successfully manage an engineering project. Know-how in this case means the skill, background, and wisdom necessary to apply knowledge effectively in practice [6].

A project is a temporary organizational structure that has an established beginning and end date, established goals and objectives, defined responsibilities, and a defined budget and schedule.

The importance of software project management is best illustrated by the following paragraphs extracted from two US Department of Defense (DoD) reports.

A report from the STARS (Software Technology for Adaptable, Reliable Systems) initiative states, "The manager plays a major role in software and systems development and support. The difference between

SOFTWARE PROJECT MANAGEMENT

success or failure—between a project being on schedule and on budget or late and over budget—is often a function of the manager's effectiveness [7]."

In a report to the Defense Science Board Task Force on Military Software, Fred Brooks states that "... today's major problems with software development are not technical problems, but management problems [8]."

2. Introduction to Papers

This chapter includes two papers on the overall management of software projects and three papers on the management of cost and risk as specific issues in software development.

The chapter begins with the classic of all classic software engineering papers, "The Mythical Man-Month," by Dr. Fred Brooks. No collection of papers on software engineering project management would be complete without this paper. Brooks could be considered the father of modern software engineering project management; his book, *The Mythical Man-Month: Essays on Software Engineering,* written in 1975, [9] was a best seller for 20 years and was republished in 1995. This paper, or, better yet, the book should be required reading for all software project managers.

The paper (and the book) is the source of such now-famous quotes as:

- "Adding manpower to a late software project only makes it later." ("Brooks's Law")
- "How does a project get to be a year late? ...One day at a time."
- "All programmers are optimists."
- "The man-month as a unit for measuring the size of a job is a dangerous and deceptive myth."

In the second paper in this chapter, Thayer expands on MacKenzie's and other papers and applies the concept of the universality of management to developing an overview of software engineering project management.

The paper takes a top-down approach to establishing a set of project management and software engineering project management responsibilities, activities, and tasks that should be undertaken by any manager who is assigned the responsibility of managing a software engineering project. It covers the management functions of planning, organizing, staffing, directing, and controlling, and it discusses in detail activities and tasks necessary to successfully manage a software development project.

The third paper in this chapter is a short essay by Tom De Marco entitled "Why Does Software Cost So Much?" In this article, De Marco quotes Dr. Jerry Weinberg: "Compared to what?" [10] This paper posits that software really does not cost too much. He reflects on the expectations of customers and users, which are perhaps unrealistic for an engineering discipline that is less than fifty years old.

De Marco points out that a major problem in the high cost of software is the unrealistic estimates that are made at the beginning of the software project. He says the assertion that software costs too much is typically a ploy by unknowledgeable managers and customers in an attempt to coerce the project manager into either estimating or developing the software for less cost.

The next paper, by F.J. Heemstra, presents a thorough overview of the state of the art in software cost estimation. Heemstra points out that it is very easy to ask the question, "Why are software overruns on budget and schedule so prevalent?" However, the answer is not so simple.

The author thoroughly discusses why software cost estimation is so difficult. The primary reason is that there is a lack of data on completed software projects. Without this data, it becomes very difficult to make project management estimates on future software costs.

The author goes into the many factors that influence software development effort and duration. He points out that the estimator must know, among other things, the size of the software project, required quality, requirements volatility (that is, the amount and rate of change of requirements), software complexity, the level of software reuse, the amount of documentation required, and the type of application.

The author also discusses the types of software cost-estimation techniques and tools. He points out that there are two main approaches that can be distinguished from each other—the top-down and the bottom-up approaches.

Heemstra also looks at some cost estimation models beginning with the principles of these models. He then presents an overview of COCOMO, function point analysis, the Putnam model, and others. He manages to pinpoint most of the major software cost-estimation techniques available today.

The fifth and last paper in this section is an original article, "Risk Management for Software Development," written by the late Paul Rook of the Center for Software Reliability in London and completed after Rook's death by Dr. Richard Fairley. The paper defines the many aspects of risk management such as risk, risk impact, risk exposure, and risk reduction or elimination. It restates the classic definition of risk as the "potential for realization of unwanted, negative consequences of an event." It concentrates on describing the importance of the relationship between risk management and project control and illustrates the sources of risk, how risk can be tackled, and how to carry out risk assessment, risk identification, and risk analysis. Risk management planning and risk resolution are also covered.

Mr. Rook's premature death in January 1995 was a blow to his friends and colleagues, and to the technology of software reliability. He will be sorely missed. The editors thank Dick Fairley for completing this paper.

1. Koontz, H., C. O'Donnell, and H. Weihrich, *Management*, 7th ed., McGraw-Hill Book Co., New York, N.Y., 1980.

2. Cleland, D.I., and W.R. King, *Management: A Systems Approach,* McGraw-Hill Book Company, New York, N.Y., 1972.

3. MacKenzie, R.A., "The Management Process in 3-D," *Harvard Business Rev.*, Nov.-Dec. 1969, pp. 80-87.

4. Blanchard, Benjamin S. and Walter J. Fabrycky, *System Engineering and Analysis*, Prentice Hall, Inc., Englewood Cliffs, N.J., Second Ed., 1990.

5. Kerzner, Harold, *Project Management: A Systems Approach to Planning, Scheduling, and Controlling*, 3rd ed., Van Nostrand Reinhold, New York, N.Y., 1989.

6. Thayer, R.H., "Software Engineering Project Management: A Top-Down View," R.H. Thayer (ed.), *Software Engineering Project Management*, IEEE Computer Society Press, Los Alamitos, Calif., 1988

7. *Strategy for a DOD Software Initiative*, Department of Defense Report, 1 Oct.1982.

8. *Report of the Defense Science Board Task Force on Military Software*, Office of the Under Secretary of Defense for Acquisition, Department of Defense, Washington D.C., September 1987.

9. F.P. Brooks, Jr., *The Mythical Man-Month: Essays on Software Engineering*, Addison-Wesley Publishing Co., Reading, Mass., 1975. Revised edition published 1995.

10. Weinberg, G., *Quality Software Management*, Volume 1: *Systems Thinking*, Dorset House, New York, N.Y., 1992.

THE MYTHICAL MAN-MONTH

The above is an extract from the *Mythical Man-Month* by Frederick P. Brooks, Jr., copyright © 1975 by Addison-Wesley Publishing Company, Inc., Reading, Massachusetts, pages 14-26, 88-94, 153-160, and 177. Reprinted with permission. The extract was prepared by the editors of *Datamation* and published in *Datamation*, December 1974, pages 44-52.

HOW DOES A PROJECT GET TO BE A YEAR LATE? . . . . . . ONE DAY AT A TIME.

By Frederick P. Brooks, Jr.

NO SCENE FROM PREHISTORY is quite so vivid as that of the mortal struggles of great beasts in the tar pits. In the mind's eye one sees dinosaurs, mammoths, and saber-toothed tigers struggling against the grip of the tar. The fiercer the struggle, the more entangling the tar, and no beast is so strong or so skillful but that he ultimately sinks.

Large-system programming has over the past decade been such a tar pit, and many great and powerful beasts have thrashed violently in it. Most have emerged with running systems--few have met goals, schedules, and budgets. Large and small, massive or wiry, team after team has become entangled in the tar. No one thing seems to cause the difficulty—any particular paw can be pulled away. But the accumulation of simultaneous and interacting factors brings slower and slower motion. Everyone seems to have been surprised by the stickiness of the problem, and it is hard to discern the nature of it. But we must try to understand it if we are to solve it.

More software projects have gone awry for lack of calendar time than for all other causes combined. Why is this case of disaster so common?

First, our techniques of estimating are poorly developed. More seriously, they reflect an unvoiced assumption which is quite untrue, i.e., that all will go well.

Second, our estimating techniques fallaciously confuse effort with progress, hiding the assumption that men and months are interchangeable.

Third, because we are uncertain of our estimates, software managers often lack the courteous stubbornness required to make people wait for a good product.

Fourth, schedule progress is poorly monitored. Techniques proven and routine in other engineering disciplines are considered radical innovations in software engineering.

Fifth, when schedule slippage is recognized, the natural (and traditional) response is to add manpower. Like dousing a fire with gasoline, this makes matters worse, much worse. More fire requires more gasoline and thus begins a regenerative cycle which ends in disaster.

Schedule monitoring will be covered later. Let us now consider other aspects of the problem in more detail.

Optimism

All programmers are optimists. Perhaps this modern sorcery especially attracts those who believe in happy endings and fairy godmothers. Perhaps the hundreds of nitty frustrations drive away all but those who habitually focus on the end goal. Perhaps it is merely that computers are young, programmers are younger, and the young are always optimists. But however the selection process works, the result is indisputable: "This time it will surely run," or "I just found the last bug."

So the first false assumption that underlies the scheduling of systems programming is that *all will go well*, i.e., that *each task will take only as long as it "ough," to take.*

The pervasiveness of optimism among programmers deserves more than a flip analysis. Dorothy Sayers, in her excellent book, *The Mind of the*

Maker, divides creative activity into three stages: the idea, the implementation, and the interaction. A book, then, or a computer, or a program comes into existence first as an ideal construct, built outside time and space but complete in the mind of the author. It is realized in time and space by pen, ink, and paper, or by wire, silicon, and ferrite. The creation is complete when someone reads the book, uses the computer or runs the program, thereby interacting with the mind of the maker.

This description, which Miss Sayers uses to illuminate not only human creative activity but also the Christian doctrine of the Trinity, will help us in our present task. For the human makers of things, the incompletenesses and inconsistencies of our ideas become clear only during implementation. Thus it is that writing, experimentation, "working out" are essential disciplines for the theoretician.

In many creative activities the medium of execution is intractable. Lumber splits; paints smear; electrical circuits ring. These physical limitations of the medium constrain the ideas that may be expressed, and they also create unexpected difficulties in the implementation.

Implementation, then, takes time and sweat both because of the physical media and because of the inadequacies of the underlying ideas. We tend to blame the physical media for most of our implementation difficulties; for the media are not "ours" in the way the ideas are, and our pride colors our judgment.

Computer programming, however, creates with an exceedingly tractable medium. The programmer builds from pure thought-stuff: concepts and very flexible representations thereof. Because the medium is tractable, we expect few difficulties in implementation; hence our pervasive optimism. Because our ideas are faulty, we have bugs; hence our optimism is unjustified.

In a single task, the assumption that all will go well has a probabilistic effect on the schedule. It might indeed go as planned, for there is a probability distribution for the delay that will be encountered, and "no delay" has a finite probability. A large programming effort, however, consists of many tasks, some chained end-to-end. The probability that each will go well becomes vanishingly small.

The mythical man-month

The second fallacious thought mode is expressed in the very unit of effort used in estimating and scheduling: the man-month. Cost does indeed vary as the product of the number of men and the number of months. Progress does not. *Hence the man-month as a unit for measuring the size of a job is a dangerous and deceptive myth.* It implies that men and months are interchangeable.

Men and months are interchangeable commodities only when a task can be partitioned among many workers *with no communication among them* (Fig. 1). This is true of reaping wheat or picking cotton; it is not even approximately true of systems programming.

When a task cannot be partitioned

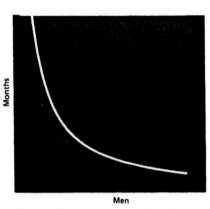

Fig. 1. The term "man-month" implies that if one man takes 10 months to do a job, 10 men can do it in one month. This may be true of picking cotton.

because of sequential constraints, the application of more effort has no effect on the schedule. The bearing of a child takes nine months, no matter how many women are assigned. Many software tasks have this characteristic because of the sequential nature of debugging.

In tasks that can be partitioned but which require communication among the subtasks, the effort of communication must be added to the amount of work to be done. Therefore the best that can be done is somewhat poorer than an even trade of men for months (Fig. 2).

The added burden of communication is made up of two parts, training and intercommunication. Each worker must be trained in the technology, the goals of the effort, the overall strategy, and the plan of work. This training cannot be partitioned, so this part of the added effort varies linearly with the number of workers.

V. S. Vyssotsky of Bell Telephone Laboratories estimates that a large project can sustain a manpower buildup of 30% per year. More than that strains and even inhibits the evolution of the essential informal structure and its communication pathways. F. J.

Corbató of MIT points out that a long project must anticipate a turnover of 20% per year, and new people must be both technically trained and integrated into the formal structure.

Intercommunication is worse. If each part of the task must be separately coordinated with each other part, the effort increases as $n(n-1)/2$. Three workers require three times as much pairwise intercommunication as two; four require six times as much as two. If, moreover, there need to be conferences among three, four, etc., workers to resolve things jointly, matters get worse yet. The added effort of communicating may fully counteract the division of the original task and bring us back to the situation of Fig. 3.

Since software construction is inherently a systems effort—an exercise in complex interrelationships—communication effort is great, and it quickly

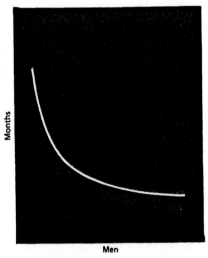

Fig. 2. Even on tasks that can be nicely partitioned among people, the additional communication required adds to the total work, increasing the schedule.

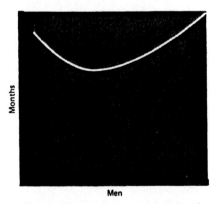

Fig. 3. Since software construction is complex, the communications overhead is great. Adding more men can lengthen, rather than shorten, the schedule.

dominates the decrease in individual task time brought about by partitioning. Adding more men then lengthens, not shortens, the schedule.

Systems test

No parts of the schedule are so thoroughly affected by sequential constraints as component debugging and system test. Furthermore, the time required depends on the number and subtlety of the errors encountered. Theoretically this number should be zero. Because of optimism, we usually expect the number of bugs to be smaller than it turns out to be. Therefore testing is usually the most mis-scheduled part of programming.

For some years I have been successfully using the following rule of thumb for scheduling a software task:

⅓ planning
⅙ coding
¼ component test and early system test
¼ system test, all components in hand.

This differs from conventional scheduling in several important ways:
1. The fraction devoted to planning is larger than normal. Even so, it is barely enough to produce a de-

of the schedule.

In examining conventionally scheduled projects, I have found that few allowed one-half of the projected schedule for testing, but that most did indeed spend half of the actual schedule for that purpose. Many of these were on schedule until and except in system testing.

Failure to allow enough time for system test, in particular, is peculiarly disastrous. Since the delay comes at the end of the schedule, no one is aware of schedule trouble until almost the delivery date. Bad news, late and without warning, is unsettling to customers and to managers.

Furthermore, delay at this point has unusually severe financial, as well as psychological, repercussions. The project is fully staffed, and cost-per-day is maximum. More seriously, the software is to support other business effort (shipping of computers, operation of new facilities, etc.) and the secondary costs of delaying these are very high, for it is almost time for software shipment. Indeed, these secondary costs may far outweigh all others. It is therefore very important to allow enough system test time in the original schedule.

two choices—wait or eat it raw. Software customers have had the same choices.

The cook has another choice; he can turn up the heat. The result is often an omelette nothing can save—burned in one part, raw in another.

Now I do not think software managers have less inherent courage and firmness than chefs, nor than other engineering managers. But false scheduling to match the patron's desired date is much more common in our discipline than elsewhere in engineering. It is very difficult to make a vigorous, plausible, and job-risking defense of an estimate that is derived by no quantitative method, supported by little data, and certified chiefly by the hunches of the managers.

Clearly two solutions are needed. We need to develop and publicize productivity figures, bug-incidence figures, estimating rules, and so on. The whole profession can only profit from sharing such data.

Until estimating is on a sounder basis, individual managers will need to stiffen their backbones, and defend their estimates with the assurance that their poor hunches are better than wish-derived estimates.

Regenerative disaster

What does one do when an essential software project is behind schedule? Add manpower, naturally. As Figs. 1 through 3 suggest, this may or may not help.

Let us consider an example. Suppose a task is estimated at 12 man-months and assigned to three men for four months, and that there are measurable mileposts A, B, C, D, which are scheduled to fall at the end of each month.

Now suppose the first milepost is not reached until two months have elapsed. What are the alternatives facing the manager?
1. Assume that the task must be done on time. Assume that only the first part of the task was misestimated. Then 9 man-months of effort remain, and two months, so 4½ men will be needed. Add 2 men to the 3 assigned.
2. Assume that the task must be done on time. Assume that the whole estimate was uniformly low. Then 18 man-months of effort remain, and two months, so 9 men will be needed. Add 6 men to the 3 assigned.
3. Reschedule. In this case, I like the advice given by an experienced hardware engineer, "Take no small slips." That is, allow enough time in the new schedule to ensure that the work can be carefully and

Fig. 4. Adding manpower to a project which is late may not help. In this case, suppose three men on a 12 man-month project were a month late. If it takes one of the three an extra month to train two new men, the project will be just as late as if no one was added.

tailed and solid specification, and not enough to include research or exploration of totally new techniques.
2. The *half* of the schedule devoted to debugging of completed code is much larger than normal.
3. The part that is easy to estimate, i.e., coding, is given only one-sixth

Gutless estimating

Observe that for the programmer, as for the chef, the urgency of the patron may govern the scheduled completion of the task, but it cannot govern the actual completion. An omelette, promised in ten minutes, may appear to be progressing nicely. But when it has not set in ten minutes, the customer has

thoroughly done, and that rescheduling will not have to be done again.

4. Trim the task. In practice this tends to happen anyway, once the team observes schedule slippage. Where the secondary costs of delay are very high, this is the only feasible action. The manager's only alternatives are to trim it formally and carefully, to reschedule, or to watch the task get silently trimmed by hasty design and incomplete testing.

In the first two cases, insisting that the unaltered task be completed in four months is disastrous. Consider the regenerative effects, for example, for the first alternative (Fig. 4 preceding page). The two new men, however competent and however quickly recruited, will require training in the task by one of the experienced men. If this takes a month, *3 man-months will have been devoted to work not in the original estimate.* Furthermore, the task, originally partitioned three ways, must be repartitioned into five parts, hence some work already done will be lost and system testing must be lengthened. So at the end of the third month, substantially more than 7 man-months of effort remain, and 5 trained people and one month are available. As Fig. 4 suggests, the product is just as late as if no one had been added.

To hope to get done in four months, considering only training time and not repartitioning and extra systems test, would require adding 4 men, not 2, at the end of the second month. To cover repartitioning and system test effects, one would have to add still other men. Now, however, one has at least a 7-man team, not a 3-man one; thus such aspects as team organization and task division are different in kind, not merely in degree.

Notice that by the end of the third month things look very black. The March 1 milestone has not been reached in spite of all the managerial effort. The temptation is very strong to repeat the cycle, adding yet more manpower. Therein lies madness.

The foregoing assumed that only the first milestone was misestimated. If on March 1 one makes the conservative assumption that the whole schedule was optimistic one wants to add 6 men just to the original task. Calculation of the training, repartitioning, system testing effects is left as an exercise for the reader. Without a doubt, the regenerative disaster will yield a poorer product later, than would rescheduling with the original three men, unaugmented.

Oversimplifying outrageously, we state Brooks' Law:

Adding manpower to a late software project makes it later.

This then is the demythologizing of the man-month. The number of months of a project depends upon its sequential constraints. The maximum number of men depends upon the number of independent subtasks. From these two quantities one can derive schedules using fewer men and more months. (The only risk is product obsolescence.) One cannot, however, get workable schedules using more men and fewer months. More software projects have gone awry for lack of calendar time than for all other causes combined.

Calling the shot

How long will a system programming job take? How much effort will be required? How does one estimate?

I have earlier suggested ratios that seem to apply to planning time, coding, component test, and system test. First, one must say that one does *not* estimate the entire task by estimating the coding portion only and then applying the ratios. The coding is only

one-sixth or so of the problem, and errors in its estimate or in the ratios could lead to ridiculous results.

Second, one must say that data for building isolated small programs are not applicable to programming systems products. For a program averaging about 3,200 words, for example, Sackman, Erikson, and Grant report an average code-plus-debug time of about 178 hours for a single programmer, a figure which would extrapolate to give an annual productivity of 35,800 statements per year. A program half that size took less than one-fourth as long, and extrapolated productivity is almost 80,000 statements per year.[1] Planning, documentation, testing, system integration, and training times must be added. The linear extrapolation of such spring figures is meaningless. Extrapolation of times for the hundred-yard dash shows that a man can run a mile in under three minutes.

Before dismissing them, however, let us note that these numbers, although not for strictly comparable problems, suggest that effort goes as a power of size *even* when no communication is involved except that of a man with his memories.

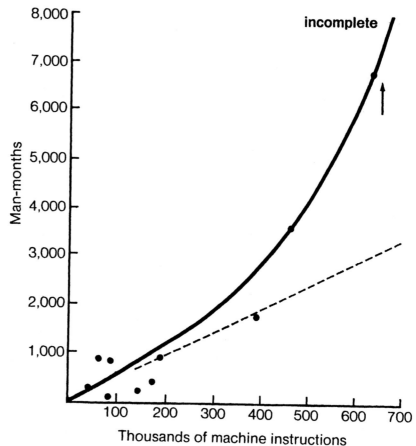

Fig. 5. As a project's complexity increases, the number of man-months required to complete it goes up exponentially.

Fig. 5 tells the sad story. It illustrates results reported from a study done by Nanus and Farr[2] at System Development Corp. This shows an exponent of 1.5; that is,

effort = (constant)×(number of instructions)[1.5]

Another SDC study reported by Weinwurm[3] also shows an exponent near 1.5.

A few studies on programmer productivity have been made, and several estimating techniques have been proposed. Morin has prepared a survey of the published data.[4] Here I shall give only a few items that seem especially illuminating.

Portman's data

Charles Portman, manager of ICL's Software Div., Computer Equipment Organization (Northwest) at Manchester, offers another useful personal insight.

He found his programming teams missing schedules by about one-half— each job was taking approximately twice as long as estimated. The estimates were very careful, done by experienced teams estimating man-hours for several hundred subtasks on a PERT chart. When the slippage pattern appeared, he asked them to keep careful daily logs of time usage. These showed that the estimating error could be entirely accounted for by the fact that his teams were only realizing 50% of the working week as actual programming and debugging time. Machine downtime, higher-priority short unrelated jobs, meetings, paperwork, company business, sickness, personal time, etc. accounted for the rest. In short, the estimates made an unrealistic assumption about the number of technical work hours per man-year. My own experience quite confirms his conclusion.

An unpublished 1964 study by E. F. Bardain shows programmers realizing only 27% productive time.[5]

	Prog. units	Number of programmers	Years	Man-years	Program words	Words/man-yr.
Operational	50	83	4	101	52,000	515
Maintenance	36	60	4	81	51,000	630
Compiler	13	9	2¼	17	38,000	2230
Translator (Data assembler)	15	13	2½	11	25,000	2270

Table 1. Data from Bell Labs indicates productivity differences between complex problems (the first two are basically control programs with many modules) and less complex ones. No one is certain how much of the difference is due to complexity, how much to the number of people involved.

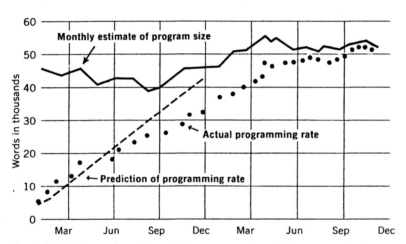

Fig. 6. Bell Labs' experience in predicting programming effort on one project.

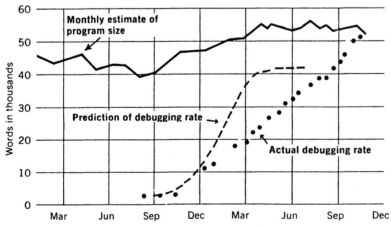

Fig. 7. Bell's predictions for debugging rates on a single project, contrasted with actual figures.

Aron's data

Joel Aron, manager of Systems Technology at IBM in Gaithersburg, Maryland, has studied programmer productivity when working on nine large systems (briefly, *large* means more than 25 programmers and 30,000 deliverable instructions). He divides such systems according to interactions among programmers (and system parts) and finds productivities as follows:

Very few interactions	10,000 instructions per man-year
Some interactions	5,000
Many interactions	1,500

The man-years do not include support and system test activities, only design and programming. When these figures are diluted by a factor of two to cover system test, they closely match Harr's data.

Harr's data

John Harr, manager of programming for the Bell Telephone Laboratories' Electronic Switching System, reported his and others' experience in a paper at the 1969 Spring Joint Computer Conference.[6] These data are shown in Table 1 and Figs. 6 and 7.

Of these, Fig. 6 is the most detailed and the most useful. The first two jobs are basically control programs; the second two are basically language translators. Productivity is stated in terms of debugged words per man-year. This includes programming, component test, and system test. It is not clear how much of the planning effort, or effort in machine support, writing, and the like, is included.

The productivities likewise fall into two classifications: those for control programs are about 600 words per man-year; those for translators are about 2,200 words per man-year. Note that all four programs are of similar size—the variation is in size of the work groups, length of time, and number of modules. Which is cause and which is effect? Did the control programs require more people because they were more complicated? Or did they require more modules and more man-months because they were assigned more people? Did they take longer because of the greater complexity, or because more people were assigned? One can't be sure. The control programs were surely more complex. These uncertainties aside, the numbers describe the real productivities achieved on a large system, using present-day programming techniques. As such they are a real contribution.

Figs. 6 and 7 show some interesting data on programming and debugging rates as compared to predicted rates.

OS/360 data

IBM OS/360 experience, while not available in the detail of Harr's data, confirms it. Productivities in range of 600-800 debugged instructions per man-year were experienced by control program groups. Productivities in the 2,000-3,000 debugged instructions per man-year were achieved by language translator groups. These include planning done by the group, coding component test, system test, and some support activities. They are comparable to Harr's data, so far as I can tell.

Aron's data, Harr's data, and the os/360 data all confirm striking differences in productivity related to the complexity and difficulty of the task itself. My guideline in the morass of estimating complexity is that compilers are three times as bad as normal batch application programs, and operating systems are three times as bad as compilers.

Corbató's data

Both Harr's data and os/360 data are for assembly language programming. Little data seem to have been published on system programming productivity using higher-level languages. Corbató of MIT's Project MAC reports, however, a mean productivity of 1,200 lines of debugged PL/I statements per man-year on the MULTICS system (between 1 and 2 million words)[7]

This number is very exciting. Like the other projects, MULTICS includes control programs and language transla-

tors. Like the others, it is producing a system programming product, tested and documented. The data seem to be comparable in terms of kind of effort included. And the productivity number is a good average between the control program and translator productivities of other projects.

But Corbató's number is *lines* per man-year, not *words!* Each statement in his system corresponds to about three-to-five words of handwritten code! This suggests two important conclusions:

- Productivity seems constant in terms of elementary statements, a conclusion that is reasonable in terms of the thought a statement requires and the errors it may include.
- Programming productivity may be increased as much as five times when a suitable high-level language is used. To back up these conclusions, W. M. Taliaffero also reports a constant productivity of 2,400 statements/year in Assembler, FORTRAN, and COBOL.[8] E. A. Nelson has shown a 3-to-1 productivity improvement for high-level language, although his standard deviations are wide.[9]

Hatching a catastrophe

When one hears of disastrous schedule slippage in a project, he imagines that a series of major calamities must have befallen it. Usually, however, the disaster is due to termites, not tornadoes; and the schedule has slipped imperceptibly but inexorably. Indeed, major calamities are easier to handle; one responds with major force, radical reorganization, the invention of new approaches. The whole team rises to the occasion.

But the day-by-day slippage is harder to recognize, harder to prevent, harder to make up. Yesterday a key man was sick, and a meeting couldn't be held. Today the machines are all down, because lightning struck the building's power transformer. Tomorrow the disc routines won't start testing, because the first disc is a week late from the factory. Snow, jury duty, family problems, emergency meetings with customers, executive audits—the list goes on and on. Each one only postpones some activity by a half-day or a day. And the schedule slips, one day at a time.

How does one control a big project on a tight schedule? The first step is to *have* a schedule. Each of a list of events, called milestones, has a date. Picking the dates is an estimating problem, discussed already and crucially dependent on experience.

For picking the milestones there is

only one relevant rule. Milestones must be concrete, specific, measurable events, defined with knife-edge sharpness. Coding, for a counterexample, is "90% finished" for half of the total coding time. Debugging is "99% complete" most of the time. "Planning complete" is an event one can proclaim almost at will.[10]

Concrete milestones, on the other hand, are 100% events. "Specifications signed by architects and implementers," "source coding 100% complete, keypunched, entered into disc library," "debugged version passes all test cases." These concrete milestones demark the vague phases of planning, coding, debugging.

It is more important that milestones be sharp-edged and unambiguous than that they be easily verifiable by the boss. Rarely will a man lie about mile-

> None love
> the bearer of bad news.
> *Sophocles*

stone progress, *if* the milestone is so sharp that he can't deceive himself. But if the milestone is fuzzy, the boss often understands a different report from that which the man gives. To supplement Sophocles, no one enjoys bearing bad news, either, so it gets softened without any real intent to deceive.

Two interesting studies of estimating behavior by government contractors on large-scale development projects show that:

1. Estimates of the length of an activity made and revised carefully every two weeks before the activity starts do not significantly change as the start time draws near, no matter how wrong they ultimately turn out to be.
2. *During* the activity, *over*estimates of duration come steadily down as the activity proceeds.
3. *Underestimates* do not change significantly during the activity until about three weeks before the scheduled completion.[11]

Sharp milestones are in fact a service to the team, and one they can properly expect from a manager. The fuzzy milestone is the harder burden to live with. It is in fact a millstone that grinds down morale, for it deceives one about lost time until it is irremediable. And chronic schedule slippage is a morale-killer.

"The other piece is late"

A schedule slips a day; so what? Who gets excited about a one-day slip? We can make it up later. And the other piece ours fits into is late anyway.

A baseball manager recognizes a nonphysical talent, *hustle,* as an essential gift of great players and great teams. It is the characteristic of running faster than necessary, moving sooner than necessary, trying harder than necessary. It is essential for great programming teams, too. Hustle provides the cushion, the reserve capacity, that enables a team to cope with routine mishaps, to anticipate and forfend minor calamities. The calculated response, the measured effort, are the wet blankets that dampen hustle. As we have seen, one *must* get excited about a one-day slip. Such are the elements of catastrophe.

But not all one-day slips are equally disastrous. So some calculation of response is necessary, though hustle be dampened. How does one tell which slips matter? There is no substitute for a PERT chart or a critical-path schedule. Such a network shows who waits for what. It shows who is on the critical path, where any slip moves the end date. It also shows how much an activity can slip before it moves into the critical path.

The PERT technique, strictly speaking, is an elaboration of critical-path scheduling in which one estimates three times for every event, times corresponding to different probabilities of meeting the estimated dates. I do not find this refinement to be worth the extra effort, but for brevity I will call any critical path network a PERT chart.

The preparation of a PERT chart is the most valuable part of its use. Laying out the network, identifying the dependencies, and estimating the legs all force a great deal of very specific planning very early in a project. The first chart is always terrible, and one invents and invents in making the second one.

As the project proceeds, the PERT chart provides the answer to the demoralizing excuse, "The other piece is late anyhow." It shows how hustle is needed to keep one's own part off the critical path, and it suggests ways to make up the lost time in the other part.

Under the rug

When a first-line manager sees his small team slipping behind, he is rarely inclined to run to the boss with this woe. The team might be able to make it up, or he should be able to invent or reorganize to solve the problem. Then why worry the boss with it? So far, so good. Solving such problems is exactly what the first-line manager is there for. And the boss does have enough real worries demanding his action that he doesn't seek others. So all the dirt gets swept under the rug.

But every boss needs two kinds of information, exceptions for action and a status picture for education.[12] For that purpose he needs to know the status of all his teams. Getting a true picture of that status is hard.

The first-line manager's interests and those of the boss have an inherent conflict here. The first-line manager fears that if he reports his problem, the boss will act on it. Then his action will preempt the manager's function, diminish his authority, foul up his other plans. So as long as the manager thinks he can solve it alone, he doesn't tell the boss.

Two rug-lifting techniques are open to the boss. Both must be used. The first is to reduce the role conflict and inspire sharing of status. The other is to yank the rug back.

Reducing the role conflict

The boss must first distinguish between action information and status information. He must discipline himself *not* to act on problems his managers can solve, and *never* to act on problems when he is explicitly reviewing status. I once knew a boss who invariably picked up the phone to give orders before the end of the first para-

SYSTEM/360 SUMMARY STATUS REPORT
OS/369 LANGUAGE PROCESSORS + SERVICE PROGRAMS
AS OF FEBRUARY 01 • 1965

A=APPROVAL
C=COMPLETED

•= REVISED PLANNED DATE
NE=NOT ESTABLISHED

PROJECT	LOCATION	COMMITMNT ANNOUNCE RELEASE	OBJECTIVE AVAILABLE APPROVED	SPECS AVAILABLE APPROVED	SRL AVAILABLE APPROVED	ALPHA TEST ENTRY EXIT	COMP TEST START COMPLETE	SYS TEST START COMPLETE	BULLETIN AVAILABLE APPROVED	BETA TEST ENTRY EXIT
OPERATING SYSTEM										
12K DESIGN LEVEL (E)										
ASSEMBLY	SAN JOSE	04/--/4 12/31/5	10/28/4 C	10/13/4 C 01/11/5	11/13/4 C 11/16/4 A	01/15/5 C 02/22/5				09/01/5 11/30/5
FORTRAN	POK	04/--/4 12/31/5	10/28/4 C	10/21/4 C 01/22/5	12/17/4 C 12/19/4 A	01/15/5 C 02/22/5				09/01/5 11/30/5
COBOL	ENDICOTT	04/--/4 12/31/5	10/25/4 C	10/15/4 C 01/20/5 A	11/17/4 C 12/08/4 A	01/15/5 C 02/22/5				09/01/5 11/30/5
RPG	SAN JOSE	04/--/4 12/31/5	10/28/4 C	09/30/4 C 01/05/5 A	12/02/4 C 01/18/5 A	01/15/5 C 02/22/5				09/01/5 11/30/5
UTILITIES	TIME/LIFE	04/--/4 12/31/5	06/24/4 C		11/20/4 C 11/30/4 A					09/01/5 11/30/5
SORT 1	POK	04/--/4 12/31/5	10/28/4 C	10/19/4 C 01/11/5	11/12/4 C 11/30/4 A	01/15/5 C 03/22/5				09/01/5 11/30/5
SORT 2	POK	04/--/4 06/30/6	10/28/4 C	10/19/4 C 01/11/5	11/12/4 C 11/30/4 A	01/15/5 C 03/22/5				03/01/6 05/30/6
44K DESIGN LEVEL (F)										
ASSEMBLY	SAN JOSE	04/--/4 12/31/5	10/28/4 C	10/13/4 C 01/11/5	11.13.4 C 11/18/4 A	02/15/5 03/22/5				09/01/5 11/30/5
COBOL	TIME/LIFE	04/--/4 06/30/6	10/28/4 C	10/15/4 C 01/20/5 A	11/17/4 C 12/06/4 A	02/15/5 03/22/5				03/01/5 05/30/6
NPL	HURSLEY	04/--/4 03/31/6	10/28/4 C							
2250	KINGSTON	03/30/4 C 03/31/6	11/05/4 C	10/06/4 C 01/04/5	01/12/5 C 01/29/5	01/04/5 C 01/29/5				01/03/6 NE
2280	KINGSTON	06/30/4 C 09/30/6	11/05/4 C			04/01/5 04/30/5				01/28/6 NE
200K DESIGN LEVEL (H)										
ASSEMBLY	TIME/LIFE		10/28/4 C							
FORTRAN	POK	04/--/4 06/30/6	10/28/4 C	10/16/4 C 01/11/5	11/11/4 C 12/10/4 A	02/15/5 03/22/5				03/01/6 05/30/6
NPL	HURSLEY	04/--/4 C	10/28/4 C			07/--/5				01/--/7
NPL H	POK	04/--/4 C	03/30/4 C			02/01/5 04/01/5				10/15/5 12/15/5

Fig. 8. A report showing milestones and status in a key document in project control. This one shows some problems in OS development: specifications approval is late on some items (those without "A"); documentation (SRL) approval is overdue on another; and one (2250 support) is late coming out of alpha test.

graph in a status report. That response is guaranteed to squelch full disclosure.

Conversely, when the manager knows his boss will accept status reports without panic or preemption, he comes to give honest appraisals.

This whole process is helped if the boss labels meetings, reviews, conferences, as *status-review* meetings versus *problem-action* meetings, and controls himself accordingly. Obviously one may call a problem-action meeting as a consequence of a status meeting, if he believes a problem is out of hand. But at least everybody knows what the score is, and the boss thinks twice before grabbing the ball.

Yanking the rug off

Nevertheless, it is necessary to have review techniques by which the true status is made known, whether cooperatively or not. The PERT chart with its frequent sharp milestones is the basis for such review. On a large project one may want to review some part of it each week, making the rounds once a month or so.

A report showing milestones and actual completions is the key document. Fig. 8 (preceding page), shows an excerpt from such a report. This report shows some troubles. Specifications approval is overdue on several components. Manual (SRL) approval is overdue on another, and one is late getting out of the first state (ALPHA) of the independently conducted product test. So such a report serves as an agenda for the meeting of 1 February. Everyone knows the questions, and the component manager should be prepared to explain why it's late, when it will be finished, what steps he's taking, and what help, if any, he needs from the boss or collateral groups.

V. Vyssotsky of Bell Telephone Laboratories adds the following observation:

I have found it handy to carry both "scheduled" and "estimated" dates in the milestone report. The scheduled dates are the property of the project manager and represent a consistent work plan for the project as a whole, and one which is a priori a reasonable plan. The estimated dates are the property of the lowest level manager who has cognizance over the piece of work in question, and represents his best judgment as to when it will actually happen, given the resources he has available and when he received (or has commitments for delivery of) his prerequisite inputs. The project manager has to keep his fingers off the estimated dates, and put the emphasis on getting accurate, unbiased estimates rather than palatable optimistic estimates or self-protective conservative ones. Once this is clearly established in everyone's mind, the project manager can see quite a ways into the future where he is going to be in trouble if he doesn't do something.

The preparation of the PERT chart is a function of the boss and the managers reporting to him. Its updating, revision, and reporting requires the attention of a small (one-to-three-man) staff group which serves as an extension of the boss. Such a "Plans and Controls" team is invaluable for a large project. It has no authority except to ask all the line managers when they will have set or changed milestones, and whether milestones have been met. Since the Plans and Controls group handles all the paperwork, the burden on the line managers is reduced to the essentials—making the decisions.

We had a skilled, enthusiastic, and diplomatic Plans and Controls group on the OS/360 project, run by A. M. Pietrasanta, who devoted considerable inventive talent to devising effective but unobtrusive control methods. As a result, I found his group to be widely respected and more than tolerated. For a group whose role is inherently that of an irritant, this is quite an accomplishment.

The investment of a modest amount of skilled effort in a Plans and Controls function is very rewarding. It makes far more difference in project accomplishment than if these people worked directly on building the product programs. For the Plans and Controls group is the watchdog who renders the imperceptible delays visible and who points up the critical elements. It is the early warning system against losing a year, one day at a time.

Epilogue

The tar pit of software engineering will continue to be sticky for a long time to come. One can expect the human race to continue attempting systems just within or just beyond our reach; and software systems are perhaps the most intricate and complex of man's handiworks. The management of this complex craft will demand our best use of new languages and systems, our best adaptation of proven engineering management methods, liberal doses of common sense, and a God-given humility to recognize our fallibility and limitations.

References

1. Sackman, H., W. J. Erikson, and E. E. Grant, "Exploratory Experimentation Studies Comparing Online and Offline Programming Performance," *Communications of the ACM*, 11 (1968), 3-11.
2. Nanus, B., and L. Farr, "Some Cost Contributors to Large-Scale Programs," *AFIPS Proceedings, SJCC*, 25 (1964), 239-248.
3. Weinwurm, G. F., *Research in the Management of Computer Programming*. Report SP-2059, 1965, System Development Corp., Santa Monica.
4. Morin, L. H., *Estimation of Resources for Computer Programming Projects*, M. S. thesis, Univ. of North Carolina, Chapel Hill, 1974.
5. Quoted by D. B. Mayer and A. W. Stalnaker, "Selection and Evaluation of Computer Personnel," *Proceedings 23 ACM Conference*, 1968, 661.
6. Paper given at a panel session and not included in the *AFIPS Proceedings*.
7. Corbató, F. J., *Sensitive Issues in the Design of Multi-Use Systems*. Lecture at the opening of the Honeywell EDP Technology Center, 1968.
8. Taliaffero, W. M., "Modularity the Key to System Growth Potential," *Software*, 1 (1971), 245-257.
9. Nelson, E. A., *Management Handbook for the Estimation of Computer Programming Costs*. Report TM-3225, System Development Corp., Santa Monica, pp. 66-67.
10. Reynolds, C. H., "What's Wrong with Computer Programming Management?" in *On the Management of Computer Programming*. Ed. G. F. Weinwurm. Philadelphia: Auerbach, 1971, pp. 35-42.
11. King, W. R., and T. A. Wilson, "Subjective Time Estimates in Critical Path Planning—a Preliminary Analysis," *Management Sciences*, 13 (1967), 307-320, and sequel, W. R. King, D. M. Witterrongel, and K. D. Hezel, "On the Analysis of Critical Path Time Estimating Behavior," *Management Sciences*, 14 (1967), 79-84.
12. Brooks, F. P., and K. E. Iverson, *Automatic Data Processing, System/360 Edition*. New York: Wiley, 1969, pp. 428-430. □

Software Engineering Project Management

Richard H. Thayer
California State University, Sacramento
Sacramento, CA 95819

Abstract

This article describes the management functions of planning, organizing, staffing, directing, and controlling that are necessary to manage any enterprise or activity. The universality of these management concepts provides a framework for adapting these traditional management functions to ensure complete coverage of project management activities. From these general management functions and activities, this article derives the detailed activities and tasks that should be undertaken by any manager who is assigned the responsibility of managing a software engineering project.

This article describes those management procedures, practices, technologies, and skills necessary to successfully manage a software engineering project.

1. Introduction

This article is about management, the universality of management concepts, and the activities and tasks of software engineering project management.

Management involves the activities and tasks undertaken by one or more persons for the purpose of planning and controlling the activities of others in order to achieve objectives that could not be achieved by the others acting alone. Management functions can be categorized as planning, organizing, staffing, directing, and controlling.

Project management is a system of management procedures, practices, technologies, skill, and experience that is necessary to successfully manage an engineering project. If the project product is software, then the act of managing the project is called *software engineering project management*. The *manager* of a software engineering project is called a *software engineering project manager*, a *software project manager*, or, in many cases, just project manager.

Software engineering projects are frequently part of larger, more comprehensive projects that include equipment (hardware), facilities, personnel, procedures, as well as software. Examples include aircraft systems, accounting systems, radar systems, inventory control systems, and railroad switching systems. These *systems engineering projects* are typically managed by one or more system project managers (sometimes called *program managers*) who manage projects composed of engineers, experts in the field of the application, scientific specialists, programmers, support personnel, and others. If the software to be delivered is a "stand-alone" software system (a system that does not involve development of other non-software components), the software engineering project manager may be called the system project manager.

Universality of management is a concept that comes from management science [Koontz and O'Donnell 1972], [Fayol 1949] and means:

- Management performs the same functions (planning, organizing, staffing, directing, and controlling) regardless of position in the organization or the enterprise managed.

- Management functions are characteristic duties of managers; management practices, methods, activities, and tasks are particular to the enterprise or job managed.

The universality of management concepts allows us to apply them to software engineering project management [Thayer and Pyster 1984].

This article describes a comprehensive set of software engineering project management functions, activities, and tasks that should be undertaken by any manager who is assigned the responsibility of managing a software engineering project. It covers the management functions of planning, organizing, staffing, directing, and controlling software projects and the detailed activities and specific tasks of project management necessary to successfully manage a software engineering project.

Section 2 lists some of the major issues of software engineering that pertain to project management. Section 3 partitions the functions of management into a detailed list of management activities. Sections 4 through 8 then partition these management activities into the detailed activities and tasks of a software engineering project manager. Section 9 provides a summary of the article.

2. Major Issues of Software Engineering

Over 70 percent of software development organizations develop their software through ad hoc and unpredictable methods [Zubrow et al. 1995]. These organizations (considered to be "immature" according to the Software Engineering Institute Capability Maturity Model) do not have an objective basis for determining software cost and schedule or judging software quality. Software development processes are generally improvised by practitioners and their management during the course of the project. The company does not have any standard practices or follow any existing practices. Each manager manages according to individual preference. Proved software engineering techniques such as in-depth requirements analysis, inspections, reviews, testing, and documentation are reduced or eliminated when the project falls behind in cost, schedule and/or the customer demands more functionality without increase in budget [Paulk et al. 1996].

The "software crisis" is identified by software that is late, over budget, and fails to meet the customer's and/or user's system requirements [Gibbs 1994]. Many if not most of these problems have been blamed on inadequate or inferior software project management.

The importance of software project management is best illustrated in the following paragraphs extracted from the indicated Department of Defense (DoD) reports.

- A report from the STARS initiative (STARS: Software Technology for Adaptable, Reliable Systems) states, "The manager plays a major role in software and systems development and support. The difference between success or failure—between a project being on schedule and on budget or late and over budget—is often a function of the manager's effectiveness." [DoD Software Initiative 1983].

- A Report to the Defense Science Board Task Force on Military Software, states that "... today's major problems with software development are not technical problems, but management problems." [Brooks 1987]

- A General Accounting Office (GAO) report that investigated the cost and schedule overrun of the C-17 said, "... software development has clearly been a major problem during the first 6 years of the program. In fact, the C-17 is a good example of how not to manage software development...." [GAO/IMTEC-92-48 C-17 Aircraft Software]

3. Functions and Activities of Management

This article presents a top-down overview of software engineering project management responsibilities, activities, and tasks that should be undertaken by any manager who is assigned the responsibility of managing a software engineering project. A top-down approach is used to partition and allocate top-level functions to lower-level activities and tasks.

Table 3.1 depicts the classic management model as portrayed by such well-known authors in the field of management as Kootz and O'Donnell [1972], and others [Rue and Byars 1983], [Cleland and King 1972], [MacKenzie 1969].

According to this model, management is partitioned into five separate functions or components: *planning, organizing, staffing, directing, and controlling* (see Table 3.1 for definitions or explanations of these functions). All the activities of management, such as budgeting, scheduling, establishing authority and responsibility relationships, training, communicating, allocating responsibility, and so forth fall under one of these five headings.

Table 3.1: Major Functions of Management

Activity	Definition or Explanation
Planning	Predetermining a course of action for accomplishing organizational objectives
Organizing	Arranging the relationships among work units for accomplishing objectives and granting responsibility and authority to obtain those objectives
Staffing	Selecting and training people for positions in the organization
Directing	Creating an atmosphere that will assist and motivate people to achieve desired end results
Controlling	Establishing, measuring, and evaluating activity performance toward planned objectives

The detailed activities and tasks that are particular to a software engineering project are defined and discussed in Sections 3 through 8. Each of these sections defines and discusses one of the five functions of management along with some of the major issues of the individual functions. The management activities from Table 3.1 are partitioned into one or more levels of detailed tasks, which are then discussed and/or illustrated in the appropriate section.

4. Planning a Software Engineering Project

4.1 Introduction and Definitions

Planning a software engineering project consists of the management activities that lead to selecting, among alternatives, future courses of action for the project and a program for completing those actions.

Planning thus involves specifying the *goals* and *objectives* for a project and the *strategies, policies, plans*, and *procedures* for achieving them. "Planning is deciding in advance what to do, how to do it, when to do it, and who is to do it" [Koontz and O'Donnell 1972].

Every software engineering project should start with a good plan. Uncertainties and unknowns, both within the software project environment and from external sources, make planning necessary. The act of planning focuses attention on project goals, objectives, uncertainties, and unknowns.

Table 4.1 provides an outline of the planning activities that must be accomplished by software project managers in planning their projects. The project manager is responsible for developing numerous types of plans.

The balance of this section discusses and provides greater detail on the activities outlined in Table 4.1.

4.2 Set Objectives and Goals for the Project

The first planning step for a software engineering project is determining what the project must accomplish, when it must be accomplished, and what resources are necessary. Typically, this involves analyzing and documenting the system and software requirements. The management requirements and constraints must be determined. Management constraints are often expressed as resource and schedule limitations.

Success criteria must also be specified. Success criteria would normally include delivering a software system that satisfies the requirements, is on time, and is within costs. However, there may be other criteria. For instance, success could include winning a follow-on contract. Other criteria might include increasing the size and scope of the present contract, or increasing the profit margin by winning an incentive award.

Success criteria might also be placed in a relative hierarchy of importance. For example, being on time might be more important than being within budget.

4.3 Develop Project Strategies

Another planning activity is developing and documenting a set of management strategies (sometime called strategic policies) for a project. Strategies are defined as long-range goals and the methods to obtain those goals. These long-range goals are usually developed at a corporate level; however, the project manager can have strategic plans within an individual project. This is particularly true if it is a

Table 4.1: Planning Activities for Software Projects

Activity	Definition or Explanation
Set objectives and goals	Determine the desired outcome for the project.
Develop strategies	Decide major organizational goals and develop a general program of action for reaching those goals.
Develop policies	Make standing decisions on important recurring matters to provide a guide for decision making.
Forecast future situations	Anticipate future events or make assumptions about the future; predict future results or expectations from courses of action.
Conduct a risk assessment	Anticipate possible adverse events and problem areas; state assumptions; develop contingency plans; predict results of possible courses of action.
Determine possible courses of action	Develop, analyze, and/or evaluate different ways to conduct the project.
Make planning decisions	Evaluate and select a course of action from among alternatives.
Set procedures and rules	Establish methods, guides, and limits for accomplishing the project activity.
Develop project plans	Establish policies, procedures, rules, tasks, schedules, and resources necessary to complete the project.
Prepare budgets	Allocate estimated costs to project functions, activities, and tasks.
Document project plans	Record policy decisions, courses of action, budget, program plans, and contingency plans.

large project. An example of a strategic plan might be to develop a new area of expertise or business for the organization by conducting a project in that area.

4.4 Develop Policies for the Project

Policies are predetermined management decisions. The project manager may establish policies for the project to provide guidance to supervisors and individual team members in making routine decisions. For example, it might be a policy of the project that status reports from team leaders are due in the project manager's office by close of business each Thursday. Policies can reduce the need for interaction on every decision and provide a sense of direction for the team members. In many cases, the project manager does not develop new policies for the project, but follows the policies established at the corporate level.

4.5 Forecast Future Situations

Determining future courses of action will be based on the current status and environment as well as the project manager's vision of the future. The project manager is responsible for forecasting situations that might impact the software project.

Forecasting is addressed in two steps. The first step involves predicting the future environment of the project and the second step involves predicting how the project will respond to the predicted future. Step one involves predicting future events, such as availability of personnel, the inflation rate, or availability of new computer hardware and the impact these future events will have on the software engineering project.

The second step involves predicting future activities of the project, such as specifying future expenditures of project resources and funds. The project manager is also responsible for estimating future risks and developing contingency plans for countering those risks.

4.6 Conduct a Risk Assessment for the Project

Risk is the likelihood of a specified hazardous or undesirable event occurring within a specified period or circumstance. The concept of risk has two elements: the frequency, or probability that a specified hazard might occur and the consequences of it. Risk factors must be identified and forecasts of situations that might adversely impact the software project must be prepared [Fairley and Rook 1996]. For example, there is serious doubt that the software can be developed for the amount specified in the contract. Should this occur, the results would be a loss of profit for the development company.

Contingency plans specify the actions to be taken should a risk (a potential problem) become a real problem. The risk becomes a problem when a prede-

termined risk-indicator metric crosses a predetermined threshold. For example, the budget has been over run by 12 percent at software specifications review (SSR). The preset threshold metric was 10 percent; therefore, the appropriate contingency plan must be put in effect. [Boehm 1987]

4.7 Determine Possible Courses of Action

In most projects there is more than one way to conduct the project, but not with equal cost, equal schedule, or equal risk. It is the project manager's responsibility to examine various approaches that could achieve the project objectives and satisfy the success criteria.

4.8 Make Planning Decisions for the Project

The project manager, in consultation with higher level management, the customer, and other appropriate parties, is responsible for choosing among the many possible courses of action those that are most appropriate for meeting project goals and objectives. The project manager is responsible for making tradeoff decisions involving cost, schedule, design strategies, and risks [Bunyard and Coward 1982].

4.9 Set Procedures and Rules for the Project

The project manager establishes procedures and rules for a project. In contrast to policies, *procedures* establish customary methods and provide detailed guidance for project activities. Procedures detail the exact manner for accomplishing an activity. For example, there may be a procedure for conducting design reviews.

In another contrast, a *rule* establishes specific and definite actions to be taken or not taken with respect to a given situation. A rule allows no discretion. For example, a rule might require two people to be on duty in the machine room at all times.

Process standards (in contrast to *product standards*) can be used to establish procedures. Process standards may be adopted from the corporate standards or written for a particular project. Process standards might cover topics such as reporting methods, reviews, and documentation preparation requirements.

4.10 Develop a Software Project Plan

A project plan specifies all of the actions necessary to successfully deliver a software product.

Typically, the plan specifies:

- The *tasks* to be performed by the software development staff in order to deliver the final software product. This usually requires partitioning the project activities into small, well-specified tasks. A useful tool for representing the partitioned project is the work breakdown structure (WBS).

- The *cost* and resources necessary to accomplish each project task [Boehm 1984].

- The project *schedule* that specifies dependencies among tasks, and establishes project milestones.

For further discussion of project planning see [Miller 1978].

4.11 Prepare Budgets for the Project

Budgeting involves placing cost figures on the project plan. The project manager is responsible for determining the cost of the project and allocating the budget to project tasks. Cost is the common denominator for all elements of the project plan. Requirements for personnel, computers, travel, office space, equipment, and so forth can only be compared and cost-tradeoffs made when these requirements are measured in terms of their monetary value.

4.12 Document Project Plans

The project manager is responsible for documenting the project plan [Fairley 1987] and for preparing other plans such as the software quality assurance plan, software configuration management plan, staffing plan, and the test plan. The project plan is the primary means of communicating with other entities that interface with the project.

5. Organizing a Software Engineering Project

5.1 Introduction and Definitions

Organizing a software engineering project involves developing an effective and efficient organizational structure for assigning and completing project tasks and establishing the authority and responsibility relationships among the tasks.

Organizing involves itemizing the project activities required to achieve the objectives of the project and then arranging these activities into logical clusters. It also involves assigning groups of activities to various organizational entities and then delegating responsibility and authority needed to carry out the activities.

The purpose of an organizational structure is to "focus the efforts of many on a selected goal" [Donnelly, Gibson, and Ivancevich 1975].

Table 5.1 provides an outline of the activities that must be accomplished by the project manager in organizing a project. The remainder of this section provides greater detail concerning the activities outlined in Table 5.1.

5.2 Identify and Group Project Tasks

The manager is responsible for reviewing the project requirements, defining the various tasks to be accomplished, sizing those tasks, and grouping those tasks. Titles and organizational entities are assigned to the assembly of tasks; for example, analysis tasks, design tasks, coding tasks, and testing tasks. This information enables the project manager to select an organizational structure to control these groups.

5.3 Select an Organizational Structure for the Project

After identifying and grouping project tasks, the project manager must select an organizational structure. A software development project can be organized using one of several different and overlapping organizational types. For example:

- *Conventional organization structure*—line or staff organization.

- *Project organization structure*—functional, project, or matrix.

- *Team structure*—Egoless, chief programmer, or hierarchical.

Table 5.1: Organizing Activities for Software Project

Activity	Definition or Explanation
Identify and group project function, activities and tasks	Define, size, and categorize the project work.
Select organizational structures	Select appropriate structures to accomplish the project and to monitor, control, communicate, and coordinate.
Create organizational positions	Establish title, job descriptions, and job relationships for each project role.
Define responsibilities and authority	Define responsibilities for each organizational position and the authority to be granted for fulfilling those responsibilities.
Establish position qualifications	Define qualifications for persons to fill each position.
Document organizational decisions	Document titles, positions, job, descriptions, responsibilities, authorities, relationships, and position qualifications

The project manager may not have the luxury of selecting the best project organizational type, since this may be determined by policy at the corporate level. Regardless of who does it, an organizational structure that matches the needs and goals of the project application and environment and facilitates communication between the organizational entities should be selected.

The following paragraphs describe these organizational considerations.

5.3.1 Conventional Organizational Structures. A *line* organization has the responsibility and authority to perform the work that represents the primary mission of the larger organizational unit. In contrast, a *staff* organization is a group of functional experts that has responsibility and authority to perform special activities that help the line organization do its work. All organizations in a company are either line or staff.

5.3.2 Software Project Structures. A project structure is a temporary organizational form that has been established for the purpose of developing and building a system that is too big to be done by one or, at most, a few people. In a software engineering project, a software system is to be built. A project structure can be superimposed on a line or staff organization.

5.3.2.1 Functional Project Organization. One type of project organization is a *functional* organization; a project structure is built around a software engineering function or group of similar functions. A project is accomplished either within a functional unit or, if multifunctional, by two or more functional units, and the work product is passed from function to function as the project passes through the life-cycle phases. Figure 5.1 illustrates the tasks and lines of authority of a functional organization used to develop a software product.

5.3.2.2 Project Organization. Another type of project organization is built around each specific project; a project manager is given the responsibility, authority, and resources for conducting the project [Middleton 1967]. (The project organization is sometimes called a *projected* organization to get away from the term "project organization."). The manager must meet project goals within the resources of the organization. The project manager usually has the responsibility to hire, discharge, train, and promote people within the project. Figure 5.2 illustrates the tasks and lines of authority of a project organization. Note that the software project manager has total control over the project and the assigned software personnel.

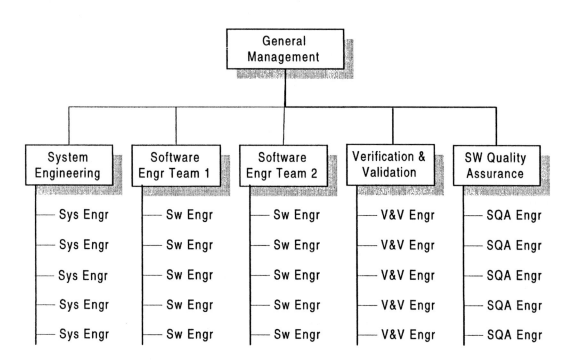

Figure 5.1: Functional Project Organization

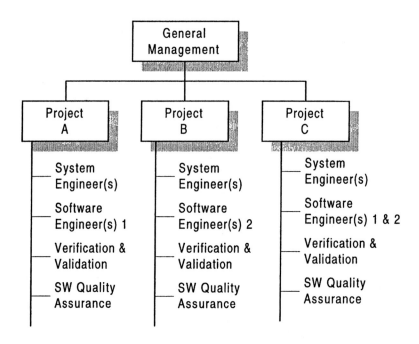

Figure 5.2: Project Organization

5.3.2.3 Matrix Project Organization. The third project organization is the *matrix* organization (sometimes called matrix project organization) and is a composite of the functional organization and the project organization [Stuckenbruck 1981]. The project manager is given responsibility and authority for completing the project. The functional managers provide the resources needed to conduct the project. In a matrix organization, the project manager usually does not have the authority to hire, discharge, train, or promote personnel within his project. Figure 5.3 illustrates the tasks and lines of authority in a matrix organization. Engineers labeled "A" are temporarily assigned to Project A, Engineers labeled "B" are temporarily assigned to Project B, Engineer labeled "C" are temporarily assigned to Project C.

Since each individual worker is "supervised" by two separates managers, the system is sometime called the "two boss" system.

Once the tasks are identified, sized, and grouped, and the organizational structure has been specified, the project manager must create job titles and position descriptions. Personnel will be recruited for the project using the job titles and position descriptions.

5.5 Define Responsibilities and Authority

Responsibility is the obligation to fulfill commitments. *Authority* is the right to make decisions and exert power. It is often stated that authority can be delegated, but responsibility cannot. [Koontz and O'Donnell 1976] support this view by defining responsibility as "the obligation owed by subordinates to their supervisors for exercising authority delegated to them in a way to accomplish results expected." Responsibility and authority for organizational activities or tasks should be assigned to the organizational position at the time the position is created or modified. The project manager is assigned and in turn assigns the responsibilities and the corresponding authorities to the various organizational positions within the project.

5.6 Establish Position Qualifications

Position qualifications must be identified for each position in the project. Position qualifications are established by considering issues such as the types of individuals needed for the project, the necessary experience in the area of the application, the required education (a B.S. in computer science or an M.S. in artificial intelligence), the required training, either before or after the project is initiated, and the required knowledge, such as FORTRAN, Lisp, or some other programming language. Establishing proper and accurate position qualifications will make it possible for the manager to correctly staff the project.

5.7 Document Organizational Structures

Lines of authority, tasks, and responsibilities should be documented in the project plan. Decisions must be justified, well documented, and made available to guide staffing of the project.

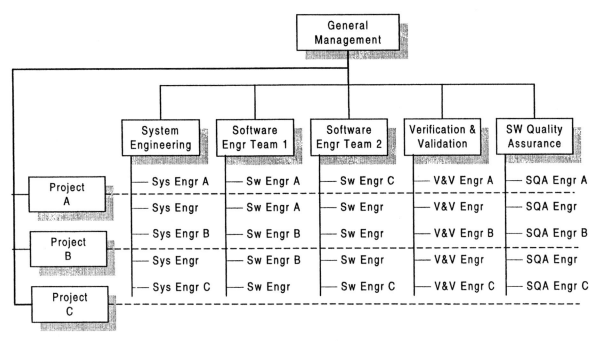

Figure 5.3: Matrix Project Organization

6. Staffing a Software Engineering Project

6.1 Introduction and Definitions

Staffing a software engineering project consists of all of the management activities that involve filling (and keeping filled) the positions that were established in the project organizational structure. This includes selecting candidates for the positions and training or otherwise developing candidates and incumbents to accomplish their tasks effectively. Staffing also involves terminating project personnel when necessary.

Staffing is not the same as organizing; staffing involves filling the roles created in the project organizational structure through selection, training, and development of personnel. The objective of staffing is to ensure that project roles are filled by personnel who are qualified (both technically and temperamentally) to occupy them.

Table 6.1 provides an outline of the activities and tasks that must be accomplished by project managers to staff their projects. The remainder of this section provides greater detail on the activities and tasks outlined in Table 6.1.

Table 6.1: Staffing Activities for Software Projects

Activity	Definition or Explanation
Fill organizational positions	Select, recruit, or promote qualified people for each project position.
Assimilate assigned personnel newly	Orient and familiarize new people with the organization, facilities, and tasks to be done on the project.
Educate or train personnel	Make up deficiencies in position qualifications through training and education.
Provide for general development	Improve knowledge, attitudes, and skills of project personnel.
Evaluate and appraise personnel	Record and analyze the quantity and quality of project work as the basis for personnel evaluations. Set performance goals and appraise personnel periodically.
Compensate	Provide wages, bonuses, benefits, or other financial remuneration commensurate with project responsibilities and performance.
Terminate assignments	Transfer or separate project personnel as necessary.
Document staffing decisions	Record staffing plans, training plans and achievements, appraisal records, and compensations recommendations

6.2 Fill Organizational Positions in a Software Project

The project manager is responsible for filling the positions that were established during organizational planning for the project. In staffing any software project, any number of factors should be considered, such as education, experience, training, motivation, commitment, and intelligence. Deficiencies in any of these factors can be offset by strengths in other factors. For example, deficiencies in education can be offset by better experience, a particular type of training, or enthusiasm for the job. Serious deficiencies should be cause for corrective action.

6.2.1 Sources of Qualified Project Individuals.

One source of qualified individuals is personnel who transfer from within the project itself. It is the project manager's prerogative to move people from one task to another within a project. Another source is transfers from other projects within the organization. This can be done anytime, but often happens when another software engineering project is either phasing down or is canceled.

Other sources of qualified personnel are new hires from other companies through such methods as job fairs, referrals, headhunters, want ads, and unsolicited resumes. New college graduates can be recruited either through interviews on campus or through referrals from recent graduates who are now company employees.

6.2.2 Selecting a Productive Software Staff. Two metrics may indicate a productive software staff:

- *Amount of experience*—An experienced staff is more productive than an inexperienced staff [Boehm 1984]. Some of the best experience comes from having worked on software projects similar to the project being staffed.

- *Diversity of experience*—Diversity of experience is a reasonable predictor of productivity [Kruesi 1982]. It is better that the individuals under consideration have done well in several jobs over a period of time rather than one job for the same time period.

Other qualities indicative of a highly productive individual are communications skills (both oral and written), a college degree (usually in a technical field), being a self-starter, and experience in the application area of the project.

6.3 Assimilate Newly Assigned Software Personnel

The manager is responsible not only for hiring the people, but also for familiarizing them with any project procedures, facilities, and plans necessary to assure their effective integration into the project. In short, the project manager is responsible for introducing new employees to the company and the company to the employees.

6.4 Educate or Train Personnel as Necessary

It is not always possible to recruit or transfer employees with exactly those skills needed for a particular project. Therefore, the manager is responsible for educating and training the assigned personnel to ensure that they can meet the project requirements.

Education differs from training. *Education* involves teaching the basics, theory, and underlying concepts of a discipline with a view toward a long-term payoff. *Training* means teaching a skill or a knowledge of how to use, operate, or make something. The skill is typically needed in the near future and has a short term payoff.

Each individual within an organization must have a *training plan* that specifies career education and training goals and the steps each person will take in achieving those goals. To be successful, top management must actively support training programs.

6.5 Provide for General Development of the Project Staff

In addition to education and training, the project manager must ensure that project staff grows with the project and company. The manager must ensure that their professional knowledge will increase and that they maintain a positive attitude toward the project, the company, and the customers.

6.6 Evaluate and Appraise Project Personnel

The project manager is also responsible for periodically evaluating and appraising personnel. An appraisal provides feedback to staff members concerning the positive and negative aspects of their performance. This feedback allows the staff member to strengthen good qualities and improve those which are negative. Appraisals should be done at regular intervals and should concentrate on the individual's performance and not on personality, unless personality issues interfere with performance [Moneysmith 1984].

6.7 Compensate the Project Personnel

The manager—sometimes directly, sometimes indirectly—is responsible for determining the salary scale and benefits of project personnel. Benefits take on many forms. Most benefits are monetary or can be equated to money. These include stock options, a company car, first class tickets for all company trips, or a year-end bonus. Some benefits are nonmonetary but appeal to the self-esteem of the individual; examples are combat medals in the military, a reserve parking place at the company plant, or an impressive title on the door.

6.8 Terminate Project Assignments

The project manager is not only responsible for hiring people, but must also terminate assignments as necessary. "Terminate" includes reassigning personnel at the end of a successful project (a pleasant termination) and dismissing personnel due to project cancellation (an unpleasant termination). Termination can also occur by firing when an employee is determined to be unsatisfactory.

6.9 Document Project Staffing Decisions

Project managers should document their staffing plan and their evaluation and training policies for all to read. Each individual within an organization should have a personal training plan reflecting course work needed and progress made. Other staffing documents that might be produced include orientation plans and schedules, salary schedules, and promotion policies. The project manager and each individual employee should have a copy of his or her annual performance objectives signed by the employee and the project manager.

7. Directing a Software Engineering Project

7.1 Introduction and Definitions

Directing a software engineering project consists of management's motivational and interpersonal aspects that encourage project personnel to understand and contribute to project goals. Once subordinates are trained and oriented, the project manager has a con-tinuing responsibility for clarifying their assignments, guiding them toward improved performance, and motivating them to work with enthusiasm and confidence toward achieving project goals.

Directing, like staffing, involves people. Directing is sometimes considered to be synonymous with leading (compare reference [Koontz and O'Donnell 1972] with reference [Koontz, O'Donnell, and Weihrich 1984]). Directing a project involves providing leadership to the project, day-to-day supervision of the project personnel, delegating authority to the lower organizational entities, coordinating activities of the project members, facilitating communications between project members and those outside the project, resolving conflicts, managing change, and documenting important decisions.

Table 7.1 provides an outline of leadership activities and tasks that must be accomplished by project managers and leadership teams for software projects. The remainder of this section discusses and provides greater detail on the activities outlined in Table 7.1.

7.2 Provide Leadership to the Project Team

The project manager provides leadership to the project management team by interpreting plans and requirements to them to ensure that everybody on the project team is working toward common goals. Leadership results from the power of the leader and his or her ability to guide and influence individuals. The project manager's power can be derived from his leadership position as project manager; this is called *positional power*. The project manager's power can also be derived from the manager's own "charm," sometimes called *charisma*; this is called *personal power*.

Table 7.1: Directing Activities for Software Projects

Activity	Definition or Explanation
Provide leadership	Create an environment in which project members can accomplish their assignments with enthusiasm and confidence.
Supervise personnel	Provide day-to-day instructions, guidance, and discipline to help project members fulfill their assigned duties.
Delegate authority	Allow project personnel to make decisions and expend resources within the limitations and constraints of their roles.
Motivate personnel	Provide a work environment in which project personnel can satisfy their psychological needs.
Build teams	Provide a work environment in which project personnel can work together toward common project goals. Set performance goals for teams as well as for individuals.
Coordinate activities	Combine project activities into effective and efficient arrangements.
Facilitate communication	Ensure a free flow of correct information among project members.
Resolve conflicts	Encourage constructive differences of opinion and help resolve the resulting conflicts.
Manage changes	Stimulate creativity and innovation in achieving project goals.
Document directing decisions	Document decisions involving delegation of authority, communication and coordination, conflict resolution, and change management.

7.3 Supervise Project Personnel

The project manager is responsible for overseeing the project members' work and providing day-to-day supervision of the personnel assigned to the project. It is the project manager's responsibility to provide guidance to and, when necessary, discipline project members to ensure that they fulfill their assigned duties.

7.4 Delegate Authority to the Appropriate Project Members

The software engineering project manager is also responsible for delegating authority to the project staff. Tasks are assigned to subgroups, teams, and individuals, and authority is delegated to these teams so that they can accomplish their tasks in an efficient and effective manner. Typically, a good project manager will always delegate authority down through the lowest possible level of the project [Raudsepp 1981].

7.5 Motivate Project Personnel

The project manager is responsible for motivating and inspiring personnel to do their best. Several motivational techniques from mainstream management are applicable to software engineering projects, such as management by objective, Maslow's hierarchy of needs [Maslow 1954], Herzberg's hygiene factors [Herzberg, Mausner, and Snyderman 1959], and sometimes just the charisma of the manager. The project manager should always acknowledge the special needs of the highly qualified, technically trained engineers and scientists who staff the project. It should also be noted that dollars will attract good software engineers to a company, but dollars will not keep them. For a further discussion of motivating software development personnel see [Fitz-enz 1978]. For another paper with a unique method of motivating computer people, see [Powell and Posner 1984].

7.6 Build Software Project Teams

As discussed in Section 5, software is built by project teams. *Team building* is the process of improving the interrelationship between team members in order to improve the efficiency and effectiveness of the team as a whole. Techniques such as team building exercises, "off-site" meetings, and group dynamics can be used to improve the capabilities of the team to be more productive as a group than the team members would be as individuals.

7.7 Coordinate Project Activities

Coordination is arranging project entities to work together toward common goals with minimum friction. Documents, policies, procedures, and so forth are viewed differently by various people. The task of the project manager is to reconcile differences in approach, effort, and schedule, and to resolve these differences for the benefit of the project.

7.8 Facilitate Communication

Along with coordination, the project manager is responsible for facilitating communication both within the project and between the project and other organizations. *Facilitate* means to expedite, ease, and assist in the progress of communication. *Communication*, in turn, is an information exchange among entities that are working toward common goals.

7.9 Resolve Conflicts

It is the project manager's responsibility to resolve conflicts among project staff members and between project staff and outside agencies in both technical and managerial matters. The project manager is not expected to be an expert in all aspects of the project; however, he or she should have the good judgment to recognize the best possible approach to solve a particular technical or managerial problem.

7.10 Manage Change that Impacts the Software Project

The project manager is responsible for encouraging independent thought and innovation in achieving project goals. A good manager must always accommodate change when change is cost-effective and beneficial to the project. [Kirchof and Adams 1986]

7.11 Document Directing Decisions

The project manager must document all tasks, assignments of authority and responsibility, and the outcome of conflict resolution. In addition, all decisions concerning lines of communication and coordination must be documented.

8. Controlling a Software Engineering Project

8.1 Introduction and Definitions

Controlling is collecting management activities used to ensure that the project goes according to plan. Performance and results are measured against plans, deviations are noted, and corrective actions are taken to ensure conformance of plans and actuals.

Control is a feedback system that provides information on how well the project is going. Control asks: Is the project on schedule? Is it within cost? Are there any potential problems that will cause slippages in meeting budget and schedule requirements? Controls also provide plans and approaches for eliminating the difference between the plans and/or standards and the actuals or results.

The control process also requires organizational structure, communication, and coordination. For example, who is responsible for assessing progress? Who will take action on reported problems?

Controlling methods and tools must be objective. Information must be quantified. The methods and tools must point out deviations from plans without regard to the particular people or positions involved. Control methods must be tailored to individual environments and managers. The methods must be flexible and adaptable to deal with the changing environment of the organization. Control also must be economical; the cost of control should not outweigh its benefits.

Control must lead to corrective action—either bringing the actual status back to plan, changing the plan, or terminating the project.

Table 8.1 provides an outline of the project management activities that must be accomplished by project managers to control their projects. The remainder of this section discusses the activities outlined in Table 8.1.

8.2 Develop Standards of Performance

The project manager is responsible for developing and specifying performance standards for the project. The project manager either develops standards and procedures for the project, adopts and uses standards developed by the parent organization, or uses standards developed by the customer or a professional society (for example see [IEEE Software Engineering Standards 1993]).

- *Standards*—A documented set of criteria used to specify, and determine the adequacy of, an action or object.

- *Software quality assurance*—A planned and systematic pattern of all actions necessary to provide adequate confidence that the item or product conforms to established technical requirements [IEEE-STD 729-1983]

- *Software configuration management*—A method for controlling and reporting on software status. SCM is the discipline of identifying the configuration of a system at discrete points in time for purposes of systematically controlling changes to this configuration and maintaining the integrity and traceability of this configuration throughout the system life cycle [Bersoff 1984].

- *Process and product metrics*—A measure of the degree to which a process or product possesses a given attribute.

8.3 Establish Monitoring and Reporting Systems

The project manager is responsible for establishing the methods of monitoring the software project and reporting project status. Monitoring and reporting systems must be specified in order to determine project status. The project manager needs feedback on the progress of the project and quality of the product to ensure that everything is going according to plan. The type, frequency, originator, and recipient of project reports must be specified. Status reporting tools to provide progress visibility, and not just resources used or time passed, must be implemented.

8.5 Measure and Analyze Results

The project manager is responsible for measuring the results of the project both during and at the end of the project. For instance, actual phase deliverables should be measured against planned phase deliverables. The measured results can be management (process) results and/or technical (product) results. An example of a process result would be the status of the project schedule. An example of a product result would be the degree to which the design specifications correctly interpreted the requirement specifications. Some of the tools and methods for measuring results are described in the following paragraphs.

Table 8.1: Controlling Activities for Software Projects

Activity	Definition or Explanation
Develop standards of performance	Set goals that will be achieved when tasks are correctly accomplished.
Establish monitoring and reporting systems	Determine necessary data, who will receive it, when they will receive it, and what they will do with it to control the project.
Measure and Analyze results	Compare achievements with standards, goals, and plans,
Initiate corrective actions	Bring requirements, plans, and actual project status into conformance
Reward and discipline	Praise, remunerate, and discipline project personnel as appropriate
Document controlling methods	Document the standards of performance, monitoring and control systems and reward and discipline mechanisms.

- *Binary tracking and work product specifications*—Specifies the objectives of the work, staffing requirements, the expected duration of the task, the resources to be used, the results to be produced, and any special considerations for the work. Binary track is the concept that a work pack is either done or not done (that is, assigned a numeric "1" or "0").

- *Unit development folders*—A specific form of development notebook that has proven to be useful and effective in collecting and organizing software products as they are produced [Ingrassia 1987].

- *Walkthroughs and inspections*—Reviews of a software product (design specifications, code, test procedures, and so on.) conducted by the peers of the group being reviewed [Ackerman 1996].

- *Independent auditing*—An independent review of a software project to determine compliance with software requirements, specifications, baselines, standards, policies, and software quality assurance plans.

8.6 Initiate Corrective Actions for the Project

If standards and requirements are not being met, the project manager must initiate corrective action. For instance, the project manager can change the plan or standard, use overtime or other procedures to get back on plan, or change the requirements, such as delivering less.

8.7 Reward and Discipline the Project Members

The project manager should reward people for meeting their standards and plans, and discipline those who without good reason do not. This should not be confused with the rewards and discipline given to workers for performing their assigned duties; that is a function of staffing. The system of rewards and discipline discussed here is a mechanism for controlling ability to meet a plan or standard.

8.8 Document Controlling Methods

The project manager must document all standards, software quality procedures, metrics and other means of measuring production and products. In addition, the manager must establish metrics for determining when corrective action must be initiated and determine in advance possible corrective action that can be taken.

9. Summary

Software engineering procedures and techniques do not alone guarantee a successful project. A good project manager can sometimes overcome or work around deficiencies in organization, staffing, budgets, standards, or other shortcomings. A poor manager stumbles over every problem, real or imaginary; no number of rules, policies, standards, or techniques will help. The methods and techniques discussed in this article, in the hands of a competent project manager, can significantly improve the probability of a successful project.

In this paper and in many other documents, the terms "project management" and "software engineering project management" are used interchangeably. This is because the management of a software engineering project and other types of projects require many of the same tools, techniques, approaches, and methods of mainstream management. The functions and general activities of management are the same at all levels; only the detailed activities and tasks are different.

References

[Ackerman 1996] F.A. Ackerman, "Software Inspections and the Cost-Effective Production of Reliable Software," in *Software Engineering,* edited by M. Dorfman and R.H. Thayer, IEEE Computer Society Press, Los Alamitos, Calif., 1996.

[Bersoff 1984] E.H. Bersoff, "Elements of Software Configuration Management," *IEEE Trans. Software Eng.,* Vol. SE-10, No. 1, Jan. 1984, pp. 79–87. Reprinted in *Tutorial: Software Engineering Project Management,* edited by R.H. Thayer, IEEE Computer Society Press, Los Alamitos, Calif., 1988.

[Boehm 1984] B.W. Boehm, "Software Engineering Economics," *IEEE Trans. Software Eng.,* Vol. SE-10, No. 1, Jan. 1984, pp. 4-21.

[Boehm 1987] B.W. Boehm, *Tutorial: Software Risk Management,* IEEE Computer Society Press, Los Alamitos, Calif., 1989.

[Brooks 1987] "Report on the Defense Science Board Task Force on Military Software," Office of the Undersecretary of Defense for Acquisition, Department of Defense, Washington, DC, Sept. 1987.

[Cleland and King, 1972] D.I. Cleland and W.R. King, *Management: A Systems Approach,* See Table 5-1: Major Management Functions as Seen by Various Authors, McGraw-Hill Book Company, New York, NY, 1972.

[DoD Software Initiative 1983] *Strategy for a DoD Software Initiative,* Department of Defense Report, 1 Oct. 1982. (An edited public version was published in *Computer,* Nov. 1983.)

[Donnelly, Gibson, and Ivancevich 1975] J.H. Donnelly, Jr., J.L. Gibson, and J.M. Ivancevich, *Fundamentals of Management: Functions, Behavior, Models,* rev. ed., Business Publications, Inc., Dallas, TX, 1975.

[Fairley 1987] R.E. Fairley, "A Guide for Preparing Software Project Management Plans," in *Tutorial: Software Engineering Project Management*, edited by R.H. Thayer, IEEE Computer Society Press, Los Alamitos, Calif., 1988.

[Fairley and Rook 1996] R.E. Fairley and P. Rook, "Risk Management for Software Development," in *Software Engineering*, edited by M. Dorfman and R.H. Thayer, IEEE Computer Society Press, Los Alamitos, Calif., 1996.

[Fayol 1949] H. Fayol, *General and Industrial Administration*, Sir Isaac Pitman & Sons, Ltd., London, 1949.

[Fitz-enz 1978] J. Fitz-enz, "Who is the DP Professional?," *Datamation*, Sept. 1978, pp. 125–128. Reprinted in *Tutorial: Software Engineering Project Management*, edited by R.H. Thayer, IEEE Computer Society Press, Los Alamitos, Calif., 1988.

[GAO/IMTEC-92-48 C-17 Aircraft Software] "Embedded Computer Systems: Significant Software Problems on C-17 Must be Addresses," General Accounting Office GAO/IMTEC-92-48, Gaithersburg, MD 20877, May 1992

[Herzberg, Mausner, and Snyderman 1959] F. Herzberg, B. Mausner, and B.B. Snyderman, *The Motivation to work*, John Wiley & Son, New York, N.Y., 1959.

[IEEE-STD 729-1983] ANSI/IEEE Std. 729-1983, *IEEE Standard Glossary of Software Engineering Terminology*, IEEE, Inc., New York, NY, 1983.

[IEEE Software Engineering Standards 1993] Hardbound Edition of Software Engineering Standards, IEEE, New York, N.Y., 1993.

[Ingrassia 1987] F.S. Ingrassia, "The Unit Development Folder (UDF): A Ten-Year Perspective," in *Tutorial: Software Engineering Project Management*, edited by R.H. Thayer, IEEE Computer Society Press, Los Alamitos, Calif., 1988.

[Kirchof and Adams 1986] N.S. Kirchof and J.R. Adams, "Conflict Management for Project Managers: An Overview," extracted from *Conflict Management for Project Managers*, Project Management Institute, Feb. 1986, pages 1-13. Reprinted in *Tutorial: Software Engineering Project Management*, edited by R.H. Thayer, IEEE Computer Society Press, Los Alamitos, Calif., 1988.

[Koontz and O'Donnell, 1972] H. Koontz and C. O'Donnell, *Principles of Management: An Analysis of Managerial Functions*, 5th ed., McGraw-Hill Book Company, New York, N.Y., 1972.

[Koontz, O'Donnell, and Weihrich 1984] H. Koontz, C. O'Donnell and H. Weihrich, *Management*, 8th ed., McGraw-Hill Book Co., New York, NY, 1984.

[Kruesi 1982] B. Kruesi, seminar on "Software Psychology," California State University, Sacramento, Fall 1982.

[MacKenzie, 1969] R.A. MacKenzie, "The Management Process in 3-D," *Harvard Business Rev.*, Vol. 47, No. 6, Nov.-Dec. 1969, pp. 80–87. Reprinted in *Tutorial: Software Engineering Project Management*, edited by R.H. Thayer, IEEE Computer Society Press, Los Alamitos, Calif., 1988.

[Maslow 1954] A.H. Maslow, *Motivation and Personality*, Harper & Brothers, New York, N.Y., 1954.

[Middleton, 1967] C.J. Middleton, "How to Set Up a Project Organization," *Harvard Business Rev.*, Nov.-Dec. 1967, pp. 73–82.

[Miller 1978] W.B. Miller, "Fundamentals of Project Management," *J. Systems Management*, Vol. 29, No. 11, Issue 211, Nov. 1978, pp. 22–29.

[Moneysmith 1984] M. Moneysmith, "I'm OK—and You're Not," *Savvy*, Apr. 1984, pp. 37-38. Reprinted in *Tutorial: Software Engineering Project Management*, edited by R.H. Thayer, IEEE Computer Society Press, Los Alamitos, Calif., 1988.

[Paulk et al., 1996] M.C. Paulk, B. Curtis, M.B. Chrissis, and C.V. Weber, "The Capability Maturity Model for Software," in *Software Engineering*, edited by M. Dorfman and R.H. Thayer, IEEE Computer Society Press, Los Alamitos, Calif., 1996.

[Powell and Posner 1984] G.N. Powell and B.Z. Posner, "Excitement and Commitment: Keys to Project Success," *Project Management J.*, Dec. 1984, pp. 39–46. Reprinted in *Tutorial: Software Engineering Project Management*, edited by R.H. Thayer, IEEE Computer Society Press, Los Alamitos, Calif., 1988.

[Raudsepp 1981] E. Raudsepp, "Delegate Your Way to Success," *Computer Decisions*, Mar. 1981, pp. 157–164. Reprinted in *Tutorial: Software Engineering Project Management*, edited by R.H. Thayer, IEEE Computer Society Press, Los Alamitos, Calif., 1988.

[Rue and Byars, 1983] L.W. Rue and L.L. Byars, *Management: Theory and Application*, Richard D. Irwin, Inc., Homewood, Ill., 60430, 1983.

[Stuckenbruck 1981] L.C. Stuckenbruck, "The Matrix Organization," *A Decade of Project Management*, Project Management Institute 1981, pp. 157–169. Reprinted in *Tutorial: Software Engineering Project Management*, edited by R.H. Thayer, IEEE Computer Society Press, Los Alamitos, Calif., 1988.

[Thayer and Pyster 1984] R.H. Thayer and A.B. Pyster, "Guest Editorial: Software Engineering Project Management," *IEEE Trans. Software Eng.*, Vol. SE-10, No. 1, Jan. 1984.

[Zubrow, et al. 1995] D. Zubrow, J. Herbsleb, W. Hayes, and D. Goldenson presentation: "Process Maturity Profile of the Software Community 1995 Update," Nov. 1995, based on data up to September 1995 for most recent assessment of 440 organizations: ML1 - 70.2%; ML2 - 18.4%; ML3 - 10.2%; ML4 - 1%; ML5 - 0.2%. Source: email, Mark Paulk, Software Engineering Institution, 14 Feb 1996.

Tom DeMarco, The Atlantic Systems Guild

WHY DOES SOFTWARE COST SO MUCH?

MANAGER

How to get people and technology to work together.

When I took over as coeditor of this department, my intent was to keep it personal. In this spirit, I've turned down several contributions, but this column captures the very kind of controversial, entertaining, and educational insights I want to relay. Tom DeMarco is the author of four books on software and management, including (with Tom Lister) the recent Dorset-House book, Peopleware: Productive Projects and Teams. *In 1986 he was awarded the J.D.Warnier Prize for lifetime contribution to the information sciences.*
— Alan Davis

IN THE ABSENCE OF MEANINGFUL standards, a new industry like ours comes to depend instead on folklore. As the industry matures, the first order of business is to recognize and question the folklore. For example, how you ask and how you answer the familiar question "Why does software cost so much?" tells much about what folklore you've grown up with.

Author and consultant Jerry Weinberg claims to have encountered this question more than any other in his long career (*Quality Software Management, Volume 1: Systems Thinking,* Dorset-House, 1992). The correct answer, he says, is "Compared to what?" There is a likable logic to that: Most of the things we do with software in the '90s are barely conceivable without software, so there is no valid basis of comparison.

Yet Jerry's answer, charming as it is, won't do you much good. At best it will just annoy the questioner. No answer is satisfactory because people don't ask that question to get an answer. "Why does software cost so much?" is not a question, it's an assertion. The assertion is that software costs too much.

The person who poses this nonquestion may seem to be motivated by intellectual curiosity: "Gee, I've always wondered, just why is it that software costs so much?" The real motivation, however, has nothing to do with curiosity and everything to do with getting the brutal assertion on the table.

It's a negotiating position: You are being put on notice that software costs are unconscionable and no budget or schedule you ask for will be considered reasonable. Your boss or user may agree to your budget, but only under *extreme* duress. Because the amount budgeted is already terribly, terribly excessive, it goes without saying that any slip or overrun is virtually a crime against nature.

In a recent interview (*Computer Design,* Aug. 1991, pp. 25-27), Cadre Technologies founder Lou Mazzucchelli observed that "software consumers are not satisfied with either the quantity or the quality of our output." Right on target. Software consumers in vast numbers are telling us that our efforts don't begin to measure up to their expectations. Software is much too expensive, takes too long to build, isn't solid enough, isn't easy enough to use — isn't good enough in any way.

I have a very grumpy question for those who complain that the software-development community hasn't measured up to their expectations: Where in hell did those expectations come from?

A LITTLE DIATRIBE. You and I and others like us built the software industry from scratch over the last 30 years. Out of thin air we made a $300 billion-a-year business. (See John E. Hopcroft and Dean B. Krafft, "Sizing the US Software Industry," *IEEE Spectrum,* Dec. 1987, pp. 58-62 to understand how I arrive at this figure.) In all of economic history, there has never been a more staggering accomplishment. $300 billion a year! Think of it. In the time it will take you to read this article, the software industry will generate something more than $12 million.

What has it taken to build this huge new industry so quickly? Hint: It wasn't just getting some programmers together and teaching them to sling code. It required the active participation of a marketplace. Somebody had to toady up huge quantities of money to buy all the software we built. And they did. Not only did they buy all we could produce at the cost we charged, they complained about not being able to buy even more, about the so-called backlog.

This growth was not the result of poor quality and poor productivity. The only conceivable explanation for the phenomenal success of the software industry is that it regularly delivered a quality and productivity far beyond the market's real expecta-

> **PEOPLE DON'T ASK THIS TO GET AN ANSWER. IT'S NOT A QUESTION, IT'S AN ASSERTION.**

Editors: Alan Davis
University of Colorado
1867 Austin Bluffs Pkwy., Suite 200
Colorado Springs, CO 80933-7150
Internet adavis@zeppo.uccs.edu

Winston Royce
TRW
1 Federal Systems Park Dr.
STC 7165U
Fairfax, VA 22030
(703) 803-5025/6
fax: (703) 803-5108

Reprinted from *IEEE Software,* Vol. 10, No. 2, Mar. 1993, pp. 89–90.

tions. But all the time that our buyers (our managers and our users) were lining up to cash in on the bargain, they were complaining. This behavior is not a recent phenomenon: They didn't congratulate us for years and years and then become upset only during the downturn in the '90s. No, they complained all the way from zero to $300 billion.

I myself am a bit peeved by this. (Perhaps you could tell.) I feel like we have accomplished wonders and been yelled at the whole time. Through their actions and their words, our buyers have sent diametrically opposed messages.

Imagine how the Wright brothers would have felt had they had a similar reception. You are Orville. It's December 7, 1904, at Kitty Hawk, North Carolina, 7:30 a.m., and you're climbing up into Flyer One. "Let 'er rip," you say, or words to that effect. The engine coughs to life. You rev it up and there is movement. There is not just movement, there is speed. Speed and bumps and wind ... by God, you're up! You've done it. You've pulled off a miracle, and the world will never be the same. You are so elated you're barely even afraid. Cool as a cucumber, you bring the flyer down.

Just as you are coming to a stop, you notice a guy in a business suit, looking sourly at his watch. He says "Orville, I'm really disappointed in this project. I had great expectations and you've let me down. Here it is nearly eight a.m. and I have to be in LA for a dinner meeting tonight. And you guys are nowhere! You haven't invented the jet engine or the flight attendant or the airport or those cocktails in tiny bottles. You've let me down completely!" This is the guy Mazzucchelli was talking about.

WHERE EXPECTATIONS COME FROM. No one expected the software industry to achieve what it has achieved. Not a single futurist predicted the extraordinary productivity and quality we have accomplished. How is it possible that the industry is performing beyond our wildest expectations while every individual project is underperforming?

It's not. Those projects aren't underperforming at all. And their consumers

know it. Pay attention to what they do, not what they say. The real message our consumers are telling us is that software is the best bargain they ever heard of. They complain to us because *they know we work harder when they do complain.* We have trained them to do this. When they complained in the past, we worked harder. We gave them more for their money (even more than the extraordinary bargain they would have gotten anyway) because they pretended to be discontent. Boy, are we dumb.

In a recent article, Albert L. Lederer and Jayesh Prasad set down some guidelines for better software cost estimating ("Nine Management Guidelines for Better Cost Estimating," *Comm ACM*, Feb. 1992, pp. 51-59). Their method involved a survey of some 400 professional software managers. What interested me was a tiny nugget tucked away in the commentary: The great majority of respondents reported that their software estimates were dismal — only about one in four projects come in at a cost "reasonably close" to the estimate. However, 43 percent said their current estimating method was "very" or "moderately" satisfactory (the two highest ratings).

What's going on here? Estimates bear little or no resemblance to reality but managers aren't dissatisfied? I think I'm beginning to understand. Maybe the purpose of the estimating process is not to come up with a realistic answer, but to come up with an *unrealistic* answer. Maybe the estimating process is not supposed to guide the manager as to what to expect. Rather, it's supposed to guide the manager as to what to *pretend* to expect.

This is the kind of process that tells your boss, for example, to set September 1994 as the expected delivery date. This "right" schedule is neither ridiculous nor feasible. That is, after all, the object of the exercise. The "right" schedule is one that is *utterly* impossible, but not *obviously* impossible.

HOW DO MANAGERS KNOW? It is a great tribute to quality software management that managers know how to set this "right" schedule. It isn't easy. In the abstract, at least, it is just as hard to predict a date that is just short

of possible as to pick one that is safe and reasonable. Both require a prediction of product size as well as a correct assessment of team capability. How do our managers learn to do this? Again, we have trained them. They watch our faces when they set schedules. If we look relieved, they know they haven't turned the screws enough. If we just giggle, they know they've gone too far.

The assertion that software costs too much is part of a cost-containment ploy. The cynical notion that a "right" schedule is one that no one has a prayer of achieving is another part of that ploy. The constant refrain that software developers just are not productive enough is a goad. It appears to work because software developers are sincere and professional and a little dopey. The problem is that our industry is overgoaded. Our work is largely incompressible. When you're under pressure, your first response is to cut out extraneous activities: chats and bull sessions.

That may indeed be productive, but that's the end of it. As the pressure continues, there is nothing more you can do. You can't work faster; that just isn't possible. You might stay later, but that has a long-term cost: Overtime applied over months and months gives only an illusion of progress that is wiped out by compensatory "undertime," burnout, disillusionment, waste, and employee turnover.

THE MORAL. As time pressure increases, the only real option is to pay for speed by reducing quality. I sometimes think, rather bitterly, that reduced quality is a conscious goal of those who pressure projects. They are saying "Loosen up, folks — learn to rush the product out the door without worrying so much about quality." This comes, of course, at the very moment that companies are paying lip service to quality as never before.

In the short run, paying for speed by reducing quality makes sense. In the long run, it will take us where it took the US automobile industry. We might win a few battles, but not the war.

If you ask the wrong question you'll never get the right answer. Instead of asking "Why does software cost so much?" we must begin to ask "What have we done to make it possible for present-day software to cost so little?" The answer to that question will help us continue the extraordinary level of achievement that has always distinguished the software industry. ◆

> CUSTOMERS COMPLAIN BECAUSE WE WORK HARDER WHEN THEY DO. BOY ARE WE DUMB.

Software cost estimation

F J Heemstra

The paper gives an overview of the state of the art of software cost estimation (SCE). The main questions to be answered in the paper are: (1) What are the reasons for overruns of budgets and planned durations? (2) What are the prerequisites for estimating? (3) How can software development effort be estimated? (4) What can software project management expect from SCE models, how accurate are estimations which are made using these kind of models, and what are the pros and cons of cost estimation models?

software, cost estimation, project control, software cost estimation model

SIMPLE QUESTIONS, DIFFICULT ANSWERS

Judging by reports from everyday practice and findings in the literature, software projects regularly get out of hand and invariably the effort expended on development exceeds the estimated effort, resulting in the software being delivered after the planned date. There is no doubt that SCE is a serious problem for software project management. At first glance the questions to be answered are simple: How much time and effort will it cost to develop the software? What are the dominating cost factors? What are the important risk factors? Unfortunately, however, the answers are neither simple nor easy.

The article gives an overview of the field of software cost estimation (SCE). Special attention is paid to the use of SCE models. These models are one of the techniques project management can use to estimate and control the effort and duration of software development. The paper starts with a description of the importance of accurate cost estimates. From this it will be clear that SCE is not easy, and management is confronted with many problems. In the following section some reasons for the problems will be highlighted, the paper going on to explain which prerequisites are necessary for an estimate to be possible. It is important to have knowledge about the product that must be developed, the development process, the development means, the development personnel, and the user organization. Also it is necessary to have available a set of estimation methods and techniques. An overview of the existing

techniques for cost estimation is given in the fifth section, and the sixth section describes the principles of cost estimation models with an overview of models available nowadays. The rest of the paper deals with one of these techniques, that is to say parametric models. The penultimate section offers a comparison of SCE models, focusing mainly on the question 'How accurate are estimates made as a result of using models?' Despite the fact that software cost estimation is in its infancy plus the shortcomings of the current SCE models, the use of models has several advantages. The last section deals with the pros and cons and gives a critical evaluation of the state of the art of the use of these models.

OVERSHOOTS OF SOFTWARE DEVELOPMENT COSTS

Estimation of effort and duration of software development has become a topic of growing importance. This is not surprising. It often happens that software is more expensive than estimated and completion is later than planned. Moreover it turns out that much software does not meet the demands of the customer. There are a number of examples of such automation projects. The development costs of the automation of the education funding in The Netherlands proved to be three times as much as expected. Delays and wrong payments are a daily occurrence (*Volkskrant*, 24 June 1987). The development of the software for the purpose of the house-rent subsidies, produced to government order, proved to be twice as much as planned (NRC *Handelsblad*, 28 February 1989). In September 1989 the Dutch media announced as front page news the results of a governmental audit concerning the automation for the police. It proved to be an expensive disaster. The development costs of a computerized identifying system were US$43 million instead of the estimated US$21 million. Furthermore the system did not answer the formulated goals. The findings of a well-known Dutch consultancy organization (Berenschot) were that the costs of the automation of the registration of the Dutch population at the municipal offices were more than twice as much as were estimated (*Volkskrant*, 5 January 1990). A few years ago the estimates of the costs were about US$25 million. New calculations show that there is a deficit of more than US$30 million.

A field study by the Eindhoven University of Technology[1] gives an overview of the present state of the art of

Faculty of Public Administration and Public Policy, Twente University, POB 217, Enschede, The Netherlands

Reprinted from *Information and Software Technology*, Vol. 34, No. 10, Oct. 1992, F.J. Heemstra, "Software Cost Estimation," pp. 627–639, 1992, with kind permission from Elsevier Science–NL, Sara Burgerhartstraat 25; 1055 KV Amsterdam, The Netherlands.

the estimation and control of software development projects in 598 Dutch organizations. The most remarkable conclusions are:

- 35% of the participating organizations do not make an estimate
- 50% of the responding organizations record no data on an ongoing project
- 57% do not use cost-accounting
- 80% of the projects executed by the participating organizations have overruns of budgets and duration
- the mean overruns of budgets and duration are 50%

Van Lierop et al.[2] measured extensively whether development activities were executed according to plan. They investigated the reasons for the differences between plan and reality, and overall 80 development activities were measured. For all these activities 3203 hours were planned but 3838 hours were used, which means an overshoot of 20% on average of the planned number of hours. The duration of the activities (in days) proved to be 28% longer on average than planned. For all the activities 406 days of duration were planned, while the actual number of days proved to be 526.

In the literature the impression is given, mistakenly, that software development without overshoots of plans and budgets is not possible. This impression is inaccurate, and other measurements confirm this[3]. These show that 6% of all the activities had a shorter duration than planned and 58% were executed according to plan and were ready exactly on time. With regard to the development effort, it appeared that 25% of the activities needed less effort than estimated and 30% needed precisely the estimated effort. The reasons for the differences between plan and reality prove to be very specific for the development situation. In the organization where the measurements were taken the reasons were mainly related to things under-estimation of the quantity of work, underestimation of the complexity of the application, and specifications which proved to be unrealistic from a technical point of view. In other organizations, where similar measurements were taken, other reasons were discovered. As a result, other control actions are, of course, necessary. This conclusion fits well with the results of research carried out by Beers[4]. Thirty experienced software developers, project managers, and others, were asked to give the reasons for unsuccessful software projects. The answers can be summarized briefly as 'many minds, many thoughts'. It was not possible to indicate just one reason. A long list of all kinds of reasons were given.

It is alarming that it is so difficult for organizations to control the development of software. This is sufficient reason to emphasize that software development cost estimation and control should take its place as a fully fledged branch within discipline of software development.

WHAT MAKES SOFTWARE COST ESTIMATION SO DIFFICULT?

The main question, when confronting the above-mentioned problems, is what it is that makes software cost estimation so difficult. There are many reasons and, without going into detail, some can be listed as follows:

(1) There is a lack of data on completed software projects. This kind of data can support project management in making estimates.
(2) Estimates are often done hurriedly, without an appreciation for the effort required to do a credible job. In addition, too often it is the case that an estimate is needed before clear specifications of the system requirements have been produced. Therefore, a typical situation is that estimators are being pressured to write an estimate too quickly for a system that they do not fully understand.
(3) Clear, complete and reliable specifications are difficult to formulate, especially at the start of a project. Changes, adaptations and additions are more the rule than the exception: as a consequence plans and budgets must be adapted too.
(4) Characteristics of software and software development make estimating difficult. For example, the level of abstraction, complexity, measurability of product and process, innovative aspects, etc.
(5) A great number of factors have an influence on the effort and time to develop software. These factors are called 'cost drivers'. Examples are size and complexity of the software, commitment and participation of the user organization, experience of the development team. In general these cost drivers are difficult to determine in operation.
(6) Rapid changes in information technology (IT) and the methodology of software development are a problem for a stabilization of the estimation process. For example, it is difficult to predict the influence of new workbenches, fourth and fifth generation languages, prototyping strategies, and so on.
(7) An estimator (mostly the project manager) cannot have much experience in developing estimates, especially for large projects. How many 'large' projects can someone manage in, for example, 10 years?
(8) An apparent bias of software developers towards underestimation. An estimator is likely to consider how long a certain portion of the software would take and then to extrapolate this estimate to the rest of the system, ignoring the non-linear aspects of software development, for example co-ordination and management.
(9) The estimator estimates the time it would take to perform the task personally, ignoring the fact that a lot of work will be done by less experienced people, and junior staff with a lower productivity rate.

(10) There exists a serious mis-assumption of a linear relation between the required capacity per unit of time and the available time. This would mean that software developed by 25 people in two years could be accomplished by 50 people in one year. The assumption is seriously wrong. According to Brooks[5] the crucial corollary is: 'Adding people to a late project only makes it later'.

(11) The estimator tends to reduce the estimates to some degree, in order to make the bid more acceptable.

PREREQUISITES FOR SOFTWARE COST ESTIMATION

There are many ways to get to grips with the SCE problems. From an organizational perspective there are numerous ways to improve software project management: allocation of responsibilities; decision-making; organizing project work; monitoring and auditing of development tasks. Also software cost estimation can be looked at from a sociological and psychological point of view. This refers, for example, to commitment, organizing group cohesion, style of leadership, and so on. The technical side of the job is also an important issue to take into consideration. For example, the availability of good equipment such as design, programming, test and documentation tools, hardware facilities, etc.

There are many factors that have an influence on the effort and duration of software development. Several prerequisites must be fulfilled to address the problems listed above and to guarantee a sound basis for predicting effort, duration and the capacity to develop the software. These prerequisites are:

Insight in the characteristics of:

- the product (software) that has to be developed   WHAT
- the production means   WITH WHAT
- the production personnel   WHO
- the organization of the production   HOW
- the user/user organization   FOR WHOM

Availability of:

- Techniques and tools for software cost estimation.

In this section the attention will be focused on the WHAT, WITH WHAT, WHO, HOW and FOR WHOM factors, referred to as cost drivers in the literature. In the next section, SCE techniques and tools will be discussed.

There are many cost drivers. A study by Noth and Kretzschmar[6] found that more than 1200 different drivers were mentioned. Although there was considerable overlap in meaning, it is impossible to take them all into consideration during SCE. It is important for an organization to consider what are the most dominant cost factors. Within the context of this paper it is impossible to give an extended overview of the overwhelming number of drivers, so concentration will be on:

- a way of structuring the cost drivers
- listing the drivers which are commonly regarded as important
- some general considerations

Table 1 presents a structure of cost drivers in five categories. For each category the most important drivers are listed. From the literature and practice it is known that it is not easy to handle the cost drivers. When making an estimate one has to know which cost drivers are the most important in the specific situation, what the values are of the drivers, and what the influences are on effort and duration. In answering these questions it is important to pay attention to several issues:

Definition There is a lack of clear and accepted definitions for drivers, such as size, quality, complexity, experience, etc.

Quantification The majority of the cost drivers are hard to quantify. Often one has to use measures such as many, moderate, few, etc.

Table 1. A structure of important cost drivers[7]

WHAT (product)	WITH WHAT (means)	WHO (personnel)	HOW (project)	FOR WHOM (user)
Size of the software	Computer constraints —execution time	Quality of personnel	Requirements project duration	Participation
Required quality	—response time —memory capacity		—stretch out —compression	Number of users
Requirements volatility	User of tools	Experience of personnel	Basis for	Stability of user organization,
Software complexity	Use of modern programming techniques	Quality management	project control —matrix org.	procedures, way of working
Level of reuse	—information hiding	Availability for project	—project org. —prototyping	Experience of user
Amount of documentation	—chief prog. team —structured program		—incremental —linear devel.	with automation, level of education
Type of application	—top-down design		—software devel.	in automation

Objectivity Subjectivity is a potential risk factor. What may be complex for developer A is not complex for developer B.

Correlation It is difficult to consider one driver by itself. A change in the value of driver A may have consequences in the values of several other cost drivers. This is a difficulty from the viewpoint of measurability.

Relation between driver and effort For estimation it is important to predict the relation between, for example, software size and the required effort, a specified quality level and required effort, etc. From the literature we know that there is little clarity about these relations.

Calibration It is impossible to talk about 'the most important' cost drivers in isolation. It differs from situation to situation.

Effectivity and efficiency There is conflict between effectivity and efficiency. From an effectivity perspective it is worthwhile to pay a lot of attention to, for example, user participation. For the efficiency of a project it is justifiable to avoid user involvement.

Human factors Almost all research agrees on the dominating influence of cost drivers, such as experience and quality of the personnel. This means that investment in 'good' developers is important.

Reuse In many studies reuse is regarded as (one of) the most important factors to increase productivity[8-10].

SOFTWARE COST ESTIMATION: TECHNIQUES AND TOOLS

In the literature you can find a great number of techniques for estimating software development costs. Most of them are a combination of the following primary techniques[11]:

(1) Estimates made by an expert.
(2) Estimates based on reasoning by analogy.
(3) Estimates based on Price-to-Win.
(4) Estimates based on available capacity.
(5) Estimates based on the use of parametric models.

Furthermore two main approaches can be distinguished:

(1) Top-down
In the top-down approach the estimation of the overall project is derived from the global characteristics of the product. The total estimated cost is then split up among the various components.
(2) Bottom-up
In the bottom-up approach the cost of each individual component is estimated by the person who will be responsible for developing the component. The individual estimated costs are summed to get the overall cost estimate of the project.

The reliability of estimates based on expert judgement (1) depends a great deal to the degree in which a new project conforms with the experience and the ability of the expert to remember facts of historical projects. Mostly the estimates are qualitative and not objective. An important problem in using this method is that it is difficult for someone else to reproduce and use the knowledge and experience of an expert. This can lead to misleading situations where the rules of thumb of an expert are becoming general rules and used in inapplicable situations. Despite the disadvantages, this technique is usually used in situations where a first indication of effort and time is needed, especially in the first phases of software development in which the specifications of the product are vague and continually adapted.

The foundation of a cost estimation technique based on reasoning by analogy (2) is an analysed database of similar historical projects or similar project parts or modules. To find a similarity between a new project and one or more completed projects it is necessary to collect and record data and characteristics of old projects.

The Price-to-Win (3) technique can hardly be called an SCE technique. Primarily commercial motives play an important part in using this approach. It is remarkable that the estimates of organizations which use Price-to-Win are no less accurate than organizations which use other methods[7].

The basis of the estimation method which regards SCE as a capacity (4) problem is the availability of means, especially of personnel. An example is: 'Regarding our capacity planning, three men are available for the new project over the next four months. So the planned effort will be 12 man months'. If the specifications of the software are not clear, this method can be successful. An unfavourable side-effect is that in situations of overestimation the planned effort will be used completely. This effect is based on Parkinson's law that 'Work expands to fill the available volume'.

In parametric models (5) the development time and effort is estimated as a function of a number of variables. These variables represent the most important cost drivers. The nucleus of an estimation model is a number of algorithms and parameters. The values of the parameters and the kind of algorithms are, to a significant extent, based on the contents of a database of completed projects. In the next section a more comprehensive explanation of estimation models is given.

As mentioned earlier only 65% of the organizations which participated on the field study estimate a software project. Table 2 shows the frequency of use of the different techniques. The figures show that most organizations make use of data from past projects in some way. Obviously this works on an informal basis, because only 50% of the participating organizations record data from completed projects. Estimates based on expert judgement and the capacity method prove to be quite popular despite the disadvantages of these methods.

Table 2. Use of cost estimation techniques (an organization can use more than one technique)

	Use (%)
Expert judgement	25.5
Analogy method	60.8
Price-to-Win	8.9
Capacity problem	20.8
Parametric models	13.7

The next sections of this paper focus on the use of SCE models. There was a rapid growth of models in the 1970s. In the 1980s and the 1990s, however, few new models have been developed despite the increasing importance of controlling and estimating software development. Most of the 1970 models are of no interest to present industrial practitioners. There is a tendency towards automated versions (tools) of (combinations or refinements) existing models. An important question is whether this kind of model can solve all of the problems discussed above.

SOFTWARE COST ESTIMATION MODELS

In this section, one estimation technique, namely SCE models, will be discussed and the principles of SCE models described, making a distinction between sizing and productivity models. The characteristics of some well-known models will also be given.

The principles of SCE models

Most models found nowadays are two-stage models[7]. The first stage is a sizer and the second stage provides a productivity adjustment factor.

In the first stage an estimate regarding the size of the product to be developed is obtained. In practice several sizing techniques are used. The most well-known sizers nowadays are function points[12] and lines of code[11]. But other sizing techniques like 'software science'[13] and DeMarco's Bang method[14,15], have been defined. The result of a sizing model is the size/volume of the software to be developed, expressed as the number of lines of source code, number of statements, or the number of functions points.

In the second stage it is estimated how much time and effort it will cost to develop the software of the estimated size. First, the estimate of the size is converted into an estimate in nominal man-months of effort. As this nominal effort takes no advantage of knowledge con-

cerning the specific characteristics of the software-product, the way the software-product will be developed and the production means, a number of cost influencing factors (cost drivers) are added to the model. The effect of these cost drivers must be estimated. This effect is often called a productivity adjustment factor. Application of this correction factor to the nominal estimation of effort provides a more realistic estimate.

Some models, like FPA[16], are focused more on the sizing stage. Others, like the well-known COCOMO model[11] on the productivity stage and some tools, such as Before You Leap[17] combine two models to cover both stages. Figure 1 shows the two stages in SCE models.

Figure 2 shows the sizing and the productivity stages in the context of general cost estimation. In Figure 2 five components of the general cost estimation structure are shown. Besides the sizing and productivity components, a phase distribution and sensitivity/risk analysis component are distinguished. In the phase distribution component the total effort and duration is split up over the phases and activities of a project. This division has to be based on empirical data of past projects. The sensitivity and risk analysis phase supports project management — especially at the start of a project when the uncertainty is great — in determining the risk factors of a project and the sensitivity of the estimates to the cost drivers settings. Again data on past projects provide an important input for this component. Before using a model for the first time validation is necessary, and it may also be necessary to calibrate the model. Mostly the environment in which the SCE model has been developed and the database of completed projects on which the model is based will differ from the project characteristics of the environment(s) in which the model is to be used. To make validation and calibration possible, data on historical projects have to be available in an organization. As already mentioned, this information is often lacking.

Most of the tools implementing SCE models do not support project management in all of these steps. The seven steps are:

(1) Creation of database of completed projects.
(2) Size estimation.
(3) Productivity estimation.
(4) Phase distribution.
(5) Sensitivity and risk analysis.
(6) Validation.
(7) Calibration.

Calibration and risk and sensitivity analysis are especially lacking.

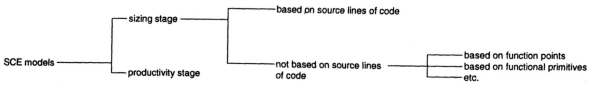

Figure 1. Structuring of SCE models

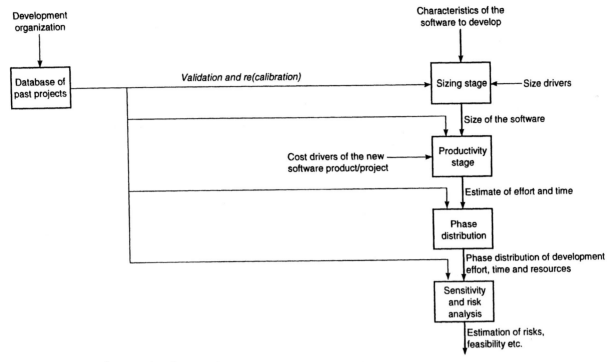

Figure 2. General cost estimation structure

An overview of SCE models

In the past 10 years a number of SCE models have been developed. This section does not give an exhaustive treatment of all the models: the overview is limited to one example of a sizing model, one productivity model, some models which are relevant from an historical point of view, well documented and within the experience of the author, and some models which introduce new ideas.

The COnstructive COst MOdel (COCOMO)

COCOMO[11,18] is the best documented and most transparent model currently available. The main focus in COCOMO is upon estimating the influence of 15 cost drivers on the development effort. Before this can be done, an estimate of the software size must be available. COCOMO does not support the sizing estimation stage: it only gives several equations based on 63 completed projects at TRW. The equations represent the relations between size and effort and between effort and development time. The equations are shown in Table 3. A distinction is made between three development modes: the organic mode (stable development environment, less innovative, relatively small size); the embedded mode (developing within tight constraints, innovative, complex, high volatility of requirements); and the semi-detached mode (between organic and embedded mode).

The nominal effort is adjusted by the influence of 15 cost drivers. In Table 4 the 15 COCOMO cost drivers are listed with the adjustment for each driver value. For example: where the required reliability of the software is

determined to be very high, the nominal effort has to be multiplied by 1.40. Furthermore COCOMO provides tables to apportion the adjusted estimated effort and development over the project phases and, in the detailed version of the model, to refine the adjustment for each phase. For example: the quality of the programmer has less influence in the feasibility phase than in the design phase. Thus phase dependent adjustment factors are used in the detailed model.

Function point analysis (FPA)

FPA has been developed by Albrecht[16] of IBM, and made widely available through the user groups *Guide and Share*. Albrecht was looking for a method to measure productivity in software development. For that purpose he developed FPA as an alternative measure to the number of lines of code. The method is programming language or fourth generation tool independent. The method has been refined several times by Rudolph[19,20], Albrecht and Gaffney[12], and Symons[21,22]. The principle of FPA is simple and is based on the number of 'functions' the software has to fulfil. These functions are

Table 3. The relation between the nominal effort and size and between development time and effort. KDSI = number of delivered source instructions/1000

Development mode	Man-month (nominal)	Development time (nominal)
Organic	$3.2*KDSI^{1.05}$	$2.5*MM (nom)^{0.38}$
Semi-detached	$3.0*KDSI^{1.12}$	$2.5*MM (nom)^{0.35}$
Embedded	$2.8*KDSI^{1.20}$	$2.5*MM (nom)^{0.32}$

Table 4. The COCOMO cost drivers and their influence on the nominal effort

Cost drivers	Value of the cost drivers					
	Very low	Low	Average	High	Very high	Extra high
Required reliability	0.75	0.88	1.00	1.15	1.40	
Database size		0.94	1.00	1.08	1.16	
Complexity software	0.70	0.85	1.00	1.15	1.30	1.65
Constraints execution time			1.00	1.11	1.30	1.66
Memory constraints			1.00	1.06	1.21	1.56
Hardware volatility		0.87	1.00	1.15	1.30	
Response time constraints		0.87	1.00	1.07	1.15	
Quality analysts	1.46	1.19	1.00	0.86	0.71	
Experience with application	1.29	1.13	1.00	0.91	0.82	
Quality programmers	1.42	1.17	1.00	0.86	0.70	
Hardware experience	1.21	1.10	1.00	0.90		
Programming language experience	1.14	1.07	1.00	0.95		
Use modern programming techniques	1.24	1.10	1.00	0.91	0.82	
Use software tools	1.24	1.10	1.00	0.91	0.83	
Project duration constraints	1.23	1.08	1.00	1.04	1.10	

related to the types of data the software uses and generates. Within FPA the software is characterized by the five functions:

- the external input type
- the external output type
- the external inquiry type
- the logical internal file type
- the external interface file type

For each of these five types the number of simple, average and complex occurrences that are expected in the software is estimated. By weighting each number with an appropriate weight a number is obtained, the unadjusted number of function points. This indication for nominal size is then adjusted, using 14 technical characteristics. Figure 3 gives an overview of function point analysis.

PRICE-S

The PRICE-S model (Programming Review of Information Costing and Evaluation — Software) is developed and supported by RCA PRICE Systems. An important disadvantage with regard to COCOMO and FPA is that the underlying concepts and ideas are not publicly defined and the users are presented with the model as a black box. The user of PRICE sends the input to a time-sharing computer in the USA, UK, or France and gets back his estimates immediately. Despite this disadvantage and the high rental price, there are many users, especially in America. There is, however, an important motivation for American companies to use the model. The US Department of Defense demands a PRICE estimate for all quotations for a software project. PRICE has separate sizer and productivity function.

The PUTNAM model

This SCE model was developed by Putnam in 1974[23]. He based his model on the work of Norden[34]. For many projects at IBM, Norden plotted frequency distributions, in which he showed how many people were allocated to the development and maintenance of a software product during the life-cycle. The curves he made fitted very well with the Rayleigh curves. His findings were merely empirical. He found no explanations for the shape of the effort curve. On the assumptions of Norden, Putnam formulated his model. There is not enough space in this paper to explain the principles of the model and the reader is referred to Putnam[23,24], Putnam and Fitzsimmons[25] and Londeix[26].

Before You Leap (BYL)

BYL is a commercial package based on a link-up between FPA and COCOMO[17]. BYL starts with a calculation of the amount of net function points. This amount is then translated into source lines of code, taking in account the language used. For Cobol, for instance, one function point is equal to 105 SLOC, for LISP 64, etc. This estimate of the size in SLOC is precisely the necessary input for COCOMO and the COCOMO part of BYL, taking into account the influence on effort of the 15 COCOMO cost drivers, calculates the estimates of costs and time-scale.

Estimacs

Estimacs has been developed by H. Rubin[27-29] and Computer Associates[30], and is available as a software package. The model consists of nine modules: a function point module; a risk module; an effort module (to estimate development and maintenance effort), etc. The most important and extensive module is Effort. The user has to answer 25 input questions. These questions are partly related to the complexity of the user-organization and partly to the complexity and size of the software to be developed. The way Estimacs translates the input to an estimation of effort is not clear. Like many other models, Estimacs is a 'closed model'.

Function count		←—— Max range: Factor * 2 ——→			
		Level of information processing function			
Type ID	Description	Simple	Average	Complex	Total
IT	External input	--*3 = --	--*4 = ---	--*6 = ---	-----
OT	External output	--*4 = --	--*5 = ---	--*7 = ---	-----
FT	Logical internal file	--*7 = --	--*10 = --	--*15 = --	-----
EI	External interface file	--*5 = --	--*7 = ---	--*10 = --	-----
QT	External inquiry	--*3 = --	--*4 = ---	--*6 = ---	-----
FC		Total unadjusted function points			

↑ Maximum range factor 2.5 ↓

General information processing characteristics

	Characteristics	DI		Characteristics	DI
C1	Data communications	---	C8	On-line update	---
C2	Distributed functions	---	C9	Complex processing	---
C3	Performance	---	C10	Re-usability	---
C4	Heavily used configuration	---	C11	Installation ease	---
C5	Transaction rate	---	C12	Operational ease	---
C6	On-line data entry	---	C13	Multiple sites	---
C7	End-user efficiency	---	C14	Facilitate change	---
PC				Total degree of influence	---

DI	Values				
Not present or no influence		= 0	Average influence		= 3
Insignificant influence		= 1	Significant influence		= 4
Moderate influence		= 2	Strong influence, throughout		= 5

FC	(Function count)	≡	Total unadjusted function points
PC	(Process complexity)	≡	Total degree of influence
PCA	(Process complexity adjustment)	=	$0.65 + 0.01 * PC$
FP	(Function point measure)	=	$FC * PCA$

Figure 3. Overview of function point analysis

SPQR-20

SPQR stands for Software Productivity, Quality and Reliability. The model has been developed by C. Jones[31]. SPQR claims to be applicable for all kinds of software projects as well as an estimate of duration, costs and effort to develop software; the model also gives an estimate of maintenance costs. SPQR uses FPA to size the volume of a program. The model is based on an extensive database of past projects. There are four versions of model, SPQR 10, 20, 50 and 100 (the numbers stand for the number of questions the model user has to answer and gives an indication of the degree of refinement of the versions). SPQR-20 is the only commercially available version at the moment, not marketed by C. Jones any more but overtaken by his Checkmark product.

BIS-Estimator

BIS-Estimator is completely different from the previously described models. According to the documentation[32] the model claims to be a 'knowledge-based tool'. This cannot be fully confirmed, because the principles of the model are secret for the most part. The model starts with a 'soft' estimate. This is a rough estimate of duration and effort based on (far too few) input questions. Next a 'hard' estimate is made for each phase. Based on the estimates by phase, by means of extrapolation, an estimate of the complete project is made. The 'hard' estimate has to be made at the start of and/or during each phase. The model has facilities to base the estimate upon a comparison with a number of projects, selected by the model user. A positive feature of the model is the evolutionary approach. This means that the estimation process changes during software development. As a result of the kind of questions, data and considerations, an estimate is based on the model changes for each phase.

Several models and computerized versions (tools) are available, but just a few of these have been described briefly above. Without going into detail, Table 5 gives a more extensive list of models and tools. The reader is referred to publications in the literature for a more comprehensive description of each. The models in the list are in chronological order (year of publication). The first 11 are ancient models and of no current interest to practitioners.

COMPARISON OF SCE MODELS

During the past few years several empirical studies have been carried out to validate the various SCE models. Validation is important but difficult to do, because of the demand to capture large amounts of data about completed software projects. As mentioned before, data collection is not common in the software community. It is labour and time-intensive and requires an attitude not only focused on the constructive part but also on the analytical part of software engineering. Furthermore data collection, usable for validating SCE, is limited to a relative small number of software development organizations. Only a few organizations realize large software projects each year. Nevertheless, a number of validation research investigations have been carried out. In this section some of them will be discussed.

The models discussed earlier differ considerably. Experiments show that estimates made by the different models for the same project vary strongly. Furthermore the estimates differ very much from the real development cost and duration. To give an opinion upon the quality of SCE models, it must be known what kind of demands have to be made upon these models. In Table 6 an overview of these demands/requirements is presented. These requirements are a part of an evaluation method for SCE models. This method has been developed by Heemstra, Kusters and van Genuchten[1] and used to

Table 5. SCE models and tools with references

Model	Source
SDC	Nelson, E A *Management handbook for the estimation of computer programming costs*, AD-A648750, Systems Development Corporation (1966)
TRW Wolverton	Wolverton, R W 'The cost of development large-scale software' *IEEE Trans. on computers*, Vol c-23, No 6 (June 1974)
TELECOTE	Frederic, B C *A professional model for estimating computer program development costs*. Telecote Research Inc. (1974)
BOEING	Black, R K D, Curnow, R P, Katz, R and Gray, M D 'BCS software production data' *Final technical report*, *RADC-TR-77-116*, Boeing Computer Services Inc. (March 1977)
IBM/FSD	Walston, C E and Felix, C P 'A method of programming measurement and estimating' *IBM System J*. Vol 16 (1977)
DOTY	Herd, J R, Postak, J N, Russell, W E and Stewart, K R 'Software cost estimation — study results. *Final technical report*, *RA-DC-TR-77-220*, Vol 1, DOTY Associates, Inc., Rockville, MD (1977)
ESDI	Duquette, J A and Bourbon, G A 'ESD, A computerized model for estimating software life cycle costs' *FSD-TR-235* Vol 1 (April 1978)
SLIM	Putnam, L H 'A general empirical solution to the macro software sizing and estimating problem' *IEEE Trans. Soft. Eng.* SE-4, 4 (1978)
Surbock	Surbock, E K *Management software development* Projekten Berlin (1978) (In German)
GRC	Carriere, W M and Thibodeau, R 'Development of a logistic software cost estimating technique for foreign military sales' *GRC Report CR-3-839* (1979)
Grumman	Sandler, G and Bachowitz, B 'Software cost models — Grumman experience' *IEEE, quantitative software model conference* (1979)
PRICE-S	Freiman, F R and Park, R E 'The Price software cost model: RCA government systems division' *IEEE* (1979)
FPA	Albrecht, A J 'Measuring application development productivity' *Proc. of Joint SHARE/GUIDE/IBM application development symp.* (October 1979)
SLICE	Kustanowitz, A L 'System life cycle estimation (SLICE): a new approach to estimating resources for application program development' *IEEE first international computer software and application conference, Chicago* (1980)
FAST	Freiman, F R 'The FAST methodology' *J. of parametrics*, Vol 1 No 2 (1981)
Baily/Basili	Bailey, J W and Basili V R 'A meta-model for software development resource expenditures' *Proc. 5th Int. Conf. Soft. Engin., IEEE* (1981)
COCOMO	Boehm, B W *Software engineering economics* Prentice-Hall (1981)
SOFTCOST	Tausworthe, R C 'Deep space network software cost estimation model' Publication 81-7, *Jet Propulsion Laboratory*, Pasadena, CA (1981)
BANG	DeMarco, T *Controlling software projects: management, measurement and estimation* Yourdon Press, New York (1982)
JS 3/System-4/Seer	Jensen, R W 'An improved macrolevel software development resource estimation model' *Proc. 5th ISPA Conf.* St Louis MO (1983)
COPMO	Thebaut, S M and Shen, V Y 'An analytic resource model for large-scale software development' *Inf. Proc. Management*, Vol 20 No 1–2 (1984)
GECOMO	Gecomo 'Software tools for professionals' *GEC Software Documentation*, G & C Company, London (1985)
ESTIMACS	Computer Associates. CA-Estimacs *User Guide*, Release 5.0 (July 1986)
BYL	Before You Leap. *User's Guide*, Gordon Group (1986)
SPQR/Checkmark	Jones, C *Programming productivity* McGraw-Hill (1986)
Jeffery	Jeffery, D R 'A software development productivity model for MIS environments' *J. of Systems and Software* 7 (1987)
ESTIMATE/1	Estimate/1. Documentative Method/1: Automated Project Estimating Aid. Arthur Anderson (1987)
BIS	BIS/Estimator. User Manual, version 4.4, BIS Applied System Ltd (1987)
SECOMO	Goethert, W B 'SECOMO' in Boehm, B W *Documentation of the seminar: software cost estimation using COCOMO and ADA COCOMO*, SAL, London. 1988' ITT Research Institute, Data & Analysis Center for Software.

Table 6. Requirements for SCE models

Model requirements	Application requirements	Implementation requirements
Linked to software control method	Possibilities for calibration	User-friendliness of the tool
Applicability at the start of a project	Accuracy of the estimations	Possibilities for sensitivity analyses
Fit with the data that is available during development		Possibilities for risk analysis
Possible to adjust estimate due to changing objectives		Open model, is it possible to see how the results were obtained
Definition of domain model is suitable for		Clarity of input definition
		Completeness and detail of output

evaluate the eight models described above. The results of that evaluation are presented in Table 7 and described in more detail in Heemstra[7]. From the table it can be seen that there are only few plusses. The conclusion is that the quality of the models is poor and much improvement is necessary. The accuracy of the estimations were evaluated by several tests. The way the tests were executed and the results obtained will be described. The objectives of the tests were:

- to determine the accuracy of the estimate using SCE models in a semi-realistic situation
- to determine whether these models will be accepted by project management

After a severe selection procedure only two SCE models remained. These were the BYL and Estimacs models. During the tests 14 experienced project leaders were asked to make a number of estimates for a project that had actually been carried out. The project was described as if it was at the start of the project. The project leaders had to make three estimates. The first estimate of effort and duration (the 'manual' estimate) was made on the basis of the project leaders' knowledge and experience. Next, two estimates were made using the models selected. In conclusion, a final estimate was made on the basis of the project leaders' knowledge and experience together with the model estimates. Each estimate was evaluated directly using a questionnaire, and the tests ended with a discussion session. The results are presented in Table 8.

The real effort and duration were eight man-months and six months. The main conclusions of the experiment were that on the basis of the differences found between the estimates and reality, it has not been shown that the selected models can be used for a reliable estimation tool at an early stage of software development. All in all, the project leaders were not wildly enthusiastic about these tools, but they were, nevertheless, felt to be acceptable as a check-list and as a means of communication. It should be mentioned that the selected project is small. Most models are calibrated on data from medium/large projects.

Kemerer[33] shows that estimates of different models can differ considerably. For each model he investigated the difference between actual and estimated number of man-months. He used COCOMO, Estimacs, FPA and Putnam's model to estimate the required effort of 15 already realized projects. From Table 9 it can be seen that for both COCOMO and Putnam's model there were sharp overestimations. FPA and Estimacs gave distinctly better results with overshoots of 100% and 85%, respectively. A similar study was carried out by Rubin[29]. A project description was sent to Jensen (Jensen's model), Greene (Putnam's model SLIM) and Rook (GECOMO) and to himself (Rubin's model Estimacs).

Table 7. Evaluation of models

Requirements	Models							
	COCOMO	PRICE	PUTNAM	FPA	BYL	ESTIMACS	SPQR	BIS
Model requirements								
Linked to software control method	− −	− −	− −	− −	− −	+ +	− −	− −
Applicable at an early stage	− −	− −	− −	+	+	+ +	+	−
Using available data	+	− −	− −	− −	− −	− −	− −	+ +
Adjustment to objectives	+	+	+	− −	− −	+	+ +	− −
Definition of scope/domain	+	−	−	+ +	−	−	−	+ +
Application requirements								
Calibration	−	− −	− −	−	+	+	−	−
Accuracy	nt	nt	nt	nt	t	t	nt	nt
Implementation requirements								
User friendliness	+ +	−	+	+	+ +	+	+	+
Sensitivity analysis	− −	+	− −	− −	+ +	+ +	−	−
Risk analysis	− −	− −	− −	− −	+ +	+ +	+	− −
Open model/traceability	+ +	− −	+ +	+ +	+ +	−	−	+
Definition input	+ +	−	+ +	−	+	+	+	+
Completeness and detail output	+	+ +	−	−	+ +	+ +	+ +	+ +

+ + = satisfies the requirement; + = sufficient; − = insufficient; − − = the model does not satisfy the requirement; nt = the model was not tested on accuracy; t = the models were tested

Table 8. Some results of the tests. Duration is given in months, effort in man-months

Variable	μ	σ
Effort		
Manual estimate	28.4	18.3
BYL estimate	27.7	14.0
Estimacs estimate	48.5	13.9
Final estimate	27.7	12.8
Duration		
Manual estimate	11.2	3.7
BYL estimate	8.5	2.4
Final estimate	12.1	3.4

Table 9. Estimates of the actual and estimated number of man-months using four different models

Models	Averages for all projects		
	Actual number of MM	Estimated number of MM	(Estimated divided by actual) * 100%
GECOMO	219.25	1291.75	607.85
Putnam	219.25	2060.17	771.87
FPA	260.30	533.23	167.29
Estimacs	287.97	354.77	85.48

The main purpose was to compare and contrast the different sort of information required by the four models. Also a comparison was made between the estimates obtained using the models, that is to say the number of man-months and the duration for the development of the selected project. From Table 10 it can be seen that the estimates vary significantly. Also Rubin's explanation is that the models are based on different databases of completed projects and have not been calibrated and the four participants made different assumptions in choosing the settings of the cost drivers.

THE IMPORTANCE OF SCE MODELS

The field study, mentioned earlier in the paper, shows that SCE models are currently not generally accepted in organizations surveyed. Only 51 of the 364 organizations that estimate software development use models. An analysis showed that these 51 model-users make no better estimates than the non-model-users. These results are disappointing at first glance. It does not mean, however, that it makes no sense to spend further research effort on models. All the investigations mentioned before agree that the poor quality is primarily due to using the models wrongly. For example: use of models requires organizational bounded data of past projects. Most of the time models are used without calibration. If models cannot be adapted the result will be less accurate estimates. The majority of the models do not support calibration.

It is worth while to promote the development of better estimation tools, despite the shortcomings of the existing models. In this section some arguments are put forward that underline the necessity to invest more effort and time in the development of SCE models.

In making an estimate, especially at an early stage of development, a lot of uncertainty and fuzziness exists. It is not known which cost drivers play a part in the estimation and what the influence of the cost drivers will be. There are many participants involved in the project (project manager, customer, developer, user, etc.). Often they all have their own hidden agendas and goals conflicting with each other (minimalization of the costs, maximalization of the quality, minimalization of the duration, optimal use of

employees, etc.). For project management it is difficult to predict the progress of a project in such fuzzy situations. To make point estimations like 'duration will be 321 man-months of which 110 for analysis, 70 for design, etc.', will be of less importance. Such exact figures do not fit in with the nature of the problem. Project management will be more interested in a number of scenarios from which alternatives can be chosen and in the sensitiveness of an estimation to specific cost drivers. For example: what will be the result on the duration of the addition of two more analysts to the project: what will be the influence on effort if the available development time will be decreased sharply; what will be the result on effort and duration if the complexity of the software to be developed has been estimated too high or too low, etc. An approach of the estimation problem like this gives project management more insight and feeling for alternative solutions. Furthermore this approach offers a proper basis for project control. If an estimate proves to be sensible for changes of a specific cost driver, this provides a warning for project management to pay full attention to this cost driver during development.

Often project management will be confronted with little tolerance in defined duration, price and quality. In such cases project management wants support in choosing the values of the decision variables. What are the available possible choices to meet the given objectives. Which personnel in combination with which tools and by means of which kind of project organization are suitable as possible solutions. The conclusion is that there is no need for a rigid 'calculation tool'. This does not fit with the characteristics of the estimation problem, namely uncertainty, fuzziness, little structuring, and unclear and incomplete specifications.

An important prerequisite for successful estimation is the development, acceptance and use of a uniform set of

Table 10. Comparison of SCE models by Rubin[29]

		Effort	Duration
Mode	Jensen	940 MM	31 m
	Putnam	200 MM	17 m
	GECOMO	363 MM	23 m
	Estimacs	17 100 hrs	16 m

MM = man-months; m = months

definitions and standards. This results in agreements such as:

- How many times an estimate is made for a project. For example: five times for each project that costs more than 12 man-months.
- In what phases during execution an estimate is made. For example: during the feasibility study, during the specification phase and after finishing the design.
- Which employees are involved in the estimation process. For example: project management, customers, developers.
- What will be estimated. For example: all development activities with regard to the phases feasibility, specification, design, etc. or all activities including training, documentation, etc.
- The output of an estimate. For example: costs in dollars, effort in man-months, duration in months.
- The factors which can be regarded as the most important cost drivers and have to be recorded. For example: size, reliability, type of application, quality of personnel, etc.
- A set of definitions. For example: volume will be expressed in function points, documentation contains of . . . , high complexity means . . . , etc.

The result will be a comprehensive list of standardized agreements. It is important that these are really applied in the subsequent project. An SCE model that meets requirements such as a set of clear definitions, measurable and relevant cost drivers, flexibility with regards to other control methods, etc. will result in a more structural approach to software cost estimation and control.

CONCLUSIONS AND RECOMMENDATIONS

In this final section some concrete guidelines for controlling and estimating software development will be offered. Most of these guidelines have been discussed at different levels of detail in the previous sections.

Determine the level of uncertainty

High uncertainty needs another approach of cost estimation and control than does low uncertainty. High uncertainty corresponds with risk analysis, estimating and margins, exploration oriented problem-solving, expert-oriented estimating techniques, etc. Low uncertainty corresponds with cost estimation models (calculation tools), experiences from past projects, realization oriented problem-solving, the estimate is regarded as a norm, etc.

Cost estimation and data collection

Collection of data of completed projects is necessary for successful cost estimation. Cost models, estimation by analogy and experts require such data. It is no solution

to use data collected from other organizations. The relevant data are different for each organization.

Use more than one estimation technique

A lot of research shows that the quality of the current estimation techniques is poor. The lack of accurate and reliable estimation techniques combined with the financial, technical, organizational and social risks of software projects, require a frequent estimation during the development of an application and the use of more than one estimation technique. More and different techniques are required, especially at the milestones of the development phases. The level of knowledge of the software whose cost we are trying to estimate is growing during a project. A possibility is to use another model during a project, because more information and more *accurate* information is available; a cascade of techniques — for example Wide Band Delphi, Estimacs, DeMarco, COCOMO — is a possible solution.

Cost estimation needs commitment

Software development has to be done by highly qualified professionals. For such people some characteristics are relevant, such as:

- individuality in work performance is important
- a good professional result of their work is important
- professionals want to be consulted in decisions, work planning, the desired result, etc.
- professionals do not want to be disturbed by management during the execution of their work

It is not wise to confront professional developers with a plan and estimate without any consultation. A hierarchical leadership is not suitable. In consulting the developers not only their expertise is used but also their involvement in the estimation process is increased. This results in a higher commitment than is necessary for the success of a project.

Cost estimation: a management problem

Software cost estimation is often wrongly regarded as a technical problem that can be solved with calculation models, a set of metrics and procedures. However, the opposite is true. The 'human aspects' are much more important. The quality, experience and composition of the project team, the degree in which the project leader can motivate, kindle enthusiasm and commit his developers, has more influence on delivering the software in time and within budget than the use of rigid calculations.

REFERENCES

1 **Heemstra, F J, Kusters, R and van Genuchten, M** 'Selections of software cost estimation models' *Report TUE/BDK* University of Technology Eindhoven (1989)

2 **Lierop van, F L G, Volkers, R S A, Genuchten, M van and Heemstra, F J** 'Has someone seen the software?' *Informatie* Vol 33 No 3 (1991) (In Dutch)

3 **Genuchten, van M I J M** 'Towards a software factory' *PhD Thesis*, University of Technology Eindhoven (1991)

4 **Beers** 'Problems, planning and knowledge, a study of the processes behind success and failure of an automation project' *PhD Series in general management, No 1* Faculty Industrial Engineering/Rotterdam School of Management, Erasmus University Rotterdam (1991) (In Dutch)

5 **Brooks, F B** *The mythical manmonth. Essays on software engineering* Addison-Wesley (1975)

6 **Noth, T and Kretzschmar, M** *Estimation of software development projects* Springer-Verlag (1984) (In German)

7 **Heemstra, F J** *How expensive is software? Estimation and control of software-development* Kluwer (1989) (In Dutch)

8 **Druffel, L E** 'Strategies for a DoD Software initiative' *CSS DUSD(RAT)* Washington, DC (1982)

9 **Conte, S D, Dunsmore, H F and Shen, V Y** *Software engineering metrics and models* Benjamin Cummins (1986)

10 **Reifer, D J** 'The economics of software reuse' *Proc. 14th Annual ISPA Conf.*, New Orleans (May 1991)

11 **Boehm, B W** *Software engineering economics* Prentice-Hall (1981)

12 **Albrecht, A J and Gaffney, J E** 'Software function, source lines of code, and development effort prediction: a software science validation' *IEEE Trans. Soft. Eng.* Vol SE-9 No 6 (1983)

13 **Halstead, M H** *Elements of software science* North-Holland (1977)

14 **DeMarco, T** *Controlling software projects: management, measurement and estimation* Yourdon Press, New York (1982)

15 **DeMarco, T** 'An algorithm for sizing software products' *Performance Evaluation Review* 12 pp 13–22 (1984)

16 **Albrecht, A J** 'Measuring application development productivity' *Proc. Joint SHARE/GUIDE/IBM application development symp.* (October 1979)

17 **Gordon** 'Before You Leap' *User's Guide* Gordon Group (1986)

18 **Boehm, B W** 'Software engineering economics' *IEEE Trans. Soft. Eng.* Vol 10 No 1 (January 1984)

19 **Rudolph, E E** 'Productivity in computer application development, Department of Management Studies' *Working paper No 9* University of Auckland (March 1983)

20 **Rudolph, E E** 'Function point analyses, cookbook' own edition from Rudolph (March 1983)

21 **Symons, C R** 'Function point analysis: difficulties and improvements' *IEEE Trans. Soft. Eng.* Vol 14 No 1 (January 1988)

22 **Symons, C R** *Software sizing and estimating—MARK II FPA* Wiley (1991)

23 **Putnam, L H** 'A general empirical solution to the macro software sizing and estimating problem' *IEEE Trans. Soft. Eng.* SE-4, 4 (1978)

24 **Putnam, L** 'Software costing estimating and life cycle control' *IEEE Computer Society Press* (1980)

25 **Putnam, L H and Fitzsimmons, A** 'Estimating software costs' *Datamation* (Sept. Oct. Nov. 1979)

26 **Londeix, B** *Cost estimation for software development* Addison-Wesley (1987)

27 **Rubin, H A** 'Interactive macro-estimation of software life cycle parameters via personal computer: a technique for improving customer/developer communication' *Proc. Symp. on application & assessment of automated tools for software development, IEEE*, San Francisco (1983)

28 **Rubin, H A** 'Macro and micro-estimation of maintenance effort: the estimacs maintenance models' *IEEE* (1984)

29 **Rubin, H A** 'A comparison of cost estimation tools' *Proc. 8th Int. Conf. Soft. Eng. IEEE* (1985)

30 **Computer Associates** CA-Estimacs *User Guide* Release 5.0 (July 1986)

31 **Jones, C** *Programming productivity* McGraw-Hill (1986)

32 **BIS/Estimator** *User manual version 4.4.* BIS Applied System Ltd. (1987)

33 **Kemerer, C F** 'An empirical validation of software cost estimation models' *Communications of the ACM* Vol 30 No 5 (May 1987)

34 **Norden, P V** *Useful tools for project management* (Operations research in research and development) Wiley (1963)

Risk Management for Software Development

Richard Fairley
Colorado Technical University
Colorado Springs, Colorado, USA

Paul Rook
The Centre for Software Reliability
City University, Northampton Square, London, UK

Keywords: Risk, Risk Management, Software Risk, Risk Exposure, Risk Factors

A risk is a potential problem; a problem is a risk that has materialized. By a problem, we mean an undesirable situation that will require time and resources to correct. In some cases the problem, should it occur, may be uncorrectable. A risk, being a potential problem, is characterized by:

- The probability that an undesired event might occur (0<P<1)
- A loss associated with occurrence of the undesired event

The loss associated with an undesired event is referred to as the *risk impact*. Sometimes, it is possible to quantify the loss in measurable terms, such as dollars or human lives. In other cases the loss is intangible; for example, loss of credibility or good will. In cases where loss can be quantified, the product of (probability * risk impact) is referred to as the *risk exposure*.

Probability and impact typically vary with time and circumstances. A small risk may become a large one, and conversely, a large risk may, with passing time, become a non-risk. For example, the probability of failing to achieve a desired result falls to zero upon attainment of the desired result. Furthermore, some risk factors may be interdependent so that reducing the probability and/or cost of one may increase the probability and/or cost of another. With hindsight, it will be determined that some potential problems occurred and others did not.

When we are dealing with risk in this general sense, it is not always easy to distinguish between single events, multiple events, continuous events, and interdependent events, or between cause and effect. In considering an undertaking, many risks may be identified. Systematic risk management requires that initial apprehensions be turned into specific root causes, and that the probabilities and potential losses be established. The specific outcome we wish to avoid must be explicitly stated in order to identify possible courses of action for risk reduction.

The first step in risk management for software development is to organize the development effort as a well-defined project having a schedule, a budget, a set of objectives to be achieved, and a set of skills needed to accomplish the work. Project objectives must be translated into a set of targets that cover, at least, cost (or effort), schedule, and product functionality, performance, and quality attributes.

In setting targets for a project, a subproject, or a development phase the following must be considered:

- *Constraints.* A constraint is an external condition imposed by forces over which project management has no control. There may be constraints on time, money, personnel, and other aspects of the work. There may also be design constraints imposed on the product. When a constraint is broken it may result in financial loss or cancellation of the project.

- *Estimates.* An estimate is a prediction of expected outcomes under certain circumstances. An estimate should be made for each of the project targets. Estimates should include ranges of values with associated probabilities, confidence levels, and most importantly, analyses of the assumptions underlying the estimates. Estimates must incorporate the process and product constraints placed on the project.

- *Types of targets.* Targets are set by the customer and by project management and specified in the project plan. Targets should include negotiated considerations of project constraints, and the estimate ranges and probabilities. These negotiations may involve the customer, management, and development staff.

- *Conditional minimax targets.* There may be a project attribute (cost, schedule, functionality, performance) that management and the customer desire to optimize. However, it may be that optimizing this target should only be achieved provided all other targets are achieved. Consequently, the optimization criteria must incorporate the full set of targets; otherwise, the desired attribute will be minimized or maximized at the expense of other attributes.

Risks are thus viewed as potential problems that, should they occur, will impact project targets. If there are no quantified targets, then there is no danger that the targets will not be achieved; risk management is meaningless unless targets are defined in measurable terms.

Identifying the risk factors for the various project targets allows risks to be traced through subsequent risk management plans, risk monitoring and reporting procedures, and corrective action.

Risk Management and Project Management

The goal of traditional project management is to control pervasive risks that might hinder the development of a satisfactory product on time and within budget. Traditional project management uses systematic procedures to estimate and plan the work, lead and direct the staff, monitor progress, and control the project by replanning and reassigning resources as necessary. This remains the fundamental basis for project management and is not invalidated by any consideration of risk management. However, on its own, traditional project management is a recipe for "problem management" in that difficult decisions are addressed and actions taken only when problems arise. In this sense, project management is reactive, whereas risk management is proactive.

Risk Management consists of Risk Assessment followed by Risk Control (see Figure 1). Risk assessment provides informed decisions based on systematic assessment of things that might go wrong, the associated probabilities, and the severities of the impacts. Risk control is concerned with developing strategies and plans to abate the major risk factors, to resolve

those risks that do become problems, and to continuously reassess risk. Real risk management occurs when significant decision making, planning, resources, money, and effort are expended to reduce the probabilities and/or impacts of identified risk factors. The extent to which time and effort are invested in these processes can be used as a test to determine whether risk management is being accomplished over and above traditional project management.

Risk management is not synonymous with project management, nor is it a replacement for project management, or something entirely separate. Rather, it is an explicit augmentation and extension of traditional project management, closely intertwined with the information gathering and decision making functions of project management. When a project is successful, it is not because there were no problems, but because the problems were overcome. Risk management does not guarantee success, but has the primary goal of identifying and responding to potential problems with sufficient lead time to avoid crisis situations, so that it becomes possible to conduct a project that meets its targets.

Types of Risks

Risks can be categorized as Contractual/Environmental, Management/Process, Resources/Personnel, and Technical/Operational. The introduction of systematic risk management requires managers to abandon the idea that all risks on a technically difficult project are technical in nature. While some risks should indeed be identified as technical risks, there are also risks in the use of resources (especially personnel), risks in the way of working the project (management/process) and, just as importantly, risks to the project which are beyond the control of project management (contractual/environmental).

Figure 2 lists these four types of risk with some examples of each. All identified risks must be correctly typed. If risks that come from other sources are misidentified as technical risks, there is a danger they will be passed down from the management level to become the responsibility of the technical staff, who may not be able to control them. The result may be that these risk factors are not explicitly managed until they have become significant problems. Ensuring that all risks are fully addressed by management, the customer, and the developers requires explicit identification of the processes, team structures, responsibilities and authorities, and environmental/contractual factors. This is properly the domain of good traditional project management in any case, and a necessary prerequisite for successful risk control.

388

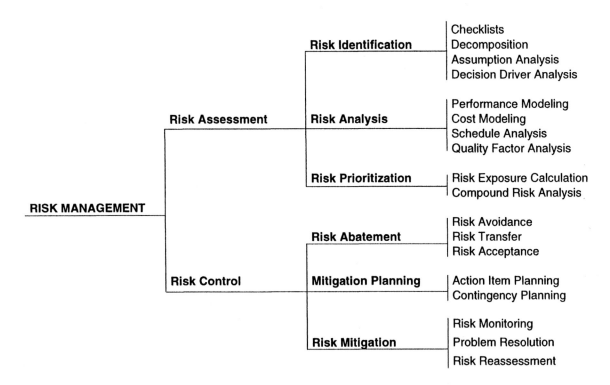

Figure 1. A Taxonomy for Risk Management (adapted from [Boehm89])

Contractual/Environmental	Management/Process	Personnel	Technical
"...to suffer the slings and arrows of outrageous fortune, or to take arms against a sea of troubles..."	"It is best to do things systematically since we are only human and disorder is our worst enemy"	"though all men be made of one metal, yet they be not cast all in one mold"	"The best laid plans..." Requirements changes
Unreasonable customers Nonperforming vendors and sub-contractors	Unclear responsibilities and authorities Ill-defined procedures	Wrong people available –lack of skills –lack of training –lack of expertise	–customer changes mind –hidden implications emerge Failure to meet requirements
Dependencies on and demands from other projects Inappropriate corporate policies	Inadequate control of development process Inadequate support facilities and services	Lack of staff continuity Incorrect staffing –too many people for the current task	–cannot produce a feasible design –acceptance tests fail Problems or errors detected
Change in management priorities	Lack of "visibility"	–too few people for the current tasks	–inconsistent design –missing components –inadequate time for testing

Figure 2. Sources of Risk

For purposes of risk control, risk factors fall into two categories:

- *Generic risks* are those risk factors common to all software projects. For example, costly late fixes (dealt with by early requirements and design verification), error-prone products (dealt with by verification, validation, and in-cremental testing throughout the life cycle), uncontrolled development processes (dealt with by planning and control based on well-defined processes), uncontrolled product (dealt with by configuration management and quality assurance), and poor communications (dealt with by documentation, reviews, and technical interchange meetings)

Over time, methods of reducing generic risks have become institutionalized in the tools and techniques used; for example, in project planning, configuration management, and verification and validation. In this sense, traditional software engineering and project management can be viewed as systematic approaches to controlling generic risk factors. Reduction of generic risk is evidenced in the choice of the overall development process (prototyping, incremental development, evolutionary development, design to cost, and so on) and the choice of methods, tools, and techniques used within that process.

Significant expenditures may be incurred in setting up a development process, acquiring tools, and training the managers and technical staff to cope with the generic risks inherent in a particular line of business. The outcomes of these risk reduction activities are the process(es), project plan(s), and work activities for each project. Generic risks for each phase of a software development project are controlled by explicitly designing the work processes of those phases.

- *Project-specific risks* are potential problems inherent to a particular project (for instance, insufficient personnel, key personnel not available when needed, unrealistic schedule and/or budget, inadequate requirements, shortfalls in externally supplied components or services, reliance on advances in the state of the art, and so on). Project-specific risks are dealt with in a Risk Management Plan which identifies the actions to be carried out should certain events occur. Risk management plans are especially useful when the customer, management, and developers agree that the project represents a risky undertaking.

A Risk Management Plan may contain both Action Plans and Contingency Plans. An action plan represents a decision to engage in a risk reduction activity that is to be conducted without further consideration; for example, acquiring training in a particular method or technique, acquiring work stations and software tools, or purchasing desks and work spaces. Like all plans, an action plan must specify a well-defined set of tasks, a schedule, a budget, and the responsibility and authority assigned to each involved person. A contingency plan is a risk reduction activity to be engaged in

at some future time, should circumstances warrant; for example, rescoping the work or adding people should the schedule slip more than two weeks, or buying more memory or reducing functionality should the memory budget exceed its allocation by more than ten percent.

A contingency plan should contain the items illustrated by example in Figure 3. As illustrated in Figure 3, a contingency plan should describe the risk factor(s) dealt with by the plan, possible alternative courses of action to mitigate the risk factor(s) should it (they) become problem(s), the constraints on contingent actions, the risks created by the various possible alternatives, the risk indicator metric(s), the threshold value(s) of the indicator metric(s) that indicate the potential problem has become a real problem, the reset level for the indicator metric(s) that will signal resolution of the problem, the resources to be applied during the contingent action, the maximum duration of the contingency plan (after which the project goes into crisis mode), and the responsible party who will track the indicator metric(s) and implement the contingency plan. A project enters crisis mode when the maximum duration of a contingency plan is exceeded. A crisis is a "show-stopper;" all available resources are focused on solving the problem until the crisis is resolved or the project is rescoped or terminated.

Choosing the development process to be used is an essential risk reduction technique and is just as important as the risk reduction techniques identified in the risk management plan.

Various process models are summarized by Boehm [BOEHM89] as follows:

- *Buy COTS*: Buying a Commercial-Off-The-Shelf (COTS) product is a simple approach often overlooked in the enthusiasm to design and build something new, or because of the problems involved in administrative procedures required to buy rather than build. (Major risks for the COTS approach include failure to satisfy user needs, lack of compatibility with other system components, and the difficulties of integrating multiple COTS packages [Fairley94].)

- *Waterfall*: The sequential, single-pass requirements-design-code-test-maintain model.

- *Risk Reduction/Waterfall*: The waterfall model, preceded by one or more phases focused on reducing the risks of poorly understood requirements or architecture, technology uncertainties, potential performance shortfall, robustness issues, and so on.

1. Risk Factors:　Software Size (256K limit)
　　　　　　　　　Processing Time (100 microsecond loop)
2. Alternatives:　Prototyping
　　　　　　　　　Memory Overlays
　　　　　　　　　Buy Memory
　　　　　　　　　Faster Processor
　　　　　　　　　Incremental Development plus Technical
　　　　　　　　　　　Performance Measurement (ID + TPM)
3. Constraints:　Schedule and Budget
4. Risk Created:　Prototype: how to scale results?
　　　　　　　　　Overlays: execution time penalty
　　　　　　　　　Memory: hardware architectural constraints
　　　　　　　　　Processor: customer constraint
　　　　　　　　　ID + TPM:　　reduced functionality
　　　　　　　　　　　　　　　　unmaintainable product
5. Selected Approach:　　Incremental Development plus TPM
　　　　　　　　　　　　　　　　–partition design into a series of incremental builds
　　　　　　　　　　　　　　　　–allocate 90% of memory and exection time to product functions
　　　　　　　　　　　　　　　　–pursue incremental development based on partitioning
　　　　　　　　　　　　　　　　–use TPM tracking on the memory and timing budgets
6. Risk Indicator Metrics:　Cost Performance Indices (CPI) for memory and timing budgets
7. Thresholds for Contingent Action: either CPI > 1.10
8. Reset Levels: CPI < 1.05
9. Resources to be Applied:　　unlimited overtime for Sue Jones and Bill Williams
10. Maximum Duration: 2 weeks
11. Responsible Party: Sue Jones

Figure 3. A Contingency Plan

- *Capabilities-to-Requirements*: This model reverses the usual requirements-to-capabilities sequence inherent in the waterfall model. It begins with an assessment of the envelope of capabilities available from COTS or other reusable components, and then involves adjusting the requirements wherever possible to capitalize on the existing capabilities.

- *Transform*: This model relies on the availability of a generator that can automatically transform the specifications into code. If such a capability spans the system's growth envelope, the transform model may be most appropriate.

- *Evolutionary Development*: This approach involves developing an initial approximation to a desired software product, and evolving it into a final product based on feedback from users. This is a highly effective, low-risk approach if the system's growth envelope is covered by a 4GL, or if the system requirements are poorly understood but, the architecture of similar systems is well-understood, lowering the risk that the system will evolve into a configuration poorly supported by the architecture.

- *Evolutionary Prototyping*: This model is similar to evolutionary development, except that a prototype-quality system (low robustness) is acceptable.

- *Incremental Development*: This approach involves organizing a project into a series of builds that incrementally add increasing capabilities to the growing system. In contrast to the prototyping models, an incremental model requires that the requirements and architecture be (mostly) understood up-front and that the design be partitioned into a series of incremental builds. This is the preferred approach in many situations because, in contrast to the waterfall model, incremental integration and frequent demonstrations of progress are possible. Incremental development also lowers the risks of insufficient development personnel and failure to meet a fixed delivery date (with, perhaps, less than full capability).

- *Design-to-Cost and/or Design-to-Schedule*: This approach involves prioritizing the desired system capabilities, pruning the requirements to fit the time and money available, and organizing the architecture to facilitate dropping lower-priority capabilities if it is determined that those capabilities cannot be realized within the available budget and/or schedule.

These last two process models (incremental development and design-to-cost/schedule) can often be combined with other process model alternatives.

Boehm lists the following factors as critical decision drivers for choosing a process model:

- *Growth envelope*: This refers to the foreseeable limits of growth to a system's size and diversity over the course of its life cycle. A high-growth envelope implies high risk of using limited-domain implementation strategy such as commercial-off-the-shelf products or 4GLs.

- *Available technologies*: Alternatively, technologies such as commercial off-the-shelf products, application generators, or 4GL capabilities that do cover a system's growth envelope may determine the most attractive process model. (A related process model is the "capabilities-to-requirements" model, in which the availability of powerful, easy-to-adapt capabilities or reusable components strongly influences the system requirements.)

- *Knowledge of requirements*: Ill-defined requirements imply process models that incorporate the user-feedback loops of prototyping and evolutionary development, as opposed to the waterfall model which has a high risk of developing software that does not satisfy user requirements.

- *Architecture understanding*: The lower the level of understanding of system architecture, the higher the risk of a pure top-down waterfall approach. On the other hand, a high level of architecture understanding lowers one of the risks of evolutionary development: that the system will evolve in directions that the architecture cannot support.

- *Robustness*: Systems that must be highly robust and error-free encounter high risks from informal process models such as evolutionary prototyping. More rigorous process models such as the incremental model reduce these risks, although the incremental model may need to be preceded by less formal prototyping phases to address requirements understanding or architecture-understanding risks.

- *Budget and schedule limitations*: May require a design-to-cost or design-to-schedule approach.

- *High-risk system nucleus*: May dictate an evolutionary or incremental development approach.

Risk Management Procedures

The origins of risk management date from the 1800s when the concept of risk exposure (probability * cost) was used in the insurance industry to analyze data collected about fires and deaths. By the 1950s, decision theory and probabilistic modeling were being taught as academic subjects. Use of risk management in the petrochemical and construction industries dates from about 1980; recognition of risk management as an element of software engineering dates from about 1990. In the 1990s risk management is being applied to many diverse disciplines. In each discipline, the basic concepts of identifying, analyzing, planning, and controlling risks are used, although the terminology and procedures vary among disciplines. Figure 1 shows a suitable structure for risk management in a software development environment (adapted from [Boehm89]). As illustrated there, risk assessment is distinguished from risk control.

Risk Assessment (Risk Identification, Risk Analysis, and Risk Prioritization)

Risk Assessment deals with determining the threats to a project, with particular emphasis placed on identifying, analyzing, and prioritizing major risk factors that might become problems.

The three explicit steps of Risk Assessment involve (i) identifying risk factors so that they are brought to the attention and understanding of senior engineers, managers, and customers; (ii) analyzing the risk factors so that numerical values can be assigned to the risk impacts, probabilities, and cost and benefits of alternative courses of action; and (iii) determining which risk factors have the highest priority for the expenditure of time and effort (money) to reduce their probabilities and/or impacts.

Risk Identification

The techniques of risk identification rely on expertise and experience to identify specific risk factors for a project. Risk identification techniques include:

- risk-factor checklists
- cause-effect diagrams
- development process audits and capability assessments
- decomposition of plans to determine task dependencies
- decomposition of the design to find technical risk factors
- investigation of interface details
- examination of assumptions and decision drivers
- worst case scenarios
- group consensus techniques
- prototyping
- benchmarking
- simulation and modeling

Risk identification is improved by relying on past experience, often in the form of checklists (sometimes structured and quantified with weightings from historical data). The most useful checklists are those derived from local experience.

Customers and users, in addition to managers, lead engineers, and the development staff, need to be involved in the risk identification process. When a number of different organizations are involved in a development project, it is necessary to integrate the different perceptions—technical and organizational—of the different parties.

Risk Analysis

The primary issue in risk analysis is developing solid, numerical values for the probabilities and impacts of various risk factors. These numbers can be developed by examining historical data, by using cost estimation tools, and by converting expert judgment into numbers (for instance, Low -> $0 < P < 0.3$; Medium -> $0.3 < P < 0.7$; High -> $0.7 < P < 1.0$).

Risk analysis techniques to be used depend on the types of risks being considered:

- *Risk of technical failure.* Techniques for analyzing technical risks include performance modeling, decision analysis, and cost-benefit analysis. Influence diagrams (fishbone or Ishikawa diagrams) can be used to identify areas of insufficient technical information. Various types of modeling, including simulation, benchmarking, and prototyping, can be used to analyze technical risk factors.

- *Risk of cost failure.* Techniques for analyzing cost risks include algorithmic cost models [Fairley93] and analysis of project assumptions. Monte Carlo simulation can be used to provide statistical ranges of cost based on probability distributions for the cost drivers [Fairley94].

- *Risk of schedule failure.* Techniques for analyzing schedule risks include algorithmic scheduling models, critical path methods, and PERT analysis. Probabilistic techniques, such as PERT and Monte Carlo simulation can provide ranges of probabilities for achieving various project milestones (including project completion) based on probabilistic values for the duration of the individual project tasks and the sequencing dependencies among those tasks.

- *Risk of operational failure.* Techniques for analyzing the risk of operational failure include performance modeling, reliability modeling, and quality factor analysis. By operational failure, we mean the risk that a project may produce a system that does not satisfy operational needs (that is, it does not possess the functional, performance, or other quality attributes the customer and users want and need). By operational risk, we do not mean the risk of hazard from a system in operation. Hazard is an intrinsic property or condition of a system that has the potential to cause an accident (hazard analysis constitutes a separate body of knowledge).

A risk factor may correspond to a single event, to a number of discrete events (any one of which may occur), or to a continuous distribution of possible events. Assessing the probabilities of discrete events and deriving probability distributions for continuous events is the most difficult part of risk analysis. Techniques available for determining these probabilities include expert judgment (especially expert group consensus techniques such as the Wideband Delphi technique), historical data, analogy, worst-case analysis, and what-if analysis. In many cases, these techniques provide a constructive framework for quantifying guesses (which is not all bad, provided the guesses are educated guesses). The best techniques are based on analysis of recorded data from past projects in the local environment.

Risk Prioritization

The purpose of risk prioritization is to choose,

from the list of identified risk factors, a prioritized subset of manageable proportions. The obvious choices for the most important risk factors are, theoretically, those with the largest risk exposures. In practice, however, the decision is more complex.

The following are some factors to consider in selecting the risk items to be included the prioritized list:

- Size of the risk exposure of the risk factor relative to the size of the target

- Size of the risk exposure of the risk factor relative to the largest risk exposure of any risk factor.

- Confidence level of the risk assessor in the reliability of the risk assessment carried out for the risk factor.

- Risk exposure range (ER), where:

  $$RER = (RE_{maximum} - RE_{minimum})/RE_{nominal}$$
  and $Re_{maximum}$, $Re_{minimum}$, and $RE_{nominal}$ are the largest, smallest, and nominal values of risk exposures among the identified risk factors. Projects having a wide risk exposure range require careful prioritization of the list. It is not necessary to perform a detailed risk analysis for a project having a small estimate range, provided the risk assessors have adequate confidence in their estimates.

- Compound risks—a risk factor that is conditioned on another risk factor that is of high priority should also be ranked high on the list.
- Maximum number of risk factors that can be interpreted and acted upon.

In selecting the risk factors to place on the prioritized list, we must not forget the objective, which is to choose those risk factors that are primary candidates for 1) immediate risk-abating actions (rather than waiting until they later become problems) or 2) are of such concern that contingency plans should be developed to trigger explicit actions should they become problems (that is, when a risk indicator metric crosses a predetermined threshold, such as a schedule delay of more than two weeks or a performance shortfall of more than 100 milliseconds).

The prioritized list is a dynamic subset of the total list of risk factors. Risk assessment should be a continuous, on-going activity, and both the total list and the prioritized, managed list will change as the project progresses. Risk factors will disappear as their threat vanishes, new risks will be identified, and risk exposures will change with the passage of time or as the result of reducing or eliminating the risks.

Risk Control (Risk Abatement Strategies, Risk Mitigation Planning, Risk Mitigation)

The conceptual basis of risk control, as in all control theory, is the feedback loop. Initial action plans are executed to reduce risk, and contingency plans are developed to trigger further risk-mitigating actions upon occurrence of certain events. As a project progresses, the operation is monitored to verify that risk factors are indeed being controlled and, if not, the project is redirected as appropriate, thus closing the control loop. The controller is the project manager who works with the project team to meet project targets by assessing risk and acting on the prioritized risk factors to protect against their possible consequences.

Risk control depends on the risk assessment procedures put in place at the beginning of a project. It is difficult to incorporate risk control into a project that has encountered problems as a result of the lack of risk assessment. The three explicit steps of risk control are (1) determining the best strategies for abating assessed risks, (2) producing risk mitigation plans, and (3) mitigating risks.

Risk Abatement Strategies

In choosing where to expend effort, time, and money on risk-reducing activities, we need to first consider areas where we do not know enough about the risks involved—or even do not know what we don't know—and proceed to gain information by prototyping, simulation, surveys, benchmarks, reference checks, examining local history, consulting experts, and so on.

In dealing with known, assessed risks there are three strategies for risk abatement:

- *Risk avoidance*, for example, by reducing functionality or performance requirements, or buying more hardware—thus eliminating the source of the risk.

- *Risk transfer*, for example, by reallocating functionality or performance requirements into hardware, moving complexity into the human element, subcontracting to specialists, or realigning authority and responsibility.

- *Risk acceptance*, by which a risk factor is acknowledged, and responsibility accepted by all affected parties, with the understanding that the accepted risk will be explicitly managed and that, in spite of our best efforts, the project might encounter significant difficulties.

Risk transfer can be a risky strategy. If, for example, there is significant risk that a specialty subcontractor may fail to deliver a satisfactory component, that problem (should it materialize) will affect the outcome of the project. We must take care to distinguish risk transfer situations from those where we retain responsibility for the outcome and those where the transfer of risk results in a transfer of responsibility as well.

Risk abatement strategies are often based on expert judgment and local experience. For example, Figure 4 illustrates the top-ten risk factors identified by Boehm in his work environment at TRW, along with risk management techniques for abating those risks [Boehm89]. Depending on your work environment, the relative priorities among the risk factors in Figure 4 (and others not on the list) may be different. For example, item 6 in Figure 4 might be the most difficult risk factor in your environment; lack of well defined development processes (not on the list in Figure 4) might be a significant risk factor in your environment.

The costs as well as the benefits of alternative courses of action must be considered; it is not sensible to spend more on risk reduction than the cost to fix the resulting problem, should it materialize. The cost incurred is the cost of the risk-reducing action and the benefit gained is the reduction of risk exposure that results from the action. Cost/benefit decisions can be based on calculations of risk reduction leverage, where:

Risk Reduction Leverage = $(RE_{Before} - RE_{After})$/Risk Reduction Cost

RE_{Before} is the risk exposure before initiating the risk reduction activity and RE_{After} is the risk exposure afterwards.

In addition to providing a rationale for choosing among alternative courses of action, risk reduction leverage can be used to decide "How much is enough?" when an activity is seen to be good (such as reviews and tests at every stage of product development) but very expensive when carried to extremes. It is clear that difficult decisions will only be made early enough and firmly enough when the risk reduction leverage calculations have sufficient credibility to support those decisions.

Risk Mitigation Planning

It is important to coordinate and reconcile the effects of various risk mitigation plans on the schedule and planned utilization of resources. This is typically done by developing the risk management plan and the risk abatement strategies and then comparing the initial risk exposure for the project to the adjusted risk exposure, taking into account the effect of the proposed risk reduction plans and their associated costs.

For example, on a project having a budget of $1M and a risk factor having an original risk exposure of $500K, implementing various risk mitigation strategies and plans, at a cost of $100K, might reduce the adjusted risk exposure to $50K. The project now has a budget/plan of, effectively, $900K with a risk exposure of $50K, which is a much less risky project. However, some other risk exposures may have increased due to the budget reduction for some of the tasks; they will have to be re-estimated or the lowest-priority requirements may have to be eliminated. Iterative reworking of all the action plans and contingency plans must be accomplished. Also note that real technical insight and real re-estimation is required, not just some playing around with risk exposure numbers.

RISK ITEM	RISK REDUCTION TECHNIQUE
1. Personnel shortfalls	Staffing with top talent; job matching; team building; training; prescheduling key people
2. Unrealistic schedules and budgets	Multisource estimates; design to cost; software reuse; requirements scrubbing
3. Wrong software functions	Mission analysis; Ops-Concept; user surveys; prototyping; early users' manual
4. Wrong user interface	Operational scenarios; prototyping; task analysis; user characterization
5. Gold plating	Requirements scrubbing; prototyping; cost/benefit analysis; design to cost
6. Continuing changes in requirements	High change threshold; information hiding; incremental development (defer changes to later)
7. Shortfalls in externally supplied components	Benchmarking; inspections; reference checking; compatibility analysis
8. Shortfalls in externally performed tasks	Reference checking; preaward audits; award-fee contracts; competitive design or prototyping; teambuilding
9. Real-time performance shortfalls	Simulation; benchmarking; modeling; prototyping; instrumentation; tuning
10. Straining computer science capabilities	Technical analysis; cost/benefit analysis; prototyping; reference checking

Figure 4. A Checklist of Software Risk Items and Risk Reduction Techniques

If systematic risk management is to be used to control risks to a project, then the estimates on which the project plan is based should not be padded for contingency. Estimates should be based on expected costs, with the assumptions clearly defined. This provides a baseline cost estimate for the project.

Each chance of an assumption being invalid is treated as a risk factor, with assessed probability and cost/schedule impact. For a high risk project, it is highly probable that the project cannot be completed within the baseline cost estimate; an extra budgetary reserve is necessary for successful project completion. The size of this reserve is usually more a matter for negotiation than true analysis based on risk exposure. Having been agreed to and allocated to the project manager's budget, this reserve is usually referred to as the "management reserve." The reserve is used by the project manager to support implementation of risk management plans and to cover unforeseen eventualities (the unknown unknowns) which require resource expenditure. A similar procedure can be applied for schedule contingency.

The management reserve can, in theory, be defined statistically to cover a reasonable percentage of the costs that would be required to deal with foreseeable project uncertainties—the 'known unknowns'. In practice, this reserve is usually negotiated downward, which creates an additional risk; that is, the risk of insufficient funds for the risk management plans. Also, having been allocated to the project, the reserve does not have the senior management's immediate attention. Major schedule delays may be introduced when the project manager has to finally go back and ask for more money or time.

An alternative approach is for the agreed-to reserve to be held outside the project (by the customer or senior management) even though inalienably committed to the project. When the project manager needs to call on the reserve, a case must be made that the perceived risk can be best mitigated by an action involving expenditure from the reserve. This encourages, in fact ensures, continuing communication between the project manager and the funding organization on the basis of management of risk.

In financial terms, the total unmitigated risk exposure for the project can be calculated from the sum of the risk exposures for all identified risk factors. The reduced risk exposure is calculated following the risk reduction activities, using the costs of those activities and the resulting risk exposure for each risk factor (calculated from the probability of occurrence and the cost impact). The resulting total risk exposure is compared with the project budget, profit margin, and commercial exposure for the organization. This can form the basis of effective communication with senior management, financial controllers, and the customer.

However, this approach treats total risk exposure in only its simplest form (a summation assumes that the cost and schedule impacts of each risk factor are independent; this may or may not be a valid assumption). More detailed analysis of interdependencies among risk factors may be required.

Decision makers also need information on the time element. The potential loss caused by a schedule delay may happen as a lump sum at a point in time, it may have a pattern of expenditure, or there may be a choice on the timing of actions, and there will be predictions of occurrence of external events. Similarly, the proposed courses of action to reduce or prevent the loss will have time-based costs and triggers for decisions which themselves will be timed (perhaps related to the reporting and decision-making processes). The combination of possibilities can be expressed as a time-based cash flow. Thus risk exposure may need to be shown as a time-based graph, or a series of graphs.

Risk Mitigation

According to the taxonomy presented in Figure 1, risk mitigation includes risk monitoring, problem resolution, and risk reassessment. If adequate risk assessment and risk reduction are accomplished at the start of a project and on a continuing basis, then, as the project progresses, the action plans and contingency plans actions should, for the most part, have the intended effect of mitigating the risk factors.

Risk monitoring (and reporting) on a regular, continuing basis have the goals of identifying risks that are about to become, or have become, problems, determining whether risks and problems are being successfully resolved, and gaining insight to identify new risk factors as they arise.

Two useful techniques for risk monitoring and reporting are Risk Item Tracking Forms and Top-Ten Risk Lists. Figures 5 and 6 provide an example of a risk item tracking form. This form consists of two parts: the risk item registry and the risk mitigation progress report. As illustrated in Figure 5, the risk registry form provides fields for identifying a risk factor, describing it, assessing it, and developing a mitigation plan to control it. The risk status and date fields provide a mechanism for tracking the progress of risk resolution. As illustrated at the bottom of Figure 5, there are several possible Risk Status Values. Figure 6 illustrates a mechanism for tracking progress on working the mitigation plan identified in Figure 5 by date and the responsible party. As indicated in Figure 6, there are several possible status values for the mitigating action.

RISK NO:	TITLE:	STATUS	DATE
Risk Item Description:			
Author_____Date_____			
Assessment/Alternatives Considered:			
Risk Owner_____Date_____			
Mitigation Plan:			
Planned Manager's Start Date_____Approval_____Date_____			

Possible Risk Status Values: IDENTIFIED
            ASSESSED
            PLANNED
            CONTINGENT
            PROBLEM
            CRISIS
            RESOLVED
            CLOSED

Figure 5. Risk Item Tracking Form

DATE	MITIGATION STATUS	ACTIONS COMPLETED	NEXT ACTIONS TO BE TAKEN	BY WHOM

Possible Risk Mitigation Status Values: PLANNED
               CONTINGENT
               AUTHORIZED
               IN PROGRESS
               LATE
               FAILED
               ALTERNATIVE PLAN
               SUCCEEDED
               UNNECESSARY
               OVERTAKEN BY EVENTS
               INCORPORATED IN PROJECT PLAN

Figure 6. A Risk Mitigation Tracking Form

Risk items to be included in the risk registry can be brought to the attention of lead engineers, project managers, and other decision makers using one or more "Top-Ten Risk Item Lists." A Top-Ten List is illustrated in Figure 7. In some organizations, Top-Ten lists are used at all levels, from the individual development team, to the subsystem manager, to the project manager, to the department manager, to the vice-president, to the customer/developer interface. Each group has a different list, depending on their responsibilities; for example, the project manager's list is a prioritized aggregation of top ten reports from the team leaders plus other risks at the project level; the department manager's list includes a prioritized aggregation of project managers' lists and other risks at the department level, and so forth. Reporting is upward through the management chain. If possible, a risk factor is mitigated within the group that identifies it, and reported to the next level. A risk that cannot be mitigated within the bounds of authority of the group that identifies it is promoted to the next level for mitigation.

Each item on a top-ten risk list should have a corresponding risk item tracking form, as illustrated in Figures 5 and 6. The top-ten list should be updated, and the status of risk tracking reviewed weekly at the team and project levels. In the absence of severe risks and problems, the lists at the department level and higher levels should be reviewed and updated monthly.

The term "Top-Ten" implies exactly ten risk items at each reporting level, but in fact, there is no particular best size for the reported list. If the true number of risk items is less than ten, then the report should concentrate on what is important without padding out the list. Ten serious risk items is about as many as a group can cope with, but if there are genuinely more, each should be reported, together with one further item that indicates there are so many risk factors that the project may be in serious trouble.

Communication at the senior management and customer levels using risk, including financial impact in terms of risk exposure, is much more effective than attempting to report progress against deterministic plans. Progress reporting against plans, and updates to plans, must still be done, but that should underpin the dominant theme of reporting in terms of risk. Attempting to communicate with senior management and the customer only on the basis of progress against plans is inadequate for high risk projects (which includes most software projects).

Risk Reassessment is a continuous process. The risk management control loop depends on risk monitoring which leads to corrective action, risk reassessment, and adjustments to risk management plans to stay in control of the evolving risk factors. Further iterations through full risk assessment will be needed on an ad-hoc basis as new risks arise, as well as at regularly scheduled intervals.

Implementation of Risk Management at the Organizational Level

Organizations that deal with advanced technology are increasingly mandating risk management plans on their development projects—the key driver being the use of systematic risk management as a means of relating technical and team/process risks at the project level to company/consortium/customer/commercial/mission risk. Communications with senior management and the customer that are based on risk enables them to understand the financial and strategic implications of risky technical undertakings in a way that they could not before. Understanding risks in financial and strategic terms also provides a basis for risk sharing between the developer and the customer.

Organizations that successfully introduce risk management incorporate:

- Explicit definition of their development and management processes
- Communication based on risk
- Risk reporting to senior management
- A corporate policy for risk management on projects that includes:
  - risk management plans developed at the planning stage of a project and incorporated into the overall project plan
  - project-specific tailoring of the development process and the risk reduction and risk control techniques to be used
  - risks explicitly reviewed on a regular, on-going basis

Deming's principles teach us that improvements must be based on analyzing how the work is done (that is, the development and management processes) rather than merely analyzing the resulting products. This applies not only to quality and productivity, but also to successful risk management [Deming86].

Documenting the development process implies level three of the SEI process maturity model [Humphrey89] and an engineering infrastructure with codes of practice supported by standards, procedures, and training. SEI Level 3 is the first level at which tool support is introduced to support the process (as opposed to tool support for activities within the process). Without tool support, it is only rarely and with difficulty that there is much communication outside

RANK THIS WEEK	RANK LAST WEEK	WEEKS ON LIST	RISK ITEM	POTENTIAL CONSEQUENCE	RISK RESOLUTION PROGRESS
1	4	2	Replacement for sensor-control software team leader	Delay in coding with lower quality - less reliable operation	Desired replacement unavailable
2	6	2	Requested changes in user interface	Will delay delivery date if not finished for demo next week	Two additional people assigned and working
3	2	5	Compiler problem	Delay in completing coding of hardware drivers	New release of compiler appears to solve most problems but must be fully checked out
4	3	6	Availability of work stations for system test	Delay in software system testing	Procurement delay being discussed with vendor
5	5	3	Hardware testbed definition	Must be completed by end of month to avoid system integration delay	Work being completed; review meeting is scheduled
6	1	3	Fault tolerance requirements impact on performance	Performance problem could require major change to hw/sw architecture with severe impact on schedule and budget	Latest prototype demonstrates performance within specifications but fault tolerance still to be determined
7	-	1	Delay in specification of tele-comm interface	Could delay procurement of hardware subsystem for integration	Meeting scheduled to consider alternatives
8	8	4	Unavailability of technical editor	Insufficient time to produce high quality manuals	Staffing requirement placed with job agency
-	7	4	CM assistant needed	Inadequate support for increasing workload	Experienced CM assistant has joined team on full-time basis
-	9	5	Inability to reuse database software	Increase in planned development effort	Uncertainty resolved in latest prototype

Figure 7. Example of a Top-Ten Risk Item Report

the various project teams on how the work is being done and the risks being identified and mitigated.

Summary

The use of risk management as a common basis for communication at all levels throughout an organization provides for:

- identifying risks
- systematic risk analysis (putting numbers on probabilities and impacts)
- prioritizing risks and evaluating alternative courses of action for risk reduction
- developing risk abatement strategies
- developing action plans and contingency plans for accepted risks
- systematic monitoring and control of accepted risks
- on-going identification of new risk factors
- routine reporting of progress in terms of risk in addition to reporting progress against the project plan
- linkage from project level risks to company/customer/commercial/mission risks

Accepting risk-oriented reporting indicates new corporate attitudes about risk management. Our earlier discussion of the time-based effects of decisions and cash-flow in terms of risk penalty can also be portrayed in terms of probability of benefit as the result of decisions, actions, or expenditures (opportunity being the converse of risk).

In many organizations the effective application of risk management depends on highly motivated individuals who understand risk management and who hold key positions in the organization. It is our hope that, in the future, risk management will become a routine way of doing business at all levels and in all organizations rather than the special domain of a concerned few.

Acknowledgment

The first draft of this paper was prepared by Paul Rook before his untimely death. He is missed as a friend and colleague.

References

[Boehm89] B.W. Boehm, *Tutorial on Software Risk Management*, IEEE Computer Society Press, Los Alamitos, Calif., 1989.

[Boehm93] B.W. Boehm, *Tutorial on Software Process Models and Software Cost Models*, 8th Int'l COCOMO Meeting, Pittsburgh, Oct 1993.

[Charette89] R.N. Charette, *Software Engineering Risk Analysis and Management*, McGraw-Hill, New York, 1989.

[Charette90] R.N. Charette, *Application Strategies for Risk Analysis*, McGraw-Hill, New York, 1990.

[Deming86] W.E. Deming, *Out of the Crisis*, Cambridge, Mass., MIT Center for Advanced Engineering Study, 1986.

[Fairley91] R.E. Fairley, *Risk Management of Software Projects Tutorial*, at 13th ICSE Conference, Austin, 1991.

[Fairley93a] R.E. Fairley, "A Case Study in Managing Technical Risks for Software Projects," *Proc. 2nd SEI Risk Conf.*, 1993.

[Fairley93b] R.E. Fairley, "How Software Cost Models Deal with Risk," *Proc. 4th ESCOM Conf.*, 1993.

[Fairley94] R.E. Fairley, "Risk Management for Software Projects," *IEEE Software*, Vol. 11, No. 3, 1994.

[Humphrey89] W.S. Humphrey, *Managing the Software Process*, Addison Wesley, Reading, Mass., 1989.

Chapter 11

Software Development Process

1. Introduction to Chapter

A *life cycle model* is a model of the phases or activities that start when a software product is conceived and end when the product is no longer available for use. It depicts the relationships among the major milestones, baselines, reviews, and project deliverables that span the life of the system. The software life cycle typically includes a requirements phase, design phase, implementation (coding and unit testing) phase, integration and testing phase, installation and checkout phase, operation and maintenance phase, and, sometimes, retirement phase. Depending on the life cycle selected, these phases or activities may occur once in a prescribed sequence, or may occur several times in varying sequence.

The first software life cycle model was the "waterfall model," developed by Dr. Winston W. Royce. His original model is shown in Figure 11.1. This and other life cycle models are described in the papers in this chapter.

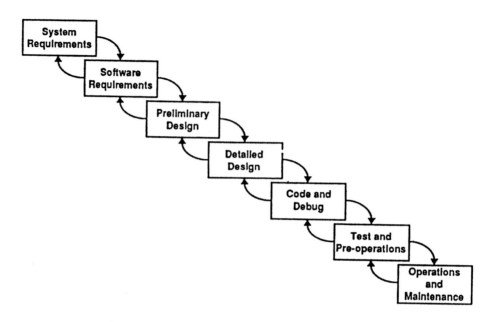

Figure 11.1. Waterfall model

A *process model* is a description of the sub-activities or tasks within a phase or activity, the dependencies among them, and the conditions that must exist before the tasks can begin or be considered complete. The process model may also include information about the performer(s) of a sub-activity or task. A process model can thus be considered as a more detailed statement of a life cycle model. Hence, any number of process models can be compatible with one life cycle model and, if the activities that make up two or more life cycle models are the same or similar, a process model may support more than one life cycle model.

2. Introduction to Papers

The first paper in this chapter is an overview of life cycle models by Edward Comer entitled "Alternative Life Cycle Models." The word alternative is used to separate the models discussed by Comer from the conventional or classical models based on Royce's Waterfall model. Comer describes the conventional life cycle models as well as the original Waterfall model. Because of the growing complexity of software systems, many practitioners feel the need to have different life cycle models available than the conventional requirements, design, implementation, and testing model.

These alternative models are radically different from the conventional model and include such approaches as rapid prototyping, incremental devel-opment, evolutionary prototyping, the reuse of previously developed software, and automated software synthesis. Comer points out that many of these alternative models are not yet standardized and are still being developed. (It should be noted that the current US Mil-Std 498, "Software Development and Documentation," recognizes, among others, three life cycle models: the conventional Waterfall, the incremental, and evolutionary development.) Comer's paper also discusses in summary form Barry Boehm's spiral model (see next paper).

The second paper, "A Spiral Model of Software Development and Enhancement," by Barry Boehm, was, when published, a revolutionary new look at the software development life cycle. An earlier version of this paper was presented by Boehm at a workshop on software requirements in early 1985. The spiral is a more general software development model than those typically in use today and treats as special cases the waterfall and other popular software development paradigms. (Boehm has referred to the spiral model as a "process model generator"—given the conditions and constraints of a particular software development project, the Spiral Model can be used to generate the correct process for that project.)

Whereas the waterfall is "documentation driven," the spiral model focuses on risk management. At the completion of each phase or major activity of software development, the spiral model prompts the developers to review objectives, alternatives, and constraints, to evaluate alternatives and risks, and to determine the nature of the next phase (prototyping, specification-driven, and so forth).

The third and final paper in this chapter is by Mark Paulk, Bill Curtis, and Mary Beth Chrissis of the Software Engineering Institute (SEI) and Charles Weber of Loral Federal Systems (formerly IBM Federal Systems and now part of Lockheed Martin). The paper is an update of a 1993 article [1] that introduced the SEI's Capability Maturity Model for Software (CMM), Version 1.1, and described its rationale and contents. During development of CMM Version 1.1, Weber was a resident affiliate at the SEI.

The CMM, and the process improvement efforts it fostered, represents perhaps the most important real change in the past 20 years in the way large-scale, mission-critical software is developed. Until the mid-1980s, efforts to improve the quality of software products and the cost and schedule of developing the products were focused almost entirely on technology (methods and tools) and people (hiring, educating, and training). A third aspect, the process by which software is developed and maintained, was neglected; its recognition as a factor of equal importance to the other two is largely due to the SEI.

The CMM is the result of about seven years of work on quantitative methods by which a software developer, or a potential customer of that developer, could determine the maturity of the developer's process. The US Department of Defense (DoD) sponsored the SEI's work; the SEI in turn convinced the DoD that process maturity should be a factor in the selection of contractors to develop software for DoD.

The CMM defines five levels of process maturity through which a software developer must move in order to become truly effective:

1. Initial (ad hoc, chaotic; process not defined and followed)
2. Repeatable (basic software management processes in place, defined and followed at the project level)
3. Defined (standard process defined at organization [company or division] level and tailored for use by projects)
4. Managed (measurements taken and used to improve product quality)
5. Optimizing (measurements used to improve process; error prevention)

The CMM has become a driving force in the US and elsewhere in the world for the improvement of software development processes. Many companies and US government agencies strive to improve their software engineering through the use of the goals and activities associated with this model. At the present time, achievement of Level 3 is the goal of many development organizations, although some have achieved Level 4 and a handful are reported to be at Level 5.

1. Paulk, Mark C., Bill Curtis, Mary Beth Chrissis, and Charles V. Weber, "Capability Maturity Model, Version 1.1," *IEEE Software*, Vol. 10, No. 4, July 1993, pp. 18–27.

Alternative Software Life Cycle Models

Edward R. Comer

Software Productivity Solutions, Melbourne, Florida

The classic waterfall model for the software life cycle (See Fig. 2.3.1) was defined as early as 1970 by Dr. Winston Royce [1] to help cope with the growing complexity of the aerospace software products being tackled. During the past 5–10 years, alternative, radically different life cycle models have been proposed, including rapid throwaway prototypes, incremental development, evolutionary prototypes, reusable software, and automated software synthesis. Although most of these alternatives are still maturing, many of their aspects have been integrated with the basic life cycle model to form hybrid life cycle models. In fact, the most recent life cycle models are actually hybrid models, including DoD-STD-2167A [2], the NASA Information System Life Cycle [3], and Barry Boehm's Spiral Model [4]. The following sections define a software life cycle model, introduce alternative life cycle models, and present an approach for contrasting and evaluating alternative life cycle models.

Introduction

Software development, for any application, is an expensive and risky endeavor. Critical software errors often remain in deployed software systems. Software maintenance is expensive and, too, error-prone. The software development process is often ad hoc and chaotic.

Aerospace systems offer special challenges for embedded software that make its development even more difficult, such as real-time, multi-mission, distributed, or autonomous.

The classic waterfall model for the software life cycle (see Figure 2.3.1) was defined as early as 1970 by Dr. Winston Royce [1] to help cope with the growing complexity of the aerospace software projects being tackled. With several years of experience with developing software for spacecraft mission planning, commanding and post-mission analysis, Dr. Royce had experienced different degrees of success with respect

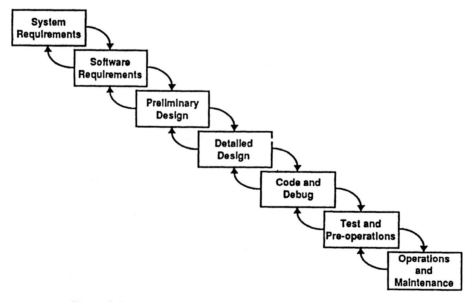

Figure 2.3.1 Waterfall life cycle model of software development

to "arriving at an operational state, on-time, and within costs" [1]. The resulting sequence of steps that he outlined, with various refinements and minor modifications, became the road map for the software development process for the last two decades.

During the past five to ten years, alternative, radically different life cycle models have been proposed, including rapid throwaway prototypes, incremental development, evolutionary prototypes, reusable software, and automated software synthesis. While most of these alternatives are still maturing, many of their aspects have been integrated with the basic life cycle model to form hybrid life cycle models. In fact, the most recent life cycle models are actually hybrid models, including DOD-STD2167A [2], the NASA Information System Life Cycle [3], and Barry Boehm's Spiral Model [4].

The following sections define a software life cycle model, introduce alternative life cycle models, and present an approach for contrasting and evaluating alternative life cycle models.

Definition of a Life Cycle Model

While the concept of a life cycle of software development is well known in the aerospace community, there are numerous misconceptions about its intent and purpose. A life cycle model is not a definition of the process a software development organization follows; the actual process is typically far more complex and includes many activities not depicted in the life cycle model. A life cycle model is not a methodology; it does not provide rules or representations for development.

Instead, we define a software life cycle model to be a *reference model* for a software development process, in the same manner that the Open Systems Interconnection (OSI) model [5] is a reference model for protocols for computer system communication. Such a reference model:

1. provides a common basis for the definition and coordination of specific project and organization software process standards, allowing these standards to be placed into perspective within the overall life cycle reference model;

2. describes the major functions, or activities, involved in software development and the terms used to define those functions;

3. highlights important aspects or features that are deemed to be important for common understanding and focus.

While a life cycle model is insufficient to represent a definition of a software development process, or to describe the methodologies applied for software development, it does serve as a reference model for these processes and methodologies. Indeed, the intent of standard DoD [2] and NASA [3] life cycles is to provide a common framework for contractor-specific processes and methodologies.

Alternative Life Cycle Models

Waterfall Model

The waterfall model documented in 1970 by Royce [1] and later refined by Boehm [6] in 1976 is the most popular and proven of the alternative life cycles. Figure 2.3.1 illustrates a waterfall model, defining the major steps, or phases, and their approximate sequence. A *phase* consists of a set of activities to accomplish the goals of that phase [3]. Additional arrows are added to represent the inherent feedback that occurs between these phases.

Most software development processes in aerospace corporations or mandated by governmental agencies have followed some basic variation of the waterfall model, although there are a variety of different names for each of the phases. Thus, the requirements phase is often called user needs analysis, system analysis, or specification; the preliminary design phase is often called high-level design, top-level design, software architectural definition, or specification; the detailed design phase is often called program design, module design, lower-level design, algorithmic design, or just plain design, etc.

In 1984, McDermid and Ripkin [7] noted that waterfall life cycle models, such as depicted in Figure 2.3.1, are too simple and abstract to deal with an embedded software development project's problem of developing, adopting, or assembling a coherent methodology. Their variant of the waterfall model, shown in Figure 2.3.2, highlights several important issues:

1. The level and purpose of the various representations are identified.

2. Activities are viewed as transformations from high level representations to low level representations.

3. Verification within a representation and between representations is explicitly shown.

4. Iterations around representations occur, as errors are discovered and changes are identified; this includes both fine and coarse iterations.

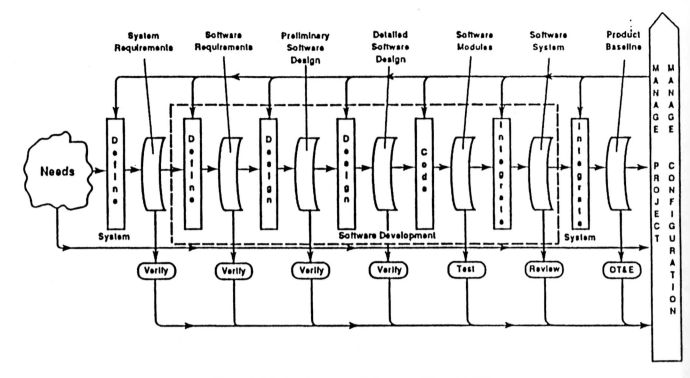

Figure 2.3.2 Another view of the waterfall model [7]

5. Project and configuration control is a special activity; this problem is compounded the presence of iteration.

Development processes based upon the waterfall model have been commonplace for aerospace software development. The use of a waterfall life cycle model:

1. encourages one to specify what the system is supposed to do (i.e., to define the requirements) before thinking about how to build the system (i.e., designing);

2. encourages one to plan how components are going to interact (i.e., designing) before building the components (i.e., coding);

3. enables project managers to track progress more accurately and to uncover possible slippages early;

4. demands that the development process generate a series of documents which can later be utilized to test and maintain the system;

5. enables the organization that will develop the system to be more structured and manageable.

Much of the motivation behind waterfall life cycle models was to provide structure to avoid the problems of the "undisciplined hacker" [6].

Rapid, Throwaway Prototypes

The rapid, throwaway prototype, made popular by Gomaa and Scott [8] in 1981, focuses on ensuring that the software product being proposed really meets the users' needs. Difficulties are often experienced using a waterfall model in the initial step of deriving a requirements specification:

1. Requirements specification documents have problems with correctness, completeness and ambiguity.

2. Errors in requirements specification are usually the last to be detected and the most costly to correct.

3. There is a communication gap between the software system developer and the user. This results in difficulties of the developer truly understanding the user's needs and difficulties of the user in understanding and approving a requirements specification.

Gomaa and Scott found that both the quality of the requirements specification and the communication of user needs can be improved by developing a prototype of the proposed system [8].

The approach is to construct a "quick and dirty" partial implementation of the system prior to (or during) the requirements phase. The potential users utilize this prototype for a period of time and supply feedback to the developers concerning its strengths and weaknesses. This feedback is then used to modify the software requirements specification to reflect the real user needs.

At this point, the developers can proceed with the actual system design and implementation with confidence that they are building the "right" system (except in those cases where the user needs evolve). An extension of this approach uses a series of throwaway prototypes [6], culminating in full-scale development.

Incremental Development

Incremental development [9] is the process for constructing a partial, but deployment-ready, implementation build of a system and incrementally adding increased functionality or performance. Two variants of this approach, shown in Figure 2.3.3, differ only in the level of requirements analysis accomplished at the start. One approach is only to define the requirements for the immediate next build, the other is to initially define and allocate the requirements for all builds.

Incremental development has received government recognition as an acceptable, or even desirable, alternative to the classic waterfall life cycle. Such an approach has been proposed in a 1987 Joint Logistics Commanders (JLC) guidebook for command and control systems [10] and discussed in the NASA Information System Life Cycle and Documentation Standards [3] for their aerospace applications.

An incremental development approach reduces the costs incurred before an initial capability is achieved and defines an approach for the "incremental definition, funding, development, fielding, support and operational testing of an operational capability to satisfy the evolving requirement" [10]. It also produces an operational system more quickly, and it thus reduces the possibility that the user needs will change during the development process.

Experience with the incremental development life cycle for aerospace applications has shown that the approach provides better visibility into the development to better assess progress and has been shown to decrease risk and to increase reliability and productivity in the development process [3]. The approach is compatible with the philosophy of "build a little, test a little" that is popular in the Ada community. Incremental development does require the use of a flexible system architecture to facilitate incremental enhancement and expansion [10] and increases the configuration management support required during the development process [3].

Evolutionary Prototypes

Evolutionary prototyping extends the concept of incremental development to its ultimate conclusion, viewing the software life cycle as a set of numerous prototypes that are evolved through successive experimentation and refinement to meet the user's needs. The approach, described by Giddings in 1984 [11], addresses the inherent problem of truly satisfying user needs and the problem of evolving a software system as the needs of the application domain change. This aspect can be important for many applications, including aerospace systems, that have a very long operational life time, often two or three decades.

In an evolutionary prototyping life cycle, shown in Figure 2.3.4, the developers construct a partial implementation of the system which meets known requirements. The prototype is then experimentally used by its users in order to understand the full requirements better. The usage observations are analyzed and used as the basis for the next evolution of the prototype. This cycle continues until a prototype is considered by the users to be acceptable for operational deployment. Future evolution of the application requirements can be addressed by continuing this evolutionary development process.

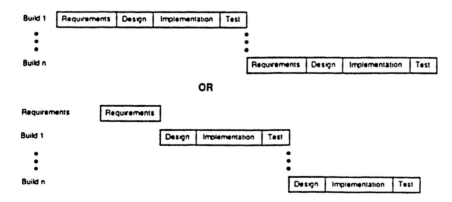

Figure 2.3.3 Incremental development life cycle models

407

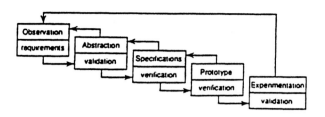

Figure 2.3.4 Evolutionary prototyping life cycle [11]

Whereas incremental development implies a high level of understanding of the requirements up front, implementing subsets of increasing capability, evolutionary prototyping implies that we do not know up front all of our requirements, but need to experiment with an operational system in order to learn them. Note that in the case of throwaway prototypes we are likely to implement only those aspects of the system that are poorly understood, but that in the case of evolutionary prototypes we are more likely to start with those system aspects that are best understood and thus build upon our strengths.

Evolutionary prototyping has challenges in scaling up to very large systems, ensuring process visibility and control, avoiding the negative effects of "information sclerosis," and avoiding the "'undisciplined hacker' approach that the waterfall and other models were trying to correct" [4]. Information sclerosis is a "syndrome familiar to operational information-based systems, in which temporary work-arounds for software deficiencies increasingly solidify into unchangeable constraints on evolution" [4].

For complex aerospace applications, it is not reasonable at this time to expect evolutionary application of prototypes to be particularly "rapid" because reliability, adaptability, maintainability, and performance (RAMP) are major forces behind making such system developments expensive and time-consuming. Since the technology is not yet available to *retrofit* RAMP requirements, they would have to be implemented up front, thus forcing software development costs high and schedules to their limit. Evolutionary prototypes will become more practical in the future as automated techniques for retrofitting RAMP requirements are developed [12].

Reusable Software

Whereas prototyping attempts to reduce development costs through partial implementations leading to a better understanding of requirements, reusable software is the discipline of attempting to reduce development costs by incorporating designs, programs, modules, and data into new software products [13]. Because the emphasis of reusable software is on a dif-

ferent approach for constructing software rather than specifying it, the approach is compatible with prototyping approaches.

The software industry is guilty of continuously reinventing the wheel. Reusability has achieved only limited application, mostly in business applications. There are few tools available to help reuse software designs or code from previous projects. Clearly, what is needed are techniques to analyze application domains for reusability potential, create reusable components, techniques, and tools to store and retrieve reusable components, and component specification and classification techniques to help catalog and locate relevant components. The net effect of reusing components would be shorter development schedules (by using wheels rather than reinventing them) and more reliable software (by using components that been previously "shaken down").

A life cycle incorporating reusable software is a major objective of the government's Ada initiative. Many of the features of the language supporting abstract data types and generics are designed to directly support the development and effective usage of reusable modules.

The most significant work in reusable software for aerospace applications is the Common Ada Missile Packages (CAMP) effort [14]. In a multi-phased Air Force program, McDonnell Douglas provided a comprehensive demonstration of a reusable software life cycle. The effort accomplished a domain analysis of missile software, identified commonalities of that application, specified and constructed a set of over 200 Ada "parts," developed tools to support reusability, and finally accomplished a missile software development using the developed reusable software parts.

Automated Software Synthesis

Automated software synthesis is a term used to describe the automated transformation of formal requirements specifications into operational code [15]. Such an approach, shown in Figure 2.3.5, relies heavily on automated tools. Formal specifications are created and maintained by users using specification tools. The formal specifications become prototypes for the

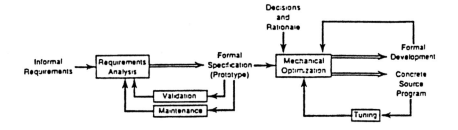

Figure 2.3.5 Automated software synthesis life cycle [15]

desired system that are used to refine the specification. Implementation of a production software system is accomplished using a highly automated transformational programming approach from the formal specification.

Transformational programming [16] is a methodology of program construction by successive application of transformation rules. The individual transitions between the various versions of the program are made by applying correctness-preserving transformation rules, stating with the formal specification. It is guaranteed that the final version of the program will satisfy the initial specification.

Fully automatic transformation clearly is best. Unfortunately, such a solution may not be feasible because of the wide gap between high-level specification languages and implementations. A partially automated solution is more feasible, in the form of an automated assistant. [15]

Automated software synthesis is an active research area [16]. To become practical for aerospace applications, there are two significant technologies that must be matured: tools for derivation of formal specifications using informal specifications and prototyping, and tools for automatic transformation of formal specifications into optimized code. Both are still highly experimental.

User derivation and maintenance of a specification, rather than code, has many advantages. The user as the systems analyst, with the aid of prototyping via an executable specification, can completely and accurately determine what the system will do and evolve the system as the application requirements change. Because implementations can be easily transformed from updated specifications, enhancement can be accomplished easier and more frequently; "it will stay 'soft' and modifiable rather than become ossified and brittle with age" [15].

Evaluation of Alternative Life Cycle Models

It is difficult to compare and contrast these new models of software development because their disciples often use different terminology, and the models often have little in common except their beginnings (marked by a recognition that a problem exists) and ends (marked by the existence of a software solution). This section provides a framework originally described by Davis et al. in 1988 [12] which can serve 1) as a basis for analyzing the similarities and differences among alternative life cycle models; 2) as a tool for software engineering researchers to help describe the probable impacts of a new life cycle model; and 3) as a means to help software practitioners decide on an appropriate life cycle model to utilize on a particular project or in a particular application area.

Life Cycle Model Evaluation Paradigm

For every application beyond the trivial, user needs are constantly evolving. Thus, the system being constructed is always aiming at a moving target. This is the primary reason for delayed schedules (caused by trying to make the software meet a new requirement it was not designed to meet) and software that fails to meet customer expectations (because the developers "froze" the requirements and failed to acknowledge the inevitable changes).

Figure 2.3.6 shows graphically how users' needs evolve over time. It is recognized that the function shown is neither linear nor continuous in reality. Please note that the scale on the X axis is not shown (the units can be either months or years), but could be assumed to be nonuniform, containing areas of compression and expansion. The units of the scale on the Y axis are also not shown, but are assumed to be some measure of the amount of functionality (such as De-Marco's "Bangs for the Buck" [17]). However, none of the observations made are dependent on either the uniformity of the axes or the linearity or continuity of the curve shown in Figure 2.3.6.

Figure 2.3.7 shows what happens during a conventional waterfall life cycle software development. At time t_0, a need for a software system is recognized and a development effort commences with relatively incomplete knowledge of the real user needs. At time

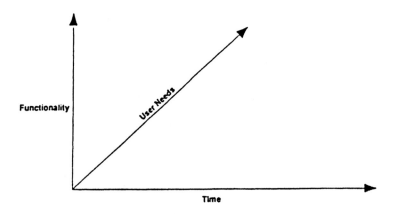

Figure 2.3.6 Constantly evolving user needs [12]

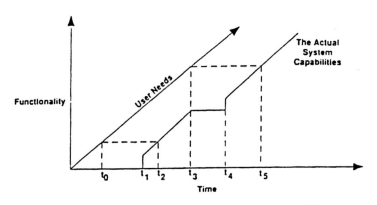

Figure 2.3.7 Evaluation of waterfall model in satisfying evolving user needs [12]

t_1, the development effort has produced an operational product, but not only does it not satisfy the current t_1 needs, it does not even satisfy the old t_0 needs because of a poor understanding of those needs in the first place. The product now undergoes a series of enhancements (between times t_1 and t_3), which eventually enable it to satisfy the original requirements (at t_2) and then some. At some later point in time t_3, the cost of enhancement is so great that the decision is made to build a new system (once again based on poorly understood requirements), development of the product is completed at time t_4, and the cycle repeats itself.

A number of useful metrics can now be defined based on the paradigm defined above. These metrics can later be used to compare and contrast sets of alternative life cycle approaches. These metrics are portrayed graphically in Figure 2.3.8 and are described below [12].

1. A *shortfall is* a measure of how far the operational system, at any time *t*, is from meeting the actual requirements at time *t*. This is the attribute that most people are referring to when they ask "Does this system meet my needs?"

2. *Lateness is* a measure of the time that elapses between the appearance of a new requirement and its satisfaction. Of course, recognizing that new requirements are not necessarily implemented in the order in which they appear, lateness actually measures the time delay associated with achievement of a level of functionality.

3. The *adaptability* is the rate at which the software solution can adapt to new requirements, as measured by the slope of the solution curve.

4. The *longevity* is the time a system solution is adaptable to change and remains viable, i.e., the time from system creation through the time it is replaced.

5. *Inappropriateness* is the shaded area between the user needs and the solution curves in Figure 2.3.8 and thus captures the behavior of

410

shortfall over time. The ultimately "appropriate" model would exhibit a zero area, meaning that new requirements are instantly satisfied.

Each of the alternative life cycle models defined earlier is now analyzed with respect to the paradigm described above.

Rapid, Throwaway Prototypes

The use of a rapid throwaway prototype early in the development life cycle increases the likelihood that customers and developers will have a better understanding of the real user needs that existed at time t_0. Thus, its use does not radically affect the life cycle

model per se, but does increase the impact of the resulting system. This is shown in Figure 2.3.9, where the vertical line (i.e., the increase in functionality provided by the system upon deployment) at time t_1 is longer than in the waterfall approach.

Figure 2.3.9 also shows the rapid prototype itself as a short vertical line providing limited and experimental capability soon after time t_0. There is no reason to believe that the length of time during which the product can be efficiently enhanced without replacement is any different than with the waterfall approach. Therefore, this period of time for the rapid prototype-based development (i.e., t_3 minus t_1) is shown in Figure 2.3.9 the same as for the waterfall developed product.

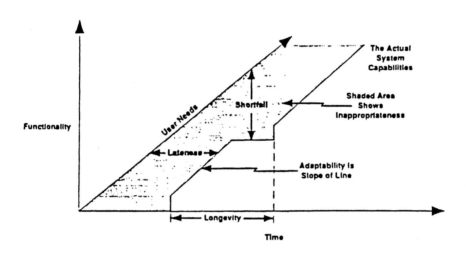

Figure 2.3.8 Life cycle evaluation metrics [12]

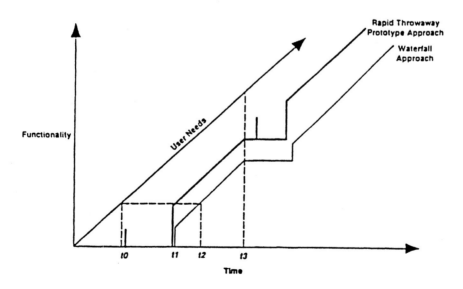

Figure 2.3.9 Comparison of rapid prototyping vs waterfall life cycle [12]

Incremental Development

When using incremental development, software is deliberately built to satisfy fewer requirements initially, but is constructed in such a way as to facilitate the incorporation of new requirements and thus achieve higher adaptability. This approach has two effects: 1) the initial development time is reduced because of the reduced level of functionality, and 2) the software can be enhanced more easily and for a longer period of time.

Figure 2.3.10 shows how this approach compares to the waterfall life cycle. Note that the initial development time is less than for the waterfall approach, that the initial functionality (A) is less than for the waterfall approach (B), and that the increased adaptability is indicated by a higher slope of the curve A-C than that for the waterfall approach (line B-D). The stair-step aspect of the graph indicates a series of well-defined, planned, discrete builds of the system.

Evolutionary Prototypes

This approach is an extension of the incremental development. Here, the number and frequency of operational prototypes increases. The emphasis is on evolving toward a solution in a more continuous fashion, instead of by a discrete number of system builds.

With such an approach, an initial prototype emerges rapidly, presumably demonstrating functionality where the requirements are well understood (in contrast to the throwaway prototypes, where one usually implements poorly understood aspects first) and providing an overall framework for the software. Each successive prototype explores a new area of user need,

while refining the previous functions. As a result, the solution evolves closer and closer to the user needs (see Figure 2.3.11). In time, it too will have to be redone or undergo major restructuring in order to continue to evolve.

As with the incremental development approach, the slope (line A-C) is steeper than in the waterfall approach (line B-D) because the evolvable prototype was designed to be far more adaptable. Also, the line A-C in Figure 2.3.7 is not stepped like line A-C in Figure 2.3.6 because of the replacement of well-defined and well-planned system "builds" with a continuous influx of new, and perhaps experimental, functionality.

Reusable Software

Reuse of existing software components has the potential to decrease the initial development time for software significantly. Figure 2.3.12 shows how this approach compares to conventional waterfall development. No parameters are changed, except for the development times.

Automated Software Synthesis

In the ultimate application of this approach, as an engineer recognizes the requirements, these are specified in some type of formal specification and the system is automatically synthesized. This approach has two dramatic effects: 1) the development time is greatly reduced, and 2) the development costs are reduced so much that adapting "old" systems is rarely more meritorious than resynthesizing the entire system. Thus, the longevity of any version is low, and the

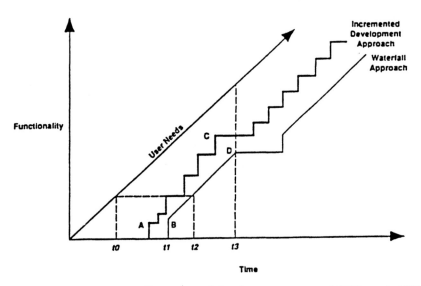

Figure 2.3.10 Comparison of incremental development vs waterfall life cycle [12]

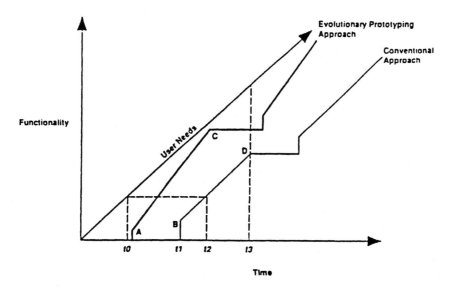

Figure 2.3.11 Comparison of evolutionary prototyping vs waterfall life cycle [12]

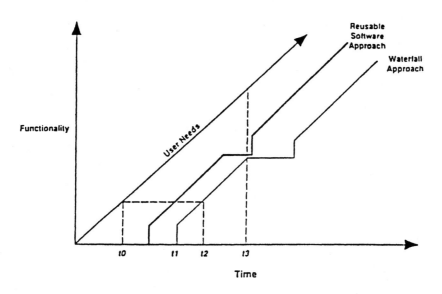

Figure 2.3.12 Comparison of reusable software vs waterfall life cycle [12]

result is a stair-step graph, as shown in Figure 2.3.13, where the horizontal segments represent the time the system is utilized and the time needed to upgrade the requirements. The vertical segments represent the additional functionality offered by each new generation.

Defining, Selecting, or Adapting a Life Cycle Model

The various life cycle alternatives reflect different approaches for improving the software development process. The life cycle model evaluation paradigm [12] provides insight into how we might define, select or adapt a life cycle model to improve our process.

Currently, many project managers make this selection based on fuzzy perceptions and past experiences or blindly follow life cycle standards. The evaluation paradigm presented points to some application aspects that should affect selection of a life cycle approach:

1. requirements volatility (that is, the likelihood that the requirements will change);

2. the "shape" of requirements volatility (such as discrete leaps, based on brand new threats; or gradual changes, as with a need to do things faster);

3. the longevity of the application; and

413

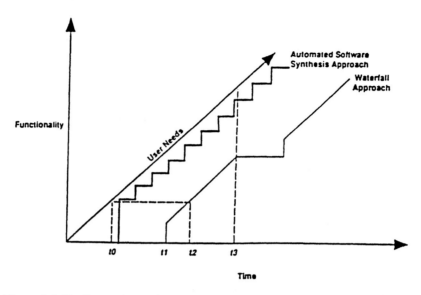

Figure 2.3.13 Comparison of automated software vs waterfall life cycle [12]

4. the availability of resources to develop or effect changes (i.e., it may be easier to get resources up front than to devote significant resources for enhancements).

References

[1] Royce, W.W., "Managing the Development of Large Software Systems: Concepts and Techniques," *1970 WESCON Technical Papers,* Vol. 14, Western Electronic Show and Convention, 1970.

[2] *Defense System Software Development,* DOD-STD-2167A Military Standard, Feb. 29, 1988.

[3] *Information System Life Cycle and Documentation Standards,* Release 4.3, NASA Office of Safety, Reliability, Maintainability, and Quality Assurance, Software Management and Assurance Program (SMAP), Washington, D.C., Feb. 28, 1989.

[4] Boehm, B.W., "A Spiral Model of Software Development and Enhancement," *ACM SIGSOFT Software Eng. Notes,* Vol. 11, No. 4, Aug. 1986, pp. 14–24.

[5] Information Processing Systems—Open Systems Interconnection (OSI)--Basic Reference Model, International Standards Organization ISO-7498-1984, Oct. 15, 1984.

[6] Boehm, B.W., "Software Engineering," *IEEE Trans. Computers,* Vol. C-25, Dec. 1976, pp. 1226–1241.

[7] McDermid, J. and Ripken, K., *Life Cycle Support in the Ada Environment,* Cambridge University Press, Cambridge, UK, 1984.

[8] Gomaa, H. and Scott, D., "Prototyping as a Tool in the Specification of User Requirements," *Proc. 5th IEEE Int'l Conf. Software Eng.,* 1981, pp. 333–342.

[9] Hirsch, E., "Evolutionary Acquisition of Command and Control Systems," *Program Manager,* Nov-Dec 1985, pp. 18–22.

[10] Joint Logistics Commanders Guidance for the Use of an Evolutionary Acquisition (EA) Strategy in Acquiring Command and Control Systems, Defense Systems Management College, Fort Belvoir, VA, 1987.

[11] Giddings, R.V., "Accommodating Uncertainty in Software Design," *Comm. ACM,* Vol. 27, No. 5, May 1984, pp. 428–434.

[12] Davis, A.M., Bersoff, E.H., and Comer, E.R., "A Strategy for Comparing Alternative Software Development Life Cycle Models," *IEEE Trans. Software Eng.,* Vol. 14, No. 10, Oct. 1988, pp. 1453–1461.

[13] Jones, T.C., "Reusability in Programming: A Survey of the State of the Art," *IEEE Trans. Software Eng.,* Vol. SE-10, Sept. 1984, pp. 488–494.

[14] McNicholl, D.G., Palmer, C., and Cohen, S., *Common Ada Missile Packages (CAMP),* Vol. I and II, McDonnell Douglas, AFATL-TR-85-93, May 1986.

[15] Balzer, R., Cheatham, T.E., Jr., and Green, C., "Software Technology in the 1990's: Using a New Paradigm," *Computer,* Nov. 1983, pp. 39–45.

[16] Partsch, H. and Steinbruggen, R., "Program Transformation Systems," *ACM Computing Surveys,* Vol. 16, No. 3, Sept. 1983, pp. 199–236.

[17] DeMarco, T., *Controlling Software Projects,* Yourdon Press, New York, 1982.

A Spiral Model of Software Development and Enhancement

Barry W. Boehm, TRW Defense Systems Group

"Stop the life cycle—I want to get off!"
"Life-cycle Concept Considered Harmful."
"The waterfall model is dead."
"No, it isn't, but it should be."

These statements exemplify the current debate about software life-cycle process models. The topic has recently received a great deal of attention.

The Defense Science Board Task Force Report on Military Software[1] issued in 1987 highlighted the concern that traditional software process models were discouraging more effective approaches to software development such as prototyping and software reuse. The Computer Society has sponsored tutorials and workshops on software process models that have helped clarify many of the issues and stimulated advances in the field (see "Further reading").

The spiral model presented in this article is one candidate for improving the software process model situation. The major distinguishing feature of the spiral model is that it creates a *risk-driven* approach to the software process rather than a primarily *document-driven* or *code-driven* process. It incorporates many of the strengths of other models and resolves many of their difficulties.

This article opens with a short description of software process models and the issues they address. Subsequent sections outline the process steps involved in the

This evolving risk-driven approach provides a new framework for guiding the software process.

spiral model; illustrate the application of the spiral model to a software project, using the TRW Software Productivity Project as an example; summarize the primary advantages and implications involved in using the spiral model and the primary difficulties in using it at its current incomplete level of elaboration; and present resulting conclusions.

Background on software process models

The primary functions of a software process model are to determine the *order of the stages* involved in software development and evolution and to establish the *transition criteria* for progressing from one stage to the next. These include completion criteria for the current stage plus choice criteria and entrance criteria for the next stage. Thus, a process model addresses the following software project questions:

(1) What shall we do next?
(2) How long shall we continue to do it?

Consequently, a process model differs from a software method (often called a methodology) in that a method's primary focus is on how to navigate through each phase (determining data, control, or "uses" hierarchies; partitioning functions; allocating requirements) and how to represent phase products (structure charts; stimulus-response threads; state transition diagrams).

Why are software process models important? Primarily because they provide guidance on the order (phases, increments, prototypes, validation tasks, etc.) in which a project should carry out its major tasks. Many software projects, as the next section shows, have come to grief because they pursued their various development and evolution phases in the wrong order.

Evolution of process models. Before concentrating in depth on the spiral model, we should take a look at a number of others: the code-and-fix model, the stagewise model and the waterfall model, the evolutionary development model, and the transform model.

The code-and-fix model. The basic model used in the earliest days of software

Reprinted from *Computer*, Vol. 21, No. 5, May 1988, pp. 61–72.

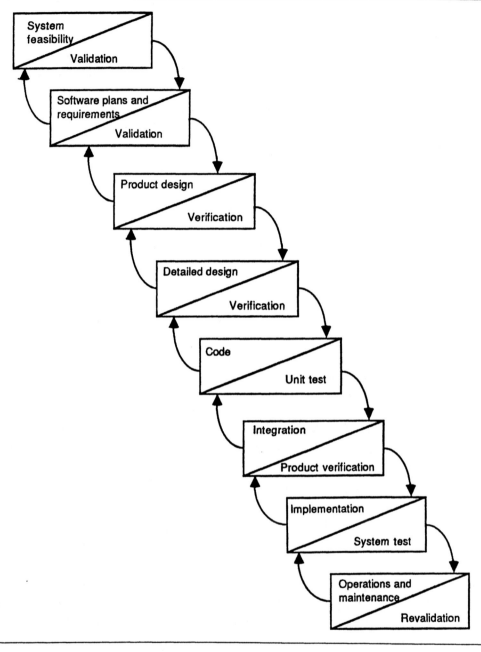

Figure 1. The waterfall model of the software life cycle.

development contained two steps:

(1) Write some code.

(2) Fix the problems in the code.

Thus, the order of the steps was to do some coding first and to think about the requirements, design, test, and maintenance later. This model has three pri-

mary difficulties:

(a) After a number of fixes, the code became so poorly structured that subsequent fixes were very expensive. This underscored the need for a design phase prior to coding.

(b) Frequently, even well-designed soft-

ware was such a poor match to users' needs that it was either rejected outright or expensively redeveloped. This made the need for a requirements phase prior to design evident.

(c) Code was expensive to fix because of poor preparation for testing and modification. This made it clear that explicit recognition of these phases, as well as test-and-evolution planning and preparation tasks in the early phases, were needed.

The stagewise and waterfall models. As early as 1956, experience on large software systems such as the Semi-Automated Ground Environment (SAGE) had led to the recognition of these problems and to the development of a stagewise model[2] to address them. This model stipulated that software be developed in successive stages (operational plan, operational specifications, coding specifications, coding, parameter testing, assembly testing, shakedown, system evaluation).

The waterfall model,[3] illustrated in Figure 1, was a highly influential 1970 refinement of the stagewise model. It provided two primary enhancements to the stagewise model:

(1) Recognition of the feedback loops between stages, and a guideline to confine the feedback loops to successive stages to minimize the expensive rework involved in feedback across many stages.

(2) An initial incorporation of prototyping in the software life cycle, via a "build it twice" step running in parallel with requirements analysis and design.

The waterfall model's approach helped eliminate many difficulties previously encountered on software projects. The waterfall model has become the basis for most software acquisition standards in government and industry. Some of its initial difficulties have been addressed by adding extensions to cover incremental development, parallel developments, program families, accommodation of evolutionary changes, formal software development and verification, and stagewise validation and risk analysis.

However, even with extensive revisions and refinements, the waterfall model's basic scheme has encountered some more fundamental difficulties, and these have led to the formulation of alternative process models.

A primary source of difficulty with the waterfall model has been its emphasis on fully elaborated documents as completion criteria for early requirements and design phases. For some classes of software, such as compilers or secure operating systems, this is the most effective way to proceed. However, it does not work well for many classes of software, particularly interactive

---

The waterfall model has become the basis for most software acquisition standards.

---

end-user applications. Document-driven standards have pushed many projects to write elaborate specifications of poorly understood user interfaces and decision-support functions, followed by the design and development of large quantities of unusable code.

These projects are examples of how waterfall-model projects have come to grief by pursuing stages in the wrong order. Furthermore, in areas supported by fourth-generation languages (spreadsheet or small business applications), it is clearly unnecessary to write elaborate specifications for one's application before implementing it.

The evolutionary development model. The above concerns led to the formulation of the *evolutionary development* model,[4] whose stages consist of expanding increments of an operational software product, with the directions of evolution being determined by operational experience.

The evolutionary development model is ideally matched to a fourth-generation language application and well matched to situations in which users say, "I can't tell you what I want, but I'll know it when I see it." It gives users a rapid initial operational capability and provides a realistic operational basis for determining subsequent product improvements.

Nonetheless, evolutionary development also has its difficulties. It is generally difficult to distinguish it from the old code-and-fix model, whose spaghetti code and lack of planning were the initial motivation for the waterfall model. It is also based on the often-unrealistic assumption that the user's operational system will be flexible enough to accommodate unplanned evolution paths. This assumption is unjustified in three primary circumstances:

(1) Circumstances in which several independently evolved applications must subsequently be closely integrated.

(2) "Information-sclerosis" cases, in which temporary work-arounds for software deficiencies increasingly solidify into

unchangeable constraints on evolution. The following comment is a typical example: "It's nice that you could change those equipment codes to make them more intelligible for us, but the Codes Committee just met and established the current codes as company standards."

(3) Bridging situations, in which the new software is incrementally replacing a large existing system. If the existing system is poorly modularized, it is difficult to provide a good sequence of "bridges" between the old software and the expanding increments of new software.

Under such conditions, evolutionary development projects have come to grief by pursuing stages in the wrong order: evolving a lot of hard-to-change code before addressing long-range architectural and usage considerations.

The transform model. The "spaghetti code" difficulties of the evolutionary development and code-and-fix models can also become a difficulty in various classes of waterfall-model applications, in which code is optimized for performance and becomes increasingly hard to modify. The transform model[5] has been proposed as a solution to this dilemma.

The transform model assumes the existence of a capability to automatically convert a formal specification of a software product into a program satisfying the specification. The steps then prescribed by the transform model are

- a formal specification of the best initial understanding of the desired product;
- automatic transformation of the specification into code;
- an iterative loop, if necessary, to improve the performance of the resulting code by giving optimization guidance to the transformation system;
- exercise of the resulting product; and
- an outer iterative loop to adjust the specification based on the resulting operational experience, and to rederive, reoptimize, and exercise the adjusted software product.

The transform model thus bypasses the difficulty of having to modify code that has become poorly structured through repeated reoptimizations, since the modifications are made to the specification. It also avoids the extra time and expense involved in the intermediate design, code, and test activities.

Still, the transform model has various

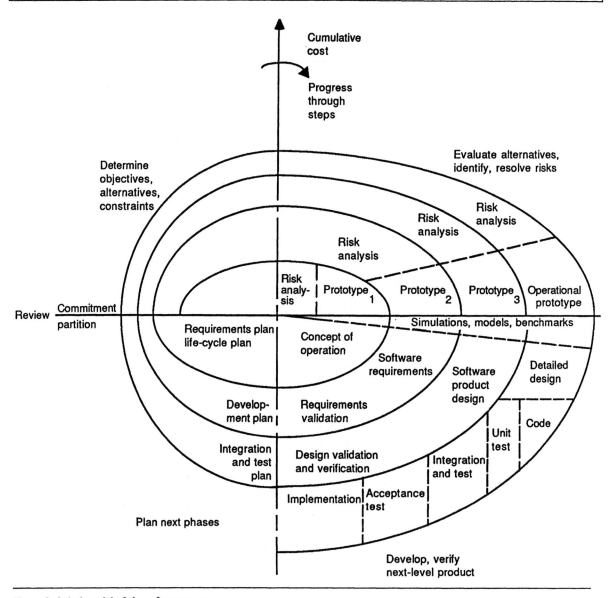

Figure 2. Spiral model of the software process.

difficulties. Automatic transformation capabilities are only available for small products in a few limited areas: spreadsheets, small fourth-generation language applications, and limited computer-science domains. The transform model also shares some of the difficulties of the evolutionary development model, such as the assumption that users' operational systems will always be flexible enough to support unplanned evolution paths.

Additionally, it would face a formidable knowledge-base-maintenance problem in dealing with the rapidly increasing and evolving supply of reusable software components and commercial software products. (Simply consider the problem of tracking the costs, performance, and features of all commercial database management systems, and automatically choosing the best one to implement each new or changed specification.)

The spiral model

The spiral model of the software process (see Figure 2) has been evolving for several years, based on experience with various refinements of the waterfall model as applied to large government software projects. As will be discussed, the spiral model can accommodate most previous models as special cases and further provides guidance as to which combination of previous models best fits a given software situation. Development of the TRW Software Productivity System (TRW-SPS), described in the next section, is its most complete application to date.

The radial dimension in Figure 2 represents the cumulative cost incurred in accomplishing the steps to date; the angular dimension represents the progress made in completing each cycle of the spiral. (The model reflects the underlying concept that each cycle involves a progression that addresses the same sequence of steps, for each portion of the product and for each of its levels of elaboration, from an overall concept of operation document down to the coding of each individual program.) Note that some artistic license has been taken with the increasing cumulative cost dimension to enhance legibility of the steps in Figure 2.

A typical cycle of the spiral. Each cycle of the spiral begins with the identification of

- the objectives of the portion of the product being elaborated (performance, functionality, ability to accommodate change, etc.);
- the alternative means of implementing this portion of the product (design A, design B, reuse, buy, etc.); and
- the constraints imposed on the application of the alternatives (cost, schedule, interface, etc.).

The next step is to evaluate the alternatives relative to the objectives and constraints. Frequently, this process will identify areas of uncertainty that are significant sources of project risk. If so, the next step should involve the formulation of a cost-effective strategy for resolving the sources of risk. This may involve prototyping, simulation, benchmarking, reference checking, administering user questionnaires, analytic modeling, or combinations of these and other risk-resolution techniques.

Once the risks are evaluated, the next step is determined by the relative remaining risks. If performance or user-interface risks strongly dominate program development or internal interface-control risks, the next step may be an evolutionary development one: a minimal effort to specify the overall nature of the product, a plan for the next level of prototyping, and the development of a more detailed prototype to continue to resolve the major risk issues.

If this prototype is operationally useful and robust enough to serve as a low-risk base for future product evolution, the subsequent risk-driven steps would be the evolving series of evolutionary prototypes going toward the right in Figure 2. In this case, the option of writing specifications would be addressed but not exercised. Thus, risk considerations can lead to a project implementing only a subset of all the potential steps in the model.

On the other hand, if previous prototyping efforts have already resolved all of the performance or user-interface risks, and program development or interface-control risks dominate, the next step follows the basic waterfall approach (concept of operation, software requirements, preliminary design, etc. in Figure 2), modified as appropriate to incorporate incremental development. Each level of software specification in the figure is then followed by a validation step and the preparation of plans for the succeeding cycle. In this case, the options to prototype, simulate, model, etc. are addressed but not exercised, leading to the use of a different subset of steps.

This risk-driven subsetting of the spiral model steps allows the model to accommodate any appropriate mixture of a specification-oriented, prototype-oriented, simulation-oriented, automatic transformation-oriented, or other approach to software development. In such cases, the appropriate mixed strategy is chosen by considering the relative magnitude of the program risks and the relative effectiveness of the various techniques in resolving the risks. In a similar way, risk-management considerations can determine the amount of time and effort that should be devoted to such other project activities as planning, configuration management, quality assurance, formal verification, and testing. In particular, risk-driven specifications (as discussed in the next section) can have varying degrees of completeness, formality, and granularity, depending on the relative risks of doing too little or too much specification.

An important feature of the spiral model, as with most other models, is that each cycle is completed by a review involving the primary people or organizations concerned with the product. This review covers all products developed during the previous cycle, including the plans for the next cycle and the resources required to carry them out. The review's major objective is to ensure that all concerned parties are mutually committed to the approach for the next phase.

The plans for succeeding phases may also include a partition of the product into increments for successive development or components to be developed by individual organizations or persons. For the latter case, visualize a series of parallel spiral cycles, one for each component, adding a third dimension to the concept presented in Figure 2. For example, separate spirals can be evolving for separate software components or increments. Thus, the review-and-commitment step may range from an individual walk-through of the design of a single programmer's component to a major requirements review involving developer, customer, user, and maintenance organizations.

Initiating and terminating the spiral. Four fundamental questions arise in considering this presentation of the spiral model:

(1) How does the spiral ever get started?
(2) How do you get off the spiral when it is appropriate to terminate a project early?
(3) Why does the spiral end so abruptly?
(4) What happens to software enhancement (or maintenance)?

The answer to these questions involves an observation that the spiral model applies equally well to development or enhancement efforts. In either case, the spiral gets started by a hypothesis that a particular operational mission (or set of missions) could be improved by a software effort. The spiral process then involves a test of this hypothesis: at any time, if the hypothesis fails the test (for example, if delays cause a software product to miss its market window, or if a superior commercial product becomes available), the spiral is terminated. Otherwise, it terminates with the installation of new or modified software, and the hypothesis is tested by observing the effect on the operational mission. Usually, experience with the operational mission leads to further hypotheses about software improvements, and a new maintenance spiral is initiated to test the hypothesis. Initiation, termination, and iteration of the tasks and products of previous cycles are thus implicitly defined in the spiral model (although they're not included in Figure 2 to simplify its presentation).

Using the spiral model

The various rounds and activities involved in the spiral model are best understood through use of an example. The spiral model was used in the definition and development of the TRW Software Productivity System (TRW-SPS), an integrated software engineering environment.[6] The initial mission opportunity coincided with a corporate initiative to improve productivity in all appropriate corporate operations and an initial hypothesis that software engineering was an attractive area to investigate. This led to a small, extra "Round 0" circuit of the spiral to determine the feasibility of increasing software productivity at a reasonable corporate cost. (Very large or complex software projects will frequently precede the "concept of operation" round of the spiral with one or more smaller rounds to establish feasibility and to reduce the range of alternative solutions quickly and inexpensively.)

Tables 1, 2, and 3 summarize the application of the spiral model to the first three rounds of defining the SPS. The major features of each round are subsequently discussed and are followed by some examples from later rounds, such as preliminary and detailed design.

Round 0: Feasibility study. This study involved five part-time participants over a two- to three-month period. As indicated in Table 1, the objectives and constraints were expressed at a very high level and in qualitative terms like "significantly increase," "at reasonable cost," etc.

Some of the alternatives considered, primarily those in the "technology" area, could lead to development of a software product, but the possible attractiveness of a number of non-software alternatives in the management, personnel, and facilities areas could have led to a conclusion not to embark on a software development activity.

The primary risk areas involved possible situations in which the company would invest a good deal only to find that

- resulting productivity gains were not significant, or

- potentially high-leverage improvements were not compatible with some aspects of the "TRW culture."

The risk-resolution activities undertaken in Round 0 were primarily surveys and analyses, including structured interviews of software developers and managers, an initial analysis of productivity leverage factors identified by the constructive cost model (Cocomo)[7]; and an analysis of previous projects at TRW exhibiting high levels of productivity.

The risk analysis results indicated that significant productivity gains could be achieved at a reasonable cost by pursuing an integrated set of initiatives in the four major areas. However, some candidate solutions, such as a software support environment based on a single, corporate, maxicomputer-based time-sharing system, were found to be in conflict with TRW constraints requiring support of different levels of security-classified projects. Thus, even at a very high level of generality of objectives and constraints, Round 0 was able to answer basic feasibility questions and eliminate significant classes of candidate solutions.

The plan for Round 1 involved commitment of 12 man-months compared to the two man-months invested in Round 0 (during these rounds, all participants were part-time). Round 1 here corresponded fairly well to the initial round of the spiral model shown in Figure 2, in that its intent was to produce a concept of operation and a basic life-cycle plan for implementing whatever preferred alternative emerged.

Round 1: Concept of operations. Table 2 summarizes Round 1 of the spiral along the lines given in Table 1 for Round 0. The features of Round 1 compare to those of Round 0 as follows:

- The level of investment was greater (12 versus 2 man-months).

- The objectives and constraints were more specific ("double software productivity in five years at a cost of $10,000 a person" versus "significantly increase productivity at a reasonable cost").

- Additional constraints surfaced, such as the preference for TRW products (particularly, a TRW-developed local area network (LAN) system).

- The alternatives were more detailed ("SREM, PSL/PSA or SADT, as requirements tools etc." versus "tools"; "private/shared" terminals, "smart/dumb" terminals versus "workstations").

- The risk areas identified were more specific ("TRW LAN price-performance

Table 1. Spiral model usage: TRW Software Productivity System, Round 0.

Objectives	Significantly increase software productivity
Constraints	At reasonable cost
	Within context of TRW culture
	• Government contracts, high tech., people oriented, security
Alternatives	Management: Project organization, policies, planning, control
	Personnel: Staffing, incentives, training
	Technology: Tools, workstations, methods, reuse
	Facilities: Offices, communications
Risks	May be no high-leverage improvements
	Improvements may violate constraints
Risk resolution	Internal surveys
	Analyze cost model
	Analyze exceptional projects
	Literature search
Risk resolution results	Some alternatives infeasible
	• Single time-sharing system: Security
	Mix of alternatives can produce significant gains
	• Factor of two in five years
	Need further study to determine best mix
Plan for next phase	Six-person task force for six months
	More extensive surveys and analysis
	• Internal, external, economic
	Develop concept of operation, economic rationale
Commitment	Fund next phase

420

within a $10,000-per-person investment constraint" versus "improvements may violate reasonable-cost constraint").

• The risk-resolution activities were more extensive (including the benchmarking and analysis of a prototype TRW LAN being developed for another project).

• The result was a fairly specific operational concept document, involving private offices tailored to software work patterns and personal terminals connected to VAX superminis via the TRW LAN. Some choices were specifically deferred to the next round, such as the choice of operating system and specific tools.

• The life-cycle plan and the plan for the next phase involved a partitioning into separate activities to address management improvements, facilities development, and development of the first increment of a software development environment.

• The commitment step involved more than just an agreement with the plan. It committed to apply the environment to an upcoming 100-person testbed software project and to develop an environment focusing on the testbed project's needs. It also specified forming a representative steering group to ensure that the separate activities were well-coordinated and that the environment would not be overly optimized around the testbed project.

Although the plan recommended developing a prototype environment, it also recommended that the project employ requirements specifications and design specifications in a risk-driven way. Thus, the development of the environment followed the succeeding rounds of the spiral model.

Round 2: Top-level requirements specification. Table 3 shows the corresponding steps involved during Round 2 defining the software productivity system. Round 2 decisions and their rationale were covered in earlier work[6]; here, we will summarize the considerations dealing with risk management and the use of the spiral model:

• The initial risk-identification activities during Round 2 showed that several system requirements hinged on the decision between a host-target system or a fully portable tool set and the decision between VMS and Unix as the host operating system. These requirements included the functions needed to provide a user-friendly front-end, the operating system to be used by the workstations, and the functions necessary to support a host-target

operation. To keep these requirements in synchronization with the others, a special minispiral was initiated to address and resolve these issues. The resulting review led to a commitment to a host-target operation using Unix on the host system, at a point early enough to work the OS-dependent requirements in a timely fashion.

• Addressing the risks of mismatches to the user-project's needs and priorities resulted in substantial participation of the user-project personnel in the requirements definition activity. This led to several significant redirections of the requirements, particularly toward supporting the early phases of the software life-cycle into which the user project was embarking, such as an adaptation of the software requirements engineering methodology (SREM) tools

for requirements specification and analysis.

It is also interesting to note that the form of Tables 1, 2, and 3 was originally developed for presentation purposes, but subsequently became a standard "spiral model template" used on later projects. These templates are useful not only for organizing project activities, but also as a residual design-rationale record. Design rationale information is of paramount importance in assessing the potential reusability of software components on future projects. Another important point to note is that the use of the template was indeed uniform across the three cycles, showing that the spiral steps can be and were uniformly followed at successively detailed levels of product definition.

Table 2. Spiral model usage: TRW Software Productivity System, Round 1.

Objectives	Double software productivity in five years
Constraints	$10,000 per person investment Within context of TRW culture • Government contracts, high tech., people oriented, security Preference for TRW products
Alternatives	Office: Private/modular/. . . Communication: LAN/star/concentrators/. . . Terminals: Private/shared; smart/dumb Tools: SREM/PSL-PSA/. . .; PDL/SADT/. . . CPU: IBM/DEC/CDC/. . .
Risks	May miss high-leverage options TRW LAN price/performance Workstation cost
Risk resolution	Extensive external surveys, visits TRW LAN benchmarking Workstation price projections
Risk resolution results	Operations concept: Private offices, TRW LAN, personal terminals, VAX Begin with primarily dumb terminals; experiment with smart workstations Defer operating system, tools selection
Plan for next phase	Partition effort into software development environment (SDE), facilities, management Develop first-cut, prototype SDE • Design-to-cost: 15-person team for one year Plan for external usage
Commitment	Develop prototype SDE Commit an upcoming project to use SDE Commit the SDE to support the project Form representative steering group

Succeeding rounds. It will be useful to illustrate some examples of how the spiral model is used to handle situations arising in the preliminary design and detailed design of components of the SPS: the preliminary design specification for the requirements traceability tool (RTT), and a detailed design rework or go-back on the unit development folder (UDF) tool.

The RTT preliminary design specification. The RTT establishes the traceability between itemized software requirements specifications, design elements, code elements, and test cases. It also supports various associated query, analysis, and report generation capabilities. The preliminary design specification for the RTT (and most of the other SPS tools) looks different from the usual preliminary design specification, which tends to show a uniform level of elaboration of all components of the design. Instead, the level of detail of the RTT specification is risk-driven.

In areas involving a high risk if the design turned out to be wrong, the design was carried down to the detailed design level, usually with the aid of rapid prototyping. These areas included working out the implications of "undo" options and dealing with the effects of control keys used to escape from various program levels.

In areas involving a moderate risk if the design was wrong, the design was carried down to a preliminary-design level. These areas included the basic command options for the tool and the schemata for the requirements traceability database. Here again, the ease of rapid prototyping with Unix shell scripts supported a good deal of user-interface prototyping.

In areas involving a low risk if the design was wrong, very little design elaboration was done. These areas included details of all the help message options and all the report-generation options, once the nature of these options was established in some example instances.

A detailed design go-back. The UDF tool collects into an electronic "folder" all artifacts involved in the development of a single-programmer software unit (typically 500 to 1,000 instructions): unit requirements, design, code, test cases, test results, and documentation. It also includes a management template for tracking the programmer's scheduled and actual completion of each artifact.

An alternative considered during detailed design of the UDF tool was reuse of portions of the RTT to provide pointers to the requirements and preliminary design specifications of the unit being developed. This turned out to be an extremely attractive alternative, not only for avoiding duplicate software development but also for bringing to the surface several issues involving many-to-many mappings between requirements, design, and code that had not been considered in designing the UDF tool. These led to a rethinking of the UDF tool requirements and preliminary design, which avoided a great deal of code rework that would have been necessary if the detailed design of the UDF tool had proceeded in a purely deductive, top-down fashion from the original UDF requirements specification. The resulting go-back led to a significantly different, less costly, and more capable UDF tool, incorporating the RTT in its "uses-hierarchy."

Spiral model features. These two examples illustrate several features of the spiral approach.

• It fosters the development of specifications that are not necessarily uniform, exhaustive, or formal, in that they defer detailed elaboration of low-risk software elements and avoid unnecessary breakage in their design until the high-risk elements of the design are stabilized.

• It incorporates prototyping as a risk-reduction option at any stage of development. In fact, prototyping and reuse risk analyses were often used in the process of going from detailed design into code.

• It accommodates reworks or go-backs to earlier stages as more attractive alternatives are identified or as new risk issues need resolution.

Overall, risk-driven documents, particularly specifications and plans, are important features of the spiral model. Great amounts of detail are not necessary unless the absence of such detail jeopardizes the

Table 3. Spiral model usage: TRW Software Productivity System, Round 2.

Objectives	User-friendly system
	Integrated software, office-automation tools
	Support all project personnel
	Support all life-cycle phases
Constraints	Customer-deliverable SDE $\Rightarrow$ Portability
	Stable, reliable service
Alternatives	OS: VMS/AT&T Unix/Berkeley Unix/ISC
	Host-target/fully portable tool set
	Workstations: Zenith/LSI-11/. . .
Risks	Mismatch to user-project needs, priorities
	User-unfriendly system
	• 12-language syndrome; experts-only
	Unix performance, support
	Workstation/mainframe compatibility
Risk resolution	User-project surveys, requirements participation
	Survey of Unix-using organizations
	Workstation study
Risk resolution results	Top-level requirements specification
	Host-target with Unix host
	Unix-based workstations
	Build user-friendly front end for Unix
	Initial focus on tools to support early phases
Plan for next phase	Overall development plan
	• for tools: SREM, RTT, PDL, office automation tools
	• for front end: Support tools
	• for LAN: Equipment, facilities
Commitment	Proceed with plans

project. In some cases, such as with a product whose functionality may be determined by a choice among commercial products, a set of weighted evaluation criteria for the products may be preferable to a detailed pre-statement of functional requirements.

Results. The Software Productivity System developed and supported using the spiral model avoided the identified risks and achieved most of the system's objectives. The SPS has grown to include over 300 tools and over 1,300,000 instructions; 93 percent of the instructions were reused from previous project-developed, TRW-developed, or external-software packages. Over 25 projects have used all or portions of the system. All of the projects fully using the system have increased their productivity at least 50 percent; indeed, most have doubled their productivity (when compared with cost-estimation model predictions of their productivity using traditional methods).

However, one risk area—that projects with non-Unix target systems would not accept a Unix-based host system—was underestimated. Some projects accepted the host-target approach, but for various reasons (such as customer constraints and zero-cost target machines) a good many did not. As a result, the system was less widely used on TRW projects than expected. This and other lessons learned have been incorporated into the spiral model approach to developing TRW's next-generation software development environment.

Evaluation

Advantages. The primary advantage of the spiral model is that its range of options accommodates the good features of existing software process models, while its risk-driven approach avoids many of their difficulties. In appropriate situations, the spiral model becomes equivalent to one of the existing process models. In other situations, it provides guidance on the best mix of existing approaches to a given project; for example, its application to the TRW-SPS provided a risk-driven mix of specifying, prototyping, and evolutionary development.

The primary conditions under which the spiral model becomes equivalent to other main process models are summarized as follows:

• If a project has a low risk in such areas

All of the projects fully using the system have increased their productivity at least 50 percent.

---

as getting the wrong user interface or not meeting stringent performance requirements, and if it has a high risk in budget and schedule predictability and control, then these risk considerations drive the spiral model into an equivalence to the waterfall model.

• If a software product's requirements are very stable (implying a low risk of expensive design and code breakage due to requirements changes during development), and if the presence of errors in the software product constitutes a high risk to the mission it serves, then these risk considerations drive the spiral model to resemble the two-leg model of precise specification and formal deductive program development.

• If a project has a low risk in such areas as losing budget and schedule predictability and control, encountering large-system integration problems, or coping with information sclerosis, and if it has a high risk in such areas as getting the wrong user interface or user decision support requirements, then these risk considerations drive the spiral model into an equivalence to the evolutionary development model.

• If automated software generation capabilities are available, then the spiral model accommodates them either as options for rapid prototyping or for application of the transform model, depending on the risk considerations involved.

• If the high-risk elements of a project involve a mix of the risk items listed above, then the spiral approach will reflect an appropriate mix of the process models above (as exemplified in the TRW-SPS application). In doing so, its risk-avoidance features will generally avoid the difficulties of the other models.

The spiral model has a number of additional advantages, summarized as follows:

It focuses early attention on options involving the reuse of existing software. The steps involving the identification and evaluation of alternatives encourage these options.

It accommodates preparation for life-cycle evolution, growth, and changes of the software product. The major sources of product change are included in the product's objectives, and information-hiding approaches are attractive architectural design alternatives in that they reduce the risk of not being able to accommodate the product-charge objectives.

It provides a mechanism for incorporating software quality objectives into software product development. This mechanism derives from the emphasis on identifying all types of objectives and constraints during each round of the spiral. For example, Table 3 shows user-friendliness, portability, and reliability as specific objectives and constraints to be addressed by the SPS. In Table 1, security constraints were identified as a key risk item for the SPS.

It focuses on eliminating errors and unattractive alternatives early. The risk-analysis, validation, and commitment steps cover these considerations.

For each of the sources of project activity and resource expenditure, it answers the key question, "How much is enough?" Stated another way, "How much of requirements analysis, planning, configuration management, quality assurance, testing, formal verification, etc. should a project do?" Using the risk-driven approach, one can see that the answer is not the same for all projects and that the appropriate level of effort is determined by the level of risk incurred by not doing enough.

It does not involve separate approaches for software development and software enhancement (or maintenance). This aspect helps avoid the "second-class citizen" status frequently associated with software maintenance. It also helps avoid many of the problems that currently ensue when high-risk enhancement efforts are approached in the same way as routine maintenance efforts.

It provides a viable framework for integrated hardware-software system development. The focus on risk-management and on eliminating unattractive alternatives early and inexpensively is equally applicable to hardware and software.

Difficulties. The full spiral model can be successfully applied in many situations, but some difficulties must be addressed before it can be called a mature, universally applicable model. The three primary challenges involve matching to contract software, relying on risk-assessment expertise, and the need for further elaboration of spiral model steps.

Matching to contract software. The spiral model currently works well on internal software developments like the TRW-SPS, but it needs further work to match it to the world of contract software acquisition.

Internal software developments have a great deal of flexibility and freedom to accommodate stage-by-stage commitments, to defer commitments to specific options, to establish minispirals to resolve critical-path items, to adjust levels of effort, or to accommodate such practices as prototyping, evolutionary development, or design-to-cost. The world of contract software acquisition has a harder time achieving these degrees of flexibility and freedom without losing accountability and control, and a harder time defining contracts whose deliverables are not well specified in advance.

Recently, a good deal of progress has been made in establishing more flexible contract mechanisms, such as the use of competitive front-end contracts for concept definition or prototype fly-offs, the use of level-of-effort and award-fee contracts for evolutionary development, and the use of design-to-cost contracts. Although these have been generally successful, the procedures for using them still need to be worked out to the point that acquisition managers feel fully comfortable using them.

Table 4. A prioritized top-ten list of software risk items.

Risk item	Risk management techniques
1. Personnel shortfalls	Staffing with top talent, job matching; teambuilding; morale building; cross-training; pre-scheduling key people
2. Unrealistic schedules and budgets	Detailed, multisource cost and schedule estimation; design to cost; incremental development; software reuse; requirements scrubbing
3. Developing the wrong software functions	Organization analysis; mission analysis; ops-concept formulation; user surveys; prototyping; early users' manuals
4. Developing the wrong user interface	Task analysis; prototyping; scenarios; user characterization (functionality, style, workload)
5. Gold plating	Requirements scrubbing; prototyping; cost-benefit analysis; design to cost
6. Continuing stream of requirement changes	High change threshold; information hiding; incremental development (defer changes to later increments)
7. Shortfalls in externally furnished components	Benchmarking; inspections; reference checking; compatibility analysis
8. Shortfalls in externally performed tasks	Reference checking; pre-award audits; award-fee contracts; competitive design or prototyping; teambuilding
9. Real-time performance shortfalls	Simulation; benchmarking; modeling; prototyping; instrumentation; tuning
10. Straining computer-science capabilities	Technical analysis; cost-benefit analysis; prototyping; reference checking

Relying on risk-assessment expertise. The spiral model places a great deal of reliance on the ability of software developers to identify and manage sources of project risk.

A good example of this is the spiral model's risk-driven specification, which carries high-risk elements down to a great deal of detail and leaves low-risk elements to be elaborated in later stages; by this time, there is less risk of breakage.

However, a team of inexperienced or low-balling developers may also produce a specification with a different pattern of variation in levels of detail: a great elaboration of detail for the well-understood, low-risk elements, and little elaboration of the poorly understood, high-risk elements. Unless there is an insightful review of such a specification by experienced development or acquisition personnel, this type of project will give an illusion of progress during a period in which it is actually heading for disaster.

Another concern is that a risk-driven specification will also be people-dependent. For example, a design produced by an expert may be implemented by non-experts. In this case, the expert, who does not need a great deal of detailed documentation, must produce enough additional documentation to keep the non-experts from going astray. Reviewers of the specification must also be

Table 5. Software Risk Management Plan.

1.	Identify the project's top 10 risk items.
2.	Present a plan for resolving each risk item.
3.	Update list of top risk items, plan, and results monthly.
4.	Highlight risk-item status in monthly project reviews. • Compare with previous month's rankings, status.
5.	Initiate appropriate corrective actions.

sensitive to these concerns.

With a conventional, document-driven approach, the requirement to carry all aspects of the specification to a uniform level of detail eliminates some potential problems and permits adequate review of some aspects by inexperienced reviewers. But it also creates a large drain on the time of the scarce experts, who must dig for the critical issues within a large mass of noncritical detail. Furthermore, if the high-risk elements have been glossed over by impressive-sounding references to poorly understood capabilities (such as a new synchronization concept or a commercial DBMS), there is an even greater risk that the conventional approach will give the illusion of progress in situations that are actually heading for disaster.

Need for further elaboration of spiral model steps. In general, the spiral model process steps need further elaboration to ensure that all software development participants are operating in a consistent context.

Some examples of this are the need for more detailed definitions of the nature of spiral model specifications and milestones, the nature and objectives of spiral model reviews, techniques for estimating and synchronizing schedules, and the nature of spiral model status indicators and cost-versus-progress tracking procedures. Another need is for guidelines and checklists to identify the most likely sources of project risk and the most effective risk-resolution techniques for each source of risk.

Highly experienced people can successfully use the spiral approach without these elaborations. However, for large-scale use in situations where people bring widely differing experience bases to the project, added levels of elaboration—such as have been accumulated over the years for document-driven approaches—are important in ensuring consistent interpretation and use of the spiral approach across the project.

Efforts to apply and refine the spiral model have focused on creating a discipline of software risk management, including techniques for risk identification, risk analysis, risk prioritization, risk-management planning, and risk-element tracking. The prioritized top-ten list of software risk items given in Table 4 is one result of this activity. Another example is the risk management plan discussed in the next section.

Implications: The Risk Management Plan. Even if an organization is not ready to adopt the entire spiral approach, one characteristic technique that can easily be adapted to any life-cycle model provides many of the benefits of the spiral approach. This is the Risk Management Plan summarized in Table 5. This plan basically ensures that each project makes an early identification of its top risk items (the number 10 is not an absolute requirement), develops a strategy for resolving the risk items, identifies and sets down an agenda to resolve new risk items as they surface, and highlights progress versus plans in monthly reviews.

The Risk Management Plan has been used successfully at TRW and other organizations. Its use has ensured appropriate focus on early prototyping, simulation, benchmarking, key-person staffing measures, and other early risk-resolution techniques that have helped avoid many potential project "show-stoppers." The recent US Department of Defense standard on software management, DoD-Std-2167, requires that developers produce and use risk management plans, as does its counterpart US Air Force regulation, AFR 800-14.

Overall, the Risk Management Plan and the maturing set of techniques for software risk management provide a foundation for tailoring spiral model concepts into the more established software acquisition and development procedures.

W e can draw four conclusions from the data presented:

(1) The risk-driven nature of the spiral model is more adaptable to the full range of software project situations than are the primarily document-driven approaches such as the waterfall model or the primarily code-driven approaches such as evolutionary development. It is particularly applicable to very large, complex, ambitious software systems.

(2) The spiral model has been quite successful in its largest application to date: the development and enhancement of the TRW-SPS. Overall, it achieved a high level of software support environment capability in a very short time and provided the flexibility necessary to accommodate a high dynamic range of technical alternatives and user objectives.

(3) The spiral model is not yet as fully elaborated as the more established models. Therefore, the spiral model can be applied by experienced personnel, but it needs further elaboration in such areas as contract-

ing, specifications, milestones, reviews, scheduling, status monitoring, and risk-area identification to be fully usable in all situations.

(4) Partial implementations of the spiral model, such as the Risk Management Plan, are compatible with most current process models and are very helpful in overcoming major sources of project risk. □

Acknowledgments

I would like to thank Frank Belz, Lolo Penedo, George Spadaro, Bob Williams, Bob Balzer, Gillian Frewin, Peter Hamer, Manny Lehman, Lee Osterweil, Dave Parnas, Bill Riddle, Steve Squires, and Dick Thayer, along with the *Computer* reviewers of this article, for their stimulating and insightful comments and discussions of earlier versions of the article, and Nancy Donato for producing its several versions.

References

1. F.P. Brooks et al., *Defense Science Board Task Force Report on Military Software*, Office of the Under Secretary of Defense for Acquisition, Washington, DC 20301, Sept. 1987.

2. H.D. Benington, "Production of Large Computer Programs," *Proc. ONR Symp. Advanced Programming Methods for Digital Computers*, June 1956, pp. 15-27. Also available in *Annals of the History of Computing*, Oct. 1983, pp. 350-361, and *Proc. Ninth Int'l Conf. Software Engineering*, Computer Society Press, 1987.

3. W.W. Royce, "Managing the Development of Large Software Systems: Concepts and Techniques," *Proc. Wescon*, Aug. 1970. Also available in *Proc. ICSE 9*, Computer Society Press, 1987.

4. D.D. McCracken and M.A. Jackson, "Life-Cycle Concept Considered Harmful," *ACM Software Engineering Notes*, Apr. 1982, pp. 29-32.

5. R. Balzer, T.E. Cheatham, and C. Green, "Software Technology in the 1990s: Using a New Paradigm," *Computer*, Nov. 1983, pp. 39-45.

6. B.W. Boehm et al., "A Software Development Environment for Improving Productivity," *Computer*, June 1984, pp. 30-44.

7. B.W. Boehm, *Software Engineering Economics*, Prentice-Hall, 1981, Chap. 33.

Further reading

The software process model field has an interesting history, and a great deal of stimulating work has been produced recently in this specialized area. Besides the references that appear at the end of the accompanying article, here are some additional good sources of insight:

Overall process model issues and results

Agresti's tutorial volume provides a good overview and set of key articles. The three recent *Software Process Workshop Proceedings* provide access to much of the recent work in the area.

Agresti, W.W., *New Paradigms for Software Development*, IEEE Catalog No. EH0245-1, 1986.

Dowson, M., ed., *Proc. Third Int'l Software Process Workshop*, IEEE Catalog No. TH0184-2, Nov. 1986.

Potts, C., ed., *Proc. Software Process Workshop*, IEEE Catalog No. 84CH2044-6, Feb. 1984.

Wileden, J.C., and M. Dowson, eds., Proc. Int'l Workshop Software Process and Software Environments, *ACM Software Engineering Notes*, Aug. 1986.

Alternative process models

More detailed information on waterfall-type approaches is given in:

Evans, M.W., P. Piazza, and J.P. Dolkas, *Principles of Productive Software Management*, John Wiley & Sons, 1983.

Hice, G.F., W.J. Turner, and L.F. Cashwell, *System Development Methodology*, North Holland, 1974 (2nd ed., 1981).

More detailed information on evolutionary development is provided in:

Gilb, T., *Principles of Software Engineering Management*, Addison Wesley, 1988 (currently in publication).

Some additional process model approaches with useful features and insights may be found in:

Lehman, M.M., and L.A. Belady, *Program Evolution: Processes of Software Change*, Academic Press, 1985.

Osterweil, L., "Software Processes are Software, Too," *Proc. ICSE 9*, IEEE Catalog No. 87CH2432-3, Mar. 1987, pp. 2-13.

Radice, R.A., et al., "A Programming Process Architecture," *IBM Systems J.*, Vol. 24, No.2, 1985, pp. 79-90.

Spiral and spiral-type models

Some further treatments of spiral model issues and practices are:

Belz, F.C., "Applying the Spiral Model: Observations on Developing System Software in Ada," *Proc. 1986 Annual Conf. on Ada Technology,* Atlanta, 1986, pp. 57-66.

Boehm, B.W., and F.C. Belz, "Applying Process Programming to the Spiral Model," *Proc. Fourth Software Process Workshop*, IEEE, May 1988.

Iivari, J., "A Hierarchical Spiral Model for the Software Process," *ACM Software Engineering Notes,* Jan. 1987, pp. 35-37.

Some similar cyclic spiral-type process models from other fields are described in:

Carlsson, B., P. Keane, and J.B. Martin, "R&D Organizations as Learning Systems," *Sloan Management Review,* Spring 1976, pp. 1-15.

Fisher, R., and W. Ury, *Getting to Yes*, Houghton Mifflin, 1981; Penguin Books, 1983, pp. 68-71.

Kolb, D.A., "On Management and the Learning Process," MIT Sloan School Working Article 652-73, Cambridge, Mass., 1973.

Software risk management

The discipline of software risk management provides a bridge between spiral model concepts and currently established software acquisition and development procedures.

Boehm, B.W., "Software Risk Management Tutorial," Computer Society, Apr. 1988.

Risk Assessment Techniques, Defense Systems Management College, Ft. Belvoir, Va. 22060, July 1983.

The Capability Maturity Model for Software

Mark C. Paulk

Software Engineering Institute
Carnegie Mellon University
Pittsburgh, PA 15213-3890

Bill Curtis

TeraQuest Metrics, Inc.
P.O. Box 200490
Austin, TX 78720-0490

Mary Beth Chrissis

Software Engineering Institute
Carnegie Mellon University
Pittsburgh, PA 15213-3890

Charles V. Weber

Lockheed Martin Federal Systems Company
6304 Spine Road
Boulder, CO 80301

Abstract

This paper provides an overview of the latest version of the Capability Maturity Model[SM] for Software, CMM[SM] v1.1. CMM v1.1 describes the software engineering and management practices that characterize organizations as they mature their processes for developing and maintaining software. This paper stresses the need for a process maturity framework to prioritize improvement actions, describes the five maturity levels, key process areas, and their common features, and discusses future directions for the CMM.

Keywords: capability maturity model, CMM, software process improvement, process capability, maturity level, key process area, software process assessment, software capability evaluation.

1 Introduction

After decades of unfulfilled promises about productivity and quality gains from applying new software methodologies and technologies, organizations are realizing that their fundamental problem is the inability to manage the software process. In many organizations, projects are often excessively late and over budget, and the benefits of better methods and tools cannot be realized in the maelstrom of an undisciplined, chaotic project.

In November 1986, the Software Engineering Institute (SEI), with assistance from the Mitre Corporation, began developing a process maturity framework that would help organizations improve their software process. In September 1987, the SEI released a brief description of the process maturity framework, which was later expanded in Watts Humphrey's book, *Managing the Software Process* [Humphrey89]. Two methods, software process assessment[1] and software capability evaluation[2] were developed to appraise software process maturity.

After four years of experience with the software

---

[1] A software process assessment is an appraisal by a trained team of software professionals to determine the state of an organization's current software process, to determine the high-priority software process-related issues facing an organization, and to obtain the organizational support for software process improvement.

[2] A software capability evaluation is an appraisal by a trained team of professionals to identify contractors who are qualified to perform the software work or to monitor the state of the software process used on an existing software effort.

process maturity framework, the SEI evolved the maturity framework into the Capability Maturity Model for Software (CMM or SW-CMM[3]). The CMM presents sets of recommended practices in a number of key process areas that have been shown to enhance software process capability. The CMM is based on knowledge acquired from software process assessments and extensive feedback from both industry and government.

The CMM provides software organizations with guidance on how to gain control of their processes for developing and maintaining software and how to evolve toward a culture of software engineering and management excellence. The CMM was designed to guide software organizations in selecting process improvement strategies by determining current process maturity and identifying the most critical issues for software quality and process improvement. By focusing on a limited set of activities and working aggressively to achieve them, an organization can steadily improve its organization-wide software process to enable continuous and lasting gains in software process capability.

The initial release of the CMM, version 1.0, was reviewed and used by the software community during 1991 and 1992. The current version of the CMM, version 1.1, was released in 1993 [Paulk95a] and is the result of extensive feedback from the software community. The CMM has evolved significantly since 1986 [Paulk95b], and the SEI is currently working on version 2.

1.1 Immature Versus Mature Software Organizations

Setting sensible goals for process improvement requires an understanding of the difference between immature and mature software organizations. In an immature software organization, software processes are generally improvised by practitioners and their management during the course of the project. Even if a software process has been specified, it is not rigorously followed or enforced. The immature software organization is reactionary, and managers are usually focused on solving immediate crises (better known as fire fighting). Schedules and budgets are routinely exceeded because they are not based on realistic esti-

mates. When hard deadlines are imposed, product functionality and quality are often compromised to meet the schedule.

In an immature organization, there is no objective basis for judging product quality or for solving product or process problems. Therefore, product quality is difficult to predict. Activities intended to enhance quality such as reviews and testing are often curtailed or eliminated when projects fall behind schedule.

On the other hand, a mature software organization possesses an organization-wide ability for managing software development and maintenance processes. The software process is accurately communicated to both existing staff and new employees, and work activities are carried out according to the planned process. The mandated processes are usable and consistent with the way the work actually gets done. These defined processes are updated when necessary, and improvements are developed through controlled pilot-tests and/or cost benefit analyses. Roles and responsibilities within the defined process are clear throughout the project and across the organization.

In a mature organization, managers monitor the quality of the software products and the process that produced them. There is an objective, quantitative basis for judging product quality and analyzing problems with the product and process. Schedules and budgets are based on historical performance and are realistic; the expected results for cost, schedule, functionality, and quality of the product are usually achieved. In general, a disciplined process is consistently followed because all of the participants understand the value of doing so, and the necessary infrastructure exists to support the process.

1.2 Fundamental Concepts Underlying Process Maturity

A *software process* can be defined as a set of activities, methods, practices, and transformations that people use to develop and maintain software and the associated products (for instance, project plans, design documents, code, test cases, and user manuals). As an organization matures, the software process becomes better defined and more consistently implemented throughout the organization.

Software process capability describes the range of expected results that can be achieved by following a software process. An organization's software process capability is one way of predicting the most likely outcome to expect from the next software project the organization undertakes.

Software process performance represents the actual results achieved by following a software process. Thus, software process performance focuses on

---

[3] A number of CMMs inspired by the CMM for Software have now been developed, including the Systems Engineering CMM [Bate95] and the People CMM [Curtis95]. Additional CMMs are being developed on software acquisition and integrated product development. To minimize confusion, we are starting to use SW-CMM to distinguish the original CMM for Software, but since this paper focuses on software engineering, we will use the CMM acronym.

the results achieved, while software process capability focuses on results expected.

Software process maturity is the extent to which a specific process is explicitly defined, managed, measured, controlled, and effective. Maturity implies a potential for growth in capability and indicates both the richness of an organization's software process and the consistency with which it is applied in projects throughout the organization.

As a software organization gains in software process maturity, it institutionalizes its software process via policies, standards, and organizational structures. Institutionalization entails building an infrastructure and a corporate culture that supports the methods, practices, and procedures of the business so that they endure after those who originally defined them have gone.

2   The Five Levels of Software Process Maturity

Continuous process improvement is based on many small, evolutionary steps rather than revolutionary innovations. The staged structure of the CMM is based on principles of product quality espoused by Walter Shewart, W. Edwards Deming, Joseph Juran, and Philip Crosby. The CMM provides a framework for organizing these evolutionary steps into five maturity levels that lay successive foundations for continuous process improvement. These five maturity levels define an ordinal scale for measuring the maturity of an organization's software process and for evaluating its software process capability. The levels also help an organization prioritize its improvement efforts.

A *maturity level* is a well-defined evolutionary plateau toward achieving a mature software process. Each maturity level comprises a set of process goals that, when satisfied, stabilize an important component of the software process. Achieving each level of the maturity framework establishes a higher level of process capability for the organization.

Organizing the CMM into the five levels shown in Figure 2.1 prioritizes improvement actions for increasing software process maturity. The labeled arrows in Figure 2.1 indicate the type of process capability being institutionalized by the organization at each step of the maturity framework.

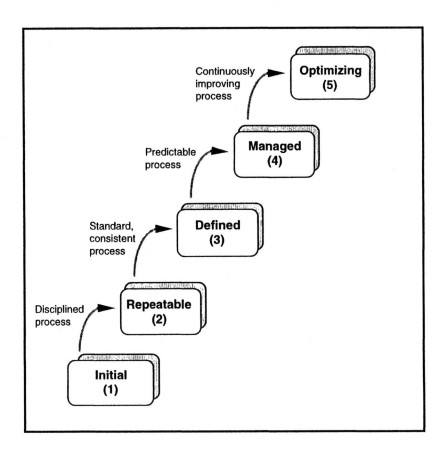

Figure 2.1   The five levels of software process maturity

The five levels can be briefly described as:

1) Initial	The software process is characterized as ad hoc, and occasionally even chaotic. Few processes are defined, and success depends on individual effort and heroics.
2) Repeatable	Basic project management processes are established to track cost, schedule, and functionality. The necessary process discipline is in place to repeat earlier successes on projects with similar applications.
3) Defined	The software process for both management and engineering activities is documented, standardized, and integrated into a standard software process for the organization. All projects use an approved, tailored version of the organization's standard software process for developing and maintaining software.
4) Managed	Detailed measures of the software process and product quality are collected. Both the software process and products are quantitatively understood and controlled.
5) Optimizing	Continuous process improvement is enabled by quantitative feedback from the process and from piloting innovative ideas and technologies.

These five levels reflect the fact that the CMM is a model for improving the capability of software organizations. The priorities in the CMM, as expressed by these levels, are not directed at individual projects. A project that is in trouble might well prioritize its problems differently than the taxonomy given by the CMM. Its solutions might be of limited value to the rest of the organization, because other projects might have different problems or because other projects could not take advantage of its solutions if they lack the necessary foundation to implement the solutions. The CMM focuses on processes that are of value across the organization.

2.1 Behavioral Characterization of the Maturity Levels

Maturity Levels 2 through 5 can be characterized through the activities performed by the organization to establish or improve the software process, by activities performed on each project, and by the resulting process capability across projects. A behavioral characterization of Level 1 is included to establish a base of comparison for process improvements at higher maturity levels.

2.1.1 Level 1—The Initial Level

At the Initial Level, the organization typically does not provide a stable environment for developing and maintaining software. Over-commitment is a characteristic of Level 1 organizations, and such organizations frequently have difficulty making commitments that the staff can meet with an orderly engineering process, resulting in a series of crises. During a crisis, projects typically abandon planned procedures and revert to coding and testing. Success depends on hav-

ing an exceptional manager and a seasoned and effective software team. Occasionally, capable and forceful software managers can withstand the pressures to take shortcuts in the software process; but when they leave the project, their stabilizing influence leaves with them. Even a strong engineering process cannot overcome the instability created by the absence of sound management practices.

In spite of this ad hoc, even chaotic, process, Level 1 organizations frequently develop products that work, even though they may exceed the budget and schedule. Success in Level 1 organizations depends on the competence and heroics of the people in the organization[4] and cannot be repeated unless the same competent individuals are assigned to the next project. Thus, at Level 1, capability is a characteristic of the individuals, not of the organization.

2.1.2 Level 2—The Repeatable Level

At the Repeatable Level, policies for managing a software project and procedures to implement those policies are established. Planning and managing new projects is based on experience with similar projects. Process capability is enhanced by establishing basic process management discipline on a project by project basis. Projects implement effective processes that are defined, documented, practiced, trained, measured, enforced, and able to improve.

Projects in Level 2 organizations have installed basic software management controls. Realistic project commitments are made, based on the results observed on previous projects and on the requirements of the current project. The software managers for a project

---

[4] Selecting, hiring, developing, and retaining competent people are significant issues for organizations at all levels of maturity, but they are largely outside the scope of the CMM.

430

track software costs, schedules, and functionality; problems in meeting commitments are identified when they arise. Software requirements and the work products developed to satisfy them are baselined, and their integrity is controlled. Software project standards are defined, and the organization ensures they are faithfully followed. The software project works with its subcontractors, if any, to establish an effective customer-supplier relationship.

Processes may differ among projects in a Level 2 organization. The organizational requirement for achieving Level 2 is that there are policies that guide the projects in establishing the appropriate management processes.

The software process capability of Level 2 organizations can be summarized as disciplined because software project planning and tracking are stable and earlier successes can be repeated. The project's process is under the effective control of a project management system, following realistic plans based on the performance of previous projects.

2.1.3   Level 3—The Defined Level

At the Defined Level, a standard process (or processes) for developing and maintaining software is documented and used across the organization. This standard process includes both software engineering and management processes, which are integrated into a coherent whole. This standard process is referred to throughout the CMM as the *organization's standard software process*. Processes established at Level 3 are used (and changed, as appropriate) to help the software managers and technical staff perform more effectively. The organization exploits effective software engineering practices when standardizing its software processes. A group such as a software engineering process group or SEPG is responsible for the organization's software process activities. An organization-wide training program is implemented to ensure that the staff and managers have the knowledge and skills required to fulfill their assigned roles.

Projects tailor the organization's standard software process to develop their own defined software process, which accounts for the unique characteristics of the project. This tailored process is referred to in the CMM as the *project's defined software process*. It is the process used in performing the project's activities. A defined software process contains a coherent, integrated set of well-defined software engineering and management processes. A well-defined process includes readiness criteria, inputs, standards and procedures for performing the work, verification mechanisms (such as peer reviews), outputs, and completion criteria. Because the software process is well defined,

management has good insight into technical progress on the project.

The software process capability of Level 3 organizations can be summarized as standard and consistent because both software engineering and management activities are stable and repeatable. Within established product lines, cost, schedule, and functionality are under control, and software quality is tracked. This process capability is based on a common, organization-wide understanding of the activities, roles, and responsibilities in a defined software process.

2.1.4   Level 4—The Managed Level

At the Managed Level, the organization sets quantitative quality goals for both software products and processes. Productivity and quality are measured for important software process activities across all projects as part of an organizational measurement program. An organization-wide software process database is used to collect and analyze the data available from the projects' defined software processes. Software processes are instrumented with well-defined and consistent measurements. These measurements establish the quantitative foundation for evaluating the projects' software processes and products.

Projects achieve control over their products and processes by narrowing the variation in their process performance to fall within acceptable quantitative boundaries. Meaningful variations in process performance can be distinguished from random variation (noise), particularly within established product lines. The risks involved in moving up the learning curve of a new application domain are known and carefully managed.

The software process capability of Level 4 organizations can be summarized as being quantified and predictable because the process is measured and operates within quantitative limits. This level of process capability allows an organization to predict trends in process and product quality within the quantitative bounds of these limits. Because the process is both stable and measured, when some exceptional circumstance occurs, the "special cause" of the variation can be identified and addressed. When the pre-defined limits are exceeded, actions are taken to understand and correct the situation. Software products are of predictably high quality.

2.1.5   Level 5—The Optimizing Level

At the Optimizing Level, the entire organization is focused on continuous process improvement. The organization has the means to identify weaknesses and strengthen the process proactively, with the goals of preventing defects and improving efficiency. Data on process effectiveness are used to perform cost/benefit analyses of new technologies and proposed changes to the organization's software process. Innovations that exploit the best software engineering practices are identified and transferred throughout the organization.

Software teams in Level 5 organizations analyze defects to determine their causes, evaluate software processes to prevent known types of defects from recurring, and disseminate lessons learned throughout the organization.

There is chronic waste, in the form of rework, in any system simply due to random variation. Organized efforts to remove waste result in changing the system by addressing "common causes" of inefficiency. While efforts to reduce waste occur at all maturity levels, it is the focus of Level 5.

The software process capability of Level 5 organizations can be characterized as continuously improving because Level 5 organizations are continuously striving to improve the range of their process capability, thereby improving the process performance of their projects. Improvements occur both by incremental advancements in the existing process and by innovations using new technologies and methods. Technology and process improvements are planned and managed as ordinary business activities.

2.2 Process Capability and the Prediction of Performance

An organization's software process maturity helps predict a project's ability to meet its goals. Projects in Level 1 organizations experience wide variations in achieving cost, schedule, functionality, and quality targets. Figure 2.2 illustrates the kinds of improvements expected in predictability, control, and effectiveness in the form of a probability density for the likely performance of a particular project with respect to targets, such as cycle time, cost, and quality.

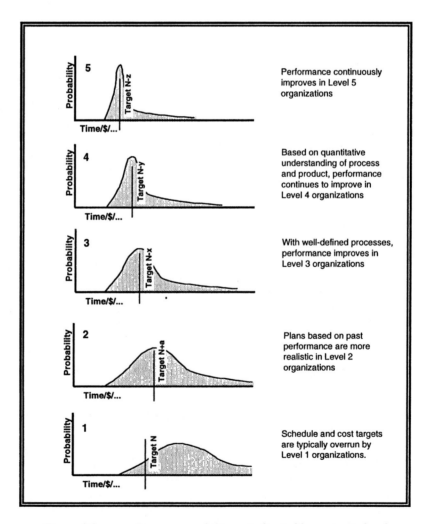

Figure 2.2   Process capability as indicated by maturity level

The first improvement expected as an organization matures is in predictability. As maturity increases, the difference between targeted results and actual results decreases across projects. For instance, Level 1 organizations often miss their originally scheduled delivery dates by a wide margin, whereas higher maturity level organizations should be able to meet targeted dates with increased accuracy.

The second improvement is in control. As maturity increases, the variability of actual results around targeted results decreases. For instance, in Level 1 organizations delivery dates for projects of similar size are unpredictable and vary widely. Similar projects in a higher maturity level organization, however, will be delivered within a smaller range.

The third improvement is in effectiveness. Targeted results improve as the maturity of the organization increases. That is, as a software organization matures, costs decrease, development time becomes shorter, and productivity and quality increase. In a Level 1 organization, development time can be quite long because of the amount of rework that must be performed to correct mistakes. In contrast, higher maturity level organizations have increased process effectiveness and reduced costly rework, allowing development time to be shortened.

The improvements in predicting a project's results represented in Figure 2.2 assume that the software project's outcomes become more predictable as noise, often in the form of rework, is removed from the software process. Unprecedented systems complicate the picture since new technologies and applications lower the process capability by increasing variability. Even in the case of unprecedented systems, the management and engineering practices characteristic of more mature organizations help identify and address problems earlier than for less mature organizations. In some cases a mature process means that "failed" projects are identified early in the software life cycle and investment in a lost cause is minimized.

The documented case studies of software process improvement indicate that there are significant improvements in both quality and productivity as a result of the improvement effort [Herbsleb94, Lawlis95, Goldenson95, Hayes95]. The return on investment seems to typically be in the 4:1 to 8:1 range for successful process improvement efforts, with increases in productivity ranging from 9-67 percent and decreases in cycle time ranging from 15-23 percent reported [Herbsleb94].

2.3 Skipping Maturity Levels

Trying to skip maturity levels may be counterproductive because each maturity level in the CMM forms a foundation from which to achieve the next level. The CMM identifies the levels through which an organization should evolve to establish a culture of software engineering excellence. Organizations can institute specific process improvements at any time they choose, even before they are prepared to advance to the level at which the specific practice is recommended. However, organizations should understand that the stability of these improvements is at greater risk since the foundation for their successful institutionalization has not been completed. Processes without the proper foundation fail at the very point they are needed most—under stress.

For instance, a well-defined software process that is characteristic of a Level 3 organization, can be placed at great risk if management makes a poorly planned schedule commitment or fails to control changes to the baselined requirements. Similarly, many organizations have collected the detailed data characteristic of Level 4, only to find that the data were uninterpretable because of inconsistent software processes.

At the same time, it must be recognized that process improvement efforts should focus on the needs of the organization in the context of its business environment, and higher-level practices may address the current needs of an organization or project. For example, when prescribing what steps an organization should take to move from Level 1 to Level 2, one frequent recommendation is to establish a software engineering process group (SEPG), which is an attribute of Level 3 organizations. While an SEPG is not a necessary characteristic of a Level 2 organization, they can be a useful part of the prescription for achieving Level 2.

3 Operational Definition of the Capability Maturity Model

The CMM is a framework representing a path of improvements recommended for software organizations that want to increase their software process capability. The intent is that the CMM is at a sufficient level of abstraction that it does not unduly constrain how the software process is implemented by an organization. The CMM describes what we would normally expect in a software process, regardless of how the process is implemented.

This operational elaboration of the CMM is designed to support the many ways it will be used. There are at least five uses of the CMM that are supported:

- Senior management will use the CMM to understand the activities necessary to launch a software process improvement program in their organization.

- Appraisal method developers will use the CMM to develop CMM-based appraisal methods that meet specific needs.

- Evaluation teams will use the CMM to identify the risks of selecting among different contractors for awarding business and to monitor contracts.

- Assessment teams will use the CMM to identify strengths and weaknesses in the organization.

- Technical staff and process improvement groups, such as an SEPG, will use the CMM as a guide to help them define and improve the software process in their organization.

Because of the diverse uses of the CMM, it must be decomposed in sufficient detail that actual process recommendations can be derived from the structure of the maturity levels. This decomposition also indicates the key processes and their structure that characterize software process maturity and software process capability.

3.1 Internal Structure of the Maturity Levels

Each maturity level, with the exception of Level 1, has been decomposed into constituent parts. The decomposition of each maturity level ranges from abstract summaries of each level down to their operational definition in the key practices, as shown in Figure 3.1. Each maturity level is composed of several key process areas. Each key process area is organized into five sections called common features. The common features specify the key practices that, when collectively addressed, accomplish the goals of the key process area.

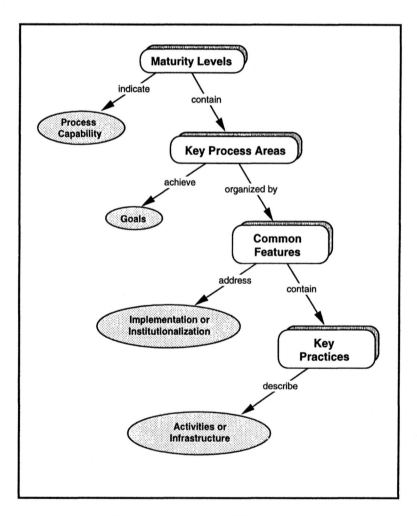

Figure 3.1   The CMM structure

3.2   Maturity Levels

A maturity level is a well-defined evolutionary plateau toward achieving a mature software process. Each maturity level indicates a level of process capability, as was illustrated in Figure 2.2. For instance, at Level 2 the process capability of an organization has been elevated from ad hoc to disciplined by establishing sound project management controls.

3.3   Key Process Areas

Except for Level 1, each maturity level is decomposed into several key process areas that indicate where an organization should focus on to improve its software process. Key process areas identify the issues that must be addressed to achieve a maturity level.

Each *key process area* identifies a cluster of related activities that, when performed collectively, achieve a set of goals considered important for enhancing process capability. The key process areas have been defined to reside at a single maturity level as shown in Figure 3.2. The path to achieving the goals of a key process area may differ across projects based on differences in application domains or environments. Nevertheless, all the goals of a key process area must be achieved for the organization to satisfy that key process area.

The adjective "key" implies that there are process areas (and processes) that are not key to achieving a maturity level. The CMM does not describe in detail all the process areas that are involved with developing and maintaining software. Certain process areas have been identified as key determiners of process capability, and these are the ones described in the CMM.

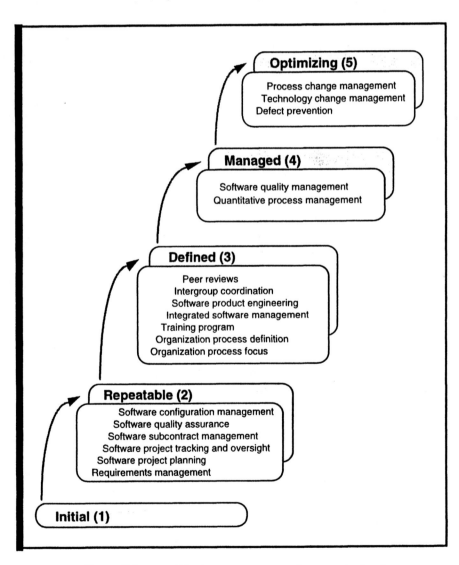

Figure 3.2   The key process areas by maturity level

The key process areas are the requirements for achieving a maturity level. To achieve a maturity level, the key process areas for that level and the lower levels must be satisfied (or not applicable, such as Software Subcontract Management when there are no subcontractors).

The specific practices to be executed in each key process area will evolve as the organization achieves higher levels of process maturity. For instance, many of the project estimating capabilities described in the Software Project Planning key process area at Level 2 must evolve to handle the additional project data available at Level 3, as described in Integrated Software Management.

The key process areas at Level 2 focus on the software project's concerns related to establishing basic project management controls.

- Requirements Management: establish a common understanding between the customer and the software project of the customer's requirements that will be addressed by the software project. This agreement with the customer is the basis for planning and managing the software project.

- Software Project Planning: establish reasonable plans for performing the software engineering and for managing the software project. These plans are the necessary foundation for managing the software project.

- Software Project Tracking and Oversight: establish adequate visibility into actual progress so that management can take effective actions when the software project's performance deviates significantly from the software plans.

- Software Subcontract Management: select qualified software subcontractors and manage them effectively.

- Software Quality Assurance: provide management with appropriate visibility into the process being used by the software project and of the products being built.

- Software Configuration Management: establish and maintain the integrity of the products of the software project throughout the project's software life cycle.

The key process areas at Level 3 address both project and organizational issues, as the organization establishes an infrastructure that institutionalizes effective software engineering and management processes across all projects.

- Organization Process Focus: establish the organizational responsibility for software process activities that improve the organization's overall software process capability.

- Organization Process Definition: develop and maintain a usable set of software process assets that improve process performance across the projects and provides a basis for defining meaningful data for quantitative process management. These assets provide a stable foundation that can be institutionalized via mechanisms such as training.

- Training Program: develop the skills and knowledge of individuals so they can perform their roles effectively and efficiently. Training is an organizational responsibility, but the software projects should identify their needed skills and provide the necessary training when the project's needs are unique.

- Integrated Software Management: integrate the software engineering and management activities into a coherent, defined software process that is tailored from the organization's standard software process and related process assets. This tailoring is based on the business environment and technical needs of the project.

- Software Product Engineering: consistently perform a well-defined engineering process that integrates all the software engineering activities to produce correct, consistent software products effectively and efficiently. Software Product Engineering describes the technical activities of the project, for instance requirements analysis, design, code, and test.

- Intergroup Coordination: establish a means for the software engineering group to participate actively with the other engineering groups so the project is better able to satisfy the customer's needs effectively and efficiently.

- Peer Reviews: remove defects from the software work products early and efficiently. An important corollary effect is to develop a better understanding of the software work products and of the defects that can be prevented. The peer review is an important and effective engineering method that can be implemented via inspections, structured walkthroughs, or a number of other collegial review methods.

The key process areas at Level 4 focus on establishing a quantitative understanding of both the software process and the software work products being built.

- Quantitative Process Management: control process performance of the software project quantitatively. Software process performance represents the actual results achieved from following a software process. The focus is on identifying special causes of variation within a measurably stable process and correcting, as appropriate, the circumstances that drove the transient variation to occur.

- Software Quality Management: develop a quantitative understanding of the quality of the project's software products and achieve specific quality goals.

The key process areas at Level 5 cover the issues that both the organization and the projects must address to implement continuous and measurable software process improvement.

- Defect Prevention: identify the causes of defects and prevent them from recurring. The software project analyzes defects, identifies their causes, and changes its defined software process.

- Technology Change Management: identify beneficial new technologies (such as tools, methods, and processes) and transfer them into the organization in an orderly manner. The focus of Technology Change Management is on performing innovation efficiently in an ever-changing world.

- Process Change Management: continually improve the software processes used in the organization with the intent of improving software quality, increasing productivity, and decreasing the cycle time for product development.

3.4   Goals and Key Practices

Goals summarize the key practices of a key process area and can be used to determine whether an organization or project has effectively implemented the key process area. The goals signify the scope, boundaries, and intent of each key process area. Satisfaction of a key process area is determined by achievement of the goals.

Key practices describe the activities and infrastructure that contribute most to the effective implementation and institutionalization of the key process area. Each key practice consists of a single sentence, often followed by a more detailed description, which may include examples and elaboration. These key practices, also referred to as the top-level key practices, state the fundamental policies, procedures, and activities for the key process area. The components of the detailed description are frequently referred to as subpractices. The key practices describe "what" is to be done, but they should not be interpreted as mandating "how" the goals should be achieved. Alternative practices may accomplish the goals of the key process area. The key practices should be interpreted rationally to judge whether the goals of the key process area are effectively, although perhaps differently, achieved.

4   Future Directions of the CMM

Achieving higher levels of software process maturity is incremental and requires a long-term commitment to continuous process improvement. Software organizations may take ten years or more to build the foundation for, and a culture oriented toward, continuous process improvement. Although a decade-long process improvement program is foreign to most U.S. companies, this level of effort is required to produce mature software organizations.

The CMM is not a silver bullet and does not address all of the issues that are important for successful projects. For example, it does not currently address expertise in particular application domains, advocate specific software technologies, or suggest how to select, hire, motivate, and retain competent people. Although these issues are crucial to a project's success, they have not been integrated into the CMM.

The CMM has evolved since 1986 [Paulk95b] and will continue to evolve. Feedback from the use of the CMM in software process assessments, software capability evaluations, and process improvement programs, the continuing evolution of the field of software engineering, and the changing business environment all contribute to the need for a "living CMM." To achieve a reasonable balance between the need for stability by organizations using the CMM in software process improvement and the need for continual improvement, we anticipate a 5-year cycle for major revisions of the CMM. Version 2 of the CMM is planned for the 1997 time frame.

The SEI is also working with the International Standards Organization (ISO) in its efforts to build international standards for software process assessment, improvement, and capability determination [Dorling93, Konrad95]. This effort will integrate concepts from many different process improvement methods. The development of the ISO standards (and the contributions of other methods) will influence CMM v2, even as the SEI's process work will influence the activities of the ISO.

5 Conclusion

The CMM represents a "common sense engineering" approach to software process improvement. The maturity levels, key process areas, common features, and key practices have been extensively discussed and reviewed within the software community. While the CMM is not perfect, it does represent a broad consensus of the software community and is a useful tool for guiding software process improvement efforts.

The CMM provides a conceptual structure for improving the management and development of software products in a disciplined and consistent way. It does not guarantee that software products will be successfully built or that all problems in software engineering will be adequately resolved. However, current reports from CMM-based improvement programs indicate that it can improve the likelihood with which a software organization can achieve its cost, quality, and productivity goals.

The CMM identifies practices for a mature software process and provides examples of the state-of-the-practice (and in some cases, the state-of-the-art), but it is not meant to be either exhaustive or dictatorial. The CMM identifies the characteristics of an effective software process, but the mature organization addresses all issues essential to a successful project, including people and technology, as well as process.

6 References

Bate95   Roger Bate, et al, "A Systems Engineering Capability Maturity Model, Version 1.1," Software Engineering Institute, CMU/SEI-95-MM-003, Nov. 1995.

Dorling93   Alec Dorling, "Software Process Improvement and Capability dEtermination," *Software Quality J.*, Vol. 2, No. 4, Dec. 1993, pp. 209–224.

Curtis95   Bill Curtis, William E. Hefley, and Sally Miller, "People Capability Maturity Model," Software Engineering Institute, CMU/SEI-95-MM-02, Sept. 1995.

Goldenson95   Dennis R. Goldenson and James D. Herbsleb, "After the Appraisal: A Systematic Survey of Process Improvement, Its Benefits, and Factors that Influence Suc

cess," Software Engineering Institute, CMU/SEI-95-TR-009, Aug. 1995.

Hayes95   Will Hayes and Dave Zubrow, "Moving On Up: Data and Experience Doing CMM-Based Process Improvement," Software Engineering Institute, CMU/SEI-95-TR-008, Aug. 1995.

Herbsleb94   James Herbsleb, et al., "Benefits of CMM-Based Software Process Improvement: Initial Results," Software Engineering Institute, CMU/SEI-94-TR-13, Aug. 1994.

Humphrey89   W.S. Humphrey, *Managing the Software Process*, Addison-Wesley, Reading, Mass., 1989.

Konrad95   Michael D. Konrad, Mark C. Paulk, and Allan W. Graydon, "An Overview of SPICE's Model for Process Management," *Proc. 5th Int'l Conf. Software Quality*, 1995.

Lawlis95   Patricia K. Lawlis, Robert M. Flowe, and James B. Thordahl, "A Correlational Study of the CMM and Software Development Performance," *Crosstalk: The Journal of Defense Software Engineering*, Vol. 8, No. 9, Sept. 1995, pp. 21–25.

Paulk95a   Carnegie Mellon University, Software Engineering Institute (Principal Contributors and Editors: Mark C. Paulk, Charles V. Weber, Bill Curtis, and Mary Beth Chrissis), *The Capability Maturity Model: Guidelines for Improving the Software Process*, Addison-Wesley Publishing Company, Reading, Mass., 1995.

Paulk95b   Mark C. Paulk, "The Evolution of the SEI's Capability Maturity Model for Software," *Software Process: Improvement and Practice*, Pilot Issue, Spring 1995.

For Further Information

For further information regarding the CMM and its associated products, including training on the CMM and how to perform software process assessments and software capability evaluations, contact:

SEI Customer Relations
Software Engineering Institute
Carnegie Mellon University
Pittsburgh, PA 15213-3890
(412) 268-5800
Internet: customer-relations@sei.cmu.edu

Chapter 12

Software Technology

1. Introduction to Chapter

This chapter introduces a number of different and somewhat independent technologies that can be applied to many aspects of the software development process. It includes such topics as reverse engineering, re-engineering, reuse, prototyping, CASE tools, and metrics.

Reverse engineering is the process of reconstructing products developed earlier in the life cycle from products later in the life cycle, for example, deriving the program requirements or design from the code. It involves analyzing a subject system to: (1) identify the system's components and their interrelationships, and (2) create a representation of the system in another form or at a higher level of abstraction.

Re-engineering is the examination and alteration of a subject system to reconstitute it in a new form, and the subsequent implementation of the new form. Re-engineering generally includes some form of reverse engineering (to achieve a more abstract description) followed by some form of forward engineering or restructuring. For example, existing code is reverse engineered in order to obtain requirements and/or design, and new (better structured, designed, and documented) code is then generated. A re-engineered software system typically performs the same functions after the re-engineering as before.

Reuse is the act of using an existing software product in a new project. It is a software development strategy that attempts to reduce development costs and to improve software quality by incorporating previ-

SOFTWARE TECHNOLOGY

DIGERNESS '91

439

ously proven work products such as designs and code into a new software product. The net effect of reusing software work products would be shorter development schedules (because components do not have to be re-invented) and more reliable software (because the components have previously been used successfully).

In engineering, a *prototype* is a full-scale model and the functional form of a new system or subsystem. (A prototype does not have to be the complete system; only the part of interest.) A software prototype would be a computer program that implements some part of the system requirements. This prototype can be used to assist in defining requirements or evaluating alternatives. Examples of the use of prototypes include determining how to obtain the required accuracy in real-time performance, or evaluating user interface suitability. The process of building the prototype will also expose and eliminate a number of the ambiguities, inconsistencies, blind spots, and misunderstandings incorporated in the specifications, or the statement or concept of the project that exists when the prototyping takes place.

It has been argued that software people misuse the term prototype, which causes confusion particularly among people trained in some form of hardware engineering. The following short paper by Gregory explains the problem.

On Prototypes vs. Mockups
S.T. Gregory [1]

Over the last several years, an increasing amount of attention has been given to a subject commonly referred to as rapid prototyping. The discussions tend to refer to the creation of programs that have user interfaces similar to the desired final product, but that are incomplete or severely restricted functionally. I have always contended that the Computer Science jargon should contain true (as opposed to false) cognates from English or the general engineering jargon. Thus, I would like to point out that the term prototype in this context is inappropriate. A more accurate term would be mock-up.

In non-computer science usage, a prototype is a hand-crafted version of a final production model. It has all of the production model's functionality. Webster's New World Dictionary of the American Language, Second College Edition, defines a prototype as "a perfect example of a particular type."

A mock-up, on the other hand, resembles the final product only at a surface level. It has little of the eventual functionality, and is often used near the beginning of a project to ensure that the customer's requirements are understood. According to the same dictionary, a mock-up is a "scale model [...] of a structure or apparatus used for instructional or experimental purposes."

Perhaps, in the future, authors will think more carefully before choosing to use the word prototype, and will pay more attention to which words they appropriate to have specialized meanings in our field.

Samuel T. Gregory University of Virginia Dept. Computer Science, Thornton Hall Charlottesville, VA 22903

A *CASE* (Computer Aided Software Engineering) *tool* is an automated software engineering tool that can assist software engineers in analyzing, designing, coding, testing, and documenting a software system and managing a software project. John Manley of the University of Pittsburgh is apparently the first person to use the acronym "CASE" for computer-aided software engineering. [2,3]

A *metric* is a measure of the degree to which a process or product possesses a given attribute. Besides process and product metrics, other definitions of types of metrics are (adapted from IEEE Std 610.12-1990 [4]):

- *Software quality metric*—A quantitative measure of the degree to which software possesses a given attribute that affects its quality. Examples are: reliability, maintainability, portability

- *Software quantity metric*—A quantitative measure of some physical attribute of software. Examples are: lines of code, function points, pages of documentation

- *Management metric*—A management indicator that can be used to measure management activities such as budget spent, value earned, costs overrun, and schedule slippage

In the early 1980s, the US Air Force's Rome Air Development Center (now known as Rome Laboratories) developed a set of software metrics called quality factors that represent the product attributes most desired by customers [5]. These metrics have become part of our metrics environment and as such are used in many developments of software systems. These metrics are:

correctness	reliability
efficiency	integrity
usability	survivability
maintainability	verifiability
flexibility	portability
reusability	interoperability
expandability	

Perhaps the most important software quality attribute is software reliability. Software reliability measures the extent to which the software will perform without any failures within a specified time period [6].

Other important attributes not on the RADC list include safety, security, complexity, and user friendliness.

An important set of metrics for software management was developed by the MITRE Corporation for the US Air Force Electronic Systems Division (ESD; now Electronic Systems Center) [7]. These ten metrics are considered by many to be the best set of management metrics available today. They are:

- Software size metric
- Software personnel metric
- Software volatility metric
- Computer resources utilization metric
- Design complexity metric
- Schedule progress metric
- Design progress metric
- Computer software unit (CSU) development progress metric
- Testing progress metric
- Incremental release content metric

Another set of management metrics was published by the US Air Force Systems Command (now part of the Air Force Materiel Command) in 1986 [8]. This set included:

- Computer resource utilization
- Software development manpower
- Requirements definition and stability
- Software progress (development and test)
- Cost and schedule deviations
- Software development tools

Measurement has been an integral part of the Software Engineering Institute's process improvement project. The first set of guidelines published by this project [9] included 10 metrics at process maturity level 2:

- Planned versus actual staffing profiles
- Software size versus time
- Statistics on software code and test errors
- Actual versus planned units designed
- Actual versus planned units completing unit testing
- Actual versus planned units integrated
- Target computer memory utilization
- Target computer throughput utilization
- Target computer I/O channel utilization
- Software build/release content

With the publication in 1993 of the Software Engineering Institute's Capability Maturity Model for Software [10], measurement became one of the "common features" that are part of every Key Process Area at all maturity levels. The paper by Paulk, Curtis, Chrissis, and Weber in the preceding chapter provides an overview of the SEI's model of process maturity and the role of metrics in this model.

One of the major issues in applying any of the new technologies or methodologies is the technology transfer gap. The technology transfer gap is the time interval (measured in years) between the development of a new product, tool, or technique and its use by the consumers of that product, tool, or technique. Redwine and Riddle [11] have concluded that the technology transfer gap is in the range of 15 to 18 years.

2. Introduction to Papers

The first article, by Patrick Hall and Lingzi Jin, on the re-engineering and reuse of software, is an original paper that explores the current use of re-engineering, reuse, and, as a side issue, reverse engineering. Production of software is expensive, and the authors point out that, with the cost of hardware decreasing, we need to increase productivity in software development. Software re-engineering and reuse is a method of increasing software development productivity. This paper provides historical background behind reuse and re-engineering and discusses, as a necessity of re-engineering, the need for reverse engineering.

The second paper, "Prototyping: Alternative System Development Methodologies," by J.M. Carey, explains what prototyping is, as well as pointing out that it has become a popular alternative to traditional software development methodologies. The paper discusses the various definitions of prototyping, looks at the advantages and disadvantages of using a prototyping approach, and looks at one positive and one negative case study of prototyping in an industrial setting.

From Carey's point of view, prototyping is a process of quickly building a model of the final software system, used primarily as communication tool to assist in meeting the information needs of the user. Software prototyping became popular with the advent of Fourth Generation Languages (4GLs) (also called application generators). The author points out some of the advantages of prototyping, including faster development time, easier end use and learning, reduced cost of development, decreased backlogs, and enhanced user/analyst communications. Some of the disadvantages of prototyping are also discussed, including fostering of undue expectations on the part of the user.

The third paper in this section, by Alfonso Fuggetta, is on the classification of CASE technology. The purpose of this paper is to provide a survey and a classification system to help categorize CASE tools. Some of the tools looked at by the author are editing tools, programming tools, configuration management tools, verification/validation tools, project management tools, metrics and measurement tools, and some miscellaneous tools.

The fourth paper, written by Ronald Nusenoff and Dennis Bunde of Loral Corporation (now part of Lockheed Martin), describes how Loral's Software Productivity Laboratory (SPL) makes use of metrics to improve its software engineering process maturity. The SPL has developed a metrics guidebook to define a set of standards for software metrics and to specify procedures for collecting and analyzing metrics data. The SPL also developed a spreadsheet tool to provide automated support for metrics generation, collection, graphical representation, and analysis.

These Loral corporate metrics were defined to map to the corporate development methodology. Both were part of the program being developed to advance Loral Corporation to Levels 4 and 5 on the SEI's process maturity scale. The paper demonstrates Loral's commitment to process improvement, as defined by the SEI, and Loral's belief in the close relationship of process and metrics.

The Loral metrics were based on the MITRE software management metrics [12]. The paper compares the MITRE and Loral metrics to those defined in the SEI's 1987 software maturity questionnaire [13], the precursor to the CMM. Loral used the 1987 document as the basis for its process improvement efforts because most of the work was done before publication of the CMM in 1993.

The last very short paper in this section, by Barry Boehm, is entitled "Industrial Software Metrics Top Ten List." This is an interesting list of metrics developed by Dr. Boehm in the late 1980s. The value of this list is that these metrics are well established and each one of them affects our ability to deliver software on time and within budget. This very short list has been circulated around the industry for years and has proved to be useful to any software engineering practitioner. For the most part they still appear to be valid today.

1. Gregory, J.T., "On Prototypes vs. Mockups," ACM SIGSOFT, *Software Engineering Notes*, Vol. 9, No. 5., Oct. 1984, p. 13.

2. Manley, J.H., "Computer Aided Software Engineering (CASE): Foundation for Software Factories," *Proc. IEEE COMPCON '84 Fall Computer Conf. Small Computer (R)Evolution* IEEE Computer Society Press, Los Alamitos. Calif., 1984, pp. 84–91.

3. Manley, J.H., "Computer Aided Software Engineering," *Selected Conference Papers, 10th Ann. Federal DP Expo & Conf.*, Interface Control Group, Inc., Vienna, VA, 1984.

4. IEEE Standard 610.12-1990, *IEEE Standard Glossary of Software Engineering Terminology*, The Institute of Electrical and Electronics Engineers, Inc., Piscataway, NJ, 1990.

5. Software Quality Measures for Distributed Systems (Vol I), Software Quality Measures for Distributed Systems: Guide Book for Software Quality Measurements (Vol II), and Software Quality Measures for Distributed Systems: Impact on Software Quality (Vol III), TR RADC-TR-175, Rome Air Development Center, Griffiss AFB, NY, 1983.

6. Bowen, T.P., G.B. Wigle, and J.T. Tsai, Specification of Software Quality Attributes: Vol. 1, Final Technical Report; Vol. 2, Software Quality Specifications Guidebook; Vol. 3, Software Quality Evaluation Guidebook; RADC TR-85-37, prepared by Boeing Aerospace Company for Rome Air Development Center, Griffiss AFB, NY, Feb. 1985.

7. Schultz, H.P., *Software Management Metrics*, ESD TR-88-001, prepared by The MITRE Corporation for the U.S. Air Force, Electronic Systems Division, Hanscom AFB, MA, 1988.

8. "Air Force Systems Command Software Management Indicators: Management Insight," AFSC Pamphlet 800-43, 31 Jan. 1986

9. Humphrey, W.S., and W.L. Sweet, "A Method for Assessing the Software Development Capability of Contractors," CMU/SEI-87-TR-23, Sept. 1987.

10. Paulk, Mark C., et al., "Key Practices of the Capability Maturity Model, Version 1.1," CMU/SEI-93-TR-25, Feb. 1993.

11. Redwine, S. T., Jr., and W. E. Riddle, "Software Technology Maturation," *Proc. 8th Int'l Conf. Software Eng.*, IEEE Computer Society Press, Los Alamitos, Calif., 1985, pp. 189–200.

The Re-engineering and Reuse of Software[1]

Patrick A.V. Hall[2] and Lingzi Jin[3]

Abstract

Since software re-engineering and reuse have matured and the major technical problems have been solved, the emphasis is now on introducing reuse and re-engineering into practice as a management activity. Re-engineering methods predominantly address the code level, but for full effect we should understand the main purpose for which software was built: the application domain. Reuse methods focus on library organization and on standards for component production, with much interest in object-oriented methods. Similarly, in order to reuse software effectively, we need to understand the application domain so that we can choose the appropriate parts, organize these effectively into libraries, and deploy the library components to solve new problems. This leads us to domain analysis. Although management, social, and economic issues remain to be solved, current developments suggest reuse and re-engineering will be re-absorbed into main-stream practice.

1 Introduction

Software re-engineering and reuse are concerned with maximizing software usage for any given development effort. The production of software is expensive, and with the decrease in the cost of hardware and the increase in hardware capability, we have been led to ever more ambitious development projects, while qualified and experienced software development staff are in short supply. How can we keep up with this demand for more software? How can we maximize the usage we obtain from software? One response has been to re-engineer software for further use, to reuse the software, and to produce software for widespread reuse from the start.

Figure 1 illustrates the problem. During software development, many alternative ideas and designs are considered and rejected, and thrown away, even though they may have great use in other applications. Tools may be built and discarded, and test cases used and then set aside. At the end of its useful life, the

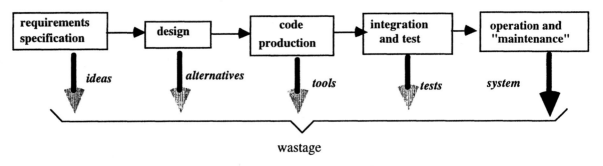

Figure 1. Software development and the products wasted during and at the end of the process.

---

[1] This review of the area is updated from many previous reviews of the area cited in the references.

[2] Department of Computing, Open University, Milton Keynes, England, MK7 6AA

[3] Now with Department of Computer Science, Nanjing University , Nanjing, PR China, 210093

complete system itself may be thrown away. It is the objective of software reverse engineering and reuse to recover some of this investment. We define the basic terms below, in preparation for the later fuller description of the areas in the body of the paper.

1.1 Re-engineering

Within the development of software, some 60 to 70 percent of total life-cycle costs are spent on "maintenance"—the activities undertaken after software is first delivered to remove bugs, change it to meet the real requirements, and enhance it to meet new or changing requirements (see Swanson and Beath, 1989). In order to make changes, we have to first understand the software, often involving 47 to 60 percent of the maintenance effort because of inadequate software documentation. Often, the maintenance effort is forced to rely on the code itself. This means that 30 to 35 percent of total life cycle costs are consumed in trying to understand the software after it has been delivered in order to make changes. Anything that we do to alleviate this situation will reduce costs. The tools and methods used to understand software are known generically as reverse engineering. Reverse engineering may be applied as required, or it may be applied in anticipation of changes as part of a preventative maintenance activity to reconstruct all the necessary documentation to support future maintenance and change.

Having reverse engineered a complete system, it may be necessary to clean up the software or restructure it to meet current standards. We may even re-implement the system by forward engineering it in a newer version of the programming language or some other language (for example in moving from C to C++), or onto new hardware and a new operating system (for example, moving to the latest version of Windows). This complete cycle of reverse engineering followed by forward engineering is called re-engineering.

1.2 Reuse

One method proposed for making a significant improvement in productivity and quality is software reuse: using a given piece of software to solve more than one problem. Frequently, this is taken to mean the reuse of program components like library subroutines in more than one application. However, reuse can also be applied much more broadly to include the redeployment of designs, ideas, or even the skills and experience of people. Re-engineering can be viewed as a form of reuse, because we take a complete system and improve it and then redeploy it. Reverse engi-

neering and re-engineering are more important within reuse because of the help they give in creating components.

The creation of components is sometimes known as component engineering. Components can be extracted from existing software using reverse engineering techniques to describe the existing software and identify the modules within it. These modules would then be candidates for reuse. Of course, we would not simply use the modules as we find them, but re-engineer them to the quality standards that we would now expect. The alternative is to create new components from scratch, sometimes referred to as design-for-reuse.

We need to select components that will be useful in the application area concerned and need to know how to use these in meeting a user requirement. The activity of understanding an application area is known as domain analysis. Domain analysis is also important for reverse engineering because we need to know what we might expect to find before we analyze a system to understand what it actually contains.

Component collections are often surprisingly small, perhaps a few hundred, but they can be very large. While small collections can be remembered by the re-user or supported by paper catalogues, large collections of many thousands of components need to be organized within a component library using specially tailored library management methods.

We also need to have methods for using components effectively. This is often known as design-with-reuse. Here the most effective approach is the use of architectural components or frameworks, an approach which originated in a couple of European projects and has since become an integral part of object-oriented methods.

1.3 The organization of this paper

Reuse and re-engineering have been with us since the beginning of computing, but have only gained prominence over the past 10 years or so. The area has now matured, all major technical barriers have been solved, and the emphasis is almost universally on management making it happen. Some recent developments indicate that the area is turning full circle and is likely to dissipate into routine practice and other areas of computing.

In this article, we will start with a review of the history of the area and look at what the traditional practice has been before we review the two major strands of the area, Reverse Engineering and Re-engineering and Software Reuse. We then move to the more general consideration of domain modeling and how this fits in.

Next we consider the non-technical issues of management, economics, and social groups. While reuse programs depend upon the development of the technology as discussed above, they cannot succeed solely because of the technology. Software engineers, either as producers of software, or as managers, frequently resist ideas of reuse, because they cannot see the benefits of reuse. A number of issues are discussed.

Finally we look back at progress to date, and at two significant papers which indicate how things might develop from here.

2. Historical background

The reuse of software has been with us from the beginning through the publication of algorithms, the use of high level programming languages, and the use of packages, as has been pointed out by many people (see Standish 1984 and Hall 1987).

Reuse through the publication of algorithms and designs has been very important for the development of computing. Textbooks published on a certain area indicate its maturity and are an important vehicle for promoting reuse. Indeed, it is at this level of abstraction that ideas are most transferable and form the cornerstone of our educational systems. As will be seen later, recent work by Arango, Shoen, and Pettengill (1993) is returning us to these origins.

However, it is the consideration of high level programming languages as examples of reuse that is the most illuminating. In high level languages, many frequently used combinations of instructions at the assembly level (for example, for subroutine entry and exit with parameter passing) have been packaged into single constructs at the higher level. A high level language gives a notation for selecting these constructs and composing them to build software systems. Facilities are provided for user created components to be stored and reused, for example through subroutines and macros. This is not the usual way of viewing programming languages and compilers, which are usually seen as "tools" rather than as the engineering foundations of software production. This view of programming languages emphasizes the unique nature of software, the great diversity that its components might take, and the very flexible way they might be interconnected. This programming language orientation has continued through module interconnection languages (see section 4), and has reached its apotheosis with the introduction of domain specific languages and associated compilers in the work of Batory and O'Malley (1992).

Similarly, procuring standard packages is an important example of reuse, and the availability of a wide range of products is again an indicator of the maturity of an area of technology. Capers Jones (1984) made a thorough appraisal of this. Packages which are rigidly defined are seldom useful—some flexibility is essential. This flexibility is provided through a range of capabilities, from simple parameterization and configuration following some elaborate build script (as is usually done for operating systems), to the modification of the package at the source level. The interconnection of the packages during systems integration then becomes the important process of design with reuse, with standard patterns of interconnection being the frameworks that guide this.

Re-engineering and reverse engineering have also been with us since high level languages and compilers were invented. Very early on there were automatic flow-charting tools—a kind of reverse engineering—and with the need to keep software systems in operation with changing hardware, re-engineering appeared. Cross-reference listings of variables were provided with compilers to help understand the large pieces of software. Systems for converting from file based systems to database systems and between database systems also appeared.

The first part of traditional systems analysis describes the current system. That is reverse engineering, though what is different now is that the current system is a computer system and descriptions of it are available in machine readable form. We could in principle use computer tools to assist us in the conventional system analysis phase of describing the current system. The description involves abstractions that remove the detail and reveal the essential nature of the current system and the subsequent development of the new system, using conventional development processes, then makes the total process re-engineering.

When connecting one piece of software to another through an interface, we need to know in great detail the representation of the data that crosses the interface and what it means in terms of the functions that are performed on it. Frequently the supplier's documentation is inadequate, and so we examine the software by running critical test cases to probe the interface or, as a last resort, looking at the code itself. Again, this is reverse engineering.

However, none of these were addressed explicitly as reuse and re-engineering until relatively late. Reuse as a concept was introduced in 1968 in the celebrated paper by McIlroy (1976), but only took hold much later in the Draco research project in the late 1970's (see Neighbours 1984), and in the many projects that followed. Reverse engineering and re-engineering as concepts seem to have crept into software development in the early 1980's, driven by the commercial need to sustain COBOL "legacy" systems and with emerging products that facilitate the maintenance of COBOL.

3. Reverse Engineering and Re-engineering

Reverse Engineering is a general area that embraces several subtly different ideas. The January 1990 issue of *IEEE Software* is devoted to Software Maintenance and Reverse Engineering. Our use of terms is consistent with that given by Chikofsky (1990) in that special issue of *Software*, though other terms are in use, such as re-documentation, design recovery, or program understanding.

3.1 Current Solutions

At any exhibition of tools that support software development, you will discover many suppliers offering Reverse Engineering tools. Rock-Evans and Hales (1990) gave a very comprehensive survey of these tools. This survey happens to be a UK publication, but a survey report produced anywhere else in the world would be very similar. While many of these tools originate in the US, many also come from elsewhere within the increasingly global CASE tool market. What are the real capabilities of these tools?

Many tools are really very simple, having been in use for many decades, and it is surprising to see these being offered now as if they were new. Outlining tools would list the functions contained within the software, giving the function names, arguments and data types, and possibly the key data structures manipulated and leading comments. The internal operation of the procedures may also be condensed in the form of a flow diagram to show its essential structure. Cross-references between modules may also be extracted, perhaps showing which procedures call which other procedures and use which data structures and distinguishing defining occurrences from places where the data structures are used. All of this may be put together in some diagrammatic form exploiting the bit-map graphics technology of modern platforms and perhaps hypertext technology.

Method and CASE suppliers will commonly include tools to reverse the software to their own notations. Early tools here were for PSL/PSA, and more recently this has been done for dataflow diagrams (Excelerator) and data structures (Bachman).

All of these commercial offerings seem relatively conventional, and the really hard problems, like re-engineering assembly programs, are left aside as activities that require essential human interaction.

Because of these hard research problems, there has been much recent activity in exploring both formal transformations and less formal pattern matching methods. The formal approaches seem to have been mostly a European interest, while the informal approaches have been mostly in the US.

3.2 Formal transformations

Formal transformations have usually been viewed as tools of forward engineering, for example transforming a simple but inefficient algorithm into one that is equivalent but more efficient, such as replacing recursion by iteration. However, these transformations can be used in reverse to simplify a well engineered and efficient, but complex and obscure, algorithm. In the process of simplification, details of the software may be removed, such as the decisions that were taken to enhance efficiency. In doing these transformations, we then progress backwards along the software development lifecycle to produce design descriptions and specifications.

Extracting flow diagrams from code is an example of the reversing from code to design. A recent example of this is the paper by Cimitile and de Carlini (1991). However, the objective here is not to produce flow diagrams—after all that had been done 20 years earlier—but to establish an intermediate representation that would serve for transformations

Other projects seek to move from code, possibly Assembler, all the way to formal specifications, typically in Z (see Spivey 1989). One example of this is the work of Martin Ward (1988), who transforms the code into an intermediate "wide-spectrum-language" and then transforms the code into Z. Ward's system is not automatic, but an interactive system which provides the user with a selection of candidate transformations which the user then applies to progressively move towards an acceptable specification. Intermediate states are removed until a pure function mapping inputs to outputs has been abstracted.

A similar system using a different intermediate language has been developed by Lano and others as part of the REDO project (see Lano and Breuer 1989, Lano, Breuer and Haughton 1993, and van Zuylen 1993). The method proposed by Lano, Breuer and Haughton reverse engineers COBOL applications back to specifications. Under manual guidance, the process consists of three stages:

1. Translation from COBOL to their intermediate language Uniform to obtain a restricted subset of constructs.

2. Transform from Uniform to a functional description language. Dataflow diagrams are used to group variables together to create prototype objects (in the sense of object-

oriented approaches). Equational descriptions of the functionality are abstracted from the code. Some simplification to obtain the normal form of the representation may be necessary.

3. The functional descriptions are combined together with the outline objects to derive a specification in Z, or an object oriented version of this, Z++.

With the widescale availability of parallel hardware, there has been considerable activity at parallelising both FORTRAN and COBOL program (see Harrison, Gens, and Gifford 1993). This is a form of re-engineering recognized in this paper, though the community that undertakes this work seems seldom to appreciate this and takes a narrow compilation view of the problem. To parallelize effectively, it may be necessary to reverse the sequential code right back to its specification where parallelism may be natural.

3.3 The importance of informal information

The importance of other information in the Reverse Engineering of code was pointed out by Ted Biggerstaff in 1989. Figure 2(a) shows an example in which all the identifiers have been replaced by meaningless numbers and letters, and all the comments have been stripped out. What we get is the machine's-eye view of the code, but to us it is incomprehensible. Figure 2(b) shows the code with the identifiers re-inserted, making it much more understandable. From the chosen identifiers we can immediately see this has something to do with symbol tables and can guess about the structure of the code and the way it operates. What we are doing is using a higher level of understanding of the problem domain being addressed to understand the code. With the comments replaced we would find ourselves even more capable of understanding what is happening.

From this simple example we see that we are concerned with several dimensions of analysis. There is the traditional technical dimension of notations and their inter-relationship. There are layers of abstraction that go from the application, to a generic view of computing problems, to the methods we use for the architectural description and design of software, to the particular constructs we use in program code. And then there are the degrees of formality of representation, from the very formal descriptions associated with program code and the newly emerging formal description techniques to the other extreme of very informal representations of knowledge contained within peoples heads.

3.4 Recognizing higher level domain concepts

We have seen that the important part of the whole reverse engineering process is recognizing the known higher level domain concepts in the code.

One method for doing this is matching patterns (also called schemas, templates, cliches, or plans) against the code. The pattern could be the occurrence of a loop and some particular instructions somewhere inside. The whole process could be quite complicated, since in matching several things we could get overlapping matches and have to decide which match to accept. This is the approach taken in the programmers apprentice at MIT (see Rich and Wells, 1990), and that at Arthur Anderson and the University of Illinois (Kozaczynski and Ning 1989, Harandi and Ning 1990, Kozaczynski, Ning, and Engberts 1992). Figure 3 shows the general approach of Harandi and Ning.

A different approach has been the recognition of "objects" in the sense of object-oriented programming. Can particular data items and the functions that operate on them be identified? One method by Garnett and Mariani (1989) looks for data declarations in C and procedures where these appear as arguments, then groups these together. Lano and others on the REDO project (see section 3.2 above) have examined COBOL code and focused on the major files used, grouping these with associated variables and procedures. Both these approaches focus on the code, and the names of the objects would arise accidentally from the data-item names or file names in the code. If these are "meaningful," then the code will have been reversed into a domain model, though clearly the names and other informal information do guide the transformation into objects.

(a) Concepts or "plans" are looked for in the code. The rules show how a particular combination of constructs is taken as evidence that some larger concept is present, for example P52, where a particular combination of assignments indicates a swap.

(b) Sample of a description of software produced by their system. The collection of concepts recognized are displayed within a hierarchy. Note how verbose this description is, with its complete audit trail of how the Bubble sort was recognized.

Throughout this discussion we have had to assume that we knew what we might find in the code we were reverse engineering. Reverse engineering can only take place in the context of a particular domain. This

(a) a machine-eye view of code

```
var
        v001: array[1..v009] of record
                        v002: char;
                        v003: integer;
                end;
        v005, v006: integer;
   function f002 (v004: char): integer;
        var
                v007, v008: integer;
   begin
        v008 := 0;
        for v007 := 1 to v005 do
             if v001[v007].v002 = v004 then
                     begin
                            v008 := v001[v007].v003;
                            leave;
                     end;
        f002 := v008;
   end;
```

(b) the human-eye view of the code—meaningful identifiers added: comments would add yet more information

```
var
        symboltable: array[1..tablesize] of record
                        symbol: char;
                        location: integer;
                end;
        lastsym, symmax: integer;
   function STlookup (sym: char): integer;
        var
                i, loctn: integer;
   begin
        loctn := 0;
        for i := 1 to lastsym do
             if symboltable[i].symbol = sym then
                     begin
                            loctn := symboltable[i].location;
                            leave;
                     end;
        STlookup := loctn;
   end;
```

Figure 2. The importance of informal information in the understanding of software.
The example here is part of simple compiler used for teaching purposes

(a)   *Concepts or "plans" are looked for in the code. The rules show how a particular combination of constructs is taken as evidence that some larger concept is present, for example P52, where a particular combination of assignments indicates a swap.*

P50:   If there exists a decremental FOR-LOOP event
        then there exists a DEC-COUNTER event
P51:   If there exists an incremental FOR-LOOP event
        then there exists an INC-COUNTER event
P52:   If there exists an ASSIGN event from ?V1 to ?T
        which precedes an ASSIGN ?T to ?V2 event and
        another ASSIGN ?V2 to ?V1 event on a control path
        (c-precede)
        then there eists a SIMPLE-SWAP(?V1,?V2) event

P57:   If a FORWARD-MAP-ENUMERATOR event c-encloses
        GUARDED-MAP-SWAP event
        then there exists a FILTERED SEQUENTIAL-MAP-SW
        event
P58:   If a DEC_COUNTER event c-encloses an
        FILTERED-SEQEUNTIAL-MAP-SWAP event
        then there exists a BUBBLE-SORT-MAP event

(b)   *Sample of a description of software produced by their system. The collection of concepts recognized are displayed within a hierarchy. Note how verbose this description is, with its complete audit trail of how the Bubble sort was recognized.*

This program implements a BUBBLE-SORT-MAP event at
lines ... which sorts the map A using a bubble sort
algorithm,
It consists of:
1:      A DEC-COUNTER event at lines (203 245) which
        decrementally changes the value in K from N-1 to 1.
        It consists of:
        1.1:   A FOR-LOOP event at lines (230 245).
2.   A FILTERED-SEQUENTIAL-MAP-SWAP-MAP even
        lines ... which sequentially switches the adjacent
        elements in a map A if A(J-1)>A(J), indexed by J
        from 1 to K
        It consists of:
        2.1:   *etcetera   etcetera*

Figure 3. Analysis approach of Harandi and Ning to understanding a bubble sort program.

450

knowledge is captured within a domain model, but domain models have to be produced themselves. This is the subject of the later section on domain analysis.

4. Software Reuse

4.1 The reuse process

The general idea of software reuse is that it is a component repository from which reusable components may be extracted. Figure 4 shows the general idea. To be able to reuse software components, we need:

- a building-up phase when reusable software is identified and brought together into a library (shown on the left side of Figure 4), component engineering; and

- a design-with-reuse phase when reusable software is selected from the library on the basis of system requirements and reused in the construction of a new software system (shown on the right side of Figure 4). New components may be designed for this system and added into the library.

There is also a need to consider more general knowledge about the area or domain of application of the components, as shown at the bottom left of Figure 4. The knowledge helps us identify suitable components and to structure the component library to aid retrieval (for example with an index or a thesaurus). This domain analysis will be discussed in more detail later.

This overall process could be refined to show more internal details. We will see some of these details in the following sections. A formal process model could be created and enacted under the control of appropriate work-flow software; some Esprit projects, notably RECYCLE, are in the process of doing this.

Integrating reuse within any particular lifecycle of software development is required. In analyzing and designing new systems, the possibility of reuse needs to be considered and the appropriate library components incorporated; new elements of software that are needed should also be considered as candidates for the library and added to it. The REBOOT project has done this for a number of standard development methodologies, from the Clean Room to Structured Analysis and Design (Karlsson 1995).

4.2 Component models

The central ingredient for reuse is the component. Figure 5 gives a visualization of components and their points of connection. Note that in this general view of components, they have multiple interfaces. Components have to be interconnected; in Figure 5 this would take the form of "plugging" the components together as permitted by the type of plug and socket. The equivalent of plugging components together in software is procedure calling, possibly with the additional use of program code to convert data. The programming language used for this purpose is sometimes known as a module interconnection language, introduced by De Remer and Kron in 1976 (see Prieto-Diaz and Neighbors 1986 for a survey).

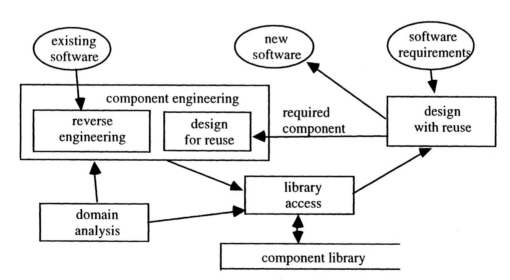

Figure 4. The Reuse Process, built round a component library into which components are added after component engineering, and from which components are taken during design-with-reuse.

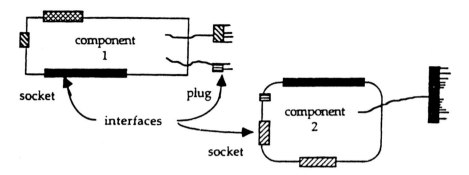

Figure 5. Software components—a diagrammatic representation, showing their interfaces. Plugs show interfaces called (required), while sockets show interfaces offered (provided). Where the shading is the same, the interfaces are of the same type, and plugs can be connected to sockets of the same type.

Deciding which components should be built is guided by domain analysis. When the component is extracted from existing software, reverse engineering is used to identify the component and to abstract the specification. Alternatively, as shown in figure 4, we could create useful software components when developing new software, a process called "design for reuse." We would focus extra effort on developing the new reusable parts to maximize the cost and quality benefits derived from the reuse of these parts within the domain.

Each reusable component should be given a clear specification and description of the principles and concepts underlying the component, independent of any particular implementation. Quality information should be recorded, for example the levels of inspection or proof undertaken, the level of testing carried out, and the results of various metrics. Other administrative information should also be recorded, such as who produced the component and when, its revision history, and a reference site (see Moineau et al. 1990 and Karlsson 1995).

In all cases it is essential to create as general a component as possible, while avoiding over-generalisation which could make specific uses difficult to specialize and inefficient in execution. This requires that generalizations and inductions are made over several more specific components, a process for which no general guidance is available as yet. The general-purpose component would be suitably parameterized, so that particular uses are easily specialized from the generic part.

Very formal models can be created; the most sophisticated are probably those of Goguen (1986), Cramer et al. (1991), and Tracz (1993), but all models have more or less equivalent capabilities for precisely defining the component interfaces and function. These definitions will identify a number of other external components. Interfaces as depicted in Figure 5 can also be viewed as components. Generic parameters will be components. Decomposition will be in terms of an implementation using other components, and in an object-oriented approach, there will be hierarchical subclass relationships to other component classes. It is clear that the particular external connections are interchangeable, and how a particular interconnection is articulated is an issue for the designer of the component.

Object-oriented methods are seen as important for reuse (see Booch 1987, 1991 and Cox 1986, 1990). The objects are the components, providing the encapsulation that is necessary, while inheritance structures provide the contexts for reuse to take place and one important method for actually effecting the reuse. Cox has called reusable parts "software integrated circuits," basing his proposals on object-oriented methods. OO methods are being applied industrially (see Harris 1991), and several ESPRIT projects are taking an object-oriented approach to reuse, for example, REBOOT (see Morel and Faget 1993), ITHACA-2 (Ader et al. 1990, Nierstrasz et al. 1991), and BUSINESS CLASS. This motivation continues with current developments in Object Oriented methods, frameworks, and patterns (see Gamma et al. 1993).

An important issue is the size or granularity of the components—are they small like scientific subroutines, or large like word-processing packages? Clearly there is a place for both, but the requirements for description and storage may be very different. With large components the collection may be quite small and amenable to searching by hand, while small components such as those in the NAG library of numerical routines or the Smalltalk library may lead to very large libraries which require computer support for finding a particular component.

4.3 Storing and Retrieving Reusable Software

Having identified software which is potentially reusable and described in such a way that anyone wishing to reuse it would be able to do so, the problem arises as to how to organize the total collection of all such software and related descriptions. Such a library can be structured by classifying the reusable software in various ways. A good system of classification not only provides the basis for cataloguing the software, but also provides a means for finding a particular piece of software held in the library. One could even view the classification system as a domain model.

Large collections of software present similar problems of classification to those of Information Retrieval (see Salton and McGill 1983). This has proved an attractive area for the research community, with many applications of library classification methods to software component libraries (see Frakes and Nejmeh 1985, Prieto-Diaz and Freeman 1987, Wood and Sommerville 1988, Prieto-Diaz 1991, and Maarek et al. 1991). The faceted classification method of Prieto-Diaz and Freeman (1987) is the current favorite. Albrechtson (1990) has also surveyed the field.

So far software libraries have been very small—typically only a few hundred components, though some special cases like Ada and Smalltalk have a few thousand. The Eiffel libraries have only 300 classes containing some 5,000 visible operations (Meyer 1990). With such small collections, the need for sophisticated library search facilities must be in doubt.

4.4 Designing Software using Reusable Parts

Given a statement of requirements or a detailed specification, or even a high level design, we will need to match this with the reusable software held in a library. We could find a single component that would fully, or almost fully, satisfy our requirement, but might only find a collection of components which, when suitably interconnected, would satisfy the requirement.

The first case is already a common problem in package selection, though this important part of commercial software practice is almost entirely ignored by system development methodologies. What we have to do here is match the requirements or specification against the specifications in the library, using the retrieval mechanisms described above. Exact matching of precise (formal) specifications will in general be undecidable (that is, impossible), and we therefore must necessarily reduce our descriptions for search purposes, accepting that we can only find near matches. Further, even if we could match precisely, we need to recognize that if we cannot find an exact match, we can always customize by adding extra software "shells," or even by modifying code (sometimes called white-box reuse and discussed later). Thus, we would be quite content to accept partial or approximate matches, with some further manual process

required to select the most suitable of the retrieved components.

If some combination of several components could satisfy our requirements, we need to decompose our requirements in some way. One way is clearly an extension of the first, looking for some sub-match of library components to the requirements by searching strings for substrings or graphs for subgraphs. We know of no work in this area.

Alternatively, we could first decompose the requirements into parts, and then search for these in the library; that is, do a high level design. One way to do this would be to use stereotypical designs, often called frameworks, such as those used in some approaches to object oriented design (Wirfs-Brock and Johnson 1990) and described for the ESPRIT Practitioner project (Hall et al. 1990). Frameworks are now well established in object-oriented software development, and the Choices operating system (Campbell et al. 1987) is based on these principles. In OO approaches, a framework is a collection of interconnected objects (abstract classes) which defines the overall architecture of the system. The framework is instantiated by supplying concrete classes to match the abstract classes of the framework. These could be selections of classes that are already available, or they could be created specially in conformance to the abstract class.

Note that the use of a framework is equivalent to the reuse of a design, but it is still code! While many people claim code reuse is irrelevant and that higher level design and specification reuse carries the benefits, frameworks actually help these ideas become concrete and become a special form of code reuse.

The most recent development in the frameworks arena is the use of design patterns. These are small configurations of components which work together to achieve particular ends, but which could not themselves be encapsulated as a component. Rather, they show how to use components and how to build frameworks. The leading book in the field is that of Gamma, Helm, Johnson, and Vlissides (1993), though patterns have been the subject of many conferences and workshops, and many other books are now appearing.

Having selected a component (or set of components) for reuse, it is necessary to adapt the component for its intended use by composing it with other components and new software to achieve the desired results. Adaptation or specialization could vary from modification of sources to the provision of parameter values to a generic package to instantiate it for a particular use, as in Ada or in fully polymorphic languages such as ML. Modifying sources, sometimes known as white-box reuse, is done as a last resort, for this could compromise the quality of the component, and quality was one of the main motivations for software reuse.

To compose components we need a language for building systems. This could be the simple linkage mechanisms of the programming language being used, or the mechanisms available at the command language level, such as pipes in the UNIX shell. However, the language for system building could be developed specifically for module interconnection, either as part of a larger programming system such as Conic (Sloman et al. 1985) or C/MESA (Lauer et al. 1979), or could even be an independent language, such as INTERCOL (Tichy 1980). These module interconnection languages (MILs) enable the consistency of interconnection to be checked by strong typing: a good survey has been given by Prieto-Diaz and Neighbours (1986).

When specialized and connected together, the available code components will probably be insufficient to meet the full requirements and other original code may be necessary, perhaps to transform the outputs from one component to the required form of inputs to another, or perhaps to add other functions not available from the component library.

4. Domain Analysis

In both Reverse Engineering and in Reuse, we have seen that a proper understanding of the application domain is essential. We termed the process of obtaining this understanding domain analysis. To do this we need to identify the major concepts of the area and identify the relationships between these concepts. The importance of this was first identified in the DRACO project (Freeman 1987, Prieto-Diaz and Freeman 1987). The fruits of this analysis are a domain model or domain language.

There will be a number of domain models, ranging from application specific domains like steel rolling mills to generic applications like continuous process control systems, or from generic technology like real-time distributed systems and data base systems to programming domains of procedure call, variables, and assignments.

In Reverse Engineering possible components or concepts are determined by the higher level domain model and the software (code, design description, or whatever) is searched to identify parts which could be components. Having identified potential components, these will be transformed, generalized, and compared against a base of already discovered components until a candidate component has been demonstrated. We can then abstract to the higher level of description and replace the component discovered by the higher level concept. The demonstration that a component is present could be very formal, involving proof techniques

or it could involve access to a human to obtain confirmation. It could also involve the execution of code against some critical test case which will confirm or refute the hypothesis. This continues by finding and confirming/discarding the components as the software is progressively understood in terms of the higher level domain language and moving up levels of language as the reverse engineering progresses.

In Software Reuse domain understanding is important in a number of ways. One way was to guide the production of components. These could be reverse engineered out of existing systems, as described above, or components could be produced from scratch. The important components in the domain are indicated by the domain model. These components then need to be organized in a way that is helpful to designers; again, domain understanding is important, typically being captured as a thesaurus. Components need to be assembled into particular systems—often these will be stereotypical solutions or frameworks-again manifesting domain understanding.

The notations used for domain analysis could be conceptual dependencies (Schank 1972) or, similarly, simply some form of data analysis using entity-relationship models (see Teory and Fry 1982 and Nijssen and Halpin 1989). They could even be thesauri (see Aitchison and Gilchrist 1971 and Townley and Gee, 1980). Object-oriented methods have also been proposed. The process of domain analysis has much in common with knowledge acquisition, but needs further development (see Simos 1988 and Prieto-Diaz 1990). In its most general form, domain analysis could be viewed as an attempt to formalize scientific method, an enterprise that is doomed to failure.

What constitutes an adequate domain model is the subject of much debate. We need compact and precise modeling methods that have an adequate expressive power, and a strong case against entity-relationship models has been made (Carasik et al. 1990) on the basis of its inadequacy for modeling natural language. However, this does seem to miss the issue of whether or not it is adequate for the required modeling task. Entity relationship models have been widely used and found adequate, particularly when extended with inheritance in what is sometimes called structurally object-oriented systems. Whether fully object-oriented methods will prove adequate remains to be seen, though clearly they are the premier candidates for use in domain models.

Domain models and design frameworks are converging in domain specific software architectures. A workshop was held by DARPA in 1990 and the idea of domain specific software architectures recurs from time to time as a means of leveraging specific applications and encapulating commercial assets (Tracz 1995).

5. Implementing software reuse and re-engineering

In order to promote reuse, it is not sufficient to establish the correct technical environment; we must also address other non-technical issues, such as managerial practices and the legal constraints of a particular community.

5.1 Reuse methods

A number of reuse methods have emerged and there is an increasing volume of literature describing the successful introduction of reuse into companies (see Matsumoto 1993 and Kruzela and Brorsson 1992). NATO has developed a reuse policy, and the US armed forces are mandating reuse similar to the way they earlier mandated the use of Ada.

Basili's approach (1990, 1991) is proving popular. This approach focuses on the comprehensive or full reuse of requirements, design, and code from any earlier versions and the reuse of processes and other knowledge. It includes a reuse model (Basili 1991), characterization schemes, and a supporting environment model. Each reuse candidate is characterized as a series of descriptors: name, function, use, type, granularity, representation, input/output, dependencies, application domain, solution domain, and object domain. Required objects are also described in the same way. Reuse consists of transforming existing reuse candidates into required objects and comprises four basic activities: identification, evaluation, modification, and integration. The categories for each reuse activity are name, function, type, mechanism, input/output, dependencies, experience transfer, and reuse quality. The important components of the supporting environment model are the project organization and the experience factory. Each project is carried out according to the quality improvement paradigm consisting of the following steps: plan, execute, and package. At each step, reuse requirements are identified and matches made against reuse candidates available in the experience base. In the final step, a decision is made as to which experiences are worth recording in the experience base.

A comprehensive methodology has been developed within the REBOOT project which will enable reuse to be added to any existing method. Pilot studies have been made of integrating reuse into the cleanroom method and object oriented methods. A reuse handbook has been published (Karlsson 1995).

5.2 Personnel issues

People who work in software production like producing software and will develop software rather than look for existing ideas, algorithms, or code. They use all sorts of personally persuasive arguments:

- "Reinventing software is fun!"
- "Why buy when you can build?"
- "Having seen the commercial product, I know I could build it better."
- "If somebody else built it, could you really trust it?"
- "In acquiring software from outside, there is always some compromise required; it never does exactly what is wanted."
- "If you build it yourself, you can control its future development; it will always do what you want."

The ability to build software yourself, be it by an individual software engineer, by a project, or by the organization as a whole, is an enormous barrier to reuse. Contrast this with electronic engineering, where the cost of designing and fabricating your own microprocessor is so enormous, and requires such specialized equipment, that it is only undertaken in very special circumstances—the margin between buying and building is very many orders of magnitude. The margins between buying and building software are not so great, except in the large volume micro-computer marketplace. In other cases, a first shot development could be as cheap as acquiring the software from elsewhere.

For the individual, the cost of acquisition consists of finding the requisite software, and we can address this through the various technical measures discussed above, as well as by the continued training and education of the individual so that more abstract entities will also be reused. The use of networks, with global information access mechanisms like Gopher, WWW, and Internet, has led to the wider dissemination of information, and the Esprit project EUROWARE has investigated the problems of offering a commercial service using these network technologies. A follow-on project, IECASE, has found that there was commercial potential here, particularly if associated with support services.

It is the ratio of cost to benefit that counts, and in addition to reducing the cost, we could also increase the benefit. If reuse does enhance productivity, then at least at the project and company levels there are payoffs. But what about the individual? What extra benefit does he/she get from reuse?

The Japanese practice of changing the monetary and status rewards for individuals is worth considering. Firstly, those who provide software for others to reuse could receive some form of royalty for this reuse, encouraging both the production of general purpose elements suitably proven and packaged for reuse, but also encouraging the promotion of the element's availability. The actual reuse should be encouraged, perhaps through piecework where the reward for the job was assessed without reuse in mind, or perhaps through a royalty on reuse for the reuser as well as the supplier. The status of people who succeed in reuse could be enhanced, possibly with the position of manager of the library of reusable components being made a highly rewarded and sought after post. This status and reward should be comparable with systems architects and database administrators which are highly sought after and respected jobs and are very similar in their intent. See for example the writings of Yoshiro Matsumoto (1981, 1992).

There is no doubt that for reuse to be successful, some form of cultural shift is necessary, with people's and institutional attitudes changing.

5.2 Economics of Reuse

The payoff for reuse occurs only after the item's initial production. Projects are usually established simply to look after the initial development of a software system, with their performance being judged solely by the costs and timescales of the project. Frequently there are quality problems resulting from this practice which become the responsibility of the maintenance team. This management practice does encourage reuse to reduce project costs, but does not encourage the production of reusable components for other projects because there are no benefits. Again, some form of royalty payable to the project might be appropriate as long as company accounting practices agreed. Alternatively, the Reusable Components Manager could be given a budget to invest in the production of components, either by subsidizing their production on projects or creating them speculatively.

A preliminary economic analysis appropriate to individual organizations has been given by Lubars (1986) and taken further by Gaffney and Durek (1989). Wolff (1990) and Barnes and Bollinger (1991) view this as an investment activity. Clearly commercial decisions concerning investment in components is very similar to investment in research and development, and company policies in these two areas could be usefully related. Accounting practices will often treat software as a consumable, and not as a capital asset, and this needs to be looked into.

Software reuse between organizations, both nationally and internationally, currently takes place through the production and sale of packages. The experience of the software packages industry is important in understanding how the reuse industry could be expanded to include reusable components.

If you build it in-house, you may be in total control of its development, but unaware of other costs. Maintenance of in-house software is likely to be more expensive since the software is likely to be less robust and it may be subject to uncontrolled voluntary "improvements" that are not required and add to cost.

Preparing software for reuse as a component does require extra effort and this extra effort needs to be rewarded. In the open market this reward would be some form of royalty or license fee. There may be problems in enforcing these payments, and disputes within the industry are frequent. However, libraries of mathematical routines have been marketed successfully for many years by the Numerical Algorithms Group in Oxford, and one person has produced a set of Ada components and is selling them (Booch 1987).

It is clear that to avoid some of these problems, a software components industry should be high-volume and low-cost, producing robust and stable products with low or zero maintenance costs. The margins between buying over building should be so great that one would never contemplate building when a component was available for purchase.

5.3 Legal issues

Illegal copying of software is a problem (see Suhler et al. 1986). Copyright protection of software is emerging, but clearly needs to be practiced internationally and improved. Many software producers appear to accept this situation and seek to earn revenue from their software in other ways, such as selling manuals or books about using it, or by selling training services. But the problem is more subtle than that.

The ability to reverse engineer software brings about conflicts concerning the market for software products. On the one hand the suppliers of software products should be protected against their products being illegally copied, not just at the level of software piracy, but at the level of rival products developed. Reverse engineering makes it possible to work back from executable code to design descriptions of exactly how the software works, and then to re-engineer the software with selected additions to form the rival product. In Europe the CEC has issued a directive making this illegal (see Lee 1992).

However, we also want an open market so that third party suppliers of software can provide products that connect to those of others, particularly the big suppliers. To do this, public interfaces need to be used and adequately documented, although in practice they often are not. All too frequently, when interfacing two pieces of software, some level of reverse engineering needs to be undertaken, and this seems to be a legitimate activity in the interests of open markets. This conflicts with the CEC directive which forbids any reverse engineering.

To maintain competitive advantage, some parts of a company's software may always be proprietary. The proprietary software may not even be sophisticated but comparable to the way application specific integrated circuits are used in hardware designs to make designs difficult to reproduce. We must always expect some level of non-reuse.

Software is not a commodity. It does not become an asset of a company that purchases it. Software may be written off in the first year after purchase, whereas hardware may be written off over 3 to 5 years or more. Software may not be allowed to be sold. For example, a computer manufacturer has required that purchasers of second-hand hardware relicense the software. There is no market in second-hand software; indeed, the very idea seems mildly ridiculous. Could this be changed? One could envisage some legal remedies to remove the restrictions and monopolistic practices. Could we get as far as enabling competitive third-party software maintenance? This whole area is receiving much more serious attention now that trading assets on the Internet is seen to have great potential, providing that intellectual assets can be suitably protected.

6 Conclusions

We have seen the development over the past 25 years of the practice of reverse engineering, re-engineering, and software reuse. Reuse is concerned with accumulating libraries of components, which could be designs and specifications, as well as code. Reverse engineering is the abstraction of design and specification descriptions of existing software to increase the life of the software. It is usually a prelude to restructuring and forward engineering, which together constitute re-engineering. Reverse engineering is also one method for obtaining components.

The technology for these is now well established, and while it is the focus of on-going research, there is really no technical barrier to reuse and re-engineering. We saw how the issue now is implementing the practices in this area.

Recently there have been two developments that point the way forward. The first is a research program by Batory and O'Malley (1992) who have separately developed sets of components for databases and communications respectively, together with a set of tools for composing particular configurations of their components to meet a particular need. They call their approach generative reuse. It can be seen as a domain specific language and compiler, and is a re-absorption of reuse into language technology, which we saw at the start of this paper as one of the origins of reuse.

The second is a program of reuse implementation at Schlumberger, reported by Arango et al. (1993). Here, instead of developing software components, they have written technology handbooks to document the corporation's expertise in their market areas. When this paper was presented at the international reuse workshop in Lucca, Italy in March 1993, it was awarded the prize for the best paper, so the program committee considered this a very important development for reuse. Recall the discussion at the start of this paper, that one of the conventional forms of reuse had been through the educational process? Here we see a further example of this conventional process, though the education is within company and proprietary.

In the implementation of reuse, existing methods are having reuse added into them. This is yet another example of the acceptance of reuse as part of the normal process of software development.

Does this mean that reuse, and reverse engineering and re-engineering, have now become established as part of the normal processes of software development? Should we now anticipate the demise of these areas as a separate branch of study?

7 Bibliography and References

Abbott, B., T. Bapty, C. Biegl, G. Karsai, and J. Sztipanovits, "Model-Based Software Synthesis," *IEEE Software,* May 1993, pp. 42–52.

Ader, M., O. Nierstrasz, S. McMahon, G. Mueller, and A.-K. Proefrock, "The ITHACA Technology: A Landscape for Object-Oriented Application Development," *ESPRIT '90 Conf. Proc.,* 1990.

Aitchison, J. and A. Gilchrist, *Thesaurus Construction: A practical Manual,* Aslib, 1971.

Albrechtson, H., "Software Information Systems: Information Retrieval Techniques," in *Software Reuse and Reverse Engineering in Practice,* Unicom seminar, Dec 1990.

AMICE ESPRIT Consortium, ed., *Open System Architecture for CIM,* Springer-Verlag, 1989.

Arango, G., E., Shoen, and R. Pettengill, "Design as Evolution and Reuse," *Advances in Software Reuse: Selected Papers from the 2nd Int'l Workshop on Software Reusability,* IEEE Computer Society Press, Los Alamitos, Calif., 1993, pp. 9–18.

Arnold, R.S., *Tutorial on Software Restructuring,* IEEE Computer Society Press, Los Alamitos, Calif., 1986.

Barnes, B.H and T.B. Bollinger, "Making Reuse Cost-Effective," *IEEE Software*, Jan. 1991, pp. 13–24.

Basili, V.R., "Viewing Maintenance as Reuse-Oriented Software Development," *IEEE Software*, Jan. 1990, pp. 19–25.

Basili, V.R. and H.D. Rombach, "Support for Comprehensive Reuse," *Software Eng. J.*, Sept. 1991, pp. 303–316.

Batory, D. and S. O'Malley, "The Design and Implementation of Hierarchical Software Systems with Reusable Components," *ACM Trans. Software Eng. and Methodology.* Vol. 1. No. 4, 1992, pp. 355–398.

BCS Displays Group, *Proc. Systems Integration and Data Exchange,* 1990.

Biggerstaff, T.J., "Design Recovery for Maintenance and Reuse, *Computer*, July 1989, pp. 36–49.

Bollinger T.B. and S.L. Pfleeger, "Economics of Reuse: Issues and Alternatives," *Information and Software Technology,* Dec. 1990.

Booch, G., *Software Components with Ada, Structures, Tools and Subsystems,* Benjamin/Cummings Publishing Company, 1987.

Booch, G., *Object Oriented Design with Applications,* Benjamin/Cummings Publishing Company, 1991.

Callis, F.W. and B.J. Cornelius, "Two Module Factoring Techniques," *Software Maintenance: Research and Practice,* Vol. 1, 1989, pp. 81–89.

Campbell, R, G. Johnston, and V. Russo, "Choices (Class Hierarchical Open Interface for Custom Embedded Systems)," *ACM Operating Systems Rev.*, Vol. 21, No. 3, July 1987, pp. 9–17.

Carasik, R.P., S.M. Johnson, D.A. Patterson, and G.A. Von Glahn, "Towards a Domain Description Grammar: An Application of Linguistic Semantics," *ACM SIGSOFT Software Eng. Notes,* Vol. 15, No. 5, Oct. 1990, pp. 28–43.

Chikofsky, E.J. and, J.H. Cross, II, "Reverse Engineering and Design Recovery: A Taxonomy," *IEEE Software,* Jan. 1990, pp. 13–17.

Cimitile, A. and U. Decarlini, "Reverse Engineering—Algorithms for Program Graph Production," *Software—Practice & Experience*, Vol. 21, No. 5, 1991, pp. 519–537.

Cox, B.J., *Object-Oriented Programming,* Addison-Wesley, Reading, Mass., 1986.

Cox, B.J., "There is a Silver Bullet," *Byte*, Vol. 15, No. 10, 1990, pp. 209–218.

Cramer, J., W. Fey, G. Michael, and M. Große-Rhode, "Towards a Formally Based Component Description Language—A Foundation for Reuse," *Structured Programming*, Vol. 12, No. 2, 1991, pp. 91–110.

DARPA. *Proc. 1990 Workshop on Domain-Specific Software Architectures*, available from the DSSA Program Manager, DARPA/ISTO, 1400 Wilson Blvd., Arlington, VA 22209.

De Remer, F. and H.H. Kron, "Programming in the Large versus Programming in the Small," *IEEE Trans. Software Eng.*, June 1976, pp. 312–327.

Dulay, N., J. Kramer, J. Magee, M. Sloman, and K. Twiddle, *The Conic Configuration Language*, Version 1.3, Imperial College London, Research Report DOC 84/20, Aug. 1985.

Fickas, S. and B.R. Helm, "Knowledge Representation and Reasoning in the Design of Composite Systems," *IEEE Trans. Software Eng.*, Vol. 18, No. 6, June 1992, pp. 470–482.

Frakes, W.B. and B.A. Nejmeh, "Software Reuse Through Information Retrieval," *SIGIR Forum,* Vol. 21, 1986–1987, pp. 1–2.

Freeman, P., "A Conceptual Analysis of the Draco Approach to Constructing Software Systems," *IEEE Trans. Software Eng.,* 1987 and included in *IEEE Tutorial: Software Reusability*, IEEE Computer Society Press, Los Alamitos, Calif., 1987.

Gaffney, J.E., Jr., and T.A. Durek, "Software Reuse—Key to Enhanced Productivity: Some Quantitative Models," *Information and Software Technology.* Vol. 31, No. 5, June 1989, pp. 258–267.

Gamma, E., R. Helm, R. Johnson, and J. Vlissides, *Design Patterns: Elements of Reusable Object-Oriented Software,* Addison Wesley, Reading, Mass., 1995.

Garnett, E.S. and J.A. Mariani, *Software Reclamation*, Dept of Computing, University of Lancaster, 1989.

Goguen, J.A., "Reusing and Interconnecting Software Components," *Computer*, Feb. 1986, pp. 16–28.

Goldberg, A. and D. Robson, *Smalltalk-80: The Language and Its Implementation*, Addison-Wesley, Reading, Mass., 1983.

Hall, P., "Software Reuse, Reverse Engineering, and Re-engineering," *Unicom Seminar Software Reuse and Reverse Engineering in Practice,* 1990.

Hall, P., C. Boldyreff, P. Elzer, J. Keilmann, L. Olsen, and J. Witt, "PRACTITIONER: Pragmatic Support for the Reuse of Concepts in Existing Software," *ancillary papers at ESPRIT Week, 1990*

Hall, P.A.V., "SOFTWARE COMPONENTS Reuse—Getting More Out of Your Code," *Information and Software Technology,* Butterworths, Jan/Feb 1987. Reprinted in *Software Reuse: Emerging Technology*, Will Tracz, ed., IEEE Computer Society Press, Los Alamitos, Calif., 1988.

Harandi, M.T. and J.Q. Ning, "Knowledge-Based Program Analysis," *IEEE Software*, Jan. 1990, pp. 74–81.

Harris, K.R., "Using Object-Oriented Methods to Develop Reusable Software for Test and Measurement Systems: A Case Study," *Proc. 1st Int'l Workshop on Software Reusability,* 1991, pp. 71–78.

Harrison,W., C. Gens, and B. Gifford, "pRETS: a parallel Reverse-engineering ToolSet for FORTRAN," *J. Software Maintenance,* Vol. 5, 1993, pp. 37–57.

IEEE Trans. Software Eng., Special Issue on Software Reusability. Vol. SE-10, No. 5, Sept. 1984.

Jones, T.C., "Reusability in Programming: A Survey of the State of the Art," in (IEEE 84), pp. 488–494.

Karlsson, E.-A., *Software Reuse—A Holistic Approach,* Wiley, New York, N.Y., 1995.

Katsoulakis, Takis, "An Overview of the Esprit project REDO, Maintenance Validation Documentation of Software Systems," *Proc. ESPRIT Conf.,* 1990.

Kozaczynski, W. and J.Q. Ning, "SRE: A Knowledge-based Environment for Large-Scale Software Re-engineering Activities," *Proc. Int'l Conf. Software Eng.,* IEEE Computer Society Press, Los Alamitos, Calif., 1989, pp. 113–122.

Kolodner, J.L. (ed.), *Proc. Case-based Reasoning Workshop,* Darpa 1989.

Kozaczynski, W., J. Ning,, and A. Engberts, "Program Concept Recognition and Transformation," *IEEE Trans. Software Eng.,* Vol. 18, No. 12, 1992, pp. 1065–1075.

Kramer, J. and J. Magee, "Dynamic Configuration for Distributed Systems," *IEEE Trans. Software Eng.,* Vol. SE-11, No. 4, Apr. 1985, pp. 424–436.

Kruzela, I and M. Brorsson, "Human Aspects and Organizational Issues of Software Reuse," in *Software Reuse and Reverse Engineering in Practice,* P.A.V. Hall, (ed.), Chapman & Hall, London, U.K., 1992, pp. 521–534.

Lanergan, R.G. and C.A. Grasso, *Software Engineering with Reusable Designs and Code,* in (IEEE 1984), pp. 498–501.

Lano, K. and P.T. Breuer, *From Programs to Z Specifications,* Z User's Meeting, Dec 1989.

Lano, K., P.T. Breuer, and H. Haughton, "Reverse-engineering COBOL via Formal Methods," *J. Software Maintenance,* Vol. 5, No. 1, Mar. 1993, pp. 13–35.

Lauer, H.C. and E.H. Satterthwaite, "The Impact of MESA on System Design," *Proc. 4th Int'l Conf. Software Eng.,* IEEE Computer Society Press, Los Alamitos, Calif., 1979, pp. 174–182.

Lee, M.K.O., "The Legal position of Reverse Software Engineering in the UK," *Unicom Seminar Software Reuse and Reverse Engineering in Practice,* Chapman & Hall, London, UK, 1992, pp. 559–572.

Lehman, M.M. and N.V. Stenning, "Concepts of an Integrated Project Support Environment," *Data Processing,* Vol. 27, No. 3, Apr. 1985.

Littlewood, B., "Software Reliability Model for Modular Program Structure," *IEEE Trans. Reliability,* Vol. R-28, 1979, pp. 241–246.

Lubars, M.D, "Affording Higher Software Reliability Through Software Reusability," *ACM SIGSOFT Software Eng. Notes,* Vol. 11, No. 5, Oct. 1986.

Lupton, P., "Promoting Forward Simulation," *Proc. 5th Ann. Z User meeting,* 1990. To be published in the BCS and Springer in their workshop series.

Maarek, Y.S., D.M. Berry, and G.E. Kaiser, "An Information Retrieval Approach for Automatically Constructing Software Libraries," *IEEE Trans. Software Eng.,* Vol. 17, No. 8, Aug. 1991, pp. 800–813.

Matsumoto, Y, *The Japanese Software Factory,* Academic Press, New York, N.Y., 1992.

Matsumoto, Y., "Experiences from Software Reuse in Industrial Process Control Applications. Advances in Software Reuse," *Proc. 2nd Int'l Workshop Software Reusability,* IEEE Computer Society Press, Los Alamitos, Calif., 1993, pp. 186–195.

Matsumoto, Y, O. Sasaki, S. Nakajima, K. Takezawa, S. Yamamoto, and T. Tanaka, "SWB System: a Software Factory," in *Software Engineering Environments,* Huenke, ed., North-Holland, Amsterdam, The Netherlands, 1981, pp. 305–318.

McIllroy, M.D., "Mass-Produced Software Components" in *Software Engineering Concepts and Techniques,* Petrocelli/Charter, Belgium, 1976, pp. 88–98.

McWilliams, G., "Users see a CASE Advance in Reverse Engineering Tools," *Datamation,* Feb. 1, 1988, pp. 30–36.

Meyer, B., "Lessons from the Design of the Eiffel Libraries," *Comm. ACM,* Vol. 33, No. 9, 1990, pp. 69–88.

Moineau, Th., J. Abadir, and E. Rames, "Towards a Generic and Extensible Reuse Environment," *Proc. SE '90 Conf.,* Cambridge University Press, 1990.

Morel, J. and J. Faget, "The REBOOT Environment," *Advances in Software Reuse: Selected Papers Proc. 2nd Int'l Workshop Software Reusability,* IEEE Computer Society Press, Los Alamitos, Calif., 1993, pp. 80–88.

Neighbors, J., *The Draco Approach to Constructing Software from Reusable Components,* in (IEEE 84).

Nierstrasz, O,. D. Tsichritzis, V. de May, and M. Stadelmann, "Objects + Scripts = Applications," *ESPRIT '91 Conf. Proc.*

Nijssen, G.M. and T.A. Halpin, *Conceptual Schema and Relational Database Design,* Prentice Hall, Englewood Cliffs, N.J., 1989.

Prieto-Diaz, R. and P. Freeman, "Classifying Software for Reusability," *IEEE Software,* Jan. 1987, pp. 6–16.

Prieto-Diaz, R., "Domain Analysis: an Introduction," *Software Engineering Notes,* Vol. 15, No. 2, Apr. 1990, pp. 47–54.

Prieto-Diaz, R. and J. Neighbors, "Module Interconnection Languages," *J. System Sciences*, Vol. 6, No. 4, Nov. 1986, pp. 307–334.

Prieto-Diaz, R., "Implementing Faceted Classification for Software Reuse," *Comm. ACM,* Vol. 34, No. 5, 1991, pp. 88–97.

Rich, C. and L.M. Wills, "Recognising a Program's Design: A Graph-Parsing Approach," *IEEE Software*, Jan. 1990, pp. 82–89.

Rock-Evans, R. and K. Hales, *Reverse Engineering: Markets, Methods and Tools*, Ovum 1990.

Salton and M. McGill, *Introduction to Modern Information Retrieval,* McGraw-Hill, New York, N.Y., 1983.

Simos, M.A., position paper for the *Proc. Workshop on Tools and Environments for Reuse,* 1988.

Sloman, M., J. Kramer, and J. Magee, "The Conic Toolkit for Building Distributed Systems," *Proc. 6th IFAC Distributed Computer Control Systems Workshop,* Pergamon Press, London, U.K., 1985.

Sneed, H. and G. Jandrasics, "Software Recycling," *Proc. Software Maintenance Conf.,* IEEE Computer Society Press, Los Alamitos, Calif., 1987.

Sneed, H.M. and G. Jandrasics, "Inverse Transformation from Code to Specification," *Proc. Software Tools '89,* Blenhiem Online, 1989, pp. 82–90.

Spivey, M., *The Z Notation,* Prentice-Hall, Englewood Cliffs, N.J., 1989.

Standish, T.A., *An Essay on Software Reuse,* in (IEEE 1984), pp. 494–497.

Suhler, P.A., N. Bagherzadeh, M. Malek, and N. Iscoe, "Software Authorisation Systems," *IEEE Software,* Jan. 1986, pp. 34 et seq.

Swanson, E.B. and C.M. Beath, *Maintaining Information Systems in Organisations,* Wiley, New York, N.Y., 1989.

Teory, T.J. and J.P. Fry, *Design of Database Structures,* Prentice Hall, Englewood Cliffs, N.J., 1982.

Tichy, W.F., "Software Development Control Based on Module Interconnection," *Proc. 4th Int'l Software Eng. Conf.,* IEEE Computer Society Press, Los Alamitos, Calif., 1979, pp. 29–41.

Tichy, W.F., *Software Development Control Based on Systems Structure Description,* PhD thesis, Carnegie-Mellon University, Computer Science Department, Jan. 1980.

Townley, H.M. and R.D. Gee,, *Thesaurus Making. Grow Your Own Word-Stock,* Andre Deutsch, 1980.

Tracz, W., "LILEANNA: A Parameterized Programming Language," *Advances in Software Reuse: Proc. Selected Papers 2nd Int'l Workshop Software Reusability,* IEEE Computer Society Press, Los Alamitos, Calif., 1993, pp. 66–70.

van Zuylen H.J., (ed.), *The REDO Compendium: Reverse Engineering for Software Maintenance,* Wiley, New York, N.Y., 1993.

Ward, M., *Transforming a Program into a Specification,* Computer Science Technical Report 88/1, University of Durham, Jan. 1988.

Waters, R.C., "Program Translation via Abstraction and Reimplementation," *IEEE Trans. Software Eng,* Vol. 14, No. 8, Aug. 1988, pp. 1207–1228.

Wegner, P., "Capital-Intensive Software Technology," *IEEE Software,* July 1984, pp. 7–45.

Wirfs-Brock, R.J. and R.E. Johnson, "Surveying Current Research into Object-Oriented Design," *Comm. ACM,* Vol. 33, No. 9, Sept. 1990, pp. 104–124.

Wolff, F., "Long-term Controlling of Software Reuse," PRACTITIONER working paper BrU-0100, Brunel University, Sept. 1990.

Wood, M. and I. Sommerville, "An information Retrieval System for Software Components," *Software Engineering J.,* Sept 1988, pp. 199–207.

Yau, S.S. and J.J. Tsai, "Knowledge Representation of Software Component Interconnection Information for Large-Scale Software Modifications," *IEEE Trans. Software Eng.,* Vol. 13, No. 3, Mar. 1987, pp. 355–361.

Prototyping: alternative systems development methodology

J M Carey

Prototyping has become a popular alternative to traditional systems development methodologies. The paper explores the various definitions of prototyping to determine its advantages and disadvantages and to present a systematic methodology for incorporating the prototyping process into the existing system development process within an organization. In addition, one negative and one positive case study of prototyping within industrial settings is included.

system development methodologies, prototyping, software life-cycle

In recent years, use of prototyping has increased dramatically for both the requirements definition phase of the systems development life-cycle and rapid building of end-user systems[1]. The increase has been primarily due to the advent of fourth-generation language (4GL) application generators.

A study of Texas-based computer facilities showed that prototyping was more widely used than almost any offline, structured, software-development tools, such as dataflow diagrams and decision tables[1].

This paper explores the definition of prototyping, the advantages and disadvantages of using this technique, and how to determine when a prototyping approach is appropriate.

CONSENSUS DEFINITION

If various analysts and programmers were asked to define prototyping, the responses would vary considerably, depending on experience and training. Prototyping has taken on a variety of meanings and uses and has been variously defined as follows:

'a strategy for determining requirements wherein user needs are extracted, presented, and defined by building a working model of the ultimate system – quickly and in context' (p 25)[2]

'Prototyping is based on building a model of the

system to be developed. The initial model should include the major program modules, the data base, screens, reports and inputs and outputs that the system will use for communicating with other, interface systems' (p 69)[3]

'working models used to check accuracy of designs before committing to full-scale production' (p 79)[4]

'The idea behind prototyping is to include users in the development cycle' (p 93)[5]

What do these definitions have in common? First, prototyping is seen as a model of the final system, much like in the automobile industry where prototype or model cars are built and tested before full-scale production is attempted. In prototyping a software system, only parts of the system are developed, with a key emphasis on the user interfaces, such as menus, screens, reports, and source documents. The prototype is then a shell of the final system with no calculations and data behind the interfaces. The final system is either built from scratch using the prototype as a model or evolved from the prototype.

Second, the emphasis is on user involvement in the software development process. In the traditional software development life-cycle, communication between analysts and users occurs early in the cycle to determine information needs, then the analysts work, in isolation, to develop the system and seldom interact with the users until system delivery and production. As users have little input into the development process, the resultant system is often dissatisfactory and difficult to learn and use. Prototyping provides a 'hands-on' communication tool to allow the analyst to determine user needs and ensure ongoing communication throughout the development process, thus ensuring that the system is the 'right' one for the user.

Third, prototyping produces an information system faster than using the traditional life-cycle approach. When users are frustrated by the development backlog that exists in most organizations, speed of delivery can be a great selling point. This is often called 'rapid prototyping' by proponents and 'quick and dirty' by opponents.

Taking these three underlying ideas and incorporating them into one gives the following consensus definition:

'Prototyping' is the process of quickly building a model of the final software system, which is used

Arizona State University – West Campus, P.O. Box 37100, Phoenix, AZ 85069–7100, USA.

Paper submitted: 19 April 1989.
Revised version received: 12 September 1989.

primarily as a communication tool to assess and meet the information needs of the user.

RATIONALE FOR PROTOTYPING

The traditional software development approach has several inherent problems, which prototyping attempts to address. These problems include the following[2,6]:

- Users seldom have clear, concise understanding of their informational needs. Therefore, they cannot prespecify the requirements. Once they begin to use a system, however, it is clear to them where the problems lie.
- The traditional function specification is a narrative description of an information system that is technical and time consuming to read. Static graphic techniques (such as dataflow diagrams, and data dictionary entries found in the structured approach) once thought to be the solution to communication cannot demonstrate the workings of a live dynamic system[7].
- The larger the development team, including user representatives, the more difficult communication becomes[8]. Semantic barriers and lack of physical proximity and time inhibit the ability of all members of the team to have a common understanding of the system being developed.
- Even if systems developed in the traditional manner function correctly, they may be difficult to learn and use.
- Both traditional and structured approaches emphasize documentation, which is time consuming and as the system changes may not be accurate[9].
- Systems being developed today are more complex, have a larger mission, and require many months to complete. The traditional approach has not served to shorten delivery time, in fact it may unduly lengthen the time required due to the emphasis on documentation[9].
- Because of the large number of people/months involved and time-consuming methods, traditional approaches not only seem to deliver late systems that do not please the user, they are also costly.
- Most large companies have a long backlog of projects awaiting initiation, while the users who requested them are frustrated, disillusioned, and ready to revolt.

All of these problems suggest that some revolutionary technique is needed. Prototyping is one technique that attempts to address these problems and provide possible solutions.

PROTOTYPING ENVIRONMENTS

There are two major types of prototyping environments[5,10]. One is a complete and integrated application-generator environment or automated development environment (ADE), which can produce quick, inte-

grated menus, reports, and screens and is tied to a database. Examples are R:base 5000 or System V for the microcomputer and NOMAD2 for the mainframe.

A prototyping toolkit comprises the other environment. The toolkit is a collection of unintegrated tools that aid the rapid building of the separate pieces of a system, such as screen painters, data dictionaries, and report generators. Together, these tools are often referred to as analysts' or programmers' 'workbench'.

The following 'workbench' tools can aid the prototyping process:

- text editors
- screen generators
- report generators
- relational databases
- fourth-generation languages (4GLs)
- spreadsheets
- data dictionaries coupled to database management systems
- *ad hoc* query languages
- security
- statistical packages
- back-up routines
- documentation generators
- online help
- interactive testing system

If purchased separately, these tools are initially expensive when compared with the traditional method of coding in a third-generation language (3GL) such as COBOL. Also, before jumping into prototyping, a training period for both development team and users is required.

Acquiring the tools or environment is just the first step. Once the environment for building a prototype has been created and staff and users thoroughly trained in the use of prototyping tools, a systematic methodology should be adopted that is tailored to the specific organization and then followed to ensure that the system that results from the prototyping technique is both usable and correct. All too often, companies purchase prototyping packages and jump into prototyping without trying to determine when and how to use the technique.

The following five steps are suggested by Klinger[6], manager of laboratory systems and programming at Ortho Pharmaceutical Corporation, as a successful approach to the use of prototyping:

- Assess each application individually. Would prototyping provide gains?
- Look at the environment and then develop and document a formal prototyping life-cycle that fits it.
- Acquire appropriate software tools and train the staff.
- Decide how the software development process will be managed and controlled.
- Train end-users in the procedures that will be followed during the prototyping life-cycle.

ITERATIVE (TYPE I) VERSUS THROWAWAY (TYPE II) PROTOTYPING

One confusion in defining prototyping arises from the existence of two distinct types of prototyping that are used by various companies. These two basic approaches to prototyping are iterative and throwaway. The iterative approach (Type I) uses the prototype as the final system after a series of evolutionary changes based on user feedback. The throwaway approach (Type II) uses the prototype built in a 4GL as a model for the final system, with the final system coded in a 3GL.

In the Type I (iterative) approach, the life-cycle consists of the following stages[6]:

- training
- project planning
- rapid analysis
- database development
- prototype iteration
- modelling
- detailed design
- implementation
- maintenance

The inclusion of training and project planning is unique. These stages are seldom mentioned in the traditional life-cycle. The modelling stage is also unique and important. It is at this stage that the prototype system is tested through benchmarking to make sure it performs within acceptable standards. Possible replacement code may be needed at bottlenecks in the prototype. Sometimes 3GL code may be substituted for any original 4GL that has been determined as inefficient. Figure 1 shows the system development life-cycle incorporating Type I prototyping.

In the Type II (throwaway) approach, some iteration occurs and the steps of analysis, design, coding, testing, and modification may be repeated many times until all of the users' requirements are identified and met. Once the prototyping phase is complete, then the prototype serves as a model for final production system, but is discarded at the project delivery[6]. The throwaway prototyping approach generally adheres to the traditional life-cycle once the prototype has been developed. Figure 2 illustrates the system development life-cycle incorporating the Type II prototyping technique.

ADVANTAGES OF PROTOTYPING

Prototyping is being used in industry with varying degrees of success. Proponents of prototyping cite the following positive attributes:

- Systems can be developed much faster[11].
- Systems are easier for end-users to learn and use.
- Programming and analysis effort is much less (less humanpower needed).
- Development backlogs can be decreased[12].
- Prototyping facilitates end-user involvement.
- System implementation is easier because users know what to expect.

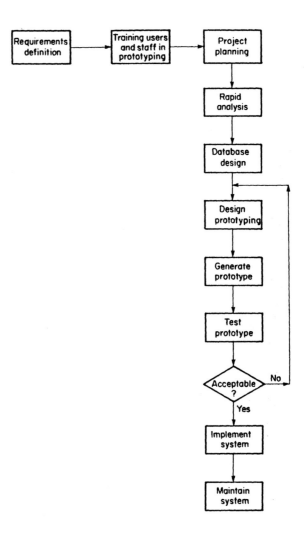

Figure 1. System development life-cycle using Type I (iterative) prototyping

- Prototyping enhances user/analyst communication.
- User requirements are easier to determine.
- Development costs are reduced.
- The resultant system is the 'right' system and needs little changing.

All of these positive attributes make prototyping sound like the system development dream, like the answer to all analyst's and user's problems. Indeed, many organizations have adapted some use of prototyping within their development life-cycle. However, there is a downside to prototyping.

DISADVANTAGES OF PROTOTYPING

Undue user expectations[13] The ability of the systems group to develop a prototype so quickly may raise undue expectations on the part of the user. They see the shell and may not understand that it is not the finished system. They may have been waiting for this system for months or even years and are so anxious to get something in place that being so close and yet so far may frustrate them even more.

Inconsistencies between prototype and final system If the prototype is a throwaway type, the end system may not be exactly like the prototype. In other words, what the user sees may not be what the user gets. It is up to the analyst to communicate any differences between the prototype and the end system; if the user is forewarned, the negative reaction may be ameliorated. It is advisable to ensure that the resultant system be as close to the prototype as possible to avoid this potential problem.

Encouragement of end-user computing The availability of prototyping software both in the organization and on the general market may encourage end-users to begin to develop their own systems when their needs are not being met by data-processing staff. While end-user involvement in system development is positive, end-user computing (development of systems by end-users) may have some negative ramifications for system integration and database integrity.

Final system inefficiencies[14] Large, complex systems that require voluminous numbers of transactions may not be good candidates for the iterative prototyping technique. 4GLs have a reputation for generating less than optimal code in terms of efficiency and throughput. Care must be taken to predetermine whether the new system should be written with an application generator/ prototyping tool or prototyped in a 4GL and then coded in a 3GL for maximum efficiency. A discussion of how to make these determinations is included in the next section.

Lack of attention to good human factors[5] The use of application generators as prototyping tools does not ensure that the resultant systems will adhere to human-factors guidelines. In fact, many application generators have rather inflexible screen and menu formats, which often inhibit the use of good human-factors techniques unless additional background code is written (defeating the purpose of the application generator).

Inattention to proper analysis Because prototyping application generators are relatively easy to use and produce quick results, analysts are tempted to plunge into prototyping before sufficient analysis has taken place. This may result in a system that looks good, with adequate user interfaces, but that is not truly functional. This is how the reputation of 'quick and dirty' prototypes came about. To avoid this pitfall, a well defined methodology that stipulates the stages of prototyping is necessary.

DETERMINATION OF WHEN TO PROTOTYPE

Some form of prototyping may be used in the development of all systems from large and complex to small and simple. Determination of whether to use the iterative prototyping technique, which will evolve into the final system, or the throwaway type, which may be used primarily to model the user interfaces, however, is dependent on several variables.

If the system in question has the following characteristics, it may be a prime candidate for iterative prototyping[3,6]:

- is dynamic (always changing)
- is transaction-processing based
- contains extensive user dialogues
- is small versus large
- is well defined
- is online
- 'is' the business (i.e., billing, record management, transaction-driven, predetermined structure)

On the other hand, if the system exhibits the following characteristics, iterative prototyping is unlikely to enhance the final system[3,6]:

- is stable
- is decision-support based

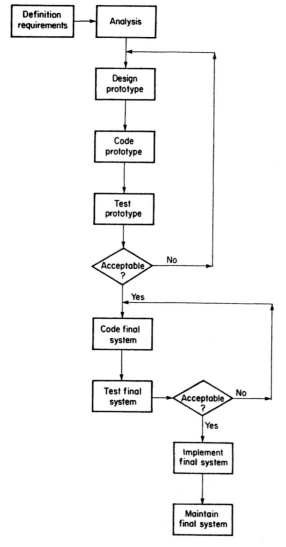

Figure 2. Traditional system development life-cycle with Type II (throwaway) prototyping

- contains much *ad hoc* retrieval and reporting
- is of no predictable form
- is ill defined
- is batch
- makes little use of user dialogues
- is large and complex
- is real-time
- does extensive number crunching
- is 'about' the business rather than directly involved in transaction processing (i.e., decision support and expert systems)

METHODOLOGY

Type I or Type II prototyping can be effectively used when developing information systems; the key to success is carefully determining which prototype type to use and then following a well defined methodology.

The methodology should include thorough requirements definition and design stages before any prototyping is attempted. The prototype should then be defined, coded, tested, and used to refine the requirements and design and put to use as a Type I or Type II prototype. During the refinement process, user comments and responses can be solicited and used to alter any unsatisfactory portions of the prototype. Once the user(s) and analyst are satisfied with the prototype, then the prototype can either be retained and expanded to become the final system or used as a model for the final system that is developed in a 3GL.

There are four phases that are inherent in the development and completion of a prototype[15].

Determination of key aspects of system to be prototyped
The three main areas that are often prototyped include the user interface, uncertain or vague system functions, and time and memory requirements. Any or all three of these aspects can be prototyped.

User interface The most common area to be prototyped. Many prototyping tools are specifically aimed at rapid development of menus, screens, and reports. This is the aspect that the user must understand and accept for the system to be successful.

Uncertain system functions Often, the development of a new system includes some functional processing that may not be well understood by any team members. This uncertain area is a probable candidate for prototyping. The development of a working model allows the team to make sure that the solution they are proposing will indeed satisfy the requirements and perform effectively. The involvement of the user will not be as heavy for this type of prototype as for the user interface. The user may not fully understand the calculations and output. The user may be able to provide both test input and output data, however, to verify the model.

Time and memory requirements The exercise of these aspects may be more appropriately termed a simulation instead of a prototype. Many systems may be characterized by huge volumes of transactions and data manipulations. Standards for interactive response times and

memory use can be established, and the prototype/simulation is exercised to ensure that the system can accomplish the functional tasks within the standards range.

Building the prototype
Many tools are available for building prototypes, as already mentioned. The prototype is initially built quite rapidly using one or more of the prototyping tools.

Testing the prototype
The prototype is tested and debugged based on user and performance feedback.

Using the prototype as a model
The prototype is used as a model for the final system (Type II) or as the base for the final system (Type I).

Adherence to a strict methodology will help to ensure the success of the prototyping approach and will combat the 'quick and dirty' system development that sometimes results from prototyping in a haphazard manner.

INCORPORATING HUMAN-FACTORS GUIDELINES INTO PROTOTYPING

Even though prototyping provides an excellent method of analyst/user communication, there is nothing inherent in the prototyping tools to ensure adherence to good human-factors guidelines. Therefore, analyst/programmers should have additional training in this critical area. Human factors in systems and the issue of 'user friendliness' or 'usability' has been recognised recently as a determinant of system success. Just because a system is technically sound does not mean that it will be easy to learn and use. The following human-factors guidelines[16] should be adhered to as part of the system design phase.

Know your users Users today range from novice to expert. There are many variables that can help profile users, including previous exposure to computers, the nature of the task they are attempting to perform on the system, level of training, how often they use the system in question, level in the organization, amount of dependency on the computer, etc. One of the first tasks of the analyst should be to profile the user population.

Use selection not entry Whenever possible, allow the user to select information from possible options on the screen rather than require the user to remember what to do next. Humans forget and have enough task variables in their short-term memory to worry about without having to memorize how to get the system to function. The only problem with selection not entry is that it may slow up the experienced user. In order not to frustrate this type of user, program selections to accept multiple keystrokes that will allow the experienced user to sidestep the selection process.

Make the system behave predictably Consistent design of function keys and options will lead to ease of learning and use. Switching and interchanging will lead to frustration and abandonment of the system.

Make the system as unobtrusive as possible The focus of any computer session should be on the work task rather than on the system itself. Some aspects of the interface, such as blinking, reverse video, colour use, and audibles can be distracting rather than meaningful, especially when the user is doing routine data entry and has to be involved with the system on an extended daily basis. These attention-getting devices may be helpful as 'training wheels' during the learning process, but probably should be removed once the user is 'up' on the system.

Use display inertia when carrying out user requests The display should change as little as possible. This helps to prevent user distraction.

Conserve muscle power A single keystroke or depression of a function key is usually faster and less cumbersome than multiple keystrokes, particularly for the intermittent user who is not a proficient typist.

Use meaningful error messages If the user makes a mistake, advise on what the mistake was and how to correct it. Avoid negative, patronizing messages. Simply state the problem and how to correct it.

Allow for reversing of actions Protect the users from the system and the system from the users. Create a suspense file that can be altered and verified before the database is altered; this will help to ensure database integrity. Allow failsafe exits from the system at any time.

This list is not all inclusive, of course. There are many other sources for user-interface design guidelines[17]. Incorporating these guidelines into interface designs and using prototypes to communicate user requirements will help to ensure system success.

TWO CASE STUDIES WITH PROTOTYPING

Case 1: New Jersey Division of Motor Vehicles[14]

From 1983 to 1985, the State of New Jersey Division of Motor Vehicles contracted Price Waterhouse and Company to build its primary information system. A new 4GL named Ideal from Applied Data Research (ADR) Inc. was used to develop the system. When the system was delivered, the response times were so slow that the backlogs generated from using the system resulted in thousands of motorists driving with invalid registrations or licences. Overtime pay to employees amounted to hundreds of thousands of dollars. In short, at delivery time, the system was declared a total disaster.

Why was Ideal chosen as the language for this development project? First, time pressures dictated speedy completion of the project and, second, the Systems and Communications (SAC) Division of the State of New Jersey had already acquired ADR's Datacom/DB, which supported Ideal as a 4GL. The decision was made by Price Waterhouse to use Ideal, against the recommendations of several members of the SAC.

Robert Moybohm, the SAC's deputy director, had earlier evaluated Ideal for possible use in other, smaller projects and determined:

- Ideal would not be able to handle the development of large, online systems. He ran some benchmark tests against COBOL programs and Ideal ran three times slower on simple processing.
- Ideal did not offer index processing, a performance-related feature that had been the initial reason that SAC purchased the Datacom/DB system in the first place.
- Ideal did not allow computer-to-computer interfacing. The large system would need to interface with 59 other computers. This fact alone should have precluded the selection of Ideal.

Why did Price Waterhouse choose Ideal? What went wrong? From the beginning, poor decisions were made about the system development process. Ideal was a brand-new product and was not well tested. The development staff had no experience using any 4GL and considerable time was spent learning and making mistakes. All along the development cycle, it became apparent that the system was not going to meet performance requirements, yet no one was able to stop the process and change to a 3GL or determine how to combat the performance problems. It seems that one of the driving forces was the fact that the development team was locked into a fixed-cost contract and delivery date and that every month after deadline would incur a stiff financial penalty. So a decision was made to deliver a nonperforming system within the deadline rather than a late, but functional, one.

After failed implementation of the new system and the resultant flurry of irate users died down, an attempt was made to rectify the problem. It was determined that only about 58 of the 800 program modules needed to be converted to COBOL to meet acceptable, response-time criteria. Eight modules were responsible for the nightly batch updates. The other 50 modules were online programs that were handling 85% of the system's transaction volume. It was not merely a simple line-by-line conversion; many modules had to be redesigned to achieve performance requirements.

The impact of a failed system on the motorists of New Jersey could have been avoided by running the old system in parallel with the new system until the problems were rectified. Instead, due primarily to costs and inadequate hardware resources, direct cutover implementation was used as a strategy. Consequently, the failure of the new system was evident to everyone in the state of New Jersey, not just to internal staff.

Was Type I (iterative) prototyping with a 4GL the wrong choice for the New Jersey Division of Motor Vehicles? Given the volume of transactions, and the development team's inexperience, the answer must be yes. A more effective approach would have been to use the Type II (throwaway) approach, using the 4GL to model the system, rather than use the Type I (iterative) approach to develop the end system.

Case 2: Town and Country Credit Line (TCCL)

In early 1988, Town and Country Credit Line (TCCL) decided to develop a system to enhance their competitive advantage over other banking cards. TCCL has long seen itself as the leader in banking card technology. (The actual nature of the system is proprietary at this time and the name of the company has been changed.) TCCL decided to explore the costs and benefits of using CASE technology to enhance delivery time for new systems. They chose a service request system as an eight-week pilot project to accomplish this purpose. They hired outside programmer/consultants who had experience in the use of CASE technology and purchased IEF (Information Engineering Facility) from Texas Instruments.

The decision to develop the service request system as a pilot was based on the following:

- the estimated short time required to deliver this product to the user community (it was perceived to be a system with a fairly narrow scope)
- the time the user community had been promised the system with no delivery
- it was felt that this system would give the development team the 'biggest bang for the dollar' (quote from project manager)
- it was felt that this system would provide the user community with a system that would dramatically enhance productivity while simplifying complex choices

Why did they not just use traditional methods to develop this system? The system had features that they felt would be very difficult to design and produce using traditional methods. These features were interprocedure communication and linking of procedures.

Because CASE technology was new to the organization, the pilot project would additionally serve to provide a knowledge base within the team to make accurate estimates for projects that use the CASE tool, and give each team member an opportunity to gain 'hands-on' experience with all phases of the CASE tool, and in doing so provide understanding of the limitations and capabilities of the CASE tool.

Two consultants were hired to provide support during the pilot project as the team had no experience with IEF. One consultant provided guidance on the methodology and project management, the other on IEF itself.

Training of the resident staff members was limited. At the beginning of the pilot project, only two team members out of nine had any training beyond Business Area Analysis and Business System Design. No team members had any training or experience with IEF technical design and construction. One team member had no training in CASE and IEF at all.

The system was developed by breaking it into its logical business components and then distributing one task to each group. The system was developed within the eight-week deadline and performs the required tasks efficiently and effectively with user acceptance. Two problems were encountered during the development pro-

cess. One was related to the CASE technology and the other to the nature of the system. As the CASE technology was new to the organization, a learning curve was encountered. The competence of the team and a willingness to work additional hours helped to overcome this problem. The other problem was a lack of communication between groups. The groups sometimes went off on inconsistent tangents and some work had to be redone. Once the product is familiar to the team, and less time is spent on learning IEF, scheduled full-team meetings could alleviate this problem.

IEF divides the development process into seven steps:

- ISP (Information Strategy Planning). Allows identification of areas of concern and establishment of direction.
- BAA (Business Area Analysis). Areas of concern are analysed for entity relationship and process dependency.
- BSD (Business System Design). The processes are packaged into procedures that are user interactive.
- TD (Technical Design). The conversion of BAA/BSD designs into specific database tables (such as DB2), CICS transactions, and COBOL II code.
- Construction. The generation of source and executable code and database definition and access statements.
- Transition. Loading data into the databases, determination of conversion strategies.
- Production. Actual implementation and ongoing use of the system.

Throughout these phases, testing also occurs. Unit or program testing is performed by individual team members. System testing occurs when the entire system is operational. User acceptance testing occurs at various points in the development process.

Some problems occurred with the interfaces between systems. Once these problems were solved, the end system performed adequately in terms of efficiency and effectiveness measures. The users were pleased with the system and it is currently functional.

Why was this prototyping effort successful, whereas the effort made by the New Jersey Division of Motor Vehicles unsuccessful? One of the main advantages is five years of advancement in prototyping tools. Ideal is less integrated and much less sophisticated than IEF. Also TCCL has had a chance to learn from other companies' mistakes. As prototyping software tools become more and more sophisticated, the inefficiencies will be reduced dramatically.

SUMMARY

Prototyping is the process of quickly building a model of the final software system, which is used primarily as a communication tool to assess and meet the information needs of the user.

Prototyping came about with the advent of 4GLs, which enabled application or code generation. The reasons for the success of prototyping arise from the problems encountered in the use of the traditional development of software systems using 3GLs.

Prototyping environments are divided into two major types: complete application generator environments and toolkit or 'workbench' environments.

There are two major types of prototyping approaches: iterative (Type I) and throwaway (Type II). In the iterative approach, the prototype is changed and modified according to user requirements until the prototype evolves into the final system. In the throwaway approach, the prototype serves as a model for the final system, which is eventually coded in a 3GL or procedural language.

Some advantages of prototyping include: faster development time, easier end use and learning, less humanpower to develop systems, decreased backlogs, and enhanced user/analyst communication. Some disadvantages of prototyping include: the fostering of undue expectations on the part of the user, what the user sees may not be what the user gets, and availability of application-generator software may encourage end-user computing.

Not all systems are good candidates for the prototyping approach. Care should be taken to determine whether the system in question exhibits characteristics that make prototyping a viable option.

No current prototyping tools ensure that good human-factors guidelines will be exhibited in the final system. Analysts should be aware of these guidelines and build systems that adhere to them, regardless of the use of prototyping tools.

Prototyping is a powerful and widely used approach to system development. Systems built with the use of prototyping can be highly successful if a strict methodology is adhered to and thorough analysis and requirements definition takes place before prototyping is attempted.

REFERENCES

1 **Carey, J M and McLeod, Jr, R** 'Use of system development methodology and tools' *J. Syst. Manage.* Vol 39 No 3 (1987) pp 30–35
2 **Boar, B** 'Application prototyping: a life cycle perspective' *J. Syst. Manage.* Vol 37 (1986) pp 25–31
3 **Lantz, K** 'The prototyping methodology: designing right the first time' *Computerworld* Vol 20 (1986) pp 69–74
4 **Staff** 'The next generation' *Banker* Vol 136 (1986) pp 79–81
5 **Stahl, B** 'The trouble with application generators' *Datamation* Vol 32 (1986) pp 93–94
6 **Klinger, D E** 'Rapid prototyping revisited' *Datamation* Vol 32 (1986) pp 131–132
7 **Yourdon, E** *Managing the structured techniques* Yourdon Press, New York, NY, USA (1976)
8 **Brooks, F P** 'The mythical man-month' (chapter 2) in **Brooks, F P** (ed) *The mythical man-month essays on software engineering* Addison-Wesley, Reading, MA, USA (1979) pp 11–26
9 **Boehm, B W** 'Structured programming: problems, pitfalls, and payoffs' *TRW Software Series TRW-SS-76-06* TRW Defence Systems, Redondo Beach, CA, USA (1976)
10 **Sprague, R H and McNurlin, B C** *Information systems management in practice* Prentice Hall, Englewood Cliffs, NJ, USA (1986)
11 **Boehm, B W** *IEEE Trans. Soft. Eng.* (1984)
12 **Goyette, R** 'Fourth generation systems soothe end user unrest' *Data Manage.* Vol 24 (1986) pp 30–32
13 **Kull, D** 'Designs on development' *Computer Decisions* Vol 17 (1985) pp 86–88
14 **Kull, D** 'Anatomy of a 4GL disaster' *Computer Decisions* Vol 18 (1986) pp 58–65
15 **Harrison, T S** 'Techniques and issues in rapid prototyping' *J. Syst. Manage.* Vol 36 (1985) pp 8–13
16 **Sena, J A and Smith, M L** 'Applying software engineering principles to the user application interface' (chapter 6) in **Carey, J M (ed)** *Human factors in management information systems* Ablex, Norwood, NJ, USA (1988) pp 103–116
17 **Shneiderman, B** *Designing the user interface* Addison-Wesley, Reading, MA, USA (1986)

BIBLIOGRAPHY

Doke, E R and Myers, L A 'The 4GL: on its way to becoming an industry standard?' *Data Manage.* Vol 25 (1987) pp 10–12
Duncan, M 'But what about quality?' *Datamation* Vol 32 (1986) pp 135–6
Staff 'Why software prototyping works' *Datamation* Vol 33 (1987) pp 97–103

A Classification of CASE Technology

Alfonso Fuggetta, Politecnico di Milano and CEFRIEL

The he design, implementation, delivery, and maintenance of software are complex and expensive activities that need improvement and better control. Among the technologies proposed to achieve these goals is CASE (computer-aided software engineering): computerized applications supporting and partially automating software-production activities.[1] Hundreds of CASE products are commercially available, offering a wide spectrum of functionalities.

The evolution and proliferation of such tools has forced CASE researchers to address a new challenging topic: How can they develop more integrated and easier to use CASE tools? In response, they have conceived and introduced new products that extend traditional operating-system functionalities to provide more advanced services, such as sophisticated process-control mechanisms and enhanced database-management functionalities.

Another growing research area is the development of technologies to support formal definition and automation of the software process, the total set of activities, rules, methodologies, organizational structures, and tools used during software production. Developers generally agree it is not possible to identify an optimal, universal, and general-purpose process. Rather, each organization must design and evolve the process according to its own needs, market, and customers. To better manage and support software processes, researchers and practitioners need new means to describe and assess them. Moreover, the descriptions must be usable by a computerized tool to guide, control, and, whenever possible, automate software-process activities. This research has produced its first results, and several industrial products have appeared on the market.

The availability of a large number of products is contributing to the improvement and wide diffusion of software-engineering practice. However, this product proliferation is creating critical problems.

It is more difficult to assess the real capabilities and features of many products on the market, and to understand how they are related to each other functionally and technologically. The terminology is often confusing or misleading. For example, terms such as tool, workbench, toolset, and environment are given very different meanings and interpretations. It is difficult, therefore, to develop a clear and systematic classification of the available technology for effective assessment and acquisition.

The variety of CASE products available today is daunting. This survey provides a classification to help in assessing products ranging from tools and environments to enabling technology.

Reprinted from *Computer*, Vol. 26, No. 12, Dec. 1993, pp. 25–38. Copyright © 1993 by The Institute of Electrical and Electronics Engineers, Inc. All rights reserved.

Critical issues in classification schemes

The basic choices and purpose of the classification scheme for CASE technology I propose in this article can be criticized in many ways. First, the acronym CASE is associated with many different definitions often less general than the one I use here.

Sodhi, for example, proposes the following definition: "Computer-Aided Software Engineering (CASE) encompasses a collection of automated tools and methods that assist software engineering in the phases of the software development life cycle."[1] This definition takes into account only the production-process technology.

Next, Pressman defines CASE as follows: "The workshop for software engineering is called an integrated project support environment, and the toolset that fills the workshop is CASE."[2] The author also includes what he calls framework tools: products supporting infrastructure development. This definition extends the scope of CASE.

And Forte and McCulley define CASE this way: "We take CASE literally, that is, CASE is software engineering enhanced by automated tools (i.e. computer-aided). . . To us, it's all part of a coordinated approach to the design and production of systems and products containing software."[3]

Finally, Sommerville proposes a CASE definition similar to the one I present in this article: "Computer-aided software engineering is the term for software tool support for the software engineering process."[4] These examples show that the term CASE is assuming a wider meaning and becoming associated with the computer-aided support offered to the entire software process.

A second criticism is that the goal of this type of classification and its approaches are shallow. It is not easy to agree on the levels of abstraction of the reference framework used to classify CASE products, or on the products' assignments to the identified classes. Moreover, it is difficult to find the right focus to technically profile the different classes of products.

Nonetheless, the need for a conceptual framework and a classification of available technology is increasing. Practitioners and researchers need to assess and compare existing technology. Customers (software-production organizations) need to have a clear overview of the available technology and its potential benefits. Educators and consultants need a solid conceptual basis

for their presentations of the state of the art in the field.

Pressman makes a significant observation on this issue:[2] "A number of risks are inherent whenever we attempt to categorize CASE tools. . . Confusion (or antagonism) can be created by placing a specific tool within one category when others might believe it belongs in another category. Some readers may feel that an entire category has been omitted — thereby eliminating an entire set of tools for inclusions in the overall CASE environment. In addition, simple categorization tends to be flat. . . But even with these risks, it is necessary to create a taxonomy of CASE tools — to better understand the breadth of CASE and to better appreciate where such tools can be applied in the software engineering process."

Pressman's words point to a particularly important problem that deserves some additional comments. An ideal classification should define an equivalence relation on the considered domain. Then it becomes possible to partition the domain in equivalent classes and assign each element in the domain to just one class. An entity's class precisely and unambiguously characterizes it for easy comparison and assessment.

Often, however, it is not possible to find such an equivalence relation, and an entity might span different classes. This risk is particularly real with CASE products. Their functionalities and characteristics are not standardized, so it may be quite difficult to assign a given product to a unique class. Nevertheless, an effective classification should aim at limiting these situations to retain its overall soundness and usefulness.

References

1. J. Sodhi, *Software Eng.: Methods, Management, and CASE Tools*, McGraw-Hill, Blue Ridge Summit, Pa., 1991.

2. R.S. Pressman, *Software Eng. — A Practitioner's Approach*, McGraw-Hill, New York, 1992.

3. *CASE Outlook: Guide to Products and Services*, G. Forte and K. McCulley, eds., CASE Consulting Group, Lake Oswego, Ore., 1991.

4. I. Sommerville, *Software Eng.*, Addison-Wesley, Reading, Mass., 1992.

In this article, I propose a classification with more precise definitions for these terms. To avoid any misunderstanding, I use the term "product" to identify any object in the classification.

Even the development of a precise classification can introduce additional conceptual and practical problems that make such efforts useless or even dangerous. The criteria must clarify the rationale, purposes, and limitations of the proposed approach. The level of abstraction must strike a balance between analysis and synthesis, and avoid the introduction of useless details or vague concepts.

My classification of products supporting the software process is based on a general framework derived from the work of Conradi et al.[2] Figure 1 shows the framework. The software process is decomposed in two subprocesses: a *production process* and a *metaprocess*.

The production process includes all activities, rules, methodologies, organizational structures, and tools used to conceive, design, develop, deliver, and maintain a software product. A production process must be defined, assessed, and evolved through a systematic and continuing metaprocess.

The purpose of the metaprocess is the acquisition and exploitation of new products supporting software-production activities and, more generally, the improvement and innovation of the procedures, rules, and technologies used to deliver the organization's artifacts. In the last decade, efforts aimed at understanding the metaprocess include those of the Software Engineering Institute, whose well-known Capability Maturity Model[3] defines five levels of process maturity and provides guidelines to progressively improve it.

The production process can be supported and partially automated by the *production-process technology* — aids to software developers to specify, build, and maintain a software product. In an organization, the specific technology and related procedures and guidelines used to support the production process are called *production-process support*.

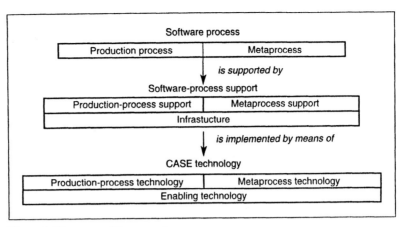

Figure 1. The general framework.

The metaprocess can be automated and supported as well with a *metaprocess technology* used to create the *metapro-cess support* — the specific aids used in an organization's metaprocess to automate and guide metaprocess activities.

Related work

One of the first and most important classification attempts was that of Dart et al.,[1] who presented a taxonomy of the trends that have produced state-of-the-art software-development environments. They defined a software-development environment as "an environment that augments or automates *all* the activities comprising the software development cycle." The aim of their classification was to understand the evolution of the principles on which environments have been built.

The taxonomy identified four basic categories:

• *Language-centered environments* built around one language (for example, Interlisp, Smalltalk, or Rational). They are highly interactive, but offer limited support for programming in the large.
• *Structure-centered environments* incorporating the idea of environment generation (for example, Mentor, Cornell Program Synthesizer, and Gandalf). These environments let users directly manipulate the grammar of a programming language to produce structure-oriented tools, such as syntax-directed editors.
• *Toolkit environments* consisting of small tools intended primarily to support the coding phase (for example, Unix PWB and VMS VAX Set). They do not offer any control of the way the tools are applied.
• *Method-based environments* centered around specific methodologies for software development, such as structured analysis and design techniques or object-oriented design (for example, Excelerator, TAGS, and Software Through Pictures).

This pioneering article has several merits, but its scope is limited. It does not offer any finer grained classification of existing products, nor does it take into account the metaprocess and enabling technologies. Moreover, it tends to consider at the same level of abstraction entities that are quite different (for example, complete environments like Interlisp and Smalltalk, and more specialized products like Excelerator).

Forte and McCulley's more recent classification[2] introduces a *tool taxonomy* on two levels. (The term "tool" identifies any product considered in the Forte and McCulley classification.) At the first level, the taxonomy proposes the following classification domains to characterize a tool: application areas targeted by the tool, tasks supported in the development cycle, methods and notations, hardware platforms, operating systems, databases and transaction processing subsystems supported by the tool, network and communication protocols, and programming languages supported by the tool.

At the second level, the authors specify attributes for each domain. Figure A shows the description of the development-tasks domain. This scheme partitions the total set of CASE tools in two main classes: vertical and horizontal tools.

Vertical tools are used in a specific life-cycle phase or activity (for example, testing), while horizontal tools are used throughout the entire software process. The merit of this classification lies in the richness of the domains to characterize tools. Moreover, it is implemented in a tool called Tool Finder, which lets users retrieve product descriptions from an electronic archive.

Unfortunately, the classification does not take into account the conceptual architecture of the software process (as I discuss in the main text). It is not easy to classify tools according to the breadth of support offered to the production process. For instance, Forte and McCulley classify a compiler under the construction task, along with other more complex and sophisticated products (workbenches supporting coding, debugging, and incremental linking). They classify tool integration and process modeling in different horizontal tasks, but provide no hints for understanding their mutual dependencies or their relationships with other classes of products. Moreover, the division between vertical and horizontal tasks becomes unclear if we consider unconventional life cycles not based on the waterfall model.

Production-process and metaprocess supports are based on a common *infrastructure* that provides services and functionalities for their operation in an integrated and homogeneous environment. The infrastructure can be implemented using operating-system services and more advanced and recent products for, say, process control and database management. The products supporting infrastructure implementation are globally identified under the term *enabling technology*. The infrastructure, production-process support, and metaprocess support constitute the *software-process support*.

The classification I propose in this article considers all products in the production-process technology, metaprocess technology, and enabling technology. Globally, these products represent CASE technology.

Refining the reference framework

To refine the framework presented in the previous section, I further classify CASE products used in the production process according to the breadth of support they offer. A production process may be viewed as a set of elementary *tasks* to be accomplished to produce a software application. Examples of tasks are compiling, editing, and generating test cases from requirements specifications.

Tasks are grouped to form *activities*, sets of tasks supporting coarse-grained parts of the software-production process. For example, coding is an activity that includes editing, compiling, debugging, and so on. The activity concept is not to be confused with the phases of a waterfall life cycle. Activities are not necessarily carried out in strict sequence: They can be composed to form any type of life cycle.

According to these definitions, I classify CASE products in the production-process technology in three categories:

(1) *Tools* support only specific tasks in the software process.
(2) *Workbenches* support only one or a few activities.
(3) *Environments* support (a large part of) the software process.

Workbenches and environments are generally built as collections of tools. Tools can therefore be either standalone products or components of workbenches and environments. For exam-

---

Pressman's classification[3] is based on the identification of these different functions supported by CASE products: business systems planning, project management, support (documentation, database, configuration management, and so on), analysis and design, programming, integration and testing, prototyping, maintenance, and framework (support for environment development). Even in this case, however, little help is given for understanding the architecture of the software-process support. Moreover, Pressman does not take metaprocess technology into account.

In another important classification, Sommerville[4] defines CASE tools as the basic building blocks used to create a "software engineering environment." He classifies CASE tools according to the functions they offer and the process activities they support. CASE tools are integrated by an environment infrastructure. Integration can be achieved along four different dimensions: data integration (sharing of information), user-interface integration (common interface paradigms and mechanisms), control integration (mechanisms to control the invocation and execution of tools and applications), and process integration (integration in a defined process model). Environments are collections of tools classified in three different categories:

• *Programming environments* support programming activities, but provide limited support for software analysis and design.
• *CASE workbenches* provide support for analysis and design, but little support for coding and testing.
• *Software-engineering environments* comprise tools for all activities in the software process.

Sommerville proposes a reference framework with two levels of tool aggregations: *stand-alone tools* and *environments*.

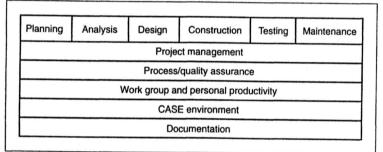

Figure A. Development tasks in Forte and McCulley's classification.[2]

Moreover, he relates important concepts such as process integration and environment infrastructure. The classification I present in this article inherits several of these concepts and further refines the idea of a layered classification scheme.

A different type of effort is represented by the *Reference Model for Frameworks of Software Engineering Environments*, jointly developed by the European Computer Manufacturers Association (ECMA) and the National Institute of Standards and Technology.[5,6] This reference model "is a conceptual and functional basis for describing and comparing existing SEEs or SEE components."[6] (SEE stands for software-engineering environment.) Thus, it is not a classification of CASE technology, but it is important because it defines the framework for constructing, operating, and evolving a software-engineering environment. The framework is a set of interrelated services for object management, process management, user interfaces, communication, tools, policy enforcement, framework administration, and configuration.

A software-engineering environment in the ECMA model is similar to the software-process support presented in the main text. The ECMA model's goals and scope, however, are quite different: It is oriented more to the definition of the ideal func-

ple, most computer manufacturers sell tools such as compilers as stand-alone products.[1] They may also integrate compilers with other tools to support both coding and debugging. (In this section, I use "integrate" in its informal and intuitive sense.) In general, these products also include a debugger, an editor, and an incremental linker. Compilers are also very often marketed as standard components of environments (for example, the C compiler in the Unix PWB environment). Some kinds of tools are seldom available as stand-alone products. For example, graphical editors for dataflow or SADT (structured analysis and design technique) diagrams are usually embedded in products also offering other components to support analysis and design.

The distinction among tools, workbenches, and environments further extends Sommerville's classification,[4] which includes only two levels of granularity: tools and environments. Fernström, Närfelt, and Ohlsson[5] advocate a different approach based on four levels of granularity: service, tool, toolset, and environment. In their classification, the term "toolset" is equivalent to workbench, while "service" identifies an operation embedded in a tool.

Production-process support may be built by adopting and integrating one or more tools, workbenches, and environments. In general, it is composed of an environment, which acts as the "backbone." It can be further extended by introducing additional tools and workbenches to fully cover the production process. (All products mentioned in this article are examples. No evaluation is associated with their citation. Readers should refer to specialized publications[1] for a complete presentation of existing products.)

Tools

A CASE tool is a software component supporting a specific task in the software-production process. Table 1 classifies such tools.

Editing tools. Editing tools (editors) can be classified in two subclasses: *textual editors* and *graphical editors*. The first subclass includes traditional text editors and word processors used to produce textual documents such as programs, textual specifications, and documentation. Editors in the second subclass are used to produce documents

---

tionalities to be offered by the infrastructure, so it does not discuss in much detail the characteristics of CASE technology. Also, it does not present a detailed classification of tools (in the ECMA terminology) and does not evaluate the different philosophies adopted by existing environments.

ECMA concepts can be easily recognized in the classification I propose in this article. My infrastructure takes into account all the ECMA services, except for process-management services, which I consider as a separate entity in the production-process and metaprocess supports.

Perry and Kaiser's more general approach[7] for analyzing software-development environments is based on a general model consisting of three components: structures, mechanisms, and policies. Structures are the objects on which mechanisms operate. Mechanisms are the basic functionalities offered by tools. Policies are the procedures, rules, and guidelines offered to and imposed on software developers by environments. An environment can be described by specifying these three components. Classes of environments can be identified by considering analogies and commonalities. For example, toolkit environments[1] can be described by the following model:

```
Toolkit environment =
    (
    {file system/object-management system},
    {assorted construction tools},
    {laissez-faire}
    )
```

To describe the problems of scale in software production, the authors introduce a metaphor that distinguishes four different classes of environments: individual, family, city, and state. Environments in the individual class emphasize software-construction activities and are dominated by mechanisms. Family-class environments address coordination and are dominated by structures. The city class emphasizes co-operation among software developers and is dominated by policies. Finally, environments in the state class address the commonality issue and are dominated by higher order policies.

This classification identifies the components useful in evaluating a software-development environment. Moreover, the metaphor characterizes the different problems that software-development projects must address when scaling up. The model is less useful when applied to classifying the large variety of commercial products, since it considers only environments and does not provide any categorizations for other types of products.

In conclusion, even if the classifications available so far have substantially contributed to the state of the art, they are still incomplete. Much work is needed to provide an effective and comprehensive reference framework and the related classification scheme.

References

1. S.A. Dart et al., "Software Development Environments," *Computer*, Vol. 20, No. 11, Nov. 1987, pp. 18-28.

2. *CASE Outlook: Guide to Products and Services*, G. Forte and K. McCulley, eds., CASE Consulting Group, Lake Oswego, Ore., 1991.

3. R.S. Pressman, *Software Eng. — A Practitioner's Approach*, McGraw-Hill, New York, 1992.

4. I. Sommerville, *Software Eng.*, Addison-Wesley, Reading, Mass., 1992.

5. "Reference Model for Frameworks of Software Engineering Environments," jointly published as ECMA Tech. Report TR/55, European Computer Manufacturers Assoc., Geneva, and NIST Special Publication 500-201, Nat'l Inst. of Standards and Technology, Gaithersburg, Md., 1991.

6. M. Chen and R.J. Norman, "A Framework for Integrated CASE," *IEEE Software*, Vol. 9, No. 2, Mar. 1992, pp. 18-22.

7. D.E. Perry and G.E. Kaiser, "Models of Software Development Environments," *IEEE Trans. Software Eng.*, Vol. 17, No. 3, Mar. 1991, pp. 283-295.

using graphical symbols. Typical examples are general drawing and painting tools (such as MacDraw), tools to enter graphical specifications (for example, those based on dataflow diagrams), and

Table 1. Classes of CASE tools.

Class	Subclass
Editing	Graphical editors
	Textual editors
Programming	Coding and debugging
	• Assemblers
	• Compilers
	• Cross-assemblers
	• Cross-compilers
	• Debuggers
	• Interpreters
	• Linkage editors
	• Precompilers/preprocessors
	Code generators
	• Compiler generators
	Code restructurers
Verification and validation	Static analyzers
	• Cross-reference generators
	• Flowcharters
	• Standards enforcers
	• Syntax checkers
	Dynamic analyzers
	• Program instrumentors
	• Tracers/profilers
	Comparators
	Symbolic executors
	Emulators/simulators
	Correctness proof assistants
	Test-case generators
	Test-management tools
Configuration management	Configuration- and version-management tools
	Configuration builders
	Change-control monitors
	Librarians
Metrics and measurement	Code analyzers
	Execution monitors/ timing analyzers
Project management	Cost-estimation tools
	Project-planning tools
	Conference desks
	E-mail
	Bulletin boards
	Project agendas
	Project notebooks
Miscellaneous tools	Hypertext systems
	Spreadsheets

tools to paint the forms and layouts constituting an application's user interface.

Examples of textual and graphical editors are Pmate, a text editor for professional programmers running on MS-DOS personal computers; MacBubbles, a Macintosh-based editing tool for Yourdon-DeMarco diagrams; and DV Draw, an editor that creates several types of graphical output.

Syntax-directed editors are an important category of textual editor. Two examples are Key-one and DEC LSE — Language Sensitive Editor.

Programming tools. These tools are used to support coding and code restructuring. The three main subclasses are *coding and debugging tools*, *code generators*, and *code restructurers*.

The first subclass includes traditional tools used to compile, run, and debug a program. Examples are the numerous traditional compilers and interpreters available on the market, interactive tester/debuggers such as Via/Smartest, and cross-compilers such as HP Cross Compilers, a family of Unix-based C cross-compilers.

The second class includes tools that generate code starting from a high-level description of the application. Typical examples are compiler generators and Cobol generators. Compiler generators (for example, yacc/lex) automatically build lexical analyzers and parsers starting from the formal description of the language syntax. Cobol generators produce Cobol starting from a high-level program description (for example, the VAX Cobol Generator).

The third subclass includes tools used to restructure existing programs. These tools can analyze, reformat, and in some cases improve existing source code by performing actions such as elimination of "gotos" and unreachable portions of code. Examples of such tools are AdaReformat and Via/Renaissance.

Verification and validation tools. This class includes tools that support program validation and verification. Validation aims at ensuring that the product's functions are what the customer really wants, while verification aims at ensuring that the product under construction meets the requirements definition. This class has many subclasses:[6]

- *Static and dynamic analyzers* analyze a computer program without executing the program (static) or by monitoring program execution (dynamic).
- *Comparators* equate two files to identify commonalities or differences. Typically, they are used to compare test results with the expected program outputs.
- *Symbolic executors* simulate program execution using symbols rather than actual values for input data and produce outputs expressed as symbolic expressions.
- *Emulators/simulators* imitate all or part of a computer system. They accept the same data, provide the same functionalities, and achieve the same results as the imitated system.
- *Correctness proof assistants* support formal techniques to prove mathematically that a program satisfies its specifications or that a specification satisfies given properties.
- *Test-case generators* take as input a computer program and a selection of test criteria, and generate test input data that meet these criteria.
- *Test-management tools* support testing by managing test results, test checklists, regression tests, test coverage metrics, and so on.

Examples of such tools are AdaXRef, a cross-reference generator; Q/Auditor, a standards enforcer; lint-Plus, a syntax checker; Instrumentation Tool, a program instrumentor; CICS Simulcast, an execution tracer; Playback, a test-result comparator; and HP Basic Branch Analyzer, a test-coverage tool. (See the detailed classification scheme in Table 1.)

Configuration-management tools. Configuration-management techniques coordinate and control the construction of a system composed of many parts.[7] Software development and management can greatly benefit from configuration management, which can be decomposed into the following tasks:

- *Version management.* During software development, more than one version of each software item is produced. Versions must be managed so subsequent work incorporates the correct version.
- *Item identification.* Each software item must be unambiguously identifiable. Software-process agents (all people working in the software process) must be able to retrieve specific software items to build and rebuild coherent configurations of the product under development.
- *Configuration building.* A software product is a complex collection of versioned software items. Building a product requires invocation of operations such as preprocessing, compiling, and linking on a possibly large set of software items.
- *Change control.* Changes to a software item may have an impact on other components. Moreover, if several programmers can access the same software items, control is necessary to synchronize their activity to prevent the creation of inconsistent or erroneous versions of software items.
- *Library management.* All the software items relevant in a software process must be subject to effective storage and retrieval policies.

Products that support specific configuration-management tasks — such as configuration building (for example, make, MMS, and Pmaker), version management (SCCS and CMS), and library management (Plib86) —

do not offer comprehensive and integrated support to all tasks. Most configuration-management tools in this classification constitute the first generation. The second generation of configuration-management products offers much wider support by integrating into a single product most functionalities offered by the individual tools considered here.

Metrics and measurement tools. Tools that collect data on programs and program execution fall into two subclasses:

- tools to analyze the source code and compute several source-code metrics (for example, to evaluate code complexity according to Halstead's or McCabe's metrics), and
- tools to monitor the execution of programs and collect runtime statistics.

Examples of such tools are Performance Architek and HP Apollo DPAK.

Project-management tools. Several types of products support project management. A first subclass includes products used to estimate software-production costs. These tools typically implement techniques such as Cocomo (Constructive cost model) or function points, and provide user-friendly interfaces to specify project information and analyze estimation results.

A second subclass comprises tools supporting project planning — that is, project scheduling, resource assignment, and project tracking. These tools are based on well-known concepts and notations such as WBS (work breakdown structure), Gantt, and PERT (program

evaluation and review technique) charts.

A third subclass includes tools to support communication and coordination among project team members. Some permit on-line and deferred interaction among people — for example, teleconferencing systems (also called conference desks), e-mail systems, and electronic bulletin boards. Other tools are project agendas used to coordinate activities and meetings.

Examples of these tools are CA-Estimacs (cost estimation), MacProject (project planning), VAX Notes (conference desk), and DateBook (distributed agenda).

Miscellaneous tools. Products difficult to classify include spreadsheets and hypertext systems.

A spreadsheet can be used as a project-management tool to perform what-if analysis or to develop models of the development process (for example, by implementing the Cocomo model). Spreadsheets can also be used for programming. Several applications have been developed using spreadsheet languages, particularly in business administration and marketing. These applications are marketed as add-ons to standard products such as Excel. For example, Computerized Classic Accounting is an integrated accounting system developed for the Macintosh version of Excel.

Hypertext systems can replace desktop publishing systems for authoring advanced documentation. They can also be used as programming tools to develop prototypes or even final applications. Many applications for the Macintosh have been developed using HyperCard — for example, Client, a personal data manager, and MindLink, an idea processor.

Integration in CASE products

The need for integration in CASE technology is increasingly acknowledged by researchers and practitioners.[1] According to Thomas and Nejmeh, integration can be analyzed in four dimensions:[2]

- *Data integration* ensures that all the information in the environment is managed as a consistent whole, regardless of how parts of it are operated on and transformed.
- *Control integration* permits the flexible combination of an environment's functions according to project preferences and the underlying processes and environment supports.
- *Presentation integration* improves user interaction with the environment by reducing users' cognitive load.

- *Process integration* ensures that tools interact effectively in support of a defined process.

We can identify several levels of integration according to the degree of technology exploitation along these four dimensions. For example, Brown and McDermid define five levels of integration, focusing on functionalities and features that support data and control integration.[3]

References

1. *IEEE Software* special issue on integrated CASE, Vol. 9, No. 2, Mar. 1992.

2. I. Thomas and B.A. Nejmeh, "Definition of Tool Integration for Environments," *IEEE Software*, Vol. 9, No. 2, Mar. 1992, pp. 29-35.

3. A.W. Brown and J.A. McDermid, "Learning from IPSE's Mistakes," *IEEE Software*, Vol. 9, No. 2, Mar. 1992, pp. 23-28.

Workbenches

Workbenches integrate in a single application several tools supporting specific software-process activities. Hence, they achieve

- a homogeneous and consistent interface (presentation integration),
- easy invocation of tools and tool chains (control integration), and
- access to a common data set, managed in a centralized way (data integration).

Some products can enforce predefined procedures and policies within the workbench (process integration).

Table 2 shows eight classes of workbenches.

Business planning and modeling workbenches. This class includes products to support the identification and description of a complex business. They are used to build high-level enterprise models to assess the general requirements and information flows, and identify priorities in the development of information systems.

The tools integrated in such products include graphical editors (to provide diagrams and structured charts), report generators, and cross-reference generators. For example, PC Prism integrates tools to create enterprise models and automatically generate documentation from the information stored in its repository.

The borderline between this class of products and analysis and design workbenches is often quite fuzzy.

Analysis and design workbenches. Products for analysis and design activities constitute an important class of workbenches. In fact, very often the term CASE is used to denote just this class of products. Since the term CASE has a wider meaning, "upper" CASE is more properly used to denote this class of tools, which are used in the early stages of the software process. Today's upper CASE workbenches automate most of the analysis and design methodologies developed in the past decades such as SA/SD (structured analysis/structured design), object-oriented analysis and design, and Jackson System Development.

An upper CASE workbench usually includes one or more editors to create and modify specifications, and other tools to analyze, simulate, and transform them. For example, Excelerator has editors to create dataflow diagrams, structure charts, and entity-relationship diagrams. It also includes an editor and a simulator to create and test mock-ups of system inputs and outputs (forms and reports), as well as a code generator to produce skeletal Cobol source code starting from structure charts. Software Through Pictures includes several graphical editors to support the creation, for example, of control-flow diagrams, process-activation tables, and state-transition diagrams. It also includes code- and documentation-generation facilities.

The functionalities these workbenches offer depend heavily on the notations on which they are centered: If the adopted notation is not formally defined, a workbench can provide only editing and document-production facilities. Using a formal notation permits a higher degree of automation.

Table 3 shows a further classification of this class of workbenches according to level of formality, supported application, and activities covered.

Level of formality. Analysis and design workbenches support notations at different levels of formality:

- *Informal.* Structured English and other informal, textual notations, whose syntax and semantics are not formally defined.
- *Semiformal.* Notations for which it is possible to build syntax checkers. Such notations still lack a precise semantics. Dataflow diagrams are a typical example.
- *Formal.* Notations whose syntax and semantics are formally defined. Finite-state machines, Petri nets, and Statecharts are examples.

Supported applications. No notation can universally support the specification of all types of applications. In each project, the software engineer must be allowed to choose the most suitable notation — or combination of notations.

For assessment and selection, notations fall in two main categories:

(1) notations for data-intensive applications, such as banking or accounting systems (for example, dataflow and entity-relationship diagrams), and

Table 2. Classes of CASE workbenches.

Class	Sample Products
Business planning and modeling	PC Prism
Analysis and design	Excelerator Statemate Software Through Pictures
User-interface development	HP Interface Architect DEC VUIT
Programming	CodeCenter
Verification and validation	Battlemap Logiscope
Maintenance and reverse engineering	Recoder Rigi Hindsight SmartSystem
Configuration management	PCMS CCC SCLM DSEE
Project management	Coordinator DEC Plan Synchronize

Table 3. A sampling of "upper" CASE workbenches.

Sample Products	Examples of Notations Supported	Level of Formality	Class of Applications Supported	Activities Covered
Excelerator	Dataflow diagrams Entity-relationship diagrams	Semiformal	General purpose	Both
Teamwork	Dataflow diagrams Ward and Mellor	Semiformal	General purpose	Both
Statemate	Statecharts	Formal	Control intensive	Both
TAGS	Input/Output Requirements Language	Formal	Control intensive	Both
ASA	Integrated System Definition Language Finite State Machine	Formal	Control intensive	Analysis
GEODE	Specification Description Language	Formal	Control intensive	Design
ER-Designer	Entity-relationship diagrams	Semiformal	Data intensive	Both
IEW	Dataflow diagrams Entity-relationship diagrams	Semiformal	General purpose	Both
STP	Dataflow diagrams Object-oriented structured design	Formal and semiformal	General purpose	Both

(2) notations for control-intensive applications, such as avionics and control systems (for example, finite-state machines, Statecharts, and Petri nets).

According to this distinction, analysis and design workbenches can be grouped in three subclasses:

- workbenches for data-intensive applications (for example, Excelerator),
- workbenches for control-intensive applications (for example, Statemate), and
- general-purpose workbenches — products that support notations for both types of applications (for example, Teamwork).

Activities covered. I call these products analysis and design workbenches because most cover both activities. However, some cover only one. Thus, I classify analysis and design workbenches as analysis only, design only, or both.

User-interface-development workbenches. This class of CASE workbenches is distinct from the others already presented. Its products do not help with specific software-process activities but rather with user-interface design and development.

Many authors have suggested that the user interface is the most critical part of some programs. Kay has even argued that in many cases the user interface *is* the program.[8] Effective support for user-interface design and development is important.

The products in this class exploit the capabilities of modern workstations and graphical environments such as Motif or Windows. They let the developer easily create and test user-interface components and integrate them with the application program.

Typically, a user-interface workbench offers

- graphical editors to paint windows, dialog boxes, icons, and other user-interface components;
- simulators to test the developed in-

terface before integrating it with the application;
- code generators to produce the code to be integrated with the application; and
- runtime libraries to support the generation of executable code.

Examples are DEC VUIT and HP Interface Architect, both developed for the Motif standard interface.

Programming workbenches. The workbenches in this class evolved from the basic programming tools and provide integrated facilities supporting programming:

- a text editor to create and modify the source code,
- a compiler and linker to create the executable code, and
- a debugger.

For effective user interaction with the different tools, programming workbenches provide an integrated and consistent interface, and manage all information created during work sessions (source-code files, intermediate files, object- and executable-code files, and so on). Often, the workbench integrates the compiler with an interpreter or an incremental linker to speed the transition from editing to testing.

Examples of programming workbenches are Turbo C++, Turbo Pascal, and CodeCenter.

Verification and validation workbenches. This class of workbenches includes products that help with module and system testing. Products in this class often integrate several tools from both the metrics and measurement class and the verification and validation class. The functionalities offered by both classes jointly analyze the quality of code and support actual verification and validation.

A typical verification and validation workbench includes

- static analyzers to evaluate complexity metrics and call and control graphs,
- cross-reference and report generators,
- a tool to instrument a program and a tracer to support dynamic analysis, and
- a test-case generator and a test-management tool to produce, store, and manage test data, test results, and checklists.

Act and Logiscope are typical products.

Maintenance and reverse-engineering workbenches. In the past, software engineers often assumed that maintenance had only to do with fixing bugs. This approach proved inadequate for evolving software according to changes in the supported business environment, changes in the available technology, and new requirements from the customer. Now maintenance must be a component of the "forward" development process.

For maintenance, software engineers use the same tools and workbenches they normally use for development. They have to modify requirement specifications, designs, and application source code. They have to repeat the testing procedure to verify that the new version of the application can be released into service. And, with appropriate configuration-management techniques, they

have to manage the artifacts of the process (documents, source code, makefiles, and so on).

Even if most maintenance is performed with the same techniques and products used during software development, some more specific tasks must be approached with ad hoc techniques and tools — in particular, techniques identified as *reverse engineering*. Müller et al. describe this discipline as "the process of extracting system abstraction and design information out of existing software systems."[9]

This goal has not been completely fulfilled. Perhaps it will be impossible to fully achieve the automatic derivation of analysis and design information from code. Such an operation requires higher level information to be synthesized from low-level descriptions (the program statements), and it appears that this can be done only by humans with knowledge of the application.

Several available maintenance and reverse-engineering workbenches provide interesting and seemingly effective features. An example is Recoder, one of the first commercial reverse-engineering workbenches. It includes a code restructurer, a flowcharter, and a cross-reference generator. It analyzes unstructured and hard-to-read Cobol programs and produces new, more readable and modifiable versions. Rigi, another reverse-engineering workbench, can build a program's call graph and suggest possible clustering techniques to achieve strong cohesion and low coupling.

Other sample workbenches in this class are Ensemble and Hindsight.

Configuration-management workbenches. The workbenches in this class integrate tools supporting version control, configuration building, and change control. For example, the HP Apollo DSEE workbench integrates a history manager to store versions of source elements, a configuration manager to define and build configurations, and a task manager and monitor manager to control the process of changing a software item. Thus, the single product integrates and substantially extends most features offered by tools such as make, SCCS, and RCS.

A few products in this class also offer more advanced functionalities to support process modeling. For example, software-process managers can tailor

PCMS according to policies and roles they specify. Policies and roles are described through the possible states of a software item and the operations applied to them to change their state.

Other examples of configuration-management workbenches are CCC and SCLM.

Project-management workbenches. There are very few products in this class. Most potential candidates address only specific project-management tasks, and it seems more appropriate to classify them as tools.

Coordinator integrates several project-management functionalities based on an extended theoretical study of how people operate in a structured and complex organization. It lets development team members create typed messages — that is, messages with a precise meaning, requiring a specific action of the addressee (for example, requests for information or submissions of a proposal for approval). Also, Coordinator keeps track of

- the activities a person has to complete,
- temporal relations among significant actions to be completed by the organization, and
- actions that must be scheduled periodically during the project lifetime.

Other examples of project-management workbenches are Synchronize and DEC Plan. Synchronize includes several tools such as a distributed agenda, memo-distribution facilities, distributed to-do lists, and a meeting scheduler. DEC Plan offers functionalities similar to Synchronize, and also addresses project-planning and task-assignment problems.

Environments

An environment is a collection of tools and workbenches that support the software process. Some of the names I use to identify the different classes in Table 4 come from existing terminology — for example, "toolkit and "language-centered environments."[10]

Toolkits. Toolkits are loosely integrated collections of products easily extended by aggregating different tools

478

Table 4. Classes of CASE environments.

Class	Sample Products
Toolkits	Unix Programmer's Work Bench
Language-centered	Interlisp Smalltalk Rational KEE
Integrated	IBM AD/Cycle DEC Cohesion
Fourth generation	Informix 4GL Focus
Process-centered	East Enterprise II Process Wise Process Weaver Arcadia

and workbenches. Unlike workbenches, toolkits support different activities in the software-production process, but their support is very often limited to programming, configuration management, and project management (and project-management support is generally limited to message handling). Typically, toolkits are environments extended from basic sets of operating-system tools; the Unix Programmer's Work Bench and the VMS VAX Set are two examples.

Toolkits' loose integration requires users to activate tools by explicit invocation or simple control mechanisms such as redirection and pipes in Unix. The shared files users access for data exchange are very often unstructured or in formats that need explicit conversion so different tools can access them (via import and export operations). Because the only constraint for adding a new component is the formats of the files read or created by other tools or workbenches, toolkits can be easily and incrementally extended.

Toolkits do not impose any particular constraint on the process that users follow. Users interact through a general-purpose interface (for example, the shell or the command-language interpreter) that leaves them free to decide which procedures or operations to activate.

Language-centered environments. Examples of environments centered around a specific language are Interlisp, Smalltalk, Rational, and KEE, developed respectively for Lisp, Smalltalk (the language and the environment have the same name), Ada, and Lisp again.[11]

The peculiarity of this class of products is that very often the environment itself is written in the language for which it was developed, thus letting users customize and extend the environment and reuse part of it in the applications under development. The main drawback is that integrating code in different languages may not be feasible. Smalltalk is an environment that suffers from this problem. These environments can hardly be extended to support different programming languages, and they are often concentrated on the edit-compile-debug cycle, with little or no support for large-scale software development.

Language-centered environments offer a good level of presentation and control integration: Users are presented with a consistent interface and are given several mechanisms supporting automatic tool invocation and switching among tools (for example, among the editor, compiler, and debugger). However, these environments suffer from a lack of process and data integration. They are based on structured internal representations (usually abstract trees), but these mechanisms are invisible or hard for users to access for extending or customizing the environment with other products.

Integrated environments. The environments in this class are called "integrated" because, with some limitations, they operate using standard mechanisms so users can integrate tools and workbenches. These environments achieve presentation integration by providing uniform, consistent, and coherent tool and workbench interfaces: All products in the environment are operated through a unique interface concept. They achieve data integration through the *repository* concept: They have a specialized database managing all information produced and accessed in the environment.

The database is structured according to a high-level model of the environment, so users can develop tools and workbenches that access and exchange structured information instead of pure byte streams. This greatly enhances the functionalities and level of integration

offered to the user. Control integration is achieved through powerful mechanisms to invoke tools and workbenches from within other components of the environment.

Such mechanisms can also encapsulate[12] a tool not written to make use of any of the environment framework services. They surround the tool with software that acts as a layer between the tool and the framework. Integrated environments do not explicitly tackle process integration. This distinguishes them from the process-centered environments discussed later.

The infrastructure needed to create an integrated environment is generally more sophisticated than traditional operating-system services. Later, I discuss *integrating platforms* — extensions to operating-system services that provide the tool builder with advanced features.

The DEC Cohesion and IBM AD/Cycle integrated environments provide basic tools and workbenches, and an integrating platform that lets other companies enrich the environment with additional products. For example, DEC Cohesion is based on an integrating platform offering tool encapsulation, a repository, and user-interface-management and tool-integration facilities (ACA Services, CDD Repository, and DEC Fuse). It includes several tools and workbenches to support production-process activities (DEC Set, DEC VUIT, DEC Plan, and DEC Design), and it can be extended with third-party products.

Fourth-generation environments. Fourth-generation environments were precursors to and, in a sense, are a subclass of integrated environments. They are sets of tools and workbenches supporting the development of a specific class of program: electronic data processing and business-oriented applications. At least four characteristics distinguish these applications:

(1) The application's operations are usually quite simple, while the structure of the information to be manipulated is rather complex.
(2) The user interface is critical. Typically, it is composed of many forms and layouts used to input, display, and modify the information stored in the database.
(3) The application requirements are very often not clearly defined and can be

detailed only through the development of prototypes (very often, mock-ups of the user interface).

(4) The software process to produce such applications is generally evolutionary.

Fourth-generation environments were the first integrated environments. In general, they include an editor, an interpreter and/or a compiler for a specialized language, a debugger, database access facilities, a form editor, a simulator, simple configuration-management tools, document-handling facilities, and, in some cases, a code generator to produce programs in traditional languages such as Cobol. Often, these components are integrated through a consistent interface, data are stored in a central, proprietary repository, and built-in triggers activate tools when specific events occur in the environment.

However, fourth-generation environments provide a low degree of process integration, and ad hoc nonstandard mechanisms support the other dimensions of integration. In many cases, for example, programs and other application-related information are stored in proprietary databases. This makes it difficult (or even impossible) for other manufacturers to extend the environment with new products and components. To overcome this problem, most of these environments are migrating to standard platforms for evolution into true integrated environments.

I defined these products as "fourth-generation environments" instead of the more traditional "fourth-generation languages" to emphasize that they are more than compilers or interpreters for specific languages: They are collections of tools to manage the design, development, and maintenance of large electronic data processing applications.

Table 5 presents a more detailed division of fourth-generation environments into three classes. *Production systems* are oriented to the development of banking or accounting systems with strong performance requirements. These environments replace traditional Cobol-based environments and fall into two subclasses: *language-based systems* and *Cobol generators.* The former are based on a language that is directly compiled

Table 5. Fourth-generation environments.

Class	Sample Products
Production systems	
• Language-based systems	Natural 2
	Informix
	4GL/OnLine
• Cobol generators	Pacbase
	Transform
Infocenter systems	Focus
	Ramis
End-user systems	Filemaker

or interpreted. The latter are products that start with a high-level description of the application and generate Cobol source code for new applications to integrate with existing ones. Natural 2 is a language-based system; Pacbase is a Cobol generator.

Infocenter systems support the infocenter department of an organization in extracting and manipulating the information managed by the main electronic data processing application. To ensure high performance, the main system is usually developed using a production system. Typically, infocenter systems do not provide the same level of performance, but offer more flexible facilities to produce, say, nonstandard reports for management, based on the information stored in the main database. A typical example in this class is Ramis.

End-user systems support end users in directly defining their database and access functionalities. They provide predefined functions and forms that users customize easily through interactive facilities, without writing traditional programs. Many products developed for the Macintosh and MS-DOS personal computers can be included in this class. A typical example is Filemaker Pro (running on the Macintosh).

Process-centered environments. A process-centered environment is based on a formal definition of the software process. A computerized application called a *process driver* or *process engine* uses this definition to guide development activities by automating process fragments, automatically invoking tools and workbenches, enforcing specific policies, and assisting programmers, analysts, and project managers in their

work.[13] Thus, these environments focus on process integration. This does not mean they do not address other integration dimensions. Rather, other integration issues are the starting points for process integration.

A process engineer or process modeler (that is, someone who can analyze a process and describe it formally) produces the formal definition of the production process (called the *process model*), using specialized tools with functionalities to define, analyze, and manage it. Thus a process-centered environment operates by interpreting a process model created by specialized tools. Several research prototypes and even products on the market support both the creation and the execution of a process model. These products are therefore *environment generators*, since they can create different, customized environments that follow the procedures and policies enforced by the process model.

Process-centered environments are usually composed of parts to handle two functions:

• *Process-model execution.* The process driver interprets and executes a specific process model to operate the process-centered environment and make it available to software developers.
• *Process-model production.* Process modelers use tools to create or evolve process models.

Because of their process-model-execution function, I classify such products in Table 5 as process-centered environments, concerned with production-process technology. However, their process-model-production capabilities also qualify them as metaprocess technology.

Examples of products and research prototypes are East, Enterprise II, Process Weaver, Arcadia, Process Wise, EPOS, HPSF, Merlin, Marvel, and SPADE/S Lang (Software Process Analysis Design and Enactment/SPADE Language), whose functionalities I discuss in the later section on metaprocess technology. (EPOS, a project at Norges Tekniske Hogskole (NTH) in Trondheim, Norway, is not to be confused with an existing CASE product with the same name.)

480

Metaprocess and enabling technologies

The metaprocess and enabling technologies are important in developing effective software-process support. Metaprocess-technology products let a process manager create, operate, and improve production-process support. Enabling technology provides the basic mechanisms to integrate the different products in both the production-process and the metaprocess technologies.

Metaprocess technology. Toward the beginning of this article, I defined the metaprocess as the set of activities, procedures, roles, and computerized aids used to create, maintain, and further improve the production process. The metaprocess is similar to the software processes. Process managers must conceive, design, verify, use, assess, and maintain a production process (the output of the metaprocess).

To achieve these goals, process managers may be able to use traditional production-process technology — in particular, analysis and design workbenches. For instance, they can create and maintain a process model using Statecharts with the support of Statemate.[14] In this way, however, it is possible to achieve only a quite limited goal: A process model created through traditional CASE products such as Statemate can be used only as a vehicle to communicate process rules and procedures, or to document and assess the existing practice. It cannot automatically generate more advanced environments and production-process supports.

Researchers have tried to develop technologies and methodologies to provide these advanced process supports. The first results were the structure-centered environment generators[10] (for example, Gandalf and the Cornell Program Synthesizer). These meta-environments can produce a set of tools starting from a formal description of the grammar of the language to be supported. Their initial aim was to produce a syntax-directed editor, but their scope has been progressively augmented to support more production-process tasks. These products are therefore environment generators, classified as metaprocess technology.

Recent work on process-centered environments and process modeling (discussed previously) has produced many research prototypes and a few commercial products,[15,16] whose goals I summarize:

- *Process modeling.* The development of notations to describe rules, activities, organizational structures, procedures, deliverables, and CASE products that constitute (or are used in) a software process, and the development of tools to validate and simulate the resulting model.
- *Process instantiation and enactment.* The development of runtime monitors and interpreters to execute or enact a software-process model — that is, to provide guidance to the people, tools, and workbenches involved in the process — and, whenever possible, to automate software-process activities. The resulting support to the production process is called a process-centered environment.
- *Process evolution.* Development of tools to support process-model evolution during the process lifetime.

The results of this research are encouraging, but several problems such as the process-model evolution have not yet been effectively solved. Nevertheless, some commercial products are available and, most important, the industrial community is becoming increasingly aware of the relevance of metaprocess technology.

Enabling technologies. Developing the complex products described in the previous sections requires services more sophisticated than the basic file-system-management and process-control mechanisms traditionally provided by operating systems. CASE products need functionalities such as advanced database-management systems to create and manage the repository, and sophisticated user-interface-management systems to design and develop graphical, easy-to-learn user interfaces for tools and workbenches.

To tackle these problems systematically and effectively, several industries and computer manufacturers are developing a new class of products that provide standard extensions to traditional operating systems (especially Unix). Built on top of the operating system, these products provide the tool developer with runtime libraries implementing several advanced features. Typical examples of this class are the already-mentioned DEC Cohesion Platform, HP SoftBench, and Atherton Software Backplane. Another example is PCTE (Portable Common Tool Environment), which is actually a standard interface definition, not a product. Currently, several existing or forthcoming products comply with this standard: the initial implementation by Emeraude, the Oracle-based version by Verilog, and implementations by DEC and IBM.

A key feature of these *integrating platforms* is their support for the creation of logically integrated but physically distributed systems. The development of personal computers, workstations, and local area network technology has made distributed implementations particularly suitable for advanced software-development environments. Hence, platform designers conceive and implement all the services for a distributed architecture. Moreover, the same services are very often available on different operating systems (for example, Unix, OSF/1, NT, and MS-DOS) to make the creation of heterogeneous architectures possible.

Standardization is a key aspect for such products. CASE developers can embed most of the functionalities offered by a platform in an application by adopting ad hoc components and products already available on the market. However, to develop distributed, highly integrated, and heterogeneous systems, they must identify standard mechanisms that ensure the required degree of product interoperability. (Interoperability is "the ability of two or more systems or components to exchange information and to use the information that has been exchanged."[6])

Besides the repository- and user-interface-management mechanisms, integrating platforms offer (or soon will offer) other key functionalities:

- *Advanced process-control mechanisms.* These let CASE developers encapsulate tools and workbenches, and invoke and control them through standard methods and event-generation mechanisms. Examples are the HP Encapsulator and the ACA Services offered by the DEC Cohesion Platform.
- *Support for the creation of multimedia products.* These features extend the functionalities offered by

traditional user-interface workbenches and let designers create advanced multimedia tools such as video documentation facilities and visual e-mail systems. A product offering these functionalities is the Multimedia Development Kit for Microsoft Windows.

- *Support for the creation of cooperating CASE tools and workbenches.* Typical examples of such applications are on-line agendas and concurrent/distributed editing tools. For example, DEC Fuse, Sun ToolTalk, and HP BMS give the tool developer a message-handling facility to support the integration and cooperation of CASE products.

The total value of the CASE technology market has grown from an estimated $2 billion in 1990 to $5 billion in 1993. Despite the recession Western countries have experienced in recent years, the CASE tool growth rate for the next couple of years is expected to be between 20 and 30 percent.[1]

Such high rates are justified because the total cost for human resources in software production amounts to about $250 billion per year. Therefore, even a modest increase in productivity would significantly reduce costs.[1] For this reason, CASE technology will play a key role in the information technology market, and many new products will appear.

The availability of such a large number of products and the complexity of the technologies used in software-development organizations make a reference framework for market evaluation and technology transfer essential. Moreover, it is important to facilitate comparison and exchange of experiences with other information-technology areas, such as VLSI design, factory automation, and office automation, where there have been similar efforts.

I have proposed concepts to bring in focus the state of the art of CASE technology. Attempts to classify and organize according to complex concepts may lead to extreme simplifications or, conversely, useless details. Moreover, the rapid changes in this area will quickly make some observations obsolete. As a result, this work will need to be updated incrementally as the technology develops. My aim in this article is to provide a reference framework and an initial classification of existing technology as a solid starting point for such a continuous updating. ∎

Acknowledgments

I thank Carlo Ghezzi and the anonymous referees for their stimulating and helpful comments.

References

1. *CASE Outlook: Guide to Products and Services,* G. Forte and K. McCulley, eds., CASE Consulting Group, Lake Oswego, Ore., 1991.

2. R. Conradi et al., "Towards a Reference Framework of Process Concepts," *Proc. Second European Workshop Software Process Technology,* Springer-Verlag, Berlin, 1992.

3. M.C. Paulk et al., "Capability Maturity Model for Software," Tech. Report CMU/SEI-91-TR-24, Software Eng. Inst., Carnegie Mellon Univ., Pittsburgh, 1991.

4. I. Sommerville, *Software Eng.,* Addison-Wesley, Reading, Mass., 1992.

5. C. Fernström, K.-H. Närfelt, and L. Ohlsson, "Software Factory Principles, Architectures, and Experiments," *IEEE Software,* Vol. 9, No. 2, Mar. 1992, pp. 36-44.

6. "Standard Glossary of Software Engineering Terminology," in *Software Eng. Standards,* IEEE, Spring 1991, pp. 7-38.

7. D. Whitgift, *Methods and Tools for Software Configuration Management,* John Wiley, New York, 1991.

8. A. Kay, invited address at the 11th Int'l Conf. Software Eng., 1989.

9. H.A. Müller et al., "A Reverse Engineering Environment Based on Spatial and Visual Software Interconnection Models," *Proc. Fifth ACM SIGSoft Symp. Software Development Environments,* ACM Press, New York, 1992, pp. 88-98.

10. S.A. Dart et al., "Software Development Environments," *Computer,* Vol. 20, No. 11, Nov. 1987, pp. 18-28.

11. *Integrated Programming Environments,* D.R. Barstow, H.E. Shrobe, and E. Sandewall, eds., McGraw-Hill, New York, 1984.

12. "Reference Model for Frameworks of Software Engineering Environments," jointly published as ECMA Tech. Report TR/55, European Computer Manufacturers Assoc., Geneva, and NIST Special Publication 500-201, Nat'l Inst. of Standards and Technology, Gaithersburg, Md., 1991.

13. M.M. Lehman, "Process Models, Process Programs, Programming Support," *Proc. Ninth Int'l Conf. Software Eng.,* IEEE CS Press, Los Alamitos, Calif., Order No. 767, 1987, pp. 14-16.

14. M.I. Kellner, "Software Process Modeling: Value and Experience," *SEI Tech. Rev.,* Software Eng. Inst., Carnegie Mellon Univ., Pittsburgh, 1989, pp. 23-54.

15. C. Liu and R. Conradi, "Process Modeling Paradigms: An Evaluation," *Proc. First European Workshop on Software Process Modeling,* Italian Nat'l Assoc. for Computer Science, Milan, Italy, 1991, pp. 39-52.

16. P. Armenise et al., "A Survey and Assessment of Software Process Representation Formalisms," to be published in *Int'l J. Software Eng. and Knowledge Eng.*

Alfonso Fuggetta is an associate professor of computer science at Politecnico di Milano and a senior researcher at CEFRIEL, the Italian acronym for the Center for Research and Education in Information Technology, established in 1988 by a consortium of universities, public administrations, and information-technology industries. His research interests are software-process modeling and management, CASE products, and executable specifications.

Fuggetta is chairman of the steering committee of the European Software Engineering Conference (ESEC) and a member of the steering committee of the European Workshop on Software Process Technology. He is a member of the board of directors of AICA, the Italian National Society for Computer Science, and of the Technical Committee on Software Quality Certification of Istituto Marchio Qualità. Fuggetta is also a member of IEEE and ACM.

Readers can contact Fuggetta at Dipartimento di Elettronica e Informazione, Politecnico di Milano, P.za Leonardo da Vinci, 32, 20133 Milano, Italy, e-mail fuggetta@IPMEL2.elet.polimi.it.

A Guidebook and a Spreadsheet Tool for a Corporate Metrics Program

Ronald E. Nusenoff and Dennis C. Bunde

Loral Software Productivity Laboratory, San Jose, California

A metrics guidebook and a spreadsheet tool have been developed at the Loral Software Productivity Laboratory as a start–up kit to enable Loral divisions and projects to implement the Loral corporate metrics program. The metrics guidebook defines a standard set of software metrics and specifies procedures for collection and analysis of metrics data. Guidelines are provided for revising schedules, resource allocations, and project procedures in light of the analysis of metrics data. The corporate-, division-, and project-level roles and responsibilities for metrics activities are discussed. The spreadsheet tool provides automated support for metrics generation, collection, graphical representation, and analysis.

This article explains the guidelines that were followed in constructing a guidebook and a spreadsheet tool that would both motivate and enable divisions and projects to implement the corporate metrics program. Metrics use is motivated at the division level as a means of developing a metrics database which will improve the organization's development and bidding capabilities, while motivating individual projects requires more emphasis on the role of metrics in monitoring and controlling project progress. Corporate metrics were tied to previous software metrics collection activities and to other data already collected and used within the organization and were mapped to Software Engineering Institute (SEI) level 2 and 3 maturity level requirements.

Guidelines for division and project tailoring of corporate metrics were provided. The corporate metrics were defined to map to the corporate development methodology, and so tailoring of that methodology by divisions or projects requires corresponding tailoring of the corporate metrics. Automated support for metrics collection and analysis, which also must be tailorable, was found to be a critical factor in enabling division and project implementation of corporate metrics. Feedback from divisions and projects that imple-mented the corporate metrics program is being used to improve the current program and extend it to cover SEI level 4 and 5 maturity level requirements.

1. INTRODUCTION

In a corporate software metrics program, a set of metrics, collection procedures, and analysis procedures are defined and then implemented throughout the company. A corporate metrics program presupposes a corporate standard software development methodology. A software development methodology consists of a process model which specifies all of the activities involved in software development, plus the individual methods, practices, and procedures which instantiate the steps of the process model. When a standard methodology has been specified, software development can be a defined, repeatable process rather than an ad hoc activity reinvented for each new project. Projects that follow the methodology can be planned, monitored, and controlled through the use of metrics which will have been defined in terms of the components of the methodology.

Projects that adopt a corporate metrics program need a guidebook (*Webster's Ninth New Collegiate Dictionary* defines a guidebook as a "handbook; esp: a book of information for travelers") that tells them how to implement this program. This guidebook should be a user–oriented handbook containing metrics definitions, collection and analysis procedures and tools, and guidelines for corrective actions. Projects also need automated support for metrics collection and analysis. This article explains guidelines we have found useful in constructing a metrics guidebook and a spreadsheet tool for the Loral Corporation corporate metrics program. Section 2 of this paper provides background on our metrics program. Section 3 covers the issues of enabling and motivating company divisions and projects to use metrics. Section 4 covers guidelines for

Address correspondence to Ronald E. Nusenoff, Octel Communication Corporation, 1001 Murphy Ranch Road, Milpitas, CA 95035

Reprinted from *J. Systems and Software*, Vol. 23, R.E. Nusenoff and D.C. Bunde, "A Guidebook and a Spreadsheet Tool for a Corporate Metrics Program," pp. 245–255, 1993, with kind permission from Elsevier Science–NL, Sara Burgerhartstraat 25; 1055 KV Amsterdam, The Netherlands.

defining a set of metrics. Section 5 covers guidelines about providing automated support for metrics collection and analysis. Section 6 discusses guidelines we are following in getting the guidebook and spreadsheet tool adopted on projects at Loral divisions. Section 7 describes the next steps planned in our metrics program.

2. BACKGROUND

The Loral Software Productivity Laboratory (SPL) is a central organization responsible for the formulation of a corporate standard software development methodology employing modern software engineering disciplines and techniques and meeting the software development requirements of Loral customers [1]. The SPL is also responsible for developing a corporate computer-aided software environment (CORCASE), which supports and enforces this methodology, and a software total quality management (TQM) program.

We have chosen the Software Engineering Institute (SEI) capability maturity model and associated assessment methodology as a framework for our software TQM program [2]. The levels within the SEI model provide the specific measurable goals which have been missing from previous TQM initiatives. The SEI maturity level hierarchy is shown in Figure 1. The three lower levels of the SEI capability maturity model are based on empirical observations about the best current software engineering and management practices. These practices are organized into levels 1–3 in a manner that provides a road map for increasing software development process capability maturity. The SEI has been conducting process assessments since 1987 and has found 81% of organizations assessed to be at level 1, 12% at level 2, and 7% at level 3. No level 4 or 5 organizations have been identified. Levels 4 and 5, therefore, represent a view of what software organizations beyond the current state of the practice might look like.

A central activity of the TQM program is the definition and implementation of a corporate software development metrics program. The goal of this metrics program is to improve contract bidding, software project management, and software engineering practices by enabling software project managers to measure, monitor, predict, and control project progress, costs, and quality. The SPL metrics program currently addresses the metrics required to achieve SEI levels 2 and 3. What characterizes the advance from a level 1 to a level 2 capability is the introduction and enforcement of formal engineering management controls and procedures, which are prerequisites to the availability and validity of schedule and effort metrics data. All software project managers must control projects using well-defined procedures for scheduling, effort and size estimation, collection of schedule and effort metrics, configuration management of baselines, and quality assurance monitoring. The advance from level 2 to level 3 is characterized by the introduction of a defined software development process in which all software engineers are formally trained in the process and its associated engineering methods. The advance to level 3 does not introduce substantial metrics collection requirements beyond those of level

Level	Characteristic	Key Challenges	Result
5 **Optimizing**	Improvement fed back into process	Still human intensive process Maintain organization at optimizing level	**Productivity & Quality**
4 **Managed**	(Quantitative) Measured process	Changing technology Problem analysis Problem prevention	
3 **Defined**	(Qualitative) Process defined and institutionalized	Process measurement Process analysis Quantitative quality plans	
2 **Repeatable**	(Intuitive) Process dependent on individuals	Training Technical practices • reviews, testing Process focus • standards, process groups	
1 **Initial**	(Ad hoc/chaotic)	Project management Project planning Configuration management Software quality assurance	**Risk**

Figure 1. SEI maturity level hierarchy.

484

2, but the defined process provides a stable baseline of technical activities which can be measured.

We divide these SEI level 2 and 3 metrics (which we call management metrics) into two types: schedule and effort, and quality. Schedule and effort metrics are used to detect variance between planned and actual progress and labor costs. A software schedule represents the planned progress of a project. Schedule metrics summarize project progress information so that the software manager can detect and compensate for unplanned schedule trends. Effort is the labor portion of software cost; it does not take into account overhead, travel, and capital expenses. Effort metrics summarize effort information so that the software manager can detect adverse trends and control software costs.

Schedule and cost variance are signals that future completion dates and the overall project budget are at risk. Further analysis is required to determine the causes of schedule and cost variances so management can adjust plans and take actions to maintain control of the project. Significant analysis of schedule and effort metrics requires plotting of collected values together with project estimates on a regular basis. This enables the identification of trends in both the measured data and its variance from estimates. These trends can be extrapolated to provide more reasonable revised estimates. Comparison with data and trends from previous projects can be used to predict where a current project is going. Where metrics are known to correlate, i.e., changes in one metric cause changes in others, comparisons of data are used to isolate problems and identify corrective actions.

Quality metrics are quantitative measures available during the software development process. They are indicators of final product quality (e.g., correctness, reliability, maintainability) and allow managers to predict and influence final product quality. The quality of the final product can be predicted by measuring the quality of the process used to produce it and of the products generated along the way. Measuring the quality of the process and its products provides early warning signs that there will be cost and schedule problems before they actually occur. Once a quality metrics data base has been established, quality data expectations can be established by reference to data and trends observed on previous projects.

Quality metrics include errors detected, the stability of requirements/design/code, and the complexity of requirements/design/code. Number of errors detected is a measure of intermediate product quality and of the quality of the error detec-

tion process. Detected error data is a predictor of remaining errors, which is an indicator of system reliability and correctness. Design and code inspections, test reviews, and software problem/change reports are the primary sources of error data. Instability in intermediate products is measured by software problem/change reports. Large numbers of reports against a baselined intermediate product are a signal that subsequent products based on it could be delayed. The complexity of system components is an indicator of system maintainability. Increases in measured complexity across the development phases indicate that additional effort will be required later.

3. ENABLING AND MOTIVATING METRICS USE

Guideline 1: Produce and Publish a Metrics Guidebook

The first major step of the Loral metrics program has been the production of a metrics guidebook [3]. Individual projects have neither the time nor the resources to develop a metrics program. They need a start-up kit that enables them to implement a well-defined program. The metrics guidebook defines a standard set of software metrics and specifies procedures for collection and analysis of metrics data. Guidelines are provided for revising schedules, resource allocations, and project procedures in light of the analysis of metrics data. The corporate-, division-, and project-level roles and responsibilities for metrics activities are discussed. Automated support for metrics generation, collection, and analysis, which includes a spreadsheet tool for organizing and graphically representing metrics data, is explained.

Guideline 2: Provide Motivation for Implementing Metrics

Metrics are still neither well understood nor widely applied within the software industry, despite extensive literature which provides a good case for the use of software metrics in terms of increases in quality and productivity [4–8]. Fear and/or loathing is a typical reaction to metrics from upper management ("the only thing metrics adds to a project is cost"), project management ("we couldn't pass data on up even if we believed it"), and engineers ("they're going to measure *us*"). Such reactions made us realize that the guidebook must do more than describe how company divisions and projects can implement metrics collection and analysis; it also must provide motivation for doing so.

At the division level, a motivating goal for metrics use can be the development of a division metrics data base. The data base provides an empirical foundation for future project estimations, analysis, and predictions. Historical data is used to analyze measurements of current projects to predict subsequent progress and suggest adjustments to current plans and schedules. Data collected from projects is used to validate and refine the metrics data base. Project data is also used to measure how well the division's version of the corporate methodology is working and the effect of either changing it or introducing new methods or technology.

SEI maturity level has also become a significant motivating factor at the company division level. The Department of Defense and other government agencies are phasing in use of SEI capability maturity levels as a criteria for contract awards. Government agencies have been using the SEI model to evaluate contractors during the contract bidding stage. The government's rule of thumb may soon be, try to find a level 3 contractor and do not deal with a level 1 contractor. The improvement of SEI maturity level was selected as the incentive for implementing a software TQM program at Loral. The SEI model was used to derive requirements for capability improvement and actions to meet those requirements. The metrics involved in advancing to SEI levels 2 and 3 are minimum requirements for the Loral management metrics program. Our inter-

pretation of SEI level 2 and 3 metrics collection requirements is given in Figure 2. The SEI question numbers in parentheses are taken from the original SEI technical report [2].

Motivation at the project level is a different issue than motivation at the division level. Once a project has started, the main motivation for using metrics has to be that it will enable the project manager to monitor and control project progress, costs, and quality. In the early stages of the corporate metrics program, there will at best be disjoint historical data rather than a corporate metrics data base to use as an empirical basis for estimations and planning. The fact that a pioneer project's implementation of the corporate metrics plan will produce data to help future projects does nothing to help the pioneers in their current endeavors.

4. DEFINING A SET OF METRICS

Guideline 3: Align Metrics with External Requirements

Guideline 4: Relate Metrics Program to Previous Metrics Collection

The Loral management metrics were selected based on literature research and investigation into current metrics activities at Loral divisions. The 10 metrics presented in "Software Management Metrics" [9]

SEI Level 2 Metrics Collection Requirements

Plot planned and actual staffing over time. (2.2.1)

Plot computer software configuration item (CSCI) size versus time. (2.2.2)

Record number and type of code and test errors. (2.2.4)

Plot planned and actual number of software units for which design reviews have been completed, versus time. (2.2.7)

Plot planned and actual computer software units (CSUs) for which unit testing has been completed, versus time. (2.2.8)

Plot planned and actual CSUs for which integration testing has been completed, versus time. (2.2.9)

Plot estimated and actual target computer memory utilization versus time. (2.2.10)

Plot estimated and actual target computer central processing unit (CPU) utilization versus time. (2.2.11)

Plot actual target computer input/output (I/O) channel utilization versus time. (2.2.12)

Plot planned and actual CSCI test progress versus time. (2.2.18)

Plot software build size versus time. (2.2.19)

SEI Level 3 Metrics Collection Requirements

Record number and type of software design errors. (2.2.3)

Figure 2. SEI metrics collection requirements.

were selected as a primary model. The software management metrics were defined by The MITRE Corporation for the Electronic Systems Division of the Air Force Systems Command, based on three years of government and industry experiences in the collection and analysis of the 8 metrics presented in "Software Reporting Metrics" [10]. A comparison of the two sets of MITRE metrics is given in Figure 3. The MITRE metrics are collected and reported at monthly intervals. They are plotted in a format showing the past 12 months of planned and actual data and the next 5 months of planned data.

The MITRE metrics are a reasonable starting point for the Loral metrics program for several reasons. They cover all phases of the software development process as defined in Department of Defense standard 2167A, from which the Loral software development process model is derived. The SEI level 2 metrics were based on the first MITRE set of eight metrics. The only SEI level 2 and 3 metrics not covered by the MITRE metrics are the numbers and types of design, code, and test errors. These data are collected during design, code, and test case inspections. A metrics program which included all of the

Metric Name	Status	Description
Software complexity	deleted	initially plotted complexity of the 10 percent most complex CSUs. Complexity was estimated on a scale from 1 to 6, as found in Boehm [13]. This metric was replaced by design complexity.
Software Size	same	plots new, modified, and reused SLOCs for each CSCI as well as for the total system.
Software Personnel	same	plots total and experienced numbers of personnel, planned and actual, plus unplanned personnel losses.
Software Volatility	modified	plots total number of software requirements, cumulative number of requirements changes, and numbers of new and open software requirements action items. Initially was a plot of the number of lines of code affected by ECPs.
Computer Resource Utilization	same	plots planned spare and estimated/actual percentages of utilization for target computer CPU timing, memory, and I/O channels.
Design Complexity	new	plots the average design complexity of the 10 percent most complex CSUs, CSCs, and CSCIs. It is based on McCabe's measure of complexity.
Schedule Progress	new	plots estimated schedule to completion based on the delivery of software work packages defined in the Work Breakdown Structure.
Design Progress	new	plots planned and actual numbers of software requirements from system design documents which been completely documented in software requirements documents, and in software design documents.
CSU Development Progress	same	plots planned and actual numbers of CSUs designed, tested, and integrated.
Testing Progress	same	plots planned and actual numbers of CSCI and system tests completed, numbers of new and open SPRs, and number of SPRs per 1000 SLOC.
Incremental Release Content	same	plots planned and actual estimates of release date and number of CSUs included in each software release.

Figure 3. MITRE metrics comparison.

MITRE metrics, plus data from design, code, and test case inspections, would meet all of the SEI level 2 and 3 metrics collection requirements. Finally, the original MITRE metrics have been a model for much of the metrics collection currently practiced by Loral divisions and are required by several government customers.

Mapping of SEI metrics collection requirements and MITRE metrics to the Loral metrics is shown in Figure 4. Each of the SEI level 2 and 3 questions is mapped to a recommended Loral metric. Nine of the 10 MITRE software management metrics map at least partially to one or more Loral metrics.

Guideline 5: Tailor Metrics to Fit the Activities and Methods of the Methodology

Guideline 6: Specify Concrete Criteria for Applying Metrics

We needed to tailor several of the MITRE metrics to fit them to the Loral software development methodology. MITRE used software problem reports as part of the testing progress metric and software action items as part of the software volatility metric. Loral methodology includes a software problem change report (SP/CR) system which is used for all configuration-controlled software and documents starting with the software requirements documents. It therefore seemed appropriate to define an SP/CR metric that corresponds to this system.

A corollary of guideline 5 is that defining metrics may suggest simple yet useful modifications to the corporate methodology. It would be useful to know when errors are introduced into the process, but the current SP/CR forms do not contain an entry for when a problem was introduced. This information is already determined when an SP/CR is assigned for resolution, but is not recorded in a readily collectable manner. It has therefore been suggested that a problem introduction entry, defined relative to the earliest document needing changes, be added to the SP/CR form.

A general rule we followed in defining management metrics to fit the corporate software development methodology was to establish concrete binary

Loral Metric	Mitre Metric	SEI Question
Schedule Progress	Schedule Progress	—
Software Cost	—	—
Software Size	Software Size (T)	2.2.2
Staffing Profile	Software Personnel	2.2.1
CSU Development Progress	CSU Development Progress (T) Incremental Release Content(T)	2.2.7, 2.2.8 2.2.9, 2.2.19
CSCI Test Progress	Testing Progress	2.2.18
Requirements Volatility	Software Volatility (T)	—
SP/CR	Testing Progress Software Volatility (T)	—
Computer Resource Utilization	Computer Resource Utilization	2.2.10, 2.2.11, 2.2.12
Inspection Defects/Hours	—	2.2.4, 2.2.3
Module Complexity	Design Complexity (T)	—
		(T) = significant tailoring

Figure 4. Mapping of MITRE and SEI to Loral metrics.

criteria for applying metrics. For example, the completion criterion for the design of a computer software unit (CSU) had to be an all-or-nothing affair, with no partial (e.g., 90%) criterion accepted. The criterion we found within the methodology was that CSU design is finished if the detailed design inspection has been completed. This is the point at which the design is placed under configuration control. On the other hand, the MITRE design progress metric, which tracks the allocation of software requirements from system design documents to software requirements documents to design documents, was not adopted because its units are neither precisely defined nor readily collectable. Before baselining a document, it is not obvious how to count incrementally the number of individual requirements allocated within that document.

When projects have acquired experience using CORCASE analysis and design tools, we intend to introduce metrics based on discrete units which can be counted directly by these tools. These metrics should provide measures of the progress between the analysis and design phases and a means of tracking the evolution of system complexity. Detailed ongoing measurement of system complexity has long been advocated by DeMarco [4]. Streamlined versions of this approach have been advanced by Card [11] and by the Software Productivity Consortium [12].

Guideline 7: Relate Metrics to Other Data Already Collected and Used

The schedule progress metric calculates the estimated schedule to complete each month by multiplying the planned project schedule by the ratio of the budgeted cost of work scheduled (BCWS) to the budgeted cost of work performed (BCWP). BCWP and BCWS are based on an earned value assigned to each discrete task in a project, as described in Boehm's *Software Engineering Economics* [13]. The difference between BCWS and BWCP is the schedule variance for the entire project. What was needed to complement this overall schedule variance metric was an overall cost variance metric. We found that many Loral divisions use financial reporting systems that plot budget at completion (BAC), which is the budgeted cost to complete a project, along with a monthly estimate at completion (EAC). EAC is calculated by multiplying BAC by the ratio of the project's current expenditures to the earned value of the tasks actually completed (i.e., the ratio of actual cost of work performed (ACWP) to (BCWP). We

adopted this as our cost metric because it uses data already collected and used throughout the company.

The software size metric uses counting rules for added, modified, reused, and removed source statements presented in the IEEE *Standard for Software Productivity Metrics* [14]. These rules had already been adopted by metrics working groups at the SEI, the Software Productivity Consortium, and by at least one Loral division. This same division also develops some code for reuse, and we have adopted their suggestion that such code be tracked separately from other newly developed code.

Guideline 8: Provide Tailoring Guidelines for Metrics

No set of definitions will fit every project perfectly. Divisions and projects that tailor the corporate methodology according to customer requirements, division standards, or business area may also need to tailor their implementation of metrics. Where we were aware of established division procedures that implied changes to the metrics definitions or analysis guidelines, we included them in the guidebook as tailoring guidelines. One Loral division uses a series of quality point reviews during the development process rather than the corporate standard inspection process. Quality point reviews generate metrics which replace our inspection metric and supplement the SP/CR metric.

5. TOOL SUPPORT FOR A METRICS PROGRAM

Guideline 9: Make Collection Nonintrusive — Automate if Possible

Much of the current resistance to metrics use on projects is based on the concern that the benefits to be gained from the analysis of metrics data will not compensate for the effort required to collect the data. The key to overcoming this resistance is to point out that most of the data that need to be collected for metrics purposes are already collected for other purposes. Most of the metrics data items recommended for collection in the guidebook are either generated automatically within CORCASE or are already being entered manually into the system independent of their use for metrics.

A detailed table was prepared listing each primitive (i.e., noncalculated) metrics data item along with the tool or other source that generates it and its location within the CORCASE data base. Most data used in estimating, planning, and tracking schedules, cost, and personnel resources is either generated by or manually entered through a Loral proprietary project management software package. Although this package does not currently handle data on actual labor hours worked, those data are available from the time card accounting system. Software size and complexity data are generated using language-dependent source code processing tools and are already recorded in electronic module software development files. Data related to numbers of and changes to requirements are already recorded in a requirements data base. Resource spare capability requirements would also be stored in the requirements data base. Data related to SP/CRs are generated and managed within an automated software problem reporting system, which also contains some data on requirements changes. Inspection data are already entered by the inspection moderators into a spreadsheet which generates statistics and graphs based on the collected data.

Guideline 10: Provide Automated Analysis Templates and Tools

The problem with much metrics data collection is that the data are merely collected. Analysis of collected values, calculation of derived values, trend extrapolation, and graphical representation require a tool that can do the work and a template that provides a common format. A management metrics spreadsheet was developed which provides an organized format for recording collected metrics data together with automatic generation of metrics graphs. This spreadsheet was developed using Wingz, a commercial spreadsheet program which is included as a productivity tool in CORCASE. A spreadsheet template was set up to record and graph the metrics recommended in the guidebook. The spreadsheet template contains labels for all data to be entered, formulas that calculate derived values, and some explanatory text describing the contents of the data cells. When planned and actual data are entered in the appropriate cells, derived values are calculated and the accompanying graphs are automatically created and updated. An empty copy of this spreadsheet can be copied to create a spreadsheet for a project. A copy of the spreadsheet template with 18 months of data was also provided as part of a tutorial on how to use the spreadsheet. The layout of the spreadsheet template, along with brief descriptions of each labelled area, is given in Figure 5. A utility was added to the spreadsheet to provide printout of graphs without spreadsheet row and column headers. A sample of this printout is given in Figure 6.

Collection of metrics data for insertion into the metrics spreadsheet within CORCASE is presently a manual process performed by a project metrics coordinator. Metrics collection and insertion into the management metrics spreadsheet will be automated in later releases of CORCASE. A metrics collection utility will be written for use by the metrics coordinators which will collect all of the metrics data items, generate a report listing the collected items, and insert the collected data items into a specified spreadsheet upon request.

Guideline 11: Make the Tools and Templates Tailorable and Portable

As with the metrics definitions, the analysis tool may need to be adjusted to fit the needs of divisions or individual projects. We included instructions for adding metrics definitions, calculations, and graphs to the spreadsheet template. We have converted the spreadsheet template from the SUNView version of Wingz on which it was developed to an X Window version. We have also successfully converted a metrics spreadsheet file into Lotus and Excel formats (even the graphs converted over), which makes it accessible to those divisions and projects that are already committed to using those packages. In the interest of portability, we avoided using any unique special features of the Wingz program.

6. ONGOING GUIDELINES IN TECHNOLOGY TRANSFER

Guideline 12: Locate Metrics Technology Transfer Point Above the Project Level

The initial criterion of success for a corporate metrics program is that it be adopted by projects at different divisions of the company. (The second criterion is that it is subsequently adopted by other projects at those divisions.) Personnel in corporate-level organizations generally have limited access to personnel at the project level, and project personnel generally do not have the position and funding to sponsor the establishment of a metrics program (or generally, any new methods). We have so far found that implementation of the metrics program at the division level is best accomplished through a division software engineering process group (SEPG) [7]. As a corporate-level organization, the SPL tailors and integrates state-of-the-practice methods and tools into a corporate methodology. The division SEPG

INTRODUCTION
General comments which describe the spreadsheet.
RAW DATA
Rows for entry of project data. The first cell (column A) of each row contains the text string naming the data. The first row of this area contains the project calendar in text strings.
METRICS FORMULAS
Formulas for calculating values to be graphed. Column A contains the text string naming the value to be calculated. Copies of the formula are contained in all remaining cells of the row, up to the column for the last month of the project calendar.
GRAPH WINDOW DEFINITION
Rows for entry of current project month and software start month, and a formula to calculate which 18 months of data to store in the Graph Data area. Data is stored for the current month, the 11 previous months, and the 6 subsequent months.
GRAPH DATA
Rows of 19 columns each for storage of pointers used to create graphs. All rows for a given graph must be consecutive. Column A of the first row for each graph contains a pointer to the graph title. Column A of the subsequent data rows contains a pointer to the name of the data for that row. Columns B..S of the first rows use an INDEX function to access the required 18 columns of the project calendar. Columns B..S of the data rows use the INDEX function to access either raw data from the Raw Data area, or calculated values from the Metrics Formulas area.
GRAPH AXIS LABELS
Rows for storage of text strings to be used as labels for the graph axes. A new label can be added to any empty cell in this area.
GRAPHS
Area in which graphs using rows from Graph Data area are located.

Figure 5. Layout of the management metrics spreadsheet.

then tailors this methodology to meet the requirements of the division customers and business area. In the case of a metrics program, the SEPG would tailor the corporate metrics definitions, procedures, and tools to keep metrics in alignment with the division version of the corporate software development methodology. The SEPG is also responsible for using metrics data and analysis from projects for developing and maintaining a division metrics data base and a division cost model, for passing data base information back to the corporate data base, and for implementing enhancements to the corporate metrics program.

Each project should have a metrics coordinator who consolidates project metrics data and prepares reports and analysis for the project manager to review. The position of metrics coordinator may not be a full-time position, but requires an experienced engineer who is well versed in the corporate or division methodology. This position might best be filled by a person from the SEPG who is matrixed into several projects as metrics coordinator. This person from the SEPG could be someone who works on the division metrics data base. Using SEPG personnel as metrics coordinators would be an instance of the collaborative technology transfer method [15], in which end users are involved in developing the technology, rather than the more traditional transfer-and-feedback mechanism which most corporate–level organizations use.

Guideline 13: Find a Pilot Project

The best way to test a metrics guidebook and spreadsheet tool is to find a real development project on which to use them. Testing with a pilot

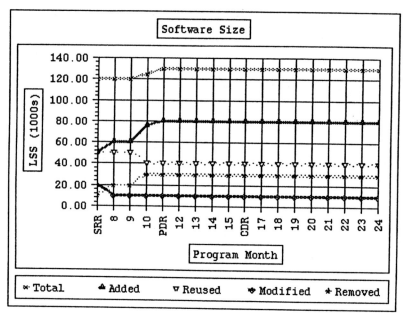

Figure 6. Sample spreadsheet graph printout.

project will uncover errors, omissions, and ambiguities more efficiently than one more review or simulation. It will also provide a practitioner's viewpoint as to what is useful, what is not, and what else is needed.

Guideline 14: Be Ready to Train and Consult

Even with the existence of a division SEPG, the corporate-level organization's job is not done. Some SEPGs may be as small as two people or may be staffed by project personnel devoting personal time to the effort. Even with a well-funded SEPG, comments and questions on the guidebook and on how to use the tool should come back. No metrics guidebook can anticipate all of the questions and even have all of the answers to the expected questions. Few (if any) tools can be used effectively without some expert guidance. No comments, questions, or corrections coming back is a bad sign: it means that users did not read the guidebook and did not try the tool.

7. NEXT STEPS

The program defined in our metrics guidebook has been implemented at four Loral divisions. The corporate metrics guidebook was used as the basis for division metrics standards, and the spreadsheet template has been modified to accommodate division tailoring of the corporate metrics definitions and

procedures. Two divisions are using the Wingz spreadsheet and two divisions are using Excel versions. Several other divisions have requested soft copies of the spreadsheet. Up to this point, the availability of personnel and resources to experiment with the spreadsheet tool has been a critical factor in getting the corporate program implemented at the division level.

Loral software projects that use the metrics, procedures, and tools defined and explained in the management metrics guidebook will provide us with feedback in the form of spreadsheets and commentary on their use of analysis guidelines and corrective actions. We plan to develop a corporate management metrics data base using the spreadsheet format and will validate and refine the metrics and procedures contained in the guidebook. Changes in the corporate software development methodology will be reflected in the corporate metrics program as required.

We also plan to develop a process improvement metrics guidebook, based on SEI levels 4 and 5, which will provide methods, guidelines, and tools for stabilizing and improving the methodology. SEI level 4 metrics address improvement of the implementation of the defined process which was established in advancing to SEI level 3. Process performance variations are measured and their causes identified. The metrics required to advance to SEI level 5 address improvement of the defined process itself. The effects of planned changes to the process are measured and compared with the predicted values of the unchanged process.

REFERENCES

1. Loral Corporation Policy on the Development of Software, Policy Letter SW-01, San Jose, California, December 14, 1990.
2. W. S. Humphrey, and W. L. Sweet, A Method for Assessing the Software Engineering Capability of Contractors, Software Engineering Institute Technical Report CMU/SEI-87-TR-23, Pittsburgh, Pennsylvania, 1987.
3. D. Bunde and R. Nusenoff, Management Metrics Guidebook, Loral Software Productivity Laboratory Technical Report SPL_SEGB_9A-91008-M, San Jose, California, 1991.
4. T. DeMarco, *Controlling Software Projects*, Englewood Cliffs, New Jersey, Yourdon Press, 1982.
5. R. B. Grady and D. L. Caswell, *Software Metrics*: *Establishing a Company-Wide Program*, Prentice-Hall, Englewood Cliffs, New Jersey, 1987.
6. V. R. Basili and H. D. Rombach, The TAME Project: Towards Improvement-Oriented Software Environments, *IEEE Trans. Software Eng.* 14, 758–773 (1988).
7. W. S. Humphrey, *Managing the Software Process*, Addison-Wesley, Reading, Massachussetts, 1989.
8. F. McGarry et al., Experiences in the software engineering laboratory (SEL) applying software measurement, in *Proceedings of the Fourteenth Annual Software Engineering Workshop*, SEL-89-007, Goddard Space Flight Center, Greenbelt, Maryland, 1989.
9. H. P. Schultz, Software Management Metrics, MITRE Technical Report ESD-TR-88-001, Bedford, Massachusetts, 1988.
10. R. J. Coles et al., Software Reporting Metrics, MITRE Technical Report ESD-TR-85-145, Bedford, Massachusetts, 1985.
11. D. N. Card and R. L. Glass, *Measuring Software Design Quality*, Prentice-Hall, Englewood Cliffs, New Jersey, 1990.
12. J. E. Gaffney and R. Werling, Estimating Software Size from Counts of Externals, A Generalization of Function Points, Software Productivity Consortium Technical Report SPC_91094, Herndon, Virginia, 1991.
13. B. W. Boehm, *Software Engineering Economics*, Prentice-Hall, Englewood Cliffs, New Jersey, 1981.
14. Standard for Software Productivity Metrics, P1045/D4.0, Draft, IEEE, New York, New York, 1990.
15. J. D. Babcock, L. A. Belady, and N. C. Gore, The evolution of technology transfer at MCC's software technology program: From didactic to dialectic, *12th International Conference on Software Engineering*, IEEE Computer Society Press, Los Alamitos, California, 1990, pp. 290–299.

Industrial software metrics top 10 list

Barry Boehm, TRW, Inc.

I am always fascinated by top 10 lists. So, when Vincent Shen asked me to write a piece for this department, I decided to present my candidate top 10 list of software metric relationships, in terms of their value in industrial situations. Here they are, in rough priority order:

1. *Finding and fixing a software problem after delivery is 100 times more expensive than finding and fixing it during the requirements and early design phases.*

This insight has been a major driver in focusing industrial software practice on thorough requirements analysis and design, on early verification and validation, and on up-front prototyping and simulation to avoid costly downstream fixes.

2. *You can compress a software development schedule up to 25 percent of nominal, but no more.*

There is a remarkably consistent cube-root relationship for the most effective schedule T_{dev} for a single-increment, industrial-grade software development project: $T_{dev} = 2.5 \times MM^{1/3}$ where T_{dev} is in months and MM is the required development in man-months.

Equally remarkable is the fact that virtually no industrial-grade projects have been able to compress this schedule more than 25 percent. Thus, if your project is estimated to require $512MM$, your best schedule is $2.5 \times 512^{1/3}$, or 20, months. If your boss or customer wants the product in 15 months, you will barely make it if you add some extra resources and plan well. If he wants it in 12 months, you should gracefully but firmly suggest reducing the scope or doing an incremental development.

3. *For every dollar you spend on software development you will spend two dollars on software maintenance.*

A lot of industry and government organizations created major maintenance embarrassments before they realized this and instituted thorough software life-cycle planning. This insight has also stimulated a healthy emphasis on developing high-quality software products to reduce maintenance costs.

4. *Software development and maintenance costs are primarily a function of the number of source instructions in the product.*

This was the major stimulus for migrating from assembly languages to higher order languages. It is now a major stimulus for developing and using very high-level languages and fourth-generation languages to reduce software costs.

5. *Variations between people account for the biggest differences in software productivity.*

Studies of large projects have shown that 90th-percentile teams of software people typically outproduce 15th-percentile teams by factors of four to five. Studies of individual programmers have shown productivity ranges of up to 26:1. The moral: Do everything you can to get the best people working on *your* project.

6. *The overall ratio of computer software to hardware costs has gone from 15:85 in 1955 to 85:15 in 1985, and it is still growing.*

This relationship has done more than anything else to focus management attention and resources on improving the software process.

7. *Only about 15 percent of software product-development effort is devoted to programming.*

In the early days, there was a 40-20-40 rule: 40 percent of the development effort for analysis and design, 20 percent for programming, and 40 percent for integration and test. Now, the best project practices achieve a 60-15-25 distribution. Overall, this relationship has been very effective in getting industrial practice to treat software product development as more than just programming.

8. *Software systems and software products each typically cost three times as much per instruction to fully develop as does an individual software program. Software-system products cost nine times as much.*

A software system contains many software modules written by different people. A software-system product is such a system that is released for external use. The discovery of this cost-tripling relationship has saved many people from unrealistically extrapolating their personal programming productivity experience into unachievable budgets and schedules for software-system products.

9. *Walkthroughs catch 60 percent of the errors.*

The structured walkthrough (software inspection) has been the most cost-effective technique to date for eliminating software errors. It also has significant side benefits in team building and in ensuring backup knowledge if a designer or programmer leaves the project.

I had a hard time picking number 10. I ended up with a composite choice:

10. *Many software phenomena follow a Pareto distribution: 80 percent of the contribution comes from 20 percent of the contributors.*

Knowing this can help a project focus on the 20 percent of the subset that provides 80 percent of the leverage for improvement. Some examples:

- 20 percent of the modules contribute 80 percent of the cost,
- 20 percent of the modules contribute 80 percent of the errors (not necessarily the same ones),
- 20 percent of the errors consume 80 percent of the cost to fix,
- 20 percent of the modules consume 80 percent of the execution time, and
- 20 percent of the tools experience 80 percent of the tool usage.

I think it has been a strong credit to the software metrics field that it has been able to determine and corroborate these and many other useful software metric relationships. And there are many useful new ones coming along. I look forward to reading about them in this department.

Reprinted from *IEEE Software*, Vol. 4, No. 5, Sept. 1987, pp. 84–85.

Chapter 13

Software Engineering Education

1. Introduction to Chapter

Efforts to establish a curriculum in software engineering began soon after the definition of software engineering as a separate discipline in 1968. A workshop organized in 1976 by Peter Freeman and Anthony Wasserman was a major influence in curriculum design [1]. The first published curriculum was a masters degree program authored by Richard Fairley under the auspices of the Association for Computing Machinery (ACM) and published in 1978 [2]. Since that time, the IEEE Computer Society and the ACM have published computer science curricula, including software engineering material [3].

In 1987, 1989, and 1991 the Software Engineering Institute (SEI) published model curricula for masters programs in software engineering [4, 5, 6] and has been working toward future undergraduate curricula. While software engineering is part of many undergraduate computer science curricula, and there are some undergraduate degrees or specializations in software engineering, most degree programs exist at the masters level. Continuing education for practicing professionals is also an area of emphasis.

As of this writing, software engineering education is an important part of an effort by IEEE and ACM to establish software engineering as a profession [7]. The Steering Committee for this effort has constituted three task forces, concerned with:

- the body of knowledge of software engineering

- ethics and professional practices

- curriculum

All three task forces have educational implications: the professional and ethical material that practitioners should know, and the approach for imparting that knowledge, at undergraduate, graduate, and professional levels.

SOFTWARE ENGINEERING EDUCATION

DIGERNESS 96

2. Introduction to Paper

There is only one paper in this chapter on software engineering education. The paper, by the well-known computer scientist David Parnas, addresses a broader topic, "Education for Computer Professionals." Dr. Parnas developed the concept of information hiding and has a large number of other noteworthy achievements [8, 9, 10]

Parnas believes that present-day computer science education is inadequate. He says that computer science graduates are employed to produce useful artifacts, often software systems, and that their education must therefore emphasize classical engineering and other fundamentals such as mathematics and science, rather than programming languages and compiler theory (topics of interest when computer science first became an independent discipline) and the research interests of computer science faculty. Computer science graduates do not possess the fundamental knowledge needed to sustain them during their professional careers; the material they learn quickly becomes obsolete. He cites computer system researchers and implementers who would prefer to take graduates in engineering, mathematics, or even history and train them in programming rather than hire computer science graduates.

Based on the above assertions and beliefs, Parnas outlines a curriculum for computing professionals. It includes:

- Mathematics (calculus, discrete mathematics, logic, linear algebra, graph theory, differential equations, probability and statistics, optimization, and linear analysis)

- Science (physics and chemistry)

- Engineering (electricity and magnetism, circuit theory, mechanics, systems and control theory, information theory, digital systems and logic design, and signal processing)

- Computing science (programming, documentation, algorithms and data structures, process control, and system architecture and networks)

He also believes in the value of cooperative education, in which students spend time in industry developing "a real product and getting feedback from interested users."

While Parnas does not propose a course or courses called "Software Engineering" as part of an undergraduate program, many elementary aspects of the material in this Tutorial appear in the computing science courses he does recommend. Other topics, such as system engineering, requirements, configuration management, quality assurance, and management topics, are, in Parnas's view, not part of an undergraduate education in computer science.

1. Wasserman, Anthony L. and Peter Freeman, eds., *Software Engineering Education: Needs and Objectives*, Springer-Verlag, New York, N.Y., 1976.

2. Fairley, Richard E., "Toward Model Curricula in Software Engineering," *SIGSCE Bulletin*, Vol. 10, No. 3, Aug. 1978.

3. ACM/IEEE-CS Joint Curriculum Task Force, *Computing Curricula 1991*, ACM, New York, N.Y., 1991.

4. Ford, Gary A., Norman E. Gibbs, and James E. Tomayko, *Software Engineering Education: an Interim Report from the Software Engineering Institute*, CMU/SEI-TR-87-109, Carnegie Mellon University, Pittsburgh, Pa., 1987.

5. Ardis, Mark A., and Gary A. Ford, *1989 SEI Report on Graduate Software Engineering Education*, CMU/SEI-89-TR-2, Carnegie Mellon University, Pittsburgh, Pa., 1989

6. Ford, Gary A., *1991 SEI Report on Graduate Software Engineering Education*, CMU/SEI-91-TR-2, Carnegie Mellon University, Pittsburgh, Pa., 1991.

7. Barbacci, Mario, "Panel presents first four recommendations aimed at establishing software engineering as a profession," *Computer*, Feb. 1994, pp. 80–81. Since this report, ACM has joined the effort.

8. Parnas, D.L., and P.C. Clements, "A Rational Design Process: How and Why to Fake It," *IEEE Trans. Software Eng.*, Vol. SE-12, No. 2, Feb. 1986, pp. 251–257.

9. Parnas, D.L., "On the Criteria to be Used in Decomposing Systems into Modules," *Comm. ACM*, Vol. 15, No. 12, Dec. 1972, pp. 1053–1058.

10. Parnas, David L., "Software Aspects of Strategic Defense Systems," *American Scientist*, Vol. 73, Sept.-Oct. 1985, pp. 432–440.

Education for Computing Professionals

David Lorge Parnas
Queen's University

E ngineering is often defined as the use of scientific knowledge and principles for practical purposes. While the original usage restricted the word to the building of roads, bridges, and objects of military use, today's usage is more general and includes chemical, electronic, and even mathematical engineering. All use science and technology to solve practical problems, usually by designing useful products.

Most engineers today have a university-level education. Government and professional societies enforce standards by accrediting educational programs and examining those people who seek the title "Professional Engineer." Certification is intended to protect public safety by making certain that engineers have a solid grounding in fundamental science and mathematics, are aware of their professional responsibilities, and are trained to be thorough and complete in their analysis. In each of these aspects, engineers differ sharply from technicians, who are trained to follow established procedures but do not take responsibility for the correctness of those procedures.

Engineering education differs from traditional "liberal arts" education as well. Engineering students are much more restricted in their choice of courses; this en-

Computing science graduates are ending up in engineering jobs. CS programs must therefore return to a classical engineering approach that emphasizes fundamentals rather than the latest fads.

sures that all graduate engineers have had exposure to those fields that are fundamental to their profession. Engineering education also stresses finding good, as contrasted with workable, designs. Where a scientist may be happy with a device that validates his theory, an engineer is taught to make sure that the device is efficient,

reliable, safe, easy to use, and robust. Finally, engineers learn that even the most intellectually challenging assignments require a great deal of boring "dog work."

It has been a quarter century since universities began to establish academic programs in computing science. Graduates of these programs are usually employed by industry and government to build useful objects, often computer programs. Their products control aircraft, automobile components, power plants, and telephone circuits. Their programs keep banking records and assist in the control of air traffic. Software helps engineers design buildings, bridges, trucks, etc. In other words, these nonengineering graduates of CS programs produce useful artifacts; their work is engineering. It is time to ask whether this back door to engineering is in the best interests of the students, their employers, and society.

I have written this article to discuss a trend, not to single out any particular department's curriculum or any particular committee report. Each new curriculum proposal includes more "new" computer science and, unavoidably, less "classical" material. In this article I reject that trend and propose a program whose starting point is programs that were in place when computing science began.

Reprinted from *Computer*, Vol. 23, No. 1, Jan. 1990, pp. 17–22.

An historical debate

In the early 1960s, those of us who were interested in computing began to press for the establishment of computing science departments. Much to my surprise, there was strong opposition, based in part on the argument that graduates of a program specializing in such a new (and, consequently, shallow) field would not learn the fundamental mathematical and engineering principles that should form its basis. Both mathematicians and electrical engineers argued that computing science was an integral part of their own fields. They felt that students should major in one of those fields and take some computing courses near the end of their academic careers, rather than get an education in computing science as such. They predicted that graduates of CS programs would understand neither mathematics nor engineering; consequently, they would not be prepared to apply mathematical and engineering fundamentals to the design of computing systems.

My colleagues and I argued that computing science was rapidly gaining importance and that computing majors would be able to study the older fields with emphasis on those areas that were relevant to computing. Our intent was to build a program incorporating many mathematics and engineering courses along with a few CS courses. Unfortunately, most departments abandoned such approaches rather early. Both faculty and students were impatient to get to the "good stuff." The fundamentals were compressed into quick, shallow courses that taught only those results deemed immediately relevant to computing theory.

The state of graduate CS education

Nearly 25 years later, I have reluctantly concluded that our opponents were right. As I look at CS departments around the world, I am appalled at what my younger colleagues — those with their education in computing science — don't know. Those who work in theoretical computing science seem to lack an appreciation for the simplicity and elegance of mature mathematics. They build complex models more reminiscent of programs written by bad programmers than the elegant models I saw in my mathematics courses. Computing scientists often invent new mathemat-

ics where old mathematics would suffice. They repeatedly patch their models rather than rethink them when new problems arise.

Further, many of those who work in the more practical areas of computing science seem to lack an appreciation for the routine systematic analysis that is essential to professional engineering. They are attracted to flashy topics that promise revolutionary changes and are impatient with evolutionary developments. They eschew engineering's systematic planning, documentation, and validation. In violation of the most fundamental precepts of engineering design, some "practical" computing scientists advocate that implementors begin programming before the problem is understood. Discussions of documentation and practical testing issues are considered inappropriate in most CS departments.

Traditional engineering fosters cooperation between theory and practice. The theory learned in mathematics and science classes is applied in engineering classes. In computing science, though, theory and practice have diverged. While classical mathematical topics, such as graph theory, continue to have applications in computing, most of the material in CS theory courses is not relevant in practice. Much theory concentrates on machines with infinite capacity, although such machines are not, and never will be, available. Academic departments and large conferences are often battlegrounds for the "theoretical" and "applied" groups. Such battles are a sure sign that something is wrong.

As the opponents of computing science predicted, most CS PhDs are not scientists; they neither understand nor apply the methods of experimental science. They are neither mathematicians nor engineers. There are exceptions, of course, but they stand out so clearly that they "prove the rule."

The state of undergraduate CS education

The preparation of CS undergraduates is even worse than that of graduate students. CS graduates are very weak on fundamental science; their knowledge of technology is focused on the very narrow areas of programming, programming languages, compilers, and operating systems. Most importantly, they are never exposed to the discipline associated with engineering. They confuse existence proofs with products, toys with useful tools. They accept the bizarre inconsistencies and unpredictable behavior of current tools as normal. They build systems of great complexity without systematic analysis. They don't understand how to design a product to make such analysis possible. Whereas most engineers have had a course in engineering drawing (also known as engineering graphics), few CS graduates have had any introduction to design documentation.

Most CS graduates are involved in the construction of information and communications systems. These systems are highly dependent on information representation and transmission, but the graduates working on them are almost completely ignorant of information theory. For example, CS graduates are not conscious of the difference between the information unit "bit" and the storage unit, which is properly called a "binary digit." As a result, conversations on important practical issues, such as the design of data representations, proceed on an intuitive ad hoc level that engineers would consider unprofessional.

Although most CS graduates have been exposed to logic, the topic's treatment is usually quite shallow. The students are familiar with the symbol manipulation rules of predicate calculus but are usually unable to apply logic in practical circumstances. For example, most graduates cannot use quantifiers properly to "translate" informal statements into formal ones, perhaps because their instructors prefer inventing new logics to applying conventional ones. Mathematicians can successfully invent formalisms, but engineers usually succeed by finding new ways to use existing formalisms.

Because they lack knowledge of logic and communications concepts, CS graduates use fuzzy words like "knowledge" without the vaguest idea of how to define

498

such a term or distinguish it from older concepts like "data" and "information." They talk of building "reasoning" systems without being able to distinguish reasoning from mechanical deduction or simple search techniques. The use of such fuzzy terms is not merely sloppy wording; it prevents the graduate from doing the systematic analyses made possible by precise definitions.

Reliability requirements are forcing the introduction of redundancy in computer systems. Unfortunately, current CS graduates are usually unfamiliar with all but the most naive approaches to redundancy. They often build systems that are needlessly expensive but allow common mode failures. Many CS graduates have not been taught the fundamentals needed to perform reliability analyses on the systems they design. Few of them understand concepts such as "single error correction/ double error detection." Familiarity with such concepts is essential to the design of reliable computing systems.

Public safety is seriously affected by the fact that many CS graduates program parts of such control systems as those that run nuclear plants or adjust flight surfaces on aircraft. Unfortunately, I do not know of a single CS program that requires its students to take a course in control theory. The basic concepts of feedback and stability are understood only on an intuitive level at best. Neither the graduates nor most of their teachers know of the work in control theory that is applicable to the design of real-time systems.

Some graduates work in the production of signal processing systems. Unfortunately, signal processing is not offered in most CS programs; in fact, many departments will not allow a student to take such a course for CS credit. Signal processing deals with issues that are fundamental to the science and application of computing, but it is neglected in most programs.

Although many CS programs began with numerical analysis, most of our graduates have no understanding of the problems of arithmetic with finite representations of real numbers. Numerical analysis is, at best, an option in most CS programs.

What went wrong?

Most CS departments were formed by multidisciplinary teams comprising mathematicians interested in computing, electrical engineers who had built or used

computers, and physicists who had been computer users. Each had favorite topics for inclusion in the educational program, but not everything could be included. So, the set of topics was often the intersection of what the founders knew, not the union. Often, several topics were combined into a single course that forced shallow treatment of each.

The research interests of the founding scientists distorted the educational programs. At the time computing became an academic discipline, researchers were preoccupied with language design, language definition, and compiler construction. One insightful paper speculated that the next 1,700 PhD theses would introduce the next 1,700 programming languages. It might have been more accurate to predict 700 languages, 500 theories of language semantics, and 500 compiler-compilers.

Soon, "artificial intelligence" became a popular term with American funding agencies, and the CS field expanded to include a variety of esoteric topics described by anthropomorphic buzzwords. Cut off from the departments of mathematics and electrical engineering by the usual university divisions, CS graduates came to view their field as consisting primarily of those topics that were research interests in their department. The breadth that would have come from being in one of the older, broader departments was missing.

Today, it is clear that CS departments were formed too soon. Computing science focuses too heavily on the narrow research interests of its founding fathers. Very little computing science is of such fundamental importance that it should be taught to undergraduates. Most CS programs have replaced fundamental engineering and mathematics with newer material that quickly becomes obsolete.

CS programs have become so inbred that the separation between academic computing science and the way computers

are actually used has become too great. CS programs do not provide graduates with the fundamental knowledge needed for long-term professional growth.

What is the result?

In recent years, I have talked to a number of top industry researchers and implementors who are reluctant to hire CS graduates at any level. They prefer to take engineers or mathematicians, even history majors, and teach them programming. The manager of one safety-critical programming project stated with evident pride that his product was produced by engineers, "not just computer scientists." The rapid growth of the industry assures that our graduates get jobs, but experienced managers are very doubtful about the usefulness of their education.

As engineers in other fields are becoming more dependent on computing devices in their own professional practice, they are also becoming more concerned about the lack of professionalism in the products they use. They would rather write their own programs than trust the programs of our graduates.

As awareness of the inadequacies of CS education grows, as people begin to realize that programming languages and compiler technology are not relevant background for the people they hire, our students may have trouble getting jobs. The main problem now is that their education has not prepared them for the work they actually do.

A new program for computing professionals

While the critics of the original CS programs were quite accurate in their predictions, I still believe that a special educational program for computing professionals is needed. When we look at the programs produced by engineers and scientists who did not have such an education, we see that they are quite naive about many of the things we have learned in 25 years of computing science. For example, new programs in the defense industry are written in the same unsystematic style found in programs written in the 1950s and 1960s. Our graduates should be able to do better.

I believe the program proposed below would provide a good education for com-

> The manager of one safety-critical project stated with evident pride that his product was produced by engineers, "not just computer scientists."

puting professionals. It is designed to draw heavily on the offerings of other departments, and it emphasizes mature fundamentals to prepare our graduates for a life of learning in a dynamic field. Wherever possible, the courses should be existing courses that can be shared with mathematicians and engineers. Students should meet the strict requirements of engineering schools, and the programs should be as rigid as those in other engineering disciplines.

Basic mathematics. The products of most computing professionals are so abstract that the field could well be called "mathematical engineering." In fact, this is the title used at some Dutch universities. Computing professionals need to know how to use mathematics, although they rarely need to invent it. Some computer scientists have suggested that their students need only discrete mathematics, not the mathematics of continuous functions. However, while discrete mathematics is used in theoretical computing science, many practical applications use computers to approximate piecewise continuous functions. Computer professionals need a full introduction to mathematics; they should not be restricted to those items taught as theoretical computing science.

Calculus. All computing professionals should take the standard two- or four-semester calculus sequence taken by other engineers. This is the basic preparation for understanding how to deal with dynamic systems in the continuous domain. Many computer applications are best understood as approximations or improvements of dynamic analog systems. Computer professionals require the full sequence.

Discrete mathematics. CS students should join mathematics students in a course on such fundamentals as set theory, functions, relations, graphs, and combinatorics. In current computing courses, students view these topics as notations for describing computations and do not understand mathematics as an independent deductive system.

Logic. Logic is fundamental to many of the notations and concepts in computing science. Students should have a deeper understanding than that usually provided by CS logic courses or a few lectures on logic in some other course. I propose a two-semester sequence, taken with mathematics students, covering such advanced topics as decision procedures and higher order logics. The relationship between

logic, set theory, lambda calculus, etc. should be thoroughly explored. Applications to computing should not be discussed.

Linear algebra. This should be covered in the standard one-semester course for engineers offered by the mathematics department.

Graph theory. Graphs offer useful representations of a wide variety of computing problems. Students who understand graph theoretic algorithms will find them useful in a variety of fields. An optional second course could deal with the application of this theory in computing practice.

Differential equations. This also should be covered in the usual one-semester course offered by mathematics departments for engineers. Many modern computer systems are approximations to analog circuits, for which this analysis is essential.

Probability and applied statistics. The reliability and adequacy of testing is a major concern in modern computing applications. Probability theory is also a fundamental tool in situations where random noise is present in communications. Everyone who works as an engineer should have at least a one-semester course on this topic; a two-semester sequence would be better for many.

Optimization. Linear and nonlinear programming are major applications for large computers. A course in this area would make students aware of the complexity of search spaces and the need to precisely define objective functions. One need not look very far into the class of programs known as "expert systems" to find areas where optimization concepts should have been applied.

Numerical analysis. This topic could be taught as either computing science or mathematics. (It is described below under "Computing science.")

Basic science. Computing professionals need the same knowledge of basic science as engineers. A basic course in chem-

istry and a two-semester sequence in physics should be the minimal requirement for all technical students.

Engineering topics. Computing professionals are engineers and should be educated as such. Computers and software are now replacing more conventional technologies, but the people who design the new systems need to understand fundamental engineering systems as well as did the engineers who designed those older systems.

Engineering electricity and magnetism. This topic should be covered in the standard one-semester course taken by electrical engineers.

Electric circuits. This also should be covered in the standard one-semester course for electrical engineers.

Mechanics. An understanding of mechanics is essential to a study of practical robotics, automated manufacturing, etc. This topic, too, should be covered in the standard, one-semester, electrical engineering course.

Systems and control theory. This standard two-semester sequence for electrical engineers should emphasize the use of differential equations, transforms, and complex analyses to predict the behavior of control systems. The course should also discuss the discrete analogues of methods for dealing with continuous functions.

Information theory. This is one of the most fundamental and important areas for computing professionals. In addition to the standard one-semester course for electrical engineers, a second course on applications in computer design would be useful as an elective.

Digital system principles/logic design. This topic could be covered under either computing science or electrical engineering. (It is described below under "Computing science.")

Signal processing. This area should be examined in a one-semester course introducing the concepts of noise, filters, signal recognition, frequency response, digital approximations, highly parallel algorithms, and specialized processors.

Computing science. Before the advent of CS departments, engineering and science students were expected to learn programming and programming languages on their own or through noncredit courses. Computers were compared to slide rules and calculators: tools that university students could learn to use. Engineering and science faculty felt that courses in programming and programming languages would not have the deep intellectual content of mathematics or physics courses. We responded that we would teach computing science, not programming or specific languages.

Unfortunately, many of today's courses prove the critics correct. The content of many courses would change dramatically if the programming language being used underwent a major change. The courses proposed below assume that students are capable programmers and avoid discussions of programming languages.

Systematic programming. This would be taught in a two-semester sequence covering finite-state machines, formal languages and their applications, program state spaces, the nature of programs, program structures, partitioning the state space, program composition, iteration, program organization, program design documentation, systematic verification, etc. Students should be competent programmers as a prerequisite to this course.

Computer system documentation. This one-semester course would teach formal methods to document computer system designs, with emphasis on methods that apply to both digital and integrated digital/analog systems.

Design and analysis of algorithms and data structures. This course would discuss comparative analysis of algorithms and data structures as well as theoretical models of problem complexity and computability. Students would learn to predict the performance of their programs and to chose algorithms and data structures that give optimal performance.

Process control. This integrated treatment of the theoretic hardware, software, and control problems of process control systems would include hardware characteristics, operating systems for real-time applications, the process concept, synchronization, and scheduling theory. Students would learn how to prove that their systems will meet deadlines and how to design for fail-safe behavior. A course in control theory should be a prerequisite.

Computing systems architecture and networks. This fairly standard course, now taught in both electrical engineering and CS departments, would cover the structure of a computer and multicomputer networks, communications bus design, network performance analysis, etc. A knowledge of assembly language should be assumed. Students should be

> **Inadequate analyses and unsystematic work are often rewarded and reinforced by high grades.**

taught to avoid buzzwords and discuss the quantitative characteristics of the systems they study.

Numerical analysis. This course, which could be taught as either computing science or mathematics, would cover the study of calculations using finite approximations to real numbers and would teach round-off, error propagation, conditioning of matrices, etc.

Digital system principles/logic design. This standard one-semester course for electrical engineers should cover the basics of combinational circuit design, memory design, error correction, error detection, and reliability analysis. The emphasis should be on systematic procedures. The course could be offered as either computing science or electrical engineering.

As in any academic program, the above program includes compromises. Many topics, such as databases, compilers, and operating systems, were considered and omitted because of time limitations. It is not that these areas are uninteresting, but rather that I have chosen the oldest, most mature, most fundamental topics over those that are relatively recent and likely to be invalidated by changes in technology. Some may find the program old-fashioned. I prefer to call it long-lasting.

One obvious exception to the "older is better" rule is the course on computer system documentation. I would like to think that its inclusion reflects its importance, but it may simply reflect my own research interests.

The program is rather full and far more closely resembles a heavily packed engineering program than the liberal arts program to which CS educators have become accustomed. The educational philosophy issues behind this traditional split are clearly outside the scope of this article. Personally, I would welcome a five-year undergraduate engineering degree to allow a broader education, but would find it

irresponsible to make substantial reductions in the technical content of four-year programs.

Projects versus cooperative education

CS students are burdened by many courses that require hours of struggle with computing systems. Programming assignments include small programs in introductory courses, larger programs in advanced courses, and still-larger projects that comprise the main content of entire courses. This "practical content" is both excessive and inadequate. Much effort is spent learning the language and fighting the system. A great deal of time is wasted correcting picayune errors while fundamental problems are ignored. "Practical details" consume time better spent on the theoretical or intellectual content of the course.

Also, the programs that students write are seldom used by others and rarely tested extensively. Students do not get the feedback that comes from having a product used, abused, rejected, and modified. This lack of feedback is very bad education. Students and faculty often believe they have done a very good job when they have not. Inadequate analyses and unsystematic work are often rewarded and reinforced by high grades.

There is no doubt that students cannot learn programming without writing programs, but we should not be teaching programming. Small assignments should have the same role as problems in a mathematics class and often should be graded the same way. The computer and the person grading the program both provide feedback, but the computer is often quite demanding about arbitrary details while ignoring substantial weaknesses in the program. The person who grades the program should be tolerant on matters of arbitrary conventions but should pay attention to the fundamental issues.

Properly run cooperative education programs provide the desired transition between academia and employment. Students produce a real product and get feedback from interested users. Review and guidance from faculty advisors is essential to integrate the work experience with the educational program. Project courses can and should be replaced by such a program. The use of the computer in academic courses can be greatly reduced.

Student needs versus faculty interests

I do not expect these remarks and proposals to be popular with the faculty of CS departments. We all have considerable emotional investment in the things we have learned and intellectual investment in the things we teach. Many faculty want to teach courses in their research areas in the hope of finding students to work on their projects. Moreover, my criticism of the education we now provide is unavoidably a criticism of the preparation of my younger colleagues.

A university's primary responsibilities are to its students and society at large. It is unfortunate that they are often run for the comfort and happiness of the teachers and administrators. In this matter, the interests of our students and society coincide. It is not in the students' interest to make them perform engineering without being prepared for that responsibility. Nor is it in their interest to give them an education that prepares them only to be technicians. Too many graduates end up "maintaining" commercial software products, which is analogous to electrical engineers climbing poles to replace cables on microwave towers.

My industrial colleagues often complain that CS students are not prepared for the jobs they have to do. I must emphasize that my proposals will not produce graduates who can immediately take over the responsibilities of an employee who has left or been promoted. That is not the role of a university. Universities should not be concerned with teaching the latest network protocol, programming language, or operating system feature. Graduates need the fundamentals that will allow a lifetime of learning new developments; the program I have proposed provides those fundamentals better than most current CS programs.

CS departments should reconsider the trade-off in their courses between mature material and new developments. It is time for them to reconsider their role, to ask whether the education of computing professionals should not be the responsibility of engineering schools. ∎

Acknowledgments

I have developed these views through a great many conversations with engineers, mathematicians, and computer professionals around the world. The contributors are too numerous to mention. Selim Akl, David Lamb, and John van Schouwen made helpful suggestions about earlier drafts. The referees made several helpful comments.

A Software Engineering Bibliography

David Budgen and Pearl Brereton

These pages list some of the source material that we use for classes that we teach on Software Engineering and also identify some papers and books that refer to particular topics in greater depth. The list does not purport to be comprehensive, but it does provide pointers to most of the key papers and texts. (For a comprehensive set of references, the list in Ian Sommerville's book is about as good a source as will be found anywhere.)

1. Know your Journals

While relevant papers are published in a wide range of journals, some are specifically targeted at Software Engineering themes. Key journals to be aware of are:

ACM Software Engineering Notes. Essentially a 'fast print' journal used for short and topical papers.

Communications of the ACM. (CACM) At one time this published some quite technical papers, but in recent years it has changed its slant somewhat and now tends to publish more review-style papers. These often provide a very readable introduction to a topic.

IEEE Software. Similar to the CACM, but almost entirely review-style papers.

Computer. More general than *IEEE Software*, the papers are more technical in nature while still being well presented and readable.

IEEE Transactions on Software Engineering. (TSE) Publishes fairly 'heavy' technical papers. Standards are generally high, but a bit uneven over the years.

Information & Software Technology. Publishes some quite readable and useful papers, including some that are tutorial in style. Papers on Software Engineering form a large part of its content.

Journal of Systems & Software. Another fairly 'heavy' journal that concentrates mostly on research papers. Again, the content is a bit uneven.

Software Engineering Journal. UK-based (published by the IEE in conjunction with the BCS). Quite technical in terms of the content of most of the papers.

Software—Practice & Experience. Papers tend to be quite long and technical. Widely read in industry, it seeks papers that report on experience with new ideas.

Software Maintenance: Research & Practice. Some useful papers that provide tutorial or survey introductions to aspects of maintenance.

Other, more specialist journals (for example, the *Journal of Object Oriented Programming Systems*) are also available, and so the above list is not meant to describe all of the journals that might usefully be consulted.

Many papers are published in conference proceedings. A particularly relevant series is the *Proceedings of the International Conferences on Software Engineering*, published jointly by IEEE/ACM. The IEEE also publishes a number of tutorials on particular topics that are essentially collections of the main reference papers for the given topic. Tutorials often provide a useful source for finding a paper without needing to locate a copy of (possibly) obscure journal issues.

2. General Textbooks

In the ideal, we suggest that *everyone* should read the following book at least once, in order to understand just what our courses are addressing:

The Mythical Man-Month, F.P. Brooks, Jr., Addison-Wesley, 1982

This is a collection of quite readable essays drawn on Professor Brooks' experiences with the earliest large-scale software development. A twentieth anniversary edition has recently been produced and an interesting excerpt from this is published as:

"The Mythical Man-Month After 20 Years," F.P. Brooks, Jr., *IEEE Software*, Sept. 1995, pp. 57–60.

Our current "preferred" overview books are:

1. *Software Engineering*, (5th ed.), I. Sommerville, Addison-Wesley, 1995.
2. *Software Engineering Principles and Practice*, Hans Van Vliet, Wiley, 1993.

Another good book is:

Software Engineering: A Practitioner's Approach (Third Ed.), R. Pressman, McGraw-Hill, 1987

and a book which takes a more business-oriented view of Software Engineering is:

The New Software Engineering, S. Conger, Wadsworth, 1994

3. The Software Problem

There are many papers and books that deal with the crises that have been occurring for the last twenty years or so in producing large software-based systems. The various papers (and the book) produced by Barry Boehm of TRW are particularly influential. A useful overview of some current trends in tackling the issues involved is provided in:

"Programming in the Large," C.V Ramamoorthy, V. Garg, and A. Prakash, *IEEE Trans. Software Eng.*, Vol. SE-12, July 1986, pp. 769–783.

Operational lifetimes—a survey by J.F. Green et al., "Dynamic Planning and Software Maintenance—A Fiscal Approach," Naval Postgraduate School, US Dept. of Commerce, NTIS, 1981, suggested that mean lifetimes for programs were climbing steeply. Over the period of a decade, the mean lifetime had climbed from three years to seven or eight years.
Human capacity to process information—the classical paper on this, frequently cited (and probably rarely read) is:

"The Magical Number Seven, Plus-or-minus Two: Some limits on our Capacity for Processing Information," J. Miller, *Psychological Rev.*, Vol. 63, 1956, pp. 81–97.

Later authors have pointed out that Miller's paper is really concerned with *events*, rather than with discrete items of information (such as the use of a variable), but the concept seems intuitively attractive nonetheless.

The following paper by Brooks contains some good points for debate:

"No Silver Bullet: Essence and Accidents of Software Engineering," F.P. Brooks, Jr., *Computer*, Vol. 20, No. 4, Apr. 1987, pp. 10–19.

and some of these are answered by David Harel in:

"Biting the Silver Bullet: Toward a Brighter Future for System Development," D. Harel, *Computer*, Vol. 25, No. 1, Jan. 1992, pp. 8–20.

Both papers are eminently readable.

4. The Software Lifecycle

The texts by Sommerville, Van Vliet, and Pressman, as well as most other introductory books, discuss this. The specific details of the phases may vary, but the overall flow usually doesn't. The lifecycle isn't necessarily an asset, and two papers that challenge its usefulness are:

1. "Life Cycle Concept Considered Harmful," D.D. McCracken and M.A. Jackson, *ACM Software Eng. Notes*, Vol. SE7, No. 2, 1982, pp. 29–32.
2. "Stop the Life-Cycle, I Want to Get Off," G.R. Gladden, *ACM Software Eng. Notes*, Vol. SE7, No. 2, 1982, pp. 35–39.

There are various other opinions expressed for and against in the issues of *Software Engineering Notes* immediately following the one containing these papers.

Barry Boehm has advocated the use of the *Spiral Model* for describing the software development process. A good description of this is in:

"A Spiral Model of Software Development and Enhancement," B.W. Boehm, *Computer*, Vol. 21, May 1988, pp. 61–72.

5. Configuration Management

A recent book giving good coverage is:

Configuration Management, W Tichy, Editor, Wiley, 1994

and a useful review paper is provided by:

"Concepts in Configuration Management Systems," S. Dart, *Proc.3rd Int'l Workshop in SCM*, ACM Press, New York, 1991.

6. The Design Problem

A book that (not surprisingly) covers much of the coursework in this area is:

Software Design, D. Budgen, Addison-Wesley, 1993

Three papers that describe studies conducted on software designers are:

1. "The Role of Domain Experience in Software Design," B. Adelson and E. Soloway, *IEEE Trans. Software Eng.*, Vol. SE-11, No. 11, Nov. 1985, pp. 1351–1360.
2. "A Field Study of the Software Design Process for Large Systems," B. Curtis, H. Krasner, and N. Iscoe, *Comm. ACM*, Vol. 31, No. 11, Nov. 1988, pp. 1268–1287.
3. "Requirements Specification: Learning Object, Process, and Data Methodologies," I. Vessey and S. Conger, *Comm. ACM*, Vol. 37, May 1994, pp. 102–113.

An interesting (and readable) paper that discusses the role of documentation and, in particular, whether we should document what was done or what should have been done is:

"A Rational Design Process: How and Why to Fake It," D.L. Parnas and P.C. Clements, *IEEE Trans. Software Eng.*, Vol. SE-12, Feb. 1986, pp. 251–257.

7. Diagrammatical Forms for Design

A survey of diagrammatic forms and the roles they are used for in design, is in:

"Mapping the Design Information Representation Terrain," D.E. Webster, *Computer*, Dec. 1988, pp. 8–23.

8. Top-down Design Approach

The classical reference for this is:

"Program Development by Stepwise Refinement," N. Wirth, *Comm. ACM*, Vol. 14, 1971, pp. 221–227.

9. Structured Analysis and Structured Design

There are many good texts in the series of books published by Yourdon Inc., (most are now available from Prentice/Hall), although probably the best are:

1. *Structured Analysis and System Specification*, T. De Marco, Yourdon Inc, 1978.
2. *The Practical Guide to Structured Systems Design*, 2nd ed., Meilir Page-Jones, Prentice/Hall, 1988.
3. *Modern Structured Analysis*, E. Yourdon, Prentice/Hall, 1989.

10. Jackson Structured Programming (JSP)

The original (rather COBOL-flavored) reference for this is:

Principles of Program Design, M.A. Jackson, Academic Press, 1975.

There are several useful articles and examples given in:

JSP & JSD: The Jackson Approach to Software Development, 2nd ed.,

J.R. Cameron, IEEE Computer Society Press, Los Alamitos, Calif., 1988.

This is an excellent example of an IEEE tutorial.

Two good (and cheap!) introductory texts are:

1. *JSP—A Practical Method of Program Design*, L. Ingevaldsson, Chartwell-Bratt, 1986.
2. *Program Design Using JSP*, 2nd ed., M.J King and J.P. Pardoe, Macmillan, 1992

11. Jackson Structured Design (JSD)

The IEEE tutorial referenced for JSP also includes a section on JSD and the paper:

"An Overview of JSD," J.R Cameron, *IEEE Trans Software Eng.*, Vol. SE-12, Feb. 1986, pp. 222–240

provides precisely that. A good and concise book on JSD is:

Jackson System Development, A. Sutcliffe, Prentice/Hall, 1988.

12. Other Methods of Software Design

Two significant contenders here are SADT and SSADM. SADT has only recently been the subject of a book, although it has been in use for many years. This is:

SADT: Structured Analysis and Design Technique, D.A. Marca and C.L. McGowan, McGraw-Hill, 1988

For SSADM a good summary is available from:

SSADM: Application and Context, 2nd ed., E. Downs, P. Clare, and I. Coe, Prentice/Hall, 1992

13. Object-Oriented Development

A particular problem with this term is that there are different techniques describing themselves in this way! An early version of an OOD technique was outlined in the paper:

"Object-Oriented Development," G. Booch, *IEEE Trans. Software Eng.*, Vol. SE-12, Feb. 1986, pp. 211–221

although the approach described in this paper might now be more correctly described as being *object-based.* An earlier paper, on which some of Booch's work was based, is:

"Program Design by Informal English Descriptions," R.J. Abbott, *Comm. ACM,* Vol. 26, Nov. 1983, pp. 882–894.

A more recent work by Booch which gives lots of very good ideas about the object-oriented philosophy and provides an excellent framework is:

Object-Oriented Analysis and Design With Applications, G. Booch, Benjamin/Cummings, 1994.

A paper which gives a good summary of object properties and which tries to clarify the terminology is:

"The Essence of Objects: Concepts and Terms," A. Snyder, *IEEE Software,* Jan. 1993, pp. 31–42.

A recent and very good book that describes ideas about how to actually design with objects is:

Object-Oriented Development: The Fusion Method, D. Coleman et al., Prentice/Hall, 1994

For the really determined, the following paper provides details and abstracts of over 240 papers in this area:

"An Annotated Bibliography for Object-Oriented Analysis and Design," S. Webster, *Information & Software Technology*, Vol. 36, No. 9, Sept. 1994, pp. 569–582.

14. Information Hiding

The original (and much-cited) reference for this concept is:

"On the Criteria to be Used in Decomposing Systems into Modules," D.L. Parnas, *Comm. ACM*, Vol. 15, 1972, pp. 1053–1058.

To be honest, this paper is not easy reading by any means, but then the concept is not easily applied in any systematic manner either!

15. Comparison of Design Methods

There is surprisingly little literature of this form, and much of what there is can hardly be described as particularly complete. The later chapters of (Budgen, 1993) describe a number of design methods using a common framework. A much fuller comparison in a structured framework is provided in:

" 'Design Models' from Software Design Methods," D. Budgen, *Design Studies*, Vol. 16, No. 3, July 1995, pp. 293-325.

A fairly analytical look at the distinction between the object-oriented strategies and the longer-established forms is provided in:

"Object-Oriented and Conventional Analysis and Design Methodologies: Comparison and Critique," R.G. Fichman and C.F. Kemerer, *Computer*, Vol. 25, No. 10, Oct. 1992, pp. 22–39.

16. Formal Description Techniques

The study of FDTs (or less accurately, 'formal methods') is a major topic in itself. Their use is increasing, especially for 'critical' parts of systems, and everyone should really know something about their strengths and limitations. The most common need is probably to be able to *understand* a formal specification, rather than to be able to *create* one, and the following papers address that by providing some overview information as well as some simple examples.

1. "Seven Myths of Formal Methods" A. Hall, *IEEE Software*, Sept. 1990, pp. 11-19.

2. "A Specifier's Introduction to Formal Methods," J.M Wing, *Computer*, 1990, pp. 8–24.
3. "Notes on Algebraic Specifications," I.M. Bradley, *Information & Software Technology*, Vol. 31, No. 7, Sept. 1989, pp. 357–365.

17. Verification, Walkthroughs and Testing

A useful reference is:

"An Engineering Approach to Software Test Data Design," S.T. Redwine, *IEEE Trans. Software Eng.*, Vol. SE-9, 1983, pp. 191–200.

18. Programming Environments

There are plenty of research papers that cover plans for IPSE and APSE development, but these are mainly published in conference proceedings. A particular series of relevance is:

Software Engineering Environments, Ellis Horwood, 1988, 1989, 1991 (Vols 1–3)

Software Engineering Environments, IEEE Computer Society Press, Los Alamitos, Calif., 1993

with Volume 3 being particularly useful as an introduction to Process Modeling. There is also the book:

Software Engineering Environments: Automated Support for Software Engineering, Alan Brown, A.N. Earl, and J McDermid, McGraw-Hill, 1992

19. Software Maintenance

Two interesting papers covering this topic include:

1. "Problems in Application Software Maintenance," B.P. Lientz and E.B. Swanson, *Comm. ACM*, Vol. 24, No. 11, Nov. 1981, pp. 763–769.
2. "Mental Models and Software Maintenance," D.C. Littman et al., *J. Systems & Software*, Vol. 7, 1987, pp. 342–355.

Of course, there is also a specialist journal, as mentioned in the opening section.

20. Cost Modeling

A survey paper often cited is:

"Software Cost Estimation: Present and Future," S.N. Mohanty, *Software Practice & Experience*, Vol. 11, 1981, pp. 103-121

which gives a comparative review of a number of cost models. Boehm's COCOMO model is summarized in:

"Software Engineering Economics," B.W. Boehm, *IEEE Trans. Software Eng.*, Vol. SE-10, 1984, pp. 4–21

and also in the following book, although this chiefly describes the Putnam Model:

Cost Estimation for Software Development, B. Londeix, Addison-Wesley, 1987

21. Software Metrics

Recent years have produced a lot of papers on various aspects of metrics. A good survey of the field is given in:

Software Metrics: A Rigorous Approach, N.E. Fenton, Chapman & Hall, 1991.

Some papers covering important aspects are:

1. "Software Function, Source Lines of Code, and Development Effort Prediction: A Software Science Validation," A.J. Albrecht and J.E. Gaffney, *IEEE Trans. Software Eng.*, Vol. SE-9, No. 6, Nov. 1983, pp. 639–648.
2. "An Evaluation of Some Design Metrics," B. Kitchenham, L.M. Pickard, and S.J. Linkman, *Software Engineering J.*, Vol. 5, Jan. 1990, pp. 50–58.
3. "Evaluating Software Complexity Measures," E.J. Weyuker, *IEEE Trans. Software Eng.*, Vol. 14, No. 9, Sept. 1988, pp. 1357–1365.

Three recent papers which examine wider aspects about the meaning and use of metrics, and which discuss the whole question of how to measure software qualities, are:

1. "Software Measurement: A Necessary Scientific Basis," N. Fenton, *IEEE Trans. Software Eng.*, Vol. 20, No. 3, Mar. 1994, pp. 199-206.
2. "A Critique of Three Metrics," M. Shepperd and D.C. Ince, *J. Systems & Software*, Vol. 26, No. 3, Sept. 1994, pp. 197-210.

3. "Towards a Framework for Software Measurement Validation," B. Kirchenam, S.L. Pfleeger, and N. Fenton, *IEEE Trans. Software Eng.*, Vol. 21, No. 12, Dec. 1995, pp. 929–943.

Software Engineering Standards

Richard H. Thayer

Introduction

A *standard* is: (1) An approved, documented, and available set of criteria used to determine the adequacy of an action or object or (2) A document that sets forth the standards and procedures to be followed on a given project or by a given organization.

A *software engineering standard* is: (1) a set of procedures that define the processes for and/or (2) descriptions that define the quantity and quality of a product from a software engineering project.

This list of software engineering standards was compiled from numerous sources: The two primary sources were:

- *Survey of Existing and In-Progress Software Engineering Standards,* Business Planning Group, IEEE Software Engineering Standards Committee, Version 1.1, August 8, 1994.

- Thayer, R.H., and A.D. McGettrick, *Software Engineering: A European Perspective*, IEEE Computer Society Press, Los Alamitos, Calif., 1993.

This document lists the current and available national and international software engineering standards and also provides a list of the sources of these standards keyed to the individual standards. Note: many of the standards can be purchased from general standards organizations such as the American National Standards Institute and other distributor of technical documents

Standards Development Organizations

Standards generally come from many different organizations and institutions:

- International standards are standards that are issued by organizations that are international in scope, for instance, IEC or ISO.

- National and multi-national standards are created under the direction of a national standards organization, for instance, NIST, CSA, U.S. DOD, or an organization representing a group of nations, for instance, CEN.

- Professional standards are standards created by professional organizations whose primary criteria for membership are individuals in a profession, such as EE, or a group of professions, such as IEEE Computer Society or ASTM.

- Other professional standards are created by organizations whose primary criteria for membership are organizations who are interested in promoting the welfare of a particular industry, for instance, EIA or ECMA.

Acknowledgments

Thanks to my Scottish colleagues who helped me identify standards development organizations in the United Kingdom and Europe: Dr. Robin Hunter, University of Strathclyde, and Ms. Anne McCullock, University of Stirling.

Standards Sources

The standards listed in this compendium come form:

AECL—Atomic Energy Canada Limited, c/o Ontario Hydro H12 D27, 700 University Avenue, Toronto, Ontario M5G 1X6 Canada

AFNOR—Association Fraçaise de Normalisation, Tour Europe - Cedex 7, F-92049, Paris La Defense, France

AIAA—American Institute Aeronautics and Astronauts, 370 l'Enfant Promenade, S.W., Washington, DC 20024-2518 USA

ANS—American Nuclear Society, 555 N. Kensington Avenue, La Grange Park, IL 60525 USA

ANSI—American National Standards Institute, 11 W. 42nd Street, 13th Floor, New York, NY 10036 USA

ARINC—Airlines Electronic Engineering Committee, 2551 Riva Road, Annapolis, MD 21401. USA

AS—Standards Association of Australia, Standards Australia, P.O. Box 1055, Strathfield NSW, Australia 2135

ASME—American Society of Mechanical Engineers, 345 East 47th Street, New York, NY 10017, USA

ASQC—American Society for Quality Control, 310 West Wisconsin Avenue, Milwaukee. WI 53203, USA

ASTM—American Society for Testing and Materials, 1916 Race Street, Philadelphia, PA 19103, USA

ATA—Air Transport Association of America, 1709 New York Avenue, N.W., Washington DC 20006, USA

BCS—British Computer Society, P.O. Box 1454, Station Road, Swindon SN1 1TG England, U.K.

BS—British Standards Institution, Linford Wood, Milton Keynes MK14 6LE England, UK

CCITT—International Telegraph and Telephone Consultative Committee (Comité Consultantif International de Télégraphique et Téléphonie.), 12, rue de Varembé, CH-1211 Genèva 20, Switzerland

CEN—European Committee for Standardization (Comité European de Normalisation), Rue de Stassart 36, B-1050 Brussels, Belgium

CSA—Canadian Standards Association, 178 Rexdale Boulevard, Rexdale, Ontario M9W IR9 Canada

CSSC—Canadian System Security Centre, Communications Security Establishment, P.O. Box 9703 Terminal, Ottawa, Canada K1G 3Z4

DIA—U.S. Drug Information Association, P.O. Box 3113, Maple Glen, PA 19002-8113, USA

DIN—Deutsches Institut für Nomrung e.V., Burggrafenstrasse 4-10, Postfach 1107, D-1000 Berlin 30, Germany

DOD—Department of Defense, Standardization Documents Order Desk, Building 4D, 700 Robins Avenue, Philadelphia, PA 19111-5094, USA

ECMA—European Computers Manufacturing Association, Rue de Rhône 114, CH-01204, Genèva, Switzerland

EEA—Electronic and Business Equipment Association, Russell Square House ,10-12, Russell Square, London, SC1B 5AE U.K.

EIA—Electronics Industry Association, 2001 Pennsylvania Avenue, NW, Washington, DC 20006, USA

EPRI—Electric Power Research Institute, 3412 Hillview, Palo Alto, CA 94304, USA

ESA—European Space Agency, European Space Research and Technology Centre (ESTEC), European Space Agency, Postbus 299, NL-2200 AG Noordwijk, The Netherlands

FAA—Federal Aviation Authority, Department of Transportation, 800 Independence Avenue, S.W., Washington DC 20591, USA

FDA—Federal Food and Drug Administration, Washington DC 20330, USA

FIPS PUBS—Federal Information Processing Standards Publication. *Published by NIST*

GER GFMT—German Federal Ministry of Transport, Bonn, Germany

GER KBST—Federal Ministry of Interior, (Budenesministerium des Innern), KBSt, Postfach 170290, D-53198 Bonn, Germany

GER MOD—German Ministry of Defense, Riit III, Einsteinstrasse 20, D-8012 Ottobrun, Germany

GISA—German Information Security Agency (Bundesamt für Sicherheit in der Infromationstechnik (BSI)), Bundesanzeiger Verlagsges. mbH, Postfach 10 05 34, D-50445 Koein, Germany

GPA—Gas Processors Association, 6526 East 60th Street, Tulsa, OK 74145, USA

IAEA—International Atomic Energy Agency, Wagramerstrasse 5, P.O. Box 1700, A-1400 Vienna, Austria

IEC—International Electrotechical Commission, 3, rue de Varembé, P.O. Box 131, CH- 1211 Genèva 20, Switzerland

IEE—Institute of Electrical Engineers, Michael Faraday House, Six Hills Way, Stevenage, Hertfordshire, SG1 2SD England, U.K.

IEEE—The Institute of Electrical and Electronic Engineers, 445 Hoes Lane, Piscataway, NJ 08854, USA

ISA—Instrument Society of America, 67 Alexander Drive, P.O. Box 12277 Research Triangle Park, NC 27709, U S A

ISO—International Standards Organisation (International Organization for Standardisation), Central Secretariat, 1, Rue de Varembé, CH-1211 Genèva 20, Switzerland

JIS—Japanese Industrial Standards, c/o Standards Department, Agency of Industrial Science and Technology, Ministry of International Trade and Industry, 1-3-1, Kasumigaseki, Chiyoda-Ku, Tokyo 100, Japan

JPL—Jet Propulsion Laboratory, California Institute of Technology, 4800 Oak Grove Drive, Pasadena, CA 91109, USA

JTC1—Joint Technical Committee 1, Joint committee from ISO and EC for information technology. *See IEEE for additional information on standards*

NASA—National Aeronautics and Space Administration, Technical Standards Division, Washington. DC 20546, USA

NATO—North Atlantic Treaty Organization, B-01110 Brussels, Belgium

NATO DPC—NATO Defence Planning Committee, c/o North Atlantic Treaty Organization (NATO), B-1110 Brussels, Belgium

NISO—National Information Standards Organization, P.O. Box 1056, Bethseda. MD 20827, USA

NIST—National Institute for Standards and Technology, Standards and Codes Information: Room A163, Bldg. 411, Gaithersberg, MD 20899, USA

NMTBA—Association for Manufacturing Technology, 7901 West Park Drive, McLean, VA 22102, USA

NRC—Nuclear Regulatory Commission, Washington DC, 20005 USA

NSA—National Security Agency, Fort George G. Meade, MD, USA

NSAC—Nuclear Safety Analysis Center, 3412 Hillview Avenue, Palo Alto, CA 98430, USA

RTCA—Requirements and Technical Concepts for Aviation, 1140 Connecticut Avenue, N.W.. Suite 1020, Washington DC 20036, USA

SAE—Society for Automotive Engineers, 400 Commonwealth Drive, Warrendale, PA 15096, USA

SDA—Scottish Enterprises, 120 Bothwell Street, Glasgow G2 7JP Scotland, U.K. (Formerly the Scottish Development Agency)

SIS—Standardiseringskommishion i Sverige, Box 3295, S-10366 Stockholm, Sweden

SPAIN—Asociación Española de Normalización y Certificación (AENOR), Calla Fernández de la Hoz, 52, E-28010 Madrid, Spain

STRS—Stennis Technical Reports Server, NASA Stennis Space Center Technical Reports, Stennis Space Center, MS 39529

UK DOH—United Kingdom Department of Health, Skipton House, 80 London Road, London SWE1 6WL England, U.K.

UK DOTI—United Kingdom Department of Trade and Industry, Information Technology Division, 151 Buckingham Palace Road, London SW1 9SS England, U.K.

UK HSE—United Kingdom Health and Safety Executive, HSE Books, P.O. Box 1999, Sudbury, Suffolk CO10 6FS England, U.K.

UK MOD—Ministry of Defence, Directorate of Standardization, Kentigern House, 65 Brown Street, Glasgow G2 8EX Scotland, U.K.

UK NCC—United Kingdom National Computing Centre, The, Oxford House, Oxford Road, Manchester, M1 7ED England, U.K.

Software Engineering Standards

The standards listed in the compendium are divided into 21 parts and 17 are the process as defined in DIS 12207 [1]: acquisition, supply, development, operation, maintenance, documentation, configuration management, quality assurance, verification, validation, joint review, audit, management, infrastructure, improvement and training. There are also 4 additional parts that include safety, terminology, user support, and miscellaneous.

[1] DIS 12207, *Information Technology - Software Life-cycle Process*, DEC 1993

1. Acquisition Standards

AFNOR Z67-131-HOM	Manual Describing the Purchaser-Provider Relationship for the Purchasing of A Software Package
AIAA G-043-92	Guide for the Preparation of Operational Concept Documents. 32 pp.
ASTM E 623-89	Guide for Developing Functional Requirements for Computerized Laboratory Systems. 6 pp.
ASTM E 731-90	Guide for Procurement of Commercially Available Computerized Systems. 7 pp.
ASTM E1283-89	Guide for Procurement of Computer-Integrated Manufacturing systems. 13 pp.
BS 6719-86	Guide to Specifying User Requirements for a Computer-based System. 16 pp.
DIN 66 271	Information Processing: Software—Dealing with Failures in Contractual Situations
DOD AFSC 800-5	Software Development Capability/Capacity Review, 1987. 62 pp.
DOD MIL-HDBK-782	Military Handbook, Software Support Environment Acquisition. 75 pp.
DOD MIL-STD-498	Software Development and Documentation, 5 Dec 1994.
DOD MIL STD-1521B	Technical Reviews and Audits for Systems, Equipment, and Computer Programs, 4 Jun 1985. 125 pp.
DOD SEI-87-TR-23	Method for Assessing the Software Engineering Capability of a Contractor, Sep 1987.
DOD STD 2168	Military Standard - Software Quality Assurance Requirements, 29 Feb. 1988. 12 pp.
ECMA-4	Flowcharts, Dec 1966, 17 pp.
GER MOD GEN DR 220	Framework Decree for the Development and Acquisition of Material
FIPS PUB 56	Guidelines for Managing Multivendor Plug-Compatible ADP Systems
IEEE 1029-1088	Standard for Software Reviews and Audits
IEEE 1062-1993	Recommended Practice for Software Acquisition. 40 pp.
UK MOD DEF-STAN 05-21	Guide to Contractor Assessment. Computer software QA systems, Book 4
UK MOD NES 620	Requirements for Software for Use with Digital Processors, Naval Engineering Standard, Issue 3, 1986.
JPL D-4000	JPL Software Management Standards Package, Dec 1988.
NATO NAT-PRC-4	Government Evaluation of Contractor Software Quality Assurance Program
NIST S.P. 500-180	Guide to Software Acceptance
NIST S.P. 500-136	An Overview of Computer Software Acceptance Testing
NIST S.P. 500-144	Guidance on Software Package Selection
UK MOD DEFCON 143	Software Development Questionnaire—for Inclusion with Invitations to Tender. 10 pp.
UK NCC-I	STARTS Purchaser's Handbook: Procuring Software-Based Systems

2. Supply Standards

AFNOR Z67-131-HOM	Manual Describing the Purchaser-Provider Relationship for the Purchasing of A Software Package
DIN 66 271	Information Processing: Software—Dealing with Failures in Contractual Situations
DOD AFSCP 800-14	Software Quality Indicators, 20 Jan. 1987 40 pp.
DOD STD 2167A	Military Standard—Defense System Software Development, 29 Feb. 1988. 59 pp.
DOD TADSTAND E	Software Development, Documentation, and Testing Policy for Navy Mission Critical Systems. 16 pp.

3. Development Standards

AFNOR Z67-103-1 FD	Analysis Engineering
AFNOR Z67-120-HOM	Minimal Packaging Identification
AFNOR Z67-121-HOM	Minimal Packaging Identification, Part 2
AFNOR Z67-122-HOM	User Documentation for Consumer Software Packages
AIAA G 009-91	Guide for Implementing Software Development Files Conforming to DOD-Std-2167A. 16 pp.
AIAA G 031-93	Guide for Life-Cycle Development of Knowledge Based Systems with DOD-Std-2167A. 26 pp.
ANS 10.2-88	Recommended Programming Practices to Facilitate the Portability of Scientific and Engineering Computer Programs. 12 pp.
ARINC 651	Design Guidance for Integrated Modular Avionics
ASTM E 622-94	Guide for Developing Computerized Systems 31 pp.
ASTM E 623-89	Guide for Developing Functional Requirements for Computerized Laboratory Systems. 6 pp.
ASTM E 624-90	Guide for Implementation Designs for Computerized Systems, Developing. 13 pp.
ASTM E 730-85	Guide for Developing Functional Designs for Computerized Systems. 7 pp.
ASTM E1340-90	Standard Guide for Rapid Prototyping of Computerized Systems. 11 pp.
BCS-90	A Standard for Software Component Testing, ISS. 1.2. 69 pp.
BS 1646-84, Pt 4	Specification for Basic Symbols for Process Computer, Interface and Shared Display/control Functions. 8 pp.
BS 4058-80	DP Flowchart Symbols, Rules and Conventions. 32 pp.
BS 5487-82	Specification of Single-hit Decision Tables. 20 pp.
BS 5887-80	Code of Practice for Testing of Computer-Based Systems 8 pp.
BS 6078-81	Guide to the Application of Digital Computers to Nuclear Reactor Instrumentation and Control. 20 pp.
BS 6224-87	Design Structure Diagrams for use in Program Design and Other Logical Applications. 36 pp.
BS 6719-86	Guide to Specifying User Requirements for a Computer-Based System. 16 pp.
BS 6976-90	Program Constructs and Conventions for their Representations. 12 pp.
BS 7153-89	Guide for Computer System Configuration Diagram (symbols and conventions). 18 pp.
BS 7738-94	Specification for Information Systems Products Using Structured Systems Analysis and Design Method (SSADM)
BS DD 196-91	Guide for Modular Approach to Software Construction, Operation and Test (MASCOT)
CCITT Z.100-104 84	Functional Specification and Description Language (SDL)
DIN 66 001	Information Processing: Graphical Symbols and Their Application: Layout of Graphical Symbols on a Template
DIN 66 241	Information Interchange: Decision Tables Description Medium
DIN 66 261	Information Processing: Nassi-Shneiderman Flowcharts Symbols
DIN 66 262	Information Processing: Program Constructs and Conventions for Their Use
DIN 66 285	Application Software: Principles of Testing
NATO DPC 85/60355	Guide for Specifying Requirements for a Computer Based Systems
EIA CRB 1-89	Managing the Development of Artificial Intelligence Software. 20 pp.
EPRI EL 3089	Software Development and Maintenance Guidelines, Vols. 1–3. 1602 pp.
ESA PSS-05-0, Iss 2	ESA Software Engineering Standards, Feb 1991. 133 pp.

ESA PSS-05-02	Guide to the User Requirements Definition Phase, Issue 1, Oct 1991
ESA PSS-05-03	Guide to the Software Requirements Definition Phase, Issue 1, Oct 1991
ESA PSS-05-04	Guide to the Software Architectural Design Phase, Issue 1, January 1992
ESA PSS-05-05	Guide to the Software Detailed Design and Production Phase, Issue 1, May 1992
FAA STD-026	National Airspace System (NAS) Software Development. 15 pp.
FDA	Technical Reference on Software Development Activities. 42 pp.
GER MOD AU 253	Handbook: Relations between GAM-T17(V2) and V-Model
GER MOD GEN DIR 253	Handbook: Relations between GAM-T17(V2) and V-Model
GER GFMT BDLI	Testing, Documentation and Certification of Software-based Systems in Aircraft. 98 pp.
IEC 8631-89	Information Technology—Program Constructs and Conventions for Their Representations, Second Edition. 12 pp.
IEE-2	Guidelines for Assuring Testability, 1988. 88 pp.
IEEE 1008-1987	Standard for Software Unit Testing. 25 pp.
IEEE 1016-1987	Recommended Practice for Software Design Descriptions. 15 pp.
IEEE 1016.1-1993	Guide to Software Design Descriptions. 26 pp.
IEEE 1074-1991	Standard for Developing Software Life Cycle Processes. 111 pp.
IEEE 829-1991	Standard for Software Test Documentation. 47 pp.
IEEE 830-1993	Recommended Practice for Software Requirements Specifications. 32 pp.
IEEE 990-1992	Recommended Practice for Ada as a Program Design Language. 15 pp.
ISA S5.3	Graphic Symbols for Distributed Control/Shared Display Instrumentation, Logic, and Computer Systems. 14 pp.
JIS X 0121-86	Documentation Symbols and Conventions for Data Program and System Flowcharts, Program Network Charts, and System Resource Charts.
JPL D-4001	Overview and Philosophy, Dec 1988. 19 pp.
JPL D-4003	[Sub]system Requirements Analysis Phase. Dec 1988. 26 pp.
JPL D-4004	[Sub]system Functional Design Phase. Dec 1988. 21 pp.
JPL D-4005	Software Requirements Analysis Phase. Dec 1988. 26 pp.
JPL D-4006	Software Design Phase. Dec 1988. 36 pp.
JPL D-4007	Software Implementation and Test Phase, Dec 1988. 42 pp.
JPL D-4008	[Sub]system, Integration, Test, and Delivery Phase, DEC 1988. 33 pp.
JTC1 1028-79	Information Processing—Flowchart Symbols
JTC1 2636-73	Information Processing—Conventions for Incorporating Flowchart Symbols in Flowcharts.
JTC1 5806-84	Information Processing—Specification of Single-Hit Decision Tables, First Edition. 16 pp.
JTC1 5807	Documentation Symbols and Conventions for Data, Program and systems flowcharts, program network charts, and system resources charts.
JTC1 6593-85	Information Processing—Program Flow for Processing Files in Terms of Record Groups, First Edition. 9 pp.
JTC1 8631-89	Information Processing—Program Constructs and Conventions for Their Representation, Second Edition. 12 pp.
JTC1 8790	Computer System Configuration Diagram Symbols and Conventions
NATO NAT-STAN-1	Software Development Requirements
NATO NAT-STAN-6	Software Testing Requirements

NATO NAT-STAN-8	Software Specification Preparation Requirements
NIST S.P. 500-136	An Overview of Computer Software Acceptance Testing
NIST S.P. 500-148	Application Software Prototyping and Fourth Generation Languages
RTCA DO/178B-92	Software Considerations in Airborne Systems and Equipment Certification. 100 pp.
SDA SDPG	Software Development Practice Guidelines
SIS TR 321	System Development Reference Model
UK MOD NES 620	Requirements for Software for Use with Digital Processors, Naval Engineering Standard, Issue 3, 1986.

4. Operation Standards

ASTM E 626-90	Guide for Evaluating Computerized Systems. 7 pp.
ASTM E1246-88	Practice for Reporting Reliability of Clinical Laboratory Computer Systems. 6 pp.
BS 5760	Reliability of Constructed or Manufactured Systems, Equipments, and Components
BS 6238-82	Code of Practice for Performance Monitoring of Computer based Systems. 12 pp.
BS 6650-86	Code of Practice for the Control of the Operation of a Computer. 12 pp.
BS DD 198-91	Assessment of Reliability of Systems Containing Software. 82 pp.
DIN 66 273	Measurement and Rating of Data Processing Performance
FIPS PUB 72	Guidelines for the Measurement of Remote Batch Computer Service
FIPS PUB 96	Guidelines for Developing and Implementing a Charging System for Data Processing Services

5. Maintenance Standards

EPRI EL 3089	Software Development and Maintenance Guidelines, Vols. 1-3. 1602 pp.
FIPS PUB 106-1984	Guideline on Software Maintenance, Jul 1984
IEEE 1219-1993	Standard for Software Maintenance. 42 pp.

6. Documentation Standards

AFNOR Z67-100-1FD	Computer Engineering Documentation Information Systems
AFNOR Z67-122-HOM	User Documentation for Consumer Software Packages
ANS 10.3-86	Guidelines for the Documentation of Digital Computer Programs. 13 pp.
ANSI X3.88-81	Computer Program Abstracts (R 1987). 14 pp.
ASME Y14-2-77	Guidelines for Documenting of Computer Systems Used in Computer-Aided Preparation of Product Definition Data User Instructions. 9 pp.
ASME Y14-3-77	Guideline for Documenting of Computer Systems Used in Computer-Aided Preparation of Product Definition Data Design Requirements. 9 pp.
ASTM E 627-88	Guide for Documenting Computerized Systems. 6 pp.
ASTM E1029-84	Guide for Documentation of Clinical Laboratory Computer Systems. 10 pp.
ASTM E919-90	Specification for Software Documentation for a computerized System. 3 pp.
ATA 102	Specification for Computer Software Manual
BS 4884	Guidelines for Software Manuals
BS 5515-84	Code of Practice for Documentation of Computer-Based Systems. 16 pp.
BS 7137-89	Specification for User Documentation and Cover Information for Consumer Software Packages. 12 pp.

BS 7649-93	The Design and Preparation of Documentation for Users of Application Software. 104 pp.
CSA Z243.15.1-79	Basic Guidelines for the Structure of Documentation of Computer Based Systems. 16 pp.
CSA Z243.15.4-79	Basic Guidelines for the Structure of Documentation of System Design Information. 18 pp.
CSA Z243.15.5-79	Basic Guidelines for the Structure of Documentation of System Data. 15 pp.
DIN 66 230	Information Processing: Software Documentation
DIN 66 231	Information Processing: Documentation of Software Development
DIN 66 232	Information Processing: Data Documentation
DOD ICAM-1	ICAM Documentation Standards, IDS 150120000A, Air Force Materials Laboratory, 28 Dec 1981. 230 pp.
DOD ICAM-2-1980	ICAM Software Documentation Standards, NBSIR 791940®, Air Force Materials Laboratory, Feb. 1980. 191 pp.
DOD MIL STD 490A	Specification Practices, 4 Jun 1985. 115 pp.
DOD STD 7935A	Automated Data Systems (ADS) Documentation, Oct 1988. 150 pp.
FIPS PUB 105-1984	Guideline for Software Documentation Management, Jun 1984
FIPS PUB 38-1976	Guidelines for Documentation of Computer Programs, Federal Information Processing Standards Publication 38, 15 Feb 1976
FIPS PUB 64-1979	Guidelines for Documentation of Computer Programs and Automated Data Systems for the Initiation Phase, 1 Aug 1979
GPA Std 9175-81	Computer Program Documentation and Development Standards. 4 pp.
IEC TR9294-90	Information Technology—Guidelines for the Management of Software Documentation, First Edition. 12 pp.
IEE-1	Guidelines for the Documentation of Computer Software for Real-Time and Interactive Systems, 1990 2nd Edition. 116 pp.
IEEE 1063-1987	Standard for Software User Documentation 17 pp.
JIS JX 0126-87	Guidelines for the Documentation of Computer—Based Application Systems. 27 pp.
JTC1 6592-85	Information Processing—Guidelines for the Documentation of Computer-Based Application Systems, First Edition. 20 pp.
JTC1 9127-88	Information Processing—User Documentation and Cover Information for Consumer Software Packages, First Edition. 11 pp.
JTC1 9294-88	Information Processing—Guidelines for the Management of Software Documentation, First Edition. 12 pp.
NASA-STD-2100-91	NASA Software Documentation Standard, Jul 29, 1991. 172 pp.
NATO NAT-STAN-8	Software Specification Preparation Requirements
NISO Z39.67	Computer Software Description
SAE ARP 1623A-86	Guide for Preparing an ECS Computer Program User's Manual. 5 pp.
UK MOD JSP 188	Requirements for the Documentation of Software in Military Operational Real Time Computer Systems.

7. Configuration Management Standards

BS 6488-84	Code of Practice for Configuration Management of Computer-based Systems. 8 pp.
DOD ML STD 483A-1985	Configuration Management Practices for Systems, Equipment, Munitions, and Computer Programs. 4 Jun 1985.
DOD ML-STD 973	Configuration Management, 1990. 237 pp.

EIA CMB4-2-81	Configuration Identification for Digital Computer Programs. 28 pp.
EIA CMB4-3-81	Computer Software Libraries. 23 pp.
EIA CMB4-4-82	Configuration Change Control for Digital Computer Programs. 47 pp.
EIA CMB4-1A-84	Configuration Management Definitions for Digital Computer Programs. 46 pp.
EIA CMB5-A-86	Configuration Management Requirements for Subcontractors/Vendors. 42 pp.
EIA CMB6-2-88	Configuration and Data Management In-House Training Plan. 18 pp.
EIA CMB6-5-88	Textbook for Configuration Status Accounting. 69 pp.
EIA CMB6-8-89	Data Management In-House Training Course. 134 pp.
EIA CMB6-1B-90	Configuration and Data Management References. 19 pp.
EIA CMB7-1	Electronic Interchange of Configuration Management]Data. 11 pp.
EIA CMB7-2	Guideline for Transtioning Configuration Management to an Automated Environment. 17 pp.
ESA PSS-05-09	Guide to Software Configuration Management, Issue 1, Nov 1992
FAA-STD 021	Software Configuration Management, FAA-STD-021, Federal Aviation Administration. 116 pp.
IEEE 1042-1987	Guide to Software Configuration Management. 93 pp.
IEEE 828-1990	Standard for Software Configuration Plans. 10 pp.
JPL D-4011	Software Configuration Management Planning, Dec 1988. 21 pp.
UK MOD DEF-STAN 05-57/2	Configuration Management Policy and Procedures for Defence Material (Standard)
NATO NAT-PRC-2	Software Project Configuration Management Procedures
NATO STANAG 4159	Configuration Management
NIST S.P. 500-161	Software Configuration Management: An Overview
RTCA DO/178B-92	Software Considerations in Airborne Systems and Equipment Certification. 100 pp.

8. Quality Standards

AFNOR NF X50-162	Customer-Supplier Relations—Guide to the Drawing up of the Quality Assurance Handbook
AFNOR NF X50-163	Quality and Management—Typology and Use of the Documents Describing the Quality Systems
AFNOR NF X50-164	Customer-Supplier Relations—Guide to the Drawing up of a Quality Assurance Plan
AFNOR Z67-123-HOM	Compliance Approach for An Application Package
AS 3563.1-1991	Software Quality Management System, Part 1, Requirements. 10 pp.
AS 3563.2-1991	Software Quality Management System, Part 2, Implementation Guide. 40 pp.
ASME N45.2.11	Quality Assurance Requirements for the Design of Nuclear Power Plants
ASME NQA-2 1990	Quality Assurance Program Requirements for Nuclear Power Plants. 101 pp.
ASME NQA-I 1989	Quality Assurance Program Requirements for Nuclear Facilities. 69 pp.
ASQC Z-1.15 1979	Generic Guidelines for Quality Systems
BS 4778-89	Glossary of Terms used in Quality Assurance
BS 4891-72	Guide to Quality Assurance. 28 pp.
BS 5750: Pt 1	Specification for Design/Development, Production, Installation and Servicing
BS 5882-80	Specification for a Total Quality Assurance Programrne for Nuclear Power Plants. 12 pp.
BS 7165-91	Recommendations for Achievement of Quality in Software
CSA Q396.1.1-89	Quality Assurance Program for the Development of Software Used in Critical Applications
CSA Q396.1.2-89	Quality Assurance Program for Previously Developed Software Used in Critical Applications

CSA Q396.2.1-89	Quality Assurance Program for the Development of Software Used in Non-Critical Applications
CSA Q396.2.2-89	Quality Assurance Program for Previously Developed Software Used in Non-Critical Applications
DOD MIL-STD-1535B	Supplier Quality Assurance Program Requirements. 8 pp.
DOD ML-HDBK-286	Military Handbook, A Tailoring Guide for DOD-STD-2168 (Defense System SQA Programs), 14 Dec 1990. 57 pp.
DOD STD 2168	Military Standard—Software Quality Assurance Requirements, 29 Feb. 1988. 12 pp.
EEA-I	Guide to the Quality Assurance of Software
EIA CRR-2-89	Computer Resources Discourse Quality Assurance Requirements for Software Processes. 9 pp.
ESA PSS-05-11	Guide to Software Quality Assurance, Issue I, Jul 1993.
FAA STD 018a	Computer Software Quality Program Requirements, FAA-STD-018a, Federal Aviation Administration, Sep 1987. 11 pp.
FDA 90-4236	Reproduction Quality Assurance Planning: Recommendations for Medical Device Manufacturers. 19 pp.
GER KBST V Model	Software Life Cycle Model (V-Model). 500+ pp.
IAEA-1987	Quality Assurance for Computer Software
IEE-4	Software Quality Assurance: Model Procedures 1990. 107 pp.
IEEE 1298-1993	Software Quality Management System, Part 1: Requirements
IEEE 730-1989	Standard for Software Quality Assurance Plans. 12 pp.
ISO 9000, Pt. 3	Guidelines for the Application of ISO 9001 to the Development, Supply, and Maintenance of Software, 1991
ISO 9000-87	Quality Management and Quality Assurance Standards Guidelines for Selection and Use
ISO 9001-87	Quality Systems—Model for Quality Assurance in Design/development, Production, Installation and Servicing.
ISO 9002-87	Quality Systems—Model for Quality Assurance in Production and Installation
ISO 9003-87	Quality Systems—Model for Quality Assurance in Final Inspection and Test
ISO 9004-87	Quality Management and Quality Systems Elements Guidelines
UK MOD DEF STAN 05-95	Quality System Requirements for The Development, Supply and Maintenance of Software. 16 pp.
UK MOD DEF-STAN 00-16/1	Guide to the Achievement of Quality in Software. 57 pp.
UK MOD DEF-STAN 05-21	Guide to Contractor Assessment. Computer software QA systems, Book 4
NATO AQAP-13	NATO Software Quality Control System Requirements, Aug 1981
NATO AQAP-14	Guide for the evaluation of a contractor's software quality control system for compliance with AQAP 13.
NRC BR-0617	SQA Software Assurance Guidelines
NRC NUREG/CR-4640	Handbook of Software Quality Assurance Techniques Applicable to the Nuclear Industry
RTCA DO/178B-92	Software Considerations in Airborne Systems and Equipment Certification. 100 pp.
SPAIN UNE73-404	Quality Assurance in the Nuclear Installations Information Systems (Spanish) 1990
STRS STRITSE	Modeling a Software Quality Handbook (MSQH)
UK DOTI TickIT	Guide to Software Quality Management System Construction and Certification using EN29001, 30 Sep 1990.

9. Verification Standards

ANS 10.4-87	Guidelines for the Verification and Validation of Scientific and Engineering Computer Programs for the Nuclear Industry. 43 pp.

BCS-90	A Standard for Software Component Testing, ISS. 1.2. 69 pp.
BS 5887-80	Code of Practice for Testing of Computer-Based Systems. 8 pp.
DIN 66 285	Application Software: Principles of Testing
DOD TADSTAND E	Software Development, Documentation, and Testing Policy for Navy Mission Critical Systems. 16 pp.
ESA PSS-05-10	Guide to Software Verification and Validation, Issue 1, Feb 1994
FIPS PUB 132-1987	Guideline for Software Verification and Validation Plans, Nov. 1987
FIPS PUB l01-1983	Guidelines for Lifecycle Validation, Verification, and Testing of Computer Software, Jun 1983
GER GFMT BDLI	Testing, Documentation and Certification of Software-based Systems in Aircraft. 98 pp.
GER KBST V Model	Software Life Cycle Model (V-Model). 500+ pp.
IEE-2	Guidelines for Assuring Testability, 1988. 88 pp.
IEEE 1012-1992	Standard for Software Verification and Validation. 26 pp.
IEEE 1059-1993	Guide for Software Verification and Validation Plans. 121 pp.
NATO NAT-PRC-3	Software Project Verification and Validation Procedure
NATO NAT-STAN-6	Software Testing Requirements
NIST S.P. 500-165	Software Verification and Validation: Its Roles in Computer Assurance and Its Relationships with Software
NSAC 38-1981	Verification and Validation for Safety Parameter Display Systems, NSCAC-39, Nuclear Safety Analysis Center, Dec. 1981.
RTCA DO/178B-92	Software Considerations in Airborne Systems and Equipment Certification. 100 pp.

10. Validation Standards

ANS 10.4-87	Guidelines for the Verification and Validation of Scientific and Engineering Computer Programs for the Nuclear Industry. 43 pp.
BCS-90	A Standard for Software Component Testing, ISS. 1.2. 69 pp.
BS 5887-80	Code of Practice for Testing of Computer-Based Systems. 8 pp.
DM 66 285	Application Software: Principles of Testing
DOD TADSTAND E	Software Development, Documentation, and Testing Policy for Navy Mission Critical Systems. 16 pp.
ESA PSS-05-10	Guide to Software Verification and Validation, Issue 1, Feb 1994
FIPS PUB 101-1983	Guidelines for Lifecycle Validation, Verification, and Testing of Computer Software, June 1983
FIPS PUB 132-1987	Guideline for Software Verification and Validation Plans, Nov. 1987
GER KBST V Model	Software Life Cycle Model (V-Model). 500+ pp.
IEE-2	Guidelines for Assuring Testability, 1988. 88 pp.
IEEE 1002-1992	Standard Taxonomy for Software Engineering Standards. 26 pp.
IEEE 1059-1993	Guide for Software Verification and Validation Plans. 120 pp.
NATO NAT-PRC-3	Software Project Verification and Validation Procedure
NATO NAT-STAN-6	Software Testing Requirements
NIST S.P. 500-165	Software Verification and Validation: Its Roles in Computer Assurance and Its Relationships with Software
NSAC 38-1981	Verification and Validation for Safety Parameter Display Systems, NSCAC-39, Nuclear Safety Analysis Center, Dec. 1981

4.11 Joint Review Standards

DOD MIL STD 1521B	Technical Reviews and Audits for Systems, Equipment, and Computer Programs, 4 June 1985. 125 pp.
IEEE 1028-988	Standard for Software Reviews and Audits. 35 pp.
JPL D-4014	Work Implementation Planning
NATO NAT-STAN-5	Software Design Review Requirements

4.12 Audit Standards

IEEE 1028-1988	Standard for Software Reviews and Audits. 35 pp.

4.13 Problem Resolution Standards

IEEE 1044-1993	Standard Classification for Software Anomalities. 20 pp.

4.14 Management Standards

AFNOR Z67-101-1FD	Recommendations for Conducting Computer Project
ASTM E 622-94	Guide for Developing Computerized Systems. 31 pp.
ASTM E 792-87	Guide for Computer Automation in the Clinical Laboratory. 44 pp.
ASTM E1113-86	Guide for Project Definition of Computerized Systems. 6 pp.
DOD AFSCP 800-43	Software Management Indicators, 31 Jan. 1986. 27 pp.
DOD AFSCP 800-45	Software Risk Abatement, 30 September 1988. 31 pp.
DOD MIL STD 1521B	Technical Reviews and Audits for Systems, Equipment, and Computer Programs, 4 June 1985. 125 pp.
EIA CRB 1-89	Managing the Development of Artificial Intelligence Software. 20 pp.
EIA DMG-1-86	Data Management Implementation Guideline. 31 pp.
EIA DMG-2-89	Automated Data Management Guideline. 31 pp.
ESA PSS-05-08	Guide to Software Project Management Issue 1, July 1994
GER MOD PROSIS	Project Control and Information Standard
IEEE 982.1-1988	Standard Dictionary of Measures to Produce Reliable Software. 36 pp.
IEEE 982.2-1988	Guide for the use of Standard Dictionary of Measures to Produce Reliable Software. 96 pp.
IEEE 1045-1992	Standard for Software Productivity Metrics. 37 pp.
IEEE 1058.1 1987	Standard for Software Project Management Plans. 16 pp.
IEEE 1061-1992	Standard for a Software Quality Metrics Methodology. 88 pp.
IEEE 1209-1992	Recommended Practice for Evaluation and Selection of CASE Tools. 35 pp.
IEEE 1220-1994	Application and Management of the System Engineering Process
JPL D-4011	Software Management Planning, Dec 1988. 21 pp.
NATO NAT-PRC-1	Software Project Management Procedure
NATO NAT-STAN-7	Software Metric Requirements

15. Infrastructure Standards

AIAA G-010-93	Guide for Reusable Software: Assessment Criteria for Aerospace Applications. 22 pp.
DOD MIL-HDBK-59A	Computer-Aided Acquisition and Logistic Support (CALS) Program Implementation Guide. 216 pp.

DOD MIL-HDBK-347	Mission Critical Computer Resources Software Support, May 1990. 77 pp.
DOD MIL-HDBK-782	Military Handbook, Software Support Environment Acquisition. 75 pp.
ECMA 149	PCTE: Portable Common Tool Interface
ECMA 158	PCTE: C Programming Language Binding
ECMA 162	PCTE: Ada Programming Language Binding
EIA IS-81	CDIF—Framework for Modeling and Extensibility. 101 pp.
EIA IS-82	CDIF—Transfer Format Definition
EIA IS-83	CDIF—Standardized CASE Interchange Meta-Model
GER MOD GEN DIR 252	Functional Tool Requirements (Standardized Criteria Catalogue)
GER MOD AU 252	Functional Tool Requirements (Standardized Criteria Catalogue)
FIPS PUB 99-1983	Guideline: A Framework for the Evaluation and Comparison of Software Development Tools, Mar 1983
IEEE 1175	Standard for Computing System Tool Interconnections
IEEE 1209-1992	Recommended Practice for Evaluation and Selection of CASE Tools. 35 pp.
NIST S.P. 500-142	A Management Overview of Software Reuse
NIST S.P. 500-155	Management Guide to Software Reuse
UK MOD DEF STAN 00-17	Modular Approach to Software Construction, Operation, and Test—MASCOT. 5 pp.

16. Improvement Standards

DOD SEI-91-TR-24	Capability Maturity Model for Software, Aug 1991.
DOD SEI-91-TR-25	Key Practices of the Capability Maturity Model, Feb 1993. 404 pp.
IEEE 1044 1993	Standard Classification for Software Anomalities. 20 pp.
SDA STD	Software Technology Diagnostic

17. Training Standards

ASTM E 625-87	Guide for Training Users of Computerized Systems 4 pp.
EIA CMB6-2-88	Configuration and Data Management In-House Training Plan. 18 pp.
GER MOD GEN DIR 258	Functional Requirements for Dp Education and Training

18. Safety Standards

AECL STD-00-00902-001	Standard for Software Engineering of Safety Critical Software
DIA-1	Computerized Data Systems for Nonclinical Safety Assessment, 1988.
DIN V/VDE 0801	Principles for Computers in Safety-Related System, 1989 (Preliminary Standard). 172 pp.
EIA SEB6-84	A Method for Software Safety Analysis. 30 pp.
EIA SEB6-A-90	System Safety Engineering in Software Development. 140 pp.
IAEA-1993	State of the Art Report on Software Important to Safely in Nuclear Plants
IEC 880-86	Software for Computers in the Safety Systems of Nuclear Power Stations, First Edition. 134 pp.
IEC 987-87	Programmed Digital Computer Important to Safety for Nuclear Power Stations
IEE-5	Software in Safety-Related Systems, Oct. 1989.
IEEE 1228-1993	Standard for Software Safety Plans
NATO STANAG 4404	Safety Design Requirements and Guidelines for Munition Related Safety Critical Computing Systems, Mar 1989

| UK DOTI SafeIT | A Framework for Safety Standards, May 1990. 56 pp. |
| UK HSE PSE Guidelines | Programmable Electronics Systems in Safety Related Applications, 1987. |

19. Terminology Standards

AFNOR X50-106-2	Vocabularie Project Management
ASTM E1013-87a	Terminology Relating to Computerized Systems. 3 pp.
BS 4778-89	Glossary of Terms used in Quality Assurance
CSA Z243.27 1-79	Data Processing Vocabulary—Fundamental Terms. 35 pp.
CSA Z243.27 4-81	Data Processing Vocabulary—Organization of Data. 38 pp.
CSA Z243.58-92	Information Technology Vocabulary. 597 pp.
FIPS PUB 11-3	Guidelines: American National Dictionary for Information Systems
IEEE 610.12-1990	Glossary of Software Engineering Terminology. 85 pp.
JTC1 2382, Pt 20	Information Processing—Vocabulary—System Development
NMTBA	Common Words as They Relate to NC Software

20. User Support Standards

AFNOR Z67-110-1 FD	Ergonomics and Man-Computer Dialogue
AIAA R-023-92	Recommended Practice for Human-Computer Interfaces for Space System Operations. 22 pp.
DIN 66 234	VDU Work Station: Principles of Ergonomic Dialogue Design
ECMA TR 61	User Interface Taxonomy

21. Miscellaneous Standards

AFNOR X50-105	Concepts
AFNOR Z67-102-1FD	Specification for Management Applications-Software
AIAA R-013-93	Recommended Practice for Software Reliability. 70 pp.
ASTM E 792-87	Guide for Computer Automation in the Clinical Laboratory. 44 pp.
ASTM E1206-87	Guide for Computerization of Existing Equipment. 6 pp.
ASTM E1239	Guide for Description of Reservation/Registration Admission, Discharge, Transfer (R-ADT) Systems for Automated Patient Care Information Systems. 10 pp.
ASTM E1246-88	Practice for Reporting Reliability of Clinical Laboratory Computer Systems. 6 pp.
ASTM E1384	Guide for Description for Content and Structure of an Automated Primary Record of Care. 11 pp.
BS 5760	Reliability of Constructed or Manufactured Systems, Equipments, and Components
BS 6154-81	Method for Defining Syntactic Metalanguage. 14 pp.
CEN ENV 40 003-90	Computer Integrated Manufacturing (CIM): CIM Systems Architecture Framework for Modeling 26 pp.
CSSC-1	The Canadian Trusted Computer Product Evaluation Criteria, Ver. 3, Jan. 1993. 208 pp.
ESA PSS-05-01	Guide to the Software Engineering Standards, Issue 1, Oct 1991
FDA CS-91-1.1	Application of the Medical Device GMPS to Computerized Devices and Manufacturing Process. 24 pp.
FDA DS-9	Reviewer Guidance for Computer-Controlled Medical
GER MOD AU 248	Handbook DP—Security Requirements

GER MOD AU 251	Methods Standards
GER MOD GEN DIR 248	Handbook DP—Security Requirements
GER MOD GEN DIR 251	Methods Standards
GER GFMT BDLI	Testing, Documentation and Certification of Software-based Systems in Aircraft. 98 pp.
GISA ITSEC 1.2 1991	Information Technology Security Evaluation Criteria
IEC 643-79	Application of Digital Computers to Nuclear Reactor Instrumentation and Control. 33 pp.
IEE-3	The Software Inspection Handbook. 26 pp.
IEEE 1002-1992	Standard Taxonomy for Software Engineering Standards. 26 pp.
NSA Spec. 86-16	Security Guidelines for COMPSEC Software Development
SAE ARP 1570	Flight Management Computer System
UK DOH GLP	Good Laboratory Practice—The application of GLP practices to computer systems, 1989.
UK MOD DEF 5169/11	ImprovelT. 180 pp.
UK MOD DEF-STAN 00-41	Practices and Procedures for Reliability and Maintainability, Parts 1-5. 171 pp.
UK MOD NES 620	Requirements for Software for Use with Digital Processors, Naval Engineering Standard, Issue 3, 1986.

APPENDIX

Software Engineering Survey Results

The Editors of this Tutorial have many years of experience in the practice and management of software engineering. Both of us attend conferences, subscribe to journals, visit libraries both here and abroad, access information available electronically, and try to read the current software engineering literature. We know, however, that we simply cannot be aware of, much less read or even scan, all sources of software engineering information. To overcome this "handicap," we determined that we should enlist the assistance of a large number of practitioners and researchers to help us identify the articles most suitable for inclusion in the Tutorial, and to identify those areas where there is a lack of suitable articles. We then identified over 200 software engineering professionals whose opinions we should solicit, and prepared a survey to send to them.

We also felt it was important to seek out software professionals outside the United States, since they would be likely to have access to journals, conferences, and other sources of material that would be less known in the United States. While most of the individuals surveyed resided in the US, there was also a significant number from other countries, including Canada, the UK, France, Germany, Spain, the Netherlands, Australia, and New Zealand.

Since the main objective of the Tutorial was to be useful in education and training, we particularly sought out software engineering educators from industry, government, and academia. Our primary sources for the mailing list were (1) the names of educators from a list provided by the Software Engineering Institute (SEI) and (2) the attendees at the SEI's Sixth Annual Conference on Software Engineering Education. To these lists we added software engineers whom we had meet at conferences and elsewhere as well as through correspondence.

Survey material included a cover letter, a list of papers under consideration at the time, and a response form. The cover letter is reproduced at the end of this Appendix. The list of papers was divided into 13 categories, matching the chapters of the book as envisioned at that time, and amounted to an overly-ambitious Table of Contents for the book in that it included 203 papers! The response form asked whether the recipient was familiar with each paper and, if so, to rate it on a scale of 1 ("marginal") to 5 ("must include"). Recipients were also asked to list any other papers worthy of inclusion and to identify

possible authors for new papers for that category. Recipients were advised that they could nominate themselves to write new papers.

Space was also provided for recipients to make additional comments. Each recipient was asked if he/she wanted a complimentary copy of the Tutorial when it was published, and if we could use his/her name and affiliation in the Tutorial as a contributor.

The survey material was mailed in May, 1993, and responses were requested by June 30. Some addresses were determined to be incorrect and the forms had to be remailed. Some additional names were acquired. In these cases a later response date was permitted.

We received 70 responses that ranged from checking a few boxes to providing extensive comments and copies of recommended papers. Let us say at this point that the contributions were invaluable, and it would have been very difficult to compile the Tutorial without these responses. However, we were surprised to observe that

- Most responses agreed with us that there were very few papers in our list that really met the criteria
- There were very few usable suggestions for papers beyond those in the list
- There was not a large number of volunteers or ideas for authors of new papers.

We reluctantly concluded that there simply are not many good survey papers either on software engineering as a whole or on its subspecialties. (Indeed, some of the survey responses said this in so many words.) Apparently, as a field matures, papers are published on results of research and industrial practice and/or on ideas for further advances, but few are written to summarize the state of practice.

The range of opinions was surprising. It was not unusual for as many as five responses to describe a paper as a "must," while several others might specifically reject the same paper. The survey did provide a consensus on a few papers:

- Brooks, F.P., "No Silver Bullet: Essence and Accidents of Software Engineering," *Computer.* Vol. 20, No. 4, Apr. 1987, pp. 10–19.
- Parnas D.L., and P.C. Clements, "A Rational

Design Process: How and Why to Fake It," *IEEE Trans. Software Eng.*, Vol. SE 12, No. 2, Feb. 1986, pp. 251–257.

- Mills, H.D., M. Dyer, and R.C. Linger, "Cleanroom Software Engineering," *IEEE Software*, Vol. 4, No. 5, Sept. 1987, pp. 19–24.

- Fagan, M.E., "Design and Code Inspections to Reduce Errors in Program Development," *IBM Systems J.*, Vol. 15, No. 3, 1976, pp. 182–211.

- Leveson, N.G., "Software Safety: Why, What, and How," *ACM Computing Surveys*, June 1986.

- Brooks, F.P., Jr., "The Mythical Man-Month," *Datamation*, Dec. 1974, pp. 44–52

- Boehm, B.W., "Software Engineering Economics," *IEEE Trans. on Software Eng.*, Vol. SE-10, No. 1, Jan. 1984, pages 4–21.

- Boehm, B.W., "A Spiral Model of Software Development and Enhancement," *Computer*, Vol. 21, No. 5, May 1988, pp. 61–72.

- Humphrey, W.S., "Characterizing the Software Process: A Maturity Framework," *IEEE Software*, Vol. 5, No. 2, Mar. 1988, pp. 73–79.

The observant reader will note that we used less than half of these "consensus" articles. In the end the editors' judgment prevailed, particularly when we felt an article, though excellent when written, was obsolete or excessively long.

Based on the results of the survey, we reluctantly concluded that a Tutorial could not be compiled using a high percentage of existing papers and just a few new ones. The necessity of obtaining the new papers delayed publication by approximately a year, during which time we identified the areas where new papers were needed; solicited authors; and negotiated time in their busy schedules to write the papers. It goes without saying that we are grateful to these well-known and busy people for agreeing to write the papers.

The following individuals responded to the survey and agreed to allow us to acknowledge their contribution. The affiliations are those of June 1993, and may have changed since then.

Dr. A. Frank Ackerman
Institute for Zero Defect Software

Prof. Brent Auernheimer
California State University, Fresno

Dr. David Barstow
Schlumberger Corp.

Dr. Joan Bebb
TRW, Inc.

Mr. James Brownlee
Center for Systems Management

Mr. Fletcher Buckley
Martin Marietta Corp.

Prof. David Budgen
University of Keele

Capt. James Cardow
Air Force Institute of Technology

Mr. Peter Coad
Object International, Inc.

Dr. Ken Collier
Northern Arizona University

Prof. James Cross II
Auburn University

Dr. Darren Dalcher
South Bank University

Dr. Alan M. Davis
University of Colorado at Colorado Springs

Mr. Thomas Fouser
Jet Propulsion Laboratory

Dr. Lisa Friendly
First Person, Inc.

Ms. Suzanne Garcia
Lockheed Missiles & Space Co.

Mr. Robert Glass
Computing Trends

Prof. Donald Gotterbarn
East Tennessee State University

Ms. Martha Ann Griesel
Jet Propulsion Laboratory

Prof. David Gustafson
Kansas State University

Mr. Simon Harris
Swinburne University of Technology

Dr. Warren Harrison
Portland State University

Ms. Jennifer Harvey
University of South Australia

Dr. Sallie Henry
Virginia Polytechnic Institute and State University

Dr. William Howden
University of California at San Diego

Prof. Pei Hsia
University of Texas at Arlington

Dr. Robin Hunter
University of Strathclyde

Prof. Xiaoping Jia
DePaul University

Prof. Kemal Koymen
Moorhead State University

Dr. Arun Lakhotia
University of Southwestern Louisiana

Mr. Frank LaMonica
US Air Force Rome Laboratory

Mr. Pierre Y. Leduc
Universite de Sherbrooke

Prof. Michael Lutz
Rochester Institute of Technology

Mr. Jukka Marijarvi
Nokia Telecommunications

Chris D. Marlin
Flinders University

Dr. J. Luis Mate
Polytechnic University of Madrid

Dr. Ed Miller
Software Research, Inc.

Mr. John Musa
AT&T Bell Laboratories

Dr. Richard Nance
Virginia Polytechnic Institute & State University

Prof. Jeff Offutt
George Mason University

Dr. James Palmer
George Mason University

Prof. Ronald Peterson
Weber State University

Prof. Keith R. Pierce
University of Minnesota, Duluth

Dr. J.H. Poore
University of Tennessee, Knoxville

Mr. Robert Poston
Interactive Development Environments

Prof. Pierre N. Robillard
Ecole Polytechnique—Montreal

Mr. Paul Rook
City University of London

Mr. Walker Royce
TRW, Inc.

Mr. Terry Snyder
Hughes Aircraft Co.

Dr. Robert Steigerwald
US Air Force Academy

M.A. Stephens
University of Wolverhampton

Mr. Alan Sukert
Martin Marietta Corp.

Dr. Wim H. Walk
Shell Research

Dr. Anthony I. Wasserman
Interactive Development Environments

Prof. Timothy D. Wells
Rochester Institute of Technology

The editors also wish to acknowledge the assistance of Mr. Fernando Proaño, a graduate student at California State University, Sacramento, who helped reduce and analyze the survey results.

May 15, 1993

To: Instructors, practitioners, and researchers in software engineering

From: Richard Thayer and Merlin Dorfman

Subj: Survey of Software Engineering Papers

Richard Thayer and Merlin Dorfman, co-editors of two *IEEE Tutorials on Requirements Engineering*, are developing a new *Tutorial* volume on Software Engineering, containing papers describing the best current practices in the field of software engineering. The *Tutorial* will be approximately 500 pages in length, with about 400 pages consisting of new or reprinted papers, and the other 100 consisting of a glossary, references, chapter introductions, etc. The project has been approved by the IEEE Computer Society, with estimated dates of January 1994 for submission to the publisher and mid-1994 for publication.

The *Tutorial* is targeted for an upper-division or first- year graduate course in software engineering. This collection of reprints and original papers will enable instructors of software engineering to provide their students with the latest state-of-the-practice papers without the effort, inconvenience, and expense of obtaining numerous copyright clearances. This *Tutorial* can also be used in industry by organizations that are new to software development and/or wish to learn the current state of the practice. We believe this *Tutorial* will be a valuable contribution to the dissemination of software engineering knowledge.

We are asking professionals in the field of software engineering to help us select the best paper(s) in various topics, or to identify those areas where new papers are needed. This survey is being sent to approximately 400 software engineering instructors, practitioners, researchers, and authors, about two-thirds of them in the US and the remainder in Canada, Europe, and, in a few cases, the Far East. While no individual is expected to be an expert in all aspects of software engineering, we believe that the group contains sufficient expertise to make good selections in every topic.

Attached is a list of topics in software engineering, along with references to a few papers in each topic. The major purpose of listing these papers is to describe the intent of the topic subject rather than to dictate a choice of papers. May we ask you to indicate, on the *Survey Response Form*, each paper with which you are familiar by placing a check mark next to its number; and to rate with a number those papers that should be considered for inclusion in the *Tutorial*. A "1" would indicate a paper that is marginal for inclusion, while a "5" indicates a paper that should not be omitted under any circumstances. More than one paper may be recommended in a single topic. May we also ask you to add, in the indicated area after each topic, any papers that we have not listed that should be considered. We are looking for tutorial-type papers that describe the best current practice rather than unproven or speculative advances in the state of the art. The "ideal" paper is eight to ten pages in length, but it need not be from a well-known or refereed journal. Please cite a reference or, if convenient, mail us a copy. Finally, if you believe that there are no existing papers on a topic worthy of inclusion, please provide the name(s) of author(s) who are qualified to write a new paper. You may nominate yourself!

If you have a reading list for a software engineering course, we would appreciate a copy of that also.

IEEE has agreed that all participants in this survey will be provided, if they so request, a complimentary copy of the *Tutorial* when it is published. If you would like to receive a copy, please complete the enclosed request form and return it with the survey response. We have provided a postage- paid, pre-addressed envelope for return of the survey response and, if you wish, the request form. (For obvious reasons the return postage is not provided for non-U.S. participants.) Also, please keep this letter and notify us of any changes of address between now and the publication date. Finally please indicate if you wish your name and affiliation to be listed in the *Tutorial* as having contributed to the effort through participation in the Survey.

We have asked the IEEE Computer Society Press to send a copy of its current Publications Catalog to all survey recipients to ensure that you are familiar with the scope and contents of its tutorials, and we have enclosed a copy of the biographies from our *Requirements Engineering Tutorials* for those of you who are not familiar with our work.

To be sure that your inputs are available in time to be included, please return the survey by June 30, 1993. Thanks for your help.

Sincerely,

Richard H. Thayer, PhD
Professor in Computer Science
Sacramento State University, Sacramento
6540 Chiquita Way
Carmichael, CA 95608
Home tel: 916-481-5482
Home fax: 916-481-8778
Email: thayer@ecs.csus.edu

Merlin Dorfman, PhD
Technical Consultant
Lockheed Missiles & Space Co.
6072 Burnbank Place
San Jose, CA 95120
Home tel: 408-268-4219

Email: dorfman@netcom.com

Biography of Merlin Dorfman

Merlin Dorfman, PhD, is a Technical Consultant in the Space Systems Product Center, Lockheed Martin Missiles and Space Company, Sunnyvale, Calif. He specializes in systems engineering for software-intensive systems (requirements analysis, top-level architecture, and performance evaluation), in software process improvement, and in algorithm development for data processing systems. He has performed concept exploration, system implementation, and operations and maintenance of data systems and has worked on proposal teams and company-funded technology projects as well as on development contracts. He was in charge of the development of the Automated Requirements Traceability System (ARTS). He was the first chairman of Space Systems Division's Software Engineering Process Group. He represented the Lockheed Corporation on the Embedded Computer Software Committee of the Aerospace Industries Association, and was Vice-Chairman of the Committee.

Dorfman wrote and taught a four-day course, "Software Requirements and Design Specifications," for Learning Tree International of Los Angeles, Calif. He co-teaches a two-week course in Software Project Management for the Center for Systems Management of Cupertino, Calif. He has been a guest lecturer on software systems engineering at the Defense Systems Management College. He is a Fellow of the American Institute of Aeronautics and Astronautics (AIAA), a member of its System Engineering Technical Committee, past chairman of the Software Systems Technical Committee, and past Chairman of the AIAA San Francisco Section, and is currently Assistant Director of Region 6 (West Coast). He is an affiliate member of the Institute of Electrical and Electronics Engineers (IEEE) Computer Society.

He has a BS and MS from the Massachusetts Institute of Technology and a PhD from Stanford University, all in Aeronautics and Astronautics. He is a registered Professional Engineer in the states of California and Colorado and is a member of the Tau Beta Pi and Sigma Gamma Tau honorary societies.

He is co-editor of two IEEE Tutorial volumes, *System and Software Requirements Engineering* and *Standards, Guidelines, and Examples for System and Software Requirements Engineering*, and co-editor of a volume, *Aerospace Software Engineering*, in the AIAA "Progress in Aeronautics and Astronautics" Series.

Biography of Richard H. Thayer

Richard H. Thayer, PhD, is a Professor of Computer Science at California State University, Sacramento, California, United States of America. He travels widely where he consults and lectures on software requirements analysis, software engineering, project management, software engineering standards, and software quality assurance. He is a Visiting Researcher at the University of Strathclyde, Glasgow, Scotland. As an expert in software project management and requirements engineering, he is a consultant to many companies and government agencies.

Prior to this, he served over 20 years in the U.S. Air Force as a senior officer in a variety of positions associated with engineering, computer programming, research, teaching, and management in computer science and data processing. His numerous positions include six years as a supervisor and technical leader of scientific programming groups, four years directing the U.S. Air Force R&D program in computer science, and six years of managing large data processing organizations.

Thayer is a Senior Member of the IEEE Computer Society and the IEEE Software Engineering Standards Subcommittee. He is Chairperson for the Working Group for a Standard for a Concept of Operations (ConOps) document and past chairperson for the Working Group for a Standard for a Software Project Management Plans. He is a Distinguished Visitor for the IEEE Computer Society.

He is also an Associate Fellow of the American Institute of Aeronautics and Astronautics (AIAA) where he served on the AIAA Technical Committee on Computer Systems, and he is a member of the Association for Computing Machinery (ACM). He is also a registered professional engineer.

He has a BSEE and an MS degree from the University of Illinois at Urbana (1962) and a PhD from the University of California at Santa Barbara (1979) all in Electrical Engineering.

He has edited and/or co-edited numerous tutorials for the IEEE Computer Society Press: *Software Engineering Project Management* (1988), *System and Software Requirements Engineering* (1990), and *Software Engineering—A European Prospective* (1992). He is the author of over 40 technical papers and reports on software project management, software engineering, and software engineering standards and is an invited speaker at many national and international software engineering conferences and workshops.

Printed in the United States
26059LVS00001B/29-128

9 780818 676093